TRUDEAU TRANSFORMED

TRUDEAU TRANSFORMED
The Shaping of a Statesman, 1944–1965

VOLUME TWO

OF

TRUDEAU, SON OF QUEBEC, FATHER OF CANADA

MAX AND MONIQUE NEMNI
TRANSLATED BY GEORGE TOMBS

A DOUGLAS GIBSON BOOK

McCLELLAND & STEWART

English translation © 2011 by George Tombs

Published in 2011 as *Trudeau, fils du Québec, père du Canada, Tome 2: La formation d'un homme D'État* by Les Éditions de L'Homme

Cataloging data available from Library and Archives Canada

We acknowledge the financial support of the Government of Canada through the National Translation Program for Book Publishing for our translation activities.

We acknowledge the financial support of the Government of Canada through the Book Publishing Industry Development Program and that of the Government of Ontario through the Ontario Media Development Corporation's Ontario Book Initiative. We further acknowledge the support of the Canada Council for the Arts and the Ontario Arts Council for our publishing program.

Published simultaneously in the United States of America by McClelland & Stewart Ltd., P.O. Box 1030, Plattsburgh, New York 12901

Library of Congress Control Number: 2011925617

The extract from F.R. Scott's "Fort Smith" has been reprinted with the permission of William Toye, literary executor for the estate of F.R. Scott.

Typeset in Sabon by M&S, Toronto
Printed and bound in Canada

A Douglas Gibson Book

 ANCIENT FOREST FRIENDLY

This book was produced using ancient-forest friendly papers.

McClelland & Stewart Ltd.
75 Sherbourne Street
Toronto, Ontario
M5A 2P9
www.mcclelland.com

1   2   3   4   5   15   14   13   12   11

*Once again, we dedicate this book
to those very dear to our hearts:*

Our daughters,
Colette and Jacqueline
and
our grandchildren,
Julien and Rachel Laurion,
Nicolas, Zoé, and Mark Traquair,
and
to the memory of
Pierre Elliott Trudeau,
a man who sought the Truth
for the Good of his people.

*The true statesman is not one who gives orders
to his fellow-citizens so much as he is one
who devotes himself to their service.*

— PIERRE ELLIOTT TRUDEAU,
Vrai, 1958

CONTENTS

IN SEARCH OF THE STATESMAN

For Canadians, the adoption of the Charter of Rights and Freedoms in 1982 marks the birth of modern-day Canada.
— JEAN-FRANÇOIS LISÉE,
La Presse, June 30, 2010[*]

WHAT, ANOTHER BOOK ON TRUDEAU? Haven't there been enough already – and maybe even a few too many? What can we offer that is really new? The answer can be summed up in a few words: we are directing a ray of light on one particular aspect of his character. Instead of the usual wide-beam searchlight, covering long periods of Trudeau's life in their many dimensions, we propose a more focused study, both of the period and of the perspective. We believe this will help to get a clearer view of a man still regarded as an enigma.

Trudeau the chameleon, many people believe, will *always* be an enigma. Indeed, journalists, biographers, and many Canadians have been and continue to be intrigued and puzzled by Trudeau. A witty comment about him conjures up the peculiar state of confusion writers find themselves in when they set out to describe him: "Someone is going to say some day, 'Will the real Mr. Trudeau please stand up,' and about fifty-eight people will rise."[1] Quoted first by his biographer George Radwanksi in 1978, this comment has often been repeated, as if to

---

[*] Jean-François Lisée is a well-known nationalist and pro-independence journalist and author. He served as political adviser to two Parti Québécois premiers, Jacques Parizeau and Lucien Bouchard.

highlight the contradictory aspects of the man or to suggest some elusive quality that makes it practically impossible to figure him out.

We have been associated with Pierre Elliott Trudeau for nearly twenty years, first as friends over a decade, then for another ten years buried in his personal papers and publications: we could make similar comments, although we would interpret his many facets differently. Indeed, we could have written several different biographies of Trudeau.

We could have written a biography of *Trudeau-the-athlete*. Anecdotes abound on the subject. For example, we could have described the many canoe expeditions he undertook, starting at a young age, travelling up to a thousand miles in a single journey. He was an avid skier who leapt at the chance to hit the mountain trails; in his younger years, he won several medals for his prowess on skis, and he was still skiing in powder shortly before his death in 2000. He was fascinated by all manner of water sports: swimming, diving, water skiing, scuba diving – and he excelled in every one. He knew how to fly a plane and could fly solo; he loved zooming up hill and down dale on his famous Harley-Davidson; he hiked hundreds of kilometres on foot and climbed mountains. Trudeau could do vertical headstands and horizontal handstands, as photographs in several biographies attest. Once he became prime minister, frisky as ever in his fifties, he could easily shake off admirers and journalists alike by bounding up the steps in the Parliament Buildings four at a time. We could give many other examples.

Long-time friend Peter Green provides a less well known anecdote. When Trudeau was prime minister, he sometimes vacationed with his family at the Green home in Jamaica, a constable of the Royal Canadian Mounted Police always coming along for security reasons. One day Green brought a horse to the beach so the children could have fun riding. "Pierre asked the Mountie to give a demonstration for the boys. The poor guy had probably not ridden for years and stumbled around the beach on the long-suffering horse. Pierre, without saying a word, got on the horse bareback – in his swimming shorts – and gave a short demonstration of control and superb riding technique, much to the embarrassment of the Mountie."[2]

We could have told many other juicy anecdotes along these lines, without exhausting all the sports at which Trudeau excelled. By the end of this biography of *Trudeau-the-athlete,* readers would likely conclude that he could have mastered these athletic feats only by devoting all his waking hours to sports and fitness. Obviously he could never have found time for serious business, so the real Trudeau must have been *Trudeau-the-athlete,* and his purportedly vast knowledge was only a thin veneer.

But we could just as easily have written a biography of *Trudeau-the-scholar-with-a-passion-for-culture.* An insatiable reader, he devoured novels, works of history and political philosophy, as well as poetry. He was endowed with a phenomenal memory, knew several opera librettos by heart, and could declaim whole poems impromptu, in French and English. He did the rounds of museums, theatres, concerts, and exhibitions. The people he met were often startled by his encyclopaedic knowledge, as the following example illustrates. He had only just become prime minister in 1968, when he was invited along with a host of celebrities to a party in New York thrown by the artists Joyce Wieland and Michael Snow, her husband. Trudeau was evidently in his element and seemed up to date on all the latest news of the New York cultural scene, from art-house movies to avant-garde dance and jazz. When Michael Snow introduced Milford Graves to him as "the greatest jazz drummer," Trudeau instantly responded, to the amazement of his admiring audience, "And what do you make of Max Roach?"[3]

We could give many more examples highlighting his impressive knowledge of painting, sculpture, music, architecture, literature, and philosophy. And after reading these anecdotes about *Trudeau-the-scholar-with-a-passion-for-culture,* readers would be tempted to conclude that here, finally, was the real Trudeau. As if the man had spent his entire life reading, studying, and trekking through museums, historical sites, and theatres and could never have found time for any other activities, such as sports . . .

We could have chosen instead to write about *Trudeau-the-daredevil-adventurer,* who criss-crossed Asia with a backpack for nearly a year and had many thrilling adventures, including a few short stays in jail for vagrancy. He could just as easily travel in high style as put up with the shabbiest accommodations. He dined in the finest restaurants of Paris (Maxim's, La Tour d'Argent, La Pérouse). But he also sometimes slept in run-down hotels, sharing a room with total strangers or even hungry bedbugs! Here was a man eager to witness everything first-hand, to live fully.

He was hungry for challenges. In 1948, while visiting Turkey, he decided to swim across the Bosphorus Strait, which marks the southern boundary of Europe and Asia: "It wasn't that hard, but it was cold and had a bloody strong current."[4] In April 1960 at the age of forty-one, he decided to paddle a canoe with two companions from Miami to Cuba – quite a harebrained scheme. Fortunately the trio were rescued midway, when their canoe was on the point of sinking.[5]

One last example. On July 6, 1961, Trudeau was in Pamplona (the capital of Navarre in northern Spain) for the first day of the San Fermín festival. The city becomes one huge fiesta from July 6 to 14, attracting thousands of tourists from around the world. The main event of this festival is the Running of the Bulls (*encierro*): at 8 o'clock each morning from July 7 to 14, the bulls are let loose in the narrow streets and then run almost one kilometre to the bullring for the afternoon *corrida* or bullfight. Along the course, daring young participants run just ahead of the bulls. Accidents are common, due to the ferocious nature of bulls and the surge of the crowds. On July 6, Trudeau partied until three in the morning. The city was overrun with tourists, no hotel room was available, and he ended up sleeping on a bench. The following morning, he participated in the Running of the Bulls. Finding the experience electrifying, he came back for a repeat performance two days later.[6] Here was a man with a lust for adventure, someone who lived life to the hilt during his many world travels. No doubt readers of this particular book would take *Trudeau-the-daredevil-adventurer* for the real Trudeau, as if he lacked the more serious qualities befitting a statesman.

But we could also have written about *Trudeau-the-man-of-faith,* a man intent on deepening his understanding of the Bible. He could quote Scripture from memory and occasionally correct people who had specialized knowledge of biblical exegesis. He almost never missed Sunday Mass, even when travelling, recited his daily prayers, sought out opportunities for meditation, often took part in retreats, and liked to join in spiritual experiences. He read the works of most major theologians and was perfectly at ease discussing their ideas. On January 25, 1956, he was granted an audience with Pope Pius XII. In 1976, Trudeau and his wife, Margaret, obtained a second audience with Pope Paul VI, and in 1980 he and his son Justin were received in a third audience by Pope John Paul II. Many people bear witness to this side of his personality in *The Hidden Pierre Elliott Trudeau: The Faith Behind the Politics,*[7] as well as in the first chapter of *Pierre.*[8]

We could just as easily have written an account from the opposite point of view: *Trudeau-the-heretic-and-even-the-atheist.* He never hesitated to cross swords with several prelates of the French-Canadian church, telling them to mind their own business and sometimes showing them scant respect. As minister of justice, he articulated his famous credo "The state has no place in the bedrooms of the nation" and legalized acts condemned by the Pope, such as divorce or homosexuality between consenting adults. Some will say there must have been two men named Pierre Trudeau – one a devout Catholic and avid reader of the Bible, the other committing himself heart and soul to separating Church from State.

And then there was *Trudeau-the-ladies-man* . . . and they certainly loved him back. Here was a Valentino, a Don Juan, who sought the company of beautiful women, each of them more charming, intelligent, and cultivated than the next! He sometimes went out with a few women at a time, his relationships seeming like a game of musical chairs. For example, in the summer of 1964, he spent a lovely holiday in Italy with Carroll Guérin, travelling to Sardinia, scuba diving, having a blast. Then, on August 30, Carroll flew to Madrid. On the 31st, he phoned Madeleine Gobeil, who joined him in Vienna . . . and they continued travelling together. On September 21, she left for Paris by train, while he headed for Geneva, to revert to a more cerebral activity – attending the congress of the International Political Science Association.[9] Clearly, Trudeau knew how to charm women. His voluminous correspondence with them is impressive – he wrote more than two hundred letters to Thérèse Gouin alone. He kept up a correspondence with most of these women, often long after the relationships were over. Undoubtedly, some will say, here was a man who loved nothing better than chasing skirts – especially ones worn by attractive females. Some might understandably be tempted to write an entire biography about *Trudeau-the-ladies-man.*

We could go on like this for some time – which just goes to show the difficulty facing biographers who try to account for every aspect of Trudeau's personality. All the different men we have just described were actually facets of a single person. We believe that the *complexity* of his personality hides the *essence* of the man. Indeed, as we examine every detail in Trudeau's life, it can be quite difficult to understand why he put his personal freedom and fun-filled life on hold, in order to manage the destiny of the country for sixteen years. The real questions are these: Why did Canadians and particularly the people of Quebec elect and re-elect him over this period? Did they vote for the athlete, the adventurer, or the charmer? Of course not! And when he died, how can the massive and spontaneous outpouring of grief, right across the country, be explained, when he had been out of politics for over sixteen years?

Canadians did not elect a Valentino or an inveterate sportsman. They must have realized that here was a man offering them a unique vision of Canada. Which explains the visceral and excessive reactions even to this day. On December 6, 1999, the *Montreal Gazette* noted: "Loved, loathed, admired and despised. . . . Pierre Elliott Trudeau walked away from public life 15 years ago, but his lasting grip on the country remains firm: the former Prime Minister is the overwhelming winner of the Canadian Press survey to name the top Canadian newsmaker of the 20th Century." On June 30, 2010, *La Presse* noted, citing an Angus Reid poll: "And the best Canadian Prime Minister since 1968 is . . . Pierre Elliott Trudeau, according to respondents in both Quebec and Canada."

What did this man offer to Canadians? Leaving aside the more intriguing aspects of his personality, we have chosen to focus in the two volumes of our biography on two questions: What was the political thought and vision of Canada – including Quebec's place within the federation – Trudeau brought to office when first elected in 1965? How was his political philosophy shaped from the day he left Quebec to 1965? To this end, in this book, we trace his education, the various environments in which he came to maturity, and the influences to which he was subjected. We mostly follow the evolution of his thought through his writings and speeches, many of which are found in his personal papers. We would like to thank the Trudeau estate's literary executor, the Honourable Marc Lalonde, and Pierre Trudeau's son Alexandre for their generosity in allowing us access to the papers.[*]

---

[*]   All of these documents are to be found in Ottawa at Library and Archives Canada (LAC), MG26, the *Rt. Hon. Pierre Elliott Trudeau Fonds,* Series 02: *Documents Before Political Career.*

In our first volume, we followed Pierre Trudeau from kindergarten up to his departure for Harvard University. We discovered a man quite unlike the conventional portrayal: he was the perfect embodiment of what the French-Canadian elite of the time stood for. Through his Jesuit schooling, he enthusiastically adopted the values of Quebec's clerical-nationalist milieu. During World War II, he rejected all war news as "English" propaganda and came out strongly against conscription for service overseas. The Bloc Populaire made anti-conscription the war-horse of its political platform. [10] In fact, the historian Eric Amyot has written, "in the summer of 1944, General de Gaulle's representative Gabriel Bonneau described the Bloc Populaire as 'practically fascistic.'"[11] Yet Trudeau campaigned for this party until his departure for Harvard.

His intellectual mentors rejected democracy and liberalism, shared the ideas of the French far right, and approved the regimes of Pétain, Mussolini, and Franco. Trudeau himself had the greatest admiration for Charles Maurras. Despite Canadian war censorship, student newspapers such as *Le Quartier Latin,* to which he regularly contributed, never hesitated to ridicule the war and federal government policies.

On the other hand, from his earliest childhood he was brought up to believe that the elite had duties toward the people, just as he was taught there would one day come a great leader who would take the people to the promised land. He was a bright young man who took his responsibilities as a member of the elite very seriously. He knew that if he was to live up to the task ahead of him, he needed a top-notch education. He first got a law degree from the Université de Montréal, then, in autumn 1944, at the age of twenty-five, he left his upper-middle-class Outremont residence for Harvard University, to complete his education in economics and politics. That is where we left him, at the end of our first volume, *Young Trudeau.*

On November 8, 1965, twenty-one years after his departure for Harvard, Trudeau won the riding of Mount Royal, as a Liberal member of Parliament. By now, he was a passionate defender of federalism and liberal democracy. Once installed as minister of justice, he made a name for himself drafting bills that conflicted with some traditional values of the Church. And once he became prime minister, he sought to establish the "Just Society"; he provided Canada with a charter defending the inalienable rights of the person; and he laid down multiculturalism as one of the founding values of the country. In short, Trudeau earned his place in history, but he adopted positions at odds with those he had championed in 1944.

What happened between 1944 and 1965? When and how did he make this 180-degree turn?

Oddly, biographies of Trudeau generally skip lightly over this period. All note the importance of his years of studies at Harvard, Paris, and London. But did he suddenly see the light, as is commonly believed, on arriving at Harvard, with a triumphant shout of "Eureka"? It is also generally known that in 1948–49, he travelled with a backpack across the Middle East and Asia. Many of his adventures are well known. Was this straightforward adventure travel? The decade of the 1950s is quickly summarized by most biographers, even though allusions are made to his writings in Cité libre. Stephen Clarkson and Christina McCall devote a few lines to this period: "He was involved in almost every important reformist cause that came up, but he developed a reputation as someone who might escape to Europe or Asia on some new odyssey whenever an organizational job turned tedious or a group's fighting became emotionally demanding."[12] In short, Trudeau was interested in all the right causes but was unwilling to make commitments. He roamed abroad to avoid any serious work and any stressful situation.

But what form did his involvement take in all these "important reformist causes"? With regard to political involvement, the biographer George Radwanski mentions only Trudeau's participation in the Rassemblement, then his attempt "to turn the Rassemblement into an active political coalition, the Union des forces démocratiques," devoting no more than two paragraphs to the subject.[13] The journalist Michel Vastel devotes many pages to these years. And what, he asks, "was Trudeau's influence at the end of the 1950s?" According to Vastel, the answer was provided by the former publisher of Le Devoir: "'Marginal,' said Gérard Filion without hesitation."[14]

John English too adheres to the view of the relative unimportance of the fifties. He writes: "In the fifties Trudeau often appeared to be aimless, if not dilettantish. The conservative nationalists with whom he had worked in the early forties . . . dismissed him as a 'dandy,' a rich unreliable playboy who made no serious contribution to the political scene. Even Pelletier became so frustrated by Trudeau's eclectic ways and frequent journeys to exotic destinations that he inquired: 'Pierre, isn't it a disaster to be born rich?'"[15] English continues, quoting the criticism by Thérèse Casgrain, who worked alongside Trudeau, as well as feedback from journalists who noted "his lack of perseverance and sustained focus"; he even quotes Duplessis, for whom Trudeau was "lazy, spoiled and subversive." English adds that Trudeau himself seems to acknowledge he had wasted his time: "Deemed unreliable by some of his friends, lazy and ineffective by his enemies, Trudeau himself seemed to view the fifties later as a lost decade."[16]

With this kind of reputation, Trudeau seemed out of place when he arrived on the federal scene in 1965. Many people thought he would not last. A year after Trudeau's election as prime minister of Canada, a political opponent confidently predicted: "He's an amateur, a dilettante, a carefree bachelor who is happiest when he travels the world. He will soon tire of his new responsibilities."[17] Conventional wisdom holds that in the 1950s, this rich father's son was just a playboy whose sole interest was travel and other frivolous activities. He lacked perseverance, pursued no serious long-term goal, and shirked all responsibility.

We take the opposite view.

The conventional portrayal of Trudeau in the 1950s does not explain why and how he ended up rejecting the very values he had held up to 1944. Was this metamorphosis brought about by a few months and some classes at Harvard? Was his goal in life to wander around the world in search of adventure? And if he led the life of an idle dilettante in the 1950s, where did he learn the arts and crafts of statesmanship?

In this volume, we will examine the development of Trudeau's political thought from the fall of 1944, when he left Montreal to study at Harvard, until November 8, 1965, when he was elected Liberal MP for Mount Royal. We will see that the conventional portrayal of Trudeau the dilettante does not stand up to the facts. In reality, the 1950s were anything but "wasted years." Trudeau seemed to be everywhere at once. The mere act of drawing up a list of his intellectual activities and campaigns leaves us breathless, as we consider this statesman carefully preparing himself for office. To understand Trudeau's political thought as it emerges on the federal scene in 1965, we will follow in his footsteps, starting with his arrival at Harvard University, which proved to be the first step in a long and gradual metamorphosis. We hope this book will help readers better understand how this son of Quebec became the father of Canada.

Get ready for the journey! Fasten your seat belts!

Chapter 2

———◦———

THE SHOCK OF HARVARD

I always have a hundred opportunities to feel like an imbecile compared to the damn students around here.

— PIERRE ELLIOTT TRUDEAU, 1945[*]

IN THE LAST DAYS OF OCTOBER 1944, Pierre Trudeau, now twenty-five years old, left Quebec to spend two years at Harvard University in Cambridge, Massachusetts. This was the first step of a journey that lasted several years and enabled him to enter an intellectual world whose existence he did not even suspect. In fact, he not only changed cities, countries, languages, institutions, and educational systems; we can say without much exaggeration that he also changed planets, given the enormous gap between the environment he had left and the one that now awaited him. In other words, to use Plato's famous allegory, in reaching Harvard, Trudeau emerged from the cave in which he had grown up. He rushed out to discover the dazzling light of the sun, which he greeted with joy. But sometimes, when blinded by that same sunlight, he took refuge in the comfort of darkness. He also openly adopted attitudes and styles of thinking that were appropriate only back in the cave. He was thrown off balance and was now struggling within himself to reach a new equilibrium.

Let us note some of the adjustments that Trudeau had to make as he stepped off the train. First, he had to get used to life in the student residence. A year after his arrival, he still hadn't. He expressed his frustration

---

[*] Letter to Roger Rolland, December 9, 1945.

in a letter to his sweetheart, Thérèse Gouin. True, he said, a person should be flexible in life, but enough was enough. He was fed up with all the noise around him: his neighbours, blaring radios, people walking back and forth overhead, pianos below, elevators nearby, children in the street, garbage collection . . . [1] Yet he needed to be free to concentrate, because he felt totally overwhelmed by the other students, whose erudition made him feel inadequate. He wrote in *Memoirs:* "Classmates and professors alike were at an astounding level of culture and erudition,"[2] and as an example he mentioned that other students knew Roman law better than he did. However, he said, Roman law was not their specialty, whereas he had spent an entire year engrossed in it. He confided to his close friend, Roger Rolland: "I always have a hundred opportunities to feel like an imbecile compared to the damn students around here."[3] Catching up took a huge amount of effort. His classmates remember that he shut himself in his room in Perkins Hall, refusing to answer the door.[4] Between the first and second sessions, he spent a few days skiing at Mount Washington, attended a few social gatherings, went swimming, wrote to many of his friends – his favourite activity[5] – but he spent countless hours sitting at his desk. Summing up his life at Harvard, he admitted to Rolland: *"The only thing I do here is study."*[*]

Another change: Trudeau was surrounded by veterans swarming all over the campus, who no doubt were happy to have saved civilization from Nazi barbarism. The soldiers had a privileged place in the student newspaper, the *Service News.*[6] And for good reason. Of 85,756 alumni, 22,620 – or one in four – had gone to war. One in eighty-seven had died in battle.[7] Great numbers of those returning from the war registered in various universities. Starting in 1944, the universities set up several committees to manage the flow.[8] At Harvard, "1944–1945 was a year in which educators spoke more and more about 'the veteran problem.'"[9] In March 1946, nearly one freshman in two was a veteran, and administrators were concerned about a possible lack of space for non-veterans.[10] In October 1946, only 7 per cent of students in the Faculty of Law were not veterans.[11] Like many other Quebeckers, Trudeau had vigorously opposed the war and must have felt very much out of place.

---

[*]   Unless otherwise noted, in all quotations in this volume, italicized words are italicized or underlined in the original text.

His new professors bore little resemblance to the ones back home. At Harvard, most professors already were – or would become – leading experts on the world stage. They were often of European origin, some having fled the Nazi threat. The views they vigorously defended in one course were sometimes attacked, just as convincingly, in another. This dichotomy could undermine the self-assurance of students indoctrinated to believe in the monolithic nature of Truth and the Good.

How did Trudeau react to this new situation? The standard answer is that he felt liberated from the stifling climate that had oppressed him in Quebec, heaved a huge sigh of relief, and triumphantly posted a sign on his door announcing he was "Pierre Trudeau, Citizen of the World." Most biographers see in this gesture the birth of a new man. By proclaiming that the world was now his country, Trudeau distanced himself from his French-Canadian origins. Thus, for example, in 2005, André Burelle, a former speech writer to Prime Minister Trudeau, saw this name tag as a sign of "community uprooting." But, wrote Burelle, in wanting to "conceive of man without the community," Trudeau discovered that *"becoming a citizen of the world meant being a citizen of nowhere."*[12] The image of the newly liberated Trudeau, proclaiming that he rejected his French-Canadian identity, has been repeated so often that it has become a cliché.

This interpretation was plausible as long as the Trudeau of our first volume remained unknown. But now that it has been established that the young man who arrived at Harvard was a nationalist, corporatist, and revolutionary who had wanted only two years previously to make Quebec an independent country, this transformation seems a little drastic, to say the least. Which is why we ask two questions: Did the sign on the door really exist? And if so, how should it be interpreted? We were intrigued by the fact that the best-known biographies take for granted that the sign on the door really existed, without providing the source of their information. We tried to track it down and believe we have found it. In a rarely quoted book, *Trudeau Revealed by His Actions and Words,* David Somerville writes: "In Trudeau's second year, an associate from the Université de Montréal law faculty, Pierre Carignan, arrived at Harvard and looked him up. 'I went to his room in a student dormitory there. On the door was written 'Pierre Elliott Trudeau – Citizen of the World.'"[13] So it is thanks to Carignan, quoted by Somerville, that we know about the sign on the door. How long did it remain posted on the door? Nobody knows. Carignan's visit is nonetheless confirmed by Trudeau, who noted in his diary that the two met on Saturday, May 11, 1946, at 6 p.m.[14]

Hence the second question: Did Trudeau seek to renounce his French-Canadian origins? We shall let the facts speak for themselves. Throughout his stay, Trudeau continued to receive *Le Quartier Latin,* the Université de Montréal student newspaper, and he confided to Roger Rolland that he read it "with real pleasure."[15] He kept in touch with his old classmates. In another letter, he admitted: "I can say without hesitation that what has provided me with the most satisfaction during my stay at Harvard has been the letters of my friends. I know you so much better now, and I respect you so much more."[16] He also admitted often being homesick and longing to drop everything and return to Montreal. In almost all of his classes and in many lecture notes, he tried to apply his new knowledge to the French-Canadian situation. Whether in the form of lectures, articles, or notes, the many references to Quebec at Harvard continued in Paris, in London, and during his 1948–49 journey around the world. Throughout this book, we shall see that Trudeau considered himself first and foremost a French Canadian, and he was constantly concerned about the welfare of "his" people.

So why did Trudeau post the sign on his door? The answer does not lie in his papers, since he made no mention of it, but can be deduced from an analysis of the setting in which he found himself. October 24, 1945 marked the creation of the United Nations, at a time when Trudeau was studying at Harvard (its charter, however, was signed in June 1944). The world community was exhausted by war and now hoped that this new body would resolve conflicts through conciliation rather than by the force of arms. But from 1945 onwards, the deficiencies of the United Nations were already becoming obvious, and a movement of "world citizens" started up in many places. In 1948, nearly one million people declared themselves citizens of the world. The most famous case was that of the American pacifist and former Broadway actor Gary Davis. After serving in the United States Air Force during the Second World War, he publicly renounced his citizenship in Paris and proclaimed himself a "citizen of the world."

From 1945 onwards, many people were convinced that only a worldwide federation made up of "world citizens" could put an end to war. Other people found the idea very naïve. The controversy reached the spires of Harvard. For example, in a lecture at the Student Federalist

League, the 1939 Pulitzer Prize–winning literary critic Carl Clinton Van Doren promoted a "world government" that he considered more effective than the UN: "There will be no solution of the world problems until we abolish all national armies and navies," he said.[17] A letter to the editor in the Harvard students' newspaper, the *Crimson Daily,* declared: "Wars and rumors of wars can be eliminated by nothing short of an international state with *worldwide citizenship.** . . . Fans of world government do not claim it to be a panacea for all the world's ills. They do claim . . . [that] government can prevent world war."[18]

This issue appears in Trudeau's lecture notes. For example, the section entitled "The Crisis of Western Civilization" in *Dictatorship, Its History and Theory,* by Alfred Cobban,[19] inspired him to write: "*Excellent* section, drawing conclusions, etc." And he noted the sentence "We must find a force stronger than nationalism (sense of super-nationalism) since that is the source of evil." This feeling was reinforced when, during the session when Carignan visited him, he read *The New Belief in the Common Man,* by his professor Carl Joachim Friedrich, whom he greatly respected.[20] He noted that the author was confident that "the common man will become *a citizen of the world,* in a system where nations will merely be pressure groups."**

Others, such as his professor William Yandell Elliott, ridiculed this idea, which they characterized as naïve internationalism: "There are Cosmopolitans as well as Internationalists who demand a more inclusive ethical community than the nation-state. One may hear '*Citizens of the world,* unite!'*** preached with moral fervor, and a vehemence equalled only by the economic exhortation which has customarily been addressed to 'Workers of the World.'"[21] Of course, Elliott was referring ironically to the famous last sentence of Karl Marx's *Communist Manifesto:* "Workers of the world, unite!" However, as we shall see shortly, Trudeau had a hard time with Professor Elliott. In the margins of an essay that Elliott had severely criticized, Trudeau wrote "Pooh to you, Elliott!"; "Poor, stupid Elliott!" etc. Was the sign on his door intended as a snub to his professor? Did he find the idea of being a "Citizen of the World" all the more

---

*   Our italics.

**   Our italics.

***   Our italics.

attractive because Friedrich favoured it, and Elliott opposed it? Did he put the sign on his door after attending a debate on the subject? Perhaps . . . One fact remains: by proclaiming himself "Citizen of the World," Trudeau was simply taking part in the debates that were current at the time.

———◦———

Trudeau registered each year for two of the three annual sessions at Harvard: the winter session from November to February, and the spring session from February to June. Each session included four classes, two in economics and two in political science. Like most French Canadians at the time, economics was not his forte. And he knew it. Indeed, as we noted in our first volume, he enrolled at Harvard on the advice of André Laurendeau, in order to catch up in this discipline. On the other hand, his passion for political science went back to his years at Collège Brébeuf. In 1942, his plan for revolution entailed a careful reading of an impressive amount of literature in this field. Moreover, it will be remembered that in his application for admission to Harvard, he expressed a burning desire to become a statesman. He must have felt far better equipped to tackle courses in political science than in economics.

But curiously enough, he got nothing but A's in economics during his first two sessions, whereas he not only failed to get A's in political science, but actually received the lowest grade of his lifetime: a B. How can this paradox be explained? In fact, on arriving at Harvard, Trudeau was fully aware of his shortcomings in economics. Since he was convinced of the importance of this discipline for the future of Quebec, he applied himself with intelligence and diligence, making up for his lack of knowledge and obtaining brilliant results. After leaving Harvard, he would often describe his profession as economist. (Oddly, once he became prime minister, he was often criticized for his lack of interest in economics, which was attributed to his imperfect understanding of this discipline.) But political science was another matter. Not only did he not start from scratch but he believed he had already mastered the fundamentals of this discipline. His ideological beliefs seemed to rest on solid foundations. He felt threatened by new ideas. Hence his internal struggle.

Most biographies note the great influence exerted on Trudeau by eminent professors such as Brüning, Leontief, and Schumpeter. But how have the authors determined who contributed significantly to his intellectual development? Until recently, decisive influences were deduced from the relative fame of his professors. The documents tell another story. Consider the often-cited case of Heinrich Brüning.[22] This professor was chancellor of Germany from 1930 to 1932, before Franz von Papen and Adolf Hitler, and led a relentless struggle against Nazism. In May 1934, the utter rout of his political convictions had left him feeling harassed and exhausted, and risking his life, he crossed the border into the Netherlands, carrying a single suitcase. By 1937, he was teaching political science at Harvard. Since Trudeau mentioned Brüning in his memoirs, it is assumed that this most reliable eyewitness of Nazi barbarity taught our young student about this, based on first-hand experience. But was this really the case? In the fall of 1944, Trudeau attended Brüning's course "Topics in International Organization," in which the professor announced he would analyze a number of peace treaties. But Trudeau seems to have attended only the first class, taking just over a single page of notes.[23] This course does not appear on his official transcript. How can it then be assumed that Brüning had a significant influence on Trudeau?

Let us take the case of Wassily Leontief. Biographers agree on the importance of this eminent professor in our student's education. It is true that during his first year, 1944–45, Trudeau took two of Leontief's courses entitled "Economic Theory," in which he earned two A minuses. But some important facts should be remembered. When Trudeau took these courses, Leontief did not yet have the reputation he later enjoyed; he was not even a full professor, a status he acquired only in 1946. And it was not until 1948 – two years after Trudeau's departure – that Leontief founded and directed the Harvard Economic Research Project, a laboratory devoted to quantitative methods where he undertook his most important research work. As for his famous work *Input-Output Economics,* he did not publish it until 1966, twenty years after Trudeau's departure. This brilliant work earned him the Nobel Prize in Economics in 1973, by which time his former student was already prime minister of Canada! Was Trudeau impressed by this professor? We should let the facts speak for themselves. In 1993, when asked about his education at Harvard, he replied briefly: "I was learning about input-output from Leontief."[24] Whereas, in 1944–45, this theory could only be in its infancy. Trudeau's lecture notes cover political economy in general and do not indicate any particular interest in this professor or his theory. In the absence of more detailed memories, could Trudeau simply have repeated a comment that was easy to make about this economist?

There remains the case of Joseph Schumpeter. According to most authors, this illustrious representative of the so-called Austrian school of economics and a pioneer of "monetarism" left his mark on Trudeau. For example, John English considers him "the professor who left the most indelible impression."[25] Was this really the case? Trudeau took Schumpeter's course "Theory and Policy of Central Banking (European Experience)" and got an A. During the next session, he took "Topics in Economic Theory" with Gottfried Haberler, another great economist of the same Austrian school. This school was considered "right wing" and controversial because of its strict adherence to market principles, its criticism of various forms of state intervention, and the great importance it attached to monetary policy as an instrument of economic management. For all these reasons, it stood in opposition to Keynesian theory, which was considered mainstream economics at the time.

By the time Trudeau took Joseph Schumpeter's course, this professor had already published *Capitalism, Socialism and Democracy* in 1942, a work that became a classic. In his famous paradoxical expression, he argued that the strength of capitalism lies in a continual process of "creative destruction," which consists of replacing obsolete objects and modes of production with other, more technologically advanced objects and modes of production. It was on this process, he said, that the exceptional standard of living provided by the capitalist system depended, and the process flourished only in a social climate favouring free enterprise and the emergence of "entrepreneurs." However, Schumpeter believed that President Franklin D. Roosevelt's New Deal in the 1930s, with its slew of social security programs, stifled entrepreneurship and paved the way to socialism. Many colleagues at Harvard, by contrast, strongly supported these measures as well as the then very popular social theories of the British economist John Maynard Keynes, who advocated precisely this greater role for the state. Overall, Schumpeter was not appreciated by his colleagues, who considered him "idiosyncratic" and criticized his adherence to neoclassical theories, which were deemed outdated. Many colleagues disliked him on a personal level. Professor Carl Friedrich openly criticized him in class, accusing him, among other things, of using "loaded dice and name-calling."[26] Schumpeter did not have a reputation as a good teacher.[27] And on top of it all, he seemed to sympathize with the now tragic plight of the Germans. Unfortunately for him, the Allies were still traumatized by their own suffering and were not moved by the pain of the Germans. Indeed, the only colleague to make any approving comment about him was Gottfried Haberler, who belonged to the same school of thought.

The few notes that Trudeau took during this course relate to the economic crisis of the 1930s. Schumpeter attributed the crisis to the decline of entrepreneurship and the way capitalists had lost confidence in the economic system that had served them so well.[28] Nothing in his notes reveals any particular influence from this professor. Our suspicions are confirmed by his reaction to the two books he read as part of course work. He summarized a few ideas, all of them technical, from the first, *Central Banks,* by Sir Cecil Hermann Kisch and Winifred Adeline Elkin,[29] without comment. As for the second, *The Theory of Forward Exchange,* by Paul Einzig,[30] he wrote: "I skipped through a great part of it, but tried to grasp a few essentials here and there." It is hard to imagine how these facts and such unenthusiastic notes can lead to the conclusion that this professor had a decisive influence on him. It is true that Schumpeter and Gottfried Haberler were the ones to initiate Trudeau to monetarism. (This proves, as John English has rightly noted, that Keynes did not reign supreme at Harvard.) But it seems an exaggeration to attribute to Schumpeter any decisive influence. In a 1993 interview, Trudeau said: "I was learning about capitalism, socialism, and democracy from Schumpeter."[31] Once again, Trudeau was not particularly impressed by this professor, and remembering nothing in particular about him, simply enunciated the title of Schumpeter's famous book.

———◦———

Throughout his studies at Harvard, Trudeau had a total of five economics professors. If Leontief, Schumpeter, and Haberler do not appear to have made much of an impression on him, which professors did leave their mark? The other two, who are rarely mentioned: John Henry Williams and Alvin Harvey Hansen. We can start with Williams. At the time, this professor enjoyed an excellent reputation in American high finance. As an expert on banking systems and monetary policy, he served, among other things, as adviser to the Federal Reserve Bank of New York. During Trudeau's first year at Harvard, he took two sequential courses entitled "Principles of Money and Banking," in which he earned two A's. The first course covered the subject from a theoretical angle, while the second examined the monetary policies of the time. Although the course readings were difficult, Trudeau devoured them with great interest. He took ten pages of notes on *The Art of Central Banking*, by an economist well known at the time, Ralph G. Hawthry. This book had been published in 1932 and was still a classic. He was delighted to read it: "Excellent book of destructive and constructive criticism. Penetrating, thorough, clear, somewhat repetitious but not boringly so, well written and well divided. . . . Realistic not utopian in its proposed reforms."[32] Professor Williams was open-minded and did not expose his students to a single school of thought. On the contrary. He wanted to make them aware of the diversity of theoretical approaches, as is illustrated by the exam question chosen by Trudeau: "From your readings, select for discussion one or two main trends in recent monetary thinking, citing leading authors and showing points of agreement and difference."[33] Trudeau answered the question by comparing the perspectives of John Maynard Keynes, Friedrich Hayek, and Knut Wicksell.

John Maynard Keynes is widely regarded as one of the greatest economists of the twentieth century, and his ideas remain among the most prominent in the realm of economic and social thought. His theories were long central to the economic policies of industrialized countries. They fell into disfavour and were considered outdated by followers of the monetarist school, but since the economic crisis of 2008, they have enjoyed renewed popularity. Today, many statesmen advocate major state intervention, along Keynesian lines, to counteract the harmful effects of the economic cycles of the capitalist system. Friedrich Hayek, the second economist chosen by Trudeau for his exam question, favoured minimal state intervention in a handful of areas. He was likely the best-known member of the "Austrian school" and had a great reputation. Some consider him one of the twentieth century's most important economists and experts on political philosophy.[34] In 1974, his monetarist theory earned him the Nobel Prize in Economics. It should be noted that when Trudeau got a grounding in economics, Hayek was not yet as well known as Keynes. The third economist was

Knut Wicksell, from Sweden. Although less well known today than the first two, he was important in the late nineteenth and early twentieth centuries. He is acknowledged to have had a marked influence on Schumpeter, Hayek, Keynes, and many others. He called for active state intervention – a principle also defended by Keynes – while focusing on monetary policy – a principle defended by Hayek. What better example can be given than this exam question to illustrate the variety of economic perspectives to which Trudeau was exposed?

The young Trudeau had the opportunity of taking a second course with Williams, which he found even more fascinating than the first, since it focused entirely on the Bretton Woods Agreements.* It should be remembered that at the time, Germany had not yet surrendered. But its defeat was only a matter of time, and forty-four Allied nations met at Bretton Woods to draft the basis of the international post-war financial system, establish the foundation for global monetary policy, and promote the economic reconstruction of countries ravaged by war. Trudeau was thus at the heart of one of the most significant events of the twentieth century, and he studied it while it was taking place. In March 1945, when he wrote twelve pages of cramped notes, Congress was debating the ratification of these agreements. During class, Professor Williams described the meetings he attended in his capacity as adviser. He explained that the proposal submitted to Congress was a compromise between two plans: "The White Plan," named after Harry Dexter White, head of the U.S. delegation, and "the Keynes Plan," named after John Maynard Keynes, head of the British delegation. Williams mentioned a third proposal, submitted by Canada. But, he said, it was "hardly a plan, rather notes on the other two, especially on the White plan. But some good points." True to his principles, Keynes proposed to promote economic growth and "extend at the international level the banking principles that were applied at the national level."[35] He asked for "investment assistance, both on the medium and long term, for countries whose development required external support."[36] For his part, White wanted to abolish protectionism and insisted on liberalizing trade. Among other things, they disagreed about the currency to serve as the international

---

* These agreements were named after the town in New Hampshire where they were signed, July 22, 1944.

benchmark. Following negotiations, the United States guaranteed that the price of gold would be fixed at $35, which amounted to maintaining the gold standard. Consequently, the dollar became the new international currency. This system regulated world trade until 1971, when the U.S. government, under President Richard Nixon, decided to end the convertibility of dollars into gold, striking the final blow to the gold standard system.

Moreover, it was at Bretton Woods that the International Monetary Fund (IMF) and the World Bank came into being, and that the United States emerged as the leading world power, both economically and politically. It can be argued that the era of globalization dated from this meeting. It was the dawn of a new era. And ongoing debates that were so important for the future of humanity were the bread and butter of the courses offered to Trudeau and other students by a highly competent teacher. Besides, it was thanks to Williams that the young Trudeau discovered the nature of the struggle between countries before and after the war. He saw the direct relationship between economics and politics. With regard to theory, this renowned expert introduced him to the three major currents of monetary policy; with regard to practice, the professor enabled him to witness the application of theoretical principles in international politics. How many professors can offer as much to their students? How many students are fortunate enough to live through this kind of experience?

When recalling this period in 1993, Trudeau said: "There was a wonderful teacher called Williams."[37] The same year, when asked whether he had been aware of what was happening nearby in Bretton Woods, he replied: "Yes. Particularly from my professor in money and banking, Williams, who was an adviser at Bretton Woods, and who was acquainting us very much with the discussions going on there, which were to lay the groundwork for at least the 30 years to come, let's say from 1944 till Nixon, when they went off the gold standard. . . . As you know, these great institutions like the IMF [International Monetary Fund], the World Bank, and so on, they served immensely . . . in rebuilding Europe."[38] This is eloquent testimony, especially compared with the extremely rare remarks he made about Leontief and Schumpeter.

The other teacher Trudeau particularly appreciated, Alvin Harvey Hansen, was an ardent apostle of Keynesian theory. In *Full Recovery or Stagnation?*, published in 1938, he explored the ways to reduce the harmful effects of economic crises, while criticizing Hayek and the monetarist school. His course "Economic Analysis and Public Policy" was devoted mainly to the post-war period: Could economic expansion generated by the war industry last? How were veterans to be reintegrated into the economy? What should be done if a new crisis erupted? The ten pages of notes Trudeau took in class, and the twenty others he drafted on related readings, reflect both his assessment of the course and his great interest in the Keynesian theories it presented. In 1993, Trudeau still remembered this professor's ability: "I was learning about business cycles from Hansen, one of the great Keynes experts. Hansen was one of the experts of the business cycle."[39]

It was during this course that Trudeau devoted special attention to Keynes's masterwork, *The General Theory of Employment, Interest, and Money*, making extensive annotations in the margins of his personal copy.[40] According to Keynes, it was quite possible in a capitalist system to significantly reduce unemployment and better distribute wealth without resorting to socialist methods. Full employment called for policies that required "a broad extension of the traditional functions of government."[41] By contrast, it should be recalled that so-called classical theory – as defended by Hayek, Schumpeter, and Haberler – rejected any state intervention in the economy. But Keynes did not advocate unbridled intervention: "Apart from the necessity of central controls to bring about an adjustment between the propensity to consume and the inducement to invest there is no more reason to socialize the economic life than there was before."[42] Keynes added this clarification: "It is not the ownership of the instruments of production which is important for the State to assume."[43] Trudeau wrote in the margin, perhaps with some relief: "Not communist!" Keynes also argued that in spreading wealth more equitably, both nationally and internationally, "the new system might be more favourable to peace than the old has been."[44]

Clearly, the ideas developed by Keynes appealed strongly to the young Trudeau, who was passionately concerned about social justice and world peace. It should be noted that Keynes set his system within a capitalist, democratic, and liberal society. Although Trudeau was still neither a liberal nor a democrat, much less a proponent of capitalism, he found in Keynes a thinker whose ideals he shared and who proposed measures to improve the social order that were far superior to the corporatist wishful thinking he had been taught by professors in Quebec. In Paris, on March 18, 1947, he gave a presentation on unemployment as part of his studies at the Institut d'Études Politiques de Paris (commonly known as "Sciences Po"). He relied mainly on the theories of Keynes and noted in his diary, perhaps with a touch of pride, the word "Success."[45] On arriving at Harvard, Trudeau had noted with astonishment how little he knew about economics, but he left Harvard with an excellent grounding in this field. In 2005, the famous economist John Kenneth Galbraith wrote about him: "Of all the politicians I have encountered over a lifetime (and there have been many), there have been few – if any – economically more perceptive and given to affirmative policy than Pierre Trudeau."[46]

So much for the courses in economics. As we said earlier, when it came to political science, he faced challenges of a whole other order. Trudeau was confident that he knew a lot, and he was sure that his positions were based on sound principles. But his courses and readings flew in the face of what he held to be true. The views he believed he was defending rigorously, and which had earned him great admiration in Quebec, were no longer tenable. He felt destabilized and profoundly shaken but decided to seek the truth by systematically examining the philosophical, political, and moral principles that he had thought were self-evident.

The four first-year courses he took were taught by greatly accomplished professors: Charles Howard McIlwain, Merle Fainsod, Herman Finer, and William Yandell Elliott. We can start with Charles Howard McIlwain, who held a prestigious chair at Harvard and was also a great defender of liberal democracy. In 1940, even before the United States had entered the war, he had strongly denounced the Nazi and fascist threat in *Constitutionalism Ancient and Modern:* "Never in recorded history . . . has the individual been in greater danger from government than now."[47] In his course on the history of political ideas in the sixteenth century, he examined, among other things, the theory of divine right monarchy. Trudeau discovered, perhaps with some surprise, the bitter struggle waged by the papacy against monarchy, not so much in order to save souls as to control power. He wrote: "The Theory of Divine Right of Kings in England is of anti-papal origin. . . . Jesuits are regarded as par excellence the teachers of the doctrine of resistance [to the divine right of kings doctrine] because of their ardent support of papal claims. . . . The Divine Right of Kings was necessary to the political side of the Reformation . . . and it simply died when . . . politics were freed from theology."[48] Like his mentors, Trudeau had wanted to establish a theocratic regime in Quebec, but he now learned that the close relationship between Church and State affected the well-being of society. In eighteen pages of notes, he observed that the subordination of political power to ecclesiastical power was not conducive to tolerance. This idea led him to ask himself troubling questions. For example, asked McIlwain: What authority prevails, the authority of the believer or of the citizen? To this question, the professor explained, Catholics and Protestants gave different answers, reflecting the divisions within Christianity. Young Trudeau must have been puzzled by this issue. Was it possible that the duties of a good citizen could come into conflict with those of a good Catholic? McIlwain made a strong impression, as Trudeau noted in 1993: "And we had a great teacher, McIlwain, who was a professor of political history and I began to understand the roots of liberalism in a political sense."[49]

Merle Fainsod and Herman Finer jointly offered courses called "Dictatorship and Bureaucracy" and "Comparative Government," which compared democratic and totalitarian political systems. Originally from Romania, Finer had long devoted his research to the study of government and public administration in European countries. He was a great defender of "Constitutionalism."* His greatest and most monumental work was the 1,556-page, two-volume *The Theory and Practice of Modern Government*. This work was first published in 1932 and went through many editions until the late 1960s. Two ideas highlighted by Trudeau denote a change of perspective on his part. The first, written in French, reveals a budding democrat: "Why shout out against democracy in Quebec? It is

---

* In the Anglo-American tradition, "constitutionalism" is synonymous with liberal democracy.

the only system that allows us to have a different opinion from the government. We should use this freedom to choose better governments." The second idea shows he was awakening to the benefits of liberal democracy: "Constitutionalism is a luxury; right; but now that we own it don't spoil it."[50] These ideas pursued their course in Trudeau's mind. In 1962, he told Peter Gzowski that his political philosophy was largely derived from "Constitutionalism."[51]

Professor Fainsod, a notable expert on the Soviet Union, was adviser to President Roosevelt, first in 1936, then from 1941 to 1943. His major work, *How Russia Is Ruled,* became an indispensable reference in the field and underwent numerous editions after its initial publication in 1953.[52] In his lectures, Fainsod examined the rise of the nation-state, nationalism, and new forms of dictatorship. He focused on socialism, but particularly on the Bolshevik revolution and the dictatorship of the proletariat: these latter two subjects filled up half of Trudeau's twenty-nine pages of notes. Fainsod not only familiarized his students with totalitarian regimes, he made them think about the political dimension of nationalism and got them to read, among others, Alfred Cobban's 1939 work *Dictatorship, Its History and Theory.* Trudeau noted this was an "essay in political science showing how the evolution of political ideas especially since the xviith Century led logically up to the modern political world where dictatorship flourishes. It is a keen and logical analysis, with a meritorious effort to show the continuity that leads from one political trend to another."[53] In this book, Cobban opposed the Marxist view, according to which the French Revolution was characterized by the conquest of political power by the bourgeoisie. For him, the French Revolution marked instead the advent of a new ideology, nationalism, and of its use for political purposes. This nationalism, developed first of all by French revolutionaries, had become, over time, the ideological tool of choice for totalitarian regimes. Trudeau noted for the first time the possibility of a link between nationalism and totalitarianism: "The modern state has progressed from divine right of kings to the idea of popular sovereignty, from that to nationalism and from nationalism to totalitarianism."[54] He certainly found these ideas very interesting, but he remained convinced of the superiority of the French tradition: "There are a number of tedious repetitions and re-repetitions. But this seems to be the English way. . . ."

Fainsod shared Cobban's view and said Robespierre's rallying cry "Despotism of liberty against tyranny"[55] paved the way for the Jacobin dictatorship. Safeguarding the nation was the revolution's primary objective, and it justified all sacrifices. Nationalism took the place of Catholicism. And the Jacobins were new priests upholding a new Truth, who felt the duty to "spread its new doctrine with the sword." From this sprang an aggressive nationalism based on a messianic ideal. The new dictators would not fail to appreciate the power of this new ideological tool. They would use it to manipulate public opinion. The French Revolution had failed, said Fainsod, but had nonetheless exerted a profound influence. Whereas dictatorships before the Revolution had imposed the will of a single man, modern dictatorships since then claimed to act on behalf of a collective whole, whether the nation or an exploited class. Modern dictatorships alleged that their plan reflected the popular will and tried to subordinate all human activity to the control of a single political party. Never in history, maintained the professor, not even in absolute monarchies, had such an objective been sought. Hence the designation of "totalitarian" regimes. Fainsod illustrated this phenomenon by explaining the evolution of the Soviet Union. Trudeau listened carefully, took careful note of the leading ideas, and saw nationalism with new eyes.

Last but not least: "Contemporary Political Theory" was offered by William Yandell Elliott, who taught political science at Harvard for over forty years and served as adviser to several presidents of the United States until the 1970s. Like the other professors already mentioned, Elliott (1896–1979) devoted his main writings to "Constitutionalism." This is the last course we are mentioning, since it was in this course that Trudeau wrote his "Major Term Paper," getting a B, and also revealed his true state of mind.

This course was mainly based on Elliott's 1928 major work, *The Pragmatic Revolt in Politics: Syndicalism, Fascism, and the Constitutional State*. In this book, Elliott stood in radical opposition to the philosophers of the "pragmatic revolt in politics," whom he said treated society like a machine whose operations could be studied scientifically. He accused them, among other things, of rejecting any universal moral standard. Elliott particularly criticized John Dewey, a professor at Columbia University: "Mr. Dewey . . . has no norms, and [he] claims that none are needed except those which arise as facts out of experience."⁵⁶ He maintained that not everything is derived from experience: universal norms do exist. He also defended the nation-state: "The existence of the state is the necessary condition of moral freedom for the individual, because without it he is delivered over to the rule of force."⁵⁷

One would have thought that Trudeau would sympathize with Elliott's views. To start with, both accepted the principle of universal moral norms. Moreover, they both valued the nation-state. It will be remembered that in 1942, Trudeau was convinced that only an independent Quebec could guarantee the development of "human excellence of the community" and could be the "guardian of freedoms."⁵⁸ And yet, he had run-ins with his professor. How can this be explained? It is not impossible that a personality conflict was involved. However, there is no doubt that deep divisions separated professor and student. For example, both agreed on the importance of the nation-state, whereas for Elliott, only the "Constitutional State" – that is to say, a liberal and democratic society – ensured individual well-being. For Trudeau, on the other hand, only an authoritarian corporatist regime, led by a benevolent leader and nurtured by the moral values of the Church, could achieve this goal. A head-on collision was about to take place in the "Major Term Paper" called "A Theory of Political Violence."

Trudeau's fifty-nine-page typescript, the thirty pages of notes he took while researching the term paper, the corrections and comments of the professor, and Trudeau's own reactions to these comments provide unique insights into his state of mind during his first year at Harvard.⁵⁹ Moreover, additional insights are contained in the comments written in French by Louis Hartz, a doctoral student, the son of Russian immigrants who was the same age as Trudeau and had been Teaching Fellow at Harvard since his return in 1942 from a one-year trip around the world. (Could this trip have inspired Trudeau to make his own journey in 1948–49?) Hartz went on to have a brilliant career as a political scientist. Among his writings, *The Liberal Tradition in America,* published in 1955, brought him several major awards and remains a classic to this day.⁶⁰ Trudeau was likely devastated by the grade he got and asked Hartz to read the term paper that had already been annotated by Elliott and provide his own comments.

Evidently Trudeau had thrown himself heart and soul into this term paper, which was written in English, a language he spoke fluently but did not write well and in which he had never studied before. He had carefully read a good thirty books and articles, drawing heavily on his previous readings and taking detailed notes. He defined the criteria he had used to develop his bibliography in an awkward style, which suggested frequent recourse to a dictionary: "To a paper of this sort, tending to co-ordinate in a new and personal scheme data and ideas of unlimited scope, can only be appended a bibliography which is absurdly long or absurdly short. I tried to solve the dilemma by marking with an asterisk those works which might have had a direct influence in the engendering of some of my ideas." The works he had marked with an asterisk deserve closer attention. John Dewey, Elliott's arch-enemy, got an asterisk for his article "Force and Coercion."[61] In addition, Trudeau deigned to include only one of his professor's many works in the bibliography – *The Pragmatic Revolt in Politics* – just one work by the very professor who was grading his term paper. This choice was inevitable, since the course was based on this book. But Trudeau did not stoop to grant it an asterisk. Was this a provocation, a challenge, or a kind of intellectual frankness one does not often find in students?

Interestingly, Trudeau's bibliography included most of the books he had read in 1942 with his friend Jean-Baptiste Boulanger, as part of their revolutionary activity.[62] Also revisited were Jacques Maritain, André Tardieu, Robert Brasillach, Jean and Jérôme Tharaud, George Sorel, Robert Hunter, Curzio Malaparte, Robert Aron and Arnaud Dandieu, Leo Trotsky, Charles Maurras, Plato, Aristotle, and Jean-Jacques Rousseau, among others. These readings reminded him, perhaps with some nostalgia, of their revolutionary manifesto and he repeated almost word for word the manifesto's language: "National Revolution: permanent struggle that strives for the excellence of the community. The 'good' is situated in time: one must strive for it without ceasing. A struggle limited by the end it seeks, of human excellence."

Since Trudeau's term paper purported to use John Dewey's "scientific method," it is perhaps useful to summarize some important aspects of the pragmatist philosophy. John Dewey (1859–1952) drew inspiration from Darwin's theory of the evolution of species and maintained that thought is nothing other than the product of the evolution of a human function whose purpose is individual survival and community welfare. Philosophically, this "instrumental" interpretation of reason formed the crux of the disagreement between Elliott and Dewey. According to Dewey, philosophy should give up the search for absolute Reality and Truth – two fundamentals of the Western philosophical tradition – in order to study the concrete problems of social life: "Philosophy recovers itself when it ceases to be a device dealing with the problems of philosophers and becomes a method, cultivated by philosophers, for dealing with the problems of men."[63] In fact, Dewey argued, there is no "true" reality beyond that which is. The same holds for the concept of truth: "Truth *denotes* verified beliefs . . . which were the outcome of the best technique of inquiry available in some particular field."[64] For this reason, truth evolves with the progress of our knowledge. This viewpoint must have surprised Trudeau, whose whole education emphasized the permanence of the True and the Good.

Trudeau was fascinated by Dewey's thesis that it is possible to undertake a "scientific" analysis of political concepts. He applied Dewey's method to compare political concepts that seemed closely related: violence, power, force, coercion, obligation, etc. "In physics," he wrote, "the mass is an inert body. It has no movement of its own; but when subjected to some force or power, it will follow the direction represented by the impelling vector." Perfect reasoning for the inanimate world. But Trudeau applied it to politics: "Likewise in Politics, the mass of the people is an inert body with no will of its own. It obeys whatever force or power may be applied to it." This logic, defended by Maurras and Trudeau's other mentors, such as Abbé Groulx, was opposed to a fundamental principle of liberal thought, namely that the people are made up of autonomous individuals, who express their will within a political system governed by democratic laws. Trudeau was using Dewey's pragmatist method to justify the view he had defended in 1942. The language was new, but the ideas were old. In fact, for Dewey, "democracy is not an alternative to other principles of associated life. It is the idea of community life itself."[65] Trudeau did not understand that Dewey's reasoning was valid only in a democratic and liberal setting, but praised the whole article, which he found "short but very enlightening."

Trudeau went on to draw a distinction between force and violence. To the question "When does force turn into violence?," Dewey replies unequivocally: "Energy becomes violence when it defeats or frustrates purpose instead of executing or realizing it."[66] Violence is simply the misuse of force. Trudeau was won over by what he saw as a scientifically rigorous distinction between these two concepts: "This definition, terrible though it may be in its political implications, I accept implicitly because of its physical soundness." Which led him to the following conclusion: "Thus terrorism, though it constitutes violence in regard to the life of the person being assassinated, does not constitute political violence if it is *absolutely* needed to attain the accepted political end of a given nation." In other words, he believed that for the sake of the community one could condone the assassination of one or more individuals.

Pursuing his enquiry on the misuse of force, Trudeau compared terrorism and insurgency, providing a honeyed definition of terrorism: "Activity consisting in destroying the most harmful person in the government . . . in punishing the perpetrators of the notable cases of violence and arbitrariness on the part of government and the administration."[67] This led him to conclude that, "if assassinating the headman had the same effect as insurging against the whole ruling clique, then the use of insurrection would constitute violence." In other words, when terrorism is more effective than insurrection, then it is insurrection, not terrorism, that constitutes an act of violence.

Trudeau openly demonstrated his admiration for Maurras, whose work, *Si le coup de force est possible,* got an asterisk in the bibliography. He wrote: "Nationalism will fight and win many more battles. At the beginning of the xxth Century, Charles Maurras gave it a new impulse, from which a great number of nationalist governments sprang." In the margin, Elliott noted, with obvious irony: "Alone and unaided? What a man!" Stung to the quick, Trudeau retorted, "A better one than you, wy." If words could kill. . . . Trudeau had not yet shaken off his old values, and shortly later in the term paper he denounced the corruption inherent in democratic regimes: "Our godly democracies . . . have their own private tools for corrupting politics: Graft, the bribery of voters, the corrupting of officials." Farther on, he wrote: "If I were a democrat . . ." Clearly, he had not become one yet. In the margin, he added this thought: "Probably the reason I got a B." He felt that Elliott, as a supporter of the "Constitutional State," simply did not accept his criticism of democracy.

Trudeau agreed with Dewey that the exercise of political power ultimately requires the use of force. This raises an important question:
When is the use of force morally acceptable? To Trudeau, citing Dewey,
the answer was simple: "An immoral use of force is a stupid use." He
provided an example: "There is as much violence in using a sledge-ham-
mer to sink a three-inch nail, as in using a violin to do the job." Therefore,
he said, in a good political system, "sovereigns are given exactly enough
authority to govern well, but no more." For their part, the governed
agreed to obey, provided they were well governed. Quoting Charles
Maurras in French, he showed that he wasn't yet opposed to an autocratic regime: "Since we are bound to be governed, then it is only just
that we be governed properly: What should it matter if we obey one individual, a hundred or a thousand?"

What power must a good government have? Trudeau wrote that in
an ideal state the government "could only apply what little coercion is
absolutely needed for the total good." But how could one know whether
coercion was excessive? To Trudeau, only two questions needed to be
asked: Was the chosen action effective? Was it essential for achieving
the objectives being sought? He developed his point of view by offering
a few examples. Only one need be mentioned here: "Let us suppose for
instance, that the sovereign makes a law that every thief shall be skinned
alive. Then that law would be a violent one, for it clearly exceeds the
measure of coercion required." This case is uncontroversial: it is easy to
agree on the excessive severity of the punishment. But if Trudeau refused
to flay the thief alive, would he accept that the thief's hand be cut off,
a punishment meted out in some societies? What norm should be applied
to determine whether a punishment is proportionate to the crime? This
question was left hanging.

On several occasions, Louis Hartz detected ambiguity in Trudeau's
thinking about the relationship between the individual and society and
asked for clarifications in the margin: "But say whether government can
subject the individual to the community: yes or no?" Elsewhere he found
that the reasoning stood up only "if one accepts the concept of 'common
good' superior to the individual good." Hartz was right: in this essay
Trudeau actually gave primacy to the collectivity. Yet in 1991, Stephen
Clarkson and Christina McCall wrote: "According to Louis Hartz, . . .
Pierre was captivated by the basic premises of liberal political theory.

The discovery that an impressive tradition of Western thought supported his instinctive and passionate individualism was tremendously exciting to this intellectual refugee from collectivist Quebec."[68] At the time, Clarkson and McCall had no reason to doubt the words of Hartz, who had died by then. This view corresponds to the image we all have of Trudeau. However, it goes against everything we have seen during his first year at Harvard.

Trudeau stated three criteria for the implementation of his theory of political violence. First, "The method shall be chosen that is best apportioned to the desired end." Is lying, cheating, or acting unlawfully justified if these means are suitable for the achievement of objectives? Absolutely, Trudeau replied: "In my opinion, the best trick of all is to succeed in licking the opponent at his own game: for cheating is not wicked when the game is to cheat. A little more thought should be given to the taking of power by insidious infiltration or by indirect means." It is no wonder that Louis Hartz exclaimed, probably in disbelief: "This boy is quite the Machiavellian. . . ." What mattered to Trudeau was effectiveness. This made him now doubt whether revolution was the best solution for Quebec. French Canadians, he said, would work miracles if they relied more on their economic and technical capacity: "Surely, revolution is a handy tool to show through one's pocket, but a tool like the cooperative movement can be used even out in the open." In other words, Trudeau said no to revolution, but not to the *threat* of revolution (as a practical weapon that would be kept in one's pocket) since this remained a good means for advancing the cause of French Canadians. This brings to mind the "knife to the throat" strategy advocated by the political scientist Léon Dion.* Or to similar threats made by the separatist Parti Québécois.

So much for the first criterion: effectiveness. Now the second one: "That method shall be applied implacably" and, thirdly, "That method shall be subject to perfect control." Clearly, no moral imperative entered the equation. Trudeau explained: "If a fight is unavoidable, strike hard

---

* Léon Dion (1922–1997), the well-known Quebec political scientist, was adviser to Quebec politicians of all stripes. In 1990, he was disappointed by the failure of the so-called Meech Lake constitutional accord and concluded that the only way to negotiate with English Canada was by holding "a knife to its throat."

and first. If a race has been singled out as the only plausible one in the circumstances, it is sheer stupidity to begin belly-aching over its illegality. The superstitious fear of illegality has made more than one great man tremble and spoiled his aim." Accordingly, once the decision was taken, a good leader should not be burdened by ethics or legality. He should strike hard when necessary.

This led Trudeau to raise an ethical issue: "Is that to say that I believe truth to be relative? And that the strongest and most cunning force is always the most moral one? It would well seem so if I ended my paper here. I therefore urge you to recall to mind that the object of my paper was to treat of Politics, not of Ethics. I don't, by a long shot, maintain that they are independent fields; as a matter of fact I strongly believe that Politics should be subordinated to ethics, but that is not what I tried to speak on." He thus asserted unequivocally that he believed political action should comply with ethical choices. But he also knew that political compromises were inevitable, and the future unfathomable. So, he asked, what principles should guide the political actor who did not know in advance whether his decisions would have the desired effect, "since life will not wait for final solutions?"

His answer: "I can only suggest, in bringing this paper to an end, that [the statesman] must hierarchize values according to certain fundamentals inherent in human nature; and when confronted with a concrete political gesture, he can judge it accordingly to its place in the hierarchy." Once these values were stated, the political actor should then prioritize his goals. He would draw up a list of the means at his disposal. Finally, having chosen the most effective means, he would apply them ruthlessly. After that, he could act with a completely clear conscience since he was "as sure as [was] humanly possible . . . that his acts [would] be absolutely non-violent."

But Professor Elliott was still not satisfied. He wanted Trudeau to identify the core values he was referring to. He asked in the margin: "And what are they? Will any do?" Elliott did not seem to have noticed the argument that Trudeau advanced: "It is certain that there won't be a unanimous opinion as to what fundamentals are inherent in human nature; and consequently, gains will be weighed differently by different individuals." Although Trudeau was convinced of the existence of fundamental values, he had awakened to the fact that they were defined differently by different people and that a single moral code could therefore not apply. Where the political actor was concerned, Trudeau concluded that ultimately he was left to himself and should act according to his conscience: "Let every man break his bonds and free the gospel he has to teach. Truth fears no test." And, quoting the Bible he knew so well, he concluded his term paper with the words "And by their fruit ye shall know them."

Circumstances required Trudeau to play the role of the hypothetical political actor of his essay, but in real life. During the October Crisis of 1970, James Cross and Pierre Laporte were kidnapped by members of the Front de Libération du Québec (FLQ), a crowd of three thousand people demonstrated in the streets of Montreal chanting slogans supporting this illegal organization, prominent Quebec personalities such as René Lévesque and Claude Ryan called on the government to give in to terrorist demands, and fear spread through the population. Prime Minister Trudeau gave a brief interview to the CBC correspondent Tim Ralfe. When asked how far he would go in the use of force, he famously replied, "Just watch me." And this reply has repeatedly been cited as proof of his arrogance and contempt for democracy. We share the view of Nino Ricci, in his book *Extraordinary Canadians: Pierre Elliott Trudeau,* that "Just watch me" "reads completely differently when seen in its entirety than it does in the provocative clip that it got reduced to by most of the media."[69]

Actually, Tim Ralfe's question corresponded precisely to the question Trudeau raised in his theory of political violence, namely, what criteria should a person holding political power (namely, himself) use, to act appropriately "since life won't wait for final answers." Following the logic developed in his essay at Harvard, he first identified his core values: respect for the rule of law, and protection of citizens. He told Ralfe, "There's a lot of bleeding hearts around who just do not like to see people with helmets and guns. All I can say is go on and bleed. *It's more important to keep law and order in this society* than to be worried about weak-kneed people who don't like the looks of . . ."* (Trudeau did not finish his sentence). Second, he had to take stock of the means leading to his goal. When he spoke to Ralfe, this is what he was working on in Cabinet. Then, third, he would choose the most effective means to succeed and apply

---

* Our italics.

them ruthlessly. But these means depended on the circumstances, namely subsequent actions taken by the FLQ, the reaction of the population, the demands of the premier of Quebec and the mayor of Montreal, and other factors. How far would he go? He did not know. One has only to listen to the phrase "Just watch me" to realize that the tone of this reply implied neither a challenge nor a threat. When Trudeau gave this impromptu interview, he really did not know how far he would have to go. As a result, "Just watch me" amounted to "Watch me closely, and you will see." All he could say was that he would use whatever means he deemed the most effective depending on the context, and he would apply these means ruthlessly. And like his hypothetical political actor, he would have a clear conscience, since he would be as sure as he could that he was acting appropriately. One can, of course, criticize the means he chose to resolve this crisis, but not the rigour of his logic.

All the effort Trudeau devoted to this essay resulted in a B that he attributed to an ideological conflict. Was that really the case? Could a personality conflict have been involved? Could Elliott have been annoyed by the fact that Trudeau, unlike other students, had not made the slightest concession in his paper to please his professor, as shown, for example, by the way he assigned asterisks in the bibliography? Or was the problem instead, as Elliott noted, that the essay "misses the systematic analysis and application of concept"? We prefer to let readers draw their own conclusions. Whether the grade was deserved or not, this essay signals a marked shift in Trudeau's thought. Although he was still committed to many of his old beliefs, he had begun to assimilate one of the fundamental principles of liberal thought: the search for means of action that took into account the plurality of conceptions of good and truth.

———— ··· ————

At the end of his first year, Trudeau's political views had not yet undergone much profound change, but significant progress can be noted. Although he still defended corporatism and authoritarianism, he began to see the benefits of "Constitutionalism" – to understand the value of the separation of Church and State, to awaken to the dangers of nationalism, and to apply pragmatism in politics. But above all, he began to open up to the political consequences of the plurality of moral systems.

He was overcome by doubt. Were French Canadians on the wrong track altogether?

On April 13, 1945, he wrote to Roger Rolland: "The problem is that we French Canadians have no doctrine, that is to say, no common treasure of culture on which to draw, by which to reassure ourselves and in which to reimmerse ourselves. This is the essential point, and it is particularly to this that we must devote our human energies. This grounding is what we lack most: there is no soil in which our tree can take root, and we are at the mercy of all the winds that blow." He realized that French Canadians were easily indoctrinated because they could draw on no tradition of rigorous thought, the way the English-speaking peoples could and whose qualities he was beginning to appreciate. Trudeau provided a brief sketch of his critique of Quebec culture in this letter, taking it up and eventually developing it further in many of his writings. This critique reached a sort of climax in 1956, in his monumental introduction to the collective work on the asbestos strike of 1949.[70] The hundred pages he wrote, under the title "The Province of Quebec at the Time of the Strike," was like shock treatment and led to a passionate outburst of reactions. We shall discuss it in due course.

⎯⎯●⎯⎯

Doubt also overcame him where the war was concerned. Had he been wrong to oppose it? With the massive presence on campus of veterans, the study of totalitarian regimes as part of his course work, he couldn't avoid the question. Moreover, in this extremely well-informed environment, like everyone else around him, he must have been following the major events then shaking the world. Let us mention a few. From February 4 to 11, 1945, Churchill, Roosevelt, and Stalin met at Yalta to develop a common strategy for the post-war period. On February 6, in France, Robert Brasillach, an author admired by Trudeau and much of the French-Canadian intelligentsia, was executed for collaboration. On February 13, the Royal Air Force bombed the city of Dresden, reducing it to a heap of rubble. On February 23, Americans raised the flag on Iwo Jima, Japan. On April 16, Allied forces liberated their first concentration camp at Buchenwald. On April 28, Mussolini, the leader of Fascist Italy, was executed along with his mistress, Clara Petacci. In a further humiliating gesture, their corpses were then strung up by their feet in a public square in Milan. And so ended the life of *Il Duce* – the man who had for so long nourished the fantasies of Quebec's clerical-nationalist elite! (Trudeau's reaction is not known. We do know, however, that he clipped and set aside a few newspaper articles on the subject.) On May 2, the Red Army entered Berlin. On May 4, Canadian troops liberated the Netherlands.[71] On May 7, Germany surrendered unconditionally. The top leaders of a totalitarian regime that had once been considered invincible now committed suicide: between April 30 and May 23, Adolf Hitler, *der Führer,* and Heinrich Himmler, head of the SS and Gestapo, killed themselves. After murdering their six children, the propaganda minister, Joseph Goebbels, and his wife took their own lives. On August 6 and 9, 1945, by order of President Truman, atomic bombs sowed horror and devastation on Hiroshima and Nagasaki.

One could easily extend the list of successive disasters that had profoundly shaken the planet since Trudeau arrived at Harvard. He was well informed and was now convinced that the Allied struggle was legitimate. Troubled by the position he had defended with such zeal in Quebec, he wrote to Roger Rolland on April 13, 1945: "One aspect of my thinking revolved around the question of whether I did the right thing in abstaining from this war. My reason approves a thousand times, but my heart does not give me peace. And I wonder whether we are always right to follow reason. And yet . . . And yet . . ."[72] Yet Trudeau remained convinced that his opposition to conscription had been dictated by reason. This did not efface his guilt over not having fought alongside the Allies against barbarism.

This confusion was also evident in a letter addressed to Thérèse Gouin. He wondered whether he had been right to follow his conscience about the war. Besides, he added, was the true conscience rational, or was it intuitive instead?[73] He judged his own past activities harshly and wondered if the great regret of his life would be that he had never turned his eyes away from works of dubious quality, while the greatest cataclysm of all time raged just ten hours away from his desk. Since Thérèse did not even understand what he meant by "the greatest cataclysm of all time," she asked for an explanation. With hindsight, such ignorance seems bewildering. But we should remember that his girlfriend was back in Quebec. In the Quebec setting, which was Trudeau's own context till his departure for Harvard, the disasters of war were shrouded in heavy silence. On May 25, 1945, Trudeau replied dryly: "P.S. The cataclysm? It was the war, the war, the WAR!"[74] The way he repeated the word "war" and wrote it in block capitals gave the impression that he wanted to scream. The naïveté of Thérèse reminded him of his own blindness. No wonder he was irritated.

Would Trudeau find an answer to his questions? Not during his first year at Harvard. So, let us follow him during his second year. We shall focus particularly on the readings that marked him the most strongly and on the two courses he took with a recognized expert on totalitarianism and constitutionalism, Professor Carl Friedrich. This German-born author of an impressive number of scholarly works had been enjoying a brilliant career at Harvard since the 1930s. Friedrich was an excellent and politically committed teacher who actively helped Jewish professors, journalists, and other intellectuals flee Nazi Germany and other fascist countries. We shall begin with his courses.

In "Planning – Theory, Organization, Method," Trudeau deepened his knowledge of totalitarian regimes.[75] Friedrich was very critical of Nazi Germany and the Soviet Union, which he considered as two variants of totalitarianism. He abhorred the way they manipulated people's minds, on the pretext that human beings could not act appropriately of their own accord. For him, this sort of manipulation was a product of the totalitarian mind. For this reason he believed that "Freud and [the] psychoanalytic school are very near to totalitarianism. [They suppose that] people do not know what they want." Trudeau discovered that totalitarianism could reach beyond the political framework. Note that while he was becoming familiar with these aspects of totalitarianism, his girlfriend, Thérèse Gouin, was studying psychology at the Université de Montréal. Freud occupied a prominent place in her studies. We shall come to understand the importance of this detail in the next chapter.

The second course offered by Carl Friedrich, "Modern Political Thought," examined the fledgling United Nations Charter, which entered into force on October 24, 1945. No better expert could have been chosen to address this subject. Friedrich's reputation in this area was such that after the war, he participated in the drafting of the constitution of Germany as well as of the new state of Israel. So for the second time since

Trudeau had settled at Harvard, he took a course rooted in contemporary news events and given by a leading expert in the field. Friedrich
examined the UN Charter, article by article, in the light of conditions that
Immanuel Kant had considered indispensable for establishing lasting
world peace. He recalled, for example, that according to article 1 of
Kant's *Project of Perpetual Peace*, no secret treaty of peace could be held
valid in which there was tacitly reserved matter for a future war. Now,
he said, "in the meeting of foreign ministers these days, no agreement
was reached because each asked himself the question: 'How will this
affect my ability in launching a war?'" The signatories therefore did not
comply with article 1. Friedrich then analyzed Kant's "first definitive
article," stating that "you cannot have parties to a treaty of peace if they
have not constitutional government," that is to say, a government based
on the rule of law. Whereas, Friedrich noted, referring to Soviet-type
regimes, the Charter accepted such countries. After careful analysis, the
professor concluded that the UN Charter did not encourage the establishment of world government as advocated by Kant. Could there be a more
fascinating course for someone dreaming of peace? A course more rooted
in current events? Or linking theory and practice more brilliantly?

We shall now examine Trudeau's course readings. During his second
year, they helped deepen his reflection on the issues that preoccupied
him: the war, for example. We have just seen that his conscience was
troubled once he discovered what was really at stake in the war. How
could he resolve the matter? Well, by searching in his readings for arguments helping him understand whether it was right or wrong to have
opposed conscription. Some scattered notes without complete references
attest to his desire to pursue the truth. Referring to Friedrich, he noted:
"Even if the declaration of war is the prerogative of the executive
(Friedrich, p. 549), the executive is the magistrate of the people. Conscription: violation of individual rights."[76] Elsewhere, he noted that,
according to Harold Laski, his future professor at the London School of
Economics, the citizen had a moral duty to oppose the war and those
who obeyed their government simply because it had declared war ceased
to be human. He concluded: "The question is not whether it was right
or wrong for French Canadians; the question was that they had this
right (Lapointe, etc.) and that [the federal government] violated this,
replacing legality by force. So obedience is no longer a duty."

Now that he had found a valid argument in the works of authors he respected, he convinced himself once and for all that French Canadians had been tricked by their governments and were therefore right to oppose conscription. This was, and remained for him, the voice of reason. He would never acknowledge error or guilt in this respect. And like many French Canadians from Quebec, he would, whenever possible, avoid any discussion of this subject.

Evidence of this position, which he now considered firmly established, is found in his marginal reactions to *The British Commonwealth at War,* by William Yandell Elliott, which he read in February 1946. He examined with particular interest Chapters 5 and 6 on Canada. Where Ernest Lapointe's promise was concerned – that there would be no conscription – he wrote in the margin that this promise had been betrayed. On the next page, reacting to the Liberal statement that members of that party would all resign if the pro-conscription premier of Quebec, Maurice Duplessis, were re-elected, he interjected: "Blackmail!" Elsewhere, he wrote, clearly in anger: "Quebec shut up!"

Another aspect of Trudeau's attitude toward the war can be deduced from a review of a novel recommended by Friedrich in the course "Modern Political Thought." The book was *The Day of Reckoning,* a novel by Max Radin published in 1943.[77] It may seem strange at first that a professor of political science should suggest reading a book of fiction. But readers will quickly grasp the reason for this choice. The author, a Jew born in Poland in 1880 and living in the United States since the age of four, was considered "Berkeley's wise and genial professor of law." He had encyclopaedic knowledge in various fields and maintained active correspondence with scholars around the world. *The Day of Reckoning,* his only work of fiction, received rave reviews in law journals and other periodicals.[78] Thanks to the magic of the Internet, we were able to lay our hands on this now rare book. And more than sixty years after its publication, we found it was still a powerful work.

This futuristic novel was set in Luxembourg in 1945, two years after its publication. Germany had been defeated, and seven defendants, including Adolf Hitler, Joseph Goebbels, Heinrich Himmler, Joachim von Ribbentrop, and Walter Funk were being brought to justice before a United Nations tribunal. How would we react to these men who were universally recognized as monsters? Radin developed his argument around two fundamental questions. First, what court was legally competent to judge these men? And second, "is such a procedure likely to satisfy the sense of justice of an outraged world?"[79]

Radin stated bluntly that "this is not a commission to determine war-guilt and to punish it."[80] The charge was much more down to earth: these men were accused of killing three people. The French citizen, Jacques Dubosque, was shot, along with other hostages, because a German officer had been shot by the Resistance. The Czechoslovak citizen, Ian Nepomuk Studicka, was hanged because he had made supposedly derogatory remarks about the Führer, and Joseph Kolinsky, a Russian prisoner of war, was killed with a bayonet because he was Jewish. All those attending the trial could not believe their ears. In accusing the seven monsters to have committed "three little puny murders of unimportant and insignificant persons,"[81] they had the impression the court was mocking them. "The halls reverberated with loud and profanely derogatory criticism of the Court, of the procedure, of the trial in general, of the silly absurdity of singling out three minor murders to charge against this monstrous group of murderers. 'Why not Lidice?'* 'Why not Poland?' 'Four million Jews massacred in cold blood inside of six months!'" The outraged remarks of spectators in the public gallery allowed the author to recall the countless atrocities committed by the Nazis. It was clear that Radin voluntarily gave the impression that the accused had committed three common-law crimes, which would fall under the jurisprudence of the respective countries. But readers quickly realized that these crimes represented three typical cases: the execution of innocent hostages, the elimination of opponents of the cult of the Führer, and murder that was of a purely racist character.

Radin provided the defendants with an excellent lawyer who made his case with such force that one wondered if the court, in respecting the principles of the rule of law, would even be able to establish the criteria for convicting these individuals. Only toward the end of the book does Radin finally set out his own position in reporting the fictional verdict. First, he said that an international court, coming under the United Nations – which,

---

* A Czechoslovakian village near Prague, tragically known for the massacre of June 10, 1942, during which the Germans killed all men over sixteen years of age, sending the rest of the population to concentration camps.

we should remember, had still not yet seen the light of day! – was perfectly suited to judge these cases, provided it did not violate "the principles of reason and the sense of natural justice which we have inherited."[82] Second, he argued that, regardless of who was responsible for the war or who won or lost, we can judge these men by natural law, that is to say, according to a universal moral norm. Not everything is permitted, even in wartime, Radin argued passionately: "To kill an acknowledgedly innocent person except in the course of war or in self-defense is wrong, is so seriously wrong that the severest punishment would be morally justified on the basis of that inherited sense of natural justice."[83] The seven defendants were therefore sentenced to death. On the very last page, Radin wrote with a touch of black humour, showing that he was aware of the Nazi furnaces: "The Execution had been carried out by administering cyanide gas. Whether this had taken place in a lethal chamber or otherwise was not disclosed."[84]

When Friedrich recommended this book for the winter session of 1946, the entire world was closely following the Nuremberg Trials, which had been underway since October 18, 1945. Among the defendants fiction-ally portrayed by Radin, two actually ended up on trial at Nuremberg – Joachim von Ribbentrop and Walter Funk. Trudeau read this novel during the trial. Once again, he was in a ringside seat: he could make the connec-tion between this reading and one of the most significant events of con-temporary history. Which is why his reaction seems so astonishing, to say the least. Over two pages of notes, he found in general that this was "a fairly stimulating book, easy reading." He carefully summarized the argu-ments of the prosecutor and defence. But unlike the highly favourable reviews of law experts, he found the author's legal arguments weak: "Far from realizing its goal of making the trials for war criminals seem justi-fied, it raises a great many doubts – if not on humane grounds, surely on legal ones. I think that if the (hypothetical) accusation was of an individ-ual crime – murder – the trial should have been before ordinary tribunals of the state where the crime was committed." However, Radin had clearly shown that each case was actually the prototype of a crime "contrary to natural justice," that is to say, a crime condemned by any civilization worthy of the name. Trudeau, however, stated categorically, "Before inter-national court, you can only try international crimes, e.g.: who caused the war? But such a question can only be answered by history."[85] Surprisingly, the subtlety of Radin's reasoning eluded Trudeau. In describing the murders as "normal" crimes, he relegated them to the same status as the murder of a woman by a jealous husband. He did not see that beyond their banal appearance, these crimes represented typical cases of the denial of human dignity. Trudeau's comments raised troubling questions: If he maintained that an international court could prosecute only international crimes, such as "Who caused the war?," did he deem the Nuremberg Tribunal to be illegitimate? How should those responsible for Nazi atrocities be treated? Did their crimes rank among the inevitable consequences of any war?

In another of his readings, Trudeau discovered the true face of fascism. He was fascinated by *Governments of Continental Europe* by Thomson Shotwell,[86] and took twenty-two pages of notes. He wrote: "Fascist totalitarianism in the economic sphere is expressed in Corporatism. . . . In practice, party henchmen hold all the jobs, and for life." Whereas corporatism had previously been praised by his professors and the Church in Quebec, and whereas he had believed in it himself during his first year at Harvard, he now learned that it was none other than the economic arm of Nazi and fascist regimes. In July 1956, he wrote an article in *Vrai* with a provocative title: "When French Canadians Clamoured for a Mussolini."[87] In September of that year and in the same newspaper, he wrote: "Several years of social thought can practically be summed up in a single word: corporatism. It was enough that this word was uttered by the pope, and that *les Anglais* could hardly see any worth in it, for us to identify it as a universal panacea."[88]

The books recommended or written by Professor Friedrich were particularly valuable for Trudeau's thinking. For example, in *Constitutional Government and Democracy*, Friedrich emphasized the importance of the separation of powers in a liberal democracy.[89] Was it in this reference work, which Trudeau found so fascinating, that he discovered the concept of counterweights, which was to prove an essential element of his political philosophy? Trudeau continued to maintain until the end of his life that "too much provincial power is bad; too little is bad. You have to look for counterweights all the time."[90]

This book had more to inspire the young Trudeau. Friedrich argued that the main objective of "Constitutionalism" was protecting the dignity of the person "no matter how lowly. For if we ask what is the political function of a constitution, we find that the core objective is that of safeguarding each member of the political community. . . . The constitution is meant to protect the *self*." That was already enough to interest Trudeau. But imagine his delight when he discovered that "Constitutionalism" was based on Christian values: "This preoccupation with the self, rooted in Christian beliefs, eventually gave rise to the notion of rights. . . . Hence the function of a constitution may also be said to be the defining and maintaining of human rights."[91] The value of a constitution in protecting the person, an idea he encountered in Friedrich's classes and subsequently developed, would mark the thought of the future statesman. He fulfilled this ideal in 1982, by giving Canada a constitution enshrining a charter of rights and freedoms.

Friedrich made one more, and unexpected, contribution to the shaping of Trudeau's mind by including in his recommended readings *A Grammar of Politics,* by Harold Laski, the famous professor at the London School of Economics (LSE). The influence Laski exerted on Trudeau has always been stressed, and rightly so. However, contrary to popular belief, it was not in England but at Harvard that Trudeau discovered this "absolutely outstanding mind." He recalled in his *Memoirs*: "When I arrived in London I was already familiar with his many writings, most notably his *Grammar of Politics,* an encyclopaedic work that for some unknown reason no longer gets any attention."[92] In fact, Trudeau took seventeen pages of detailed notes on two of Laski's works: his masterpiece, *A Grammar of Politics,* and *The Foundation of Sovereignty and Other Essays.* Here we provide only a brief overview of what Trudeau derived from his first contact with this thinker who was engaged in active politics – an ideal he himself had long pursued – and who eventually became his mentor.

Trudeau was baffled by what he read: "[Laski's] position is not clear and you never know whether he will give precedence to the individual over the community, to the civil over the spiritual, or the reverse."[93] He further wrote, "One doesn't know what to think." Laski's position was confusing for Trudeau because here was a Marxist who nonetheless upheld the primacy of the person. Trudeau did not yet know much about Marxist thought, which was characterized in Quebec as the work of Satan. But he appreciated the novelty of these ideas: whereas his professors at Harvard focused on the concepts of freedom, democracy, and constitutionalism, Laski, using a Marxist perspective, set liberty, as well as equality, as the founding principles of justice itself. Trudeau was surprised that on the basis of such a theory, and without recourse to religious imperatives, Laski ardently defended the person and his rights. These ideals appealed strongly to him: "[Laski] is trying to create a system from scratch in which human values will be safeguarded. The result is a highly complicated and not always realistic construct, which nonetheless shows an admirable concern for collective justice. For example, he finds that equality is necessary for justice: he seeks how it can be realized in practice." Trudeau was fascinated. How ironic that he discovered this thinker, a Marxist activist who defended a socialist conception of justice, thanks to Friedrich, a conservative and anti-Marxist professor!

On May 16, 1946, Trudeau successfully passed his "General Examination for PhD in Political Economy and Government." But we uncovered no record of the choice of subject or thesis director. Was it because he was not interested in an academic career? Possibly, since in his application he said he wanted to become a statesman. And given this objective, he had undoubtedly received a thorough intellectual grounding. He had closely followed the restructuring of the post-war world, under outstanding professors. He became familiar with many schools of thought, both in economics and politics. He awoke to the potential dangers of political and social principles he held dear. Trudeau definitely emerged from his cave. A new man was gradually coming into being.

Toward the end of his time at Harvard, Trudeau decided to pursue his studies. But where? And with whom? Well, at the London School of Economics (LSE), with none other than Laski. On February 7, 1946, he informed the LSE admissions committee that he intended to register for the 1946–47 academic year.[94] On April 6, he sent his completed application to the dean of post-graduate students, while trying to land a scholarship. In June 1946, he learned that the Department of the Secretariat of the Province of Quebec had granted him a scholarship to study in England. But Trudeau did not go directly to London. He first spent a year in Paris. How can this change of program be explained? What happened is that shortly after sending his letter to the LSE, he learned that the French government provided a number of scholarships to Canadians. He found the prospect enchanting. In March, after obtaining all the information he needed, he made a formal request to René Messières, cultural attaché at the embassy of France in Canada. He wrote: "What shall I add except that I have always nourished the hope of going to France to complete my studies? You probably know the French Canadian well enough to know that this desire is quite common; but I trust that you will deign to find in my academic record evidence of my aptitude to truly benefit from my studies in France." Trudeau hurried to fill out all the forms. He explained the importance of the scholarship to Charles Coderre, secretary-treasurer to the Bar of the Province of Quebec, from whom he requested a transcript: "Need I remind you that the interest of these scholarships is not solely financial? Indeed, at the present time, the active benevolence of the French state is almost a pre-requisite for undertaking successful studies there."

Trudeau needed letters of reference and wrote to Father Robert Llewelynn, student chaplain at the Université de Montréal. He confided to the priest that after two years at Harvard, "I would like to wrap it all up with a year of study and personal development in old France. . . . Harvard was amazing for exactly two years but no more than that. And it is with joy that I will spend the summer in Canada. I am just looking forward to reconnecting with friends and buddies from home. Autonomy is a discipline, but its riches are not inexhaustible."[95] What luck that his friend Roger was also planning to study in France. Trudeau was jubilant. On April 4, he replied: "Paris in September is for-r-r-midable. Your letter leaves me practically out of breath. Seeing you so determined has made me that much more eager to go." They had to cancel the trip to Florida they had planned for the summer, in order to "be back early enough to prepare for the departure that really counts." Instead, Trudeau proposed, "Have you thought of 'Frontier College?' It would be wonderful to spend a month with lumberjacks up North." In a two-page letter on May 20, he wrote again about the intoxicating prospect of their stay in Paris, especially given that they both intended to take their motor-cycles along. Trudeau could no longer contain his joy: "Besides, I am getting fed up with Harvard. My heart is in Paris. And son of a gun, I will follow my heart, for once."

On July 24 he received a letter from the French embassy in Canada, confirming his scholarship of 50,000 francs for one year of study in Paris, and free tuition.[96] On September 21, he sailed from New York. His head full of dreams and hope, he was heading for Paris, the Mecca of French Canadians of his generation. But before crossing the pond, he spent the summer in Quebec, recharging his batteries.

Chapter 3

PARIS, JE T'AIME!

The idea of the supremacy of society over the person is reaction-
ary, counter-revolutionary.

– NICOLAS BERDYAEV, 1943[*]

BEFORE HEADING OFF FOR PARIS, Trudeau decided to volunteer with
Frontier College. Founded in 1899, this "college" uses volunteer staff to
provide literacy programs across Canada, including in the Far North. At
first glance it might seem strange that a rich young man in love, who had
a short break after slogging away at Harvard for two full years, should
consider it "wonderful" to spend a month with lumberjacks, far from
his sweetheart and his friends. Did this decision have anything to do
with his desire to become a statesman? Possibly. At Harvard, he had just
discovered that the "people" are not some amorphous mass to be channelled this way and that by their elite. So he may now have wanted to get
to know ordinary people better, to see how they lived and to learn what
their true needs were. All he had known was the posh, sheltered environment of Montreal's French-Canadian upper middle class. Frontier
College offered him the chance to rub shoulders with robust woodsmen
completely unlike the intellectuals he usually spent time with. It also
provided him with an opportunity to contribute to these people's education. The prospect of leading a hard life in the North appealed to him.

He finally set out for the Far North, but he didn't end up in a majestic
forest, among lumberjacks. Instead he headed deep down into the shafts

---

[*] N. Berdyaev, *Slavery and Freedom*, Centenary Press, 1943.

of Sullivan Consolidated Mines, in Val d'Or, Abitibi. From July 9 to August 2, he worked hard, eight-hour shifts, just like the other miners. And like them, he bought his boots, underwear, gloves, and everything else he needed from the company store.[1] On July 14, he wrote to Thérèse Gouin: "The work is hard, the men tough, the food plentiful, the night cold, the flies bad. . . ."[2] It was tough. But when the time came to leave the mine, he had experienced first-hand the hard life of mineworkers. It was an experience he never forgot. Three years later, as a Privy Council clerk in Ottawa, he wrote, "We admire civil servants and councillors. But our heart is with miners. Isn't a man worth more than any number of balanced budgets?"[3]

Enriched by this experience, he now returned to Montreal to plan his move to Paris – which was certainly not going to be easy. This was 1946, the year that marked the beginning of twenty-seven years of uninterrupted growth in France – "les trente glorieuses" – that lasted from 1946 until the first oil crisis in 1973. Even so, France was making a slow recovery from the German occupation as well as the Allied Liberation. A few months of Allied bombing raids had razed cities, blown up roads and railways, and smashed infrastructure, causing more devastation than all the years of war and occupation.

Just about everything was in short supply and had to be rationed. It would be hard to imagine nowadays a French cultural attaché reminding a young Canadian on a scholarship that he should bring enough soap with him. Yet this is the advice Trudeau was given: "You are advised to bring all the clothing, towels and soap you will need during the year."[4] Foreigners were also allowed to bring along some rationed or scarce food items, for their personal use. On arrival, they had to submit a detailed customs declaration, in order to prevent these items from finding their way to the black market. Trudeau was allowed to bring "a box containing food rationed in France and soap." His declaration included 3½ pounds of tea and coffee, 10 pounds of chocolate, 12 pounds of honey and marmalade, 15 pounds of candy, and 10 pounds of soap; the total weight of food was 73 pounds.[5]

The ever-methodical Trudeau drew up for his own use the list of clothes he was bringing along. Noteworthy were his five sport jackets, five suits, and especially his tuxedo. Clearly, he knew he would not just have to scrape by, like most poor students. And he was right. He already had a very complimentary letter of introduction, written on the letterhead of the Senate of Canada, which would open doors for him in the most distinguished circles in Paris. "We love Pierre so much," wrote Yvette Gouin, the wife of Senator Léon-Mercier Gouin and mother of Thérèse, "that our whole family considers him an adopted son."[6]

An official declaration from the Consulate General of France noted that Trudeau was also bringing "two trunks and two suitcases containing books, clothes and a pair of skis that are his personal property and not for trade."[7] If we add up the two trunks, two suitcases, and seventy-three pounds of food, it is clear that he brought an impressive amount of luggage to France. In addition, his beloved Harley-Davidson was shipped on October 30 at a cost of $26.43.[8] What a contrast between this virtual baggage train and the single rucksack he would take on his round-the-world journey in 1948–49!

On September 21, 1946, his steamship departed for France. After a nine-day crossing, he met up in Le Havre with his uncle Gordon Elliott and his aunt, who had fled occupied France and found refuge in Canada. They had returned to France after the war and had driven from Varengeville-sur-Mer in Normandy to greet him. Once he set foot on French soil, Trudeau embarked on a whirlwind of social and intellectual activities. The day after his arrival, he was already in Paris. On October 2, he went to see Jean Cocteau's play *Les parents terribles* [Intimate Relations] with his friend Roger Rolland.[9] On the 3rd, he went "with a gang" – to use his own words – to see Marcel Carné's masterpiece, *Les enfants du Paradis* [Children of Paradise]. (He had the pleasure of seeing this movie again on April 8, 1948, with his mother and Roger.) On October 4, he walked around Montmartre with Roger. On the 10th, he saw the stage adaptation of Dostoyevsky's famous novel *The Brothers Karamazov*. On the 13th, he was back in Varengeville, spending two hours in the studio of the renowned sculptor and painter Georges Braque and savouring a cake festooned with the word "Canada" in his honour. The next day he returned to Paris by car with his uncle and aunt and noted in his diary: "Tonight, we're reading Jean-Paul Sartre and eating in our room." The next day, Wednesday the 16th, he was back at Braque's place, in Varengeville. On the evening of the 17th, he heard a speech by Maurice Thorez, vice-president of the Council.*

---

* The function of president of the Council corresponds to prime minister in Canada.

Thorez served as secretary general of the French Communist Party from 1930 to 1964 and remains to this day, with the Italian Palmiro Togliatti, one of the most influential figures of Western European Communism.

Trudeau mixed with the proletariat while attending a lecture by their leader, but then moved on to the world of high finance. On October 20, he was received by the very wealthy Baron Edouard de Rothschild and his daughter, the Baroness Bathsheba. They were Jewish members of the French nobility who had to flee Paris in 1940 and had taken refuge in New York. From there, Bathsheba joined De Gaulle's Free French Forces and took part in the liberation of Paris alongside the U.S. Army. Given Trudeau's long-standing opposition to conscription, how did he feel being with the Rothschilds? We only know that the evening must have gone well, since it ended with champagne in a restaurant. The next day, Trudeau met another French-Canadian student, Marcel Rioux – who became a well-known Quebec sociologist and whom Trudeau regularly saw in Ottawa once he became a Privy Council clerk. The two friends couldn't get tickets to see Edith Piaf and the Compagnons de la chanson, so they spent the night at a tavern instead. But Trudeau managed to see Piaf the following evening with other friends.

These few pages from Trudeau's social agenda give an idea of the feverish pace of his cultural and social activities. Interestingly, his circle of friends consisted almost entirely of French Canadians, such as Roger Rolland, of course, but also Guy Viau, with whom he had made his 1,000-mile canoe expedition; Jean Gascon and Jean-Louis Roux, who studied theatre and left their mark on the Canadian scene; Andrée Desautels, the future musicologist then studying at the Paris Conservatory (Trudeau later travelled with her to Spain); and Gérard Pelletier, whom he was just getting to know and who became one of his best friends.

François Hertel, the maverick Jesuit professor and darling of young students in Quebec's *collèges classiques,* deserves special mention.[10] Other than Rolland, with whom Trudeau shared a room, Hertel was probably the person he saw most during this stay. Later, whenever Trudeau passed through Paris or Hertel returned to Quebec, the two never failed to meet up. Hertel was already in Paris by the time Trudeau got there. He settled there permanently in 1949, two years after leaving the Society of Jesus. In "Letter to My Friends," he explained with great bitterness why he had left Quebec "not as a deserter, but as a free man."[11]

He wanted, he said, "to shape free spirits; but I would have ended up creating rebels. . . . In spite of myself, my approach to education is contrary to [the Catholic Church's] official teachings." He added with a touch of sarcasm, "All of this does not legitimize certain base calumnies, especially coming from people in official positions. . . . I wonder if Catholicism as sometimes practised in Canada is not some dark clerical heresy." He was even more biting in his conclusion: "The real scandal for me . . . is that the Son of Man has come to earth to redeem us and we seem beyond redemption."

Hertel's nonconformism and eccentricity did not bother Trudeau. Quite the contrary – as long as he respected certain limits. But in 1964, Hertel went too far. In the April 9 issue of *Le Quartier Latin* appeared an article he had penned in Paris: "So if you want to kill someone . . . assassinate on my behalf a traitor, 'a genuine one of us'; that would be a productive 'job.' Deliver poor Laurendeau from his mortal existence which seems to bore him so much – he is an old man before his time and a pretty dirty old one at that." Hertel's outburst infuriated Trudeau. He scolded his former friend sharply in *Cité libre:* "I would not have thought that this man, whom I have long respected because he used to have the rare courage to reject all forms of conformity, would wind up as a church mouse in the separatist chapel. So now from Paris, beyond the reach of our criminal courts but not of our contempt, he writes: 'Assassinate for me a traitor. . . . ' Et cetera. To address such words to a public preparing to sacrifice all values – especially personal freedom and safety – to the idol of collectivism, and which has already begun to take terrorists for heroes and martyrs, is the act of a dangerously irresponsible man."[12] In 1964, the sparks flew between Trudeau and Hertel, but in Paris in 1947, their friendship was blooming. Hertel shared with Trudeau the networks he had established in exclusive literary and artistic circles. It was thanks to him that Trudeau was invited to a reception marking Etienne Gilson's elevation to the Académie française.

———◦———

From his base in Paris, just one year after the end of hostilities, Trudeau found himself in a country that had experienced the Nazi occupation and the war. What did he learn about the experience? Not much, it seems. True enough, in November 1946 at a ceremony commemorating the D-Day landing in Normandy, Trudeau along with other Canadian students got an eyeful of France's immense gratitude to Canada. Marcel Rioux wrote a long account of this commemoration in the November 30, 1946, issue of the review *Notre Temps*. Pierre de Grandpré – the future novelist and literary critic – wrote a similar piece for the January 11, 1947, issue of *Le Devoir*. Trudeau kept clippings of these articles. But apart from this set of clippings, we could find no other mention of the war in his archives. We interviewed Roger Rolland. What was being said in France about the recent events of the war? "Not much," he replied. "People seemed to avoid talking about it."

This perception is backed up by many eyewitness accounts, such as, for example, the well-known French political personality Simone Veil, a member of the Académie française since March 2010. As a Jew, she had been subjected to deportation and incarceration in concentration camps, including Birkenau and Bergen-Belsen, and "the unforgettable long march of death, a true nightmare for survivors, in biting cold temperatures of thirty degrees below zero."[13] Once she was freed at the end of the war and returned to France, she and many others felt the need to tell their stories: "We wanted to talk, but nobody would listen. . . . Nobody was interested in knowing what we had endured."[14] At Sciences Po, she writes, people "rarely expressed their opinions. Too many wounds had still not healed. Our professors exercised the same caution. . . . The rift between the two Frances – between those who had collaborated and those who had resisted – was still so deep that people took care to avoid any unnecessary controversies."[15] Writings on this period often make references to this silence. For example, in his autobiographical novel, *La soupe au pistou,* Claude Tatilon, a professor at York University in Toronto, remembers that the French did not want to talk about the war, although each person had different reasons for not talking: "After all, everyone had known [his share of horrors]. So, enough already! It was time to forget all that. . . . Better to shut up, swallow your bitterness and suffer in silence."[16]

This explains why the deeds of the Vichy government were not called into question for decades. Robert Paxton's study, *Vichy France, Old Guard and New Order, 1940–1944,* based on his doctoral dissertation (1963), was the most thorough and most damning study of that period. Published in 1972, it caused quite a controversy. Contrary to the generally accepted view, Paxton's work demonstrates that the Vichy government had not only collaborated willingly but had even cravenly anticipated German directives. We should also mention the bold and fascinating documentary by Marcel Ophüls, *The Sorrow and the Pity*. Ophüls produced the film for television in 1969, but it was rejected. When finally released in theatres in 1971, it became an immediate and resounding success. Nevertheless, the main body of important works on the German Occupation and its aftermath began to come out only in the 1990s. Let us now briefly sketch the general post-war context in which Trudeau pursued his studies, without returning to the war years, since they occurred prior to his arrival.

With the Allied victory, the hatred that had built up over the years gave rise to acts of vengeance on a huge scale: France had to be "purged" of people convicted or suspected of collaboration. This "purge" involved more than 10,000 executions, mostly after summary trials, while more than 20,000 women accused of "horizontal collaboration" (i.e., sleeping with the enemy) were publicly humiliated and had their heads shaved. According to this Manichean interpretation of the war years, the French were now categorized either as "good" people or as "bastards." (We know, however, that this categorization was overly simplistic, as illustrated, for example, in Irène Nemirovsky's poignant novel, *Suite française* [French Suite].[17]) This either/or view was very pervasive at the time; even the non-ideological and moderate author Albert Camus fell into this trap. On October 20, 1944, he wrote in *Combat* that France was made up either of "men of the Resistance" or of "men of betrayal and injustice." France could be saved only if "[these men of betrayal] still living in its midst were destroyed in order to save the nation's very soul."[18] The interlude of *épuration* (the big purge) was underway.

On January 6, 1944, the Comité national d'écrivains (National Authors' Committee) decided "unanimously to refuse to write for any newspapers, magazines and collections accepting to publish work by a writer whose attitude and writings during the occupation had brought moral or material assistance to the enemy."[19] Two names stand out in the list: Charles Maurras and Robert Brasillach. Both of them were well regarded by the clerical-nationalist elite in Quebec, including Trudeau prior to his departure for Harvard. The trials and convictions were getting underway. Maurras, well known for his vigorous campaign against the falsely accused Jewish military officer Alfred Dreyfus, had long preached anti-Semitism and other extreme right views. He was charged with placing his magazine, *L'Action française,* at the service of the "Collaborators," of supporting the adoption of a National Socialist regime in France, and, more generally, of supporting vigorously the enemies of the Resistance.[20] Given his poor health, he was not sentenced to death but, in January 1945, was condemned instead to national degradation and life imprisonment. On hearing his sentence, he shouted, "This is the revenge of Dreyfus!"[21]

That same month, the trial of the notorious Nazi sympathizer Robert Brasillach split the intelligentsia in two camps. No one doubted that he had collaborated willingly, but some felt it was unfair to come down too severely on writers, when other "collaborators," including people who had supplied weapons to the Germans, were spared. After all, they said, writers collaborated only through mere words, contrary to some other people who had committed visible and concrete harmful deeds. Jean-Paul Sartre took the opposite stand: writers, he felt, should be treated even more harshly, since they had a social responsibility, they had a "commitment" to uphold (*Ils sont engagés*). This notion of "commitment" of writers became a major concern at the time. For his part, Brasillach was convicted and executed on February 6, 1945.

To some people, the "purge" was an opportunity to settle personal accounts, which risked plunging France into a bloodbath. How could such a catastrophe be avoided? De Gaulle found the solution. "For post-war France," writes historian Tony Judt, "getting rid of the Vichy problem called for a peculiar outbreak of deliberately induced amnesia: this was indeed peculiar since it took place in broad daylight, so to speak, whereas everyone knew deep down what had really happened."[22] And so emerged the myth of a France that, from the beginning of the war, had been fully engaged in the Resistance. For this myth to take hold, the people had to agree to remain silent about the recent past.

This glorification of the Resistance was of special benefit to the Communists, since they had joined the Resistance as early as 1941, once the Soviet Union entered the war alongside the Allies. This allowed the Communists to reject any responsibility for Vichy's detestable policies. After the Liberation, they took it out on all those right-wing politicians, "corrupt" capitalists, and "reactionary" Catholics who had despised them and were now at the receiving end of public scorn. Moreover, the heroic battle of Stalingrad had greatly contributed to the Allied victory and now roused a sense of gratitude toward Moscow and the Communists. Not surprisingly, the Communist Party (PCF) took advantage of this situation and cast itself as "the party of the 75,000 partisans executed by the firing squad."[23] Support for the PCF reached a high point in the elections of October 21, 1945, where the party came first for the only time in its history. On October 24, its newspaper, *L'Humanité,* proudly displayed on the front page: "The Communist Party is the leading party of France." Communism and revolution became widely accepted ideals, while anti-Communism was loudly denounced.

But Communism, this ideology now in vogue, was atheist. Pope Pius XI had already described it as "the avowed enemy of the Church and of God Himself."[24] How can the post-war French infatuation with this ideology be explained in a predominantly Catholic country? And how did Trudeau react to Communism, given that he then was, and remained throughout his life, a practising Catholic? We have seen that he acknowledged the Church's authority throughout his life, to the point of seeking permission to read prohibited books on the *Index (Index Librorum Prohibitorum).* While in Paris, he contacted the archdiocese once again, and, on January 27, 1947, the archbishop authorized him to read prohibited books for a period of three years.[25] Three years later, almost to the day, on January 20, 1950, he sought permission from Monsignor Vachon, Archbishop of Ottawa, to read various prohibited publications: "I trust that the state of grace will help protect me from the dangers denounced by the Holy Father and the Sacred Congregation of the Index, and therefore present to you, Excellency, my humble petition requesting a dispensation for the reading of prohibited works."[26] On January 28, Monsignor Vachon granted him permission to read the publications on the *Index* as well as those that "fell under the Decree of the Holy Office last spring, condemning Marxist literature . . . *as long as these readings are absolutely necessary for the performance of your duties.*"* We should note that in 1950, when Trudeau sought this dispensation, he was thirty-one years old and working for the Privy Council, a civil service department providing significant support to the prime minister of Canada and his cabinet.

---

* Unless otherwise indicated, italicized words appearing in quotations are underlined or italicized in the original text.

To determine if Trudeau's deep faith stood out in this context, let us examine the impact of the war on relations between the French Communists and Catholics. During the occupation, the Church hierarchy had initially compromised itself by enthusiastically supporting Pétain. But, rapidly, many members of the clergy distanced themselves from the regime, secretly helped the Allies, and helped Jews and members of the Resistance. Winock also notes that "many young Catholics followed General De Gaulle whose Catholicism was well-known."[27] A new brotherhood of arms was established in the Resistance movement between Catholics, lay people, socialists, Communists, members of other faiths, free thinkers, and others. Unsurprisingly, right-wing Catholics kept their distance from Communism. But this was not the case for many left-wing Catholics such as Emmanuel Mounier and his personalist review *Esprit*. Many specialists in this field, such as E.-Martin Meunier and Jean-Philippe Warren, believe that *Esprit* has exercised a decisive influence on the artisans of the "Quiet Revolution." It is therefore worth outlining the review's post-war position.[28]

The founder and soul of *Esprit*, Emmanuel Mounier, believed that "an obscure movement of history" leads to revolution. More important in the context of the times, he claimed that "an honest analysis of France's situation shows that it is revolutionary."[29] He had no trouble outlining the major objectives of this revolution: "the expulsion of big capital, the abolition of the proletariat . . . the creation of new popular elites." This profound transformation "could not happen without violent resistance that would in turn lead to counter-violence." It certainly was not the bourgeoisie that could trigger, much less lead, such a movement: "In no case will this transformation be brought about by the chattering liberals of parliamentary democracy."[30]

This revolution required "a purge." An article in the January 1945 issue of *Esprit* explained that the purge was not just a matter of "punishing collaborators, but also all those responsible for the climate which [has] made Collaboration possible: anti-Communists, right-wing politicians and intellectuals, big business, and anti-Semites. This was a divisive issue. Some writers, like Jean Paulhan and François Mauriac – both Catholics and veterans of the Resistance – outraged by the absence of charity and compassion, denounced the excessive harshness of the proposed measures. But, in the special issue of August 1947 devoted to political justice in

France, Mounier took the opposite view, arguing that "justice in situations of crisis . . . is not a justice of individual salvation . . . but a justice of *public salvation*."[31] *Esprit* not only endorsed Marxism, Communism, and revolution but also displayed a deep sympathy toward the Soviet Union. Mounier even wrote that Russia "is doubtless the only country able to teach this withering Europe the ways of love once again, by setting the example, despite the paradox of her initial violence."[32] To the historian Goulven Boudic, this clearly demonstrated that "the director of *Esprit* does not hesitate to sweep aside the violation of individual and political rights and freedoms in the Soviet Union, which he justifies, at least temporarily, by the overarching goal of achieving an egalitarian society."[33]

So when Trudeau was in Paris, many Catholics, much like *Esprit* itself, considered themselves not only left-wing but also pro-Communist and pro-Soviet Union. Trudeau noticed it: "Young people, in particular, were truly fascinated by the Soviet model."[34] So did Gérard Pelletier, a great admirer of Mounier: "Stalinist Communism was surging across Europe, as had Christianity two thousand years earlier. . . . I must admit that Marxism, the 'great system' that claimed to solve all problems, made my head spin at the time."[35] But Trudeau remained aloof from this current; none of his records suggests any leanings whatsoever toward this ideology. After all, he was fresh out of Harvard, where he had discovered the value of liberal democracy and the dangers of dictatorships – including the Soviet variety. Pelletier remembered that Trudeau stood out from the crowd. He knew "books, events, schools of thought, historical trends, facts and statistics that gave our discussions a direction and style that for me were entirely new."[36]

In this culturally and politically effervescent milieu, Trudeau studied at the Institut d'études politiques (Sciences Po) and the Faculty of Law. In his *Memoirs,* he enthusiastically described the exciting intellectual climate of Paris; strangely, he made no mention of his studies.[37] Moreover, his personal papers contain some notes, but few comments on his teachers and classes. How can this be explained? At the time, Sciences Po offered an undergraduate program only. (A doctoral program was created in 1956.) At Harvard, not only did he complete master's and doctoral studies, but he was immersed in the intellectual, economic, and political life of the United States, which had become the new superpower. Many of his professors already enjoyed well-established reputations. Others were younger but equally brilliant and were destined for international fame. At Sciences Po, although many of his professors were well known in Europe, they had just come out of four years of occupation, which was hardly conducive to the development of science and the promotion of new ideas.

Simone Veil had studied at Sciences Po a year before Trudeau. "I soon got cracking at Sciences Po," she later recalled, "but spent little time at the Faculty of Law, where, like almost everyone else at the time, I resorted essentially to duplicated lecture notes to study. What I found fascinating at the Institute were the lectures given by personalities from different backgrounds who shared their wealth of experience with us."[38] Trudeau did much the same, as is indicated by his correspondence with the London School of Economics (LSE). Responding to his application of March 24, 1947, the dean of graduate studies at the LSE requested information about his studies in Paris, as well as two letters of reference from his professors.[39] Trudeau answered: "My stay in Paris being limited to one year, I could not take any degree at l'Institut des sciences politiques nor at the Law School. Therefore I did not pass* my exams and cannot send you any teacher's report on them. I chose to follow those lectures which would best benefit me and not those which were imposed by the official curriculum."[40] Indeed, Trudeau attended many lectures given by personalities from different backgrounds, as Simone Veil mentioned. More precisely, between October 21, the first day of class, and December 8, he attended twenty-two lectures given by sixteen different professors.

Pierre Renouvin – a celebrated historian and one of the pioneers of the political science subfield of "international relations" – gave two lectures. Trudeau must have really appreciated his second lecture, devoted to the world situation at the beginning of the twentieth century, from a European perspective; he took ten pages of notes. Among other things, Renouvin dealt with nationalism, stressing its powerful manipulative potential: "The press, public speakers etc. want to tug on the national

---

* Trudeau is using "pass" with its French meaning. Here, he wants to say he did not "write" any exams.

heartstrings. . . . The movement of nationalities tends to identify the nation with the state itself."[41] Once again, Trudeau was exposed to critiques of the use of nationalism for political purposes, along much the same lines as at Harvard.

On Thursday, October 24, he took eighteen pages of notes on "The Organization of the State." This topic, too, obviously interested him. The speaker, Jacques Donnedieu de Vabres, held an important position in the Council of State, one of the most important institutions within the French civil service. His father, Henri Donnedieu de Vabres, was one of the judges at the Nuremberg Tribunal, which had just finished its deliberations a few days earlier. This professor was therefore well placed to deal with the notion of freedom in history. "Individual liberty," Trudeau wrote down, "maintains its primacy over all forms of freedoms because it is the freedom of the mind in its most immediate sense." But the professor added: "Freedom within the individual counts for nothing: what we need is freedom within society." What would the freedom of thought be worth, if there was no way of expressing one's ideas in public? Which led the professor to say: "It is not freedom of thought as such that matters, but rather the diffusion of ideas throughout all classes." He also warned that individual liberty should not be confused with collective freedom: "Collective freedom counts for nothing [since it leads to the] dictatorship of the masses." The professor allowed, however, that collective freedoms do exist, such as the freedom of assembly. But even "within collective organizations, the law must protect the individual."

Donnedieu de Vabres proceeded to pay tribute to the British. They had created and made good use of legal instruments that achieved considerable progress in the protection of individual liberty. He explained that *habeas corpus,* established in England in 1679 to protect citizens against the King's tyranny, proclaimed that no person could be arrested without reason, and without providing him with the means to defend himself. The professor added that in the United States, the Bill of Rights guaranteed freedom of religion, speech, and the press, among other things, and in so doing protected the citizen from government abuses. Donnedieu de Vabres then provided an overview of the situation in some European countries, noting that in Nazi Germany, "all traditional values were suspended. . . . Shortly after 1933, most political and civil liberties were suspended."

Most certainly, this course reinforced Trudeau's attachment to individual liberty and the necessity to protect human rights through appropriate legislation; it also alerted him to the effectiveness and dangers of the use of nationalism for political purposes.

Among Trudeau's teachers was a dominant figure at Sciences Po: the world-renowned André Siegfried, a leading expert on America. Siegfried had been introducing his students to North American studies for a quarter of a century. He was a member of the Académie des sciences morales et politiques and since 1933 had held the chair in Geography and Economic Policy at the Collège de France, while teaching at Sciences Po. In 1945, he became the first president of the Fondation nationale des sciences politiques. A darling of French-Canadian intellectuals, he was often invited to give guest lectures in Canada. Trudeau had long been familiar with his writings, extracts of which had been required reading in some courses at Collège Jean-de-Brébeuf. He must have felt privileged to hear this great scholar in person. Siegfried gave three lectures (more than any other professor). In tracing the history of Europe in the nineteenth and twentieth centuries, he betrayed fundamental racism. Trudeau copied down: "Today, in 1946, more than in 1918, the white race is still master of the world. . . . Traditional Europe is a civilization springing from the white race, and from a certain conception of man (Socrates and Christ)."

Siegfried gave another lecture in his area of expertise, entitled "The United States and American Civilization." In 1927 he had published *Les États-Unis d'aujourd'hui* [America Comes of Age: A French Analysis], a work reprinted in 1948 without any changes. Siegfried expressed concern about the future of America. Why the concern? Simply because, according to him, the mass immigration of Jews would make the United States less Anglo-Saxon and Protestant. In New York, he wrote, in the narrow streets of the East Side, you meet "surging floods of olive-skinned Levantines or dishevelled Hebrews . . . Jews of the synagogue, just escaped from their ghetto."[42] Siegfried couldn't stand them and hastened to add: "I would probably prefer . . . some Alsatian Jew, a 'kike' from Breslau, a 'sheeny' from Lemberg or Salonika, or even – and I do not exaggerate – a Hebrew from Asia with goat eyes and patriarchal beard."[43] Could the issue be that Jews did not assimilate? Not at all, exclaimed Siegfried. The problem was that "the bearded Jew from a far-off ghetto in Eastern Europe is so Americanized that no trace of the alien remains."[44] But the Jew will always remain a Jew. He is invasive, disruptive, corrupting. "The Wandering Jew . . . forces the Christian to compete in a gruelling race." He forces him to engage in an unequal, losing battle, in the realm of intellectual arguments for argument's sake. To Siegfried, anti-Semitism "is a natural, inevitable and justified reaction."

It is hard to imagine a more racist and anti-Semitic professor. What did he have to say of some interest in his lecture on the United States? Not much that captured Trudeau's attention, judging by his two meagre pages of notes, quoting such remarks as "The most striking feature of America is the grandeur of nature. It is well beyond the human scale: Niagara Falls, the St. Lawrence River, the Rockies. . . . North Americans have a supreme faith in the power of man." In writing these lines, was Trudeau stifling a sneer? Quite probably. Indeed, a few months later, in a talk called "The Promise of Quebec," Trudeau warned his audience that his remarks would surprise "a whole generation of people in France trained by Sciences Po to believe in the imminent collapse of the American continent, where rivers, boundaries, buildings and institutions defy the 'law' of grandeur."[45] In the same ironic tone he assured his audience that "the man of America is not distracted by the macrocosm within which he tosses and turns; he understands his resources better than others do. . . . And the planet Earth is not so enormous that it prevents a man of average size from easily travelling its length and breadth." Trudeau scarcely concealed his contempt of the specious generalizations uttered by the great Professor Siegfried.

———◦◉◦———

Although Trudeau seemed to attend lectures at Sciences Po without any great enthusiasm, he rushed to UNESCO to hear the eminent personalities of the time. In the single month of November 1946, he attended five such lectures. On November 1, he heard the famous writer and existentialist philosopher Jean-Paul Sartre. On the fifth, it was the turn of the writer and adventurer André Malraux, whose hugely successful books – *Les Conquérants*, *La Condition humaine*, and *L'espoir* [The Conquerors, Man's Fate, and Man's Hope] – appealed particularly to young people. On Saturday the 9th, he attended a lecture by the writer Daniel-Rops, who was quite popular in post-war Catholic circles. On the 13th, he listened to Emmanuel Mounier. On the 28th, he attended a talk by the well-known Communist writer Louis Aragon. Sartre, Malraux, Daniel-Rops, Mounier, Aragon . . . What a fabulous month for our young student! In his memoirs, Trudeau recalled admiringly that "the beauty of the intellectual climate in Paris was that all tendencies of contemporary political thought were represented by worthy spokesmen – the Christian left, the worker priests, and proponents of orthodox Marxism or Catholicism, the existentialism of Jean-Paul Sartre, and pure liberalism."[46]

Trudeau enjoyed life to the fullest and this non-stop succession of shows and lectures obviously thrilled him. But there was something more. In the above-mentioned letter dated April 7, he explained to the dean of the LSE that "much was gained outside of the Schools by reading the literature, and meeting such men as Emmanuel Mounier, Etienne Gilson, Robert Aron." What was he reading? This inveterate reader must have spent much of his time devouring the important works of the time. But which ones? We do not know, because he left no record of his personal reading after his departure for Harvard. But in his private library, in later years, was tucked away a book he had studied carefully in Paris: *De l'esclavage et de la liberté de l'homme* (*Slavery and Freedom*). The author, Nicolas Berdyaev, is generally considered the guiding spirit of personalist philosophy.[47] This work casts an interesting light on the thought of Trudeau, and we will shortly examine it in some detail.

In his April letter to the LSE, Trudeau said he had met three prominent figures of the time. He did. First, he met Emmanuel Mounier, director of *Esprit,* in a bistro, after attending a lecture by Georges Bernanos, the well-known Catholic writer. They exchanged a few words on the lecture, which they had both found disappointing, then discussed personalism.[48] As far as the second person mentioned in his April letter, Etienne Gilson, is concerned, Trudeau had already attended several of his lectures. Gilson was renowned worldwide for his work on Thomas Aquinas and had been one of the founders of the Pontifical Institute of Medieval Studies at the University of Toronto in 1929. He held the chair of Medieval Philosophy at the Collège de France. On May 29, 1947, he was admitted to the Académie française. Two days later, Trudeau was invited along with Hertel to a reception in Gilson's honour. He also met other important people, such as the renowned Pierre Teilhard de Chardin, who became a mentor for many Christians around the world. This philosopher was trying to integrate Christian theology with theories of evolution and was trying to encourage the rise of a global consciousness, rooted in faith. Is it really surprising that Trudeau found him "tremendously impressive"?

Trudeau met the last of the three figures mentioned, Robert Aron, on several different occasions, including at the reception in honour of Gilson. Aron and Arnaud Dandieu had founded the review *L'Ordre nouveau* in the 1930s and jointly authored *La Révolution nécessaire*, which promoted a kind of corporatism.[49] Trudeau had greatly admired their works. But Aron's positions had changed since the war. He was Jewish and fled during the war to Algeria, where he joined the Free French Forces and took part in de Gaulle's first elected government after the Liberation. In 1950, he undertook extensive research on the Vichy regime, the Liberation, and other aspects of contemporary France. He was to be publicly inducted into the Académie française on April 20, 1975, but died the day before. On April 3, 1947, Trudeau made his presentation, "The Promise of Quebec," before the Robert Aron group at the École Normale. This presentation, which will be discussed below, sheds a very useful light on Trudeau's political thoughts at the time.[50]

Etienne Gilson, Pierre Teilhard de Chardin, Emmanuel Mounier, Robert Aron . . . Just imagine the delight of a twenty-seven-year-old French Canadian, rubbing shoulders with some of the heroes he had so admired back in Quebec. He was also packing in as many plays, concerts, films, and philosophical and political debates as he could manage. We can only share his delight, at a distance.

———

On December 10, 1946, Trudeau had to interrupt this whirlwind of activities to have an appendectomy at the American Hospital in Paris. Because of a shortage of anaesthetics, the surgery was painful. After a short stay in hospital and recovery in an infirmary, he returned home on December 23. But could he imagine a Christmas holiday without skiing? Impossible. Without wasting a minute, he took a night train that evening with Roger and two other friends, bound for one of the most popular ski resorts in Europe: Mégève, in the French Alps.

In 1947, an activity unrelated to his normal activities, but nonetheless time consuming, is worth mentioning. He had thirty-eight sessions of psychoanalysis between February and June.[51] Why did Trudeau consult a psychoanalyst? Could he have felt uncomfortable about himself? Possibly. He probably saw analysis as an opportunity to better understand himself, to overcome what he perceived as weaknesses in his character. Perhaps he wanted to experience something completely new, at a time when psychoanalysis was all the rage in France. At Harvard, he had read *A General Introduction to Psychoanalysis* by Sigmund Freud.[52] Later, in London, he made a careful study of *Les deux sources – consciente et inconsciente – de la morale* [The Twin Sources, Conscious and Unconscious, of Moral Life], by Charles Odier,[53] who extolled psychoanalysis for having uncovered the unconscious dimensions of morality. In 1962, Trudeau named Freud as one of the five people who had influenced him the most.[54] Finally, his relationship with his sweetheart, Thérèse Gouin, must have had an effect. She was working on her doctorate in psychology at the time and, like all other psychology students, she submitted to psychoanalysis sessions and was convinced of their value. She recommended that Trudeau do the same. The idea did not appeal particularly to him. However, as a sign of his goodwill, he attended a talk at UNESCO by Anna Freud, daughter of Sigmund Freud, as well as a seminar on love and marriage.[55] Given the increasing tensions in his and Thérèse's relationship, he agreed to submit to psychoanalysis as a "last concession."[56]

Trudeau, who never did things by halves, chose the famous Dr. Georges Parcheminey (1888–1953), who was one of nine founders of the Société psychanalytique de Paris and served as its president on two occasions. He was a true Freudian and placed great emphasis on the analysis of dreams. Trudeau took notes of his dreams with characteristic thoroughness and pencilled between the lines the psychoanalytic interpretation. We will give one example, placing in italics, between brackets, the interpretation Trudeau pencilled in: "After a dinner with Blais + 2 (young girls?) we climbed [*difficulties*] a hill in the car [*life force*] (it looked like the hill at Murray Bay) [*desiring Thérèse*]. Seems there are four packages or suitcases in the car. Car stalls 2 or 3 times, [*difficulties, lack of imagination,*] out of power or gas. We have to get out to push and get it started again. Tip is driving, [*married, settled in life. The opposite of Blais, a skirt chaser. I fall somewhere in between*]."[57]

The other dreams being on similar lines, we won't detail them here. However, Parcheminey's analysis and the discussion between psychoanalyst and patient cast new light on Trudeau at the time. We learn, for example, that at the age of twenty-seven, this man who became the Don Juan of Canadian prime ministers was still a virgin. True to his faith, he had abided by the Church's moral teachings and had had no sexual relations outside of marriage. Parcheminey attributed many of his problems (shyness, aggression, a desire to impress) to his sexual frustrations.

In April 1947, having undergone many sessions, Trudeau wrote: "We are speaking of analysis itself. My sessions are easy-going, almost restful. . . . This is because I am not making any neurotic transfer, since I have no neurotic relationship that is crying for resolution. My transfers are transient and variable, like those you would have with anyone else: you like this person, you yell at another person. . . . There can be no question of any real obsession. [Parcheminey] says I have no neurosis. . . . That I am only undergoing a character analysis that will bear fruit probably after the experiment is over by helping me better understand myself. He suggests I return until mid-May and we will apply ourselves to clarify particular aspects of my character."

That is just what psychoanalyst and patient did. In May, Trudeau noted: "During the first session, I talk about the possessive side of my character, what I call my demon of possession. At first, it meant I kept old papers, letters, wrote up facts describing my life. Preserve, collect, keep secret, don't spend, be as shy about giving as about receiving. . . . See everything, know everything. Parcheminey explains that a pregenital anal fixation has the disadvantage of turning all activity inwards, whereas normally all this energy would be directed towards action in the outside world."

Trudeau continued: "At the second meeting, Parcheminey asks what concerns me on a day-to-day basis. I start by talking about the search for the best in me, by this introspection. . . . Then I turn to aggression, which we discuss at length, for example, my love of paradox, of originality. And it becomes clear that this desire to appear independent is so strong because actually I am just the opposite, I attach too much value to what people might think. This assertiveness was useful in younger years, when I was fighting against shyness and a highly emotional nature. But it should lose its systematic character. . . . There is not necessarily any trauma underlying all of this. The best way to correct it: Be aware of it."

On June 14, after thirty-eight sessions, Parcheminey took stock of the situation. He told Trudeau there had been too much emphasis on duty during his childhood. "There was no neurosis . . . but something blocking me from the threshold of manhood has produced mechanisms that compensate through regression. . . . Parcheminey concludes that I have no complex that cannot likely be dispelled through the normal fulfilment of my masculinity, that is, through marriage. He suggests unreservedly that I stop my sessions. One or two years of married life, during which my vital energy will be able to express itself, and virility will flourish in a stable home setting, in contact with feminine tenderness, the satisfaction of my sexual appetites, etc. – all this will likely stabilize my character."

This is the result of thirty-eight long and costly sessions of psychoanalysis! Trudeau did not marry until age fifty-one. But he did strike "a reasonable accommodation" over the years between his faith and his sexual impulses. He did not remember his psychoanalyst fondly. Three years after Trudeau's sessions had ended, Roger Rolland wrote to him asking for the phone number of a few girls they knew in Paris, as a favour for a certain "Phil" who seemed to be in a bad way. On June 7, 1950, Trudeau provided the requested information, adding, "I wish Phil a lot of luck. I thought of another address he should make a point *of not* remembering: PAS 61.48.* Someone by the name of Parcheminey."

The many sessions of psychoanalysis did not hold Trudeau back from the hyperactive lifestyle he loved. On March 18, 1947, as part of a seminar at Sciences Po, he made a presentation on unemployment. In April, his mother visited him, and they travelled together, sometimes on his motorcycle. They went to the Côte d'Azur, where they attended a performance of Les Ballets Russes de Monte Carlo and indulged in other activities.

———————

We have already seen and we will see time and again how Trudeau was consistently concerned about the fate of French Canadians. The stifling atmosphere back in Quebec struck him as all the more outrageous since he was totally immersed in the intellectual freedom of Paris. Distressing evidence of Quebec's backwardness reached him through the scandal

---

* PAS 61.48 was a Paris telephone number. Phone numbers at the time were composed of three letters and four digits.

swirling around the film *Les Enfants du paradis*. To the Quebec Church of the time, movies were a profoundly corrupting influence; it prohibited young people under sixteen years of age from going to the cinema. (This prohibition was lifted only in 1961.) Starting in 1913, all films had to be submitted to a board of censors. Infidelity and adultery particularly riled censors. These were precisely the themes of Marcel Carné's masterpiece. Voted best film in the history of cinema in 1995, it tells the wonderful love story of Garance (played by the famous Arletty) and Baptiste (played by Jean-Louis Barrault, a genius of mime). Their passion endures, even after they are separately married. As might be expected, *Les Enfants du paradis* was banned in Quebec. But the French consul in Montreal secretly passed a copy to the Students Association of the Université de Montréal. A day before the screening, Premier Maurice Duplessis heard about the incident and called in a special censor, who ruled that love and marriage must be intimately linked. The board of censors accordingly stated that the film was "immoral, opposed to family values and glorified free love." The screening was cancelled.

This incident had immediate repercussions in France. When François Mauriac, a Catholic writer if there ever was one, heard about it, he could not contain his anger. On April 25, 1947, he wrote in *Combat:* "Did you know that in French Canada the censors have banned *Les Enfants du paradis,* and there has been a diplomatic incident about this supposedly obscene movie? And so many articles have been churned out there about how rotten we are! I have read them, and it is simply unbelievable! Well, I propose that massive stocks of those Delly* novels be shipped over to our dear Canadian friends: they will see that we are second to none when it comes to what they imagine to be virtue and good writing." Trudeau and his friends, including Roger Rolland, Jean-Louis Roux, Jean Gascon, and Marcel Rioux, were also outraged. Trudeau and Rolland wrote a letter of protest, which appeared in the daily *Le Canada* in April. But on May 1, the newspaper also published the acid reaction of Father Jacques Tremblay, who accused Trudeau and Rolland of all manner of vices. Stung to the quick, the two Quebeckers in Paris wrote

---

* "Delly" was the pen name of two writers, brother and sister, who wrote best-selling schmaltzy novels, particularly in the first half of the twentieth century.

a three-page reply that is notable for its bluntness: "We believe that art is part of life, and that a person has not been properly educated if he or she cannot look at the Venus de Milo without feeling scandalized. *Les Enfants du Paradis* is a work of art. . . . But in the province of Quebec, the authorities want to protect us from art itself, because art breathes flesh and we live in constant dread of the flesh. . . . Religious education in Quebec centres on a single dogma: that sexuality is the path leading to eternal damnation. . . . Accordingly, the only people being recruited for Christ are colourless virgins, flabby parishioners, retarded church-wardens and psychopaths in cassocks. But we believe that Christianity is a religion of virile men and healthy women, and we refuse to be cas-trated. We're troubled that a religion at once bold, generous and sublime, is mainly being used to educate the scrupulous, the constipated and the moronic."[58] It should come as no surprise that the editor, Guy Jasmin, told them that their incendiary reply had no place in his newspaper and he "doubted whether any French newspaper in Canada would publish it verbatim."[59] The film remained banned in Quebec for twenty years, and Trudeau's fiery response remained unpublished, as predicted.

Trudeau wrote in his memoirs that he adopted personalism while in Paris, and he mentioned Jacques Maritain and Emmanuel Mounier in connection with this.[60] Strangely, he did not mention Nicolas Berdyaev. Yet we have proof that not only did he study *Slavery and Freedom* very carefully – underlining passages, writing in notes, adding comments in the margins – but he also kept this book until the end of his life.[61] We therefore believe that a brief presentation of Berdyaev is in order.

Born in Kiev into an aristocratic family, Berdyaev (1874–1948) was a Marxist in the early 1900s but later rose up against what he called totalitarian Marxism. Since he was openly critical of the Bolshevik regime, he had to flee Russia in 1922 and settled in Paris two years later. It was here that he wrote most of his works. He was in Paris when Trudeau was there. Berdyaev considered himself resolutely personalist and socialist at the same time, but he categorically rejected the Bolshevik revolution, because it was "based on the supremacy of society over the person." He strongly believed that the "capacity to experience pain [was] inherent in every living creature . . . but not in collective realities nor in ideal values . . . such as society, nation, state, civilization, church."[62] From this basic principle he contrasted "patriotism," which he linked with personalism, to "nationalism," which he linked with individualism. Personalism, on the one hand, had "a communal tendency, it desir[ed] to establish brotherly relations among men. Individualism in social life, on the other hand, establishe[d] wolfish relations among men.[63] . . . With the triumph of nationalism the strong state dominates over the person."[64] He added, with obvious disdain: "The most mediocre and the most insignificant man feels himself exalted and raised through his share in what is 'national.'" He insisted, moreover, that the brotherhood of man does not confer any rights on the community or nation. "The 'we' is not a collective subject or substance.[65] . . . The idea of the supremacy of society over the person . . . is reactionary, counterrevolutionary."[66] The virtues of French-Canadian nationalism had been drummed into Trudeau, who had ended up believing that revolution in the name of the nation was justified, but he was now won over by Berdyaev's arguments. In 1964, he wrote an article in *Cité libre* entitled "Separatist Counter-Revolutionaries."[67]

Berdyaev also criticized nationalism on the grounds of his faith: "Christianity is a personalist and universal religion not a national, not a racial one. Every time that nationalism proclaims Germany for the Germans, France for the French, Russia for the Russians, it reveals its pagan and non-human nature. . . . Nationalism is . . . a terrible sin against the image of God in man. He who does not see a brother in man but another nationality, who, for example, refuses to see a brother in a Jew, such a one is not only not Christian, but he is losing his own proper humanity, his own human depth."[68] Trudeau had already been exposed to the dark side of nationalism and was now studying a devastating critique of this notion from a Christian perspective. He underlined the passage and wrote "important" in the margin. Berdyaev convinced him that a person could not be a nationalist and a Christian simultaneously. This explains Trudeau's later horror of slogans such as "Quebec for Quebeckers," chanted by many of his fellow Catholics in the 1960s.

Berdyaev's personalism allowed for some form of inequality between people: "I believe in a real aristocracy of the person, in the existence of men of genius and of great men who always recognize the duty of service, and feel the necessity not only to rise but also to

descend. But I do not believe in the aristocracy of a group, in an aristocracy which is founded upon social assortment. There is nothing
more repellent than contempt for the mass of the people among those
who regard themselves as the elite."[69] Trudeau liked this passage: he not
only underlined it but added a double bar in the margin. Like Berdyaev,
he would always accept the concept of an aristocracy defined in terms
of the intrinsic qualities of the person but would strive to reduce inequalities of wealth and social conditions.

According to Berdyaev, "Knowledge of truth demands a victory over
fear."[70] Trudeau applied this principle to his own life. Recounting his
journey around the world in 1948–1949, he wrote: "This trip was basically a challenge I set myself. . . . I wanted to know, for instance, whether
I could . . . travel across a war-torn country . . . without succumbing to
panic."[71] All his life, Trudeau was a lover of truth who refused to give in
to fear. Canadians, including his greatest enemies, acknowledged his
exceptional courage, which was put to the test several times during his
political career. Could this bold determination to vanquish fear have
been inspired and strengthened by reading Berdyaev?

To sum up: Berdyaev's personalism, as articulated in *Slavery and
Freedom,* had the following features: the primacy of the person over the
collectivity; the rejection of nationalism in the name of Christian values,
faith in a Christian kind of socialism emphasizing the dignity of the
person; recognition of an aristocracy based on talent rather than on
social status or wealth; ability to vanquish fear in the demanding search
of truth. There are so many similarities between these ideas and those
of Trudeau that it clearly seems to us that his personalism cannot be
properly understood without due reference to Berdyaev.

On April 3, 1947, Trudeau made a presentation before the "Robert
Aron group at the École Normale" entitled "The Promise of Quebec."[72]
This presentation throws a most interesting light on his political
thoughts and marks a major turning point in his intellectual evolution.
Here lies the kernel of the position he defended for the rest of his life.
Since his departure from Quebec, in 1944, he had devoted considera-
ble energy to learning. He had listened, read, reflected, and assessed
his old beliefs in the light of new ideas and new experiences. Yet

Quebec always remained central to his concerns. Now, three years later, he felt ready and eager to present his ideas in public. This talk was timely. As usual, he threw himself heart and soul into the enterprise, writing and rewriting his speech. We have found three versions of the typed text, each containing numerous handwritten corrections. We are using the one with the fewest corrections, without noting the small differences between it and the others.

By way of introduction, Trudeau ridiculed the grotesque description of the vastness of North America (made, as we know, by Professor Siegfried). He then brought up the unavoidable question: "Are you first of all Canadians or French Canadians?" His exasperation was evident in the biting irony of his reply: "That is the question to which the experts in fine rhetorical distinctions have applied their cunning, and which they hope will let them determine once and for all whether we are broad-minded or narrow-minded. Well, to tell you the truth, we are both Canadians and French Canadians, and actually we are also Americans because we live in America: Who is so limited that he cannot spread his vision over several horizons?"

Trudeau then announced: "I want to talk about the promise made to the world by my country, Canada, and especially my little *patrie* [homeland] of Quebec. . . ." Note the formulation which is now commonly accepted in Quebec: "Canada, my country, Quebec, *ma patrie* [my homeland]." This formulation faithfully expresses Trudeau's sense of identity. He no longer hesitated to consider himself Canadian. Nor did he hesitate to define Quebec as his homeland. The Trudeau of 1947 accepted Berdyaev's conception of patriotism, that is an emotional attachment to a group or place: "Love for one's people," Berdyaev wrote, "is a very natural and good thing." The same can be said of "love of one's native land, of one's soil, of one's people."[73] Contrary to the image being peddled about him, Trudeau would always accept, as a good thing, the emotional attachment of an individual to a particular group and to a specific place. In an interview we conducted with him in 1996, he summarized his idea of multiculturalism: "It is about recognizing that it is perfectly normal for people to want to associate with others with whom they feel certain cultural affinities, including language."[74] The idea he was already refuting here, in 1947, as he would the rest of his life, was the politicization of the concept of nation. In 1962, he proclaimed, in his pithy style, "It is not the concept of *nation* that is retrograde; it is the idea that the nation must necessarily be sovereign."[75]

Trudeau dreamed of a great future for his people. The French Canadians, he said, "have always had at heart the protection of their intellectual and spiritual autonomy." But he now understood that it was thanks to the federal system that "French Canada has developed the personality that enables it . . . to avoid becoming a mere spectator in the [planetary] game played out between peoples." He listed some of Quebec's achievements: it was the "only province of Canada that has enshrined French as an official language, the only one where the old French law still has the force of law, the only one where the Roman Church is universally established and respected." We French Canadians, he said, should take particular pride in our legal system, which corresponds to "our national character." Even if our legal system is no better than others, it "still has the merit of being our own. . . . Nobody can count without *our* procedure, *our* lawyers, *our* courts."

Trudeau was well aware that these gains had been achieved through hard work and struggle. But the situation had now changed. Living side by side had been of benefit to both the French- and English-Canadian communities: "From the encounter at the federal level of two highly distinctive national ways of life, a happy mixture often resulted. The French Canadian has a strong philosophy of life that gives him direction and hope; the English Canadian is more pragmatic. The first has a generous nature, while the second channels this virtue into socialism. The first is a person of high devotion, the second can better organize his efforts."

Toward the end of his stay in Paris, having associated with left-wing Catholic intellectuals and having carefully read the personalist Berdyaev and others, Trudeau, more than ever, saw socialism in terms of Christian social justice. But why did he think English Canadians were the ones who would usher in socialism? Probably because he now had a better grasp of the political ideas of the CCF (Co-operative Commonwealth Federation) and admired the struggles waged by this socialist party since it was founded in 1932 by the "English" of Calgary in Alberta. He also admired the fact that, once again, since January 1, 1947, the Saskatchewan CCF government, under T.C. Douglas, had pioneered the first system of compulsory and universal health insurance in Canada. To Trudeau, it was federalism that would enable French Canadians to join forces with English socialists and benefit from their experience. This was all the more important since Canada's Catholic archbishops and bishops, most of them French Canadians, had condemned the CCF in 1933.[76]

But this was not the sole advantage of federalism. By belonging to Canada, French Canadians benefited from the country's British heritage: "There is no doubt that British institutions cannot rival the crystal-clear perfection of utopian constructs; but in terms of what actually exists, we should be very pleased to have in our country a conception of politics based on respect for the individual. This ensures compliance with civil liberty protections (habeas corpus, the presumption of innocence in criminal law, for example) and political freedom (democracy based on the famous *agreement to disagree*)." Trudeau was well aware that the cohabitation of the French and English groups was not easy, since they both aspired to control the state. But he attributed this rivalry to faulty logic: people believed that to each nation should correspond its own state. "How can two different nations be identified with the same state? This problem set Canadian opinion onto three equally destructive perspectives." To Trudeau, these three perspectives were obsolete and should be scrapped. They constituted a major obstacle on Quebec's path toward a bright future.

He began with the separatist arguments: "Since Canada has two ethnic entities each with its own collective will, our country should accommodate two sovereign states. This solution might seem to be a true judgment of Solomon, since it guaranteed each of the two parties 'peace and honour.'" False, retorted Trudeau: "Such a division would only succeed in avoiding civil war while laying the conditions for future wars between nations." He believed that once the principle of dividing up a country according to ethnic criteria was accepted, it would become impossible to stop the spiral of subsequent splits demanded by new minorities. Trudeau tirelessly defended this argument until his dying breath. For example in the 1962 article "The New Treason of the Intellectuals," he reminded the separatists that "the very idea of nation-state is absurd. . . . Because every national minority will find, at the very moment of liberation, a new minority within its bosom which in turn must be allowed the right to demand its freedom."[77]

To those who maintain that this wouldn't happen in Quebec, let us remind them about the heated and hate-filled debates that raged in the aftermath of the 1995 referendum.* When the close results made it seem that the secession of Quebec was a distinct possibility, some minority groups demanded to remain part of Canada and to secede in turn from Quebec. Some did not exclude the possibility of fighting for their rights. This crisis came as no surprise to Trudeau. In 1998, recalling "The New Treason of the Intellectuals," he wrote, "I recorded that observation in 1962, more than thirty years before the movement of some anglophone and native communities to partition Quebec in the event of its separation from Canada. I'm not claiming any prophetic powers. Logic made it absolutely predictable."[78] We now know that he had actually recorded these remarks forty-five years earlier, in 1947. But he obviously could not refer to "The Promise of Quebec," which has not been published to this day.

Trudeau moved on to the second perspective typically held by the "imperialists," who were "more likely to be on the English side of the population." This group equated the state with the nation in order to "assimilate or quite simply wipe out one of the two nations (preferably not their own!)." But this, he claimed, was a perspective held by a tiny group of people: "In general, Canadians distanced themselves from the imperialist solution. Only extremists believed in this creed, that is, people living at the outer edge of normality: megalomaniacs, the paranoid and frustrated, plus a few oafish thugs who revelled in brutality." That's that for what he thinks of "imperialists"!

The third perspective fared no better – quite the contrary. This group was made up of people who naïvely believed in a "half-baked union between our two great nations [that] would create a more or less homogeneous Canadian nation and would be incorporated in a single state." Trudeau described this group as "foot soldiers lying prostrate before the English language" and "wimps always willing to compromise." Nothing less. And to achieve this fanciful Canadian nation, he declared that "all these brave fellows were pressuring us to make a

* This was the second Quebec referendum on separation. The first referendum, held in May 1980, clearly favoured Canadian unity; the question of the partition of Quebec was therefore not raised.

shameful transaction – bartering our language, faith, culture, patriotism, honour and personality for some supposed 'unity.'" It is not hard to guess that, to him, this third group comprised French Canadians who were not up to the task of defending the interests of their people. Trudeau, a true "son of Quebec," could not tolerate this contemptible point of view.

He then asked a rhetorical question: If these various solutions were so inadequate, why call his presentation "The Promise of Quebec"? What would enable Quebec to fulfil its great destiny? The answer lay in federalism. He explained: "The concept of sovereignty is four centuries old and has lost its relevance . . . in the age of the World Bank, international cartels, economic imperialism, the Communist International, interstate commissions and the atomic bomb." On the other hand, federalism "held unsuspected riches: federated nations were no longer rivals doomed to coexist in the same cage and condemned to live at the expense of one another, they were ethnic entities that pursued their national objectives in strict independence with the possibility of collaborating with each other in the pursuit of higher goals." Trudeau had high hopes in federalism. This system "would allow Quebec to define a surprisingly large role for itself among the concert of nations." Without renouncing who we are, he said, "we need to recognize that our *patrie* [homeland] is also part of an enormous country. . . . The man of the twentieth century cannot feel cramped in a country whose proud device is '*A mari usque ad mare.*'"

Federalism was not the status quo. Trudeau was sure that Quebec could and would improve the Canadian federation so that it would meet the requirements of a new age. At this point, he could no longer contain his enthusiasm and gave a quasi-mystical twist to his presentation: "And this multi-faceted social apparatus will always be aimed at the betterment of mankind, so that the man at the bottom will rise to the summit, made greater by love of his neighbour, and enriched by all the resulting interchanges. . . . Why should you only ask for the moon when you can also have the sun, stars and ocean?" One wonders if Trudeau was not presenting in Paris his own version of the apostolic mission of French Canadians. He clearly saw Quebec leading Canada toward a bright future: "Quebec will illustrate the discipline architects call 'functional.' Functional politics will not maintain the thousand prejudices inflicted by the past on the present, but will seek instead to build in the interests of the whole man." (The notion of functional politics, mentioned here for the first time, repeatedly turned up in the pages of *Cité libre*.)

Trudeau then wondered whether Quebec would fulfil this promise. But his optimism quickly prevailed. A proper understanding of federalism would put an end to the futile shifting between narrow-minded nationalism, impersonal Canadianism, and insipid pan-Americanism. Besides, he was not alone in feeling this optimism: "Many young people are preparing to teach the synthesis of heart-felt patriotism and broad-minded humanism." He stressed, however, that it was urgent to act: the struggle of these young people "will not last very long because if they do not win soon, Quebec will quickly become a reactionary obstacle along the path of progress in America." In order to succeed they would have to change their mentality: "Their struggle will be all the harder as they will have to lead a people to battle who owed its very survival to defensive actions. The Quebec people would have to make the leap from conservatism to revolution." But Trudeau said they would win out in the end, because "it is a matter of life or death, and the immense hopes and indomitable will of the Quebec people will come through."

Then a question arises: Who would help French Canadians throw off their conservatism, throw off defensive attitudes, and become revolutionaries? Traditionally, the mantle of guide had fallen on the Catholic Church. Trudeau himself had accepted that, as we saw in his 1942 project of "national revolution."[79] But by 1947, his view had changed radically. He paid a brief tribute to the Church for contributing to the well-being of French-Canadian society and defending its language and faith. Then he went on the attack. The Church had established a system of education that unfortunately resulted in "a spirit of conservatism hostile to any form of change, a form of religiosity close to Jansenism, and narrow-mindedness bordering on xenophobia." Today, he said, these characteristics "undermine the vitality of our people." The ecclesiastics had grown used to their role, "marching nobly ahead of the flock, and are now indignant about having to walk at our side: ecclesiastical guardianship over education and particularly social education has smothered us to the point where tragically we have to seek emancipation outside of the Church of Quebec. But here again, we shall prevail, and there is more evidence of this every day." He was accusing the French-Canadian Church of being an obstacle to progress. No less. Of seeking emancipation outside the Church. It is hard to imagine today just how heretical these statements were in 1947. Had Trudeau lost his faith? Not in the least. For him, "the plan of reform drafted outside of the Church is not directed against it, since the best elements of our elite (which includes several priests) are profoundly Catholic."

A year later, Trudeau wanted to publish his speech. On June 23, 1948, shortly before his departure on his round-the-world tour, he wrote to Roger Rolland, "You ask what I should do with my article 'The Promise of Quebec.' Your idea of my having it published in *La Table ronde* is very nice, but probably unrealistic. Besides I have no more time to take care of this, or even the desire to do so. Keep the article, then, and if the opportunity ever arises to publish it (in France, Canada or elsewhere), do your best." Trudeau's faithful friend worked hard at it. In November 1948, he sent a copy to *Le Devoir*. No answer came back. He pestered the deputy editor-in-chief, André Laurendeau, who finally replied on February 11, 1949: "At first I thought I could publish Pierre Elliott Trudeau's presentation, which I find very interesting as a whole. Except, however, for one paragraph, which I showed to three or four friends I consider particularly 'open-minded.' The result was negative: they told me that publishing the presentation, as is, would be wrong not only for the author but also for the newspaper." And which sentence was the cause of their torment? It was, of course, the one referring to the Church. Laurendeau quoted it, emphasizing the unacceptable words: "Ecclesiastical guardianship over education and particularly social education has smothered us to the point *where tragically we have to seek emancipation outside of the Church of Quebec*." While deploring the intellectual climate in the province, Laurendeau nonetheless felt he was "reluctantly forced to reject the entire article."[80] The efforts to silence Trudeau were just beginning.

Summer was now approaching. The time has come for us to assess Trudeau's stay in Paris. His unpublished article, "The Promise of Quebec," gives us a very good idea of his state of mind in 1947. It also casts new light on what Paris contributed to the evolution of his political thought. It is often claimed that this period was some kind of parenthesis, which allowed him to have a good time. This was just not the case.

Trudeau did not get swept up in some whirlwind of social and cultural activities. He refined his thinking, he synthesized what he had learned up to that point, and he began to articulate his ideas in public. The separatist Trudeau was now dead and buried. This "son of Quebec" who identified strongly with "his people," his "ethnic group," and his French-Canadian "nation" had now become a staunch federalist. We have seen that his entire approach to politics was carried through a Quebec perspective and was directed toward the good of his people. But after two years of study at Harvard, followed by readings and discussion in Paris, he had become convinced that federalism offered French Canadians a framework ideally suited to their needs and their fulfilment. In the same breath, he now accused the Quebec Church of hindering the progress of the people. Federalism was the future, the voice of reason, the way to reconcile patriotism and humanism. Trudeau brimmed with enthusiasm, because he had found the path Quebec should follow to achieve its enormous potential. Contemplating the future in high spirits and trusting the good sense of French Canadians, he felt that victory was at hand.

Chapter 4

"BRITISH-STYLE" SOCIALISM

When order cannot be reconciled with justice and when hatred has stifled love, the time for negotiations is over.

           – PIERRE ELLIOTT TRUDEAU, 1947*

TRUDEAU RETURNED FROM PARIS to spend his holidays in Quebec, just as he had done after leaving Harvard. Quebec was the home of his sweetheart, Thérèse Gouin, and of his passion, politics. But on June 22, 1947, shortly after his arrival in Montreal, disaster struck. Thérèse was leaving him for good.[1] On July 10, he wrote to her brother Lomer Gouin that Thérèse had removed all reason for him to live.[2] But you wouldn't have guessed it from the whirlwind of his activities. Trudeau did not hang around in Montreal. He loved to hike and took off with three friends for Lac Saint-Jean, hitching a ride as far as La Tuque, then walking the rest of the way – nearly 150 kilometres.[3] On August 19, he headed north on a motorcycle. He played tennis, went riding, and learned how to pilot an airplane. He took his first flying lesson on August 1. On September 3, he flew solo for the first time and repeated this feat twice before the holidays were over. He also visited with some old friends, such as François Lessard and Jean-Baptiste Boulanger, with whom he had wanted to launch the "national revolution," although he was now decidedly a federalist. He hung out at the Cercle universitaire de l'Université de Montréal (the Faculty Club) and visited Gérard Pelletier, whom he had got to

---

* P.E. Trudeau, "On Lawyers and Others, and Their Relationships with Justice," *Notre Temps*, November 14, 1947.

81

know better in Paris. He often associated with François Hertel, who had also just returned from Paris to spend the summer in Quebec.

But summer was going by quickly and his departure for London approaching. He was itching to present his ideas in public, just as he had done the previous April with "The Promise of Quebec." So he did the rounds of the French-Canadian intelligentsia, with an eye on future publications. On September 5, Trudeau and the omnipresent Hertel visited Abbé Groulx, the historian and leader of Quebec nationalists. He knew Groulx's ideas well and had studied them at Collège Jean-de-Brébeuf and the Université de Montréal. What did they discuss? Nobody knows. But they were no longer on the same wavelength, and Trudeau knew it. On September 8, he met the editor of Le Devoir, Gérard Filion. The next day, he went to see Léopold Richer, the passionate nationalist and former partisan of the Bloc Populaire, who had founded the review Notre Temps in 1944. The meetings with Filion and Richer bore fruit: they published Trudeau's very first articles.

Trudeau met Claude Ryan twice. Ryan had been national secretary of the French-Canadian wing of Catholic Action since 1945 and remained in this position until 1962. He went on to hold several prominent positions in Quebec, including director of Le Devoir, head of the Quebec Liberal Party, and minister of education in the government of Robert Bourassa. When the two men met in the summer of 1947, Ryan was twenty-two. He had already attracted a lot of attention in his role as secretary of Catholic Action. He worked actively to forge links with committees of young Catholics outside Quebec. Interested in this project, Trudeau accompanied Ryan to Toronto in August to attend a meeting of Catholic associations in Canada. On September 10, the two met up again in Montreal.

Some readers may remember the great animosity Ryan later bore Trudeau as prime minister. Marc Lalonde, who held several key positions in the Trudeau government, told us that "Ryan was never able to stomach Trudeau. I think it was something instinctive."[4] At first, we also believed this antipathy went way back to the beginning of their relationship. We were wrong. On September 10, 1947, Trudeau explored with Ryan the prospect of collaborating with the Catholic movements in Quebec. After the meeting, Ryan sent Trudeau a list of concrete tasks he could perform in England on behalf of the "proletarians back in Canada."

And Ryan concluded, admiringly, "It has been a revelation for us, to meet a guy like you – you are so close to us whereas so many things seemed to separate us. We know that in spite of the distance, our indefinable loyalty will nourish our relationship."[5] Two months later, Ryan's admiration for Trudeau was as strong as ever. In November, in a review he published called *Jeunesse canadienne*, Ryan wrote an article entitled "Jeunes Canadiens au Vieux Monde" – "Young Canadians in the Old World," offering brief profiles of French Canadians then pursuing graduate studies in Europe. Ryan wrote about Trudeau: "What will Pierre do, once he returns to Quebec? Providence has showered him with so much ability and knowledge that he could excel in any area: the arts, the humanities, philosophy, politics, economics, he is well-versed in all of them. He will only have to choose. What we *do* know is that he will return, and that he has remained a proud Canadian."[6]

Doesn't it seem strange that the same Ryan contributed to a 1972 collective work called *L'anti-Trudeau*, in which the preface claims that "the following articles tell us Trudeau is formalistic, idealistic, arrogant and dangerous"?[7] Dangerous. Nothing less. In 1947, Ryan was not alone in his admiration of Trudeau. At the time, most French Canadians considered him exceptionally talented, yet affable and dedicated. Although he had every reason to be a snob, he was actually a man of astonishing simplicity. Everyone knew how proud he was to be French Canadian. Trouble would start only several years later.

On September 23, 1947, Trudeau reached beyond the French-Canadian milieu. He met Frank Scott, a prominent member of the English-speaking community. Born in Quebec City in 1899, Scott was a professor of constitutional law at McGill University, a superb poet, and a committed intellectual. His anti-conscription stand had already endeared him to the French Canadians and angered his fellow anglophones.[8] Since his studies at Oxford as a Rhodes Scholar, he had become a strong proponent of Christian socialism. When Trudeau met him, he was a founding member of the Co-operative Commonwealth Federation (or CCF) and had served as its president since 1942. (In 1961, the CCF became the New Democratic Party.) We have seen that in Paris, Trudeau saluted English Canadians for having brought socialism to Canada through the CCF. Although Quebec bishops continued to warn their flock about the extreme dangers the CCF posed for their salvation,

Trudeau now knew that the party's first leader, J.S. Woodsworth (1874–1942) had been a Methodist minister and not a communist atheist. This first encounter with Scott developed into a lasting friendship. In 1981, at a symposium on Scott, Trudeau said, with great generosity, "Frank taught me everything I know."[9]

Contacts with Filion of *Le Devoir,* Richer of *Notre Temps,* Ryan of Catholic Action, Frank Scott and the CCF: clearly, Trudeau was not sweetly spending his Quebec vacation in idleness. But all good things come to an end. On September 27, 1947, he set sail on the *Empress of Canada* in first class. Destination: London.

———◦———

The England he discovered had just vanquished the Nazis, with the help of the United States and the Soviet Union and others, of course. But this victory owed a lot to the courage and stubborn determination of the British people, who had accepted deprivation and suffering without a whimper, even when Hitler's armies seemed invincible. "I have nothing to offer but blood, toil, tears, and sweat," Winston Churchill famously declared, on taking power in May 1940 at the head of the Conservative Party. "We have before us an ordeal of the most grievous kind. We have before us many, many months of struggle and suffering."[10] Unfortunately, history has shown that he was not exaggerating. In that same speech, he stressed the need for everyone to join in the common cause. He set an example, by forming a coalition government. The Labour Party leader, Clement Attlee, became deputy prime minister. An influential member of the left wing of the party, Ernest Bevin, was appointed minister of labour and national service. The nation followed suit. Thus the desperate fight against Nazism forged a strong bond among the British. It is well known how much blood and tears were spent during the long years of war. Less known is the fact that this war transformed the social and political landscape of Britain for at least two reasons: first because the state had to play a particularly important role in the economy, and second because, ironically, the war laid the foundations for Labour's victory in 1945.

In January 1940, the government took the first steps to a planned economy and intervened in areas normally considered within the citizens' private sphere. For example, it prohibited embroidery and cuffs on pants and even decreed the length of socks.[11] It imposed the rationing of almost all products. Surprisingly, these measures were very well accepted by the population; they created a sense of equality or at least reduced disparities. Rationing, for example, tended to penalize the rich while improving the plight of the poor. The government's fiscal policy, adopted to meet wartime expenditures, had the same effect. Taxes were raised to a record level. As one would expect, this measure naturally had a greater impact on the wealthy. Equally demanding on the wealthy was the government's right to requisition secondary residences when the war effort required it. Conscription also helped smooth out social differences. With the men off at war and the women working in factories or elsewhere, finding domestic help became a challenge for wealthy people. So they got used to getting their hands dirty. A spirit of equality thus found its way into social attitudes, clearing the way for greater acceptance of the notion of equality of opportunity, a cardinal principle of socialism.

A few dissenting voices were still heard. Take, for example, Friedrich Hayek – whose works Trudeau had studied in an economics course at Harvard. Hayek, a colleague of Harold Laski's at the LSE, was strongly opposed to any form of government intervention. In the best-seller *The Road to Serfdom* (1944), a work translated into many languages, Hayek sharply criticized the government's economic policy (and by "government" he meant the Labour Party) – claiming that it paved the way to "planned Socialism" of the Soviet type. Hayek not only denounced the economic inefficiency of this system, but also the inevitable servitude to which it would lead.

In general, British citizens didn't take these critiques too seriously. On the contrary, in their daily lives they welcomed the radical social transformations brought about by the coalition government's policies. With good reason, some may say. In 1942 the "Beveridge Report" (officially known as "The Treasury White Paper of 1942") paved the way to social security for all. It confidently predicted the ultimate triumph of peace and social justice after the war. Although opposition from the Conservative Party held up its immediate application in practice, "the notion that a triumphant left would, with peace, remake the world to usher in a new age of democracy and equality" made inroads.[12]

July 5, 1945, marked a historic day for Great Britain. Churchill, the lion who had stirred and rallied his people so magnificently during the darkest years of the war, was now roundly defeated in the elections. For the first time ever, the country was ruled by a majority Labour government. Under Clement Attlee, this party remained in power from 1945 to 1951, and according to many experts it formed one of the best governments in British history. The historian William D. Rubinstein, for example, maintains that "by common consent, the Labour government was one of the ablest of the twentieth century, quite possibly the very best, and the government with the most achievements to its credit, at least in peacetime."[13] According to Monica Charlot, a world-renowned specialist on Britain and professor emeritus at the Sorbonne, "Labour's social policies, implemented in just a few years, will go down in history as one of the most significant contributions of a government to the transformation of British society."[14] One of Labour's most spectacular achievements was the so-called welfare state.

However, the Labour government did not have an easy time implementing its program. On the contrary, fate seemed to be working against it. In 1946, the country faced a severe food shortage. Even bread, which had been sold without restriction during the war, was now added to the long list of rationed goods. All restaurants were prohibited from offering it to accompany main dishes.[15] At the end of 1947, almost all food was still rationed. At times, some staple products, including gasoline, were simply unavailable. Rationing lasted a long time. Tea and sugar were rationed until 1952, and the rationing of butter, bacon, and meat was not lifted until 1954.[16]

Things got even worse. In Britain, 1947 is sometimes called "annus horrendous."[17] In the midst of a global shortage of both food and coal, the country now faced the coldest winter in more than half a century. In response, the government enacted exceptional measures: "The supply of electrical power to individual homes was interrupted from 9 am to 12 pm, and again from 2 pm to 4 pm. Street lighting was removed; escalators, particularly in the Tube, and elevators were shut down; traffic lights were switched off."[18] This terrible winter was then followed by a particularly dry summer, threatening the harvest. Mother Nature was not exactly coddling Labour!

The British population was beginning to realize that Great Britain no longer held the powerful position it had enjoyed before the war. The country's external debt placed it on the verge of bankruptcy. Fortunately, in June 1947, General George C. Marshall, U.S. Secretary of State, announced, in the famous speech where he noted "the dislocation of the entire fabric of European economy," that Europe "must have substantial help . . . principally from America" for three or four years. On April 3, 1948, the European Recovery Program, better known as the Marshall Plan, came into effect. "This unexpected windfall of dollars made 1948 the year of Britain's economic recovery," writes Charlot.[19] *The Economist* of March 19, 1949, attributed much of this success to Labour: "1948 will stand as an example of what can be achieved by economic planning when it is based on clarity of thought and backed by political courage."[20]

Indeed, the government did not wait for the Marshall Plan to launch the vast program of policies that transformed British society forever. Drawing inspiration from the Beveridge Report, it embarked on the ambitious project of setting up a system of social security for the entire population. A key part of it was the National Health Service (NHS), mapped out in 1946 and established in 1948. This very avant-garde and even revolutionary reform provided all citizens with access to free health care. But the government went further. It gradually set up unemployment and workmen's compensation insurance, a retirement plan, maternity leave, and free access to legal services. In 1947, it raised the age of compulsory schooling to fifteen years.

The Labour government revolutionized the social landscape and also changed Britain's economic structures. It nationalized coal, steel, transport, and the Bank of England, for example. Notwithstanding the demobilization of three million combatants after the war, the government managed to curb unemployment. Thanks to the Marshall Plan and devaluation of the pound sterling, the external debt was reduced and was almost completely eliminated in 1949. Little wonder that this Labour government ranks as one of the best Britain has ever known. Trudeau reached London two years after Labour had come to power and witnessed first-hand the benefits of "British-style" socialism, which he considered close to his own Christian ideal. He drew many elements of his "Just Society" from the British model.

Whereas the government's domestic policy was based on "socialist" principles, this was not the case with its foreign policy. Although the Labour Party had a pro-Soviet wing, cabinet members were openly anti-Communist. So when Churchill visited the United States in 1946 and spoke of the "Iron Curtain" now dividing Europe (he coined the expression) and called for greater collaboration between Britain and the United States, Labour followed suit without reservation. It wanted to stop the spread of Communism just as much as the Conservatives did. This is why, in 1947, the foreign secretary, Ernest Bevin, endorsed the "Truman Doctrine," according to which the United States undertook to prevent any attempt at Communist expansion in Europe. Rubinstein asserts: "By the later 1940's the Attlee government had thus entered the Cold War in a full-hearted way as America's closest ally, a situation which has, in effect, continued until the present."[21] Trudeau carefully studied this anti-Communist socialism during his stay in London. He found it consistent with his beliefs. Unlike many *Cité libre* collaborators, including Gérard Pelletier, Trudeau never shared Emmanuel Mounier's sympathy with the French Communist Party.

This was the backdrop for Trudeau's entrance onto the London stage. He arrived on October 4, 1947, enrolled on the 6th at the London School of Economics, and two days later met the man who would become one of his mentors: Harold Joseph Laski. What was Trudeau's status at the LSE? He was officially "a research student at this school from October 1947 till June, 1948 in the Department of Government under the supervision of Professor Laski."[22] He signed up for eight courses. But we have found no grades, no formal assessment, no trace of any thesis. In theory Trudeau had to submit a research topic to qualify for the Ph.D. program. He probably did. Among his Paris papers we found two thesis topics written on a Lux soap wrapper: "Liberties embodied in Canadian Constitution" and "Bill of Rights not in BNA but in reality."[23] There is no further mention of these topics. In *Memoirs,* Trudeau wrote that at Harvard, he had already chosen as the topic of his doctoral thesis "the interplay between two doctrines, Christianity and Marxism, which were competing for Asians' loyalty. I chose India as my area of study."[24] However, when Laski gave him a letter of recommendation, he made no mention of any Ph.D. project: "The bearer of this letter, Mr. Pierre Trudeau, is well-known to me. He has been a member of my seminars in this school, and has won both my regard and respect for his vigour and tenacity of mind, and for his power to arrive independently at his conclusions. I recommend him with warmth and respect."[25]

Trudeau's unfinished thesis is often cited as evidence of his lack of seriousness, his dilettantism. For example, in April 2002, the journalist and Trudeau biographer Michel Vastel[26] wrote a vitriolic article attacking the CBC for failing to report that Trudeau was "a dilettante who regularly skipped classes at university, and who managed to get out of Harvard, the Sorbonne and the London School of Economics without any degree."[27] Just for the record, we should make it clear that Trudeau obtained a master's degree at Harvard and was at no time enrolled at the Sorbonne.

It is true, though, that he has no doctoral dissertation to his credit. Is this convincing evidence of his dilettantism? Not in our view. The career path Trudeau was planning to follow did not require a Ph.D. He enrolled at the LSE to further his education and get to know Harold Laski, this brilliant professor who managed to combine an academic career with active participation in politics. And in this regard, the LSE served its purpose admirably. Most of Trudeau's classes revolved around Laski. He met him regularly, every week, in one-on-one or small group discussions as part of the "Government Seminar." This gave him the chance to soak up the powerful ideas of the physically diminutive but intellectually great Laski. He took a hundred pages of notes during this professor's course, nearly twice as much as in all of his other courses combined. Throughout his life, Trudeau remembered Laski with admiration, gratitude, and emotion, as he later demonstrated in an article for the first issue of *Cité libre* in June 1950.

The historian Max Beloff has called the inter-war period "The Age of Laski."[28] Many people have asserted that countless students had had "the fires of their minds and souls lit by Harold Laski . . . one of the greatest teachers of our time."[29] He had a big hand in training many future Third World leaders, such as Jawaharlal Nehru, the leading figure of India's struggle for independence and its prime minister from 1947 to 1964. Nehru never tired of urging young Indians to study with Laski. He was not only an excellent teacher with a remarkable mastery of his subject but also very funny. At the LSE, people knew he "was lecturing when every five minutes or so a great burst of laughter could be heard through the rest of the building."[30] He loved to rub shoulders with great personalities, and he seemed to know everyone. His writing was fine and clear, his sense of humour and remarkable eloquence were legendary. Aneurin "Nye" Bevan, minister of health in the Labour government in 1945, wrote in the *Daily Herald:* "Mr. Churchill has been described as the most articulate Englishman of his day, but I would give the prize to Harold Laski."[31]

Laski's ideas evolved over time. Before the First World War, he fought for the trade-union movement and universal suffrage. In the 1920s, he met the famous couple Sidney and Beatrice Webb, founders, with George Bernard Shaw, of the LSE, and joined the Webbs' "Fabian Society," a socialist movement that included many intellectuals, such as Shaw and H.G. Wells. But he later distanced himself from them. He revealed his Marxist sympathies in a famous work, *A Grammar of Politics.* For example, he wrote (and Trudeau underlined the sentence) that *"only by means of Marxism can I explain phenomena like the state as it appears in Fascist countries. . . . It is there, nakedly and without shame, what the state, covertly and apologetically is in capitalist democracies like Great Britain or the United States."*[32] However, his Marxist inclinations did not prevent him from opposing political violence or from vigorously defending human rights and the British parliamentary system.

Laski did not try to convert students to his views, despite his great powers of persuasion and exceptional eloquence. Instead, he encouraged rigorous analysis, intellectual autonomy, and active debates. Moreover, he invited renowned speakers to defend positions flatly contradicting his own and got students to read works that directly opposed his own ideas. This is how Trudeau attended three lectures given by the well-known French sociologist, political scientist, and journalist Raymond Aron, who sharply criticized all ideological orthodoxies, especially Marxism, as well as intellectuals like Jean-Paul Sartre, who sympathized with the French Communist Party. For Aron, a classless society as promised by Marxists was neither possible nor desirable: "A classless society," Trudeau noted while listening to Aron, "would oppose an unorganized mass to an organized elite, whereas democracy is pluralistic. A classless society leaves the masses without any means of defence against the elite."[33]

One of Laski's ideas must have particularly appealed to him: that "no one can teach politics who does not know politics at first hand."[34] Some people criticized Laski for his political activities, which they claimed were incompatible with the objectivity and detachment needed for scientific analysis. But Laski took such comments in stride and remained resolutely active in politics throughout his life. He was a member of the executive committee of the Labour Party from 1937 to 1949, a year before his death, and was its chairman in 1944–1945. However, when Trudeau studied at the LSE, in 1947–1948, internal dissensions had got the better of Laski's close involvement in the party. Laski had strongly backed the nomination of Herbert Morrison as leader of the party. Bitterly disappointed that his candidate was not chosen, he launched into fierce attacks on Attlee, who was now prime minister – even though Attlee had appointed Morrison deputy minister. This meant war. On August 20, 1945, an exasperated Attlee wrote to Laski that "a period of silence on your part would be welcome."[35] Laski distanced himself.

Laski got along well with Conservatives like Winston Churchill but couldn't stand some right-wing economists like Friedrich Hayek whom he described as "fanatical individualists."[36] Moreover, he strongly opposed the school commonly called British Idealism, the most prominent members being T.H. Green (1836–1882), F.H. Bradley (1846–1924), and Bernard Bosanquet (1848–1923). This was not an idealist school that happened to be British but rather a specific philosophical movement of some notoriety in the late nineteenth and early twentieth centuries. Laski argued (wrongly, some would say) that according to these philosophers "what is willed by the state is willed a priori by the individual. No difference between the two wills, because the state wills what the individual should really will." For Laski, this was the British idealist school's major fault. It led to "the abandonment of the individual as unique and the exaltation of the Nation, which the individual must serve by identifying his aims with those of the State."

True to his educational principles, Laski had his students read the works of major philosophers of this school. Trudeau later mentioned he had been initiated to "the philosophy of T.H. Green, whose liberalism preceded the personalism of Maritain and Mounier in saying that the focal point was not the state but the individual – the individual seen as a person integrated into society, which is to say endowed with fundamental rights and essential liberties, but also with responsibilities."[37] This interpretation of Green, written in 1993, contradicts what we find in his seven pages of notes, taken down in 1947, during the "Lectures on the Principles of Political Obligation." Several times, Trudeau expressed reservations similar to Laski's: "Green starts from the postulate that all rights and duties are social in principle. . . . This conception draws him dangerously close to the Hegelian form of the state." According to Hegel, the State – and more specifically the Prussian State – represented the most complete form of individual freedom. Trudeau was clearly against Green and for Laski. In 1957, Trudeau re-examined the question of who determines the "common weal" in an article published in the review *Vrai,* published by his friend Jacques Hébert. He wrote: "Tyrants always claim that their social order is based on the common good . . . but they reserve the right to define it as they see fit."[38]

Laski also criticized the British idealist school for ignoring the fact that the state defended the interests of the ruling class. Pursuing this thought along Marxist lines, he claimed in *A Grammar of Politics* that the class struggle would inevitably lead to revolution, because history shows that "no class in possession of state power has peacefully abandoned its possession. . . . The final conflict is when the bourgeoisie conflicts with the proletariat."[39]

Was Laski promoting a Communist revolution? Not in the least. He had no sympathy for the Communist Party and was deeply attached to many features of the British political system. Let us mention three of them. Regarding the advantages and shortcomings of various electoral systems, Trudeau noted that "Laski believes in a two party system." He also stated that while he opposed the principle of an Upper House, he still wanted "the House of Lords to keep on as it is," since politicians had failed to agree on either abolishing or reforming it. And what did this Marxist make of the monarchy? It is an "ideal system. The king can't do anything but he can draw attention to things. It forces the cabinet to have second thoughts, since his opinions can't be refused without the proper forms."

In practice, Laski, the "revolutionary" Marxist, was a reformer. He had no qualms about criticizing authoritarian regimes, such as the Soviet Union: "Today Laski thinks that in Russia the dictatorship is not *of* but *over* the proletariat. Like [in] any police state, [one finds there an] inability to criticize even harmlessly."* Moreover, although he believed that the class struggle necessarily led to revolution, he advocated recourse to reforms until the revolution actually occurred. His explanation: "The operations of the modern state rarely permit of successful revolution."

---

*   Our italics.

As a result, any party intent on transforming the economic basis of society must "maintain as long as it can the constitutional order which permits it openly to recruit its strength."[40] In theory, he only wanted to delay the revolution in order to avoid chaos. But in fact, he was not eager to bring it about, since democracy, despite its flaws, was to him the best political system. Trudeau wrote: "What is the case for democratic government? H.G. Wells: 'No case that can't have the bottom knocked out in ten minutes. But no other system of government can last five.'" In fact, Laski believed so strongly in its superiority that he held out the hope that "ultimately Russia will become a democracy more real than any we know." So Laski was at once a Marxist revolutionary, a reformist, and an advocate of parliamentary democracy. Trudeau was well aware of the contradictions in his professor's ideas and mentioned them in the otherwise very flattering eulogy he wrote in 1950 in *Cité libre*.

For Laski, "the central problem of Political Science is why some people obey authority." Trudeau was fascinated. He later wrote in *Memoirs*: "At the time, . . . I wanted to know how governments work and why people obey."[41] Laski refuted the notion of a universal ethical code. Its only function, he said, was to get citizens' approval of existing norms and principles. But then, how would people know which laws to obey? Ultimately, he maintained, "the roots of valid law . . . are, and can only be, within the individual conscience."[42] Trudeau was won over. He wrote in the above-mentioned article for *Vrai*: "It is the duty of citizens, therefore, to examine their consciences on the quality of the social order they share and the political authority they acknowledge."[43] Laski stressed the important role citizens play in the political realm. He strongly believed, like Lord Acton whom he quoted, that "power always corrupts, and absolute power corrupts absolutely." So constant vigilance was required: "In any society, whatever the reason for giving authority to the government, there is a reason to protect the individual against it." Maritain, who strongly upheld the necessity of charters of rights, shared this value. Likewise Trudeau championed it throughout his life.

Laski did not adhere to a single school of thought.[44] Some of the rights he considered essential to the blossoming of individual freedoms are typical of liberal democracies: for example, freedom of expression, or the right to universal suffrage. These rights were so important for him that "even a fascist movement should be able to run candidates." Other rights he advocated, such as the right to work at a reasonable wage or for a reasonable number of hours, are usually included in socialist or "left-wing" programs.

Trudeau was particularly impressed by the way Laski connected the concepts of freedom and equality. "Freedom," Trudeau noted, "is the result of the expansion of economic well-being. In the absence of butter, increase of freedom is in jeopardy." Yet, according to Alexis de Tocqueville and Lord Acton, freedom and equality are mutually exclusive (the more egalitarian a society, the less free its citizens, and vice versa). Laski opposed this restrictive interpretation of the notion of equality: "Equality does not mean that everyone has the same talent and needs the same education, same clothes, same house, etc. . . . Equality means: 1 – Absence of special privileges . . . 2 – Adequate opportunities laid open to all." Trudeau was bowled over by this conception of justice. In the chapter wrapping up *Towards a Just Society: The Trudeau Years* (1990), he wrote: "I have long believed that freedom is the most important value of a just society and the exercise of freedom its principal characteristic."[45] But he later realized that "the value with the highest priority in the pursuit of a Just Society had become equality. Not the procrustean* kind of equality where everyone is raised or lowered to a kind of middle ground. I mean equality of opportunity."[46] Laski has left his mark. This is the notion of equality enshrined in the Charter of Rights and Freedoms, as Trudeau explained: "Undoubtedly, the two main facets [of the Charter] lay in equality of opportunity for all Canadians, regardless of the economic region in which they lived, and regardless of the language – French or English – they spoke."[47]

Imagine Trudeau's thrill in discovering that deep down Laski was a "personalist" in all but name. This atheist Marxist actually defended values similar to those of the Christian left. After reading Laski's *Liberty in the Modern State,* Trudeau summarized the main ideas: "This volume does not have many ideas that are not already in the *Grammar of Politics.* The same philosophy respecting the individual, but recognizing that society helps the individual along in his pursuit of happiness. The same

---

* In Greek mythology, Procrustes the robber attached his victims to a bed. He would cut the tall people's feet and stretch the limbs of the shorter ones to make them all fit the size of the bed.

pluralism, tinged with concepts that will be refined further, and (later) called personalism." Why did he write "and will (later) be called person-alism"? Why the future tense? Because he knew his facts. *Liberty in the Modern State,* published in 1930, actually came out before the left-wing Christian personalism of Berdyaev, Maritain, and Mounier. For Laski and the personalists, Trudeau noted, "ultimately it is only the individual conscience, 'the individual's experiences,' that can serve as a springboard for action."[48] But how in the world could he include Laski among the personalists, when he knew his professor could not be promoting "Christian" values? Because Trudeau no longer cared for labels: this Jewish Marxist could well be personalist, since he adhered to certain ideas of universal application. Similar values could be expressed in differ-ent ways. Pluralism had become part and parcel of Trudeau's thinking.

In London, Laski was front-row centre in the shaping of Trudeau's mind. But Trudeau took other courses as well. In "French Political Thought from 1789," Dorothy Maud Pickles, a specialist on France, considered this country as a fascinating laboratory for studying the relationship between Church and State. This subject was naturally dear to Trudeau's heart, which explains why he took twenty-five pages of notes. Pickles underlined the rise in the first half of the nineteenth century of a Catholicism that was both liberal and ultramontanist. To explain this unusual posi-tion, she focused on three key figures in this movement: Hugues Félicité Robert de Lamennais (1782–1854), Henri Lacordaire (1802–1861), and Charles Forbes René, Count de Montalembert (1810–1870).

The three reformers wrote in the December 7, 1830, issue of *L'Avenir,* a French journal, "We ask for the freedom of conscience or the freedom of full universal religion . . . and as far as we, Catholics, are concerned, we ask for the total separation of church and state. . . . Just as there can be nothing religious today in politics there must be nothing political in religion." When Pope Gregory XVI condemned the reformers' liberal ideas in his encyclical *Mirari Vos,* on August 15, 1832, Lacordaire and Montalembert recanted and submitted to the Pontiff's judgment. Lamennais alone stood his ground. Lacordaire condemned the pride of Lamennais, charged him with "Protestantism," and accused him of plac-ing the authority of mankind over that of the Church.

Professor Pickles focused on Lamennais, and with good reason. Today, he is widely regarded as the forerunner of liberal Catholicism. Trudeau was more and more persuaded of the need to separate Church and State, so the professor's lectures touched the right chord. Trudeau would become a new Lamennais in Quebec. Despite his unwavering faith, he fought unceasingly for the separation of Church and State and was sometimes accused of being a Protestant.

Different perspectives on the history of Christianity turned up in different courses. Trudeau wrote glowing pages, in French, about John Mackinnon Robertson (1856–1933), the author of *An Introduction to English Politics:*[49] "In order to reveal the major forces at work throughout history, [Robertson] studies a few periods of history with remarkable erudition and simplicity." Who was this long-forgotten professor who made such an impression on Trudeau? According to the biographer Martin Page, Robertson was "one of the more remarkable figures of British history, who should be rescued from oblivion, . . . a man of the highest integrity whose bluntness offended some but whose charm and candour attracted more."[50] We will quickly understand why, in 1902, his words were deemed offensive. In *A Short History of Christianity,*[51] he wrote: "Everything the gospels affirm as biographical fact is fortuitous or purposive invention." Trudeau expressed his admiration for Robertson in French: "He deflates myths and prejudices with astonishing mastery, he shows the events in their true light." Trudeau summarized these myths, this time in English: "Tries to show that Christianity does not prevent slavery, debauchery, . . . just as under paganism." And, reverting again to French, he added: "His conclusions (magnificent writing) are those of an agnostic." Trudeau was no longer bothered that an agnostic should be critical of Christianity. What mattered now was the quality of a person's ideas.

<hr />

Law, including constitutional law, was an important part of Trudeau's program. Glanville Williams (1911–1997) and H.F. Jolowicz (1890–1954) devoted their whole courses to it. In *Memoirs,* nearly half a century later, Trudeau remembered Williams as an "exceptional professor."[52] He was not alone in this assessment. At Williams's death in 1997, the London daily *The Independent* wrote that "Glanville Williams was a legal scholar in a class on his own. . . . And he was also a hugely effective law reformer – a kind of legal Asterix, whose boundless energy and unquenchable optimism led him into endless battles against unjust laws. . . . *Learning the Law* (1945), now in its 11th edition, . . . was, and still remains essential reading for any would-be law student."[53] Trudeau found one more role model to follow: a scholar coming out of the ivory tower to combat social injustice. In his course, Williams refuted the notion of "natural law," basing his critique on several schools of thought: "All conclude that there is no objective good, no objective justification of rules that we need to maintain." Laws simply reflect the value systems of a constantly evolving social context. This led him to the conclusion that "natural law . . . is simply morality expressed in legalistic language."

Williams "steered" Trudeau to the renowned Swedish jurist and philosopher "Karl Olivecrona [1897–1980] and his book *Law as Fact*."[54] According to Olivecrona, since "laws are *creations of men not of gods*," they can be studied like any other social factor. This approach to the study of law appealed to Trudeau. He was less convinced, however, of Olivecrona's claim that law is enforced not because it reflects moral demands from God but because it is perceived as necessary for life in society. Trudeau conceded that this was correct "for most of the regulatory commands of the state." But the existence of core values was to him unquestionable. Indeed, "it is belief in these fundamentals which permits man to live in society."

Trudeau took two law courses. The first was taught, as we have seen, by Williams. The second was offered by Professor H.F. Jolowicz, a highly renowned Roman law specialist. Jolowicz retraced the history of law from the fall of the Roman Empire to the U.S. Constitution, reviewing the various interpretations of the relationship between law, morality, and politics that had marked the history of Western civilization. Trudeau was delighted to learn that Kant, in spiritually neutral language, defended the Christian principles of the primacy of the person. He noted with conviction: "Kant's main postulate: no human being must be regarded as a means to an end. He must be free to use his will in order to achieve his own end. . . . Law is an umpire between competing wills."[55]

One of the course readings Trudeau pored over was *Law and Morals,* by the American Roscoe Pound. The very flattering comments, written in French, reveal his fascination with this work: "The viewpoint of each of [the major schools of legal thought over the last century] is presented with such mastery, and the quotations chosen with such erudition, that each school he studies seems to be revealing the whole truth. Pound insists that a law can only be enforced if it is part of a historical tradition: 'In general, law cannot depart far from ethical customs nor lag far behind it. For law does not enforce itself.'" Once again, Trudeau was awakening to the importance of the social context: it is not enough for a law to be good. Citizens also need to be ready to apply it. And for this to happen, the law needs to be part of a tradition and be perceived as neither too advanced nor too backward.

Thanks to the courses given by Williams and Jolowicz, and his readings of Olivecrona and Pound, Trudeau discovered the complex relationships between law, morality, and social justice. He was dazzled by this discovery and immediately sought to share his knowledge with his fellow citizens by applying what he had just learned to the Quebec context. On November 14, 1947, he sent an article to *Notre Temps* entitled "On Lawyers and Others, and Their Relationship with Justice."[56] Clearly, in this article, he was forging a synthesis of his courses at the LSE and his readings.

The article starts off with a quote from Pascal: "If magistrates had true justice, they would have no use for square caps." In other words, resorting to lawyers and judges was necessary only because injustice prevailed in society. Trudeau developed his thesis convincingly, not realizing its offensive potential: "Lawyers," he wrote, "are men of law; they have nothing to do with justice. Their role is to investigate whether the legal order has been enforced in a particular case or not. . . . This is not a dishonourable profession, but it is ridiculous for lawyers to consider themselves so superior to high school teachers." So much for lawyers' egos! "Judges too," Trudeau continued, "are concerned with legality, not justice. I am not suggesting that legality and justice never coincide, all I'm saying is that when they don't coincide, judges are forced to opt for what is legal, not for what is just." He admitted there were a few exceptions, however: in cases where the ambiguity of the law allowed for conflicting interpretations, the court had "the unusual opportunity to come down in favour of what is just." But let there be no mistake, Trudeau quickly added: "Such cases arise so rarely that it is a gross exaggeration to speak of the 'Palais de Justice.'"*

---

* The French *Palais de justice* (literally "Palace of Justice") conveys Trudeau's meaning, although "Courthouse" is used in English.

There is no doubt that lawyers and judges do not create justice. But then, who does? Well, Trudeau answered, those who make laws – in other words, politicians: "The good legislator always tends to bring law and justice closer together. He uncovers and corrects the injustices that arise within the legal order." That is, justice is in the realm of politics. Expounding on an idea he had gleaned from Pound, he explained that a law needed to be part of a tradition and be perceived as neither too advanced nor too backward: "[The good legislator] does not believe his justice to be immutable (this is the error of the Napoleonic Code), yet he must avoid the chaos of constant change. A good system of laws needs to strike a constantly shifting balance." Trudeau drew a clear distinction between law enforcement, which fell within the judicial system, and the creation of law, which is the exclusive preserve of the legislative system.

He then tried to apply these ideas to the Quebec context (as he would regularly do in future): "The Quebec legislator doesn't reach this ideal, far from it. He seems unaware of the fast evolution of the society he serves." Trudeau was sounding the alarm, stressing that action was urgently needed. If a just social order, based on laws adapted to present circumstances, was not established, then class struggle and revolution would reach Quebec, just as they were gaining ground in other parts of the world: "When too many people understand there is nothing inevitable about their filthy slums, their inadequate food or their degrading conditions of work, . . . when order cannot be reconciled with justice and when hatred has stifled love, the time for negotiations is over." Fortunately, Quebec could still avoid the worst, because it "is perhaps one of the last countries where one could still examine conflicting issues in the light of faith and reason, choose level-headedly the best in each camp and then reach a peaceful and just synthesis." Inaction would have disastrous effects on Quebec: "If our society's foundations crumbled under our feet, if the orthodoxy we believed to be eternal disappeared, if the masses turned away in disgust from the 'ruling' classes still mired in the rigidity of their super ego and antiquated laws, I wouldn't bet on the future of this French and Christian civilization in which our ancestors laid so much hope." Quebec had stagnated for too long. Laws had to be brought in line with the current needs of society. Or suffer dire consequences.

Reaction to the article came swiftly, in the form of a hot blast from Antonio Perrault, head of the editorial board of the *Revue du Barreau*.

Trudeau had deeply insulted the entire legal profession, so he flew to his colleagues' defence: "It would be hard to imagine anyone accumulating more errors, whether intentionally or unintentionally, on a single page. . . . And with such an outpouring of fallacies, some still find it surprising that confusion should reign in society, that there should be such contempt for social order and for those charged with maintaining it."[57] Perrault didn't seem to notice he had just admitted lawyers and judges were mandated to maintain social order. That's precisely my point, Trudeau could have answered, their job is to apply the law and not to create it.

This fundamental distinction between law and justice had completely escaped Perrault, whose indignation exploded in every sentence. He said he would proudly continue referring to the "Palais de justice, never mind what our profession's denigrator has to say." He concluded in a lyrical tone: "Yes sir, you are quite right: ours is not a dishonourable profession. It is even a wonderful and grand profession for lawyers who work honestly and with a clear conscience, and whose mission, despite the author's evident disdain, is closely related to Law and Justice." Roscoe Pound argued that a new law could be accepted only if it wasn't too avant-garde. He could have added that a new idea – such as Trudeau's – cannot be accepted or even understood when it is too far ahead of the intellectual tradition that it addresses.

This article is dated November 14, 1947, that is, little more than a month after Trudeau had registered at the LSE. He had already read and absorbed important ideas of professors Jolowicz and Williams, while keeping up with work in other courses; revised his position on justice and law; and drafted an article synthesizing and applying what he had learned to the Quebec context. He had even found time to write another article three weeks before. On October 24, 1947, he sent "Citadels of Orthodoxy"[58] to *Notre Temps*. It was his first piece intended for a general audience, not only students. The occasional awkward and obscure style reveals a budding polemicist. The underlying message is nonetheless striking. He consistently used "we" and "us" in his scathing criticism of French-Canadian culture. It is clear he was addressing "his" people – he was criticizing from within: "It is high time," he wrote, "that we begin simply to think. But unfortunately I can see no encouraging sign this is actually happening."

That was the first salvo. Trudeau explains how he had reached this depressing conclusion. First he paid tribute to their French-Canadian ancestors' collective struggle to resist "religious and ethnic assimilation." But then he hastened to add that this fight was collective in name only: "Everyone was fighting for his own freedom to believe, think and act." Consequently, as the danger of assimilation decreased, each individual felt less directly affected and lost his fighting spirit. Yet new "more pernicious" dangers rose on the horizon, although they weren't perceived as threatening each person. And what, according to Trudeau, were these dangers, which he considered even more destructive than religious and ethnic assimilation? His unequivocal answer: "Moral decay and political treason." Every French Canadian, he continued, felt guilty for not fighting individually against these new dangers, and "soothed his conscience by submitting to 'systems' of collective protection. We strove to codify everything that had worked for our ancestors, and then to abide slavishly by it. The era of orthodoxies had begun; . . . and since the forces of opposition to change had ensured our survival thus far, we would remain conservative until the end of time."

He went on to attack the mind-numbing orthodoxy that hindered people's ability to grow and to think for themselves. We feel safe, he said, only with the ideas "of the great minds of the past centuries. . . . No new thinking manages to penetrate our citadels of orthodoxy." And, twisting the infamous French regulation "No spitting or speaking Breton allowed,"* he wrote ironically: "No spitting or thinking allowed here." Meanwhile, he said bitterly, "the human caravan of progress has marched a hundred miles ahead, while we linger behind, still simmering in our juices." Nothing is possible as long as "we continue to huddle within our walls."

Trudeau then explained the pernicious effects of this defensive mentality: "Since we are committed to nationalism, we never really dream of loving our country. And as avowed Christians, we do not worry much about living out our faith in practice." All of which led him to a harsh conclusion: "Orthodoxy is the enemy within." He nevertheless closed

---

* This regulation is generally used as an example of the French state's repressive laws, banning Breton and other minority languages to enforce a single public language: French.

with a lyrical message of hope, worthy of the greatest French-Canadian preachers: Let us get rid of our orthodoxy, for our dogmatism and "our confidence in the state of grace will give us the audacity of apostles. And in our *patrie*, we will once again see free men taking action."

How can we explain Léopold Richer's decision to publish in *Notre Temps* this very critical article about Quebec, whereas just a year later, *Le Devoir* turned down "The Promise of Quebec"? There are probably two reasons. First, nobody in particular felt targeted by Trudeau, since he used the collective "we" in accusing all members of society of not knowing how to think and in suggesting they join the human caravan of progress. Second, and more importantly, he wasn't attacking any sacred cow head on; he wasn't arguing as he had done in "The Promise of Quebec," and continued to do on other occasions, that the Catholic Church's meddling in civic affairs smothered the people in a narrow-minded orthodoxy. When he later identified his targets more forcefully and precisely, the conservative Richer got the point and attacked him mercilessly. Trudeau, who was rarely short of words when it came to defending himself and knocking down his opponent, counterattacked, calling *Notre Temps* a "self-styled 'social and cultural' weekly."[59]

But for now, no clouds cast a shadow on their relationship. On February 5, 1948, Trudeau sent a third article to *Notre Temps*: "Reflections on a Democracy and Its Variant." A day after publication, an admiring Léopold Richer eagerly thanked Trudeau for the piece on "the Arcand incident and our democracy," assuring him that the article was attracting a lot of attention and encouraging him to write "more of these good pieces."[60] A week later, Adrien Arcand himself asked Grace Trudeau to convey his thanks to her son: "I appreciate what he has written about my fellow prisoners and myself, but I am impressed most of all by his courage, because that's what it takes to tell the truth in these times of moral terrorism (while awaiting the Red Terror)."[61]

What was this "Adrian Arcand incident" all about? First of all, who was Arcand? We saw in Volume 1 that he was a great admirer of Hitler, head of the Parti de l'unité nationale (PUN), a federalist and out-and-out Nazi party supporter, and anti-Semitic to boot. At the beginning of the Second World War, the government declared PUN activities illegal, and

Arcand was interned in New Brunswick from 1940 to 1945. Once the war ended, he sued the federal government.

Some, like historian Esther Delisle, have looked at four documents together – Trudeau's article, Richer's congratulations, Arcand's thank-you note, and Trudeau's 1942 article "Nothing Matters Now But Victory," in which he ridiculed the Nazi threat – and have then concluded that Trudeau came out "supporting Arcand, the Canadian Nazi leader." For example, in *L'imprégnation fasciste au Québec,* Delisle writes: "Apparently, Trudeau's thinking about the Second World War had hardly changed since the days when he wrote for *Le Quartier Latin.*"[62] John English, meanwhile, claims that Trudeau, by roundly criticizing the King government, showed "that his views had not changed since the war . . . and he vigorously denounced the incarceration of fascist leader Adrien Arcand."[63] English goes on to mention Arcand's letter to Madame Trudeau. But is it true that, by defending Arcand, Trudeau demonstrated he had not changed his views since the war? What did Trudeau write?

From the first lines, Trudeau praised democracy and stated that he was sure French Canadians shared his views. Had he forgotten his own speeches against democracy, which had been very well received in Montreal at the time? Not at all. But he now claimed that the problem was semantic: French Canadians simply "bore a grudge against the word democracy." Whereas, deep down, "along with the vast majority of Canadians, they cherish these values which no other form of government safeguards any better. They believe in the priceless dignity of the person [and] the inalienable right of every man to freely and fully develop his personality." Trudeau went on praising this – very Christian – form of government: "The glory of democracy is that it tends to apply these principles in the political sphere. . . . This entails the freedoms of press, assembly, speech, religious tolerance, equality before the law. . . . This kind of Christianity and of democracy our people will defend forever, heart and soul." Trudeau had definitely changed since the war. He was now a staunch democrat.

Moreover, and contrary to his former position, Trudeau no longer blamed the government for its participation in the war. Although Canada was not actually in danger, he said, "we do not blame noble souls for rushing to the defence of the oppressed." He thereby acknowledged that the war was fought to protect the oppressed. This was another significant change from his previous position. Trudeau then asked, how could it be that this war, ostensibly fought on the basis of such noble principles, "led in equal measure to fervour and cynicism, a state of mind to which I was no stranger?" (So he was admitting that he had been among the cynics.) How is it that in Quebec, people believed "that neither democracy nor Christianity was really at stake"? The answer, he argued, is that the King government's deeds were not in accord with the values advocated to justify the war. The real problem was the hypocrisy of the leaders: "The government sought obedience in the name of democracy, as the people understood it, but then governed using a style of democracy, as it alone understood." Trudeau drew up a long list of the King government's violations of democratic principles, including "government by decree, the suspension of habeas corpus, the Arcand, Houde, Chaloult incidents. . . . Lapointe's lie. . . . The manipulation of the plebiscite, or King, the king of charlatans. Using propaganda to intimidate the public. The 'nioui' policy.* . . . The gag of censorship! The end of civil liberties."

But, one might counter, didn't the state of war justify these measures? Trudeau anticipated the question: "Let nobody claim that the state of war automatically justifies the suspension of democracy rules." People should not confuse a state of war with a state of siege, he said. Indeed, when a country is under siege, when the enemy is at the gates, public consultation is impossible, and the government has to act on behalf of the people. "But this wasn't Canada's case. Far from it. The government had no excuse. Instead of establishing dialogue with its opponents," Trudeau charged, it "sent them to jail disregarding law or justice, without due process or adequate defence, without any idea of a proportionate punishment or of an independent judgment. In so doing, it violated the basic principles of the society of equals." In a true democracy, Trudeau added, no one should be imprisoned, whatever the crime, without due process of law.

We have almost reached the end of the article, and it is still not clear why some people cast him as defending Arcand the Nazi. Up till this point, as we have seen, Trudeau had only mentioned Arcand's name once, and in passing. But then he wrote: "Mr. Arcand, his attorney and

---

* "Nioui" is a French coinage referring to "ni oui, ni non" – Mackenzie King's ambiguous "neither yes, neither no" policy was perfectly reflected in the famous slogan "Conscription if necessary, but not necessarily conscription."

his co-applicants show striking public spirit in bringing these issues to court; they deserve the deep appreciation of all those who accord some importance to freedom and justice." Clearly, Trudeau was not approving Arcand's ideology. The reason he was congratulating Arcand was for bringing his case before the courts, because that is how democracy, freedom, and justice are safeguarded, even in wartime.

In taking this position, he was probably inspired by Laski. In his notes, Trudeau wrote that according to Laski, "whenever there is no immediate fear of imminent danger, freedom of speech should not be interfered with. . . . [Laski] believes that beyond reporting to the enemy information useful to him, there should be no difference in freedom of speech, except perhaps that it should be even greater in war than in peace time."[64] Undoubtedly, this article was an ode to democracy and to the rule of law. The corporatist Trudeau of the 1942 "Conscription Crisis" was now dead and buried. Although he continued to castigate the King government, he now did it on the basis of liberal and democratic principles.

Ironically, during the 1970 October Crisis, the Trudeau government dusted off the War Measures Act, which authorized the violation of individual liberties. Those who still criticize him for this apparent U-turn should remember the distinction he made in this article between a state of war and a state of siege. In October 1970, a series of terrorist acts by the Front de libération du Québec (FLQ) led Montreal mayor Jean Drapeau and Quebec premier Robert Bourassa to urge the federal government to act swiftly and without compromise. Trudeau responded to these appeals. With the full support of all the members of his Cabinet, including ministers from Quebec, he judged this to be a state of siege, saw that there was a clear and present danger, and believed that public consultation was now impossible. His assessment of the situation was widely shared by Quebeckers, over 80 per cent of whom approved his handling of the crisis.

———❦———

One may think that with his courses and his many readings and writings Trudeau had no time for social activities or sports. That's what his mother thought. In a letter dated November 1947, she wondered whether he had any friends because, she said, "you never mention anyone." According to John English, his mother was concerned "for good reason, of course. Grace had quickly realized that, in London, there was no 'circle.'"[65] Actually, his agenda proves his mother shouldn't have worried. Here are a few of his activities: less than three weeks after arriving, on Wednesday, October 22, he had a coffee with Turner of the Socialist Party; on Thursday the 23rd, he went to a "Catholic tea: Blackhurst on Black Friars"; on October 27, he dined with Louis Hartz (who had commented on his work at Harvard); October 28, he went to a dance organized by a Catholic group. On February 8, he wrote: "Anne and Amy Jennifer Hales at Letchworth [in Hertfordshire]. I'm going with Harry Buxton. We are staying over there, after a splendid day in the countryside, poetry, religious and political discussions." Besides, he must have spent a lot of time at the pool: on May 27, 1948, he took part in swimming championships at the University of London and noted proudly: "I came second in men's diving (out of nine)." Twenty years later, by which time he had become prime minister, he often dazzled the gallery with his acrobatic dives. Until the last days of his life, he continued swimming, first in the indoor pool he had installed at 24 Sussex Drive in Ottawa, then in his private residence in Montreal.

Most importantly, in addition to meeting friends and engaging in sports and social activities, Trudeau was a member of the Newman Circle. This chaplaincy, founded in Britain in 1942, was part of an international network of centres, clubs, and circles, all named after Cardinal John Henry Newman. Trudeau had already dipped into some of Newman's writings, while attending Collège Jean-de-Brébeuf in his younger years. This Catholic association aimed to bring together "men who know their religion, who enter into it, who know where they stand, who know what they hold and what they do not, who know their creed so well that they can give an account of it."[66] Newman saw that these passionate, intelligent, and well-instructed lay Christians could have an irresistible influence: "A few endowed men will rescue the world for centuries to come."[67] This Catholic association fitted Trudeau like a glove. He took part in the dances and social and spiritual activities it organized, as well as lecture programs and interventions in underprivileged neighbourhoods. He attended Mass and meetings at the Educational Resource Centre (ERC) of the Newman Circle until the end of his last session, on June 22, 1948. On January 21, it was likely at one of these meetings that a certain Jean-Pierre lent him Newman's intellectual autobiography

Apologia pro vita sua,[68] which is generally considered one of the great intellectual autobiographies of all time.

If Trudeau took notes about Newman, he didn't leave any for posterity but there is little doubt that he read it with great care. On the one hand, he later said Newman was one of the five authors who had influenced him the most. And on the other, when his fiancée Margaret Sinclair was getting ready to convert to Catholicism, he suggested Newman's *Pro vita sua* among readings he believed were more important than those recommended to her.[69] Given his close involvement in the Newman Circle and his appreciation of the person, we will briefly present Newman the theologian, historian, philosopher, preacher, novelist, poet, companion and spiritual guide, and the author of over forty books.

Newman was born in 1801 in London to a Calvinist father originally from Holland and to a mother descended from the Huguenots. From a young age, he was passionate about the Bible and religion. By the age of fifteen, he had begun to veer away from Calvinism and was ordained an Anglican priest in 1824. Starting in 1833, he became one of the leading figures of the Oxford Movement, which sought to reconcile the Church of England with its historic Roman Catholic roots. The Oxford Movement published many tracts with a view to renewing the Anglican church while positioning it midway between Catholicism and Protestantism. *The Parochial and Plain Sermons,* published in eight volumes, "remain one of the high points of Christian preaching over the last two centuries," according to the French Association of Friends of Newman.[70] Over time, however, Newman became increasingly convinced that the search for a middle position opened the door to sectarianism and weakened the Church. In 1845, he converted to Catholicism and was ordained a priest in 1846. He is acknowledged to have played a major role in the revival of Catholicism in Britain and the conversion of many Anglicans. But his conversion to Catholicism also meant many people considered him beyond the pale.

Newman maintained that the Church's structure should be neither liberal nor democratic but hierarchical and authoritarian. Otherwise, it would collapse. This explains why he rallied to the dogma of papal infallibility in 1870. In 1879, Leo XIII made him a cardinal. His thought had such a profound impact on the Church that Jean Guitton, the French Catholic philosopher, writer, and member of the Académie française, would later call him the "invisible thinker of Vatican II." In 1991, he was declared "venerable" (the first stage of sainthood) and was beatified in Birmingham on September 19, 2010.

One can easily imagine Trudeau being swept off his feet by the *Apologia pro vita sua*. This was the third major thinker, along with Bergson (a Jew) and Maritain (a Protestant), who chose to convert to Catholicism after a long search for truth. For Newman, "to be a *Christian means* to be adopted as a person by God the Father of Christ."[71] He held that Christians strive above all for intimate communion with God. Which explains his celebrated motto: "Cor ad cor loquitur" (Man speaks to God). Trudeau later became a champion of liberalism in the political sphere and always accepted, like Newman, the authority and hierarchy of the Church in matters of dogma. This explains why he willingly submitted to the *Index*. Yet, like Newman, he accorded a central place to individual conscience.

Trudeau took part in many activities in England, but at an emotional level he still longed to be back in Paris with his Canadian friends. He arrived in London in early October, but by the 16th he was headed back for Paris, likely to participate in planning a lecture series on Canada for December. Two months later, he was back in Paris again, this time giving a lecture on December 20 that will be discussed below. After a few days in the City of Light, he took off for Weisshorn, one of the highest peaks in the Swiss Alps. On January 1, after attending Mass (he almost never missed it), the former ski champion at Brébeuf took part in a championship ski race and noted with pride: "The best time was 4 min. 4 sec., and mine was 6 min. 16 sec. I am 2nd in my class, worldwide." He remained an avid skier right up till the last years of his life, when illness put an end to his passion for sports. He was back in London on January 16 but then returned to Paris two months later. On March 20, he served at the wedding Mass of his good friend, Roger Rolland. On March 22, he jumped onto his motorcycle, Andrée Desautels in tow. She was a music student he often hung out with in Paris, and the two headed off on a three-week tour through France and Spain, enjoying the "incredible beauty" of landscapes along the way.

———————————

Despite this whirlwind of studies and various other activities, Trudeau remained chiefly concerned with Quebec, as is clearly indicated by his talk

"The Promise of Quebec" and the three articles he had written for *Notre Temps*. This enduring interest is also manifested in his participation in a major public event, which reflects the state of his thinking at the time. The Cité club de Paris was organizing a series of six talks to present Canada to French students. On November 15, 1947, Jean-Louis Roux gave the first talk, entitled "Images of Canada." Jean-Paul Geoffroy followed with "A Geographic Perspective on Canada," while Roger Rolland and others spoke mainly about literature and art. On December 20, Trudeau brought the series to a close with a presentation called "Canadian Politics." The text of this lecture has not been published to this day.[72] The only public mention of it is a report from Agence France Presse, which appeared in the daily *Le Soleil*. Trudeau scribbled angrily on his clipping: "An idiotic and misleading report!"[73] So, if we want to know the real substance of his talk, we are probably better off looking at his manuscript!

The seventeen-page document is jam-packed with all kinds of information. He must have invested much time and energy in preparing the talk. His point of departure is clearly outlined from the outset: "I am going to show you a Canada at the crossroads; I will try to make you see the forces at work shaping the political future of our country." These few words alone denote a major shift in his thinking. He was now thinking not of Quebec alone, but of "our country," Canada, a country poised at the crossroads. The future of Quebec was now intimately linked to the future of Canada.

Trudeau mentioned two main reasons why Canada was a federal country and not a unitary one such as France or Great Britain. First, its ethnic composition. Canadians "are made of two fairly homogeneous groups: 49% are connected by their origins or ancestry to the British Isles, 30% are French Canadians. A third heterogeneous group makes up the remaining 20%." Next, its geography: "A country as large as Europe, and almost as diverse, is divided into five huge regions that are completely distinct from each other and have their own resources and special needs." If on the one hand one can understand that Canada had somehow to be a federal country, on the other hand, for "specific historical reasons it was prevented, at the other extreme, from *forming a confederation,* more or less loosely held together: British North America had to bond together to stave off U.S. imperialism, which was then already apparent." To tame these contradictory forces, the founders of the country formulated a wise option: "In 1867, Canadian statesmen understood that Canada could not become a unitary state, because of the regionalisms I have just mentioned. It was therefore natural for them to adopt whatever was good in the Constitution of the United States. They expressed reservations about a wholesale adoption of American principles, however, because the recent Civil War had reminded them of the need for a strong central government." Canadian federalism was based on the American model, but Canada's form of government was "a parliamentary democracy along British lines." This fortuitous mixture of American federalism and the British parliamentary system, he explained, was deeply ingrained in the BNA Act (the British North America Act). He then devoted most of his talk to this Canadian Constitution.

The first point Trudeau wanted to make was that Canada was not a colony. His impatient tone suggests he was refuting an all-too-common point of view: "You should know first of all that Canada is a sovereign country. I apologize to those who find this fact too obvious to mention, by reminding them that many of their fellow citizens are completely oblivious of it." According to the naysayers, the fact that "Canada is subject to the King of England" is proof of its being a colony. False, he retorted: "Canada and Great Britain are two equal and sovereign nations, whose king is the same man." And what proof was there of this? The proof was obvious, in the case of the Second World War. "The Crown had to be divisible, since the King of Great Britain had declared war on Germany on September 1st 1939, whereas the King of Canada maintained neutrality for nine more days." Trudeau was generally on the ball with his facts – he was right about the delay between the two declarations of war but wrong about the details. On September 3, England – and France – declared war on Germany. (On September 1, Germany had invaded Poland.) Canada declared war on September 10, seven days after Great Britain.

He then presented the Statute of Westminster, passed by the British Parliament in 1931, as further evidence that Canada was not a colony: "Today, no other government than the Government of Canada can make laws for Canadians, and this is the exact definition of sovereignty." He admitted that Canada could not amend its Constitution but explained that this situation had not arisen because of Canada's supposed colonial status. On the contrary, he explained: "Unable to agree on an amending formula, Canadians themselves requested that, in the very Act which recognized their sovereignty, a clause limiting their amending power be inserted." He cited additional evidence of Canada's sovereignty, such as the appointment of ambassadors and the recent creation of Canadian citizenship. (Canadians had previously been British subjects.) On January 3, 1947, Prime Minister Mackenzie King officially became the first-ever Canadian citizen. Trudeau himself got his first Canadian passport six months after King.

After dismissing any doubts about Canada's sovereignty, Trudeau went on to describe "our" constitutional charter in positive terms. This did not prevent him from criticizing some of its measures. He claimed, for example, that "our Senate is an odd mixture of the U.S. Senate and the British House of Lords, and, as it lacks the justification of either of these Chambers, it is perfectly useless. In my opinion, in a country of the federative type, the main justification for a second Chamber is to safe-guard the interests of federated countries." In other words, senators should represent the provinces. "But, fearing autonomist pressures, the Fathers of Confederation created a system where whole regions, rather than provinces, were represented. But worst of all, senators are appointed for life by the central government, not elected by the provinces! In short, the Senate . . . was meant to serve as a bulwark against the tumultuous waves of popular democracy. Whereas in actual fact, this bulwark mainly ensures that 96 doddering old monks spend their working hours in blissful slumber, profiting handsomely at the public trough."[74] This was a harsh criticism of the Senate. Trudeau argued forcefully for sena-tors elected by the provinces and for set terms. In the ensuing half century, some of Trudeau's critiques of the Senate have been addressed, but the status of the Chamber remains highly controversial.

Trudeau went on to present Canadian political parties, highlighting the advantages of the two-party system. He also noted the shortcomings of such a system, including the fact that "third parties, created to demand particular rights, have little chance." Another drawback is the fact that in the drive to gain and maintain power, each of the two major parties has to "appeal to the broadest range of interests, and diversity of loyalties." As a result, "political agendas must be extremely vague and unclear." It follows that "our major parties – which call themselves respectively 'con-servative' and 'liberal' – are both extremely conservative," despite some differences. For example, the Conservative Party is generally more protectionist, and the Liberal Party more supportive of free trade. All in all, however, Trudeau agreed with Laski that bipartisanship's main advantage is that it promotes government stability: "Think for a moment," he wrote, "for over half a century (1896–1948), we have only had five prime ministers (Laurier, Borden, Meighen, Bennett and King) and less than ten governments.[75] During this time, France has certainly had more than fifty!"

Trudeau recounted the history of the two parties. When the British Parliament created the Dominion of Canada in 1867, power naturally went to the Conservative Party, comprising well-established English- and French-Canadian families, which had supported the founding of the federation. "At the time," Trudeau said, "the so-called Liberal Party seemed doomed to remain out of power forever" because it was unable to gain the support of Quebeckers: "Liberalism in Canada at the time was strongly anticlerical. The *Rouges* [the Liberals] had a limited following in the intellectual community, whereas the *Bleus* (Gallicans) and *Castors** (ultramontanes) had the [Catholic] Church's support and were followed by the people."

But things changed. In the late nineteenth century, a series of events "knocked the Conservative Party off its pedestal." First, "John A. Macdonald, the Conservative party leader, died in 1891, and no man of his stature was found to succeed him." Second, "the Quebec vote was completely alienated, first by the 1885 hanging of Louis Riel,** who had defended a cause in Manitoba with which French Canadians sympathized, then, in 1890, by the way French Canadians were denied justice in the government's handling of the Manitoba Schools Question."*** Third, when

---

* The literal English rendering of this French nickname "Castors" is "Beavers."

** Louis Riel (1844–1885) is still a controversial figure today, revered by some and considered insane by others. At the head of the Métis nation, he led rebellions against the government to protect the rights of his people. He was convicted of treason and executed in 1885. After his hanging, French Canadians were enraged at the Conservative government.

*** Whereas the Manitoba Act gave equal rights to English-language Protestant schools and French-language Catholic schools, the 1890 Manitoba Schools Act abolished French as an official language and removed funding for Catholic schools.

Wilfrid Laurier became Liberal leader in 1887, not only did he manage to win the French-Canadian vote, but "thanks to his truly remarkable political acumen, [he succeeded in establishing] a coalition between Quebec, the western provinces and scattered groups, which has maintained the Liberal government in power since 1896 until the present today."

In between the lines, he wrote: "with two exceptions," without giving further details. He was thinking, no doubt, of the Conservative governments of Robert Borden (from 1911 to 1920) and Richard Bennett (1930 to 1935). He can be forgiven perhaps for neglecting the short-lived government of Arthur Meighen (July 1920 to December 1921 and June 1926 to September 1926). Nonetheless, Conservative governments were in power for a total of fifteen years. How could Trudeau mention them only after the fact, without further explanation? Because he was setting events in the context of Quebec, and these two exceptions did not contradict his basic tenet. Even when the Conservatives won, Quebeckers voted overwhelmingly for the Liberal Party. For example, in the 1917 election, in the midst of World War I, Borden's coalition government got 153 seats, but Laurier's Liberals created a tidal wave in Quebec, garnering sixty-two seats out of sixty-five.

Trudeau then turned to third parties. The difficulty these latter parties had in positioning themselves on the political scene lay in the fact they articulated narrowly localized claims, and "their leaders had neither the flair nor the chance to develop inter-regional alliances." Only one such party has understood the need to act otherwise: the CCF (Co-operative Commonwealth Federation), which could break the "age-old liberal-conservative dichotomy, and constitute a force which, in my opinion, must be taken seriously."

Why was this party likely to succeed whereas others had failed? It was because although the CCF was rooted in agrarian discontent in Western Canada, it had managed to broaden its base. According to Trudeau, "Mr. Woodsworth, the founder of the movement, was shrewd enough to fit this regional discontent into a broader ideological programme: the CCF . . . rapidly came to champion all left-wing forces. . . . Obviously, [Woodsworth] is not preaching some radical socialism wherever he goes, for fear of scaring off the farmers. . . . I have the impression that this party is patiently waiting for the day when the workers will rally behind it. This is a slow process, because Canadian unions only account for 20% of all salaried workers." His stay in London, during which he had witnessed the establishment of a type of socialism to his liking, has obviously influenced Trudeau. His meeting with Frank Scott had probably helped him understand the CCF's affinities with this type of socialism. Unsurprisingly, he said, the rise of the CCF upset the old parties, particularly the Conservatives, who "knew full well for whom the bell tolls." That was why, Trudeau said ironically, at their "National Convention in 1942, the Conservatives took on a bewildering new name – the Progressive Conservatives.* Whereas the Liberals have had the foresight of keeping a moderately left wing within their party."

To avoid his views about the CCF being misinterpreted, Trudeau explained his position: "I would be remiss if I left you with the impression that the class struggle in Marxist terms is already underway. Liberalism in Canada has not yet completely fulfilled its historic role: the momentum of the middle classes has not yet crashed against the wall of the proletariat. . . . The two opposing forces still have enough room for manoeuvre to be able to reconcile their divergent interests within the parliamentary system." Canada, he believed, could avoid the disruptions that shook the rest of the world, because "a land of abundance can afford to raise wages." His optimism was grounded in the material, cultural, and even spiritual assets of this great country, which he considered his own: "Canada is perhaps one of the last countries where one could still examine conflicting issues in the light of faith and reason, choose level-headedly the best in each camp and then reach a peaceful and just synthesis."

Attentive readers have probably noticed that these words are exactly those he used in his article "On Lawyers and Others, and Their Relationship with Justice," with one extremely important exception: the word "Quebec" has been replaced by "Canada." Trudeau emphasized, however, that acting was urgent, "and this would make the struggle exciting." Carried away by his enthusiasm, he could see promising signs in Quebec: "Hardly two months ago, during the meat packers' strike, French Canadian strikers identified with the proletarian cause, rather

---

* The official name of this party became the Progressive Conservative Party of Canada, a name it kept until 2003, when it reverted to the Conservative Party of Canada.

than the nationalist one. We live in a crucial time when new alliances are being formed, when different allegiances are coming together."

What did Trudeau mean in referring to "the proletarian cause"? Under Laski's influence, he had now come to see the important role the working class played in transforming society. And what did he mean in referring to "a crucial time when new alliances are being formed, when different allegiances are coming together"? Remember that he was writing this lecture in a British setting. He had observed first-hand the benefits of the "welfare state" and could see that this restructuring of British society had been brought about through alliances of political opponents who united in view of the common good of the British people. Trudeau was now nourishing the hope that French Canadians would also forge new allegiances and go on to great achievements. His message was neither Marxist nor revolutionary. He wanted to promote Christian socialism based largely on what he had learned of the British Labour Party.

To bring about this better world, Trudeau (using "charity" in its biblical sense of love) explained that "we need charity most of all, since charity alone can prevent political struggles from turning into social wars." He reiterated his trust in his country's potential: "All of this should be possible in a new country like Canada, since we are not prisoners of some bitter history of caste or privilege, and since our conflicts – no matter how serious – never make us forget the intrinsic dignity of our opponents." Trudeau dreamed aloud of a great and beautiful Canada in which Quebec would be a major partner, in a Canada of freedom, equal opportunity, social justice, and human dignity. Like Martin Luther King, he could have said "I have a dream." This was Trudeau the visionary, Trudeau the father of Canada, who could stir and rally the crowd, who could give them the courage to reach for the moon and the stars. This Trudeau was born in Paris on December 20, 1947. He was twenty-eight years old.

Chapter 5

─────◆─────

A POLITICAL GLOBE-TROTTER

You have to leave your homeland to thank God for having one in the first place.

— PIERRE ELLIOTT TRUDEAU,
Travel Notes, 1949

HARVARD, SCIENCES PO, the London School of Economics – what an impressive string of institutions. Harvard, the brain of the new global superpower; Paris, the Mecca of French Canadians; and London, the grand finale – the place where he encountered a man and a political system measuring up to his ideals. Quite a treat! Trudeau believed that it was at the London School of Economics that he synthesized everything he had learned so far, and "it was on those premises that I based all my future political decisions; it was that philosophy that underlay all my writings."[1]

Naturally, in saying this, he minimized what he learned in later years. But there is no doubt that his stay in England strongly shaped his thinking. He now realized that the fundamental principle of the primacy of the person was not the exclusive preserve of Christianity; he had learned that this principle needed to be enshrined in law over and above the power of government. He had always cared about individual liberty, but now, thanks to Laski and his own discovery of the "welfare state," he understood that individual liberty acquired its true meaning only when accompanied by equality of opportunity. This explains why he was drawn to a particular conception of socialism. He upheld the values of liberal democracy and was convinced that the needs of French Canadians were best met by federalism. He therefore encouraged French Canadians to enthusiastically embrace peaceful coexistence with other Canadians, giving the world a lesson in Christian love, tolerance, and justice. Brimming with hope, he wanted to share this personal discovery – the fruit of so much study and deliberation – with "his" people.

However, at the end of Trudeau's year at the LSE, he made a decision that may seem strange at first sight: instead of returning to Quebec to throw himself into political action, he decided to wander the world for a few months, in the farthest reaches of Asia. Why didn't he head home after four years of study in three countries and on two continents? To this intriguing question, biographers have offered many answers. Stephen Clarkson and Christina McCall see the journey as Trudeau's last caprice before settling down to work in a real paying job.[2] This self-proclaimed "world citizen" returned to Canada only because, to his dismay, "he still had to have a nationality."[3] For George Radwanski, meanwhile, the Asian trip was a sign of a "fundamental rootlessness."[4] Likewise, John English attributes the journey to Trudeau's ambivalence, claiming that "confusion and contradiction more than emptiness seemed to mark Trudeau's life in late 1947."[5] In short, Trudeau, rootless, aimless, and full of contradictions, ventured around the world in search of himself.

Archival documents, however, shed new light on this trip. We have already seen that Trudeau had known what he wanted to do from a very young age. Quebec had always been at the heart of his concerns. His studies had now fulfilled one overarching goal: to acquire as fine an education as possible in order to do good things for "his" people. So why didn't he head straight home after his year in London? Because he realized he knew the world in theory alone. He felt the need to flesh out this theoretical understanding with practical knowledge, by getting first-hand experience of different nationalities and situations.

A letter to his mother clearly reveals that the political dimensions of his travels were more important than simply racking up new adventures. He tells her that he had just made the hardest decision in his life. In Rangoon, Burma, he had to decide whether to head north, south, or east. But how could he choose, when he felt drawn in all directions at once? The south was out of the question, since the Dutch had declined to give him a visa to Indonesia: "It was to be expected, I suppose, considering the outrageous Imperialistic policy they are pursuing there; they don't welcome outside observers."[6] There remained the choice between the north and east. As for the north, "Mandalay, though much destroyed, has romance in its name, and getting there would have been quite an adventure with insurgents all along the line, then the Burma Road into China. . . . *If I were out for adventure, I would not have hesitated. . . . Since I am trying to understand the world's politics,*[*] I felt I couldn't honestly forego seeing Bangkok. . . . It would have been criminal to leave out Indo-China, where French colonial policy is undergoing a very critical test. So the North with its scenery and hardships, *but no politics,* was ruled out."[7] Trudeau could not have explained the objective of his trip more clearly.

Trudeau crossed war zones during this trip, sometimes at the risk of death. Many explanations have been given to his willingness to expose himself to danger. George Radwanski sees it as a way for Trudeau to prove "that his earlier avoidance of war had not been due to cowardice."[8] McCall and Clarkson say his travels allowed him to play the part of Cyrano de Bergerac, the blustering hero he had admired in his youth.[9] Our perspective is different. We have already shown in our first volume that Alexis Carrel's *L'homme cet inconnu* [Man, the Unknown] had convinced him it took a maximum of courage, physical fitness, and skills to be part of a genuine elite.[10] Carrel's life principle was probably reinforced in Paris in 1947, when he read Nicolas Berdyaev's *Slavery and Freedom*. For this personalist philosopher, knowledge of truth demanded a victory over fear, and "the fear of death is the limit of fear."[11] Much along the same lines, Trudeau wrote in *Memoirs:* "I wanted to know, for instance, . . . whether I would be able to travel across a war-torn country (there was no shortage of regional conflicts) without ever succumbing to panic."[12] His travels gave him the chance not just to observe various ways of life but also to test his courage, to overcome fear, and to cheat death. This self-appointed mission proved a success, as even his fiercest opponents would agree.

———⊙———

The years 1948 and 1949 marked a major turning point in the restructuring of the world. In Europe, several countries now found themselves behind the "Iron Curtain." In the Middle East, the recent proclamation of the State of Israel led to the first state-on-state clashes between Jews and Arabs. In Cambodia and Vietnam, decolonization was underway. The recent

---

[*]   Our italics.

partition of India led to bloodshed and chaos. China was in the last phase of a civil war from which Mao Zedong would emerge victorious. The United States and the Soviet Union, two new superpowers with diametrically opposed ideologies, were engaged in a relentless struggle to win the support of many countries and peoples. Trudeau travelled across a world in turmoil, torn by fratricidal wars, and striving to find a new balance.

Why did he decide to head for Asia? Because that was the continent undergoing the biggest political upheavals since the Second World War. Trudeau, who had become keenly aware of the problem of decolonization during his stay at the LSE, now wanted to see for himself how the various peoples of this part of the world were experiencing this process. He knew that some people in Quebec were convinced they were living in a British colony. By the time he got home again, he would have found out what life was like in a real colony and what people could expect in the aftermath of independence. He confided to his diary that in travelling he also sought "the grace to love men: not only to want to know them on an intellectual level."[13] He did not always succeed and on occasion noted the quirks of some groups and the malice or stupidity of particular individuals.

———◦———

Trudeau was wealthy and could have chosen to travel in luxury. He had been acquainted with first-class treatment since childhood, as indicated by the menu specially printed for the Trudeau family, including Grandfather Elliott, when they sailed on the *Empress of Britain* in the summer of 1933:

MENU

Caviar

Petite marmite [a soup]

Lobster Mornay

Duckling à l'orange

Peas

Braised Celery

Anna potatoes

Crêpes Suzette

Washed down with a Montrachet 1923.[14]

Mouth-watering! Remember also that he crossed the Atlantic in October 1947, bound for the LSE, in a first-class cabin on board the *Empress of Canada*. Now in Asia, however, luxury was not on the menu. All he brought along was a backpack. Why? To wrestle against "the demon of possessiveness," he confided to his diary, and against the "conceitedness of the 'big shots' of our planet." Travelling with a backpack also meant expressing his "real sympathy for the little people" and his desire for "spiritual and intellectual simplicity."

Fortunately, Trudeau had room in his backpack for copious notes, ink, pen, and even notebooks, like those he had used at Collège Jean-de-Brébeuf. The notebooks and pages are still in good condition. The notes are neatly written, which suggests he wrote drafts, because we know Trudeau rarely wrote without numerous corrections. He obviously spent a lot of time committing his observations to paper, not including those articles and letters he sent in transit. Unfortunately, he rarely dated his texts, which makes it difficult to determine exactly how much time he spent in a given country or city. His passports are not that helpful either: we have tried to retrace his route by referring to Customs stamps at the point of entry and exit, as well as police checks. We finally gave up, in the face of the profusion of such stamps, often appearing in random order, many of them illegible, or in languages and alphabets unknown to us. Consequently, our account of his journey cannot be precise.

One last remark, before turning to the notes themselves. Trudeau used English place names, even when writing in French. For example, he wrote Salzburg, not *Salzbourg,* Pakistan, not *le Pakistan,* Warsaw, not *Varsovie.* Sometimes he reproduced place names phonetically in the national language: for example, the Polish *Oswiecim* rather than the German, and better known, *Auschwitz.* He often made spelling mistakes, none of which appear here, in translation.

———◦———

Trudeau was engrossed in his analysis of the political, economic, and religious life of each place he visited, yet he also took great interest in everything around him: clothes, social conventions, food, architecture, etc. In Turkey, for example, he noted "character traits so different from Westerners. The Turks (the same goes for Arabs) never manage to talk without raising their voices, and never raise their voices without shouting." He always appreciated the beauty of women, noting in India: "After all the veils of Afghanistan and Pakistan, what a joy to see young Hindu women 'at liberty,' with their big black eyes, long jet-black hair, voluptuous and lively lips, and laughing teeth." Later he remarked that Anglo-Indians were snobbish but "what they are best at doing, especially in Bombay and Calcutta, is having daughters who are of remarkable beauty."

He was fascinated by exotic food. From time to time, once he had passed through a few countries, he provided a summary of foods under the heading "Cuisine." His eager description of various dishes, with their name in the language of the country, gives an idea how he marvelled at it all. He enjoyed new foods and drinks in Eastern Europe, but "radical change begins in Turkey," he wrote. "In bakeries you can buy light, warm puff pastry, stuffed with meat and onions or cheese. . . . Meals consisting of kebabs (i.e., roasted meat). . . . Then, in Syria and Lebanon, more of the same, only better: rice mixed with meat, roasted almonds, pistachios. Sugar pastry, baked macaroons filled with pistachios, dates." In Iraq and Transjordan, however, he was disappointed: "The food is the same as elsewhere, but everything is expensive and nothing is good." Which led him to think of a potential topic for further study on cooking: "Compare countries under the control of France, then of England . . ." This remark had less to do with reality than with the prejudices of his upbringing: these countries had not waited for French or British mandates to develop their own styles of cooking.

Trudeau wanted to immerse himself in local customs. In the words of Roger Rolland, he wanted to be "Chinese in China and Hindu in India."[15] For example, he noted in India that "people eat sitting on mats, using the *right hand*,* (the left is impure) to take little piles of mixed vegetables, with a piece of chapati (a type of pancake)." Perseverance paid off: he mastered this new art. He wrote to his mother with undisguised pride, "I am quite good at eating food by picking it up with a piece of chapati, though at first I used to cheat by using my left hand."[16]

Those of us who had the pleasure of sharing a meal with Trudeau at a Chinese restaurant were always amazed by his chopstick dexterity. In a

---

* Unless otherwise noted, the italics in the quotations given here are always underlined or italicized in the original text.

letter to his mother, he explained how he mastered this skill. On a two-day bus trip from Shangsha to Shanghai, he wrote: "I saw something of the real China. . . . I slept in a tiny Chinese hotel. . . . I sat on a stool at a round table with many other famished travelers and learned to warm my fingers, numbed, on the boiling teacup, that I might be more agile with the chopsticks. Indeed, agility was an essential if I were not to go hungry; for there is no time to lose when everyone begins digging in at the common bowl."[17] There it is! For Trudeau, chopstick dexterity was a matter of survival.

He wrote not only about food, but occasionally jotted down a few paragraphs about language and usage. Here are some examples, about traditional greetings. In Baghdad, people say "Salam alecum. Answer: Alecum salamah (Peace be with you). They greet one another with fingers on the forehead, then on the heart. (In Turkey, they kiss the father's hand, then press their forehead on it, with a genuflection.) Frequent expression: 'Inshallah' (God willing). . . . In Pakistan, greetings as among the Arabs. . . . Hindus join their hands together before the face, as a sign of vassalage. . . . Christians make the same gesture, but say: 'Jai Jesuki' (long live Jesus). . . . They added, referring to my beard Swarniji (Ji, diminutive: The wise and holy man)." In Peshawar, Pakistan: "They call me haji (Muslim pilgrim)." In Siam,[*] he noted with some delight: "This is perhaps the first country where I have not learned the 'polite' vocabulary: Thanks, hello, greetings, pardon me, etc. A beaming smile, a song, a friendly gesture are the Esperanto of this happy land."[18]

A thousand and one examples show that Trudeau carefully observed all aspects of life around him. This man, who often later was described as cold or callous, sometimes expressed his joy with youthful abandon. For example, on arriving in Kabul, he wrote: "I made it, I made it, I made it . . . Kabul, the forbidden, in the very heartland of the world. After Samarkand, this is the place whose name I found most tantalizing."[19] Further on, dazzled by the beauty of Thailand, he adopted a poetic style: "The sights I have seen both around Bangkok and Chiang Mai have made me regret for the first time in my whole trip, not having a camera. But perhaps even that regret is superfluous, for the fairy-like splendour, the stupendous colour, the tireless workmanship, the unthinkable shapes, the very abundance of exotic form could not possibly fit into a camera."[20]

---

*   Siam is the former name for Thailand. We will use Thailand from now on.

His journey involved great and small discomforts. For example, in Indochina, he complained about "confounded bats eating chocolate at the bottom of my backpack, and digging under the cloth to get at it." He also complained that "Chinese buses" were overloaded right up to the roof, making them particularly uncomfortable. He added: "Naturally, I am the only white man in this indescribable bus, jammed in between Chinese blowing their noses and spitting everywhere." His trips were often difficult and dangerous. For example, in Indochina, people had to travel in armoured trains or convoys, because transport links were liable to be cut by any guerrilla group: "These convoys are quite something. Often with a fatal ending. . . . There may be a dozen cars long (Siem Reap) or well over fifty (Saigon). . . . My heart jumped many times in these convoys." He described the uncertainty and fear whenever the bus stopped: "Was this an attack? Were we cut off from the other cars?" Travelling from Cambodia to Vietnam, he noted that "the Phnom Penh-Saigon* convoy . . . already feels like real war"; all the white people had pistols and were willing to use them, because "the Viet Minh steal from all Asians, but they smash up all Whites."

Trudeau still took time to do some sightseeing and attend various events. Overall, he was captivated by what he saw – which did not prevent him from criticizing some monuments for their lack of aesthetics. (Could the fact his brother, Tip, was an architect have something to do with it?) For example, in Angkor Wat, the largest temple complex of Angkor monuments, he noted that the great technical weakness of the building resulted "in functionally horrible architecture. They didn't know how to build vaults, and as a result the stone lintel dictated how narrow each feature had to be. . . . It would be very interesting to consider how this technical weakness, which imposed limits on minds obsessed by the need to build great things for their gods, meant they could only seek grandeur through a process of accumulation and repetition." He provided examples of this religious obsession: accumulations of prayers, of idols that all look alike, of saucers, of shells, "the accumulation of masses of lying or standing Buddhas, whose size reaches monstrous proportions."

---

* Saigon is now called Ho Chi Minh City.

Let us now retrace Trudeau's journey from the very beginning, focusing on the most important feature – the social and political content of his notes. In summer 1948, he took part in a camp of the International Union of Socialist Youth in Ebensee, Austria, accompanied by twenty-five other members of the British delegation, among them Morris Miller, a Jewish friend from the London School of Economics. They travelled by train through a devastated Germany. Extensive Allied bombing had left 20 million Germans homeless. The former supermen of Hitler's armies, at least those lucky enough to get home, were no more than "a ragged band of belatedly returning prisoners."[21] Germany was then a demoralized country in ruins and reduced to a state of total deprivation. Although he did not stop there, he witnessed on the train the servile attitude of the Germans, as they stooped before their new masters. He couldn't believe his eyes: "They are willing to swallow their pride for a cigarette. . . . These peddlers, train conductors and soldiers who now beg for a cigarette used to be the invincible warriors of the Third Reich. . . . I'm so astonished at finding myself in Germany. The world has not changed. Men still have two legs, a head, etc. But the people of this country have fought a terrible war against the people on the other side of the line. How can Christians agree to blow the head off the man in front of them?" The absurdity and immorality of the war outraged him: "I am in the camp. In my tent are Austrians, Germans. One of my mates, exactly my age, was in the Luftwaffe. He is going to be a lawyer; we have supper together. Whereas, four years ago, I would have had to kill him."[22]

Trudeau got to Salzburg and visited a "Displaced Persons" (DP) camp. Once a country fell under the Nazi yoke, a significant part of the population was placed at the service of the Reich, first locally, and later in Germany. In 1942, the French Vichy government forced hundreds of thousands of people into the Service du travail obligatoire (STO, or Compulsory Work Service).[23] In September 1944, more than 7 million foreigners worked in Germany as slaves – about 21 per cent of the national workforce.[24] At the end of the war, they had to be sent home, despite the deplorable state of the means of transportation. The retreating Germans, the Allies, and the French Resistance bombed and blew up everything they could – roads, bridges, railways, and trains. In France, for example, twelve thousand locomotives before the war had been reduced to fewer than three thousand after Germany's defeat.

For their part, Hitler and Stalin "uprooted, transplanted, expelled, deported and dispersed some 30 million people in the years 1939–1943."[25] The forced movement of peoples on this scale was unprecedented in the history of the West. Some deportees waited to return home; others had no home to return to since their country had been wiped off the map; still others were loathe to be sent back to the Soviet Union. There were millions of these "Displaced Persons" (DPs) – people of any age and condition who had to be sent home or somewhere else. In 1943, the Allies had founded the United Nations Relief and Rehabilitation Administration (UNRRA) because they could see this human tide coming. UNRRA's mission was to distribute food and clothing to refugees and to assist in their repatriation. But the situation was getting worse: whereas at the end of 1945, this organization administered nearly 250 refugee and DP camps, by June 1947, it had to handle three times as many.[26] Western countries did not openly welcome refugees and offered preferential treatment, without scruples. The most sought-after were strong men, able to work; next were women who could work as domestics; and finally, at the bottom of the scale, were orphans, the elderly, and single women with children.

The Jews were a special case. Initially, the authorities treated them like any other DPs. But in August 1945, President Truman announced that Jews had particular problems and should be placed in separate camps. According to historian Tony Judt, "There had never been any question of returning the Jews to the East – no one in the Soviet Union, Poland or anywhere else evinced the slightest interest in having them back. Nor were Jews particularly welcome in the West, especially if educated or qualified in non-manual occupations. . . . The difficulty of 'placing' the Jews of Europe was only solved by the creation of the state of Israel: between 1948 and 1951, 332,000 European Jews left for Israel."[27]

Trudeau and his friend Miller visited such a DP camp in Salzburg. The Jewish DPs there were much franker with the two young visitors than they would normally be with strangers. Why? Trudeau wrote: "Miller speaks Yiddish and I have a beard, so we are readily accepted as their own kind."[28] This was the first time he heard about the Jewish problem from the inside, and the experience brought him to write three and a half pages of notes, under the heading "Jews." He wrote: "[The Jewish DPs] are waiting. All the young people will fight for Israel, the families will emigrate to Canada, the United States and sometimes South America. . . . They can't stand living any longer in a Europe of ghettos and pogroms. . . . They have been in these camps for six months, two years, waiting for their chance to leave. But they have no right to open a business, etc. . . . The only thing they can do is trade on the black market. . . . Which is why we learned that in every city, the black market is located near the synagogue or DP camp. And from one city to the next, people give you the (approximate) address (and a vague name: Sam, Abe, etc.), so that Jewry truly constitutes an international agency for information and commerce." Trudeau also noted that there might be "a high percentage of Jews in communist parties or movements of young Marxists," but this was not the case in this particular camp: "Most of the DPs (Poland, Romania, Bulgaria, etc.) are dissatisfied and no longer want to live under Communism. They got to know the Russians during the war (in Siberia, the USSR, factories, etc.)."

He stressed the plight of these DPs: "Almost all of them are the sole survivors of entire families. . . . For example, in the camp of Lazné Housenow near Prague, 90% were young orphans." He was deeply moved by the suffering of Jews. The Warsaw ghetto, which was razed to the ground, came to his mind as well as "all the stories of torture and humiliations. And think of Auschwitz, where 5 million Europeans (half of them Jews) from all over the continent were put to death."[29] This concentration camp was discovered and liberated by the Russians on January 27, 1945, and continues to symbolize the full atrocity of Nazi genocide. In 2005, the UN declared January 27 International Holocaust Remembrance Day. Trudeau's travel notes clearly show that when he visited Auschwitz, on August 28, 1948, he was very troubled by what he saw. He wrote: "Auschwitz Concentration Camp: one of the worst Nazi camps."

He was undoubtedly moved by the Jewish problem, but his response was ambivalent. On the one hand, their suffering made him almost scream: "Really, how can we fail to cry 'have mercy on the Jews?' How can we fail to understand this quasi-chauvinistic nationalism of fighting for Israel?" But on the other hand, he still showed some traces of anti-Semitism and felt Jews were partly to blame for their fate. Confusing cause and effect, he wrote: "And yet they are not blameless either. They admit having little taste for hard manual labour. They only too readily form closed communities. Many Jews living in the Warsaw ghetto didn't speak Polish. Martha, a person he met at the camp, confessed that until the war she had never known anyone but Jews." (Someone might have asked Trudeau whether that was her own choice.) But in analyzing points in their favour, he referred to some historical causes of anti-Semitism: "Their fate was to perform unpopular tasks: they took care of loans at exorbitant rates of interest because Christians were prohibited from doing so; they formed the merchant class in Poland, since all land was still under the yoke of feudalism, and whenever things went wrong, it was easy to designate them as exploiters and scapegoats. This partly explains the harsh anti-Semitism that still characterizes the Polish people." And he added with evident dismay: "Dreadful to think this people are so Catholic. Just last year they killed forty Jews in a pogrom – Jews who had come back seeking refuge in Poland after surviving the Nazi regime." What a change since his departure from Quebec!

After taking part in the international socialist youth camp in Ebensee, from July 19 to 29, 1948 (he merely noted the names of a few people he met there),[30] he attended the congress of the World Federation of Democratic Youth (WFDY) in Otwock,* Poland, in August 1948. The federation was created on November 10, 1945, at a congress bringing together for the first time representatives of 30 million young people from sixty-three countries of various religions and political persuasions. At this congress, the WFDY solemnly pledged to fight for peace, the unity of youth of all races and all nationalities, the friendship of peoples, and the eradication of all traces of fascism. A great program, although plans for perpetual peace rarely seem to bear lasting fruit. However, from the beginning of the Cold War, almost all Western agencies had withdrawn from the WFDY, and it was primarily associated with pro-Soviet organizations.

In fact, when Trudeau attended the Otwock Congress in August 1948, the WFDY was already recognized as pro-Soviet. Since he has often been accused of sympathizing with Communist regimes, because he attended such meetings, his reactions then are worth some examination. He noted the shameless propaganda at Otwock: "Overall, the most notable feature is the drive to produce a unanimous condemnation of 'U.S. imperialism,' fascism. The meeting sticks closely to formulas, always the same formulas, nothing but formulas. . . . Some repetition could be excusable for the purposes of mass propaganda, but is inexcusable when intellectuals

---

*   Just outside Warsaw.

have come together to discuss problems, not to be railroaded into accepting solutions." Trudeau was definitely not "a fellow traveller" of Communists, unlike many French intellectuals, such as Emmanuel Mounier, for example.

———— ◦◉◦ ————

In Hungary, on learning that 70 per cent of the Communist Party was Catholic, he exclaimed: "Either they aren't good Catholics or they are forced to become party members because they wouldn't have got a job otherwise." He learned that the government was trying to restrict the role of religion in the country, but it "cannot touch the churches because the people are very Catholic. But it eliminates the influence of the clergy everywhere else. . . . People here seem to despair of ever being able to adapt socialism to Christianity, because Communism is so relentlessly materialistic." Trudeau was convinced Christianity was superior to Communism, and he drew a lesson directly for his country: "The need for Canada to bring about social Christianity: there will still be free competition. Show that our justice is as good as theirs. Here, it is no longer possible: the government has all the powers: money, police, army, government, etc." In pursuit of this goal, Trudeau did not reject the idea of an alliance with Canadian Communists, who struck him as less threatening than others: "True, conspiracy should remain a crime, but the Communist Party of *Canada* is not obviously made up of conspirators." Collaboration would be possible in Canada because Communists acted within the framework of democracy. Trudeau cited as evidence the fact that during the Ontario election, Communists advised members to vote for the CCF, except in districts where there were Communist candidates. This was only a strategic alliance, in Trudeau's opinion, and could strike some people as a Machiavellian one: "For this reason, the theory of Christian cooperation with Marxism should be considered. [Marxists] want a classless society and believe that religion, the opium of the people, will wither away on its own. As a Christian, I want a classless society because I believe that once freed from material cares, man will be more inclined to seek God."

Trudeau deplored the lack of democracy in Communist regimes in Eastern Europe. But the people he spoke to reminded him that patience was needed: democracy would grow with time. He remained unconvinced and wrote that Communists always disparaged their opponents, labelling them "reactionaries, fascists, imperialists, etc." They imposed revolution on the majority of the population, "claiming that it would be for the greater good of humanity." Trudeau admitted that certain circumstances justified imposing one's will on the majority. In other, very rare cases, revolution was justified: "Fighting the oppressors might require the suspension of some civil liberties. In short, when circumstances require action, one has to accept this need and act accordingly." But he hastened to add these were only exceptions. When the system could be improved "with the consent of the majority, then there must be no assault on the individual conscience: for every man must be left free to pursue the good as he sees fit (even when I believe this good is actually bad for him)." Gone is the appeal to the benevolent leader guiding his people toward the good. Trudeau was really embracing the values of liberal democracy!

He also wanted to see Christian socialism prevail. Even though it was well established that heavy-handed bureaucracy was one of the major weaknesses of so-called socialist countries, this did not cool his enthusiasm: "We must be willing to pay the price if it means eliminating poverty." He had encountered poverty, beggars, and cripples since the beginning of his journey, and especially in Hungary. But would Christian charity not help reduce poverty, as he had been taught in his youth? Trudeau no longer believed in this single remedy alone: "Private charity is not enough: when there is too much [misery], people end up doing nothing." He believed that political intervention was essential, it was the "duty of the State . . . to eradicate poverty." Yet he knew that charity would remain needed: "There will always be destitute people who need private alms."

Once he got to the Middle East, Trudeau wrote: "The Syrians want to reunite with Lebanon, and possibly with Iraq, to reconstitute Greater Syria, and base this claim on their common language. But while the Syrians are very anti-French, . . . and bitterly complain about the bombardment of Damascus in 1945, when the British liberated the capital from French troops, . . . the Lebanese for their part remain well-disposed towards France, which granted Lebanon independence from Syria. Lebanon is a haven for Christians in the Middle East, their stronghold. Statistics show there is a Christian majority, and the Constitution requires that the president be Christian (he is Maronite) whereas the head of the Council (?) must be Muslim.[31] Many Lebanese consider themselves very different from Arabs: this country is the Phoenicia of antiquity and their ancestors are the Phoenicians."

This short excerpt combines accurate facts with more doubtful observations and sheds some light on the sources of information Trudeau typically gathered during his journey. To place his notes in context, we will sketch some of the very complex and controversial history of this region. The Ottoman Empire had been allied with Germany during the First World War. After the defeat of the Empire, France obtained a League of Nations mandate to govern Syria and Lebanon. During the Second World War, Syria, still under French rule, came under the control of Vichy and therefore collaborated with Germany. For example, in 1941, the government authorized the German air force to refuel in Syria. That same year, de Gaulle's Free French Forces and British troops invaded the country. The Allies defeated Vichy forces in Syria after a month. At the time of the invasion, the Free French recognized the independence of Syria and Lebanon as a way of gaining the support of the local population. But this was independence in name only. From 1943 to 1945, the Free French refusal to transfer power to the Syrian government led to nationalist riots. The crisis worsened and, in 1945, General de Gaulle sent in the troops and ordered the bombing of Damascus. The British were forced to intervene.

Trudeau was right about the bombing of Damascus by French forces, which would explain anti-French sentiment, and he accurately noted that the Lebanese Constitution stipulated the president had to be a Maronite Christian and the prime minister a Sunni Muslim. He explained that the Lebanese were well disposed toward France because it "had made Lebanon independent from Syria." But he said nothing of the fact that it was thanks to French support for Christians in the Mount Lebanon region – part of Syria – that Lebanon became an independent country after the First World War. In so doing, France not only put an end to the aspirations of Syria, which did not want an independent Lebanon, but at the same time deprived Syria of outlets on the Mediterranean. Moreover, the Constitution guaranteed the political supremacy of the Christians in Lebanon. Trudeau's sympathy for the Lebanese and his antipathy for the Syrians become easier to understand. We can also guess that Trudeau's mains source of information were Christian priests and missionaries, as they often were in his travels. In Lebanon, they claimed the majority of the population was Christian. But when Trudeau wrote these lines, this claim was already being challenged. The Phoenician origin of much of the Lebanese population is even more controversial. This interpretation of history is often advanced by Christians in order to differentiate themselves from Muslims. Without getting bogged down in this debate, let us note that Phoenicia ceased to exist after the conquest of Alexander the Great, more than three hundred years before Christ.

We will now focus on Trudeau's visit to Jerusalem in the fall of 1948, because it provides a compelling illustration of the difficulty in separating myth from reality. As Trudeau's visit has been described in different ways, a comparison of these various interpretations will allow us to highlight what the versions had in common and where they contradicted one another. We will begin with the account Trudeau gave in *Memoirs*. In Amman, Transjordan (now Jordan), he learned that journalists were writing their despatches about Jerusalem without going there. The reason? "'The road between Jericho and Jerusalem has been blocked by Palestinian forces. . . . It's too risky.'"[32] Trudeau went there anyway, explaining that "I soon spotted trucks in the main square of Amman loaded with Arab volunteer soldiers who were leaving to do battle in Jerusalem. I jumped aboard one of these vehicles, already loaded with some twenty armed soldiers, and a few minutes later we were on our way. Amman was barely sixty kilometres from Jerusalem." The truck reached the centre of Jerusalem without difficulty.[33] There he visited "a Canadian Dominican whose address a priest in Beirut, had given me." He dodged Israeli-Arab crossfire, getting to the other side of the street. This meant violating a curfew, and two Arab soldiers arrested him, throwing him in prison, "in the Antonia Tower, where Pontius Pilate had judged Christ." He was informed he would be accused of spying for the Haganah, an Israeli self-defence militia, and therefore risked the death penalty. However, the Dominican helped establish his identity. After a day and night in prison, he was removed from his cell and placed on another truck loaded with Arab soldiers and bound for Amman. "Unfortunately for me," Trudeau later wrote, "the Arab soldiers who surrounded me had not heard the Dominican's testimony. As far as they were concerned, I was indeed a Jewish spy. . . . They let me know by vivid and easily understandable gestures that there was nothing to stop them from killing me and dumping my corpse into the ravine that bordered the highway. But I did my best to act confident, and they did nothing beyond turning me over to the authorities in Amman, still under arrest."[34] He was released through the intervention of the British embassy. So much for the first version.

It is easy to be captivated by the intrepid character of this story. But on second thought, how could a white-skinned, blue-eyed man who did not speak Arabic jump unnoticed onto a truck full of armed soldiers and travel sixty kilometres? (We should note a factual error in this account: members of the Arab Legion were not "volunteers" but the most professional and best-trained soldiers deployed in this war.) Once he got to Jerusalem, how could he slip away, without any of the soldiers noticing? And when taken for a spy for the Haganah, how did he escape any interrogation or abuse? These questions have yet to be answered.

A second interpretation of this journey was broadcast by Radio Canada on May 5, 1950, under the title "Portrait of Pierre Trudeau."[35] The text of this broadcast was carefully scrutinized by Trudeau, as his many annotations indicate. For example, he added "Elliott" in between Pierre and Trudeau, placed parentheses here and there, and corrected some figures. We are reproducing most of this broadcast here: "As soon as he reached the streets of Aleppo, Syria, UN officials took him for a Jewish spy, because of his black beard. Count Bernadotte had just been assassinated. . . . Three thousand Arabs chased him, pelting him with stones and shouting 'Death!' He was expelled to Lebanon where he met the brother of Father Legault and in the midst of the Jewish-Arab war, he left for Jerusalem with a Dominican from Brazil. Naturally, he no sooner reached Jerusalem than he was arrested as a spy . . . once again because of his famous beard. There was talk of sending him before a firing squad, and he got locked up in the Antonia Tower where Christ Himself was imprisoned, while the battle raged in the city. Thank God . . . he managed to meet an Arab soldier with a funny accent (from the Lower St. Lawrence).* . . . It was a Canadian! What was he doing there? Just as the firing squad was about to finish him

---

*   Trudeau added "Lower St. Lawrence" in brackets.

off, Pierre Trudeau was saved by the Dominican from Brazil and by this Canadian disguised as a Muslim. Not wanting to be outdone, he headed back to Transjordan, but his convoy was attacked by irregulars. His beard got him arrested a third time for spying. . . . When he was on the point of being shot at the roadside, he got a miraculous reprieve. In Amman, he was released and as a consolation was taken to see King Abdullah."

James Bond could not have done any better!

A third version deserves our attention: an article entitled "Where There Is No Question of Love," written on October 27, 1948 – or more than a year *before* Radio Canada broadcast the outlandish "Portrait."[36] In this article, Trudeau expressed his deepest feelings: his faith, his disappointments, and his hopes. He wrote, for example, that visiting the holy sites in Jerusalem was "the most moving experience of [his] life as a Christian." He deplored that love of one's neighbour was so rare. Over the three months of his journey, he asked, "Who is my neighbour?" and had met nothing but "hatred, distrust, fear and revenge. The Communists hate the Socialists, the Socialists despise the Christians, the Christians are suspicious of the Jews, the Jews hate the Arabs, the Arabs resent the English." A very long list followed of people, each of whom was trying to outdo the others' hatred. This ghastly "perpetual motion machine," he wrote, would shatter the world. It was imperative that men act. But they weren't ready to act, he said, because "the Christian nations – especially the Christian nations – have lost the sense of [loving] their neighbour."

Trudeau acknowledged he had also seen what goodwill could accomplish. "I saw the benefits of the Marshall Plan, the Joint Distribution Committee, the International Organization for Aid to Refugees, the Friendship Train. I saw English Catholics making sacrifices in order to help German students. . . . But what does that prove? Jews loved me, as long as they thought I was Jewish. . . . The Hungarians, Poles welcomed me into their home, as long as they thought I was sympathetic to their problems. The Arabs treated me to hospitality, as soon as I acknowledged the validity of their grievances. . . . But I had so many problems with Hungarian, Yugoslav and Romanian consulates, when they examined my 'reactionary' passport! . . . I was imprisoned so many times by the Arabs, who were sure I was a spy for the Haganah! And how cold

Catholics could be, when they saw me as no more than a vagrant scroung-
ing for food!" Trudeau was categorical: "All these people violate the
second commandment. . . . How does loving only those who are good to
you make you any different from pagans?"

After this lamentation about evil and human nature, he brought his
readers back to the Holy Land. He was tortured by the absence of neigh-
bourly love and went to Calvary and the Holy Sepulchre, "with bullets
and dumdums whistling by." And then, he wrote, "kneeling before the
Holy Presence, entering into it more than I had ever done before, I prayed
that we men might one day understand the parable of the Good Samaritan."
He thought about this prayer later that evening, when he was placed on
board a truck headed for Amman, and when at dawn as they crossed the
Jordan: "My guard was under the impression I had got up to look at
the camp on the riverbank, and stuck his gun in my back, motioning for
me to sit down again. I hate to be treated roughly, and gestured to him to
bugger off. An ill-considered move on my part. I paid a price for it! For
twenty minutes, I helplessly watched the pathetic spectacle of a dozen
Arab 'irregulars' armed to the teeth urging each other to execute me sum-
marily as a Jewish spy, since I had come without permission from
Jerusalem, and their leaders were now weakly sending me back to prison
in Amman. . . . A young warrior was particularly eager to prove his worth,
as well as his knowledge of English, and kept saying: 'You Jew . . . We kill
you . . . after . . . '" Trudeau's bluster helped get him out of the situation,
and it was a relief later to reach Amman unscathed. Returning to the
theme of the Good Samaritan, he made his *mea culpa*. He wondered
whether he would have acted the Good Samaritan himself, if he had met
this young warrior one on one: "I kept hearing the words in his mouth:
'You Jew . . . We kill you . . . after . . . ' and I happily pictured my fist
planted in the middle of his face." He concluded, sadly: "And yet, at the
time, 'Who was my neighbour?' O divine answer, when shall we hear
thee?" It is unfortunate that this article, published in *Le Devoir* more than
half a century ago, should have become a forgotten page in the history
books. It reveals a very different man.

We now have three quite different versions of the same trip to
Jerusalem. How can we figure out what really happened? The answer
lies in Trudeau's agenda and travel diary. In the diary he wrote that in
prison "A. J., my first interpreter, is the guard who had arrested me and

had lived ten years in Cuba. . . . Then came a kind young Arab woman, who said there was no Red Cross in Jerusalem. They give me tea, a good meal and I sleep in prison in the Antonia Tower, where Christ was imprisoned. . . . In the evening, all sorts of people come to the guard-house. We speak German. A guy from Saskatchewan." In his agenda, Trudeau wrote on October 7: "In Amman, Baby Haddad looks for hotel with me. We are locked up, released." On October 8: "Stand close to King Abdullah as he comes out of the mosque. . . . Offices closed, so I take the chance of going to Jerusalem without the required visa. $1.25 collective taxi, and 2½ hours. Downhill. Cross the Jordan. Jericho. Then Jerusalem, the Holy City. Walk towards the walls. At the door, I am seized, led to the guard room where I sleep (former Tower of Antonia, where I was held!). Conversations with guards, English, etc." On October 9, he wrote: "Father Martin brought in to identify me. Obtains from Father Ibrahim (military government) that I am escorted to all holy places. Very moving. All this with dum-dum bullets and 6-inch mortar shells. Left Father at his convent of St. Stephen. Come back to sleep in the guard room. Big meal at officers' mess. Eucharist at noon." On October 10: "4:00 AM Back in military truck where 'irregulars' promise to kill me as a Jew! The sun rises. I arrive safe and sound. Whew!"

Here then are the facts. They speak for themselves.

This comparative exercise highlights the part of drama in Trudeau's accounts of his travels. These fantastic stories end up creating the false image of a thrill-seeking adventurer. Regarding this famous trip to Jerusalem, two other texts, unpublished until now, are worth looking at, since they reveal Trudeau as a well-informed political analyst who pondered the Israeli-Palestinian problem, a problem that unfortunately persists to this day.

We should first briefly recall the history of the region. After the First World War, the League of Nations granted Great Britain a mandate over Palestine, stating that the British must help Jews "reconstitute their national home in that country." Jewish immigration to Palestine was organized in the 1920s. Once Hitler came to power, this immigration increased dramatically, fuelling the resentment of the local Arab population. Jews founded the Haganah (Hebrew for "defence"). Terrorist militias were also organized, such as the Irgun and Lehi (also called the "Stern Gang"), who at first attacked Arabs and then British officials starting in 1939.

In 1945, given British restrictions on immigration to Palestine, illegal immigration was organized, and renewed fighting broke out again. Great Britain was under such acute pressure that it decided to withdraw from the region, handing the fate of Palestine over to the United Nations (UN), which adopted a plan on November 29, 1947, to split Palestinian territory into two states that would remain united economically. This plan failed, and fighting between the communities intensified, with many casualties on both sides. The British Mandate ended on May 14, 1948. That very day, David Ben-Gurion proclaimed the independence of the State of Israel. The proclamation triggered the first Arab-Israeli war. The fate of the new state seemed uncertain. In June, both sides accepted the United Nations ceasefire. However, a peace plan proposed by UN mediator Count Folke Bernadotte was rejected by both camps. In September 1948, Bernadotte was killed with his driver by three members of the Stern Gang.

It was in this overheated atmosphere that Trudeau visited Jerusalem. The independence of the State of Israel had been proclaimed only a few months before. Count Bernadotte had only just been assassinated, adding to tensions. The conflict was raging, and nobody could foresee the outcome. Trudeau wrote two texts, "Memories of Jerusalem" and "The Palestinian Affair." The first seems to have been written for his personal use, while the second is undated and looks like an unfinished draft article. Since both texts deal with the same subject, we will address them together.

The Israeli-Arab war moved Trudeau deeply. He found the situation so complex that he felt "at a loss to know whether the Arabs or the Jews are right." He wrote ironically: "I always admire the way some people come out with conclusive judgments on the most diverse topics, their confidence growing in inverse proportion to the amount of information they have. Such people can be great men of action, and just as easily the biggest fools." Since he had hung out with both types of people, he couldn't resist recording "some thoughts likely to raise doubts in the minds of those blindly supporting one cause or the other."

He was indignant about the UN: "What is the UN doing? The mere fact fighting continues is proof that the arms embargo is ineffective. . . . And the fact I met so many Jews in Europe bound for Palestine . . . proves that the halt on immigration is not being respected." Who does this country belong to? Trudeau admitted it was hard to answer this question: "The historical arguments are rubbish: thirty years ago, this area was neither Jewish nor Arab, but Turkish." He briefly summarized the arguments put forward by Jews and Arabs: "Admittedly, in 1915, Great Britain promised freedom to those Arabs who would take its side in the war. But with the 1917 Balfour Declaration, Britain also promised a 'national home' for Jews. The Arabs answered that this did not imply an independent *State* and claimed the Jews aimed one day to occupy lands from the Euphrates all the way to the Nile." Rather, Trudeau asserted, it "would be much more instructive to consider this whole episode between two Semitic tribes in the light of British diplomacy."

To the historical facts we have just noted, he added Great Britain's oil-related interests: "England is absolutely masterful at playing one alliance off the other. Admittedly, the communists are trying to get a foothold (the prospect of extreme wealth alongside extreme poverty attracts them), but their party is banned (in all Arab countries) and they often lack cohesion because they lack leaders. As for the Americans, I think they would not mind having an ally in the region, like Israel. But the downside is there are many communists in Israel, just as there are many capitalists. (This is the most important cause of disunity: the Stern Gang is communist.)" Although Trudeau's analysis is well documented, he is mistaken about the Stern Gang, which was terrorist and extremist but definitely not Communist. (Ben Gurion called the Gang "fascists.") He held Jews partly responsible for the animosity to which they were subjected: "Of course, they have a lot of faults. First of all, they lay themselves open to anti-Semitism by having such a dreadfully tribal mindset: we know that wherever a Jew goes, thousands will follow, and these thousands will never assimilate to their surroundings for fear of weakening their ties with the tribe and with international Jewry. . . . They are not blameless in Palestine either. There is no need to recall the horrific violence of the Stern Gang and the Irgun."

Is Trudeau betraying here a trace of anti-Semitism? Whatever the case, he immediately returned to arguments in their favour, recalling their persecution and incorporating his previous description of the harsh conditions Jews experienced in the DP camps and around the Joint Distribution Committee (USA Relief for Jews): "Really after all that, how can we not cry out 'have mercy on the Jews' or understand the chauvinist spirit of Zionists? After such a long exile, now that they have reached a land they could consider their homeland, isn't it perfectly understandable that this people should want to shield themselves from the blows of history?" After these comments, made in 1948, we did not find the slightest trace of anti-Semitism in Trudeau's writings. It is worth recalling that he was the first Canadian prime minister to appoint Jews to important positions from which they had previously been excluded. The best-known example is Bora Laskin, the first Jew appointed Chief Justice of the Supreme Court. Many other Jews received government appointments.

Trudeau then considered the Arabs, among whom he had lived and whose souks and food he had enjoyed: "The Arabs, on the other hand, are waging a war that seems pleasant, chivalrous, but totally ineffective. In Syria, general mobilization is no sooner decreed than an exception is quickly made for Jerusalem. If it weren't for the whizzing bullets, we wouldn't know the city is under siege: you can find absolutely anything you want in the bazaars. All you can see are happy and unconcerned Arabs. They are implacable in their hatred of Jews. . . . Of course, Arabs have a dark side. On the slightest pretext, a Bedouin will rip you open. It is not unusual for a brother to kill his dishonoured sister. They get into bloody brawls. But give them the slightest reason to hold you in high esteem, and their generosity is boundless. In my experience, although I gave them a thousand reasons for suspicion, they rarely failed to show their traditional hospitality and friendliness."

On the political level, Trudeau wrote, "the Arabs are not waging a serious war, because they are divided. Abdullah of Transjordan wants to be king of Greater Syria. . . . Also, he orders his troops, trained by the Englishman Glubb Pasha,* not to advance into Palestine. He awaits the UN settlement. Other Arab countries see this as a betrayal and vow to assassinate Abdullah. But they will do nothing as long as they remain disunited."

Trudeau speculated about the future: "Would a return to the Koran mark the start of an Arab renaissance, the way some people hope? It seems unlikely; and a great leader would be needed, who would know how to command and to call for a holy war. Meanwhile, England pulls all the

---

* There is a slight factual error here: Glubb Pasha commanded the Jordanian Army; he did not train it.

strings." Trudeau was convinced that "the Arabs talk more than they act. They swear by all the attributes of Allah that they will push the Jews into the sea, but in reality they won't do anything because they're never going to agree." Which explains his harsh verdict on the outcome of fighting: "And for this reason, there does not seem to be any doubt about the question of Palestine: in spite of everything, there will be a Jewish state in Palestine; this seems to establish itself almost as a corollary of the laws of history. A clever, ambitious, tenacious, rich, materialistic people, is opposed to a divided, passive, carefree and backward people."

In 1948, Trudeau did not seem to have met Jews in Israel: he made no mention of any such encounter in his notes. On visiting Israel again in 1959, he would express his amazement: "It is hardly an exaggeration to speak of the miracle of Israel. Next to all the scorched lands of the Middle East, here you find greenery, gardens, flowers, fields of wheat, cotton, corn, here are forests of orange, cypress and eucalyptus trees."[37] He saw a few beggars, but overall, found people to be clean, well dressed, vigorous. Noting many dilapidated shacks on the road to the airport, he was "told these are North Africans who prefer not having to pay taxes, electricity, rent." (Once again, we wonder about his source of information. If he had had the opportunity to speak to the North African Jews living in these hovels, he might have heard about racism and discrimination from which Israelis are not immune.)[38] In Jerusalem, he visited the district of Orthodox Jews, presented by the tour guide as "our fanatics. They don't pay taxes, don't join the army, etc." But, Trudeau noted, "the Israelis are counting on the children to gradually be attracted to the country's cultural mainstream." He found the Israelis "a little chauvinistic. They never tire of talking about the greatness of their country, of its achievements. They compare themselves to the Arabs, and constantly vow to defend themselves if necessary, and to triumph. But they are not so expansionist as they seem to have been. They seem ready to accept a certain status quo. In the case of Jerusalem, for example, they don't expect to see the Arabs clear out. Quite simply, they would consider a kind of internationalization." More than half a century later, it is to be regretted that moderate Israelis – like the ones Trudeau was apparently quoting – have not managed to persuade other parties of the wisdom of this position.

At the end of 1948, we find Trudeau in Asia, visiting India and Pakistan, among other places. We should recall that after the war, Great Britain wanted to withdraw from India as quickly and honourably as possible and favoured a united India. But the Hindus and Muslims could not agree on a single formula for independence. Gandhi and the Congress Party sought a secular and united India. Muhammad Ali Jinnah, leader of the Muslim League, demanded partition. Seeing the partition as inevitable, Lord Louis Mountbatten, the last Viceroy of India, set about negotiating it. Partition came into effect on August 15, 1947, and Pakistan was born. It comprised two provinces more than 1,500 kilometres apart – West Pakistan (present-day Pakistan) and East Pakistan (present-day Bangladesh). Partition resulted in massive movements of population: 12 million people crossed the new borders in both directions, in search of safety. Massacres and bloodshed of unusual ferocity intensified, while the government was incapable of managing the ensuing chaos. Trudeau reached these regions just a year after partition and was stunned by the scale of these movements of population, equal to the entire "population of Canada!"³⁹

Trudeau's notes cover a wide range of topics: descriptions of landscapes, religion and politics, art, climate, populations, castes, social customs, the economy. . . . Among his informants were many missionaries, Jesuits, or people associated with Catholic Action. He seems to have had access to the most exclusive social circles. In a letter to his mother, for example, he wrote: "I attended a session of the Constituent Assembly, a very interesting one since they discussed Article 31 on economic democracy. There was a remarkable intervention by one Father D'Souza, an Indian Jesuit, elected from Madras. That evening, I went over to the Archbishop's Palace and had a very long and enlightening discussion with him (D'Souza) as well as a chat with the Archbishop who gave me his blessing and the Vicar General Monsignor Burke late of Singapore."⁴⁰

In analyzing the reasons for partition, the people he met expressed prejudices typical of their social background. In India, for example, "D'Souza blames the Muslims who are less educated, less enterprising, and he considers them less intelligent: even a Hindu who converts to Islam is soon afflicted with the disease of apathy. Too much trust in Allah? Inshallah? . . . Given the backward state of Muslim affairs, education, wealth, etc., they simply wanted a separate State that would

employ Muslims and lead them forward." In Pakistan, on the other
hand, he heard different interpretations of the causes of partition.
According to a communist bookseller in Lahore, for example, "the communists have made a tactical error by promoting Pakistan: they did not
understand this was a division sought by reactionary conservatives."
Who was right about the causes of partition – the Hindus or the
Muslims? Trudeau felt unable to decide: "According to Hindus, Pakistan
was of interest mainly to a few ambitious leaders, especially Jinnah, who
could not bear to play second fiddle in the State of India. . . . They
played on the passion of the people, raising the cry of religious persecution. . . . According to the Muslim viewpoint, Pakistan was an unfortunate necessity, given the bitterness and injustice of the Hindus, who
would always remember how [Islam had conquered India], and would
always seek to make amends for this insult, by putting down Muslims
everywhere. . . . Admittedly, I have often personally witnessed the animosity and vindictiveness of Hindus in this respect. On the other hand,
aren't there Muslims calling for holy war, taking Delhi, etc.?"

Opinions were divided on the cause of partition, but people agreed
on one thing: no one really wanted it. This partition was "certainly a
misfortune for India," Trudeau wrote. "The problem is knowing whether
this disaster was avoidable, and, now that it is an established fact,
knowing how to make the most of the situation." Just a few months
earlier, Trudeau had advocated federalism as an ideal system for French
Canadians and now saw India as a place where this solution could have
been put to the test: "We could have seen whether the project of making
India a federation with residual powers in several States would not have
allowed the Muslims to play a major role in several provinces where they
were strongly represented. . . . And before long the Muslims would have
taken the place that was rightly theirs in a united and prosperous India.
The example of French Canadians is perhaps not irrelevant. When the
destiny of a great people is involved, you need to set your sights high. . . .
Even if Hindu favouritism played against Muslims," he wrote, "I can't
convince myself that this justifies the need for a separate State, and am
inclined to attribute this need to the stupidity of some leaders (probably
the mullahs) and to the ambition of others (example: Jinnah)." With
regard to geography, partition didn't make any sense at all. "If all
Muslims more or less lived together in the same area, separatism would

have been understandable. But of these 110 million inhabitants, 49 million had to live in Hindu States, and another 70 million were divided between East (40 million) and West (30 million) Pakistan, living thousands of miles apart." Trudeau was dead right: the separation of Pakistan into two regions so far apart could not last. After a bloody struggle, East Pakistan declared its independence in 1971, becoming Bangladesh.

Trudeau devoted forty pages to India, this "country of hope and disappointment, a country of the future that is nonetheless so backward, a country of cultural and philosophical grandeur, full of human pettiness." He found the challenges India faced practically insurmountable. India's leaders faced three huge problems: the shortage of skilled leaders, corruption and the prevalence of bribery, and especially disobedience "promoted as a virtue for a quarter of a century and more." Trudeau feared that the immensely popular Congress Party would yield to autocracy: "Power corrupts . . ." he wrote, citing the famous words of Lord Acton: "Power corrupts, absolute power corrupts absolutely." But he had confidence in "Nehru, the great Nehru," who seemed aware of the danger. What was Nehru's main challenge? "Knowing how to instil democracy among a people of illiterates, whose political education consisted in asking him to demand freedom in their name."

He denounced the widespread xenophobia he saw. In the city, he said, "there is resentment towards all foreigners, the understandable legacy of 150 years of inferiority. The result is a general lack of courtesy when you ask even the most straightforward question." He found the caste mentality exasperating: "It is said that the Englishman's condescending attitude made him detestable. But what about the contempt wealthy Hindus show towards inferior Hindus – isn't it even more detestable?" As a result: "This caste mentality is so strong that it is still found among Catholics. . . . Because of these divisions, Catholic Action is impossible, and it is often impossible to train choirs."

His informants – people active in Catholic Action, often senior clergy, missionaries – highlighted the similarity between Gandhi's ideas and Christianity. For example, they said, "Gandhi's reconstruction plan is highly acceptable to Catholics. And the charter of rights contained in the current constitution is more Catholic than the UN's declaration of rights." Trudeau quoted a lecturer, who declared: "It is said 'East is East and West is West.' But that is false. The world is looking for a synthesis and India's contribution will be . . . its unending concern about the relationship between God and man."[41] Trudeau liked this point of view. However, he was disappointed to learn that Hindus were not well disposed toward Christians. Lacking any direct experience of Christians, Hindus had misconceptions about them and failed to distinguish between Catholics and Protestants. For example, they took for granted that "when a man is seen in public with a woman, that means he is fornicating with her. Which explains the low opinion Hindus have of the company Christian women keep." Trudeau found it ironic to find such opinions in "a people who deify female dancers and courtesans."

Concerning the struggle in India between Christianity and Marxism, Trudeau noted that these two ideologies targeted the same social class: the Dalits (untouchables). "The Communists and the Christians are here to remind the pariahs they share in human dignity. So . . . converts come especially from among the poor, like the Chamars, who must live just outside the village. And the work of restoring their rank as men also involves giving them a little rice when they are hungry, clothing etc." Missionaries were well aware that this resulted in "Rice Christians," in other words, people who converted for a bowl of rice. But in justifying their actions, these missionaries were quick to recall that Christ also fed the people who came to listen. Trudeau did not condemn this practice: "It seems indisputable that we have to put something in the pagan's belly before we can expect him to listen to the gospel." Too few Catholics, he wrote, understood the need above all of bringing relief to the poor: "The Protestants are a little better. So when I see 'Christian Relief' in Lahore, I know right away that this is Protestant relief. Why do we allow them to monopolize the word 'Christian'?"

The struggle between these two ideologies was not waged on equal terms: the missionaries faced obstacles the Marxists knew nothing about. Converts to Christianity were rejected by their own communities, couldn't find work, had an even harsher life. "But it is even worse for Muslims: converts are beaten, and often 'disappear.'" But this was not the sole cause of the stagnation of Catholicism in India, Trudeau wrote. Many missionaries behaved badly. The situation was worse among indigenous brothers and sisters of religious communities. That entire civilization had to change. A bewildered Trudeau then wondered: "That's just the point – how can we possibly change it within a man before ordaining him as a priest?"

He thought of a few solutions, but one in particular filled him with enthusiasm: "Let young laymen come to settle with their families in the country of their mission, to practice their profession normally, bearing witness to the Christian way of life. They would live as laymen, independently of the mission." He was fascinated by this idea, believing it offered wonderful opportunities to French Canadians: "The marginal return would be greater than in Canada, which is a Christian country. But all this is based on the assumption that the layman would remain long enough to learn the language; true vocation. They could always return home after 10–15 years. And then, what a contribution they would make from a Christian perspective!" These opportunities set him dreaming, and soon he pictured himself writing an article on the subject. The title was inspired by Baudelaire's "Invitation au voyage" [Invitation to the Voyage]. He even wrote a few lines, inspired by this famous poem: "'My child, my sister, think of the rapture of living together there,' there in the Sunderbans, among the densest population on Earth. . . . The children would have a better education than in Quebec, with four teachers for every seven students." But Trudeau was already thinking about an even more provocative title: "Anti-Quebec conspiracy: our élites are called to a mission in India." Once he got back to Quebec, he discussed the idea of founding a lay mission with friends, including Gérard Pelletier.

<hr />

On December 2, 1948, Trudeau was delighted to find himself in Kabul, the capital of Afghanistan, at that time a country little known by Canadians. We have already noted his enthusiasm in the letter he wrote to his mother: "I made it. I made it. I made it. . . ." He continued in the same vein, confiding to her that "*veni, vedi,* and now I feel I can continue my trek home with peace in my heart."[42] But in going from Lahore to Kabul, Trudeau seemed to be backtracking. To understand why his route was so tortuous, we have to remember it was hard to get visas, roads were blocked by warring factions, and there was an utter lack of transportation facilities. Freedom of movement was hindered in all kinds of ways. We should also note that while Trudeau usually chose the same means of transport as the common people, he also travelled by airplane.

Why didn't he visit Kabul, before going to India? To answer this question, we must return to India. In Delhi, Trudeau ran from one embassy to another, trying all sorts of schemes to get visas. He was delighted with an unexpected success, as he explained to his mother: "I got my Siamese visa and in the same day received permission to go to Kashmir as well as to Afghanistan, two countries no one seems able to enter. Afghanistan has always looked with suspicion on foreigners. Kashmir now is closed to everyone because of war. I worked on both angles, thinking that at the very best one would work out, and both worked. Other people I met have been trying for months to get to Kashmir, to distribute clothing to refugees."[43] Since he couldn't visit both countries, he opted for Afghanistan. So, back to Lahore, then on to Peshawar. "Peshawar has always been a centre of intrigue, tribal uprisings, provincial revolts, invasions through the Khyber Pass. . . . And things have not changed for the new state of Pakistan, with war on the North, suspicion on the East besides outstanding unsettled business with Afghanistan in the Kandahar region."[44] In Peshawar, Trudeau managed to get a lift with an American attaché headed for Kabul. In going through the Khyber Pass, they had to beware of bandits and found that "every major gulley is the site of some bloody battle which the British had to fight. Plaques of the participating regiments still plaster the walls of the pass." He was told that the nomads he saw were "greatly influenced by their 'mullahs' (priests); the mullah is not only religious, he is the wise man who teaches youngsters in the tribe how to read." Trudeau also noted the mullahs' dark side: "These mullahs constitute a reactionary force in the country, and oppose the progressive tendencies of the oligarchic and nepotistic government." The more things change, the more they stay the same. . . .

Trudeau's journey now took him back across India. He stopped in Delhi to pick up his mail, spent three days in Benares, the holy city of Hinduism, and headed east from there, to Calcutta. Then he left India for Burma (now known as Myanmar), a former British colony which had become independent on January 4, 1948. Since the 1930s, nationalist movements had been engaged in all kinds of struggles, including infighting between various factions and ethnic groups. From 1942 to 1945, Burma was occupied by Japan, which promised to grant it independence upon its victory. But the population was divided. The Communists and socialists created an anti-fascist organization that fought alongside the Allies. It was not until 1945 that the Japanese were finally driven out by Allied forces. But this did not mean peace. Infighting between Communists, socialists, and other groups continued.

Trudeau visited Rangoon, capital of Burma (until 2006). In eight pages of notes, he found nothing positive to say. He made no reference to Japanese occupation or the damage inflicted by war or the country's recent history. After listing the tribes, clans, and ethnic groups making up the Burmese people, he wrote: "I have never seen people so inclined to hatred. They hate white people and deny visas to any missionary . . . unless they get a bribe. They hate each other. No one trusts the government." And he added sarcastically: "And this complete chaos is ironically called the 'Union of Burma.' Not a day passes without the newspapers reporting a massacre, looting, etc. Some incidents are worthy of a comic opera. . . . The administration is corrupt from top to bottom." Rumour had it that "the president of the union is so fed up he wants the British to come back," but Trudeau was sure the British, with their keen sense of politics, would never return. He found the idea some people had of UN intervention completely unrealistic, given Burmese hatred of foreigners.

The situation was so complex and multi-faceted that Trudeau felt unable to make any predictions. Not much hope could be placed in the youth of the country, he felt: "They only know they hate the English and they want independence from everything." This led him to a particularly pessimistic conclusion: "Despite the law of history according to which few countries now in existence end up committing suicide, I would say Burma will surely collapse, and will splinter into as many little countries as there were before the British turned up: it will remain in this splintered state until some fascist force imposes unity by force." It was a bleak judgment that resonates even today. In 2008, Michael Enright, the host of CBC Radio's well-known *Sunday Edition,* called the Burmese regime "the worst government on Earth."[45]

Trudeau left this complete chaos and headed to Thailand. He was amazed: "Oh! If there be a paradise on earth . . ." he wrote his mother. "Oh! that I could blindfold you and instantly transport you within some sacred precinct, . . . you would swear you were dreaming."[46] Trudeau found the Thai combination of inexpensive travel (he always kept detailed accounts of the price of each train, bus or plane ticket, each hotel room, etc.) and good food irresistible: "It is also, by far, the country in the East where the cost of living is lowest, and food being delicious, I am always hungry." He then provided a long list of foods he had sampled, at all hours of the day. His notes and the long letter to his mother were ecstatic, but there was a downside: "The situation of Catholicism is not very encouraging. After 300 years of apostolic missions, there are only 100,000 Catholics in Siam."

To his amazement, he noticed there was no hunger in the country, apart perhaps from the slums of Bangkok. People here, he wrote, "can literally feed off fruit and roots. Rice overproduced, fish in every pond, a fine sawmill industry in the east." He tried to understand why the people in Thailand were so friendly, unlike the xenophobic countries he had just visited. His explanation: "Although surrounded by countries 'colonized' by Europe, this people have remained free. And they see Europeans as their equals, and are able to have human sentiments about them, devoid of hatred." Thailand is the only country in Southeast Asia never to have been colonized. (In fact, "Thailand" means "land of free men" in the Thai language.) But Trudeau did not seem aware of the country's recent past. He said nothing of the fact that, unlike Burma, which had been a theatre of war during the Second World War, Thailand was a passive ally of Japan and allowed the Japanese army to use its military bases to invade other countries in Southeast Asia.

Trudeau was concerned about Thailand's future: "The people do not understand what economic imperialism means. They don't worry about seeing big Danish, Swiss, Dutch companies, Chinese merchants, etc. "Thais don't seem to realize that these foreign investments enhance their well-being, but could bring about their servitude, "*since eternal vigilance is the price of liberty,*" Trudeau wrote. His advice for the future? "Need to make the people politically aware. This should be relatively easy since this is one of the most literate countries of the Orient, and one rarely sees even a small village without its own school." In the light of later events, Trudeau's prediction proved inaccurate. Thailand proved to be subject to military regimes, political instability, and many coups d'état. Of all the countries he visited, Thailand was the one Trudeau seemed to have the least insight into. Was it because he was completely captivated by the country's exotic charms? Could he have been influenced by the trip he made in brilliant company to Chiang Mai, Thailand's second-largest city?

We will let Trudeau describe this trip. First he noted the social status of members of his group: "The company was by worldly standards, what one would call choice. The son of the Regent, a Princess of the Royal Blood, the American cultural attaché, a couple of wealthy Muslims, the wife of a British diplomat, a fraulein, daughter of a government adviser, the French military attaché and his sister, a judge, a banker, etc." And now, what they did: "In Chiang Mai we had a grand old time, seeing everything of interest within a radius of 40 miles, and there is an astonishing amount to see. Having picnics by some golden pagoda near a water fall, swimming, exploring caves, seeing a rare relic of Buddha himself, meeting governors, dancing with princesses, eating with princes of Chiang Mai, etc. . . . Our trip to Chiang Mai coincided with the winter fair, so into the bargain, we were treated to exhibitions of the marvellous Siamese dancing and singing, we witnessed the choice of Miss Chiang Mai, besides doing a bit of dancing ourselves."[47] No wonder Trudeau's political judgment was somewhat affected.

He then headed for Saigon (now Ho Chi Minh City), in what was then called French Indochina. Until 1954, Indochina was a colony, which included Cambodia, Laos, and Viet Nam. French influence was all pervasive, from the smell of cheap wine to pastis[*] and restaurants offering "French cuisine." Trudeau particularly enjoyed "the complete (and so typically French) respect of one another's individual freedom." He was happy to see that for the first time, nobody paid attention to his beard, he could walk in sandals without socks, and he could walk around shirtless without creating a sensation. In comparing this situation to what he had seen in former British colonies, he wrote: "What a contrast with the English who are afraid of losing face in front of the indigenous population and criticize whoever 'has gone native'! The Englishman wants to demonstrate his superiority. As far as he is concerned, the native is a child under guardianship. . . . The Frenchman sometimes happens to walk over the native, because he doesn't notice the native exists." The Frenchman is an

---

[*]   Very popular in Southern France, pastis is a liqueur flavoured with aniseed.

exploiter who knows he is an intruder, which weighs on his conscience – but "the Englishman has neither delicacy nor scruple: he is more of a cool calculator, and this is to his advantage because he knows when to leave." Accordingly, Trudeau saw the French as poor colonizers leading an indecisive campaign against the Viet Minh,* which was bad for the soldiers' morale. The same indecision was found at the political level, he said. Some people wanted to hold on to the colony and its riches. On the other hand, "the communists want the French out right away, and recognition of Ho Chi Minh's Viet Minh government. But it is obvious their generosity is not entirely devoid of calculation. . . . They want to strengthen the position of communism worldwide." Trudeau was convinced that Ho Chi Minh's struggle was not "simply for national independence. . . . A Viet Minh government would be along Marxist lines . . . and wholly sympathetic to the USSR." Which explains why he concluded by deploring the fact that "justice and the call to freedom are persistently promoted by one party alone, the party of atheism and materialism."

He visited Indochina at a time when everyone knew its days were numbered. This led him to ponder the problems arising from the process of decolonization. France had to withdraw; there was no doubt about it. But it could not withdraw in any which way. If a sudden withdrawal plunged the country into chaos and misery, then France would be guilty of a further injustice. Trudeau felt France had a moral obligation, before withdrawing, to steer the population toward autonomy. It should ask itself two questions: "a) If we leave immediately, will a new imperialism simply take the place of French imperialism?" and "b) once a national government is set in place, will this government be effective, and will it be just?"

Trudeau felt the answer to the first question was obvious. It was clear to him that a new "imperialism" – necessarily Russian or Chinese – would replace French imperialism. Actually, it could only be Russian, in the short term, because Chinese imperialism provided little cause for worry. He knew the USSR could not impose "imperialism properly speaking" in Indochina, since "all Soviet propaganda and doctrine is opposed to colonialism." So how would it proceed? He surmised that the Soviet strategy consisted of educating "native experts in the USSR, who return to their country of origin when the time is ripe, spreading the good word there."

---

* A nationalist organization dominated by Communists and led by Ho Chi Minh.

This reminded him of his own suggestion to send French-Canadian laymen to live in India for a few years, and he noted with appreciation: "This variation on the 'lay missionary' tactic has its merits."

The second question concerned whether a just and effective government would be set up. In terms of effectiveness, Trudeau wrote, he couldn't predict the future, but the many examples of Viet Minh's actions on the people's behalf suggested there were good prospects of an effective government. But would it be just? Trudeau was not so sure. Even if "the Viet Minh claim to be unfailingly democratic," a number of problems such as the protection of minorities would arise if the Viet Minh were too strong. As a French Canadian, Trudeau was naturally sensitive to this problem.

His conclusion? France had to "withdraw as elegantly as possible." In the event of internal conflicts, a truce should be established and monitored by UN observers, and a campaign of intense voter education launched. This should be followed by free elections. "Only then could we hope to see a definitive end put to a war of unrivalled barbarity, which is demoralizing for both the native population and the youth of France." History has shown that France did not withdraw "elegantly." The great powers – the United States, the USSR, China – quickly took advantage of the vacuum created by France's withdrawal and reinforced their own military presence in the region. With the result everyone knows: the appalling Vietnam War, Pol Pot's barbaric Khmer Rouge regime in Cambodia . . . and an unending succession of tragedies.

———— ❦ ————

Trudeau visited China – the "real China" – exploring it by train and bus. He spent one month there, mingling with the people in the remotest parts of the country. In one little village, seeing the startled faces of children and the elderly, he concluded he must have been the only white man they had ever met. He described the exotic aspects of land and people, but his political observations interest us the most. Upon arrival, Trudeau found China in a dismal state: "The first symptom of a sick society, a very sick one, lies in the country's financial condition." Inflation was so severe that cash had become "a perishable commodity." Like everyone else, he changed his money day by day. Trudeau felt unable to make any predictions about Chinese politics, especially because people avoided answering his questions. "In my opinion," he wrote, "this comes from a fear of compromising oneself. . . . As soon as the wind veers towards Communism, it is almost impossible for me to interview anyone who dares to defend the Kuomintang."* For this reason, he added, "Communism will remain strong in China as long as Chinese people believe it is strong." He thought the United States was wrong to support the Kuomintang, since there could be no doubt about the outcome of war: "Chiang Kai-shek is finished. . . . The administration has become a system of organized corruption. . . . Ultimately, any [U.S.] aid serves only to prolong a war, by providing short-term support to the side which will eventually lose."

Why was Communism assured of victory, as Trudeau shrewdly predicted? For him, it was because "the people are under the illusion they are supporting a movement created for them rather than for high finance. And they march with the same enthusiasm as people in countries behind the Iron Curtain. Truly, the word freedom is on everyone's lips. And here as elsewhere – perhaps here more than elsewhere – because the Orientals are often more mystical – they are ready to die for a noble idea, for the happiness of future generations." Trudeau found the power of this idea paradoxical in "a philosophy which, contrastingly, acknowledges no transcendence, nothing beyond man himself."

The journey was coming to an end. Trudeau brought his thoughts together in a section of his notebook entitled "Reflections on the Orient." The pessimism that emerges is striking: "If I had to find a single word to describe these people, it would be 'selfishness.' 'Oriental politeness' is actually the biggest joke. Even when the Chinese (for example) are distressingly excessive in their politeness, there is no sign of any genuine altruism. They are only polite with people it is important for them to be polite with. . . . But when they are with a stranger, some unknown person, selfishness rears its ugly head. . . . The Orientals who have achieved some distinction complain of being treated without consideration by white people. But you should see how they are with their own people: no one is more brutal or contemptuous towards his inferiors, or more craven towards people in authority." To him, this showed the superiority of Christianity: "The

---

* Nationalist forces led by Chiang Kai-shek, engaged in a brutal struggle against Mao Zedong's communists.

difference between East and West is that in the West, we respect each other since we share inherent dignity. . . . Ever since Christ came to preach the gospel of love of one's neighbour, the practical application of this doctrine has fallen short several times. But gradually, the inviolable person is winning over new areas, one after the other." This did not imply resting on one's laurels: "We still have a lot to learn on the economic level, with regard to fair wages, reasonable profits, etc. and on the international level, with wars."

Once again, Trudeau regretted that Marxism was trumping Christianity: "It is unfortunate that the Marxists are the ones teaching us the love of our neighbour, and with each step forward on this point, they force us to take two steps backward on other points. Indeed, Marxism and socialism have so far only gained a foothold in Christian countries. Let's wait and see whether collectivism can make inroads in a country like China where the concept of selfless service to others is treated with repugnance." Trudeau doubted that Mao's victory would lead to socialism in China. Over sixty years later, this prediction still has some validity. China is a curious mixture of totalitarian communism on the political level, with unbridled capitalism on the economic level.

———◦◦◦———

After China, Trudeau reached Hong Kong, a British colony since 1842. (It remained under British administration until 1997.) Although he had seemed to enjoy the laissez-faire atmosphere in French colonies, he was now delighted to be back in a British setting: "After Indochina, what a transition to find myself once again in an English colony. . . tolerance . . . , dignity, order . . . and obviously snobbery. But again, what a fine example of Britain's political ingenuity." When he heard that Chinese here dared to testify in court against other Chinese, which they were unwilling to do in China, he concluded: "So they must be confident they are shielded from retaliation." The fact that Chinese behaved differently, depending on the political system where they lived, made him think of Hobbes, for whom the life of man in a state of nature was "poor, nasty, brutish and short." Trudeau recognized the importance of the rule of law: "Maybe this Hobbesian society . . . only exists because of a lack of real government."

He made a final stopover for a few hours in Japan, which had recently been conquered and was still under occupation. There was no time to form an opinion of the country, of course, but he had enough time to feel uneasy in a nightclub frequented by American GIs: "The Japanese are no longer polite in the way a free people would be: their eagerness to please is disturbing. . . . It upsets me when the occupying forces get priority treatment in train stations, clubs, etc. Strange paradox of teaching democracy by military means." Trudeau had made a similar remark in Germany, and, to this day, it hasn't lost its relevance.

Here he was in late March, heading home aboard the SS *President Gordon,* in third class: "I was at the bottom of the last hold, with hundreds of Chinese (immigrants or people returning to the U.S., Canada, Caribbean, etc.) and a handful of Europeans (DPs) fleeing Shanghai to avoid becoming victims of war again." He found life in the hold simply unbearable. But this "tightly-packed humanity" fortunately gave him "a chance to know so many displaced peoples better – White Russians, Austrian and German Jews, Polish Catholics." He got to see America through the eyes of all these refugees: "They are all alike, in the simplicity and almost pathetic enthusiasm with which they talk about the land of America, where they will no longer be scorned, where democratic equality will enable them to start their lives over, on a stable and permanent basis." In meeting them, he felt particularly glad to be Canadian. Without the advantages of Canadian citizenship, he wondered, would he have had the courage to act as he had? "You have to leave your homeland to be able to thank God for having one in the first place."

Home sweet home! Back in Montreal, and happy to be there, Trudeau took stock of what this journey had brought him. Undoubtedly, the biggest lesson, he said, "was to feel in my body the weight of scorn that tends to crush all the little people in every country on this planet. . . . It was enough for me to walk around in torn sleeves and with no other baggage than my beard to become at once a man of low condition." He now saw what damage this contempt had on poor people: "The more I was treated as inferior, the more heroic efforts it took not to act inferior, not to be rude or to go around looking like a hangdog. Society imposes an inferiority complex on the poor, and some people find it surprising that this complex incites a reaction of hatred and aggression." And to think that years later, some critics would argue that Trudeau's personal wealth made him completely incapable of understanding "ordinary" people!

Trudeau was convinced the problem of the poor would not be resolved, as Karl Marx thought, through class struggle. On the contrary, this struggle only increased aggression. No, he stated categorically, what was needed was "not the struggle but the brotherhood of classes. . . . The proletariat would be the worst of all dictators. . . . The contempt a poor person has for one even poorer is more dreadful than his hatred (and often his meanness) towards the rich. . . . Truly, *homo homini lupus*. ('A man is a wolf to other men.')" Love of one's neighbour was lacking not only among ordinary people, but – what was worse – among priests: "I only met one or two who were willing to take in a bedraggled type like me. . . . The higher [the priest] in the hierarchy, the likelier he is to get conceited."

There was no point, Trudeau wrote, in preaching charity to people suffering from physical and mental poverty. Progress in a given society depended on "providing more people with the conditions of happiness. These conditions are material well-being and education of the mind" whereas this was lacking in the "lower classes of all countries." Where would these indispensable conditions of happiness come from? Trudeau saw two possible sources. They could "come from above (aristocracy, totalitarianism, fascism) or from below (popular democracy)." Which source should be chosen? In 1942 he firmly believed the solution came "from above." He now rejected this for two reasons. On the one hand, those people "above" had a vested interest in maintaining their privileged position and, secondly, they did not believe in the people's ability to govern themselves. And even if "it could be proven that oligarchy provides more happiness to all than democracy, democracy would still be preferable," since every step forward would be freely desired by the citizens as a whole and not imposed by force. How more democratic can one be?

Trudeau went further: "There seems no doubt that History is moving towards a more just distribution of material possessions . . . , that is to say, moving towards socialism." Now that the masses have learned they can aspire to freedom and well-being, "they will strive for it for better or for worse, and the party of the people – socialism, communism – will eventually come out the winner." He saw the inexorable march toward socialism as the result of human progress. By increasingly getting rid of degrading work, the invention of the machine will give greater emphasis to the dignity of man: "Once toilets replace the work of Chamars in India, imagine how social degradation will disappear." But as the people are emancipated, they "must have philosophers and technicians." It is therefore essential for "good men to espouse the cause of the people. For if the people are bound to win in any case, it is eminently desirable that they win honestly, and that their victory produce honest fruit." Where will these "good men" come from? Trudeau's answer: "I strongly believe in the wisdom of the middle class that is disparagingly called 'bourgeois.'" He warned, however, "we must ensure that the proletariat rises to a middle-class condition on its own, since one should never rely on others to fulfill one's own good." Gone is his former contempt of the bourgeoisie. He was counting on them in the march toward socialism. But in the final analysis, it is the proletariat, in becoming better educated, who would improve their own lot.

Did this entail working within a group or social class? No, Trudeau replied: "One should not associate one's destiny with a single social group, such as labour unions and agricultural cooperatives: one should instead develop a policy for the entire nation, not for this or that part of it." What party offered the best prospect of developing a policy for the entire nation? We should recall that a few months earlier, he had high hopes in the CCF. He now believed that in Canada, "a party like the Liberals, slowly moving leftwards, could in theory be the best party to lead the nation as a whole towards the people's society of the future." He acknowledged that internal dissent would dampen their enthusiasm: "The Liberals' commendable desire to borrow the best aspects of socialism is clashing, and will inevitably clash, with the opposition of parties representing financial interests."

According to some biographers, including John English, Trudeau still did not have clear aims and objectives when he reached the end of his journey: "In the late 1940s, Trudeau was still not clear about his destiny."[48] As evidence, English cites "Reflections on a Democracy and Its Variant" in Notre Temps, an article that, as we have tried to show, actually defended democracy.[49] According to English, this article "illustrates the contradictions that existed in his understanding of the future of Quebec."[50] He stresses the ambiguity in Trudeau's thought: "His chords were not yet in tune."[51] Based on what we have presented so far, it seems to us that from Harvard onwards, Trudeau methodically did his best to acquire the tools needed to play a useful role in improving his province. On returning from his travels, he wanted to participate in making Quebec, within Canada, a society whose concern for social justice, humanism, and ability to live peaceably with others would serve as a model for the world. But for democracy – and possibly Christian socialism – to reign in Quebec, the people needed to be educated. Trudeau did not yet know the actual form his commitment would take. But his objective was crystal clear.

Chapter 6

—◆—

LET THE FIGHT BEGIN!

The time has come to throw to the winds those many prejudices with which the past has encumbered the present, and to build for the new man. Let's batter down the totems; let's break the taboos.

— PIERRE ELLIOTT TRUDEAU[*]

END OF MARCH, 1949. After over a month in China, Trudeau headed back to Montreal. He felt ambivalent about leaving the Orient: "I would have preferred waiting to see Shanghai taken by the Reds," he noted in his diary, "but they had been in talks for a month, and I wanted to get back in time for Canada's federal elections."[1] The last ones having been held June 11, 1945, new elections were looming on the horizon. (They were held June 27.) They signalled big changes to the political landscape. For the first time in thirty years, the ruling Liberal Party was no longer led by William Lyon Mackenzie King, and the new party leader, Louis St. Laurent, was a French Canadian.

On arriving in Montreal, Trudeau the globetrotter seemed like a rare bird. How many French Canadians of the time had visited even a few of the many exotic places he had explored? He was greeted as a hero, with both admiration and curiosity. His return was reported in the press, and journalists eagerly sought out his opinions on the state of the world. No sooner did he get off the train than *Le Devoir* published an exclusive

---

[*] P.E. Trudeau, "Politique fonctionnelle," *Cité libre,* June 1950, reprinted in P.E. Trudeau, *Against the Current: Selected Writings 1939–1996,* Toronto, McClelland & Stewart, 1996, p. 28.

interview on April 13: "Five Minutes with . . . Pierre Trudeau – Around the World in 580 days." Alert readers would have noticed that not even 365 days had elapsed between July 1948 and April 1949. But we must resign ourselves to the fact that hype and inflated claims are more often than not associated with Trudeau. In June 1949, a report published by the Jeunesse indépendante catholique stretched out *Le Devoir*'s 580 days to two full years.[2]

And what, according to Trudeau, was the state of the world? He gave different accounts to different people, sometimes repeating what he had previously said, or adding to it, but other times contradicting himself. We will try to distill the essence of his thinking by examining three stories that appeared after his return to Montreal: the article from *Le Devoir* of Wednesday, April 13, an interview in *Le Petit Journal*[3] published on June 12 and conducted by Roger Rolland (who now had a doctorate from the University of Paris), and "Where Is the World Headed?" a detailed report of a talk he gave on June 22 at Lake Stukely in the Eastern Townships, as part of the civic summer school organized by the Jeunesse indépendante catholique of Montreal.[4]

Trudeau had just returned to Montreal and still felt the bitterness he had noted in his travel diary. He told *Le Devoir* that "overall, you can find great distrust and even hatred in practically all countries, with the exception of America. I was thrown into jail just about everywhere: the Jews took me for an Arab spy, the Arabs for a Jew, Muslims for a Hindu, Chinese Communists for a nationalist, etc." But two months later, in the interview with Rolland, he preferred to leave hatred and dissension behind: "Instead of focusing on differences, I was attracted most of all by similarities; rather than zero in on what divides us, I sought out what unites us, our shared humanity."

He believed two important ideologies were at loggerheads in the world: Communism and Christianity. Why did he single out just these two? Because "these are the only two that appeal directly to the masses and offer the prospect of an ideal life culminating in earthly and spiritual happiness."[5] In a world in turmoil, he had witnessed first-hand "the determination of the masses to throw off the yoke of all tyrannies. Everywhere in the world, ordinary people are becoming increasingly aware of their own strength and human dignity." Which of the two ideologies could bring about this liberation? For Trudeau, the answer was self-evident:

"I see no reason to believe that the dictatorship of the proletariat – considering the means it needs in order to establish itself – is any fairer or more just than capitalism." No! Class struggle would not improve the welfare of the people. The real solution lay in replacing hatred with understanding, with love of one's neighbour. Only Christianity could save the planet, because "Christ alone offered us the means to bring all men together as perfect friends. The revolution of the future should be a revolution of brotherhood, or it should not be at all.[6] . . . Only Christianity offers true freedom to the human spirit, freedom both of the person and of the world. Lived Christianity is a social religion, which alone provides an answer to all problems. [It is a religion] where there is neither Jew nor Gentile, neither slave nor freeman, but all are one in Christ Jesus."[7]

Trudeau was not naïve. He knew from experience that this "social" Christianity had still to be fulfilled, that Christian love was sorely lacking. And he was unimpressed by allegations that Catholic missionaries knew the meaning of loving their neighbour! He still harboured bitter memories of their supposed charity. A year after his return, a letter in Le Devoir from Brother Cécilius-Marie gave him the chance to pour his heart out about "a long withheld opinion of Catholic hospitality." The brother had harshly criticized Jacques Hébert for admitting, in one of his many travel columns, that he had sought "lodging at the YMCA in Bangkok rather than with the Brothers of St. Gabriel."[8] This criticism infuriated Trudeau. On January 22, 1951, he wrote to André Laurendeau: "When I got to Bangkok myself, carrying a rucksack, my feet muddy and my wallet empty, I had to turn to the Thai and Chinese YMCA for a friendly and generous reception."[9] He listed the barriers that poor people encountered when they knocked on the doors of Catholic religious communities: boredom, suspicion, misunderstanding, contempt, cowardice . . . Well aware that his comments would generate a lot of criticism, Trudeau concluded with a pre-emptive strike: "This letter will not be well received, and people may fling all kinds of comments at me: that I look strange, that I am generalizing, that I have no right to judge the heroic members of religious orders living in misery among unbelievers in foreign lands. As for my appearance and manners, suffice it to say they did not scare off Protestants at the YMCA." And, driving the nail a little deeper, he concluded: "Is the situation really so different on our own continent? People looking for considerate and organized charity are better off seeking out the company of Protestants. Do many Catholic lodging-houses offer brotherhood and hospitality to travellers without luggage?" Laurendeau sent this letter to his boss, Gérard Filion, publisher of Le Devoir, who penned an explosive response to Trudeau: "Considering that disgusting beard you hauled all the way across Asia, it would take more than Christian charity for people to take you in."[10] Needless to say, the letter of January 22 was not published.

The clerical elite quickly realized that Trudeau had changed substantially between his departure for Harvard five years earlier and his return to Montreal. He now held views seen as quite radical in Quebec. It is clear from this letter that he was now prepared to denounce the failings of some members of religious orders. Gradually, he would confront "these clergymen" who took on the role of guardians, wielding power over the Quebec people as if they were wards incapable of caring for themselves. He later denounced the clergy's pernicious usurpation of "control in areas where members of religious orders clearly lacked appropriate means and expertise."[11] But he wasn't there yet. At first, he merely questioned some aspects of Church orthodoxy in Quebec, notably as it pertained to authority. He had already discovered that everywhere in the world, man seeks "to throw off the yoke of all tyrannies." To this discovery he now added a powerful new idea: "Instead of considering authority as emanating from God and exercised by his ministers, man considers himself the sole authority."[12] We can imagine all the commotion such a statement was likely to stir up.

When Trudeau returned to the fold, he had the impression time had stood still: "I found myself back in the Quebec of the 1940s with all its numerous weaknesses and problems. Maurice Duplessis had been governing the province when I left in 1944; he was still governing it when I got back. . . . And Quebec had stayed . . . marginal, isolated, out of step with the evolution of the world. . . . I found that the same antiquated elites were still in power in virtually every social realm, where they busily maintained a stifling intellectual climate."[13] He was definitely shocked, but he was not surprised. When in London, he had already criticized the "citadels of orthodoxy." His travel journal shows that he closely followed politics in Canada, and especially in his home province of Quebec.

Maurice Duplessis, leader of the Union Nationale, back to power in 1944, was re-elected in 1948. He won handily at the polls again in 1952 and 1956, and had it not been for his death in 1959, he would very likely have won again in 1960. Duplessis – commonly called the "*chef*" (or the "boss" in English) – remains to this day one of the most colourful figures in Quebec history. Most studies cast his regime in an unfavourable light, with the notable exception of two highly flattering biographies: Robert Rumilly's *Maurice Duplessis et son temps,* published in 1973, and Conrad Black's *Duplessis,* published initially in 1977 and re-edited in 1998 under the title *Render Unto Caesar – The Life and Legacy of Maurice Duplessis.*[14]

In 1981, the political scientist Gérard Boismenu published a thorough study of the Duplessis years from a class struggle perspective, calling into question conventional interpretations of this era, including the use of the term "*la Grande noirceur*" or "the Great Darkness."[15] Since then, debates have raged about the true nature of "Duplessisme" – the Duplessis ideology and style of governance. Three sociologists, Jacques Beauchemin, Gilles Bourque, and Jules Duchastel, have continued along this path, focusing on the "liberalism" of the Duplessis regime (by which they mean the pro-capitalist and free-market ethos of the regime). Many scholars oppose this revisionist view, among them the historians Michael D. Behiels and Jacques Rouillard, and the sociologist Dorval Brunelle. We agree with Gérard Boismenu that using the expression "*Grande noirceur*" to describe this era "makes it harder to gain a true understanding of the paradoxical complexities of the period and tends to portray the Quiet Revolution as an instantaneous phenomenon."[16] We do not, however, intend to take part in the debate on the "liberalism" of the Duplessis regime, which would stray too far from our subject. Readers interested in an overview of the various positions on this question should refer to the proceedings of an interdisciplinary symposium held at McGill University in the fall of 1996 to commemorate the sixtieth anniversary of the Union Nationale's first government. Published under the title *Entre la Grande noirceur et la société libérale* [Between the Great Darkness and Liberal Society], this collective work was edited by the political scientist Alain Gagnon and the historian Michel Sarra-Bournet.[17] It brings together the papers of many specialists and eyewitnesses articulating a wide range of positions current nowadays.

Trudeau took part indirectly in the debate on "Duplessisme." He criticized the Union Nationale for reasons that merit our attention, although he naturally did so without referring to the concepts of "*la Grande noirceur*" or "liberal society." He insisted that "the fact that this party is conservative is not a reason to reject it." To him, its major short-comings lay elsewhere: "It is a despicable and false party, because it bases its power on prejudices (a mean-spirited and aggressive national-ism, a constipated religiosity). This is all well and good for social climb-ers, but they should realize they are helping to maintain falsehood in society. . . . They are true reactionaries."[18]

We cannot truly understand the Union Nationale without assessing the personality of its leader. In this regard, the testimony of Pierre Laporte – who was murdered by members of the FLQ during the October Crisis of 1970 – provides useful insights, since he followed Duplessis closely as a journalist for *Le Devoir* throughout this period. A year after the death of the "*chef,*" he wrote *The True Face of Duplessis,* providing vivid memo-ries of the man who "delighted or enraged an entire generation."[19] It is generally accepted – even by his fiercest opponents – that Duplessis was a sharp-witted speaker, often funny and sometimes cruel. A few examples will illustrate his special talent. According to Laporte, "During a debate Godbout declared: 'The Union Nationale elected more members than we did but it was the Liberal party that drew an over-all majority [in the 1944 elections]. Laurendeau spoke next: 'We of the Bloc populaire practically hold the balance of power in the Legislative Assembly.' Duplessis, the last speaker in the debate, concluded: 'Great! The Liberal party has had the most votes. The Bloc Populaire holds the balance of power. And we . . . well, we *are* in power. So that should make everybody happy!'"[20] Laporte mentions many other examples, including the following: "He rarely missed a chance to say to a French visitor: 'You know, we French-Canadians are improved Frenchmen.'"[21] A last example of his spirited and somewhat cruel rejoinders is found in the memoirs of Jacques Hébert, whose weekly *Vrai* fought Duplessis relentlessly: "Duplessis wanted to prevent a Liberal member of the Legislative Assembly of Quebec from speaking. The Liberal member cried out: 'This is like the guillotine!' The 'chef' retorted: 'To be guillotined, you need first of all to have a head on your shoulders!'"[22]

Duplessis reigned supreme, snubbing or silencing his ministers in public, making decisions without consulting them, yet managing never to incur their wrath. In fact, according to Laporte, several of his ministers "would readily have been cut to pieces for their Chief." How can this be explained? In Laporte's view, Duplessis "was a born leader. He exercised a magnetism that turned his Ministers into happy slaves. This explains that men of normal intelligence accepted being treated as nonentities."[23] Despite this magnetism, Duplessis was the object of far more scathing criticism than of admiration. For example, in an article marking the fiftieth anniversary of Duplessis's death, the journalist Jean-François Nadeau recalls André Laurendeau's scathing critique of February 1959: "The most pernicious thing about the Duplessis regime is the pervasively arbitrary character of its decisions, the desire to take no heed of generally accepted and fixed rules, the inclination to govern according to the leader's whims. This arbitrariness shows up in a multitude of shapes and forms: contracts without tenders, grants without transparency, as well as reprisals against individuals. When combined with intolerance, then everyone's freedom is at risk."[24]

According to Laporte, Duplessis controlled everything, down to the smallest expenses, rewarding some people while punishing others: "He looked into the background of civil servants, to determine whether they belonged to the Liberal or Union Nationale party before authorizing salary increases. He could block a civil servant's promotion because, 20 years earlier, he had been a candidate or a friend of an opposing party. These are but some of the tactics used by this man who was at once generous and petty."[25] Similarly, in 1997, Gérard Boismenu claimed that "Maurice Duplessis, with his staff, closely controlled the elaboration of political strategies, the administration of economic policies, the coordination and implementation of policies and even the civil service. In practical terms, far from limiting itself to establish the policy guidelines of his government, he was also deeply involved in their implementation by overseeing the administration of all departments, distributing contracts personally and overseeing all government spending. First and foremost, Duplessis personally established a hierarchy of political and economic affairs, in both their global and immediate dimensions."[26] Enough to make even Louis XIV jealous!

Political scientist Réjean Pelletier, who studied Quebec's electoral process, analyzed the Union Nationale's 1948 campaign slogan: "Liberals give to foreigners, Duplessis gives to his province." Pelletier shrewdly noted that "this slogan mixes up federal and provincial Liberals, just as it treats Duplessis and the Union Nationale as a single entity: in fact the leader embodies the party and virtually the state itself, and reigns over 'his' province. The confusion and merged identities here are total, but a single name, a single personality emerges, just as it would have in the era of absolute monarchs: Duplessis."[27] In fact, Duplessis had the sole power to decide whether a bridge or highway would be built, much like Francis I and other kings of France, who justified their decisions with the words "It pleases us." Pierre Laporte provided several examples of this kingly style of governance, including the following: "At Shawinigan, in St. Maurice riding, he once declared that if the voters re-elected a member of the Opposition, a bridge needed for the heavy local traffic would not be built. They were warned. And when they elected a Liberal member anyway, the bridge was not built while Duplessis was alive."[28] The same went for the construction of roads, hospitals, schools . . .

In 1958 Trudeau criticized the Union Nationale's campaign slogan "Duplessis gives to his province" for many of the same reasons as Réjean Pelletier, but in a different style. He wrote in *Vrai* that political morality was incompatible with the idea that "a prime minister *gives* bridges, roads, schools to his province. These are works that society needs, that it gives to itself and pays for through taxes. A prime minister gives nothing at all. . . . A bad statesman, then, is one who refuses to serve the community and goes so far as to obstruct the mechanisms by which society governs itself. Either a region needs a bridge, a road, a school, or it doesn't. If it doesn't need them, the statesman has no right to promise them. If it does, he has no right to refuse them. The Hon. Maurice Duplessis and Paul Sauvé* are therefore bad statesmen when they say to voters: 'Vote for so-and-so and we'll give you a bridge.' These servants who lay down conditions rather than doing what they are paid to do are bad servants: they ought to be kicked out."[29]

The electoral campaigns of Duplessis were always dominated by two themes: the fight against Communism and the defence of provincial autonomy. We will not dwell on the second theme, which primarily served as a battle cry and a means of rallying the people against what were presented

---

* Strongman Paul Sauvé had been minister of Social Welfare and Youth since 1946. When Duplessis died suddenly, Sauvé became leader of the Union Nationale and premier of Quebec for just 112 days, since he died suddenly in turn, on January 2, 1960.

as Ottawa's tentacles. Duplessis was the first politician to use the slogan "*Maîtres chez nous*" or "Masters of our own house" – a slogan later taken up by Jean Lesage's Liberals in 1962. The struggle for autonomy was presented in dramatic life-or-death terms, the better to castigate any political opponents. For example, in the campaign preceding the elections of July 28, 1948, Duplessis presented his party as follows: "The Union Nationale candidates . . . represent, in this struggle, those who in the past as well as today want to keep our national traditions intact. We stand for patriotism, the preservation of our rights and traditions, and indeed for our survival as a people, whereas the Liberals only stand for denial, centralization and the extinction of our most cherished traditions."[30]

The first theme, the struggle against communism, led to repressive laws. Duplessis was obsessed by Communists. He saw them hidden behind every door. His political opponents were regularly accused of being Communists, and even disasters such as the collapse of the Trois-Rivières bridge were blamed on Communists. According to Gérard Boismenu,[31] "As far as communists were concerned, [the Duplessis government] was on a permanent war footing." On March 24, 1937, his government adopted the "Padlock Law," which gave the governmental authorities the right to order "the closing of any house" and therefore to place padlocks on the house, keeping it hermetically sealed.* The law stated that "it shall be unlawful to print, to publish in any manner whatsoever or to distribute in the Province any newspaper, periodical, pamphlet, circular, document or writing propagating or tending to propagate communism or bolshevism." The problem was that the law nowhere made clear what was meant by Communism or bolshevism. That these terms remained vague in the text of the law was vintage Duplessis. He used the Padlock Law in his campaign against the Jehovah's Witnesses and especially against his *bête noire,* the trade unions.

Jacques Rouillard, a specialist of Quebec's trade union movement, wrote that in 1944, and "until the death of Duplessis in 1959, [his government] sought to limit the scope and the bargaining power of unions. It thus deprived groups of public sector employees of the right to

---

* This law, adopted during the first Duplessis mandate (1936–1939), was shelved by Premier Godbout's Liberal government (1939–1944). On returning to power, Duplessis put it back in operation.

unionize or to strike, sought to prohibit the closed shop and all forms of union security, wanted to remove all communists within the leadership of trade unions, impeded improvements to the Labour Relations Act, and promptly brought in the provincial police to restore public order during labour disputes."[32] We will have the opportunity to return to the merciless struggle waged by Duplessis against labour, since Trudeau became a passionate and forceful advocate of trade unions. While these were the premier's main target, no opponent, no group that stood up to him was immune. Organizations accused of Communism included *Cité libre,* naturally; *Le Devoir,* which Duplessis considered "bolshevist";[33] and even the provincial Liberals. The federal government was riddled with Communists as well: "In Ottawa, there are communists in the public service. The government in Ottawa is blind to this, and has allowed communists to infiltrate the National Film Board, the Media, External Affairs and even the office of the Prime Minister."[34]

Draping himself in ideological and political paternalism, Duplessis presented himself as the champion of stability and tradition. In fact, he stood for the farmers and encouraged big corporations to exploit the province's natural resources with cheap labour. But his style of governance cannot be reduced to the deeds of a single person. Paul-André Linteau, René Durocher, Jean-Claude Robert, and François Ricard note cogently that "the ideas of Duplessis were widely shared by some of the traditional elites and the clergy, whose grip on Quebec society was increasingly threatened by the process of modernization."[35] So when Duplessis went tooth and nail after the Jehovah's Witnesses, he got the backing of the Assembly of Catholic Bishops of the Province of Quebec on December 26, 1946.[36] That same year, "Cardinal Villeneuve, Archbishop of Quebec, wrote that the Jehovah's Witnesses 'only claim to follow the *Bible* as a way of better promoting their anti-religious fanaticism and their spirit of sedition.'"[37]

This alliance between State and Church suited both parties. Duplessis left the administration of social affairs entirely to the Church. Education, public health, and social welfare were all in the hands of the Church – the Quebec Ministry of Education was finally created in 1964! Since Duplessis held the purse strings, he could rightly boast that the bishops ate out of his hand.

Understandably, on returning from his world travels, Trudeau deplored "the stifling intellectual climate" prevailing in Quebec. He found this state of affairs appalling, but he nevertheless saw a glimmer of hope in the "bubbling of ideas that already, in a very timid way, presaged the changes to come."[38] What was he referring to? Most likely, among other things, to a manifesto published in 1948, and to the courageous struggles of the trade union movement.

Let's start with the manifesto. On August 9 the *Refus Global* (or *Total Refusal*) had appeared. It was a bold and explosive document written by Paul-Emile Borduas, a painter and teacher at the École du meuble, and countersigned by fifteen other artists, including the famous painter Jean-Paul Riopelle.[39] This document is a compelling "cry of revolt" from people who were suffocating and demanding freedom in all spheres of endeavour, including the expression of their art. They denounced the mind-numbing effects of religion and tradition. Ever since Canada had fallen under the British crown, they said, the defeated and beleaguered French-Canadian people, in their efforts to remain French and Catholic, were "clutching the skirts of priests who've become the sole guardians of faith, knowledge, truth and our national heritage." As a result of this dependence and withdrawal into themselves, the people have been "shielded from the universal, albeit perilous, evolution of ideas, educated by well-intentioned but misguided teachers who distorted the major facts of history whenever they found it impractical to keep us totally ignorant." The authors blamed Quebec's institutions of learning, "heirs to the automatic, infallible papal authority" of being "past masters of obscurantism." In the view of the artists signing the manifesto, French Canadians were particularly fond of going to Paris because they could find there a chance to "catch up on a belated sexual education." Religion and tradition had been useful, initially, since they had ensured the survival of the people, but they had now become the cause of the current catastrophic situation. Hence the artists' cry of revolt: "To hell with holy water and the French-Canadian toque! Whatever they once gave, they were now taking back, a thousand fold."

But all was not lost, said the manifesto, since people were increasingly daring to read books prohibited by the Index, bringing "a little relief and hope. Shame at our hopeless bondage is giving way to pride in a liberty that could be won with vigorous struggle." But opening up to humanity meant transcending first the barrier of religion: "Only beyond Christianity, which has become a closed door, can we reach the burning brotherhood of humanity." Only then, the authors declared pointedly, will "fear in its many forms no longer rule the land." There followed a particularly long list of the many forms this fear took: "fear of prejudice – of public opinion – of persecution – of general reprobation; fear of being alone without God or a society that inevitably isolates us; fear of ourselves – of our brothers – of poverty; fear of the established order – of absurd laws; fear of fresh relations; . . . fear of opening the floodgates of our faith in man – in the society of the future," etc. Fear, they said, had given way to overpowering mental anguish, which in turn had yielded to nausea.

These hypersensitive artists suffered for all humanity, which was subjected to various forms of cruelty: "Who could not . . . moan at the endless lists of concentration-camp torments? Who would not be chilled to the bone at descriptions of Spanish jails, gratuitous reprisals, cold-blooded revenge?" Enough was enough! "We must break with the conventions of society once and for all, and reject its utilitarian spirit." In the face of all these false values, there could only be a *Refus global* – a total refusal – hence the manifesto's title: "We refuse to close our eyes to vice and fraud perpetrated in the name of knowledge. . . . We refuse to keep silent. . . . Enough brutal assassination of the present and the future under repeated clubbing from the past."

In conclusion, the signatories made a resounding appeal to the entire population of Quebec: "Let those tempted by the spirit of adventure join us. . . . We will not rest or falter. Hand in hand with others thirsting for a better life, no matter how long it takes, regardless of support or persecution, we will joyfully respond to a savage need for liberation."

Over sixty years later, we are still moved by this heart-rending cry, this need for oxygen. Unfortunately for the signatories, it was only many years later that their call of distress was heard, understood, and appreciated. When the manifesto appeared in August 1948, in a modest print run of four hundred copies, it outraged the authorities and shocked the public. More than one hundred articles appeared, in various newspapers and magazines, including one by Gérard Pelletier,[40] sharply criticizing Borduas and his manifesto, particularly for the harsh words aimed at the Church. Borduas was fired by the École du meuble, although he had been working there for eleven years. Unable to find employment in Quebec, he was forced into exile in Paris.

When the manifesto came out, Trudeau was on the far side of the world. But through Hertel he had personally known Borduas for several years. During his stay in Paris, he had also attended an exhibition of abstract works by French-Canadian painters, including Borduas and Jean-Paul Riopelle. Learning upon his return – or perhaps earlier – about this courageous manifesto, he must have been pleased that a small group of artists was already struggling against the "citadels of orthodoxy" he had denounced while studying in London. Was it to show his solidarity with Borduas that he bought a painting from him on May 19, 1949, for two hundred dollars? This wouldn't have been the first time he quietly used his money to help people in need or to help causes he supported.

The other encouraging sign, which Trudeau felt boded well for the future, came from the working class. He was happy to see that in Quebec, as elsewhere in the world, the worker was "becoming increasingly aware of his own strength and human dignity." Long before his departure, there had been labour struggles, strikes, and work stoppages. For example, there were about 150 strikes between 1931 and 1941, and 200 more between 1942 and 1944, in the thick of war.[41] But at the time, Trudeau was immersed in the conservative ideology of Quebec society, and the trade union movement could just as easily never have existed. His teachers at Brébeuf and his professors at the Université de Montréal taught him repeatedly that industrialization jeopardized the core values of Quebec society. It was therefore better to promote a "return to the land" than to defend the working class.

Unfortunately for these prophets facing backward, Montreal had by the late nineteenth century become "Canada's leading commercial, industrial and financial metropolis."[42] The rural population was increasingly deserting the countryside to seek work in town. The rise of industrialization was inevitably accompanied by conflict. Workers became organized, joined trade unions in order to defend their rights, and struggled to improve their working conditions, which were often harsh, especially under the Duplessis regime.

When Trudeau returned home, a new conflict was rocking Quebec: the famous strike in Asbestos and Thetford Mines, south of Quebec City. The strike was part of a long series of major labour struggles. Without going too far back, we may note the strike in 1946 of five Dominion Textile mills in Montreal and Valleyfield (on the South Shore of the St. Lawrence River). The conflict was quickly settled in Montreal but continued to simmer in Valleyfield. On August 13, a confrontation between strikers and police turned into a riot. Many leaders were arrested, among them the well-known trade union activist Madeleine Parent. After striking for a hundred days, the workers got significantly better wages and working conditions.

In 1947, a new strike broke out, involving six thousand unionized employees of Dominion Textile in Sherbrooke and Magog, in the Eastern Townships; in Drummondville, east of Montreal; and in Montmorency, near Quebec City. Textile workers struck in Louiseville, in the St. Maurice region on the North Shore of the St. Lawrence River. Certified members of the United Textile Workers of America working for Dominion Ayers in Lachute, northwest of Montreal, struck for five months. Also in 1947, 1,500 members of the International Meat Packers Union working for big corporations such as Canada Packers and Swift went out on strike, while in 1948, 1,200 members of the furniture makers union struck for ninety-three days in Victoriaville, near Drummondville.

So, as has often been noted, the Asbestos strike was not the first strike in Quebec history. It was not even the strike that enabled union members to rack up the greatest gains. In addition, it is generally acknowledged that Trudeau played a secondary role. Whatever the case, not only did the strike attain an almost mythical status in Quebec history, but Trudeau's name came to be forever associated with it. How can this be explained? We should draw a distinction between the conflict itself and the later book edited by Trudeau, bringing together the contributions of several authors. This book was published in 1956 and had an enormous impact, becoming a classic in the contemporary history of Quebec.[43] The ninety-one pages (in the original French edition) of Chapter 1, "The Province of Quebec at the Time of the Strike," and the epilogue of twenty-five pages (in the original French edition), both by Trudeau, came as a bombshell and set off a tidal wave of reactions. But this book was published in 1956, whereas the Asbestos strike itself took place in 1949. By the time the book came out, Trudeau's ideas had been maturing for seven years. Also note-worthy is the fact that his introduction was not about the strike itself, but provided, rather, an ideological, economic, and political overview of Quebec society at the time. It is therefore important to distinguish between the event, which we examine in this chapter, and the book itself, which will be discussed below, in Chapter 12.

———————

Fortune always seemed to smile on Trudeau: he had benefited from unique life experiences, some of which we have already mentioned. And now he had returned to Quebec from abroad, at a time generally regarded as one of the most significant in Quebec history. In 1999, major celebrations were held marking the fiftieth anniversary of the Asbestos strike. François Vaudreuil, president of the Congress of Democratic Trade Unions (commonly referred to by its French acronym CSD), and Rodrigue Chartier, president of the Asbestos Miners' Union, claimed that the strike had "changed the history of trade unionism in Quebec forever."[44] Jacques Rouillard, on the other hand, argued that this interpretation should "be put into perspective," since some people tend to blow the strike up out of proportion.[45] He acknowledged, nevertheless, that the strike "has come to represent the stubborn resistance of workers against the union-busting attitude of employers and the Duplessis government."[46] He added that Gérard Pelletier's articles in *Le Devoir* and the book on the Asbestos strike edited by Pierre Trudeau led to greater public sympathy for labour, "from which workers benefited in the 1960s and 1970s." The government then adopted "a series of laws placing Quebec in the forefront of labour relations and social security."[47]

The strike figures prominently not only in most studies dealing with trade unionism but also with those examining the origins of the "Quiet Revolution" and the history of the Church in Quebec. For example, according to the historian Irving Abella, a specialist of the Canadian labour movement, "The Asbestos strike was the 'first shot of the Quiet Revolution' and a decisive event both for the history of the province and for the modern trade-union movement in Quebec."[48] Michael Behiels, a historian specializing in this period, noted in his book *Prelude to Quebec's Quiet Revolution* that the Asbestos strike was "an event which symbolized the maturation of the Catholic labour movement."[49] In 1971, the political scientist Gérard Bergeron ranked the Asbestos strike among the four major events in Quebec history that reflected a sort of "furor populi."[50] According to Professor Jean-Philippe Warren, this strike marks "the inclusion of workers' movements in sociological discourse."[51]

The Asbestos strike was on everyone's mind when Trudeau returned home. He was already convinced that social progress would emanate from the working class, and he wanted to observe this labour conflict up close, since it seemed to herald the beginning of a new era in Quebec. *Le Devoir* assigned the journalist Gérard Pelletier to cover the story, and Pelletier agreed to take Trudeau along, although they were not yet close friends. In Asbestos, Trudeau met Jean Marchand, who played a key role in the strike. Marchand was secretary general of the Catholic Workers Confederation of Canada (CWCC) – in French, Confédération des travailleurs catholiques du Canada (CTCC). He would become Trudeau's close friend.

Trudeau was only briefly involved in the strike. He made impassioned speeches to asbestos miners and was arrested by the police, but not much more is known about his involvement. According to Esther Delisle and Peter Malouf, Trudeau "played only a very minor, little-known role during the Asbestos strike which, notwithstanding the book of essays he edited in 1956, would not even be worth mentioning nowadays, were it not for his later political career."[52]

This judgment is only partially valid. Trudeau certainly played a relatively minor role, but this role was hardly "little-known." There is no doubt that he attracted a lot of attention through his charisma and ability to captivate the miners, who nicknamed him St. Joseph (after the patron saint of workers). His fiery rhetoric had such an impact on the strikers that Jean Marchand was worried it could lead to violence. One cannot therefore claim that Trudeau's name is associated with the strike only because of his later political career. With regard to the book mentioned by Delisle and Malouf, Trudeau did far more than just bring various contributions together into a single volume. As we will see in Chapter 12, his contributions were the most incisive, the most widely discussed, and the most often quoted, long before he became prime minister.

By the time Pelletier and Trudeau arrived on the scene, negotiations had started between the unions and the mining companies operating in Asbestos and Thetford Mines. But they soon stalled and were particularly harsh in Asbestos with the Canadian Johns Manville Co. At the now historic union meeting of February 13, 1949, workers had two choices: resorting to arbitration as provided by law, or declaring an illegal strike, since they could not give the required notice of their intention to strike. Unsure of the impartiality of the arbitration committee, which they believed tended to side with the employers and the government, they opted, in the superheated atmosphere of the meeting, for an illegal strike. That night marked the beginning of a very bitter four-month struggle that was resolved only on July 1, 1949.

Nowadays, people refer to the "Asbestos strike" although workers struck in both Asbestos and Thetford Mines. Why is that? The strike in Thetford Mines was "quiet, almost monotonous," whereas in Asbestos it was "rocked by incidents, violent outbursts and practically a pitched battle."[53] In 1951, Jean-Paul Geoffroy, a member of *Cité libre*'s editorial team, wrote that "the conflict reached a point of exceptional intensity" in Asbestos.[54] He also noted that in Asbestos, a small town of eight thousand inhabitants, the mine was the only employer. The long-lasting strike therefore "took hold of the town, . . . and commanded everyone's attention." Its effects reached into every household: "Men only took one meal a day. Rents were not paid; suppliers whose credit had run out were on the verge of bankruptcy."[55]

What were the miners' grievances? Their first demand was "the elimination of asbestos dust inside and outside the mills." In this regard, Delisle and Malouf should be commended for the important job they have done bringing to light the passionate struggle of the investigative journalist Burton LeDoux, who denounced the incurable and usually fatal diseases contracted by miners as a result of long-term exposure to asbestos dust.[56] But this was not the strikers' only demand. Far from it. They also wanted better wages and, in line with the social doctrine of the Church that called for collaboration between employers and their employees, the right to participate in the administration of the company. For example, they demanded "consultation with the union in all cases of promotion, transfers, dismissals."

What was the outcome of four months of bitter struggle? Answers to this question vary depending on one's perspective on the conflict and whether one considers gains in the short or long term. For our purposes, a few key results may be noted. With regard to wages, the strikers became the highest-paid workers in the mining industry. Although elimination of asbestos dust was one of the most hotly debated issues during the strike, the final settlement read as follows: "The Company recognizes that the asbestos dust is harmful. It states that it is prepared to continue the work, which it has already begun (to eliminate it). . . . This clause may not in any way be interpreted as a contractual obligation on the part of the Company."[57] The company was already lining up an escape route. According to *Le Front ouvrier* of February 4, 1950, the company claimed it "took steps to improve its system of dust elimination and air purification, setting aside approximately $500,000 for the purpose."[58] But it actually did very little to improve working conditions, and many workers of that generation lost their lives to disease. In 1974, Dr. Irving J. Selikoff, a leading authority on the subject, said Quebec's asbestos mines were the unhealthiest in the world. As for the unions' demand to participate in the management of the company, they ran into a brick wall. The employers claimed this demand was a direct encroachment on their basic rights and even violated the principle of private property itself. Such a demand could be inspired only by socialism, not to mention communism. It seems, therefore, that the strike did not result in long-lasting gains, despite the hard struggles of the miners and those supporting them, such as the tireless Burton LeDoux.[59] Rodolphe Hamel was one of the main leaders of the strike. In 1974, by which time he had become president of the National Federation of Mining Union Employees, he recalled bitterly: "We came to an agreement on our hands and knees, we settled in order to save our skin."

So why has this strike acquired such a mythical place in Quebec's history? A combination of factors explains it: the activism and courage of the workers, and the enthusiastic and unprecedented solidarity demonstrated by the Church, the trade union movement, the general public, and the strikers. The Church's support seemed all the more surprising since it had traditionally promoted obedience to the law and respect of "Authority." Yet Labour Minister Antonio Barrette declared the strike illegal, and rightly so, since the workers did not file notice of their intention to strike within the proper time frame. But the government's underhand tactics show it was also at fault: on February 22, the Labour Relations Board exceeded its authority and broke the law by revoking the certification of the unions. This meant, in theory, that it revoked their right to negotiate. But that was not all. The government also swept aside any idea of acting as an impartial arbiter. As Abbé Gérard Dion wrote in "The Church and the Conflict in the Asbestos Industry," the government "openly and publicly expressed its opinion on each of the union demands (wages, sanitary working conditions, Rand formula) upholding company positions."[60] And yet, most members of the Church supported an illegal strike declared by unions whose certification had been revoked and ignored the fact that all union demands had been denounced by the government. This position was, to say the least, unprecedented, and to explain it we will have to go back in time.

We have seen in our first volume that the Church in Quebec, drawing inspiration from the encyclicals *Rerum Novarum* (1891) and *Quadragesimo Anno* (1931), promoted corporatism in response to the severe economic crisis of the 1930s. The Church believed that this social arrangement encouraged effective collaboration between employers and workers, thus bringing an end to the class struggle and to the labour strife raging in society. It was thought to offer the best of all possible worlds, avoiding the shortcomings of other evil systems, such as capitalism, democracy, socialism, or communism. In order to counteract the growing appeal of international unions,* the Catholic Church in Quebec drew on teachings of the Vatican to set up unions of its own. Among their primary objectives was workers' participation in the management of companies. But the war upset everything. On the one hand, it became abundantly clear that fascist regimes, such as the Vichy government, had actually resorted to corporatism in order to ban trade unions, including Christian ones. On the other hand, the collapse of fascist regimes meant that the corporatist model had lost its lustre. As a result, according to Jacques Rouillard, "for the younger generation of leaders and chaplains who rose to leadership of the CTCC right after the war, the professional corporation . . . looked like an outdated ideal, the inevitable arch enemy of the free trade-union movement."[61] Taking a leaf from left-leaning French Catholic thinkers, union leaders no longer clung to the ideal of the "professional corporation" but sought instead to expand the role of workers within the company.

It was becoming all the more urgent for the Quebec Church to update its social doctrine since the very notion of a Catholic trade union was falling into disfavour, in an increasingly industrialized world, with an ever more diverse workforce. Starting in 1943, as a way of blocking the expansion of international unions, the Canadian and Catholic Confederation of Labour formally recognized that all members, whatever their religion, had

---

* International unions are actually the Quebec affiliates of non-denominational American and Canadian labour federations.

the same rights. The Church remained silent on this issue, although it deplored the rise of secularization. In the view of Abbé Dion, the Church realized that the Asbestos strike could affect the survival of the Catholic trade union movement: "If the CCCL could not summon the economic strength to fight for what it deemed to be the interests of the workers and emerge with honour, its days were plainly numbered. . . . The Church could not allow an institution it had established and fostered for nearly forty years to be sabotaged in a few months."[62] This explains the Church's major shift, throwing its support behind the strikers *against* the government, that is, against political authority.

All union chaplains rallied behind the miners. For its part, the Church's Sacerdotal Commission of Social Studies issued a statement entitled "Let Us Help the Asbestos Workers," appealing urgently "to all associations" and calling on them "to cooperate with religious authorities in the organization of a collection for the stricken families."[63] The Archbishop of Montreal, Mgr. Joseph Charbonneau, the Archbishop of Quebec, Mgr. Maurice Roy, the Bishop of Sherbrooke, Mgr. Philippe Desranleau, and the Bishop of St. Hyacinthe, Mgr. Arthur Douville, all prelates and members of the Episcopal Commission on Social Issues, fully backed this appeal. They set up collections to help the strikers every Sunday at all Masses and in all diocese. The people responded generously. The sum of $167,558.24 was collected – an impressive amount at the time – and had a decisive effect on the sequence of events, since it enabled the miners to continue striking.

The strikers received more than material assistance; they also received the moral support of many ecclesiastics. On April 20, 1949, the influential Abbé Groulx, who was not particularly known for sympathizing with workers, wrote in *Le Devoir* that the strikers "are not fighting merely for food and wages. They are fighting, in fact, for their lives and the lives of their sons and daughters, in a murderous industry. . . . Some people are claiming . . . that they might well be patient for a while. Who displays such heroic patience in the face of sickness and death?"[64] As for Archbishop Charbonneau, his vigorous support of the strikers definitely contributed to the huge problems he later faced. In a sermon on May 1 at Notre Dame Basilica, he fervently proclaimed: "The working class is a victim of a conspiracy which seeks to crush it, and when there is a conspiracy to crush the working class, the Church has a duty to intervene. . . .

We are more attached to man than to capital. This is why the clergy decided to intervene."[65] The same day that Mgr. Charbonneau made this stunning statement in Montreal, Mgr. Desranleau of Sherbrooke practically incited the strikers to revolution, which he deemed fully consistent with the papal encyclicals: "The primary cause [of extreme poverty] is not new. Popes Pius xi and Pius xii loudly proclaimed this truth. . . . It is greed. . . . Capitalism is the cause of all our wretchedness. We must work hard to replace it. . . . You have taken up the struggle against this threat. Do not give up."[66] One could well imagine revolutionaries uttering words like these, in their call for the final emancipation of the working class. But coming from prelates who had previously been preaching obedience? This was a revolution!

All union chaplains sided with the strikers, but none of them as passionately as Abbé Camirand: "I know the miners at Asbestos well, for I am their union chaplain. . . . They have not temporarily deprived themselves and their children of a livelihood for the fun of it, but because they have been driven to it by unspeakable tactics of provocation. If I were a miner, I would be on strike myself and, in the present circumstances, I would have a clear conscience. I may add that though I am not a miner, I am with them all the way, and they know it."[67] But, on the employer's side, the Johns Manville Co. increased production by hiring hundreds of scabs, and then on April 20 it threatened to evict striking miners from the lodgings they rented from the company. Father Camirand said the company would have to pass over his dead body first before it could remove a single stick of furniture.[68] Could the chaplain's words have prompted the minister of labour to intervene the following day, asking the company to "reconsider this decision and to cancel the eviction notices"?[69]

The same day, April 21, in the midst of a fiery demonstration pitting the strikers against the scabs, Gérard Pelletier of Le Devoir and Pierre Trudeau reached Asbestos. Given the highly charged atmosphere, no wonder they had altercations with the police. What exactly was Trudeau doing in Asbestos? What we know was reported by others, many years after the fact. He himself never gave a clear explanation of what he was doing there. He noted in his diary that on the evening of April 21, he made a speech to the strikers; on the 22nd he was arrested, and that evening he noted the theme of his speech: "Down with the scabs!" and "Death to the bastards!"[70] One can easily guess Trudeau's fiery rhetoric and sympathize with Jean Marchand's understandable concern. On the 23rd, Trudeau returned to Montreal, putting an end to his physical presence in Asbestos. But his struggle for the miners, trade unionism, and the working class in Quebec was only just beginning.

As time went by, increasingly frequent and intense acts of violence were committed on both sides – by strikers and by the police. And yet the Church generally continued to side with the workers. This solid and unflinching support was reflected in the population as a whole: support came in from all sides. Under the guidance of Father Jacques Cousineau, students at the Université de Montréal launched a fundraising campaign. Students from Université Laval, the Alliance of Catholic Teachers, and other groups followed suit. Many Quebec, Canadian, and even American unions provided moral and material support to the strikers. An example: at the end of May, the Canadian railway workers union sent the miners seven tons of food.

As could be expected, business people and the Duplessis government were dismayed by the unprecedented activism of church members, coupled with a hitherto unheard-of level of solidarity between the general public and the strikers. On April 22, Canadian Johns Manville president Lewis H. Brown vented his anger in every English- and French-language newspaper: "It is surprising and a source of disappointment that some spokesmen in the Church appear to be supporting strike leaders who seem intent upon usurping the functions of management and thereby the property rights of thousands of owners."[71] The company believed that by supporting the unions to such an extent, the Church had moved away from its traditional position of siding with authority. The government came to the same conclusion. According to Boismenu, "This period marked a turning point in relations between the Church and the government."[72] Duplessis was also well aware of this shift and decided to turn the screws on the Church: "The discretionary award of grants to multiple religious institutions enabled the Premier to exert tighter controls on the political behaviour of the lower as well as the higher clergy."[73]

But the Quebec Church was not monolithic, and it would be wrong to suggest there was a complete ideological shift. Behind the Church's apparent unanimity, two groups were actually warring. The "modernists" – such as the Dominican Father Georges-Henri Lévesque, dean of the Faculty of Social Sciences of Université Laval, or the Archbishop of

Montreal, Mgr. Joseph Charbonneau – were influenced by "left-wing" Catholic movements in France: they wanted to adapt their teachings and social actions to the rapid industrialization of Quebec. The traditionalists, meanwhile – including the very conservative Archbishop of Rimouski Mgr. Georges Courchesne, whose sermon was quoted earlier – clung to the old principles. They vigorously opposed a movement they felt was excessively influenced by English and Protestant ideas, by the materialism of the Humanities, as well as by "left-wing" Catholics in France. But for now, the Church presented a common front. The settling of accounts would come later.

The strike finally came to an end, thanks to the Church's intervention. On June 13, 1949, the Archbishop of Quebec, Mgr. Maurice Roy was named chief mediator. On July 1, everything was settled. The people's shouts of joy carried from the asbestos mining region well beyond Quebec's borders, and even beyond Canada itself. In Washington DC, for example, the newspaper *Labor* reported that "there was dancing in the streets of the little town of Asbestos when one of the most unusual strikes in the history of the Dominion labor movement was settled this week through negotiations personally conducted by Archbishop Maurice Roy of the Roman Catholic Church."[74]

Once the crisis was over, tensions within the Church came to the fore. Traditionalists massed behind Mgr. Courchesne. His archdiocese of Rimouski represented Quebec's staunchly conservative countryside. On the other hand, Mgr. Charbonneau spoke in terms of class struggle, as for example in the sermon quoted above. It is not really surprising that he should have thrown his support behind the working class. After all, Montreal was an industrial and commercial metropolis, driving Quebec into the industrial age. Mgr. Charbonneau was well aware that the nostalgic hearkening for a French-Canadian people rooted in the land was nothing but a pipe dream. He knew the difficult living conditions of workers first-hand. No wonder he wanted to help them. But as archbishop, his pro–working-class perspective pushed the Quebec Church into a new direction and met with the Vatican's disapproval since "class collaboration" had long been the cornerstone of corporatism. Traditionalists had no stomach for this shift to the left. In a dramatic turn of events, Charbonneau suddenly left Montreal on February 9, 1950, bound for Victoria, British Columbia. He was allegedly suffering from health problems. Newspapers reported merely the official explanation of his sudden departure. But everyone suspected that illness was only a pretext and that the radiantly healthy archbishop was actually being "punished."

It all looked fishy to Trudeau. On April 19, 1950, he wrote about "the disgusting treatment of Archbishop Charbonneau" to Roger Rolland, who was now a professor at the University of British Columbia in Vancouver: "By the way, why don't you pay him a visit in Vancouver, so we can have a clear conscience about the matter? If his health is good, as everyone says, then we'll have to accuse Mgr. Antoniotti, Roman prelate, Apostolic Delegate, Prince of the Church and successor of the apostles, of lying like a cad. It is high time the Church of Christ took greater care of souls and the Truth, and *completely* withdrew from politics."[75] By the month of May, Trudeau no longer had any doubts that the Church's official line was a lie. Boiling with rage, he wrote a draft article on behalf of the editorial board of *Cité libre,* whose first issue was coming out in June. "What is unacceptable," he wrote, "is to be lied to. We lay people do not accept that our priests lie to us about the Church. . . . It is always infuriating to be taken for suckers. . . . There is never a valid reason for lying. And just because one is a bishop or archbishop doesn't make the reasons for lying any more compelling. In fact, the boorishness of lying only becomes that much more disgraceful."[76] The *Cité libre* editorial board felt the draft was inappropriate, especially for the first issue of the magazine. "Draft replaced by Pelletier," Trudeau wrote on his copy. Instead, under the title "Question," a watered-down and more "politically correct" version of the article appeared in *Cité libre:* "'Why did Mgr. Charbonneau leave Montreal?' . . . We know perfectly well that our question will remain unanswered. So then we must ask another: 'Why should the departure of our Archbishop be shrouded in shameful silence and awkward lies which aren't fooling anyone? Is this really required by Church policies?' We believe that any truth, no matter how painful, would have been preferable."[77]

Why didn't Trudeau publish his article under his own name? We know he was not faint of heart. The problem was that starting in September 1949, he had been working at the Privy Council in Ottawa. Thus he was not free to express his views publicly. He tried to publish something, although in a roundabout way. In a letter to *Le Devoir,* dated May 12 and signed "Civil Servant," he explained that "civil servants are not allowed to have political opinions." As a result, "*Le Devoir,* which has such sound and strong opinions, is required reading for civil servants." But this compliment was followed by a sharp reprimand: "A critique, however, is in order: Isn't it odd that *Le Devoir* did not complain about the lies used to explain the recent departure of a distinguished prelate? What cowardly prudence incited you to betray two such faithful friends: Truth and Mgr. Charbonneau?"[78] Trudeau accused *Le Devoir* of a dual betrayal. Nothing less. Whether Filion fell off his chair while reading this letter is not known. We do know, however, that Trudeau's letter was never published

It is well known today that beyond Trudeau's support for the striking miners, what especially infuriated traditionalists such as Mgr. Ferdinand Vandry, and especially Mgr. Courchesne, was essentially the "left-wing" ideas of Mgr. Charbonneau – the so-called red archbishop. Indeed, the historian Paul-André Linteau noted in *Histoire de Montréal depuis la Confédération* that the Archbishop of Montreal "represented new trends arising within the Church. He promoted the more active participation of lay people in the diocese and gave new impetus to Catholic Action. He was convinced of the need to renew the structures of the Church in Montreal, taking into account the particularities of the metropolis."[79] The time to settle accounts came once the strike was over. Mgr. Courchesne went in person to Rome to present a memorandum accusing Mgr. Charbonneau and his followers "of no longer being in communion with the hierarchy, of preparing a schism within the Church of Quebec by splitting off from the other bishops and thus breaching Episcopal unity, and preaching a left-wing form of social Catholicism."[80] The conservative wing of the Church won this battle. On January 2, 1950, Rome ordered Mgr. Charbonneau to resign. This decision could not be appealed.

According to Father Georges-Henri Lévesque, Archbishop Charbonneau was also subjected to these critiques for reasons that may strike modern readers as bizarre. In an interview, Father Lévesque told us Charbonneau was accused of having "an English way of thinking. Nobody said so openly. . . . He had been in the Diocese of Hearst, Ontario, and he had been educated in the great seminary in Ottawa, among English-speaking people."[81] Father Lévesque knew quite well what he was talking about. During this very same period, between 1949 and 1951, when he was de facto vice-president of the Royal Commission on National Development of the Arts, Letters and Sciences – known as the "Massey Commission" – he was also accused of being in the pay of the English. Starting in the 1960s, Trudeau too was accused of having "an English way of thinking." For people dishing out this kind of talk, no explanation was necessary: once a French Canadian took on an English way of thinking, he deserved to be shunned.

Mgr. Charbonneau's dismissal meant that Mgr. Courchesne and the traditionalists still held the upper hand. However, the Asbestos strike clearly showed that a rift was opening in the foundations of the Church, a rift that filled "left-wing" Catholics with hope. They began to anticipate a future alliance with progressive elements of the clergy and a way of freeing French Canadians from the crushing yoke of traditionalism. They persevered in this quest and ultimately succeeded, bringing together the forces that transformed Quebec society forever.

While Trudeau has often been presented as a solitary person, after returning from his travels he in fact led a very active social life. His diaries show that he had one or more appointments almost every day. On April 29, he went to Quebec City, stopping at the Dominican Monastery to meet Father Georges-Henri Lévesque, dean of the Faculty of Social Sciences at Université Laval, which he founded in 1938 (it was first a School and became a Faculty in 1943). Trudeau wanted to get to know him. Before leaving for Harvard, Trudeau had never shown any particular interest in this Dominican priest, and it is easy to understand why. Father Lévesque was one of the first leading intellectuals to abandon his corporatist ideas. He now stood for avant-garde positions diametrically opposed to the Jesuits and the intellectual mentors Trudeau originally admired. Whereas conservative prelates preached obedience, Father Lévesque expounded the view that "freedom also comes from God." Whereas traditionalist clergy in the 1930s fiercely defended the need for agricultural cooperatives to remain strictly Catholic, he laughingly told us in 1999: "I said there was no such thing as Catholic butter and Protestant butter." He then told us, in a more serious tone, that his struggle for "non-denominational" agricultural cooperatives (he took credit for coining the term "non-denominational") turned many of the traditionalist hierarchy of the Church against him: "I was reported to

Rome for that. They tried to put me on the *Index*, to have me condemned by the conference of universities, for example. But this didn't
happen. I was lucky."[82] Among his many powerful opponents were
Mgr. Courchesne, Abbé Groulx, and especially Mgr. Vandry, rector of
his university. Nowadays, Father Lévesque and the Faculty of Social
Sciences he founded are recognized for their important contribution to
the wave of reforms called the "Quiet Revolution."

Trudeau admired this man's courage and pioneering positions and
he wanted to meet him, hence his trip to Quebec. The visit also gave him
the opportunity to get to know some of the professors of this progressive
faculty, such as Maurice Lamontagne and Jean-Charles Falardeau.[83] From
then on, Trudeau participated in many activities of the Faculty of Social
Sciences, and he established a lasting relationship with Lamontagne,
Falardeau, and some of their colleagues. A brilliant sociologist, Jean-
Charles Falardeau (1914–1989) wrote the preface to *The Asbestos
Strike*. Maurice Lamontagne (1917–1983), a Harvard graduate and economics professor, later pursued a long career in federal politics: he served
as economic adviser to Lester B. Pearson, when the latter was Leader of
the Opposition in Ottawa – then as president of the Privy Council, minister of federal-provincial relations, and finally as senator from 1967
until his death in 1983. In 1954, he wrote *Le fédéralisme canadien: évolution et problèmes* [Canadian Federalism: Trends and Problems],[84] a
work that incurred the wrath of the nationalist elite. We will compare
Trudeau's and Lamontagne's conceptions of federalism in Chapter 11.

———◦———

Let us go on with Trudeau's activities in 1949. We know that he had
been attracted to socialism ever since he studied in Paris and London.
He had shown an interest in the CCF (Co-operative Commonwealth
Federation) even before leaving Canada for London, when he met Frank
Scott. A well-known intellectual and poet who combined academic life
at McGill Law School and political action, Scott had been national president of the CCF since 1942 and remained in this position until 1950.
Shortly after returning from his world travels, Trudeau saw him again
for lunch, on May 17, 1949. Four days later, they lunched again, this
time with Eugene Forsey (1904–1991), a constitutional expert and professor at Carleton University in Ottawa whom he was meeting for the

first time. Like Trudeau, Forsey had adopted democratic socialism during his stay in England. His interest in the CCF went back a long way; he had been a delegate at the founding congress of the movement, in Regina, in 1933. He had even run unsuccessfully as a CCF candidate in the Ottawa area. As a constitutional expert, he was long considered one of the most respected political commentators in Canada. Trudeau appointed him a senator in 1970.

On the afternoon of May 21, Trudeau met Scott again, along with a few other people, including Gérard Pelletier. That evening he called on Thérèse Casgrain (1896–1981), president of the Quebec wing of the CCF. This indefatigable lady had long campaigned for women and the poor and remained, to the end of her life, a zealous advocate of social justice. She received eleven honorary doctorates and several prestigious awards. Frank Scott, Eugene Forsey, Thérèse Casgrain . . . Now that he was back home, Trudeau was meeting the leading figures of the CCF, who welcomed him with open arms. The next day, he spent the evening at the Pelletier home, discussing an issue that had been close to his heart since his travels in Asia: the creation of an organization of lay missionaries.

So, in just over a month, Trudeau went to Asbestos to get a first-hand view of one of the most famous strikes in Quebec history and to address the miners; he went to Quebec City to meet a Dominican priest – one of the most progressive men of the province – as well as two leading professors at the Faculty of Social Sciences, who would play a prominent role in the history of Quebec; he spent a lot of time with senior members of the CCF; and he even started thinking about a project involving lay missionaries.

In the federal election of June 27, 1949, which Trudeau had not wanted to miss, Louis St. Laurent's Liberals scored a decisive victory – going from the 125 seats they obtained in the 1945 election to 190 seats, while George A. Drew's Conservatives dropped from sixty-seven seats in 1945 to forty-one seats.[85] On June 27, Gérard Filion expressed concern in *Le Devoir*. This situation troubled him since "under the parliamentary system, the Opposition has an important role to play." His solution? "Creation of a social and republican movement. Public opinion is closer than we think to the idea of the total emancipation of Canada, the breaking-off of all colonial ties binding us to Great Britain."[86] And he cited the examples of Ireland, India, and South Africa, all of which were moving in that direction.

But Trudeau was imbued with the idea of social justice and felt Filion was flat wrong. On July 6, 1949, he replied that a strong opposition party was definitely needed, but that it should be positioned to the left of the Liberals and should focus on economic and social issues.[87] He believed that when Filion called for a "republican and social" movement, he really meant "national" since the "social" question had almost no appeal for him. For Trudeau, that was the nub of the problem: the only people who would respond to Filion's call were conservative nationalists, who wanted to "liberate the people from British imperialism, but not from economic imperialism," from which they personally benefited.

What proofs did Trudeau provide that Filion had little interest in the "social" question? He gave him two. First, "the adjective 'social' disappears in the middle of your sentences on the republic." Second, "you take the trouble to show that you care far more for republican independence than for social emancipation: aren't you citing the examples of Ireland, India and South Africa, three countries where the fiercest republicanism is also unfortunately identified with reactionary regimes?" This is why, according to Trudeau, "left-wing" nationalists would not let themselves be tempted by these proposals. Numerous reforms were "absolutely necessary" in Quebec, but they could not be brought about by the old parties "as both parties are essentially bound up with high finance, and have a vested interest in preserving the status quo . . . whereas a new party resting solely on democratic and popular foundations would be able to tackle all the reforms that a Christian society is entitled to expect from its government."

This first piece Trudeau wrote since his return to Quebec illustrates the evolution of his political thoughts. He now had no qualms displaying his willingness to establish a democratic and left-leaning party in Quebec, which would respond to the real needs of a Christian society. To achieve "absolutely necessary" reforms leading to social justice, he envisaged an alliance with Canadians in other provinces. He thought the fight against British imperialism could wait. His first priority was the struggle for social justice.

———◦———

Shortly after writing this letter, "in one of the surprising moves that mark Trudeau's life," writes John English, "he left Quebec. . . . To the shock of Pelletier and other friends, Pierre Trudeau departed for Ottawa and became a civil servant."[88] Gérard Pelletier, likewise, said he never quite understood why Trudeau had gone to Ottawa. Several biographers have sought to justify this decision, which seemed to have been taken on a whim. John English, for example, wrote that Trudeau would not have wanted to teach at the Université de Montréal, given the previous negative experience he had had while studying there. He added that no doubt Trudeau also wanted to get away from his mother, with whom his ties were too close for a man of thirty years: "If Trudeau was to consolidate his new-found independence, he no doubt sensed that he should not return to his family home."[89]

It is not impossible that these factors played a role. But we should note that upon his return from Ottawa, Trudeau tried several times to get a job at the Université de Montréal – in vain. (He got to work there only after Duplessis had died.) And if he really wanted to leave his mother, why didn't he seek a posting as a university professor in some other Canadian city? Besides, on his return from Ottawa, he lived with his mother, in the Outremont family home, for another fifteen years.

We believe the explanation lies elsewhere. We only need to consider the personal path he had followed since his days at Collège Jean-de-Brébeuf to realize that this decision involved more than either an escape or a whim. When he was twenty-five, he had written in his Harvard University application: "I shall make Statesmanship my profession and, if God permit, I shall know my profession well."[90] He was determined to combine theory and practice, and so he had begun by getting the best possible theoretical training at three of the most prestigious universities in the Western world. Next, he was dead set on seeing the practical problems of various peoples first-hand, so he travelled to the far side of the planet. As he said himself: "This journey . . . gave me the opportunity to become intimately acquainted with political and economic problems in almost all countries in Europe and Asia."[91]

But ultimately, there was still something missing in his training: he had no direct experience of the Canadian political system. He certainly couldn't get such training in Quebec, by working for the Duplessis government. Duplessis wouldn't have allowed him to do so anyway. And, since Canada was a federation, his best option was the federal government. While he had no plans to pursue a career in public service, he thought this experience would complete his training. In fact, his private papers indicate clearly that he decided to explore his chances of landing a job in a government department as soon as he returned to Montreal.

On June 2, 1949, less than two months after his return, he got the following reply from Pierre Dumas, who worked in the office of the Under Secretary of State for External Affairs: "My dear old Pierre, I spoke to Jules Léger about the possibility of a job as secretary in the Prime Minister's Office. Jules appeared very interested."[92] Jules Léger, brother of the famous Cardinal Léger, had worked at the Department of External Affairs since 1940. In 1954, he became the first French-speaking Under Secretary of this department and would thereafter enjoy a brilliant career in Canadian diplomacy. Trudeau appointed him Governor General of Canada in 1974. On June 8, Pierre Dumas wrote another letter: "I mentioned your name to Paul Pelletier at the Privy Council. He was very interested, and although there is no vacancy at the moment, he suggested it might be possible to add a secretary to the staff of the Privy Council. He needs to discuss the matter shortly with Mr. Norman Robertson." The latter was then Clerk of the Privy Council and Secretary to the Cabinet. Pierre Dumas added: "I also spoke to Mr. René Garneau, who already knows you by reputation. . . . He assures me that you will have preference over any other candidate."[93] Trudeau replied the following week: "When I met René Garneau, he was already very much in favour of my application, thanks to you. Unfortunately, he didn't see anything of interest for me in his sector. However, he'll look into possibilities at the Privy Council." Trudeau explained why he no longer wanted to work in the Prime Minister's Office: "Becoming attached to a party leader, no matter how worthy he may be, implies a kind of commitment I do not feel able to give fully at this time." Only the Privy Council interested him. If that failed, he said, "I'll probably go to the National Film Board."[94] On August 19, he sat for the oral examination of the Civil Service Commission. On the 25th he had a few interviews, after which he was offered not one position, but two – it was up to him to decide: one was in the Ministry of Finance and the other in the Privy Council. "I opt for the Privy Council," he confided to his diary.[95]

On August 31, he was named a "civil servant of the Privy Council, Class 1, with an annual salary of $2,880."[96] Class 1 meant starting at the bottom of the ladder. He was the lone assistant of Gordon Robertson (not to be confused with the boss, Norman Robertson). Gordon Robertson, in Class 6, was a member of the Cabinet Office and worked as head of the Economics Division in the Privy Council. Before starting his new job, Trudeau took a twelve-day holiday with his friend Charles Lussier in Murray Bay (now called La Malbaie), on the north shore of the St. Lawrence River about 150 kilometres downstream east of Quebec City; in 1976, he appointed Lussier head of the Canada Council for the Arts. On September 13, at 7:30 in the evening, in driving rain, Pierre Trudeau arrived in Ottawa. And the next day would be his first as a junior civil servant.

Chapter 7

———◈———

GRADUATE COURSE IN
APPLIED FEDERALISM

*We admire civil servants and advisers. But our heart is with the
mine workers. Isn't a man worth more than all balanced budgets?*
— PIERRE ELLIOTT TRUDEAU[*]

MOST OF TRUDEAU'S BIOGRAPHERS claim he did not like Ottawa. We
would probably draw the same conclusion if we just referred to the
city itself. As a French Canadian, Trudeau felt alienated and lonely in
Ottawa, which at the time seemed to him a dull, provincial, and above
all an English city. He struck up a friendship with Marcel Rioux, whom
he had often seen in Paris. Rioux was another "exile," working as a
researcher at the Museum of Man in Ottawa. He had a wife and family,
and often invited Trudeau home. The two friends did not share the same
intellectual background, but as Jules Duchastel wrote in his biography
of Rioux, "they completed one another. They had very different personalities but they had great respect and a high regard for each other. . . .
What brought them together was above all the open-mindedness they
felt was lacking in Quebec, the desire to change things."[1] Their friendship lasted a good fifteen years, as is shown, for example, by the personal inscription Trudeau wrote in 1956 on the copy of *The Asbestos
Strike* he gave him: "To my friend Marcel Rioux, a distinguished anthropophagite and jolly good fellow."[2]

---

[*] This remark is undated, but since it was written on the letterhead of the
Privy Council, it probably dates from between 1949 and 1951.

These two comrades-in-arms had a common goal: to transform Quebec. Rioux regularly contributed to the new magazine *Cité libre*. Until the early 1960s, he also criticized nationalism, which he considered obsolete. For example, in 1955 he wrote: "The principle of nationalities – namely that each ethnic group should have its own state – no longer means anything in an increasingly united world. So is there really any point in clinging to such an outdated formula?[3] . . . The nationalists . . . are primarily concerned not with justice in general but with *their* justice, not with human progress as such but with the progress *their own* kinsfolk make, not with God, but with *their* religion. . . . It takes faith in man to rise up against the status quo and the unrealistic character of a fossilized ideology."[4]

But Rioux was gradually drawn to the nationalist and separatist current of thought. In the early 1960s, he realized "an unbridgeable rift now separated him from his friend,"[5] especially where FLQ (Front de Libération du Québec) actions were concerned. He saw the FLQ as a "liberating force," whereas Trudeau saw it as a "terrorist group." In 1964, Marcel Rioux and Fernand Dumont, both now renowned sociologists and well-known public figures in Quebec, came out in favour of independence.

But Trudeau did not break off contact with his old friend. In 1965, when he decided to stand as a Liberal candidate in Mount Royal, he made a point of meeting Rioux to let him know in person: "I wanted you to be the first to know, so you wouldn't learn about my candidacy in the press." Rioux didn't react in any way. Breaking the silence, Trudeau asked: "Have you seen Vadboncoeur lately?" Rioux answered: "Yes, last night, and we even heard of your decision before you told me. We tried to find a way to beat you. . . . So long, buddy!"[6]

They never met again. Some time later, probably shocked by Rioux's attitude, Trudeau asked his chief of staff to get Rioux to repay a debt he had contracted many years earlier. Rioux paid up – without interest.[7] After the 1980 referendum, Rioux, deeply disappointed by Trudeau's victory over the separatist option, brought out a pamphlet entitled *Taking Public Leave of a Few Bastards*.[8] Rioux's targets included Trudeau.

After soaking up the experience of Paris, London, and other enthralling cities, no wonder Trudeau showed little enthusiasm for the Ottawa of 1949, which was hardly a glamorous, pulsating metropolis. He confided his feelings to Roger Rolland, now a professor at the University of British Columbia in Vancouver: "I am delighted by the reception you got at the university, although I imagine the minute you leave the campus, you risk being swallowed up in the gloom of the Anglo-Saxon city. I feel this strongly myself." He was worried that this isolation and loneliness would turn into resentment and pettiness. So he suggested to his friend: "Let's make sure we keep in touch with regular friendly letters."⁹ Gloom, isolation, and loneliness; resentment and pettiness . . . Trudeau's discomfort was palpable. In less than six months, he had moved five times. Why? We don't know. Whatever the case, at the drop of a hat, he rolled out his Harley-Davidson or jumped into his car and raced back to Montreal.

Fortunately for Trudeau, in September 1950, a year after his arrival in the grey city of Ottawa, a sudden burst of sunshine shot across the sky. He noticed a story with a photo in the *Ottawa Citizen* about a lovely and well-read twenty-year-old Swedish woman who had just arrived to work at the Swedish embassy. Trudeau made sure he got to meet her, and one thing quickly led to another. The beautiful Helen Segerstråle fell madly in love with Trudeau, a man of considerable charm. Less than a year later, they were planning to get married, with Grace Trudeau's blessing. But dark clouds loomed on the horizon. Their relationship was not a smooth one. The rhythm of their heart-wrenching fights was occasionally broken by renewed declarations of love. Clearly, Trudeau's decision to leave the Privy Council in September 1951 and head out on a long journey didn't help things. But until then, a wedding had still not been ruled out.¹⁰

While he was far from enchanted with Ottawa's dreary character, there can be no doubt that Trudeau loved his job: "I am absolutely delighted with my work here," he wrote to Roger Rolland. "You know of course that when I had to choose between the Ministry of Finance and the Privy Council, I opted for the latter. Since then, I haven't stopped congratulating myself for this decision. . . . All things considered, there is only one job in the entire world that would get me to become a civil servant, and that's the position I have right now."¹¹ But what was he doing exactly?

This is how he described his work to Rolland: "So many people ask me what the Privy Council is that I hope you won't mind my saying a few words about it. There are fifteen of us senior officials in the Privy Council office, and our sole activity is to prepare the work of the Prime Minister and his ministers. We are a kind of secretariat working for the Cabinet. So as you can imagine there is no way to be closer to the centre of politics and the government, and the most important and varied tasks

invariably reach our desks. For example, I have so far been mainly occupied with research on constitutional reform, and on major economic
policy issues: you know how passionate I am about these two subjects.
One thing is for sure: some moves are under way in Ottawa that will
leave their mark on our history."[12] In fact, he admitted being so engrossed
in his work that sometimes he only stopped to drop into bed! The range
and depth of the records he left in the Canadian archives bear witness to
his enthusiasm and dedication. It took us a lot of stamina and perseverance to pore over the rich store of detailed documents he drafted. We
don't need to study them all here. Instead, we will examine only those
documents that enable us to follow the evolution of his thoughts.

Less than three weeks after taking office, Trudeau submitted a six-page
report to his supervisor, Gordon Robertson, entitled "On Price Support
for Commodity Surpluses."[13] This document was intended to guide government policy on fisheries and agriculture. Trudeau's report reveals that
he did not belong to just one school of economic thought. He neither
defended all-out state intervention nor a market left to its own devices:
"Price support is only a means; the end we seek should be a livable income
for every citizen. And as a means, price support cannot be used systematically; for it naturally tends to prevent equilibrium of demand and supply."

A thick and constantly renewed stack of files reached his desk. Some
of these would make a significant contribution to his future role as prime
minister. Once again, he was in the right place at the right time. Parliament
Hill was in something of a buzz when he started work. Two federal-
provincial conferences were planned for the year: the first to be held in
Ottawa from January 10 to 12, 1950, and the second in Quebec City
from September 25 to 28. They would both focus on the Constitution
and its eventual repatriation from Great Britain. Nowadays, Canadians
have grown so weary of the never-ending succession of constitutional
"crises" that they may find it hard to picture just how excited people
were about constitutional reform and repatriation, back in 1950. Don't
forget that the 1950 conferences were among the most important meetings addressing the issue since the Statute of Westminster had been
enacted in 1931, granting quasi-independence to Canada. But since
Canadian governments had failed to agree on an amending formula, the
Constitution had not been repatriated. In a bid to resolve outstanding
issues, a federal-provincial conference had taken place in December

1935, but it had proved a failure. The result was that in 1950, there was renewed hope an agreement would be reached, and Canada would finally gain full powers over its Constitution for the first time in its history.

So Trudeau was in the Privy Council office at a key moment in Canadian constitutional history. Moreover, in 1950, there were three federal-provincial conferences, two of which were devoted to constitutional issues. We will not focus on the third one, which addressed various other matters. Remember that such meetings were rare at the time. Indeed, after 1950, it was five years before a new meeting took place, and then ten years before the next one. This latter one coincided with the launch of the so-called Quiet Revolution and witnessed Premier Jean Lesage's confrontation with Conservative prime minister John G. Diefenbaker on constitutional matters. Interestingly, issues pertaining to patriation and amendment of the constitution would not surface again until the unsuccessful August-September 1964 Federal/Provincial Conference convened by the Lester B. Pearson government. It would take another eighteen years before the Trudeau government finally resolved these issues with the Constitution Act of 1982.

In 1950, Trudeau, who had just arrived on Parliament Hill, was being assigned constitutional files of major importance by his direct superior, Gordon Robertson. He was provided with many preparatory documents, including the brief tabled by Premier Duplessis, a study of various amending formulae in Canada, Australia, and the United States, as well as other documents sometimes stamped "Secret." Trudeau got down to the job, poring over a large number of books and articles on the subject. He submitted to Robertson a first draft of the report intended to assist the federal team in establishing its position in the forthcoming negotiations with the provinces. Robertson sent back the text with annotations and comments. Several versions flowed back and forth before the final report was hammered out. Robertson did not always agree with Trudeau and criticized him on some points. But his comments show how much Trudeau commanded the admiration and respect not just of his superior but also of members of Prime Minister St. Laurent's cabinet, as we will see below.

Trudeau began his report by studying a question then considered extremely important: Was Confederation based on a pact or on a law? This issue was controversial, and he knew it could greatly affect talks on repatriation of the Constitution, so he wrote a four-page document entitled "Notes

on the Compact Theory."[14] The debate surrounding this theory had flared
up again with renewed vigour since Paul Gérin-Lajoie had returned to
Quebec in 1948 with a doctorate in hand: Trudeau's brilliant former class-
mate at Collège Jean-de-Brébeuf had gone on to become a Rhodes Scholar,
studying constitutional law at Oxford University under the supervision of
the renowned constitutionalist Kenneth Clinton Wheare. His dissertation,
published in 1950 by University of Toronto Press as *Constitutional
Amendments in Canada,* had a significant impact in Canada and even in
Great Britain. It won the Quebec government's prestigious Prix David en
sciences morales et politiques. Paul Gérin-Lajoie embarked on a distinguished political career in 1960 and served as Quebec's first minister of
education in 1964, under the Liberal government of Jean Lesage.

Most politicians and intellectuals in Quebec were of the view that the
founding act of Confederation, the British North America (BNA) Act of
1867, was the result of a pact. But between which parties? There were two
interpretations. The first one claimed that the pact had been concluded by
two ethnic communities, English and French Canadians. According to the
second, the pact was established by three colonies, already known in 1867
as "provinces": Canada, New Brunswick, and Nova Scotia. As a result of
this pact, the province of "Canada" was split into two further provinces,
Quebec and Ontario, ushering in the four founding provinces of
Confederation. This second interpretation was often distorted, especially
in Quebec. For example, Premier Duplessis argued that "the Government
of Quebec, in agreement with the highest constitutional and political
authorities . . . , is of the opinion that the British North America Act is a
pact between the four founding provinces."[15] Impossible! These "four
founding provinces" could not have negotiated the terms of the BNA Act
for the simple reason that it is this same law, enacted at Westminster, that
had created them out of the three original colonies.

Whichever interpretation one preferred, it was often claimed that the
pact provided the basis for the protection of French Canadians within
Confederation. Along these lines, André Laurendeau, associate editor-
in-chief at *Le Devoir,* wrote an editorial on January 9, 1950: "Since
Confederation is and shall remain a pact between two nations, no one
should be able to get rid of the one state [Quebec] where the French
Canadian nation is in control."[16] But who in the world wanted to "get
rid" of Quebec? We don't know.

Gérin-Lajoie's thesis – masterfully defended, according to Trudeau[17] – rejected the compact theory. Trudeau did not automatically agree with this view, compelling though it might be. He wanted to reach his own conclusions, weighing the pros and cons. He noted that this theory had adherents beyond Quebec's borders, citing as evidence two of the Fathers of Confederation, John A. Macdonald and George-Etienne Cartier. He also noted that a number of experts and court judgments had sometimes interpreted the BNA Act as a pact. Yet he detected weaknesses in this perspective. Logically, he said, a pact could not be changed without the consent of the parties. History shows, however, that although the British government had consulted the four founding provinces before making any amendments, the BNA Act had always been amended by a simple act of the British Parliament in Westminster. Obviously, the British government had the discretionary power to amend this act as it saw fit, whereas the contracting parties – whether provinces or ethnic groups – had no such power. Consequently, the BNA Act had no more force than an ordinary law.

But wait, Trudeau said. It would be wrong to consider only the purely formal aspect of the act, since the spirit of the law had also to be taken into account. He pointed out that negotiations had taken place both among the three original colonies and between the two linguistic communities. The signatories of the time had publicly expressed their willingness to accommodate the linguistic and religious rights of French Canadians. He cited as evidence an excerpt from the debates leading up to the signing of the act: "John A. Macdonald prefers legislative union but finds it impracticable . . . because French Canadians would have cause to fear for their religion and nationality."[18] These considerations led Trudeau to find fault with both rigid advocates of the compact theory and those who considered the BNA Act as no more than an ordinary law. And he did not hesitate to single out people guilty of erroneous interpretations, even the prime minister himself. In a note accompanying "Notes on the Compact Theory," he pointed out to Robertson that "by altering what may be within his jurisdiction, without specifying the federal nature, [St. Laurent] is going to the extreme of the theory of law, as extremist as the theory of compact."

Just a moment! Doesn't denying the existence of a pact also mean removing the basis of the protection of French Canadians? Not at all, Gérin-Lajoie would have replied: "This compact theory has so many weaknesses that we would be wrong to use it as a basis for the rights guaranteed by the Canadian federal State. The surest foundation of these guarantees is . . . in the text of the 1867 Act of Confederation itself." According to Gérin-Lajoie, the best protection for Quebec – as for other provinces – lay in the fact that "the 1867 Constitution established a two-level state for the governing of the territory that is now Canada: one at the provincial level and the other at the federal level." As a result, each level "was granted a legislative and administrative domain for the governance of its population, a domain of its own and over which it enjoyed full autonomy."[19] It was thanks to Canada's federal structure that each province had great flexibility in managing its affairs. Trudeau agreed completely, despite the many weaknesses he found in this system. It seemed obvious to him that instead of getting bogged down in fruitless discussions, it would be far better to devote greater attention to the improvement of Canadian federalism, first by better defining the areas of competence of each level of government, then by respecting their jurisdiction.

Now that Trudeau's "Notes on the Compact Theory" had identified the preliminary pitfalls to be avoided, he threw himself into research directly related to the federal-provincial conference of January 1950. This conference would essentially focus on developing an amending procedure to be ratified by the provinces and by the central government. On December 14 he submitted a seven-page document entitled "Federalism Revisited."[20] As soon as the report reached the Prime Minister's Office, Jules Leger, then senior civil servant in the Department of External Affairs and later Governor General of Canada, wrote back: "Thanks so much. Excellent paper. All I have to do now is convince Maurice."[21] (Maurice is evidently Maurice Duplessis, the champion of Quebec autonomy.)

Trudeau reasserted, first of all, that the core principle of federalism is the sharing of sovereignty between central and regional governments. Canada was a true federation, not only because this principle is enshrined in the text of the BNA Act, but also because, in practice, the central government has never unilaterally modified the jurisdiction of the provinces and will never be able to do so in the future. Could Canada acquire a truly Canadian Constitution? From a technical point of view, quite easily, according to Trudeau. All the provinces and the central government had to do was amend the title and the preamble of the BNA Act. The real problems lay elsewhere: first, in setting up an impartial forum for the interpretation of the Constitution and, second, in finding an amending formula acceptable to both Ottawa and the provinces. And to these issues he devoted most of his report.

History has decided, he went on, that French Canadians should inherit a federal system that gave all provinces, and thus the province where they constituted the majority, a very large degree of autonomy. They thus had the flexibility needed for their full development. But for this system to work properly, it has to maintain a strict division of powers between the two levels of governments and ensure that the central government does not enjoy undue advantages. The myth of "Trudeau the die-hard centralist" has proven so pervasive that many people will be surprised to learn he ardently defended the rights of the provinces at the time. He was truly a "son of Quebec," concerned above all with the well-being of his fellow French Canadians. In fact, his position was much like Laurendeau's, who complained in Le Devoir on September 26, 1949, "of the continual encroachments by the central state in the fields of provincial jurisdiction. If this trend continues, the provincial state will become a sort of municipality, whose much-reduced autonomy will be constantly under threat. The Confederation as such will have ceased to exist." To Trudeau, it was therefore imperative to maintain the balance of powers between the two levels of governments. Moreover, in the event of a dispute, the aggrieved party should be able to lodge a complaint with an impartial arbitrator. In Canada, for historical reasons, this role fell to the Supreme Court. And that, said Trudeau, is the rub: the fact judges are appointed by the central government undermines the Court's impartiality. As a way of remedying this shortcoming, he recommended that the provinces have their say in the selection of judges. He also suggested, among other things: "The BNA Act could be amended by adding Section 101A, giving the provinces a certain measure of control over the number of Supreme Court judges, and over their mode of nomination."

Trudeau emphasized the delicate balance that a good amending formula needs to maintain: "The dilemma, which is everywhere encountered in providing a federal institution with a process of amendment, consists in safeguarding the division of jurisdiction, whilst avoiding undue rigidity." Accordingly, he proposed a three-step procedure, with increasingly rigorous requirements, depending on whether the changes in question related to a single jurisdiction, two jurisdictions, or the general population. For example, in the simplest case, affecting only one province, the amendment could be enacted "by a mere law of the legislature

concerned." However, if the goal were to change "a bill of rights, that is
to say, sections concerning matters of such vital significance to the community that upon their inviolability is founded the general will to live
together as people of one country," then the conditions for the amendment process would have to be more stringent. He proposed three procedures for adopting such an amendment, whereby it "a) is approved by
all the regional legislatures, or b) is plebiscited by all the provinces voting
separately, or c) is approved by some legislatures, and plebiscited in the
remaining provinces." Worth noting: when the Constitution was repatriated in 1982, it included a similar hierarchical amendment process but
did not include recourse to referendums. However, the records show that
during the negotiations prior to repatriation, Trudeau defended vigorously the option of recourse to referendums in some cases. [*]

In the conclusion of "Federalism Revisited," Trudeau summarized his
suggestions for improving the functioning of the Canadian federal system.
First and foremost, a more equitable sharing of sovereignty between the
two levels of government and the establishment of an impartial arbitrator
in the event of disputes. In his view, for Canada to become a truly democratic country, the Constitution needed to be repatriated; in addition, it
should include an amending procedure taking proper account of the
shared sovereignty between the two levels of government. More importantly, it had to ensure that the fundamental law of the land is the expression of the will of the people. The Canadian people should become
sovereign: "Whereas formerly the general will identified itself with the
pronouncements of the Westminster Parliament, now the sovereign people
of Canada, federally united, wish to take the Constitutional Powers unto
themselves." Brimming with enthusiasm, Trudeau longed to share with
"his" people his conviction that the proper functioning of federalism was
the answer to their problems. He took on the challenge of improving
Canada's federal system, even before leaving his job as a civil servant.

————◦————

Anyone who lived through the excruciating constitutional sagas of the
1960s, 1970s, 1980s, and 1990s doesn't need to be told that the conference

---

[*]   We would like to thank the renowned constitutionalist Alan Cairns, who
kindly shared his expertise with us on this subject.

of January 1950 did not result in any constitutional agreement. So, did the participants admit failure? Not at all! A document dated September 18, 1950, boasts a long list of achievements,[22] namely that the ministers agreed on the need to find a formula for amending the BNA Act; they agreed on the fact that a Canadian Constitution was really desirable; they agreed on the need to divide the BNA Act into six sections for the purposes of amendment; and they saw the need to study the issue of delegation of powers. Finally, they approved the creation of a committee to analyze and harmonize the views of various governments concerning the classification of sections of the BNA Act for amending purposes.

Many Canadians nowadays will likely smile at this long list of so-called positive results, which amounted to no more than agreement on general principles. But at the time, optimism was still in fashion. The repeatedly unsuccessful attempts to repatriate the Constitution have abundantly demonstrated the almost insuperable difficulty of reconciling the conflicting interests of participants, each wanting to take advantage of constitutional talks in order to grab more power. Trudeau realized this in 1950. As a civil servant in the Privy Council office, he witnessed the politics of constitutional reform up close. For many years to come, this experience would lead him to advocate "deep social reforms along the lines suggested by the progressive people in Quebec" rather than opening up the Pandora's box of constitutional reform.[23]

At the end of the federal-provincial conference of January 1950, Trudeau threw himself into preparations for the September conference. Meanwhile, he was part of a small group of French Canadians working hard to launch *Cité libre*. This magazine would play a key role in Quebec history and right across Canada, and Trudeau's name would forever be associated with it. But no one knew that yet. For now, it was just a project that Trudeau found extremely stimulating, as is revealed in the letter he wrote to Roger Rolland on April 19, 1950: "Great things are getting ready in the shadows. I think Pelletier must have slipped you a word about our magazine, which is *finally* coming together. We have already read and discussed all the articles for the first issue, and believe me, it's *utterly* exciting. It's what we always wanted. . . . You have no idea how this magazine gives shape and reality to our drive for liberation and truth. Our small team will overcome fear and superstition, and soon we will see similar groups doing the same thing across the province. It will take us a very long time to get the whole population on board. But at least *they* won't be able to say that in our lifetime truth was treated with scorn in Quebec."[*][24]

Trudeau got to know by heart the roughly two hundred kilometres separating Ottawa from Montreal. While working in the Privy Council office, he made this journey every other weekend, and sometimes more often than that, so he could take part in editorial meetings. We will get to *Cité libre* in Chapter 8. Let's return to the Privy Council and Trudeau's drafting of the document for the September meeting.

On June 2, 1950, Trudeau submitted "Theory and Practice of Federal-Provincial Cooperation" to Gordon Robertson.[25] Everybody knows, of course, that the work of civil servants is to research and provide facts relevant to policy makers. Expressing their opinions is not part of their job description. But this twenty-nine-page document could easily be mistaken for a professor's essay. After the customary travel back and forth between Trudeau and Robertson, a second version of the document appeared on September 11. Now thirty-two pages long, the revised text, written in an impersonal and bureaucratic style, had been given a new title: "Federal-Provincial Cooperation."[26] In comparing the two versions of this document, we clearly see how Trudeau, the rebellious philosopher, ultimately yielded to the bureaucratic constraints imposed on Trudeau, the civil servant. Let us examine the first draft of the document, which sheds a more interesting light on Trudeau's thinking at the time. Although we will not summarize his copious notes, it is important to note that before focusing on the Canadian case, he studied various types of federations around the world; he even sketched a brief comparative outline.

Theoretically, Trudeau said, cooperation is unnecessary in a federal system, since each level of government exercises full autonomy in its own spheres of jurisdiction. This is true . . . in theory and only in theory. He explained: "In practice . . . no federation as yet has succeeded in dividing its sovereign powers with adequacy and finality among regional and

---

[*]   Unless otherwise indicated, words given in italics are underlined or in italics in the original version.

central governments." This is why, in practice, the proper functioning of a federal system requires cooperation between the two levels of government. However, the political dynamic inherent in federalism pulls in the opposite direction, through the formation of ad hoc coalitions between governments, coalescing and dissolving according to short-term interests: "Too often their dealings with one another have been nothing but a disguised attempt to gain more power. Naturally the result has not been greater understanding, but rather the development of a persecution complex, which in turn results in increased aggressiveness."²⁷ An additional factor makes intergovernmental cooperation vital. Sometimes, in a given area, the legislative powers of a province do not coincide with its material resources. It follows that "the government most apt to legislate on a given subject cannot be relied on to administer the laws most efficiently." It is therefore important to find effective means for thwarting or at least minimizing the impact of these opposing forces.

Our system is centralized, he said, because the Fathers of Confederation, fearing that too much provincial autonomy would destroy Canada, "took every precaution to prevent the provinces from isolationist tendencies."²⁸ This is why the central government acquired disproportionate powers, compared to the provinces. First, the powers of disallowance and reservation allow it to invalidate a provincial law. Second, the power to appoint lieutenant governors, that is, representatives of the executive who have at the provincial level the same powers as the governor general at the federal level, has the effect of weakening the provincial executive. Thirdly, the power to choose and remunerate senators gives the central government too much control over the Upper Chamber.

Trudeau added that the Fathers of Confederation established spheres of shared jurisdiction between the central government and provinces. He listed areas where the division of powers, not being well defined, makes cooperation between the two levels of government particularly important. Such is the case, for example, with agriculture, immigration, and justice. It is not surprising, he wrote, that "from the very outset the provinces and the Dominion Government forged many instruments of joint action." And to show how cooperation is inherent in the spirit of federalism, Trudeau provided a detailed ten-page list of joint governmental actions.

Trudeau strove for objectivity, but he couldn't help expressing an opinion that betrayed his own bias in favour of decentralization. He highlighted the discrepancy between the responsibilities and financial resources of the provinces, a phenomenon now called "fiscal imbalance": "As ideologies moved from the liberal state towards the social-service state, the financial situation of the provinces was bound to deteriorate steadily, since under the Constitution, responsibility for the new welfare functions fell upon the provinces."[29] And he cited as an example the situation prevailing between 1921 and 1930: "While current public welfare expenditures of all governments rose 130%, three quarters of the additional burden was borne by provinces and municipalities. The inevitable result was a steady increase of provincial debt ... [which] was partly due to the fact that the federal government was busy paying for the war."[30] But his criticism went further. He underlined the harmful impact of certain grants made to the provinces: "The poorer provinces were quick to show that conditional grants were a form of blackmail which obliged them to pay more than they could afford for social improvements."[31] Was he accusing the federal government of blackmail? Clearly, Trudeau did not yet realize that neither his personal criticism nor his style was appropriate to his function. In a brief note, Robertson resolved this thorny issue diplomatically by asking Trudeau to remove these sections, since they fell under the purview of the Ministry of Finance.

Regarding royal commissions, which are supposed to illustrate cases of cooperation between the two levels of government, once again, Trudeau did not spare the central government: "There is no denying that as an instrument of intergovernmental cooperation, Royal Commissions are inherently vitiated. For they are essentially a creation of the executive branch of *one* government. . . . No conception of sovereignty, however broad, can justify that one government should exercise inquisitorial activities over acts within the jurisdiction of another government."[32] Unbelievable! Trudeau was accusing the federal government – his employer, lest we forget – of acting as an inquisitor by creating inherently flawed commissions and of meddling in matters that were none of its concern.

Which royal commission was Trudeau thinking about as he wrote these lines? Very likely the Rowell-Sirois Commission,[33] called by the federal government in 1937 as a result of the Great Depression, to address the distribution of powers between the two levels of government. Its report was tabled in May 1940, during the war, and proposed expanding the role of the central government. It recommended in particular the devolution of direct taxation to the federal government as well as the administration of social programs. This is how Unemployment Insurance ended up under federal jurisdiction. The report also recommended a system of equalization payments to redistribute cash to poorer provinces. As might be expected, the report was vigorously denounced in Quebec, which accused the federal government of encroaching on provincial jurisdictions guaranteed by the Constitution. Nonetheless, at the federal-provincial conference of January 1941, Quebec and all other provinces, with the exception of Ontario, endorsed the recommendations of the Rowell-Sirois report. Given the social benefits that would accrue from the new system, and lacking adequate financial resources to meet the pressing needs of the time, these provinces accepted the transfers of powers to the central government.

Trudeau believed that federal-provincial relations badly needed improvement. He drew a leaf from the relationships between Great Britain and her former colonies: "The Imperial Government ceased to investigate the national affairs of any country which had attained responsible status, without prior consent of the government concerned. It should follow logically that the Federal Government at Ottawa should obtain consent before inquiring into any matter falling within the ambit of provincial jurisdiction." Thus, for Trudeau, the provinces should have a status equivalent to that of an independent country, within their respective jurisdictions.

Unsurprisingly, Robertson could not accept the critical evaluation of the federal government nor the style of writing Trudeau employed, let alone his suggestion that Ottawa draw inspiration from Britain's treatment of her former colonies. He knew that a public servant must gather and present facts. Nothing more, and nothing less. He therefore annotated Trudeau's successive drafts, in order to make the final document "bureaucratically correct." After successive versions over a period of four months, the document was given its new title, "Federal-Provincial Cooperation." It was purged of Trudeau's theoretical considerations and practical suggestions. Here, for example, is how the revised version to the section on the royal commissions now read: "Provincial as well as federal Governments in Canada have long made use of Royal Commissions to investigate their respective problems, and it is a well established rule, whatever the object of the investigation, [that] due regard should be given to the representation of all interests. Consequently, when it becomes necessary to carry out an inquiry into some matter over which both the federal government and the provinces have jurisdiction, there is generally little opposition from the provincial governments to the appointment of a Royal Commission."[34] Any hint of criticism had vanished. The document now claimed that royal commissions were firmly rooted in tradition and welcomed by the provinces. In reading the perfectly neutral final text, as edited by Robertson, poor rookie Trudeau probably felt he was losing his soul, although he maintained courteous relations with Robertson until his departure. But we can easily understand how hard it must have been for Trudeau to put up with such restrictions on his freedom of expression. The fact that he was simultaneously throwing himself heart and soul into a struggle for the emancipation of Quebec in the new magazine *Cité libre* must have made the situation all the more unbearable. Unsurprisingly, after two years in the Privy Council office, he could no longer stand his bureaucratic straitjacket.

Let us return to the far more interesting first draft of the document where Trudeau defended the vital importance of cooperation between the federal and provincial governments. In support of his position, he referred to a document obviously in favour of centralization. "As the Rowell-Sirois report (II, 70) put it: 'The complexities of our social, political and commercial organization have now reached the point where the earlier view, once widely held, that all Dominion-provincial difficulties arising from disputes over jurisdiction could be settled by a strict demarcation of powers and responsibilities must be finally abandoned.'"[35] So far, so good. Cooperation, which required mutual trust and a sense of security, had become a necessity. And that's where Trudeau strongly criticized the federal government: "If the Supreme Court . . . and the Royal Commissions . . . were given a really 'federalist' mandate . . . , if relations between Ottawa and the provinces . . . were to become really a two-way avenue of exchange; then there might arise some hope of fruitful cooperation." For Trudeau, everything depended on the central government: "Confidence breeds confidence. If the provincial governments were really given cause to believe that their right to exist was not questioned, they probably would be much less intransigent regarding constitutional amendments."[36] What was he referring to when he implied that provincial governments' right to exist was threatened? We don't know. What we do know, however, is that this was a persistent concern. We saw earlier that on January 9, 1950, Laurendeau expressed this view in *Le Devoir*.

Trudeau firmly believed that it was up to the central government to demonstrate its sincerity when it claimed it wanted to establish new relationships with the provinces. "For instance," he suggested, "if the Federal Government were to indicate willingness to forsake its right of disallowance and of reservation, it is possible that in return the provinces might agree that a bill of rights be included in the Constitution."[37] Let us underline the fact that Trudeau was not suggesting the central government demonstrate its good will by ceding a right without receiving anything in return. Forty years later, in his famous October 1, 1992, Maison Egg Roll* speech on the Charlottetown constitutional accord, Trudeau blamed Brian Mulroney's Conservative government precisely for giving up powers without getting anything in return: "The sad fact is the federal government will have thrown overboard all its advantages. . . . Ottawa still had the power of disallowance and reservation. . . . But in this contract, it gives that up. And the federal government will be stripped naked. . . . It will have nothing to give in exchange."[38]

In his first draft, Trudeau fiercely defended the provinces from federal incursions into their jurisdictions. This would lead him, in one very special case, to side with his big political opponent: Premier Duplessis. In 1951, Maurice Duplessis accepted federal funding for universities, but then changed his mind and rejected it on principle, even though Quebec universities were suffering from severe underfunding. What explains Duplessis's stand? Education is within provincial jurisdiction, so federal funding would undermine Quebec's autonomy. Academics, whose faculties were strapped for cash, were outraged and blasted Duplessis's position. The French-Canadian intelligentsia rallied to their cause. Gérard Pelletier, for example, wrote an article entitled "Reflections on the State of Siege," for the February 1957 issue of Cité libre. But Trudeau went against the tide and created a sensation. In "Federal Grants to Universities," an article appearing in the same issue that was later reprinted in Federalism and the French Canadians, he agreed with Duplessis and maintained that these grants undermined provincial autonomy.

---

* The Maison Egg Roll was a Chinese restaurant in a working-class district of Montreal, where the Friends of Cité libre held their monthly gatherings for nearly twelve years. The restaurant has since disappeared.

By chance, Trudeau, who had been won over at Harvard by Carl Friedrich on the importance of a constitution and a charter of rights, found himself, on May 8, 1951, acting as secretary at a presentation of a brief by delegates of a committee for a bill of rights to the federal government. The government team included Prime Minister Louis St. Laurent and Secretary of State for External Affairs Lester B. Pearson, among others. The committee, founded in 1946, comprised members of the Association for Civil Liberties and was engaged in a campaign against abuses of power, including those perpetrated by the police. The 1951 delegation, representing two hundred individuals and fifty organizations, presented to Prime Minister St. Laurent a report examining the prospect of incorporating a charter of human rights into the Constitution. The delegation included representatives of various trade unions, teachers' associations, student movements, Christian youth groups, and others. Trudeau had already met some of these people: for example, Eugene Forsey, representing the Canadian Labour Congress, and Professor F.R. Scott, representing the Montreal Civil Liberties Association. He was impressed by the quality of the presentations made by these two intellectuals, and he would remember them again, many years later.[39]

The members of the delegation asked the government to implement recommendations of a Senate report, tabled a year earlier, which recommended among other things that "the Federal Government should adopt a Declaration of Human Rights modelled on the United Nations Universal Declaration of Human Rights." Throughout the meeting, the delegation stressed the benefits of a charter. For its part, the government stressed the difficulties that would inevitably arise from such a project. As we well know today, the meeting produced no tangible results. Nine years later, on August 10, 1960, the Conservative government of John Diefenbaker adopted a bill of rights. But this was only a federal law, which could easily be amended. It was not until thirty-one years later, in Ottawa on April 17, 1982, that a beaming Pierre Trudeau looked on as Queen Elizabeth ratified the repatriated Constitution, enshrining the Charter of Rights and Freedoms. As he dutifully took the minutes at the meeting in 1951, could Trudeau have imagined that the Charter would one day be his most important contribution to Canadian history? One thing is certain: he got first-hand knowledge, which proved invaluable in later years, on all aspects of constitutional issues during his two years in the Privy Council office.

Trudeau was fascinated by everything he was learning and was eager to share his discoveries with his fellow French Canadians. While his civil service duties kept him quite busy, he wrote articles for *Cité libre* that were inspired by his work experience. His expertise was much sought after, and he was often invited to give public talks. For example, in a letter dated July 26, 1950, the Jesuit priest Jacques Cousineau wrote: "My dear Pierre, I just wanted to remind you that you have kindly agreed to give a presentation on the current status of the federal-provincial conference on the Constitution, during the study days to be held on St. Ignace Island."[40] A few years later, relations between Father Cousineau and Trudeau would turn very sour.

Trudeau's responsibilities in the Privy Council were not limited to constitutional matters. Far from it! On October 28, 1950, he sent a memo to Robertson titled "Business pending during my vacation," enumerating all the files stacked up on his desk.[41] We will focus on a report submitted to Robertson on January 2, 1951, on an issue of major concern since the beginning of the Cold War in 1947: the Communist threat. At the time, this was a source of considerable anxiety in Western countries, Canada among them.

It is probably useful to say a few words about the "Gouzenko Affair," which created quite a stir in Canada. In September 1945, Igor Gouzenko, a clerk at the Soviet embassy in Ottawa, appeared at the office of Louis St. Laurent, then Canadian minister of justice, with documents revealing the spying activities of the Soviet Union. He requested and was granted political asylum. When word got out to the press, in February 1946, it created a scandal. A royal commission set up to investigate the allegations resulted in the arrest of thirty-nine persons, eighteen of whom were eventually convicted of a variety of offences. Particularly noteworthy is the conviction of Paul Rose, member of Parliament from the Montreal riding of Cartier, and the only Communist MP ever to sit in the House of Commons. The Gouzenko Affair ushered into Canada the era of the "Communist Menace." South of the border, "collective neurosis" is the more appropriate term to describe this fear. Starting in 1950, Wisconsin senator Joseph McCarthy engaged in a Communist witch hunt with fanatical zeal, in a drive to ferret out so-called Communist sympathizers in many public and private institutions. Understandably, in Ottawa the government undertook a comprehensive study in order to gauge the extent of this problem in Canada, and in particular within the civil service.

Trudeau wrote two documents on the subject. We will focus only on the first, "Communism in Canada," which analyzed the position of various political parties on the "Red Menace." In drafting his fifteen-page report, he systematically went through *Hansard** from 1945 onwards and studied the evolving positions of the government and opposition parties. Until 1948, the Liberal government in power did not seem overly preoccupied by Communism. Prime Minister Mackenzie King believed that the most effective way to fight Communism was to promote equality of opportunity and social justice. But suddenly, under the attacks of the opposition, he adopted a surprisingly combative tone: "Mr. King said (*Hansard*, 2307): 'There is no menace in the world greater [than Communism].'" Louis St. Laurent, then Secretary of State for External Affairs, held much the same line. However, Trudeau noted, while the Liberal government deployed tough rhetoric and a Manichean interpretation of the world, it also refused to adopt the specific measures against Communism that the opposition demanded. Louis St. Laurent took over as prime minister in 1948. Until 1950, he maintained that laws currently in force were tough enough to ensure state security. "The best method of combatting Communism," he said, "is to make democracy work as a system benefiting no particular classes or groups."

The Conservatives, Trudeau discovered, routinely condemned the Liberals for being soft on Communism. Then, from 1947 onwards, they escalated their demands for tougher legislation to fight Communism. Meanwhile, the two other opposition parties, the CCF (Co-operative Commonwealth Federation) and the Social Credit, held much the same position as the Liberals. The CCF made clear it was vehemently opposed to Communism, while stressing the need to protect human rights. Its leader, Major** James Coldwell, therefore refused to support banning the Communist Party. For its part, the Social Credit said it had always fought Communism but refused to support its criminalization. The Social Credit

---

*   *Hansard* is the official published verbatim report of proceedings of the House of Commons.

**   Major is not a military rank. It is Coldwell's first name.

leader, Solon Low, believed the government should simply prosecute individuals who commit seditious acts threatening the security of Canadians.

On January 6, 1951, Gordon Robertson expressed in writing his complete satisfaction with Trudeau's report: "Your note outlining government and opposition statements concerning communism is just what I wanted and should be very helpful." Trudeau did not display any sympathy whatsoever for Communism in his summary of the position of all parties in Canada. This should come as no surprise since we know that in London he admired Professor Harold Laski while deploring his Marxist outlook. We have also seen that during his tour of Asia he was upset about the progress of Communism, since to him Christianity had so much more to offer. But rejecting Communist ideology did not entail breaking off all relations with Communist countries. Peace in the world depended on keeping communications open with one's adversaries.

This explains why, in 1963, Trudeau disapproved of the position taken by Secretary of State for External Affairs Lester B. Pearson. His reference to Pearson – by then leader of the Liberal Party – as the "defrocked prince of peace" has attracted much attention. In fact, contrary to general belief, Trudeau was merely quoting Pierre Vadeboncœur, who had coined the expression.[42] What is less known is that in 1950, Trudeau was already at odds with Pearson's policy, especially with respect to Taiwan and Korea. Unfortunately for our maverick, he was still working as a civil servant so he had no right to express his personal opinions in public. He let off steam by sharing his misgivings with sympathetic colleagues. On April 31, 1950, he wrote to Jules Léger, in the Prime Minister's Office: "I just heard Pearson's speech in the House on Korea. Not a single original thought. A bit of current events, a lot of propaganda. . . . We are losing Asia. It is time you save Europe at least. . . . You have no doubt seen the article in *Esprit* and Étienne Gilson's three latest articles in *Le Monde*. I would like to draw your attention to two more articles: 'Clean Hands,' by Maurice Duverger in *Le Monde* of August 3rd; 'Neutrality for Europe' by Hubert Beuve-Méry, and Raymond Aron in the *New York Times Magazine* of August 13th."[43] Trudeau, who was well aware of the neutralism/Atlantism debate then raging in France, did not just criticize, he also wanted to promote reflection. So he suggested that Léger read two articles by renowned French intellectuals with opposing viewpoints. Duverger, a lawyer and political analyst, was in favour of a neutral Europe, while the journalist and sociologist Raymond Aron advocated closer cooperation between Europe and North America in political, military, and economic matters.

On April 10, 1951, Pearson gave a speech entitled "Canadian Foreign Policy in a Two-Power World," a copy of which Trudeau obtained.[44] After paying tribute to the United States, on behalf of Canada, for the struggle against Communist imperialism, Pearson gave unconditional support to its policy in Korea. The world, he said, was in a perilous state: "The situation which faces us may erupt into an explosion at any time. . . . It may be a deliberate and controlled explosion brought about by the calculated policy of the hard-faced despots in the Kremlin, men hungry for power and world domination. Or more likely it may be an accidental one. . . . We should accept without any reservation the view that the Canadian who fires his rifle in Korea or on the Elbe is defending his home as surely as if he were firing it on his own soil."

Trudeau could barely contain his indignation. On April 28, 1951, he wrote to two colleagues, first to Lester Pearson's secretary, and then to another acquaintance, sharing with much pleasure "the following comment which the Official Secrets Act may prevent me from including in my forthcoming *Grammar of Dissent* (or the *Chronicle of a Sometime Resident of Tomb Town*)."[45] Trudeau was obviously playing on words, using *Grammar of Politics* by his favourite professor, Harold Laski, to poke fun at Pearson. As for the "sometime resident of Tomb Town," he was naturally referring to the "dead" city of Ottawa, from which he sought to escape as often as possible.

The rest of the letter adopted a more serious tone. By accusing the Kremlin leadership of being power-hungry despots bent on world domination, wrote Trudeau, Pearson was in fact contradicting "the reports on the situation in Russia and China sent back by two special envoys of the Canadian government." On the one hand, "Watkin's last dispatch from Moscow (March 29th) pictured Soviet Russia as a country of war-weary, peace-desiring people, naively proud of their primitive democratic institutions, and where the government was actively engaged in improving the economy, and was even proceeding with a certain amount of demobilization." On the other hand, "Ronning's last Report from Nanking (January 24th) was along similar lines: 'The fundamental problems of China (he wrote) are finally receiving the attention of Chinese leaders, and progress is being made in their solution for the benefit of the Chinese people as a whole.'" Pearson's position could therefore in no way be justified: "Either Mr. Pearson is unacquainted with such reports, and then he is not doing his job. Or being acquainted with them, he discounts their veracity, and then he is guilty of retaining the service of two Foreign Service officers who are gullible soviet stooges. Or believing in their veracity, he still prefers to spread the belief that Communists are intent on starting a war, and then he is misleading the people."

Moreover, Pearson was gutless and his foreign policy did not promote peace: "Wars are fought with physical courage, but in these times courage of a finer temper is required to affirm one's belief in truth and justice. If Mr. Pearson had that courage, would he not acquaint the public with facts which tend to open avenues of comprehension and sympathy towards the potential enemy? Or because our world is fractured, must we regard it as our duty to rend it completely asunder?" Peace perforce involves negotiating with enemies. It was not by demonizing them and spreading lies about them, as Pearson did, that war would be avoided. On the contrary. And, with a bit of ironic flourish, he signed "Comrade Trudeau."

Was Trudeau criticizing Pearson out of sympathy for the Soviet Union and China? Was he revealing secret Communist leanings in signing the letter "Comrade Trudeau"? Clearly, the letter suggests otherwise. He was above all criticizing Pearson's subservience to the United States, the illogical character of his position, and his unwillingness to engage in dialogue with the enemy, in order to avoid war. Throughout his life, Trudeau would argue that in international relations, peace necessarily involves negotiating with adversaries and even enemies. Refusing to talk to the enemy was no way to avoid war; on the contrary, the better way was to maintain open channels of communication.

———◆———

Trudeau could not derive much satisfaction from sending a private missive here and there to fellow colleagues in government. He wanted his views on Canadian foreign policy out in the open. Fortunately, he had been intimately involved with a magazine offering him a public outlet for a year now: *Cité libre*. On April 13, 1951, he sent his colleagues an article on the war, with an accompanying letter, highlighting the thorny problem he faced: "I have come across a ministerial decree dating back to the Laurier government, from which I quote the following: 'For an official to make a public attack upon a Minister of the Government under which he serves is a proceeding . . . that cannot with propriety be overlooked . . . a grave act of indiscretion and insubordination.'" So Trudeau could not sign his article. He proposed a tactical solution to get around the problem: sign the article "*Cité libre.*" But this tactic wouldn't fly: "By putting the masthead on the cover of *Cité libre*, listing the members of the editorial team, and then signing the article on war '*Cité libre,*' [the editors] are automatically contravening the above-mentioned decree." A second solution: "Sign the article with a pseudonym which would henceforth be used to identify me in the review." And if the article caused a big stir, what would he do? "Clearly I would come forth and identify myself." But these tactics ran against his temperament, and he knew the situation could not last: "I am more and more convinced that these tactics are only stop-gap measures. Because writing this article upset me so much that I was unable to work serenely in the office." His article, "Positions on the Current War," nonetheless appeared the following month, in the issue of May 1951. Under a pseudonym? Not at all. It was signed *Cité libre.* So how did the magazine get around the ministerial decree? Quite mysteriously, and for the only time in its history, someone *forgot* to include the masthead listing all the members of the editorial board. . . . .

Trudeau presented his thesis in the opening words of the article: "War is not the greatest of evils, and we do not consider peace the ultimate benefit. Because what matters most of all is justice; and arms must sometimes be taken up to defend it. But the goal being sought is not victory itself, nor peace alone, but rather the preservation or restoration of justice."[46] Note his use of the personal pronoun "we" in place of "I." This choice was dictated by the fact the article was signed *Cité libre.* But it is clear that Trudeau was expressing his own opinion. His position had changed considerably since 1942: he now accepted that the pursuit of justice could require resorting to arms. This is why farther on in the article he considered himself a peace-seeking person and not a pacifist. He put forth a key question about Korea: "Is the huge expansion of this conflict, brought about by the intervention of the United Nations, directly geared toward achieving a greater good than the massacre which it is causing?"[47] His answer left no room for doubt: "With respect to what is good for Korea itself, the answer is clearly No. It is impossible to imagine that the blitzkrieg unleashed by the North Koreans and the subsequent unification of all Korea under a communist and even totally atheist government could produce for the combatants, non-combatants and refugees as many collective and singular injustices, as much blind slaughter, as much abominable destruction and hallucinating terror as is actually resulting from the military intervention of the United Nations."

Trudeau gave several examples from international politics to underline the injustices committed by some Western countries. American foreign policy is particularly criticized. "The Americans . . . undeniably seek emancipation and self-government for all countries. However, they also want to make sure liberated nations become American-style democracies, that is, friendly to private enterprise and large landed estates. . . . They don't realize that capitalism rings hollow in countries with 80% illiteracy rates and where the average annual income is below $40 per person. How can we not see the total failure of American diplomacy, which preaches the democratic Gospel around the world, but then denies peoples the right to use their new freedom to build an economic system that deviates from *the biggest and the best?*"[48] U.S. diplomacy, he said, had gone astray because of Americans' "delirious fear of socialism." This is why "*Cité libre* has no choice but to declare its conscientious objection to a conflict such as this one."[49] Some might ask ironically: "Are you going to fight once Soviet troops reach the Ottawa River?"[50] Trudeau had anticipated the question. He replied without flinching that he would fight "when the fratricides to which we consent in waging war are *absolutely* essential to prevent a greater evil, and when our intervention is *clearly* directed towards the restoration of justice rather than the mere will to vanquish."[51] This brings to mind an earlier paper he had written at Harvard. He then maintained, and continued to maintain, that precisely that amount of force should be applied which is needed to meet the stated objectives, in this case the restoration of justice. Nothing more, nothing less.

What conclusions did Trudeau draw about Canada's position on the Korean conflict? He saved his harshest criticism for the conclusion. He accused Pearson and Prime Minister St. Laurent of being "puppets of one of the parties involved." One had only to read Pearson's speech of February 2, 1951, in the House of Commons "to understand how pathetic vision becomes when it is used as the handmaiden of cowardice." As proof, he cited a long list of actions showing Canada's servility to the United States. Unable to refrain himself, he added: "Ye gods! Does this mean we should forever give up the hope of seeing a Canadian public figure, standing squarely on his hind legs, committing a single independent gesture? What is so sacred about maintaining the unity of Western nations that Canada should refrain from seeking the truth wherever it may lie? Is it somehow inconceivable that Canada should ever benefit from its position as a small nation to develop and promote a foreign policy based on mutual assistance rather than on domination, exploitation or rushing after commercial opportunities?"[52] Many years later, Trudeau the prime minister would not think that differently – much to the displeasure of Canada's neighbour to the south. Could the courage of Fidel Castro, head of state of a tiny island, "standing squarely on his hind legs," defying the greatest power in the world, explain at least partly why Trudeau always maintained such a friendly attitude toward him?

He shot one last bullet in his conclusion: "We would like [the government] to seek wholeheartedly to remedy the injustices we commit because of our servility toward some powers and our hatred of some others; for we would find it painful to be forced eventually to disobey, in both civil and military matters."[53]

We can now understand why he wrote to his friends at *Cité libre* that writing the article had made him "unable to work serenely in the office." It doesn't take a trained psychologist to see that this situation was untenable. On September 28, 1951, Trudeau sent his letter of resignation to the Clerk of the Privy Council, Norman Robertson,* with whom he had always maintained friendly relations marked by mutual esteem: "My work with the Privy Council has been to me a constant source of satisfaction, and not infrequently of delight. I have never ceased to be aware of the precedence in your mind of human beings over institutions, and this in itself has been a valuable lesson. As for fellow workers, I cannot imagine a more sympathetic lot. But now I feel that I can be of more use in another place. So with your permission, I shall leave the office on the 6th of October 1951."[54] And with that touch of humour

---

* Not to be confused with Gordon Robertson, his immediate superior.

that characterizes all his writings, he added: "I dare to hope that the structure of central government will not be too badly shattered by my departure." He ended with a few words in French: "Adieu grand Homme! Je vous serre la main très cordialement et avec reconnaissance." ("Farewell great man! I convey to you my cordial good wishes and my gratitude.") Norman Robertson recognized talent when he saw it and believed Trudeau had what it took to pursue a brilliant career in public service. He tried to convince him to reconsider his decision: "Why? You are useful here and we need men like you. You have a good future if you stay here. Why leave?" "Because I want to return to Quebec," Trudeau replied. " . . . Right now Quebec is where the important battles are being fought. That's where I can be most useful."[55]

With the Privy Council behind him, a major gap in Trudeau's careful training had been filled. He had attended some of the most prestigious universities, then familiarized himself with worldwide political realities and the struggles of many peoples. Then, on his return to Canada, he realized he lacked practical training in the administration of governmental affairs. Now, mission accomplished. Thus, over the years, Trudeau, free of any financial worries, had patiently and systematically acquired the knowledge needed to exercise statesmanship.

Trudeau now had to map out his future. He was a lawyer, so why not work as a labour arbitrator? He asked Jean Marchand, whom he had befriended when they fought side by side during the Asbestos strike, to look into the prospects of landing a job in this area. One thing was certain: between October 6, 1951, and November 8, 1965, when he was elected a Liberal member of Parliament, Trudeau felt free – free to vent his indignation, free to write whatever he pleased, free to openly join the editorial board of *Cité libre* and promote democratic and liberal values, free to explore parts of the planet that he had not yet visited . . . Free, free, free.

But before embarking on this new stage in his life, he needed oxygen and wide-open spaces. He was irresistibly drawn to distant lands. On October 24, he boarded the passenger liner *Ile de France,* headed on a very long journey, which put on hold his tumultuous relationship with the young and beautiful Helen Segerstråle. He also put on hold his involvement in *Cité libre,* a project that in his own words was *"utterly exciting."* But what, precisely, was *Cité libre* all about?

Chapter 8

THE BIRTH OF *CITÉ LIBRE*

Among this band of righteous men who fought to maintain the Christian sense of human dignity in the first rank of political principles, History will acknowledge with some astonishment that two of them were Marxist Jews who constantly distinguished themselves by their intelligence, valour and tireless generosity.

— PIERRE ELLIOT TRUDEAU, 1950[*]

IN 1993, THE POLITICAL SCIENTIST Léon Dion wrote: "*Cité libre* now exerts a magical attraction on many people who never read it or even held a copy in their hands."[1] Indeed, most students of this period confirm that *Cité libre* made an important contribution in ushering in what is now called the "Quiet Revolution." Others, however, consider its reputation overrated. In 1976, Georges-Émile Lapalme stated categorically: "Nowadays, people speak of *Cité libre* as if it had played some decisive role. In fact, it never played any role whatsoever."[2] Lapalme was hardly a nonentity: when *Cité libre* first came out, in 1950, he was the leader of the provincial Liberal Party and Leader of the Opposition from 1952 to 1960. By the time he wrote these caustic remarks, he had already served as vice-premier in Jean Lesage's government from 1960 to 1964, attorney-general from 1960 to 1963, and minister of cultural affairs from 1961 to 1964. One detail is worth noting, however: Lapalme and the Liberal Party were among *Cité libre*'s

---

[*] *Cité Libre*, vol. 1, no. 1, June 1950, pp. 37–38. Trudeau was honouring the memory of Léon Blum and Harold Laski.

prime targets. This example shows just how difficult it is to assess the historical significance of the magazine.

The same problem arises regarding Trudeau's role at *Cité libre*. According to Gérard Pelletier, his articles were the most sought-after: "An issue of the magazine without his name on the table of contents seemed dull even to our least demanding readers."[3] Lapalme would not, of course, agree with this judgment. He wrote contemptuously of his 1952 interview: "I remember an academic meeting: whereas I bore responsibility for a political party, he was responsible only for himself. Every word I said could potentially lead to public uproar, whereas he could say what he liked, and it would fall on deaf ears in the general public."[4] Did Trudeau shout himself hoarse in the wilderness? Did his articles generate no response whatever? Léon Dion was perhaps less extreme in his interpretation of Trudeau's influence, but he nonetheless wrote that "it was above all in *Vrai*, in 1958, that Trudeau made his meagre contribution to genuine political thought."[5] If Trudeau's writings in *Vrai* amounted only to "a meagre contribution," then what are we to make of his writings in *Cité libre* or elsewhere?

Like his colleague Léon Dion, political scientist Gérard Bergeron believed that Trudeau was seen as a "political philosopher," because in Canada the title is bandied about indiscriminately. Without his compelling personality, "his writings would never have been taken seriously."[6] Besides, he added, his articles were quickly subjected to widespread criticism in the academic world, and rightly so; while he undeniably was a skilled polemicist, he lacked creativity. Bergeron also deplored "the poverty of his bibliographic sources and the influences he acknowledged."[7] In other words, he had a lot of flair, and not much substance. Bergeron went on to say that the Quiet Revolution "took place without Trudeau,"[8] adding, however, that Trudeau was "the intellectual idol of French-speaking Quebec in the 1950s."[9] How odd . . .

Claude Ryan, long-time publisher of *Le Devoir* and leader of the Quebec Liberal Party at the time of the first referendum on Quebec's secession in May 1980, held much the same view: "A bit naively, I believe the generation of *Cité libre* came to revere Pierre Elliott Trudeau as the prototype of the 'political scientist.'* However, Trudeau . . . was never a

---

* Ryan used the English expression "political scientist" in his French text.

true master of political science. One searches in vain for any original contribution he might have made to the discipline. He did not write any systematic works on these issues."[10]

So, why did Trudeau, a so-called thinker without either originality or creativity, receive the President's Medal from the University of Western Ontario in 1958, for "Some Obstacles to Democracy in Quebec," rated the best scholarly article of the year? Why did he receive so many invitations to scholarly meetings that he had to decline many of them? And why was he made a Fellow of the Royal Society of Canada in 1964? The Royal Society is, after all, one of the most prestigious institutions in the country – not just anyone is admitted to its ranks. Given all these negative evaluations, we wonder how so many intellectuals could have so poorly gauged the quality of his thoughts that they ended up "revering" him. But let's point out an important detail: most of these critical assessments were written many years after Trudeau had entered the political arena, stirring up public passions. This seems to have affected his critics' memory – and memory is unreliable even at the best of times, since it holds up a distorting lens to reality. A single example will illustrate our contention.

Guy Cormier was one of the very first contributors to *Cité libre*. In the January 14, 1978, issue of *Le Devoir,* he claimed it was only through Gérard Pelletier's vigorous intervention that Trudeau was accepted as part of the magazine's editorial board. He remembered that at one of their early meetings, someone said: "I do not want to have Trudeau as part of the team. He is not with our people; he will never be with our people."[11] Of course, by "our people" Cormier meant "*pure laine* Quebeckers" or "French Canadians of old stock." If one were to believe Cormier, the other contributors did not accept Trudeau as a "real" French Canadian. It has been claimed so often that Trudeau had identity problems that this "truth" might seem self-evident. But was Cormier accurately reporting what that mysterious "someone" at the meeting had actually said? Not according to Pelletier. To him, Cormier was committing an error of historical perspective: "In 1950, in fact, we didn't refer to *our* people, but to *the* people." Given the strongly pro–working-class stance of the *Cité libre* team and Trudeau's upper-middle-class background, "the comrade who made the remark was afraid that Trudeau would betray a social class, not an ethnic group."[12] Pelletier added: "Our vocabulary was not nationalist."

We fully agree with Pelletier and will even go further. We maintain that until the late 1950s, the idea of Trudeau belonging to "the French-Canadian people" was not questioned, even by the most hardened nationalists. His many opponents "discovered" his middle name Elliott – the irrefutable proof of his mixed origins! – only once he assailed their own positions and interpreted French-Canadian history in a manner not at all to their liking. That is when they began noticing the shallowness of his political philosophy and the poverty of his bibliographic sources.

What was *Cité libre*? We do not plan to give an exhaustive answer to the question. But since Trudeau's name is forever associated with it, we believe that a brief outline of its positions and values, especially in its early years, is necessary. All of the original members of the editorial board came from the Jeunesse étudiante catholique. Trudeau, having attended an "elite" school, was the only exception. Pelletier recalled that "he went to school at a Jesuit shop where the Jeunesse étudiante catholique had never set foot!"[13] (This may explain the reference to his "bourgeois" – upper-middle-class – upbringing.)

The masthead of the very first issue, dated June 1950, identifies the members of the "Editorial Team" in the following order: Maurice Blain, Guy Cormier, Réginald Boisvert, Jean-Paul Geoffroy, Pierre Juneau, Roger Rolland, Gérard Pelletier, and Pierre Elliott Trudeau. Charles-A. Lussier's name was added to the list, starting in December 1951, and Pierre Vadeboncoeur's in November 1953. From February 1955 onwards, all references to the editorial board disappeared. A new administrative structure emerged, and the names of only two directors appeared: Pierre-E. Trudeau and Gérard Pelletier, followed by that of Pauline Lamy, "secretary to the editorial board." That Trudeau's name appeared ahead of Pelletier's in all subsequent issues suggests he was the key figure. However, Jean-Philippe Warren wrote in 1999 that Gérard Pelletier was the "principal founder and guiding member of *Cité libre*"[14] and that he "was generally thought of as the director of *Cité libre* who left a deep mark on the magazine."[15] Warren saw *Cité libre* through a prism that magnified Pelletier's role and attributed his positions to those of the magazine as a whole. In so doing, he greatly minimized Trudeau's contribution. But the facts tell a different story.

According to many eye-witness accounts, from June 1950 onwards, a number of people orbited around the team – Gérard Pelletier's wife, Alex Pelletier, for example – although they were not officially part of the editorial board. In our view, what is important is that a small group of individuals, including Trudeau, set out on this adventure with enthusiasm. From the very first issue, in a text signed "the Editor," but most likely the work of Pelletier, the "Citélibristes"* explained they wanted to break the silence they had had to endure for several years already: "*Cité libre* therefore proposes to serve as a meeting-point for supporters of this necessary resistance. *Cité libre* will create study groups, working sessions; it will serve as the springboard for action." Modest objectives, resolute action, threadbare finances. None of the original team members could have imagined that the magazine would survive as long as it did. In fact, *Cité libre* went through three distinct "incarnations." The first one, from 1950 to 1959, roughly coincided with the last decade of the Union Nationale regime of Maurice Duplessis. The second incarnation, from 1960 to 1965, during the Liberal regime of Jean Lesage, coincided with the rising nationalism symbolized by the slogan "Maîtres chez nous" ("Masters of our own house"), and with the euphoria of the so-called Quiet Revolution. The third incarnation, not discussed in this volume, covered the years 1991 to 2000: Anne-Marie Bourdhouxe, Gérard Pelletier's daughter, ran the magazine from 1991 to 1995, followed by us from 1995 to 2000, in a period marked by the nerve-wracking second referendum on Quebec's secession.

Cité libre announced in its very first issue that it would be a quarterly publication, and it restated this intention right up to the twenty-third and last issue of the first series, in May 1959. Despite this bold statement of intention, the magazine came out four times a year on only two occasions – in 1955 and 1958. In fact, more often than not, the magazine appeared only twice a year and was even down to one issue per year in 1956 and 1959. Given its small circulation (originally five hundred copies) and such unpredictable publication dates, it is tempting to conclude that its impact was marginal. But from the first issue, reactions flew thick and fast. Pelletier explained they were of two kinds:

---

* "Citélibriste" is the name given to contributors to the review, but also eventually to the review's most loyal readers.

"enthusiastic reception or angry disapproval."[16] *Cité libre* continued to make waves and raise passions. It was banned in many schools, where students could read it only on the sly. One of Pelletier's friends was teaching abroad and wrote to him: "Really, I don't understand it. All the Quebec papers I get here allude to *Cité libre* so often, you'd think it was a daily, though you can't even manage to come out four times a year!"[17]

"Our newspapers are overflowing with streams of rubbish," wrote Pelletier, speaking on behalf of the editorial board. "We are constantly threatened by a dogmatic vision of the world which is hard to overcome, and has nothing Christian or even living about it."[18] *Cité libre* sought to liberate French Canadians from the crushing yoke of this mind-numbing culture. This did not mean freeing them from religion; quite the contrary. All contributors bore witness to their faith and proudly upheld a Christian conception of man and society. This is not to suggest that they spoke with a single voice. Divergences arose from the first issue and raged till the very last. Let's provide some examples.

In Volume 1, Number 1, Pelletier articulated the magazine's mission as the search for holiness. His inspiration came from a chance encounter with a twenty-year-old man: "He said the word 'grace' and the word changed colour, became current and mysterious, enigmatic and fascinating. . . . The things of God came back to life and we felt flooded with light. Because a layman simply offered holiness to us."[19] To Pelletier, this was the ideal to which they ought to aspire. Two years later, in July 1952, he wrote: "We know the revival we are seeking will not be produced by our articles, but will flow instead from the degree of love all Christians invest in their lives – this includes the bishops, the clergy and the laity."[20] In 1957, he continued to attribute Quebec's political stagnation to the crisis of religion and laid his hopes for social renewal in Christianity: "Where shall we find the strength to resist the intoxication of reassuring lies? . . . I happen to think that it will be in the living sources of Christianity. . . . What the Christian finds within the Church community is the constant challenge of seeking perfection and the quest for truth."[21]

Holiness, perfection, the quest for truth. These were Pelletier's ideals, but it was not the kind of Christianity French-Canadian youth had been taught: "When the Gospel's moral demands and underlying revolutionary violence are removed from Church teachings, the Gospel itself ends up being watered down."[22] We should note here that Pelletier condones revolutionary violence. As we have seen, this position is similar to that of Mounier and his review, *Esprit*. This revolution was both spiritual and material and sought to combat the twin evils of capitalism and totalitarianism. All his life, Pelletier admired Mounier, claiming that *Cité libre* adhered to the ideals of *Esprit*. This evident admiration appeared in the very first issue of June 1950.

In March, just a few months before the birth of *Cité libre,* three notable figures died – Emmanuel Mounier, Harold Laski, and Léon Blum. The magazine paid tribute to them in two unsigned pieces. This resulted in a misunderstanding that persists to this day. Trudeau's official biographer, John English, for example, attributes these articles to Trudeau and claims they reflect his thinking: "In the June 1950 premier issue, Trudeau wrote tributes to three giants who had recently died: the French socialist leader Léon Blum and his own intellectual mentors Emmanuel Mounier and Harold Laski."[23] And since English believes Trudeau was the one to have written these articles, he also believes it was Trudeau who wrote that "[Mounier's] influence touched every page of *Cité libre*. . . . So great was his impact that the journal's founders had hoped to give him the first copy of the new magazine."

However, we had the privilege of consulting Trudeau's personal copy and discovered that he wrote by hand "GP" next to the article on Mounier and "PET" next to the article on Laski and Bloom. We thus know for certain that Pelletier wrote the tribute to Mounier, while Trudeau wrote the second one.[24] Indeed, these two texts illustrate the differences in the men's philosophical and political thoughts. For Pelletier, the principles underlying *Cité libre* came directly from Mounier. He wrote: "*Cité libre* was born under the sign of *Esprit,* and faithful to the very same values for which Mounier fought to the last. . . . The most casual reader can find on every page of *Cité libre* [evidence of] the influence exerted on each of us by *Esprit*."[25] The discovery of *Esprit* greatly satisfied Pelletier as it enriched his progressive outlook. Previously he had known only Catholic Action movements, within which he struggled against the retrograde Church of the 1930s. (In 1934, on returning from Canada to France, Jacques Maritain told Emmanuel Mounier, "During the visit, I faced obscurantism right up close."[26])

In this article, Pelletier's sense of gratitude toward Mounier is palpable: "I wonder whether non-conservative Christians will ever give enough

credit to the Christian light that *Esprit* shines ahead of them."[27] The fact
that this article was unsigned gives the impression that it reflected the
views of the entire editorial team. True, Mounier had a great influence
on Pelletier and on some other Citélibristes. But not on all of them, and
certainly not to the same extent on Trudeau. He had studied in the greatest universities of America and Europe and had drawn inspiration from
several sources. His intellectual background included Mounier among
many others. His ideals were not inspired by *Esprit*. Even his personalism owed more to Maritain and Berdyaev. One of many proofs of this is
found in the eloquent tribute he paid to the two Jewish socialists, Harold
Laski and Léon Blum.

———————

Why did Trudeau choose to honour Léon Blum, who appears nowhere
in his notes and does not seem even to have inhabited his intellectual
universe? Blum, a man of great culture, was both the first socialist and
the first Jew to serve as prime minister of France. He held the position a
first time in 1936–1937, and again in 1938 during the government of the
"Popular Front," the name generally given to the coalition of left-leaning
parties then in power. During his brief term in office, workers made significant gains: the forty-hour week, paid holidays, the right to collective
bargaining on wage claims, and many others. Blum survived the Second
World War, including two years in the Buchenwald concentration camp.
Then, from December 1946 to January 1947, he led the last provisional
government before the creation of the Fourth Republic, at the very time
when Trudeau was in Paris. Blum was hated and reviled by Charles
Maurras, Robert Brasillach, Léon Daudet, and the French anti-Semitic
extreme right, a group whose writings Trudeau and the French-Canadian
nationalist elite had read rapturously. Léon Daudet, for instance, wrote
of Blum: "We need a man, not a Jew."[28] Charles Maurras considered
him "human garbage . . . here's a man who should be shot, but in the
back."[29] In writing the tribute to Blum, was Trudeau trying to set the
record straight and show where he now stood?

Whereas Pelletier stressed what *Cité libre* and all Christians owed to
Mounier, Trudeau stressed what all humanity owed to Léon Blum and
Harold Laski: "Among this band of righteous men who fought to uphold
the Christian sense of human dignity in the first rank of political

principles, History will acknowledge with some astonishment that two of them were Marxist Jews who distinguished themselves by their intelligence, valour and unfailing generosity."[30] Could Trudeau have paid a more gracious tribute to the two men? He wanted to make clear that so-called Christian values were not the exclusive preserve of Christians. He continued in his praise: "Blum was one of the bright lights of the École Normale; Laski had already revealed precocious genius while at Oxford; they both had an admirable command of spoken and written language. But both preferred to let their energies flow towards action. Their influence extended far beyond the borders of their respective countries. Both were read, discussed and admired wherever a group of men fired by vigilant idealism committed themselves to political action."[31] Needless to say, these two men who represented the ideal Trudeau had pursued since his youth had many admirers around the world, "but most of all they had implacable enemies, and this is, in a way, the tragic sign of their greatness and of our pettiness. On both sides of the Iron Curtain, the names of Blum and Laski inspired unquenchable hatred." Why were they hated so much? Because they did not howl with the wolves, and they dared to criticize certain aspects of their own ideology: "They were somehow the enemy within, the consciences that refused to toe the line. They were socialists and yet they rejected Stalinism. They were democrats, and yet criticized capitalism."[32] Did Trudeau know that his opponents would one day also consider him "the enemy within"?

Although he was full of praise for these men, he did not forget their weaknesses: "[Blum's] positions were doubtless courageous, but sometimes lacked realism, for the same reason that Laski's sometimes lacked consistency: Since a life devoted to action prevented these idealists from dwelling on perfection, they deliberately chose to commit their errors out of overconfidence rather than excessive caution." Trudeau already knew – and life in politics would bear this out – that political action and perfectionism were incompatible. But he also knew that the struggle for justice and respect for human dignity requires action. Mistakes were bound to occur along the way.

In his article Trudeau quietly distanced himself from Mounier and *Esprit*, as he did on many later occasions. He identified the wellspring of "his" *Cité libre*: "[Laski's] door was always open to those who strove for justice, and he greeted heads of state and poor students with equal naturalness. He sought to universalize this affectionate generosity into political systems. *His huge contribution, through his writings and his deeds, has been a continuous search for the* cité libre* –, where men could live in tolerance, and ultimately love one another."[33] Trudeau's gratitude and emotion infused every sentence. Clearly for him, it was Laski – not Mounier – who personified the ideal of the *cité libre.* Jews and Christians, and people from all creeds, freely mingled in this city founded on tolerance. No need to proclaim one's beliefs.

Pelletier tirelessly maintained that *Cité libre* upheld the "personalist" values of Mounier and *Esprit,* and as a result many have concluded that personalism – a very popular school of thought among left-wing Catholics, in France and in Quebec – was necessarily linked to Mounier's thought. E.-Martin Meunier and Philippe Warren, for example, devoted many studies to the role of Catholicism in the modernization of Quebec and concluded that personalism was the cornerstone of the Quiet Revolution. The titles of some of their studies bear witness to this perspective. For example, in 1999, Warren published an article in the review *Société* entitled "Gérard Pelletier et *Cité libre:* la mystique personnaliste de la Révolution tranquille" [Gérard Pelletier and *Cité libre:* The Personalist Mysticism of the Quiet Revolution].[34] In 2002, Meunier and Warren jointly authored a work entitled *Sortir de la "Grande noirceur": L'horizon "personnaliste" de la Révolution tranquille* [Emerging from the "Great Darkness": The "Personalist" Horizon of the Quiet Revolution].[35] Warren maintained that *Esprit* had become akin to a new Bible to French Canadians. In a formula, which he acknowledged as somewhat simplistic, he claimed that "in the Catholic French Canada of the 1930s, everyone thought along the same lines as *L'Action française,* whereas twenty years later, everyone thought along the same lines as *Esprit.*"[36] Since our own study bears less on the origins of the Quiet Revolution than on the development of Trudeau's ideas, the question before us is whether, like "everyone," he thought along the same lines as *Esprit.* Since he was one of the founders of *Cité libre,* many people have jumped to the conclusion that, indeed, that was the case.

---

* Our italics.

This is the view taken by André Burelle, political adviser and French-language speechwriter to Prime Minister Trudeau from 1977 to 1984. In a book highly critical of his former boss, he claims that Trudeau had abandoned the "communitarian personalism of Mounier and Maritain" that he originally professed in *Cité libre,* in favour of a "legal, individualistic and republican liberalism, which he proudly proclaimed, at the time of the 1982 repatriation of the Constitution, as the founding principle of a new 'Canadian nation.'"[37] This, to Burelle, was proof that Trudeau once shared the "communitarian personalist" values of Mounier and Maritain. Was this really the case?

In 1990, in his article titled "The Values of a Just Society," Trudeau wrote: "The very adoption of a constitutional charter is in keeping with the purest liberalism, according to which all members of a civil society enjoy certain fundamental, inalienable rights and cannot be deprived of them by any collectivity (state or government) or on behalf of any collectivity (nation, ethnic group, religious group or other). To use Maritain's phrase, they are 'human personalities.'"[38] Here was Maritain being quoted once more. Again, in *Memoirs,* published in 1993, Trudeau wrote: "Thanks to two French thinkers, Jacques Maritain and Emmanuel Mounier, I never came to believe in the doctrine of absolute liberalism."[39] Trudeau rarely referred to Mounier, and when he did, he almost always mentioned Maritain in the same breath, to whose thoughts he showed boundless appreciation. In other words, these two thinkers, especially Maritain, helped him avoid the pitfall of precisely the type of liberalism Burelle is pinning on him.

Since Mounier and Maritain both claim to be "personalists," they are often lumped together, without drawing any distinctions. But were their ideas so similar? Did they defend the same type of personalism? And, while we're at it, what is personalism? This philosophy and movement has been thoroughly studied, so we will provide only a brief sketch. How did Trudeau define personalism? In an admittedly vague caption he claimed that it was "a philosophy that reconciles the individual and society."[40] With such a catchall definition, it would be hard to find a non-personalist philosopher! Mounier himself stressed the vagueness of this label: "We are well aware of the lazy or flashy use many will make of this label to conceal the vacuity or uncertainty of their own thinking. . . . Personalism is for us merely a useful password, a convenient collective designation for various doctrines."[41] According to Jean-Marie Domenach, director of *Esprit* from 1957 to 1976, personalism is not "a doctrine, it is not an ideology, it is an inspiration. . . . It is the idea according to which human beings can be perfected, which is the very axis of our tradition and our progress."[42] With such broad definitions, it is understandable that it has given rise to many diverse interpretations.

Goulven Boudic highlights the difficulties posed by the term "personalism" in his exhaustive study of *Esprit* in the years 1944 to 1982. He notes first that the word had been used before Mounier by authors such as Arnaud Dandieu and Denis de Rougemont and also, as we have seen, by Nicolas Berdyaev, who thoroughly examined it and made it his own. In Boudic's view, Mounier managed to impose his own definition of this term through his work and publications. However, Mounier himself stressed in *Qu'est-ce que le personnalisme?* [What Is Personalism?] that his own ideas had gone through various stages. Boudic rightly concludes: "We therefore cannot speak of a single version of personalism, but rather of a succession of periods and projects, marked by inflections and adaptations of the initial version."[43] Like Mounier himself, Burelle acknowledges the existence of several variants of personalism (atheist, existentialist, etc.), and deliberately restricts himself to the personalism of Mounier and Maritain. But in accusing Trudeau of having betrayed the "communitarian personalism" of Mounier and Maritain, he implies repeatedly in his book that these two thinkers advocated the same kind of personalism. In Quebec, most scholars have adopted this view, with rare exceptions, such as the historian John Hellman.[44] We concur with Hellman's position: indeed, Mounier and Maritain both claimed to be "personalists," yet their views were often antithetical.

Let's first look at Mounier. Since we already reviewed the core of his positions, in Chapter 3, we will merely refresh the reader's memory. Communism was at the height of its glory in France in the immediate post-war period, and Mounier and *Esprit* joined the chorus of converts. They claimed not only to be leftists but also followers of Marx, "of the Marx arriving in triumph from the East, mounted on the liberating tanks of the Red Army."[45] *Esprit* at the time was resolutely in favour of communism, the Soviet Union, and the French Communist Party. To Winock, this was the "philocommunist" stage of the review's history.[46] Mounier argued that revolution was necessary because reforms alone could not solve the problems of a frozen society. Bringing on the revolution meant resorting to extra-parliamentary means, including sweeping aside the rights and freedoms characterizing liberal democracies. In dismissing this ineffective type of democracy in favour of the far superior model of "mass democracy," the review ended up justifying the repressive policies of the Soviet regime: "In some countries [these freedoms . . .] momentarily appear to be incompatible, and when this happens, it is not a betrayal of democracy but rather a way of serving it to subordinate its formal aspects to its overarching goal which is the material and moral elevation of man – the man of the masses, and not just the man of some caste."[47] It is abundantly clear that for Mounier, "collective rights" should take precedence over individual rights in certain circumstances. We can therefore understand the attraction his "communitarian personalism" exerted on many French-Canadian intellectuals, including Burelle.

Mounier and *Esprit* were strongly opposed to liberal democracy. Boudic summarizes their position as follows: "In its capitalist attires, political liberalism is explicitly posited as an outdated system and political philosophy, the invocation of which may even denote reactionary and counter-revolutionary behaviour."[48] Mounier was openly anti-capitalist and anti-American. To him, the hoped-for personalist revolution was threatened by the United States, not the Soviet Union,[49] a view *Esprit* perpetuated even after Mounier's death. In 1952, the magazine continued to denounce "the evils which American culture is imposing on our country and which strike at the very heart of the mental and moral cohesion of the European peoples."[50] Four years later, America still took the brunt of this attack: "What can we expect from American civilization, which mocks and caricatures the spiritual traditions of the West and brings humanity down to a horizontal existence, devoid of any inner dimensions?"[51]

Unlike Mounier, Jacques Maritain loved America and knew it well.[52] He had frequently visited the United States and Canada since the early 1930s; he spent the war years in the United States; he strongly condemned the fascist Vichy regime from day one; and he zealously supported the Allied forces. He did not return to France until the Liberation in 1944. In *Le crépuscule de la civilisation* [The Twilight of Civilization], published in Montreal in 1941, he praised American democracy and was delighted to observe "the reconciliation which is now in progress, after more than a century of destructive conflict, between freedom, democracy and religion."[53] Maritain tirelessly defended the primacy of human rights as "an essential characteristic of any civilization worthy of the name." In *Les droits de l'homme* [The Rights of Man and Natural Law], published clandestinely in France in 1940, then republished in New York in 1942, he stated that "in defence of human rights, just as in the defence of liberty, we must be ready to give our lives."[54] His liberal ideas were recognized the world over and resulted in his being called on to take an active part in drafting the Universal Declaration of Human Rights of the United Nations, which was adopted in 1948 by the General Assembly of the United Nations.

Maritain was a pro-American democrat and liberal and showed no sympathy whatever for Soviet Communism or any regime sacrificing the rights of the person in the name of the community. He acknowledged, however, that "civil society is not solely made up of individuals but also of particular societies which they create."[55] Some people, including Burelle, take this statement to mean that Maritain advocated "communitarian personalism." Let us take a closer look at his position as he succinctly summarized it: "A nation is a community of people who become aware of themselves as history has made them, who treasure their own past, and who love one another as they know or imagine themselves to be. . . . The nation has rights, *which are but the rights of human persons to participate in the particular human values of a specific national heritage.*"* To him, the nation has no rights other than those conferred on each of its individual members.[56] (This, as we have seen, was also Berdyaev's position.)

To Maritain it was imperative that the nation-state be pluralistic. Constituted of particular societies, it could not and should not espouse any specific religion. After the war, the Vatican newspaper *Osservatore Romano* called on the French people to abandon the secular and anticlerical laws "which had hurt them so badly" and become a Catholic country once again. François Mauriac, the well-known profoundly catholic writer, was sharply opposed to this position: "In a country inhabited by Catholics, Protestants, Jews, atheists, rationalists, Marxists, not to mention the hope of France, the happy crowd of existentialists, and where all faiths, all refutations, all attitudes of mind have their supporters and their converts, the state (unless it is totalitarian) should remain

---

*   Our italics.

outside the sphere of influence of a particular doctrine and religion, and should dominate them all."[57] This is exactly the point of view Maritain had already supported in *Humanisme intégral* [True Humanism]. This form of pluralism, typically associated with liberalism, Maritain defended as a Christian value: "In our modern society, believers and unbelievers live together." Imposing on all the same faith is therefore "unacceptable for a Christian."[58] Trudeau would always defend this view.

This brief comparison shows that Mounier and Maritain were far from sharing the same conception of "personalism." Although Mounier was committed to the Christian principle of the primacy of the person, under certain circumstances he accepted the suppression of individual freedom in the name of "collective rights." He was hostile to capitalism and parliamentary democracy and flaunted his anti-Americanism. Maritain, on the other hand, was hostile to communism. He was a democrat and liberal, who liked America and its political system. To him, individual rights were of paramount importance. It was individuals within the nation, not the nation itself, who had rights, and these rights had to be embedded in a constitution in order to protect them from the will of their rulers. Clearly, then, to speak of a *single* philosophy shared by Mounier and Maritain is to make a much too sweeping generalization. In fact, when Trudeau and Pelletier were in Paris, Maritain and Mounier had been going their separate ways for many years. Although Maritain was one of the founders of *Esprit,* he had long stopped contributing anything to the review.

There is simply no article by Trudeau in *Cité libre,* or anywhere else, professing Burelle/Mounier-style "communitarian personalism," nor is there any particular emphasis on personalism itself as a major source of his political thought. On the other hand, while we found abundant references to Maritain in Trudeau's personal papers, there was no trace of any special appreciation of *Esprit* or of Mounier's ideas.

Indeed, when *Esprit* decided in 1952 to devote an entire issue to French Canada, Trudeau's name did not appear among the contributors.[59] A coincidence? Perhaps. But Trudeau had profound disagreements with positions taken by *Esprit,* as the following example indicates. For the television series on *Memoirs,* Trudeau had an interview, in 1993, with Jean-Marie Domenach, the director of *Esprit.* Although the conversation was conducted in a civil tone, it was marked by some tension from the very beginning.[60] Trudeau reminded him that "at a certain point, you came out strongly supporting Quebec nationalism." Domenach agreed and went on to explain that since Quebec was threatened to the core, it was right to enact laws protecting its French identity, even if they infringed on personal liberty. Like Mounier, he argued that in some cases, collective rights take precedence over those of the individual. That, he told Trudeau, is "what separated me from your perspective, because I said: 'Survival is a prerequisite.' Democracy is fine, but survival is a prerequisite. . . . If the Québécois people exist no longer, . . . then what good will democracy be?" And as a way of restoring the bond of friendship between them, Domenach added: "This is what separated us. And the fact we can say so, loud and clear, is just wonderful."

If Domenach felt it was "wonderful" to be able to talk about this divergence of opinion thirty years later, one can surmise that the wounds had not completely healed. But Trudeau would not let go. He reminded him: "And besides, we agreed on a common point, namely that the collectivity does not embody values. It is the individual, the person, who embodies values. . . . And when we talk about collective rights . . . we should not use this idea to crush individual rights." Domenach agreed but continued to defend collective rights. In 1993, the rift between the two men had not yet ended. So can it be claimed that Trudeau has betrayed the "communitarian personalism" of *Esprit* and Emmanuel Mounier? Hardly. In fact, he never adhered to this view. Like Maritain, he defended the inalienable rights of the person.

———※———

Let us stress the fact that *Cité libre* did not speak with one single voice. Far from it! While all, or nearly all, contributors believed that they were true to the Church's authentic teachings, there was a wide range of ideological perspectives in their ranks. Let us look at the first few issues of the magazine to see how this worked in practice.

As we have seen above, Pelletier based his call for action on love and holiness, arguing that "revolutionary violence" was part and parcel of the Gospel. Meanwhile, another Citélibriste, Réginald Boisvert, examined social issues from a class struggle perspective. In "Domiciles de la peur sociale" [Where Social Fear Resides], he argued that "there is nothing to be gained from reconciling the classes as if they were sisters who had got into an argument and become adversaries. Actually, the classes are not sisters. They have never been. They are born enemies. The only way to put an end to animosity is to abolish social classes altogether. There should be neither capitalists on one side, nor the proletariat on the other."[61] To this typically Marxist perspective, Boisvert added a forceful attack on clerical-nationalism, which he blamed for the social and political distress of French Canadians: "We have revelled in nationalist slogans and become seduced by them. We had lost everything but honour. We were poor, it is true, in terms of material goods, but the great river watered the land with a rich spiritual harvest: we were French and Catholic. . . . Some images exalted us, stimulated us. . . . No wonder that at the height of our nationalistic impulses, we had our fit of fascism."[62] While these words sharply criticized the nationalist clergy, they were not aimed at Catholicism as such. Like Pelletier, Boisvert firmly believed that his position was based on the Gospels, and that the deeds of some members of the Church provided grounds for hope.[63]

The magazine was full of harsh criticism of Quebec society and of the pervasive nationalism that characterized it. Pierre Vadeboncoeur was a left-wing Catholic, like practically all contributors to *Cité libre,* and attacked his society head-on: "The spiritual failure, the failure of preaching, and in politics the failure of our nationalism, are due to the fact that we thrive on myths and ideals, whose relationship to reality is only of the vaguest sort: this is the most irritating feature of our culture."[64] Like Mounier and *Esprit,* Vadeboncoeur advocated a revolution to put an end to the spiritual crisis and to the inhuman conditions of life and work.[65] And it was vital for him as for Pelletier "that Catholics should deliberately adopt revolutionary means of action."[66] But the reader should be aware that the revolution being advocated here had nothing in common with the Soviet or French Revolutions, nor even with the corporatist revolution that filled French-Canadian youth with rapture in the 1930s and 1940s. The Catholic Revolution that filled the dreams of several contributors to *Cité libre* was, and remained, an abstract concept, without any clearly defined content, without a plan of action. But, somehow, it had the magical power to conjure up a truly Christian society, without any bloodshed. It is hard to believe that this was the same Vadeboncoeur who sharply admonished French Canadians for their lack of realism.

In "Brève méditation sur l'existence canadienne-française" [Brief
Meditation on the Existence of French Canadians], Guy Cormier also
fought the conservative Church in the name of Christianity. He claimed:
"We want a Christian Quebec, but one that is Christian on the inside –
which is much more difficult to bring about – and not a politico-religious
state which oppresses consciences."[67] He claimed that his criticism was
not directed at the Catholic Church since it had never encouraged obscurantism and intellectual laziness. Instead, the Church had continually
waged war against the powers of darkness.[68] His criticism was directed at
the Church in Quebec. By confusing the spiritual and temporal realms, it
was preventing citizens from "acting like politically mature people."[69]
This habit of treating citizens like children, he said, had had dire consequences. He lambasted the clerical-nationalist elite, holding it responsible
for having spawned "the disgusting creature called the Union nationale":[70] "I know perfectly well that neither Mr. Groulx nor Mr. Laurendeau
will recognize themselves in Duplessis. You can argue with him, make fun
of his nose, but he remains your responsibility, he is part of your family.
You have begotten him, you have fed him with slogans. You have given
him the weapons he was incapable of producing himself, although he is a
genius when it comes to using them. . . . He begat the tiny microbe called
provincial autonomy, and this tiny microbe, when administered skilfully,
lulls the people to sleep and makes it possible to establish a French state
which strangely resembles a dictatorship."[71]

Quebec could not be considered a fascist province, he claimed, simply
because it lacked "essential organs, such as an army and better finances."[72]
But there should be no mistake. There is no doubt that "the key elements
of the Quebec government . . . are clearly veering towards totalitarianism,
[and] the Great Leader who currently controls the province's destinies
shows real talent for the role of dictator (Great God! We never lacked
talent!)."[73] Cormier was desperate about his province, but he took comfort
in the thought that the "State of Quebec will not reach the full stature of
a fascist state as long as the federal government is strong enough to contain
it. . . . Ottawa seems better suited to guarantee the fundamental rights of
man than Quebec does."[74] This vitriolic criticism of Duplessis and clear
defence of the "federalist" option became the hallmark of the magazine.

Interestingly this social critique went hand in hand with a heartfelt
faith in Catholicism. The sincerity of the faith of Citélibristes was one of

their strengths, since a condemnation by religious authorities would amount to a death warrant for the magazine. Pelletier remembered that the French university professors Henri Marrou and Paul Vignaux had encouraged *Cité libre* contributors to be cautious: "Your originality," Marrou said, " . . . is that . . . you are a voice within the Church, and that makes all the difference. If you are pushed outside it, no one will listen to you except the tiny group of declared non-believers."[75] It did not take long for Citélibristes to realize how apt this warning was and how precarious their situation really was.

In Volume I, we described the activities of Father Marie-Joseph d'Anjou, one of five members of the "Central Power" of the LX, the clandestine group then preparing a revolution to create an independent Catholic and corporatist *Laurentie,* or Laurentian nation. There, he got to know Trudeau, who was a zealous member of the LX. As soon as the very first issue of *Cité libre* appeared, he wrote a paternalistic critique in the Jesuit review *Relations.* He assured the team that there "is among people of my age far more sympathy for your goals, than you seem to believe: at least one of your contributors has long been aware of this fact."[76] The unnamed contributor was naturally Trudeau, as later events confirmed. But youth was not an excuse for everything, he told them: "As befits a mature mind," *Cité libre* needed to express "ideas which are of an adult, positive, constructive, and serene nature because it is sure of itself." This was the case here and there, he said, for example in "Pierre Trudeau's very tightly-argued attack on the trickery used by supporters of autonomy." But the magazine also contained a lot of nonsense, such as Guy Cormier's attack on a leading thinker in Quebec: "This nasty little speech is intended for Canon Lionel Groulx. Well, my dear child, this simply won't do!"[77]

Father d'Anjou made no bones about putting Cormier in his place. But he liked Trudeau, and to avoid any misinterpretation of his remarks, he sent him a confidential letter explaining his critique: "I know my review of the first issue of *Cité libre* was on the rough side. But it is mostly Cormier's fault, and I may have granted him too much importance. In fact, in giving him a good thrashing, I wanted to warn all of you about the danger of provoking adverse reactions from well-placed people, especially members of the clergy. It is better for me to be scolding you than . . . the authorities. Do you understand what I am saying? . . . I even made a fairly clear allusion to you, my dear Pierre, just to make sure you got my point. But enough about that! When will the second issue come out? And what theme are you going to take on? I am told you plan to focus on academic freedom. You should be careful. I am really unhappy that Maurice Blain is on the editorial board, because his muddled mind seems likely to bring you nothing but trouble (this must remain strictly between us) and he holds, on the notion of freedom, opinions which I find decidedly anti-Christian. If he expresses them in the review, I guarantee you I will come out against *Cité libre,* and once you have published a number of articles that clearly depart from Church teachings, I will eat your paper alive. But to you, Pierre, I do not need to repeat that my everlasting friendship is assured."[78] This cleverly constructed letter combines expressions of deep friendship, warnings . . . and threats. Father d'Anjou was not the only one to be disconcerted by the path the magazine was pursuing. Many clergymen kept a close eye on *Cité libre* and were ready to pounce on the magazine and "eat it alive" if it dared to go too far.

From the first issue, Trudeau stood out from the other contributors. He was a staunch Catholic like them, if not more so, but he made a point of not wearing his faith on his sleeve. In the first issue of *Cité libre* the only acknowledgment of his faith was short and mild: "We want to bear witness to the Christian and French fact in America. Fine; so be it. But let's get rid of the rest."[79] He would rarely say more than that since he firmly believed that religion was a private matter, and politics, a public one. This led him to call upon the Church to concern itself with spiritual matters, without interfering in the temporal sphere, which was not in its purview. As might be expected, these ideas did not please the clergy, to say the least. They warned the editorial board to be careful. But Trudeau didn't pay any attention. Whereas Pelletier was diplomatic and groomed his style, Trudeau did not mince words. As early as the second issue of *Cité libre,* he blasted a cannon shot at the Church. In "Functional Politics II," he argued that in Quebec, "we are conditioned to have the reflexes of slaves, bowing before established authority. We should once again become the authority ourselves." He even had the audacity to add: "The divine right of prime ministers, or bishops, simply doesn't exist: they have authority over us only if we let them."[80]

This was sacrilegious! The blast was heard throughout the province and even beyond, shaking up the prelates. Mgr. Paul-Émile Léger, Archbishop of Montreal, shared his concern with Claude Ryan. He was afraid he was going to have to come down heavily on the magazine. Ryan assured him that "the people at *Cité libre* are Christians" and persuaded him to talk to them before punishing them. Mgr. Léger followed this plan. Gérard Pelletier sent Trudeau the summons to see the archbishop, explaining his anxiety: "We will certainly be discussing that sentence you wrote about divine right, which unfortunately has taken off for a spin across the province! . . . However, since you are not a former member of Catholic Action, this makes you less irritating in their eyes but more a cause of worry for us."[81]

In his memoirs, Pelletier recalled "the incredible atmosphere of a medieval dispute" in which their conversation took place, focusing mainly on Trudeau's sentence: "'If I were to condemn the magazine for this proposition,' said the Archbishop . . . it would be with great regret, believe me.' 'And we,' interrupted Trudeau, 'would appeal to the universal Church, as is our right.' The Archbishop, disconcerted, stared strangely at Trudeau. He hesitated a moment, then went on to his next topic."[82] Phew! The journal would survive. But unfortunately for Trudeau, as we will see in the next chapter, this sentence caused problems that would persist well beyond the meeting with the archbishop.

The second issue of *Cité libre* came out in February, and it was even less to Father d'Anjou's liking. True to his promise, he sank his teeth into the magazine. His article, "The Case of *Cité libre*," was published in *Relations* in March 1951 and re-appeared the same month in *Notre Temps*. He attacked first "*Cité libre* confesse ses intentions" [*Cité libre Reveals Its Intentions*], by Gérard Pelletier, for whom he seems to have had deep antipathy. (Was it because Pelletier came out of the Catholic Action movement, which was detested by Church traditionalists?) He criticized the distasteful tone "and the thousand hackneyed jabs he made against the reactionary conformism of religion and education in Quebec."[83] For d'Anjou this "'revelation of intentions' betrayed a sense of uncertainty and even of insecurity, which the author's casual tone was designed to conceal." Pelletier defended himself with intelligence and restraint, as he would always do when standing up for the magazine and its contributors. He acted so often as spokesman and advocate for *Cité libre* that many people tended to confuse his ideas with those of the magazine and indeed of Trudeau himself.

What did Father d'Anjou dislike so intensely? First of all, the scandalous audacity of some of their arguments: "With your mind and heart, you should acknowledge that it is crazy – in the literal sense of the word – for Christians, whether laymen or not, to cast themselves as reformers of the Christendom and even of a part of it, outside of the letter and spirit of the Gospel, outside of the respect and filial piety they owe to the hierarchy." How the heck could these youngsters dare reform the Church? As for Trudeau's sentence, d'Anjou found it simply heretical: "It is especially regrettable to see such an outpouring of senseless bravado that consists in confusing the human origin of democratic power on the one hand and the truly divine power of Episcopal authority on the other. . . . I make no claim to teach a political expert like Pierre Trudeau that even the popular *designation* of the subject of civil authority does not allow the people to see themselves as the absolute *foundation* of power."[84] D'Anjou did not spare his friend. At least not in his article.

However, in a personal letter d'Anjou continued admonishing his friend: "I will never stop distinguishing between you as a person and the mistakes you make. And you allowed your pen to make a horrendous mistake in writing that the divine right of prime ministers and bishops simply doesn't exist, and all the rest. This may hold true for prime ministers, but it is heresy when applied to bishops. You knew that, I suppose, Pierre. So why did you run the risk of inserting this unnecessary and misplaced bravado in your article, which was otherwise serene and solid?"[85] Apparently, Father d'Anjou did not understand what his young friend was driving at. Trudeau was not questioning, and never would question, the divine right of priests over *spiritual matters*. But he denied them this right in *temporal matters*. In the heat of the controversy, Trudeau had not sufficiently refined his thoughts and did not make a clear enough distinction between the battle against clericalism and respect of the Church itself.

An amusing detail in this letter reveals the complex relationship between these two individuals. After having severely admonished Trudeau, d'Anjou asked: "Did you give alms during Lent?" And he added, in the most natural way, that an unwed teenage mother needed assistance. His till was empty and he wondered if Trudeau could "contribute something." On March 2, d'Anjou acknowledged Trudeau's "munificence" and his "wonderful charity."[86] He also mentioned having intervened on Trudeau's behalf with Mgr. Léger, assuring the archbishop of Trudeau's "intrinsic orthodoxy."

D'Anjou categorically disliked this second issue, which contained an article by Hertel, the famous Jesuit idolized by many young Quebecers, including Trudeau and Roger Rolland. From Paris, where he now lived, Hertel explained why he had left Quebec: "I am leaving, at least temporarily, because I am beginning to realize that despite my desire to do good, I would, in the long run, do more harm than good; my ideas are, in spite of myself, contrary to [the Church's] official teachings."[87] Roger Rolland wrote a tribute, assuring him of the gratitude of the young people he had taught: "By helping us understand Man, you made us love God. But a God who does not resemble the divinity that was imposed on us: a God of love rather than fear, a God of heaven and earth rather than a God of hell. So much so that, thanks to you, we could go directly to Him without going through Them."[88]

Going directly to God without going through His representatives? D'Anjou was stunned and found Rolland's views completely unacceptable. Such a perspective led straight to Protestantism: "Luther seduced this portion of Christendom and then corrupted it by broadly disseminating, amongst other errors, a theory of liberty."[89] All of this had led, continued d'Anjou, "at times to anarchy, at times to despotism, depending on the whims and interests that Luther-style liberty sought to conceal." The prelates of the Church in Quebec shared this opinion and would regularly accuse *Cité libre* contributors of Protestantism. Trudeau recalled on several occasions – for example, in *Memoirs* – that from a young age, he was criticized for his Protestant frame of mind. Clearly, this critique goes back to the beginnings of *Cité libre*.

In 1993, Trudeau told Jean-Marie Domenach: "My writings, as you may remember, were mostly on political issues."[90] This indeed is clearly apparent from the very first issue of *Cité libre* in "Functional Politics,"[91] where he declared: "I want to demonstrate that political science should not be magic. This is why it is important above all to purge our vocabulary of its emotional content. Nationalism, independence, bilingualism, clericalism, socialism, centralization are all words that make us jump for joy or fly into a rage, without reason."[92]

He started by tracing the historical roots of the situation. For years, he said, French Canadians had to struggle against the real danger of ethnic and religious assimilation. But the more they resisted, the more they came to believe that virtue consisted of saying no to everything. As a result, the very things they sought to protect – language and faith – ended up in a sorry state. This is because progress does not involve merely resisting, but also acting. And "what is most lacking in French Canada is a philosophy of action." And effective action must be based on facts rather than on prejudices. This means that every "major issue needs to be re-examined in a scientific spirit. For what we lack most of all is science, not emotions. . . . The time has come to borrow the 'functional discipline' from architecture, to throw to the winds the many prejudices with which the past has encumbered the present, and to build for the new man. Let's batter down the totems, let's break the taboos. Better yet, let's consider them null and void. Let us be coolly intelligent."[93]

Coolly and methodically, Trudeau examined two key concepts of Quebec politics: autonomy and centralization. He penned this very first article just as he got his job at the Privy Council and was thrilled at the first-hand experience he was getting of federal-provincial conferences as well as in other matters. He had already spoken publicly of the benefits of the federal system for French Canadians during his stay in Europe. Now that he had deepened his knowledge and acquired valuable experience in Ottawa, he wanted to convey to his readers the importance of cooperation between levels of government.

In Quebec, he said, autonomy and centralization were such emotionally charged concepts that they clouded people's judgment: "It is high time for us to make an honest and dispassionate examination of autonomy. This is not an idea but a call to arms. It is a verbal antidote to the (verbal) poison of centralization."[94] Trudeau was being especially critical of Duplessis, who used and abused this "call to arms." This simplistic view was devoid of any scientific foundation and prevented French Canadians from appreciating, in some situations, the benefits of centralization. Arguing from a Keynesian perspective, he stressed the importance of coordinating the economic policies of all governments. For example, a province should not allege autonomy as an excuse "to opt out of the economic cycle, since it would be inadmissible for a regional government to fill up its treasury with funds from other provinces that were meanwhile heroically slashing their own budgets in order to prevent a global crisis from escalating."[95] As he wrote these words, Trudeau knew that French Canadians put so much stock in autonomy that they would interpret his article as a defence of centralization. In anticipation, he countered: "If some people believe that I am preaching centralization here, they will have completely misunderstood the intent of the forego-ing paragraphs. It is high time our policies stop being one big joke, that's all I wanted to demonstrate. Which is why I singled out autonomy – just one of the many magical formulas dear to our politicians."[96]

His warning went unheeded. As he feared, his remarks were misin-terpreted. This explains his focus on provincial autonomy in a follow-up article, "Politique fonctionnelle II" [Functional Politics II]: "I had only raised the issue as a way of demonstrating how emotional and vulnerable our beliefs are; some readers concluded nonetheless that I was a central-ist, which didn't impress me much, but only served to illustrate their own obsession with outdated categories."[97] In this second article, he attempted to clarify the meaning of real autonomy and explain that "functional politics must first of all do away with prejudice."

He started with a paradox: "Why do we cling so tenaciously to auton-omy, when a handful of competent civil servants in provincial capitals, reporting to the national government, could do a better job than all pro-vincial deputations combined?"[98] The classic response of French Canadians was that "in such a bureaucracy [their] ethnic group might be poorly rep-resented, with the result that laws would be enforced without due regard to [their] specific characteristics and customs."[99] This was a valid concern, Trudeau admitted, but only up to a point. The real benefits of autonomy went well beyond the interests of any ethnic group and could bring together "all those, in any province whatsoever, who believe in freedom of the person." He went on to explain that "in an overly centralized state, . . . the government will be forced to rely on an increasingly inflated and powerful bureaucracy, in other words, less and less controllable." The result would be "that bureaucrats would exercise their inordinate powers as they saw fit."[100] It was therefore vitally important to strike a balance between autonomy and centralization. This, he said, is precisely the chief charac-teristic of our federal system, which encourages "the division of labour between the provincial governments and the federal government, which share the attributes of sovereignty. . . . Thus understood, autonomy becomes a key principle of political life in our country. . . . It is no longer a nation's call to arms, but an idea capable of rallying all those who care about good government."[101] The real problem arose, according to Trudeau, when the words "centralization" and "autonomy" were bandied around for narrow political purposes.

Trudeau's main point, therefore, was that provincial autonomy served as a counterweight to centralization. It also brought the rulers and the ruled closer to each other, facilitating the participation of citizens in the political realm. Because of this, "autonomy acts directly on the citizen and cultivates in him those civic virtues needed to preserve freedom" because "a state where citizens are uninterested in politics is doomed to slavery." For all these reasons, provincial autonomy, defined as the exclusive right to legislate in certain areas, should be regarded "as a positive good, and as a cornerstone of our democratic institutions."[102]

This, then, was "real autonomy," whereas the autonomy articulated by most politicians was "a revolting deception. Only intended to strengthen provincial power – their power! – at the expense of central power; in other words, in no way did it intend to provide citizens with a sense of civic responsibility."[103] He stated categorically: "We urgently need to understand this, above all in Quebec, since we are conditioned to have the reflexes of slaves, bowing before established authority. We should, once again, become the authority ourselves."

At this juncture came the famous passage, which offended so many people in high places: "The divine right of prime ministers, or bishops, simply doesn't exist: they have authority over us only if we let them." He continued with a rebuttal, seemingly directed at Father d'Anjou, who accused Cité libre contributors of being immature: "The day we understand these truths, we will cease to be a 'young people,' and we'll be expected to engage in more than childish babbling and adolescent rebellion."[104] Trudeau continued with a caustic attack on Duplessis, who was commonly referred to in Quebec as "*le chef*" or "the chief." On that day, he said, autonomy will no longer be treated as "as a totem worshipped by the chief . . . of a half-civilized tribe."[105]

A half-civilized tribe? Wasn't this an indication of Trudeau's contempt for the French-Canadian people, of which he was so often accused?

Not at all! We firmly trust that many Quebeckers of the early 1950s would have recognized the implied reference to the novel *Les demi-civilisés* [The Semi-Civilized], published in 1934. The author was none other than Jean-Charles Harvey, a journalist loathed by the clerical-nationalist elites, including some of Trudeau's friends, first because of his support for conscription and the federal government, and second for his outspoken critique of Marshal Pétain.[106] In this novel, Harvey defended "free love, freedom of thought, culture and the rights of the individual." He also denounced conformism and hypocrisy.[107] One understands that this book would create quite a stir. Still, the virulence of attacks on Harvey is hard to grasp. In 1962, in the introduction of the new ediiton of his novel, Harvey recalled the episode: "Towards the end of April, His Eminence Cardinal Villeneuve, Archbishop of Quebec, banned *Les demi-civilisés*. The decree was published in *La Semaine Religieuse,* and prohibited the faithful, under pain of mortal sin to read this book, to keep, lend, buy, sell, print or distribute it in any way."[108] Trudeau deliberately chose the expression "*demi-civilisés*" as a nod to the author, whose courage he admired. Jean-Charles Harvey was still alive – he died in 1967 – and must certainly have understood and appreciated this discreet tribute.

In conclusion, Trudeau reiterated the importance of striking a balance between centralization and real autonomy. To this end, he said, it was all-important to carefully delimit the spheres of jurisdiction of the federal government and the provinces. But this sharing was not something abstract: "Functional politics cannot be developed entirely in the mind: it must be translated into actions by righteous citizens." Trudeau would repeat this a thousand times over: We should act coolly, intelligently; people must act. Let us send an appeal to all the people of goodwill. That same year, "Functional Politics" appeared in English translation in *Canadian Life*. The publisher of the magazine, Alan Thomas Jr., was convinced the article would create quite a commotion. He wrote to Trudeau: "Actually your article is dynamite enough for one issue."[109] But Trudeau was far from having exhausted his supply of explosives. Not by a long shot.

———•———

Two issues of *Cité libre,* and two hard-hitting articles by Trudeau. Although no article appeared under his name in the third issue dated May 1951, we have seen above that he penned "Positions sur la présente guerre" [Positions on the Current War]. Subsequently, in both the December 1951 and the June–July 1952 issues, his name appeared only as a member of the editorial board. The reason: he was off travelling, once again, to faraway lands, although this didn't prevent him from writing. As we will see in the next chapter, he wrote ten articles for *Le Devoir:* two on Egypt, one on the Sudan, and seven more on the USSR. On returning to Montreal on July 23, 1952, he jumped right back into the fray at *Cité libre,* whose December issue would be entirely devoted to the provincial election of July 16. His article, by far the longest in the issue, was the *pièce de résistance.*

First, a few facts. The provincial Liberals under its new leader, Georges-Émile Lapalme, won twenty-three seats, compared to a mere eight in 1948. The Union Nationale, meanwhile, dropped from eighty-two seats to sixty-eight. These results did not adequately reflect the substantial support enjoyed by the Liberals, who won 45.77 per cent of the popular vote compared to 50.50 per cent for the Union Nationale. Smaller parties, including the CCF and the pro-communist Labour Progressive Party, were completely swept off the electoral map. Although Duplessis had lost many seats, he continued to command a large majority.

The December 1952 issue opened with an unsigned preliminary note, most likely written by Trudeau, announcing its intention "to sort out the key elements of the [July election], which are a tangle of ideology, interests and banditry."[110] True to their characteristic open-mindedness as well as their educational objectives, the editorial board invited people from all major competing political movements to interpret the results from their respective points of view. All of them accepted. This kind of collaboration was very rare in Quebec, and the editorial team proudly saw this as an "indication of a broad perspective and a political maturity that were very welcome."[111]

Unfortunately, most readers did not demonstrate the same maturity. Some were outraged that the magazine should publish an article by the Labour Progressive Party. On March 22, 1953, the liberal, widely read daily *La Patrie* claimed that Communists had infiltrated *Cité libre.* Since it was common knowledge that the Church and the government took this type of accusation seriously, *Cité libre* had to reply. The accusation could prove to be the young magazine's death warrant. Charles Lussier replied on behalf of the team. He reminded readers that

Cité libre was "committed to serve theological truth under the magis-
terium of the Church. . . . Those who have read and understood us,"
he added, "are aware that all members of the *Cité libre* team are active
in thoroughly Christian and anti-communist movements."[112] He then
explained the reason *Cité libre* had sought out these various contributions: "We wanted the views of all political parties involved in these
elections. . . . We were not the ones to choose these parties, the Province
was." [113] Despite Lussier's explanation, the magazine would often be
labelled extreme left wing, particularly by Robert Rumilly, the biographer and eulogist of Duplessis. More than others, Trudeau would
have to defend himself from charges, from people in authority, of being
a Communist fellow traveller.

In this issue, five contributors undertook a critical analysis of the
provincial election: Charles Lussier, Gérard Pelletier, Pierre Laporte,
Marcel Rioux, and Pierre Elliott Trudeau. We will be concerned here
only with Trudeau's article, "Reflections on Politics in French Canada."[114]
This was the first time Trudeau examined at some length French-
Canadian political culture. He would long be concerned with the subject
and developed his ideas further over time, the most complete formulation being his 1956 introduction to *The Asbestos Strike*.

The first paragraph, consisting of a single short sentence, set the tone
and substance of the article: "Our deep-seated immorality has to be
explained."[115] Trudeau had just fired another cannon shot. He quickly
added that immorality did not affect all sectors of activity: "Our ideas
on the order of society are shaped by Catholic theology, and our personal values generally bear witness to the sincerity of these views – with
one exception. In our relations with the state, we are really quite immoral:
we corrupt bureaucrats, we blackmail members of the Assembly . . . we
cheat the tax-collector. . . . And when it comes to electoral matters, our
immorality is absolutely appalling. . . . The lawyer who calls for the
maximum penalty when the parish poor-box is emptied out is proud to
have added two thousand phoney names to the electoral list. And stories
of electoral dishonesty have so filled our childhood's collective memory
that they hardly shock anyone anymore."[116]

Trudeau supported his views with some of the other contributors'
articles to this issue: "Marcel Rioux and Pierre Laporte have given us
compelling evidence of dishonest electoral practices. . . . Mr. Gélinas

has highlighted some examples of police terrorism. . . . Jean-Marie Nadeau . . . [has] drawn up a long list of fraudulent deeds perpetrated by the Union Nationale. . . . All parties deplored the depravity of our morals."[117] After providing a few examples of his own, he asked: "So we now have to put the question bluntly: how much longer will heaven continue to delegate authority in this country, working through boxers, blackmailers and professional gangsters, and using firearms sometimes loaded with blanks, resorting to theft, lies, and intimidation? In short, can we hope eventually to overcome our profound immorality?"[118]

The answer would eventually be yes, but not just yet. Four years later, right after the 1956 elections, an explosive forty-seven-page pamphlet appeared in print: *L'immoralité politique dans la province de Québec* (this pamphlet also came out in English at the time under the title *Political Immorality in the Province of Quebec*).[119] It is widely agreed that this "dynamite" greatly helped pave the way to the Quiet Revolution. It was important not only by virtue of its content, but also because its authors were both priests. Abbé Gérard Dion was director of the Department of Industrial Relations at the Faculty of Social Sciences at Université Laval and diocesan chaplain of labour-management associations in Quebec. (By the time he co-wrote this pamphlet, he had already written a chapter for the collective work on the Asbestos strike that Trudeau edited.) His co-author, Louis O'Neill, was a professor at the Séminaire de Québec and chaplain of Catholic Action at Université Laval. Years later, he joined the Parti Québécois, and in 1976, he became one of the first two priests to be elected to the National Assembly.

The fact that Dion and O'Neill openly denounced political morality in Quebec brought to light a struggle within the Church between left-wing progressives and right-wing traditionalists. On the basis of Christian values, Dion and O'Neill denounced deceitful propaganda that left ordinary people defenceless. They used strong images, claiming, for example, that "this technique, perfected by Hitler, was taken up by the Communists. It is now part of our electoral method."[120] They trotted out an impressive list of all the moral violations that people no longer found shocking: "Vote buying, corruption of the electoral law, threats of reprisals against those who do not support the 'right party,' false oaths, the corruptions of election officers, are set to become normal facets of our electoral process."[121] They gave several examples of candidates buying votes such as paying for roof repairs, hospital bills, and so on. They complained that the clergy were just as likely to accept bribes as the rest of the population: "In a parish of a Quebec City suburb a rector carried his kindness so far as to preach in his pulpit in favour of his candidate and even solicited votes from door to door."[122] They added: "The danger is all the greater since a great deal of evidence shows that the consciences of the perpetrators, including members of religious orders, are not troubled by such corrupt behaviour."[123]

Dion and O'Neill denounced "the profound immorality" of French Canadians just as forcefully as Trudeau, but they were pursuing different objectives. They wanted to remind priests of their duty and bring the lost sheep back to the fold: "We are terribly responsible before God," they wrote, "if the people end up believing that the Kingdom of God is this hodgepodge of pious sentimentality, of barefaced civic immorality and of latent Fascism."[124] Trudeau, on the other hand, was exclusively concerned with the political realm: he wanted to put an end to the reign of immorality so that Quebeckers would get a true, democratic government that would seek the common good. The first condition to achieve this goal was to understand the root cause of the problem. With this in mind he set out to trace the history of Canada, from a French-Canadian perspective.

Up to the time of the Conquest, he claimed, French Canadians had experienced only authoritarian rule. The British victory in 1759–1760 signalled the advent of parliamentary democracy. But British parliamentary government rests on two premises: first, that political parties agree to pursue the common good, although they propose different means for achieving it, and secondly, that the political minority can periodically become a majority. But tensions arose. On the one hand, there had never been an agreement between the French and English Canadians on the common good worth pursuing. On the other hand, "the alternation between majorities and minorities could never work, because the basic cleavage reflected a stable ethnic breakdown far more than ideologically motivated voting patterns."[125] And since the majority was English, French Canadians deduced, correctly, that "the government of the people by the people would not be *for* the people, but, above all, for the English-speaking part of the people."[126] Viscerally concerned with their survival, they also interpreted the common good as relating solely to their ethnic group: "They formed a community within the community. . . . which meant breaking the rules of the Canadian public weal in order to safe-guard the French-Canadian one. Cunning and compromise dictated their choice of parties or alliances. . . . Our people did not vote for or against an ideology or an economic system, but only for the champion of our ethnic rights." [127] Unfortunately, cheating is habit-forming, Trudeau lamented. Having lost a sense of moral obligation toward the common good, "everyone pursued his own interest, to the detriment of the community. In other words, our sense of civic pride was perverted: we became opportunists."[128] Ironically, the final result was that each individual did not even act in the interests of the ethnic group.

There was another reason for the historical mistrust of the French Canadians toward democracy. Since it was to them a given that "authority comes from God, people brushed aside electoral misbehaviour in democratic systems. They paid no heed to the deeper significance of the process they viewed as typically Protestant and Anglo-Saxon antics, preferring to focus on the immediate and tangible benefits, such as the gift of a bottle of whisky, the construction of a parish hall, or a contract to build a road."[129]

Trudeau drove the point home a little more: "For historical and religious reasons, we are prejudiced against the democratic system although we have not submitted it to a fair test, and this explains how, after being nationalists for generations, our ranting finally took the form of the extreme right ideology: many intellectuals embraced the views of Charles Maurras, men of action then yielded to the temptation of fascism and our people felt an enthusiasm for authoritarian governments in this country and elsewhere." Trudeau was speaking from experience. He remembered that in his youth, the clerical-nationalist elite had preached corporatism and prayed to heaven for leaders like Portugal's Salazar or Italy's Mussolini. He remembered his own admiration for Maurras. But now he had turned the page. And it was high time for French Canadians to do likewise.

They should reconsider their preconceived opinions about democracy – in fact, they really had no choice in the matter – "for the good reason that governments nowadays are constantly using taxes, social benefits and grants to redistribute the national product among various groups, and those who remain aloof or don't come out of their tent risk not being served well by the system."[130] Each group therefore had to make sure it was not left behind. Ever since the state had acquired this new role, "the crucial problem is determining who will benefit from a particular government intervention: which ethnic group, or which social class?"[131] These reflections were the backdrop for Trudeau's analysis of the July 1952 election results.

Why had Duplessis triumphed? It went without saying that the Union Nationale was extremely adept at manipulating voters. But according to Trudeau, election irregularities alone did not explain Duplessis's success. Among the many other factors, he singled out the Union Nationale's Conservative ideology, which guaranteed the solid support of the upper middle class, as well as the backing of farmers and rural dwellers. A true believer in as free a market economy as possible, Duplessis opened wide Quebec's doors to investors, many of them from the United States and English Canada. He catered to their needs through appropriate pro-business legislation, including labour laws that attempted to hamper the rise of a more militant trade-union movement. Moreover, continued Trudeau, this state of affairs was accepted by most of the elites, since "apart from a progressive minority, the clergy and nationalists were instinctively afraid of reforms that could open up cracks in monolithic Quebec."[132] This goes a long way to explaining why even though the province was by then highly industrialized the elites clung to the myth that French Canadians were a rural breed who could best solve their problems by "returning to the land." This state of affairs, claimed Trudeau, suited Big Capital to a T. So the Union Nationale could count on the financial support of big business.

At this point, Trudeau raised the issue of the cost of elections. He quoted Gérard Filion who, in *Le Devoir* of July 15, estimated "that a Quebec election costs four to five times more than in Ontario."[133] The obvious conclusion, said Trudeau, was that "as long as it takes this much money to elect a government in Quebec, the population will inevitably have policies dictated by big capital: in other words the state will continue being a tool of economic dictatorship."[134]

Who could put an end to this sorry state of affairs? Trudeau replied without hesitation: "The change, if it should come, will come from the working class."[135] Workers would sound the death knell of the Union Nationale. And he detected encouraging signs in the July 1952 election results. First: "The Union Nationale won almost exclusively in rural areas of Quebec: the party won 58 out of 67 rural or mixed constituencies, and only 10 out of 24 exclusively urban constituencies."[136] In addition, as it adhered to obsolete social systems and values, the Union Nationale neither recognized the rise of the working class nor made any attempt to win it over. Trudeau cited as proof the fact that "last November 12th, the Union Nationale government's Throne Speech . . . devoted five paragraphs to the rural class of farmers, while only reminding the working class, in a single reference, that 'performing one's duty is always the best way to guarantee one's rights.'"[137] Trudeau was hopeful because things were starting to change. With the growth of the trade union movement, workers were now forging alliances that transcended their ethnic origin: "The earth-shaking 1949 Asbestos strike made them realize that their struggle was no longer against the English, Protestants or Jews, but against big capital, more specifically against a certain idea of capitalism."[138] This explains that as soon as he left the Privy Council, Trudeau got involved in workers' education, so that they would become aware of their strength and would take a more active part in politics.

———— ◆ ————

Trudeau was passionate about politics, whether municipal, provincial, or federal, so when federal elections were held on August 10, 1953, he offered a comprehensive analysis of the results in the November issue of *Cité libre*.[139] In these elections, the Liberal Party under Louis St. Laurent was re-elected, with 171 seats, which represented a loss of nineteen seats compared to the 1949 elections. The Progressive Conservatives under George Drew won fifty-one seats, ten more than in 1949. The CCF, under M.J. Coldwell, got twenty-three seats, a gain of ten seats. The Social Credit under Solon Low won fifteen seats, five more than in 1949, and five seats went to "other" parties. In other words, the ruling party was the only one to have lost seats.

Trudeau sketched in some historical background, before going on to explain the current situation. He underlined the gains made all over the world by the popular classes during the war. Governments realized that "ordinary people ultimately bore the weight of war, were the source of the wealth of nations, put leaders in office and invested the laws with legitimacy. This is how, between 1939 and 1945, the idea of democracy made . . . enormous progress around the world."[140] Unfortunately, he continued, slowly but surely the propertied classes and media magnates convinced the working people that "their own unreasonable demands were the cause of inflation, and that labour strife only ended up benefiting demagogues. Exaggerated social benefits led to higher production costs, which in turn brought about an unfavourable balance of international payments and a devalued currency. In short, as the example of the USSR illustrated, left-wing ideas were claimed to be the root of all evils."[141] Bombarded relentlessly with this message, the people "began to doubt their own political acumen." Understandably, when such a climate of insecurity and propaganda prevails, the people generally opt for the status quo, stability, and authority.

"Things have not worked out that much differently in Canada," Trudeau wrote. "The Canadian people first became aware of their importance and strength during the war."[142] In Canada as elsewhere, he said, the government suddenly showed a lot of interest in the people, making them "understand that democracy seeks the greatest good for the greatest number. In 1940, it enacted unemployment insurance legislation, and the same year Quebec recognized women's suffrage. . . . In 1943, the Marsh Report on Social Security* was published, proposing benefits for everyone; the following year, child benefits were introduced. The government reduced illiteracy, taught trades, created jobs, built houses, let trade unions spread their wings, stabilized prices, and lavished honours on soldiers."[143] This all meant that the winds of change were blowing across the country. For example, Trudeau noted that the CCF had racked up gains, taking power in Saskatchewan in 1944 and becoming the Official Opposition in several other provinces. In Quebec, however, the left had "a nationalist rather than a social character."[144] Once the war was over, the elite in Quebec and in other places disseminated propaganda in what proved to be a successful bid to persuade the people that their unreasonable demands would lead to new problems.

Given the "resurgence of conservatism," why was the Liberal Party voted into office in August 1953 and not the Conservative Party? Trudeau

---

* In *Histoire du Québec contemporain*, historians Paul-André Linteau, René Durocher, Jean-Claude Robert, and François Ricard stated that the *Report on Social Security in Canada* (the "Marsh Report") tabled on March 16, 1943, "marked the birth of Canada's welfare state."

asked. For two main reasons: First, "the Liberal party portrayed itself during the election campaign as the more conservative of the competing parties, which was indeed the case. The Conservatives proposed shaking up federal-provincial relations, introducing tax relief, laying off government employees and even floated the idea of health insurance. The CCF reaffirmed their plans for social security and a planned economy. But the Liberals promised nothing, preferring to cast themselves as the party of the status quo. It was precisely this security, this immobility that appealed to an electorate that was beginning to have grave doubts about the efficacy of popular sovereignty."[145] Second, continued Trudeau, very often, "voters view federal elections like races where the main point is to bet on the winning horse."[146] They believe that unless they are represented "within the winning party across the land, they would have no share in the spoils of victory."[147] He then explained why St. Laurent was believed to be the horse most likely to win.

Trudeau, an advocate of democratic socialism, was well aware that the resurgence of conservatism then taking place in so many countries would prove detrimental to this ideology. It made him wonder: "Can we still say despite everything that the left has a future in Canada?"[148] Since the left in Canada was essentially embodied in the CCF, he examined the party's potential impact in various provinces. Did it stand a chance in Quebec? The figures were there to prove, he said, that support for the CCF was negligible "and did not even amount to a core of support."[149] Why was this the case? Essentially because French Canadians always defined the common good in terms of their ethnic identity. They "are faithful to their history. They only supported the Conservative Party because of Cartier; they only supported the Liberal Party because of Laurier, Lapointe and St. Laurent. They never really adhered to a Canadian party; instead, they allied themselves (for reasons of their own) with parties with a semi-detachable Quebec wing."[150] He believed that neither the nationalists (which he called the "nationally-minded") nor the socialists (which he called the "socially-minded") had any real impact on the political scene. He explained their lack of effectiveness in the following terms: "The socially-minded have strength in numbers, but a lack of traditions prevents them from translating this strength into laws. The nationally-minded are characterized above all by loyalty, but their lack of revolutionary sense prevents them from bridging the gap between past and future. When these two wings act separately they are unable to fill the political vacuum, and so they helplessly watch as the people are cast adrift, while they themselves wait to be sucked up in the maelstroms of communism on the left and fascism on the right."[151] In short, the gap between these two groups could prove catastrophic: it could open the way to the triumph of totalitarianism. Yet both of these groups have the welfare of the French-Canadian people at heart, and many nationalists are on the left. What should be done?

Trudeau's proposal struck us as so astonishing that we reread it several times. He proposed an alliance between the nationalists and the left. In his own words: "I would like to see the nationally-minded and the socially-minded work together to develop a concrete program of political action." He stressed, however, that he was only addressing people of good faith and goodwill: "I obviously am not speaking of adventurers for whom politics is a game, but rather of sincere men who take to heart *the weight of social and national injustices.*"[152] Trudeau was convinced that French Canadians were victims of injustice in Canada. While he no longer approved the methods nationalists used to undo these injustices, he still backed their claims. However, he had witnessed with his own eyes how in Great Britain, throughout the war years, unity had produced strength. He therefore concluded that since the socially-minded and the nationally-minded shared a similar conception of the common good, they should be "coolly intelligent" and form an alliance, which would naturally require mutual concessions. Trudeau was not naïve: "I have no illusions about the chances of success."[153] But he was certain about one thing: it was a risk worth taking. The election results of August 10, 1953, clearly demonstrated that action was urgently needed.

———※———

By the end of 1953, Trudeau had already penned, in *Cité libre,* two articles on "Functional Politics," one on Canada's foreign policy (1951), one on provincial elections, another one on federal elections. To top it all, he wrote an article that would launch a thorough critique of the cozy relationship between Church and State. Firmly convinced that political action was the indispensable tool for social progress, he was passionately interested in political analysis in all its forms. Over time, he became an authority on these and other issues and made regular appearances on radio and television.

In this chapter, we have taken time out from our chronological narrative in order to throw some light on *Cité libre* and provide an overview of Trudeau's role in this magazine. We left him, at the end of Chapter 7, when he resigned from the Privy Council. Then, in order to better enjoy his newly won freedom, he set sail on October 24, 1951, on the liner *Ile de France*. Let us join him there.

Chapter 9

THE HELLISH STRUGGLE OF ANTICLERICALISM

If I were granted the safe-conduct Dante apparently got, I would gladly go to hell to collect some statistics on the privation of the sight of God.

– PIERRE ELLIOTT TRUDEAU,
Le Devoir, 1952

MANY OF THE THINGS WRITTEN ABOUT the Trudeau of the 1950s give the impression he lived in Canada like a bird on a wire, poised to fly off at any moment. He seems ready to slip away without warning, on a whim and without any apparent reason, like a man constantly performing some kind of disappearing act. The truth is Trudeau actually mapped out his travels laboriously and with the utmost care. Behind this magician was a man who meticulously prepared his travels and foreign jaunts.

As an example, let's look at the visas he got between October 12 and 19, 1951. Once he left the Privy Council in Ottawa on October 6, 1951, he lost no time preparing for his trip. On October 12, 1951, he received a visa from the Greek Consulate in Montreal, writing in his passport next to the visa, "one month stay, visa valid four months." The same day, he rushed off to the Consulate of France to get a visa to visit Morocco. This time, he wrote: "Tunisia + Algeria, two month stay." In fact, whenever his visas were written in a language or alphabet other than French or English, he translated the most important details. Three days later he was back in Ottawa, where he got a one-month visa, valid for four months, from the Consulate General of Egypt. On October 16, he was still in

Ottawa and received a visa from the General Konsulat der Bundersrepublik Deutschland, valid until October 15, 1952. (He noted in English: "repeated entries till 15 October 1952, West Germany.") On October 17, he called on the "Office of the High Commissioner for the United Kingdom," where he was issued visas for short stays in Tripoli, Cyrenaica,* and Eritrea.** That same day, October 17, 1951, he was off to the Yugoslav embassy, where he got a visa for Zagreb and Dalmatia.*** He wrote: "Yugoslavia until 31 January. One month." On returning to Montreal, he rushed to the Consulate of Belgium, where he got a visa on October 19 for the Belgian Congo, valid for six months. All in all, between October 12 and 19, he zigzagged between seven separate delegations in Montreal and Ottawa, obtaining visas for eleven countries or regions.

But there is more. Trudeau noted the duration of each visa in the margins of his passport because he now had to plan his itinerary, taking into account the duration and validity dates of each visa: some visas were valid for one month, others for four, some specified the length of his stay . . . there was hardly anything spontaneous in this trip!

On March 16, 1952, Trudeau wrote to Pelletier, from Paris: "I have never in my life felt so unattached, physically and morally. . . . I'm ready to commit the greatest follies; . . . all in all, I am in a rather pitiable state."[1] These sentences have been repeatedly quoted by authors such as Michel Vastel or Léon Dion as evidence that Trudeau was wandering through life with neither ties nor responsibilities, a man subject to *ennui*. Dion wrote: "With the exception of obscure functions and fleeting occupations, . . . Trudeau's life consisted of a series of evasions. . . . During the greater part of the decade, he led an aimless existence. In 1952, he wrote: 'I am in a rather pitiable state.'"[2] So he was down in the dumps because he lived such an idle life. This view is echoed by Stephen Clarkson and Christina McCall. They write that until 1959, the people closest to Trudeau wondered if the lack of a wife or a permanent job meant he would continue "to fritter away his unusual intellectual gifts in aimless bohemianism and endless travel."[3]

---

* Cyrenaica became part of Libya in 1951.

** Located in northeast Africa along the shores of the Red Sea, Eritrea was under British rule. It became part of Ethiopia in 1952 and became independent in 1993.

*** Dalmatia, along the shores of the Adriatic, is now almost entirely in Croatia.

But the facts tell a different story. Throughout the 1950s, Trudeau had dozens of irons in the fire at the same time. So how are we to explain the famous statement "I am in a rather pitiable state," which seems to contradict our assertions? Placing his remark in context will help. Let us retrace Trudeau's steps after he left the civil service.

On October 24, 1951, with a passport loaded with visas, he boarded the passenger liner *Île de France*. As usual, he headed straight for France, and more precisely Paris, to immerse himself in French culture: be it theatre, concerts, museums, shows, or exhibits. He reconnected with old friends, Hertel among them, naturally. He wandered through the streets of Paris. What bliss! He continued on to Rome where he met Claude Ryan, then on to Naples, and its "wonderful" museum.[4] After a brief stay in Greece, he was off to Egypt. The holidays were over. He was now embarking on the serious part of his journey.

Once again, Trudeau was lucky to land in the right place at the right time. In January 1952, Egypt was rocked by a very serious political crisis that led to the coup of July 23 and King Farouk's abdication. Since the Anglo-Egyptian Treaty of 1936, Great Britain had full authority to occupy the Suez Canal zone and could continue to do so until 1956. But in 1951, the nationalists wanted to free Egypt from British rule. They also denounced government corruption and called for the overthrow of King Farouk, whom they considered, not unreasonably, a British puppet. Following unrest in Ismailia (a small town on the west bank of the Suez Canal), on January 26, 1952, British soldiers killed forty Egyptians, an act that led to massive riots in Cairo. More than two hundred fires broke out that day alone.

So here was Trudeau in Egypt, at a pivotal moment in its history, witnessing a government crisis first-hand, as well as explosive riots of a people demanding liberation. He wrote two very different freelance articles for *Le Devoir,* under the title "Letters from Egypt." In the first, he explained that one day, being fed up with constantly being asked where he was from, he regrettably told students he was British. What a disaster! A furious crowd rushed at him, forcing him to flee. This led him to a tongue-in-cheek philosophical observation: "You can show off in front of a handful of men, but never in front of a mob."[5] He quickly learned his lesson and from then on he admitted only to being "French, Russian or Hottentot." He added with a touch of irony, "I always noticed the same phenomenon: all these

nationalities are friends of the Egyptians and enemies of the British."
Hence the title of his article: "Avoid Being English . . ."

The second "Letter from Egypt" came out the following day and dealt
exclusively with politics. With a deadpan sense of humour, Trudeau began
by highlighting the disastrous effects on tourism of the ongoing riots:
"What! [the incredulous Egyptian will say] tourists refuse to come here
simply because all foreigners are suspected of spying and could be beaten
up by a suddenly uncontrollable mob?"[6] He then went on to analyze the
political situation, demonstrating a sound grasp of the recent history of
the region. The facts were accurate and the analysis insightful. England,
he said, had "been drawn into a conflict that would permanently remove
Egypt from the Anglo-American sphere of influence." However, Egypt
and Turkey were the two key countries for the defence of the Middle East.
Turkey had quickly sided with the West, but Egypt "would probably
consent to being armed by the Soviet Union (although communism is currently banned here)." It was true, he said, that "since the Anglo-Egyptian
Treaty of 1936, the British have full authority to occupy the Suez Canal
zone. And they are not ready to strike camp because of threats, particularly since they do not fear the wrath of the poorly equipped Egyptian
army, which was roundly defeated in the war against Israel. They can
easily stay in Egypt until their rights run out in 1956."

On September 1, 1951, Egypt was condemned by the UN Security
Council for blocking the entry of Israeli ships into the Suez Canal. King
Farouk and his government, whose popularity had been in sharp decline
since the defeat of 1948, indulged in some grandstanding. On October
8, he proclaimed himself King of Egypt and Sudan. His government
denounced the treaty of 1936 and ordered the British to evacuate the
Canal Zone. Trudeau offered an explanation for these robust actions:
"In my opinion, the unilateral abrogation of the treaty would never have
taken place . . . if the hand of the government had not been forced by the
fanatical sect of the Muslim Brotherhood. Using murder, terrorism and
civil unrest, the Brotherhood has forced successive cabinets to become
increasingly anti-British and pro-Islamist. The Brotherhood is well-
placed to blackmail a scandalously and notoriously corrupt oligarchy."
For this reason, the king's and government's sudden ultranationalism
"seems mainly a diversionary tactic, intended to distract public opinion
from the government's own mismanagement."

Although Trudeau did not attempt to predict the outcome of the crisis, there was no doubt in his mind "that the British have nothing to gain by stubbornly occupying Suez until the expiry of their mandate." They should call on the United Nations to find a solution. This would allow them to save "their strength and their money" and offer evidence of their good faith to the Arab world. On the other hand, if they prove obstinate, the Muslim Brotherhood "will become even more dangerous. At best, they will establish a fiercely Muslim government that will launch a pan-Islamic crusade. At worst, they will create a state of total anarchy that communism, an ever vigilant force, will not fail to exploit." However, he said, if Britain withdraws, "the Muslim Brotherhood will ultimately disappear, or become a legitimate political movement that can – hopefully – stem the current oligarchy's shameless exploitation of the people."

But the British did not withdraw, and the rest is history: in 1956, the Suez Canal was nationalized; a confrontation broke out that risked escalating into a major conflict pitting the Franco-Anglo-Israeli alliance against Soviet-backed Egypt. To name but a few of the consequences: all French and English nationals were expelled from Egypt, resulting in the almost total exodus of all the other "Europeans" – the Greeks, Italians, Armenians, Jews, etc., including many well-established old families who had lived in Egypt for generations. The Muslim Brotherhood activists pushed even harder for the establishment "of a fiercely Muslim government," posing a real threat to the present one.

Lester B. Pearson, then Secretary of State for External Affairs, played a key role in the peaceful resolution of the Suez crisis, which earned him the Nobel Peace Prize in 1957. In this regard, an unsigned article in *Cité libre*, likely written by Trudeau, is worth mentioning. Whereas he had roundly criticized Pearson's policy on Korea, in this article he commended the Canadian government for its handling of the Suez crisis and for courageously taking an independent stand on British policy.[7] We'll come back to this article in Chapter 13.

Trudeau steamed southwards up the Nile, heading from Egypt to Sudan, admiring the wilderness, and reading a book a day. But he also found time to write a new article, "Sudan for the Sudanese," posting it to *Le Devoir* during a stopover in Uganda.[8] He briefly summarized the history of Sudan, recalling that in 1899, an agreement was signed between Egypt and England providing for the joint administration of the country.

Although this accord was confirmed in the friendship treaty of 1936, it had not prevented the political machinations of both the British and the Egyptians, to maintain or increase their control over Sudan. It was in this context, he wrote, that Egypt's unilateral abrogation of the 1936 treaty should be understood: "By this brave and ingenious stroke, Farouk the Ripper would become king of Sudan and master of the Suez Canal."

This article in *Le Devoir* pales in comparison to an unpublished one, entitled "About missions," and datelined "Sudan, January 1952."[9] We don't know if it was ever mailed. One thing, however, is certain: it was not published, for obvious reasons. The first lines reflect the content and tone of the whole: "There is only one solution, I thought. Canada should expel the Jesuits, sell all their possessions and give the proceeds to the Jesuit missions. As a result, these great men would be scattered out in the sticks where their community is already doing remarkable works. It would certainly be a painful separation for those of us who have studied in their colleges, but we would accept it knowing that their teaching would be more useful in infidel countries than in oh so Christian Quebec. Economists would consider this as a straightforward question of marginal productivity. After the Jesuits, we would take care of the Franciscans, the Grey Nuns, the Holy Cross, and – why not? – the Dominicans. In the end, there would only remain communities that take the vow of poverty seriously."

Trudeau's bantering and ironic tone hardly conceals his revolt, on the one hand, against the missionaries' deplorable living conditions, which hinder their good works, and on the other hand, against the kitschy and outrageous ostentation of the Catholic Church in Quebec. He also objected to a situation that had long been of concern to him: the lack of lay people working as missionaries. The reason for their absence? "They cannot find employment, sometimes because of systematic exclusion, mostly because as breadwinners, the laity cannot accept the low wages paid to the clergy." This led him to a new thought, bordering on heresy: "As if priestly celibacy were a means for the Church to have access to cheap labour." Tax breaks granted to religious orders were also criticized: "We should abolish this obsolete practice which leads to unfair competition, and which insults the competence of these holy men in financial matters."

Why was he so flushed with anger? Because Trudeau – often considered as insensitive – was terribly upset: "I could not bear to see the abjectness, the disease and awful misery that is the normal condition of our brothers, the Christian Copts of Upper Egypt. It made me realize how purely financial barriers were preventing the Gospel from reaching a multitude of hearts hungry for faith. All it would take for remote villages to receive the sacraments is a bicycle, but there isn't any. . . . For lack of a football to attract children, youth is lost to Christianity." Meanwhile, in Canada: "We pay big bucks for statues that make our churches uglier. . . . We spend a lot so that on the Feast of Corpus Christi, the Children of one parish can outshine the children of the next one with their beautiful banners." He probably never sent this article anywhere for he must have known it was not publishable.

———◈———

Nothing we have said so far explains the famous sentence "I am in a rather pitiable state." But we are getting there. Anyone reading his articles of February 1, 2 and 5 in *Le Devoir* could hardly imagine what he was going through, physically. We find him writing in his diary, with evident dismay: "The whole time, from day one, an intolerable tooth abscess, which even aspirins, wine, and Gardenal can't soothe. At Coquilhatville,* a dentist opens the tooth, then refuses to pull it given the abscess. An injection of penicillin (Monday in Coquilhatville) makes no difference. I get back to the boat and worry that I am going nuts."

But poor Trudeau hadn't yet seen the end of his troubles. On February 8, he received three letters: the first from his mother, another from Laurendeau, and a third from Helen Segerstråle, who had changed her mind about marrying him because she found their relationship too tumultuous. Soon after Trudeau's departure, she had met someone else and now was enjoying more peace and harmony than ever before.[10] It was too much for Trudeau. Fed up, and in agony from toothache, he cried out: "Enough of this hemisphere, I am flying home."[11] He wanted to see Helen. Perhaps he could make her change her mind? But when you are in the middle of nowhere, flying to Europe is no easy task. After taking many connecting flights, he eventually landed in Stockholm, where Helen met him. "We had an aperitif," Trudeau wrote, "walked,

---

* Coquilhatville was in Belgian Congo. This city, located in the Democratic Republic of Congo, is now called Mbandaka.

talked a lot, kissed a little."[12] From mid-February until his departure on March 6, he saw Helen almost every day. They went to shows, ate together, or went for walks, but it was clear that the former lovers were now just friends. Marriage was ruled out.

So when Trudeau returned to Paris on March 13, everything seemed to be falling apart. He had quit his job in Ottawa and there was no immediate prospect for another one. He had had to leave Africa suddenly, he had suffered unbearable toothache, and, above all, his projected marriage to Helen would now not take place. No wonder that he wrote to Pelletier on March 16: "I have never in my life felt so unattached, physically and morally; . . . all in all, I am in a rather pitiable state." Who wouldn't, in his shoes?

Unaware of the context, which was unknown until now, many people have over-emphasized these words. In the process they have also overlooked the rest of the letter, which casts an interesting light on Trudeau's political ideas. Pelletier had enquired if he "would be interested in running in a provincial election, probably *in asbestos country*, with the *total support* of the unions and our chums, of course." In his letter, Trudeau replied: "Oh well! Yes." But he wasn't the type to make a blind commitment. He chided Pelletier for not providing him with "any elements that would have allowed [me] to respond intelligently. . . . If you're looking for more than a straw man; if you want a motivated candidate who acts intelligently, you have to present to me a well-thought proposal." He needed precise answers to all his questions, such as: What was meant by the "total support" of the unions? Was there a specific platform? Where would the money come from? He concluded with a biting comment: "I leave you, hoping that your next letter will be less simplistic."[13]

Pelletier explained in his memoirs where this idea came from. A little group of well-meaning union activists led by Jean Marchand knew that in the upcoming elections, expected in the summer of 1952, no party could defeat the Union Nationale of Maurice Duplessis. So they dreamed up a plan of electing two or three independent candidates, with union backing, so they would gain a voice in the government. But they knew precious little about the political game and made no concrete plans to achieve their goal. "We were dreaming," admitted Pelletier, many years later.[14] Trudeau never got answers to his questions. This unrealistic project was nipped in the bud, yet it reveals that Trudeau was interested in running for office in Quebec as early as 1952.

—◆—

This letter is dated March 16, 1952. By Easter, April 13, Trudeau was in Moscow. What was he doing there? And how did he get permission to travel behind the Iron Curtain, at the high point of the Red Scare? To find out, we must go back in time once again, to Quebec, shortly after his departure from the civil service. In October 1951, Professor Maurice Lamontagne of Université Laval received a letter from Paris, inviting him to attend a meeting in Copenhagen to prepare for an international conference to be held in Moscow.[15] The letter was signed by Alfred Sauvy, a noted French economist and demographer who had been an adviser to the Raynaud government in 1938, and once again in 1954, to the Pierre Mendès France government. Lamontagne mentioned the invitation to Trudeau, who found the idea very interesting. On October 15, Lamontagne wrote to Sauvy to explain that he was unable to go to Copenhagen, but would appreciate receiving more information on this meeting. And he added: "One of my young friends, Pierre Trudeau, will be leaving for Europe shortly, and is very interested in the Moscow meeting. If he does not arrive in time to attend the conference in Copenhagen, he will try to meet you in Paris."[16] In due course, Trudeau had a long meeting with Alfred Sauvy in Paris. And on November 12 – before his departure for Egypt – he wrote a six-page letter to Lamontagne from his hotel in Florence, recounting the conversation.[17] He felt that "people mean business in Moscow" and Sauvy "seems satisfied with the guarantees of political neutrality given in Copenhagen," since it is an international planning committee, made up of distinguished personalities, who is organizing the Moscow International Economic Conference, scheduled for April 1952.

Trudeau was satisfied. But given the Cold War psychosis then raging, he was aware of the risks participants would be running. His recent experience at the Privy Council had impressed on him the extent of public fears about Communism in Canada. Duplessis, in particular, had a fixation on Communism. Everyone should be cautious, but "we, Canadians," Trudeau wrote, "would benefit from being even more so. . . . Given our political climate, it is important to make clear we are nobody's fools." What should they do to avoid suspicion? Trudeau had an idea: invite bona fide anti-Communist participants to come along: "We should also encourage François-Albert Angers to come, as he is thinking of doing: his unflinchingly right-wing views would provide an excellent lightning rod against suspicion!"

François-Albert Angers was a well-known Quebec economist and professor at the École des Hautes Études Commerciales who overtly advocated corporatism. Corporatism, you ask? Hadn't this economic system died off with the defeat of the fascist regimes implementing it? Not quite. Since the end of the war, the Catholic Church had been shifting again to the right, under the influence of Pope Pius XII, whose positions on Nazi and fascist regimes is still highly controversial. This rightward shift was only too clear in Quebec, for example in the "Charbonneau Affair." The "leftist" archbishop of Montreal had been transferred to Victoria, British Columbia, "due to illness" and replaced by Mgr. Paul-Emile Léger. With this appointment, "the situation changed completely," writes Suzanne Clavette, in her comprehensive study *Les dessous d'Asbestos, une lutte idéologique contre la participation des travailleurs* [Behind the Scenes at Asbestos: An Ideological Struggle Against Worker Participation].[18] Mgr. Léger was a traditionalist who fully agreed with the Pope's condemnation of the new "leftist" orientations within the Church. (In 1953, Pius XII put an end to the social involvement of worker priests, alleging that this would lead them toward Marxism.) Mgr. Léger also wanted to radically transform the role of Catholic Action: "The first responsibility of Catholic Action . . . is to stir the intelligence of its members about God."[19] As Suzanne Clavette rightly notes, "This is a far cry from the social commitment and the tradition of *seeing, judging* and *taking action* which had been the hallmark of Catholic Action from its beginnings."[20]

An anti-labour wind was sweeping Quebec. For example, the Association professionnelle des industriels (the Quebec Association of Industrial Employers, a Catholic businessmen's group often referred to by its French acronym API) held its annual convention on November 14 and 15, 1949. Attending the convention were well-known figures such as François-Albert Angers; Marcel Clément, whom we will meet again later; Mgr. Maurice Roy, Archbishop of Quebec; and Premier Maurice Duplessis. The opening speech of the convention underlined the serious harm that recent strikes, including the Asbestos one, had caused to the social fabric. Members were invited "to focus on one aspect of the

Church's social doctrine, namely corporatism."²¹ François-Albert Angers and Marcel Clément came fully prepared to lead the association in this direction and unveiled an action plan. Starting from the premise that the labour movement had gained too much power, thereby threatening the balance between employers and employees, they recommended that the provincial government formulate "a law allowing the practice . . . of authentic corporatism."²²

We can therefore understand why Trudeau thought that Angers's "unflinchingly right-wing views" could serve as a lightning rod. Who could possibly accuse Angers of being a Communist? A fascist perhaps, but surely not a Communist. . . . But Trudeau wanted to do more than forestall any possible attacks. He wanted to be absolutely sure that the Moscow Conference would be a serious one. If Lamontagne deemed it necessary, he was willing to go to Prague to discuss the matter openly with key organizers. And if everything indicated that the Soviet Union was truly reaching out to the West, then Canadians simply had to be there: "I would hate people to say, rightly, that we are the ones keeping the Iron Curtain shut tight."

When he wrote this letter in November 1951, he didn't believe he would be able to stay in Europe until April. So he encouraged Lamontagne to make up his mind as soon as possible: "Since you at Laval constitute the only social sciences research group that counts in French Canada, your attitude will affect many other people. . . . The question that now matters is whether we (or you?) can go there simply as witnesses of freedom and as men of good faith." On January 16, 1952, after a lengthy correspondence, Lamontagne sent a letter to the secretary of the organizing committee along with an article from the *New York Times* indicating that the Moscow Conference struck Americans as a propaganda exercise. "In these circumstances," he said, "despite the precautions you have taken, people in North America who are willing to participate in the Conference will expose themselves to unfair but violent attacks." This convinced Lamontagne to turn down the invitation. But Trudeau accepted the challenge and headed for the conference. In spite of his busy agenda and the torments of his love life, on June 7 he sent to Laurendeau at *Le Devoir* seven despatches on his trip to Moscow. In fact, he was back in Paris on May 5, and left for Stockholm on the 19th to spend four days there. On May 29, he was back in the Swedish capital. In vain!

Helen had not changed her mind. The articles appeared in *Le Devoir* between June 14 and 21, 1952, while Trudeau was still in Europe. He returned to Quebec on July 23, after an absence of nine months.

———◦———

The seven feature articles appeared as a series under the general title "Je reviens de Moscou" [Back from Moscow].[23] In the first article, Trudeau explained why he had decided to attend the meeting, although he knew that "for many people, the Soviet Union is synonymous with hell, and nobody can set foot there without making a pact with the devil."[24] Of the many reasons he gave for attending, we will mention just three.

First, he said, the principles seemed eminently acceptable. According to the declaration made at the Copenhagen meeting, the purpose of the Moscow Conference was to study "ways to improve the lives of peoples worldwide through the peaceful cooperation of different countries and different systems and the development of economic exchanges between all countries." It welcomed "anyone who wanted to promote peaceful cooperation in the economic field, whatever his economic, political and social opinions."[25] Besides, he added, like him, "nearly 500 people, in 49 countries, representing all shades of political opinion, accepted."

He gave a second reason: "I hate, both as lawyer and economist," he wrote, "to sweep pacts aside without bothering first to examine them. Why hide the fact? If I were granted the safe-conduct Dante apparently got, I would gladly go to hell to collect some statistics on the privation of the sight of God."

And thirdly, as John Lennon sang twenty years later in "Give Peace a Chance," Trudeau argued that if we really want peace, we cannot afford to reject "even the remotest chance of bringing it about." For all these reasons, he was convinced not only that he was right to go but also that Canada should have sent "first-rate citizens."

In his second article, "Premières rencontres" [First Encounters],[26] he explained that unlike the French delegates who flew from Paris to Moscow via Prague, he decided to take the train via Austria. He had to apply for visas, which were speedily granted by the Soviets. He thought he would arrive incognito at the Prague train station at three o'clock in the morning, but was stupefied to discover that the authorities were expecting him. He appreciated the treatment he received: "They assigned me magnificent lodgings, fed me, granted me the Soviet visa and sent me on to Moscow, with exemplary speed and courtesy." On arriving in Moscow four days before the conference, he was again received with open arms and installed in a new hotel, "a masterpiece in the nouveau riche style," and granted "an interpreter, a driver and a Ziss, an amazing copy of a Chrysler luxury sedan." He nevertheless managed to shake off his minders and walked alone, travelling by subway and bus. When he told his hosts that he intended to go to Mass on Passion Sunday, they at first made fun of the fact he "still believed in such nonsense," but then they gave him all the information he needed. He went to Mass four Sundays in a row, in three different places. He also entered a synagogue and several Orthodox churches. Trudeau did not conclude, nevertheless, that religion was alive and well in the USSR: "On the main feast days, these temples are filled to overflowing – but only with elderly people. Religious freedom has not been abolished – but for lack of religious instruction, young people are being cut off from Christianity here."

Trudeau was surprised that the authorities gave in to all his requests, even when he asked to consult in libraries the works of the much-despised Leon Trotsky. He took all kinds of liberties. The tolerance of his hosts seemed boundless. But Trudeau, who had an irrepressible love of mischief, wanted to know, to quote Jean Cocteau, "how far we can go too far." So the ultimate test was to mock Stalin's personality cult. "In the city and the country," he wrote, "I was impressed to see both in public and even private places, an assortment of effigies, busts, statues, pictures, paintings, engravings, mosaics, embroidery, bas-relief, high-relief, pasteboard, ebony, ivory, marble, sculpted rice grains and what not, showing the Father of the People, the Idol of the Working Masses, the Leader of Universal Socialism, the Liberator of the Oppressed, the Head of the Party of Peace, the Philosopher of History, the Guide of Democracy, the Wise, the Eminent, the Sweet, the Hard, the Infallible, the Great Comrade Stalin: So I tenderly threw a snowball at a statue representing him in a particularly benevolent pose." Was he tossed into jail for the crime of *lèse-majesté*? Not at all. "It was a scandal," Trudeau wrote, "but my hosts were more pained than angry."

Once the conference was over, Trudeau described, in his third article, the people he had rubbed shoulders with during the two weeks he spent in the USSR. This article was appropriately entitled "Un peuple sympathique, mais conventionnel jusqu'à la nausée" [Friendly People but Nauseatingly Conventional].[27] Trudeau denounced the indoctrination of the population: "Stalinism has often been compared to a religion, but you really have to go to the USSR to feel how blind their faith is, how unflinching their hope, how inquisitorial their charity. Marx the prophet; Lenin the precursor; and Stalin made man. I do not write this in a spirit of blasphemy, but rather to get readers to understand the strength and irrational character of the movement that inspires the faithful." Trudeau knew that any generalization blurs over nuances, and that he had "just barely passed through a few large cities in four Soviet republics, and also that the number of people a person can see in a month is necessarily limited." Even so, he dared to deduce from his observation that "the people seem content with their relative prosperity."

Drawing both on the Soviet struggle against the Nazis and on what he saw first-hand, Trudeau criticized the Western perception of the Soviet Union: "Western politicians make me laugh when they portray the Russians as a people living solely in the hope of being freed from Stalin's yoke." On the contrary, "the more they feel their country threatened from outside, the more they will rally around their leaders, and harden their monolithic thinking." What solution did he propose? "A lasting peace would make the Stalinist defensive reactions meaningless, and they would have to loosen their grip over society." In other words, "Give Peace a Chance . . ." Trudeau was well aware what happened to opponents of the regime. Mass support for Stalinism should therefore be interpreted with a grain of salt: "Besides, when the choice is between believing and dying, it is not surprising to find a majority of people are believers."

In the next article, "Le citoyen soviétique demeure un 'cochon de payant'" [The Soviet Citizen Foots the Bill], Trudeau gave an unflattering account of the cost of living and the state of the Soviet economy and finances.[28] Everywhere he went, he witnessed difficult living conditions and a lack of housing and consumer goods. He noted the long line-ups in front of most stores. And to give readers a rough idea of Soviet living standards, he converted the rouble into dollars, acknowledging, however, that the rouble "is not officially traded on foreign exchange markets." Foreigners had to buy them "at a rate that has nothing to do with its official value." This guesstimate left a lot to be desired but gave some idea of the cost of housing, restaurants, and some staple foods. He clearly saw that people in the USSR had a very hard life, yet they were not miserable. Where the regime's achievements were concerned, he wondered whom they benefited most of all: "The country is no doubt making tremendous strides. But it is advancing exactly along the lines laid out by the planners, not by the citizens. . . . We will never know whether the Russians would have preferred being less cooped up in their huts, rather than traveling around in incredibly luxurious subways. So in the Soviet Union, just as in capitalist countries, the citizen still foots the bill. His only consolation lies in believing that the Soviet economy aims at the common good rather than the good of a single class. This is what the People's Democracies call 'economic democracy.'"

Trudeau devoted the fifth and sixth articles of his series to the conference itself.[29] There could be no doubt that it was the result of a Communist initiative. Was that reason enough to boycott it? Not at all, he answered: "The important thing was that the organization should remain neutral enough to allow men of all stripes, and even potential enemies, to work together. Because these are the men who will bring about peace." As expected, the speakers from the People's Democracies sang the praises of their regime, repeating one after the other that "all is for the best in the best of all possible worlds," and claiming that the economic blockade only hurt the West. Listening to them, Trudeau noted ironically, "one would inevitably have concluded that the goal of the Conference was to help the Western nations devastated by their own blockade." As to concrete results of the eight-day meeting, only a few agreements were concluded between businessmen.

This did not surprise Trudeau in the least: "It would have been naive," he wrote, "to expect more than that when the conference was boycotted by the United States, the country which so powerfully dominates world trade outside of the Soviet bloc." The important thing was to take the first steps, "to show that not all capital, not all markets are controlled by the United States." He was sorry that Canada had not yet realized that "the omnipresent dollar is not without danger for national sovereignty." But he hastened to add: "Of course, I would like an omnipresent rouble even less." On balance, he concluded that the conference was a welcome initiative of reconciliation that should not have been boycotted for the simple reason that it had been organized by the other side: "Otherwise, we would only ever make peace with countries that agreed with us." To the end of his life, Trudeau tirelessly maintained that peace inevitably involves negotiation with enemies, so we must keep the channels of communication open.

In the seventh and last article of the series, he took stock of the Soviet situation under the revealing title "Est-ce pour ça qu'on a fait trois révolutions?" [Is This Why They Launched Three Revolutions?].[30] To the burning issue at the time "Do the Soviets seek war?" he replied that he had seen more uniforms there than in any other country and found the propaganda highly effective. These two factors led him to issue a warning: in the USSR, "more than elsewhere, the people will follow the orders of their superiors." Russians, he said, are presented with a distorted image of foreign countries. They are taught, for example, that in America, material well-being is reserved for a privileged class, while in the USSR, it is for everyone. Trudeau denounced this false propaganda, providing ample evidence of social inequality in the USSR. To him, much of the hatred inculcated against the United States and the capitalist governments was "based on envy." What proof did he offer? Russians copied Americans as much as they possibly could. This could explain the popularity of Tarzan movies, for example. His conclusion showed clearly that he emphatically rejected the Soviet system: "Did they launch three revolutions, live through two wars, trigger terrible famines, liquidate millions of kulaks, purge the revolutionary old guard and imprison an unknown number of political opponents merely in order to establish a system of such commonplace inequalities, so similar to our own? . . . I do not see what the Revolution achieved, or what the Party wants to protect apart from the absolute power of the comrades in control."

Trudeau, who was testing the limits of official Soviet tolerance, finally reached them, at his own expense. The exact reason for the abrupt turnaround he experienced is unknown. The fact is that the administrative system he had found so flexible "suddenly became as stiff as a corpse," and he was coldly ordered to leave the USSR. The embassies of Poland and Germany were re-opened for him one evening, so they could quickly stamp the required visas in his passport. At six o'clock the next morning, two men arrived at his hotel, woke him up, drove him to the airport, and put him on a plane bound for Poland.[31] Farewell, USSR.

Trudeau's articles were very well received. He was flooded with invitations to present his journey. In September, in a series of four fifteen-minute talks on CBF, the French-language network of Radio-Canada, he recounted his journey behind the Iron Curtain in a light and amusing style, highlighting its human dimension.[32] These talks were published shortly afterwards in *Le Devoir*. In the October 23 issue of *Le Quartier Latin*, the student newspaper at the Université de Montréal, appeared a report on a talk he gave to the International Relations Club, under the title "Back from the USSR – Comrade Trudeau."[33] The word "comrade" was obviously intended as a joke. The students were well aware that Trudeau had been won over neither by Communism nor by the Soviet system. The author of the report, Jacques Brossard, summarized Trudeau's conclusions as follows: "The USSR is not the paradise they want us to imagine. There is no *true* equality there: besides, the Russians do not deny the many inequalities in their society, although official propaganda proclaims they are all perfectly equal. . . . *The worker is actually more important and wields more influence in our democratic countries than in the USSR.*"* Writing on behalf of the club, Yvon Côté penned an ecstatic letter of thanks to Trudeau.

Although Trudeau did not characterize the USSR as a living hell, he clearly remained highly critical of the Soviet system. At home, his message seemed to go over quite well. For several months, everything was hunky-dory. Could Lamontagne's fears have been unfounded? Had Trudeau simply been too cautious in speaking to his friend of the need to take along a right-wing lightning rod? Actually, considering the tsunami that was unleashed on Trudeau five months later, a lightning rod would have been a ridiculously inadequate defence.

In November 1952, three publications – *Nos cours, L'Action catholique,* and *Le Droit* – simultaneously printed a "detailed comment on Pierre Elliott Trudeau's articles."[34] Strangely enough, this extremely harsh full-scale attack was not even submitted to *Le Devoir,* which had published the articles so roughly challenged. Was it because, unlike *Le Devoir,* these three publications were dominated by religious conservative orders?

---

* A reminder that, unless otherwise stated, italics are in the original text.

And why did it take such a long time for this critique to come out? According to the official explanation, the author was off travelling. How odd. If the author was away travelling, that meant he must also have been away when Trudeau's articles first appeared. Who made him aware of them, and why? Did he launch into this stinging criticism on his own initiative or because someone else put him up to it? These questions bring us into the midst of a no-holds-barred fight.

The author of this "detailed review" wasn't just anyone. The Assumptionist Father Léopold Braün had been a priest in Moscow for twelve years and was fluent in several languages, including Russian. He was a rabid anti-Communist and had worked closely with the U.S. government in its fight against Communism. For Father Braün, the USSR was clearly the Evil Empire. And since Trudeau had not described it as such, he was a devilish fiend. So he had to be exorcised. And when it came to combating the devil, fair play wasn't necessary. Every line of attack was acceptable: distorting facts, making up sentences and attributing them unfairly to Trudeau, judging him on mere intent, denigrating him . . .

Even the most cursory reading of this "detailed review" – actually far longer than Trudeau's original seven pages – reveals that Father Braün did not seek just to refute Trudeau's message; he was determined to annihilate the messenger. This is clearly revealed by the expressions he used: "teems with errors and false conclusions . . . ; dares, with a scandalously offhand manner . . . ; unbelievable blunders . . . ; what an insult to the intelligence of readers of Le Devoir . . . ; ignorance . . . ; spouting this type of nonsense . . . ; parading his highly offensive incompetence. . . . What was Trudeau the so-called economist thinking . . . ? He should have kept his mouth shut . . ." Father Braün accused him of absolutely everything, including converting roubles into dollars in order to compare living standards. All of this demonstrated beyond the shadow of a doubt, in the priest's view, Trudeau's utter incompetence in economics.

It was a case of Goliath against David. On one side was a priest – with all the influence that this status gave him in Quebec – who knew Russia and the Russian language and had moreover gained considerable prestige in the United States for his role as a specialist in the fight against Communism. On the other side was a thirty-year-old man, a budding economist and sometime journalist, who described living conditions in the Soviet Union on the basis of a one-month stay there. This is a rare occasion where Trudeau seemed profoundly shaken; his reputation and future credibility depended on the outcome. He was well aware that being labelled a "Communist" or even a "socialist" was almost equivalent to a death warrant for anyone aspiring to a career in the civil service or in politics. This was no longer a war of ideas. The fact that Trudeau's opponent wore a cassock only drove him on to fight back that much harder. In a letter to Laurendeau, he concisely summed up his opinion of his opponent: "the Reverend Father Leopold Braün, A.A., and priest for eternity, is either a fool or a rogue."[35]

Trudeau was already convinced that Quebec clericalism was an obstacle to democracy. He had already denounced the lack of Christian charity of several missionaries. He had already objected to the unjust treatment of Archbishop Charbonneau and his subsequent exile to Victoria, British Columbia. In his article "Functional Politics II," he had openly challenged the principle of the divine right of bishops in the secular world. But this time, the fight was personal. His reputation was at stake. That is why he threw himself headlong into battle.

He wanted to confront his attackers face to face. On November 21 he went to Quebec City to meet the editor of *L'Action catholique,* Louis-Philippe Roy. During their encounter, Roy "was unable to keep up his bluster, and seemed much less brave in person than he was at a distance wielding his pen."[36] He agreed to publish Trudeau's reply if it was neither defamatory nor too long. Trudeau dutifully prepared his rebuttal for the three publications, barely containing his anger. His rough draft is full of strong language, and whole sentences are crossed out and rewritten. First he blamed Father Braün for quoting him "very rarely and never completely, which in itself constitutes an unfair tactic when referring to a text no one has close at hand, since it came out in newspapers far away in time and space." Furthermore "publishing this attack without first submitting it for publication to *Le Devoir,* which had printed the original story, is a violation of professional ethics."

To give an idea of Trudeau's general tone, let us quote the following: "Father Braün is supposed to speak perfect Russian, German, Polish and some other languages besides. This may well be the case. But nobody ever told us that he spoke French, which perhaps explains why he misunderstood me so totally, and wrote such an inept reply. However, every man should get his due, and I acknowledge that this priest is quite an expert at delivering insults." Trudeau went on to dissect each of what he called Father Braün's "blunders."

On December 1, 1952, he gave his reply to the three conservative publications: by registered mail to Roy at *L'Action catholique;* by hand to *Notre cours;* and by mail with an accompanying letter addressed to Camille L'Heureux, editor-in-chief of *Le Droit* in Ottawa: "I expect the respect for truth, justice and the law will incite you to publish my defence on the same page and in the same places as Father Braün's articles." On December 3, L'Heureux replied that he could not publish the response Trudeau had sent in its current form, "given the personal attacks it contains." Yet the personal attacks of Father Braün did not seem to bother him. But Trudeau was not about to give up. On December 11 he went to Ottawa, met an apparently friendly L'Heureux, and they came to an understanding. On December 15, as agreed, he sent a completely redrafted text to the newspaper. This time, L'Heureux told him on the telephone that "the Oblates were impressed by its accuracy." Trudeau's reply appeared in *Le Droit* on December 18. So one battle was won.

At *Nos cours,* things didn't go so well: far from it. Trudeau called on the Institut Pie XI and delivered his reply to the editor of the review, Father Jean-Baptiste Desrosiers, who promised to read it and publish it the following week, "if it is accepted by the Council." On December 4, Father Desrosiers sent a letter of refusal: "There is no need to convene the Council of the Institut Pie XI. Your reply is nothing but a series of half-truths." Trudeau was not deterred. He wanted to explain his position face to face. Learning that Father Braün lived at the Collège de Montréal, he turned up there. To no avail. He was told the priest was away.

Trudeau tried to see Father Desrosiers. Through sheer perseverance, he got to meet him on December 20. Their confrontation took on epic proportions. Initially, Trudeau noted in his personal papers, "the poor man tried to be conciliatory; said he was not an 'enemy.' He handed me back my text admitting he hadn't had the chance to study it thoroughly. He was sorry, he said, because he was the one who had asked Father Braün to respond to my articles." (Thus we have just learned, along with Trudeau, that Father Braün was indeed acting on behalf of Desrosiers, and perhaps of others as well.) Desrosiers tried all sorts of excuses for refusing to publish the article. But Trudeau wasn't deterred. The priest tried to give reasons for the rejection, but proved "woefully ignorant" and incapable of identifying a single error. Trudeau demanded that *Nos cours* at least publish the same article that *Le Droit* had accepted. Desrosiers refused. "Why?" Trudeau asked, insisting on an explanation. Desrosiers jumped up and screamed: "Why?" Trudeau shoved him back into his chair, urging him to remain calm.

Desrosiers finally admitted that publishing Trudeau's response would cause them great harm. If that was case, Trudeau demanded that he sign a statement admitting he didn't want to publish him. Desrosiers refused but promised not only to read more carefully the reply *Le Droit* had published but also to give Trudeau an answer by the following Tuesday. Trudeau got more aggressive: If *Nos cours* refused to publish his rebuttal, then he would bring this matter before the courts. Unaccustomed to such threats, Desrosiers "was at a loss. . . ."

And through this verbal jousting, we discover, as did Trudeau, the crux of the matter: "He finally blamed me for that sentence I had written in *Cité libre* about divine right. A few priests had read it and had all found it unacceptable." So that's how it came to this. Some clergymen had patiently built up their resentment for two years, waiting for the appropriate moment to switch to the attack mode. And to them, Father Braün emerged as the person uniquely qualified to shut Trudeau's bloody little trap, once and for all.

Were Trudeau's threats successful? On January 10, 1953, *Nos cours* published his response, and *L'action catholique* published it on January 13. Could he now declare victory? Hardly! We counted the pages. In *Nos cours*, for example, his text was reduced to two pages and was followed by a new eight-page reply by Father Braün, which was just as venomous as the first, if not more so. Desrosiers contributed four additional pages, enthusiastically backing Father Braün's views, while adding a little venom of his own. Father Desrosiers stated clearly why Trudeau was so dangerous. He had had the audacity to say in *Cité libre* that "the divine right of prime ministers or bishops, simply doesn't exist." For Desrosiers, "this short passage amounts essentially to communism, because it undermines the entire social order." Only a Communist could question the divine right of bishops! Desrosiers warned Trudeau that "he needed to come out clearly against communism."[37] This made no sense. Trudeau had not only harshly criticized the Soviet regime in his articles but had even said up front, in the first sentence of the only two pages Desrosiers was good enough to publish in this issue, "I am opposed to communism." Did Desrosiers even glance at what he published before writing his answer?

"Lie, and lie again: something of your lie will live on forever," said Voltaire. Trudeau would long be suspected of being a Communist fellow traveller, a situation that caused him many problems. For example, shortly after the "detailed review" came out, he learned that Professor Esdras Minville, director of the École des Hautes Études Commerciales at the Université de Montréal, considered Father Braün's attack to be "very serious." This opinion helped Trudeau understand why Minville seemed so "aloof when [they spoke about] a teaching position in political science."[38] Over the next eight years (until 1961), he applied several times for a professorship, and each time his candidacy was blocked by university authorities or by Premier Duplessis himself. It was well known, though, that he was at least as qualified as most other professors. But then *they* were not suspected of Communism. . . .

Enough already! Two well-known public figures who could not reasonably be accused of having Communist sympathies could no longer tolerate such a flagrant attack on justice and truth. André Laurendeau, deputy editor-in-chief of *Le Devoir,* and François-Albert Angers – the very man whom Trudeau wanted to take along to serve as a lightning rod in Moscow – expressed their outrage at these unfair tactics. The title of Laurendeau's article, which was published in *L'Action nationale,* was aptly chosen: "La chasse aux sorcières est-elle commencée?" [Has the Witch Hunt Started?].[39] Unsurprisingly, this article was published neither by *Nos cours* nor *Le Droit,* which had published Father Braün's articles. Evidently, everyone stuck to his own turf. Laurendeau denounced "the acrimonious and insulting tone adopted by this priest" in criticizing articles that were admirable for "their nuances, their remarkably subtle analysis." He detailed the profoundly dishonest means Father Braün had used to achieve his ends: in quoting any of Trudeau's sentences, Father Braün isolated it and "twisted it out of context so that it became unrecognizable." The best way to show the "exaggerated and ridiculous" character of Father Braün's attack and his distortions, Laurendeau wrote, was to put Trudeau's original sentences alongside Braün's. But there were so many distortions that it would take more than two issues of *L'Action nationale* to simply reproduce them. Laurendeau returned to the offensive in *Le Devoir* of February 28, 1953. In "An Epilogue," he accused

Father Braün of "having misinterpreted, distorted and warped Trudeau." He added that it took quite "a fanatic to refuse to hear a moderate witness." This led him to ask with concern: "In our own special way, are we becoming totalitarian?"

François-Albert Angers wrote a remarkable twenty-four-page article, entitled "Au nom de l'honnêteté et du bon sens!" [In the Name of Honesty and Common Sense].[40] He dissected each of Father Braün's accusations, for example about religion, economics, or cars, and then compared them with what Trudeau had actually written. The conclusions were obvious: Father Braün "clearly wants to find fault with Trudeau, to contradict him, even when they basically agree, by adding some little nuance or detail. Worse, to make him say things he never said, and to refute him as if he were guilty." According to Angers, Father Braün was blinded by his ideology: "[He] was so bent on combating the ideas that he expected to find, . . . that he ended up detecting them even when Trudeau was expressing the opposite view either explicitly or implicitly."

Angers came to the crux of the problem: "Basically, Trudeau is being blamed for having gone to Moscow, for having seen in Russia something other than a primitive Stone Age system, and for suggesting that there could be some benefit in maintaining limited relations between West and East." Angers was concerned: "All that communism wants in order to usher in a new era around the world is for Catholics to be divided" into warring factions. A month later, in "How P.E. Trudeau's Reports Were Distorted,"[41] Angers asserted that Father Braün's aggressive critique of a fellow Christian was hurting all Catholics. Trudeau and Angers saw eye to eye on Father Braün's tactics in this case, but once Trudeau's chapters in the collective work on the Asbestos strike came out in 1956, he and Angers found themselves at loggerheads.

Trudeau was shocked that priests had singled him out for vicious attacks. Taking advantage of their power, they were gagging him, denying him the right of reply. Fortunately, in Cité libre he could vent his frustration. The May 1953 issue of the review featured "Matériaux pour servir à une enquête sur le cléricalisme" [Materials for the Study of Clericalism], an article divided into two parts: the first part was signed by Trudeau, and the second one by Roger Rolland.[42] Rolland pleaded vigorously, although coolly, for a greater role of lay people in the life of the Church. "It is because the layman has so far been cut out of this role that he now has a hard time recognizing himself in the Canadian Church."[43]

Trudeau vented his rage. His aim was twofold: to use this controversy to struggle against clericalism and to settle accounts with Fathers Braün and Desrosiers, who had lined up the whole "arsenal of the hierarchical Church" against him.[44] He began by clarifying his own position: "Let it be understood at the outset that I am an anticlericalist. (I write this without shame, even though I firmly believe many people will assume that I am therefore anticlerical.) In other words, I believe with Maritain that 'the clergy should not directly hold the levers of strictly temporal and political action.' (*Humanisme intégral*, p. 287)."[45] Let us note, once again, this reference to Maritain. Trudeau acknowledged then, and would acknowledge to the end of his life, that "the sacrament of Holy Orders confers grace and specific powers relating solely to the position and function of the priesthood." Let us highlight the word *solely*. To Trudeau, this meant that "in addressing purely temporal problems, a cassock is of no particular help, a tonsure is no sign of immunity before the law and public opinion, and a doctorate in theology should not be mistaken for a certificate of universal infallible competence."[46] As a result, he continued, "each time a member of the clergy gets involved in temporal matters, he should do so as a citizen. . . . All men are equal in the public sphere." Therefore, a priest "may well be a theologian, but if he spouts sheer nonsense, then he must accept being contradicted and treated as a fool."[47] Once this principle is well understood and applied, "then the clergy and lay people could work more calmly to build a truly Christian church and city."[48] For Trudeau, it was clear that everyone would benefit from this healthier relationship.

———◦——

History also showed, he added, that the alliance between the Church and the State often led to anti-Christian consequences. He recalled horrors such as the Inquisition and the St. Bartholomew Massacre: "Lest we forget, all these atrocities, these degradations were committed in the name of Christ and the universal Church."[49] The comments that followed illustrate the considerable evolution of his thoughts since leaving Montreal in 1944: "We, Catholics of French origin, are still ashamed of the incredible depravities committed in the name of Catholicism during the Dreyfus Affair."[50] The young Trudeau who had written the anti-Semitic play *Dupés* at Collège Jean-de-Brébeuf in 1938, who had been influenced by the right-wing ideology of authors such as Charles Maurras and Léon Daudet, was gone forever. Now a more mature Trudeau was deploring the shameful Dreyfus Affair and drawing lessons from the past: "We should take care that hatred and persecution do not enter Canada through the gates of the Church," he wrote.[51]

So much for the article's first objective of combating clericalism. But Trudeau also wanted to settle scores with Fathers Braün and Desrosiers, who had lined up the whole "arsenal of the hierarchical Church" against him. Was all this, he wondered "because I saw beautiful parks in Moscow, and said so?"[52] He dissected their polemical attack, describing in some detail the manipulative approach the two priests had adopted. "The Church was definitely not speaking through the mouths of these bitter and vindictive men," he wrote, "these guardians of light . . . who want to turn Quebec into the last bastion of clericalism and political reactionarism, a haven for all the ideological wrecks riding the inexorable tide of History."[53]

He then turned to the publishers of the journals that had attacked him – journals oozing with "sickly-sweet religiosity": "If you disagreed with what I had published in June, why couldn't you start up a discussion on your own? Did you really need to wait five whole months to flood me with insults which any moron could have drafted in just five days? Why did you wait for our Archbishop to be absent and for the publisher of *Le Devoir* to be off traveling, to get your fascistic *combinatione*** going? Why? Because you are just a bunch of flunkeys, ready to cravenly follow the first foreign schemer who offers to think in your place."[54] If they wanted respect, they should live by the words of St. Paul: "We put no obstacle in anyone's way, so that no fault may be found with our ministry. (2 Corinthians 6.3)"[55]

---

* Captain Alfred Dreyfus (1859–1936) was a French Jew unjustly accused of treason and sentenced to perpetual exile. The Dreyfus Affair (1894–1906) revealed the rabid anti-Semitism of those who claimed he was guilty. This affair created profound cleavages then, and it remains to this day one of the darkest chapters of French history.

** This is a French form of an Italian word describing the underhand alliances politicians set up to achieve their goals. In French, this word has a strictly pejorative connotation.

This controversy would have lasting consequences. In January 1954, Edgar McInnis, president of the Canadian Institute of International Affairs, offered to cover all of Trudeau's expenses so he could attend a conference in late March in Lahore, Pakistan.[56] Trudeau accepted. To reach Lahore, he had first to obtain a visa to travel through the United States, a country in the throes of the McCarthyite Communist witch hunt. The U.S. Department of Justice replied that it would first have to review his application: "The deferred inspection may result in your temporary exclusion from admission into the United States . . . as a person whose entry may be prejudicial to the interests of the United States."[57] Could the articles by Father Braün, a man who worked so closely with the U.S. government in its fight against Communism, have helped put Trudeau on the blacklist? "Lie, and lie again . . ." However, a week later, the visa was granted.

Years went by. The "Communist" label stuck. In 1960, once again, Trudeau crossed swords with a priest. In June, he learned that Abbé Gérard Saint-Pierre had referred to "Pierre Elliott Trudeau, the Canadian Karl Marx" in the February 6 issue of Le Nouvelliste, the daily newspaper of Trois-Rivières, northeast of Montreal. Trudeau was furious to discover he was once again falsely labelled a Communist. After consulting a law firm, he concluded that there were "grounds to sue and seek compensation" and decided to start the procedures. He could take the case directly before the courts and charge Saint-Pierre as a citizen, regardless of his status as an abbé.

But Trudeau, the good Catholic who had regularly asked permission to read books listed on the Index, wanted to abide by the laws of the Church. In this case, Church law required him to seek the consent of the priest's superior before proceeding. Trudeau therefore wrote to inform the bishop of Trois-Rivières, Mgr. Georges Léon Pelletier, that he was seeking from Abbé Saint-Pierre "a public, full and unequivocal retraction of his defamatory comments." Failing which, he respectfully requested Mgr. Pelletier's authorization to institute legal proceedings. "Apart from the legal aspect of the question," he added, "I hope Your Excellency will appreciate the regrettable nature of the charge of heresy launched by one of your priests against a fellow Christian."[58]

The bishop replied on June 20: "I freely admit that the abbé's description of you is hardly complimentary, and I will let the author know this. However, after reading some of your articles, I hesitate to consider this as libel."[59] And a new blow was coming this time from Mgr. Pelletier, who shared Abbé Saint-Pierre's views. On June 30, Trudeau respectfully repeated his request for a public retraction or authorization to commence legal proceedings. No answer came back . . .

Finally, in a dramatic turn of events, the archbishop answered on September 3, 1960: "I have no objection to your suing Abbé Saint-Pierre." If Mgr. Pelletier had changed his mind, why did it take him so long to respond? He was simply using a tactic to stump Trudeau, who later explained: "The authorization to sue reached me three months to the day after I had asked for it: which is to say exactly when the statute of limitations under the laws of the Province of Quebec had just run out. In fact, according to our Press Act (337 RSQ 1941, Art. 3), a suit for damages must be brought within three months of the publication of the offending article, or of knowledge that such an article has been published."[60] Trudeau concluded bitterly: "Obviously, in the current state of affairs, it cannot always be 'blamed on the English' that 'the French Canadian Catholic' is treated as a second-class citizen and deprived of his rights, in the beautiful province of Quebec."

The struggle against clericalism has long been thought to date from the 1950s. True, the fight intensified during this decade, but it actually started much earlier. Catholic Action started up in the 1930s and consisted of two branches: Jeunesse étudiante catholique (JEC or Young Catholic Students) and Jeunesse ouvrière catholique (JOC or Young Catholic Workers). Its mission was to help young people affected by the Great Depression to play a more active role in society. The members of these two associations were intent on fulfilling their social responsibilities and sought a greater place for lay people in areas controlled by the Church, such as family affairs, health care, and education. Trudeau and *Cité libre* joined the struggle, which proved long and hard but ultimately bore fruit. In the 1960s, the laity had taken over these areas.

The so-called Quiet Revolution ushered in a new era in Quebec. Clericalism rapidly waned, and the religious and social landscape of the province underwent a remarkable upheaval: monks rushed out of their monasteries; priests left holy orders; attendance at Mass went into sharp decline; couples lived under common-law arrangements; families with ten and more children became a rarity. (In fact, over the next few years Quebec's birth rate became one of the lowest in the Western world.) Given the radical changes in religious traditions, many people have seen this revolution as a collective emancipation from – or rejection of – the Catholic Church and faith. Wrongly.

In 1985, the historian Michael Behiels rightly challenged this view and showed that those engaged in the struggle against clericalism were good Catholics who criticized the Church from within. In his classic work, *Prelude to Quebec's Quiet Revolution: Liberalism versus Neo-Nationalism, 1945–1960,* he noted, for example, that "the Citélibristes feared that Quebec had become so thoroughly imbued with clericalism at all levels that . . . Quebec society was on the verge of ceasing to be truly and effectively Catholic."[61] Behiels showed that the struggle against clericalism, perceived as the major obstacle to Quebec's modernization, was led by an alliance of intellectuals from two ideological currents. On the one hand were the "liberals," represented for example by *Cité libre,* by the historians of the so-called Laval School,[*] and by some professors at Université Laval's Faculty of Social Sciences. On the other hand were the "neo-nationalists," represented by the historians of the so-called Montreal School,[**] *Le Devoir,* and *L'Action nationale.* The alliance between "liberals" and "neo-nationalists" ended with the defeat of clericalism at the end of the 1950s.

By the 1960s, as clericalism waned, the struggle jointly waged by liberals and neo-nationalists turned inward and became increasingly bitter. From 1963 to 1968, *Cité libre* faced off against the left-wing nationalist and separatist review *Parti Pris,* which counted among its contributors former Citélibristes such as Pierre Vadeboncoeur. Trudeau, who saw separatism and all types of nationalism placing the collectivity above the individual as anti-Christian, was routinely accused of treason by the "neo-nationalists." Like Berdyaev – whom he greatly admired – he was convinced that this type of "nationalism is a terrible sin against the image of God in man." Any man who does not see the next man as his brother is not truly Christian. Like Maritain and Berdyaev, he

---

[*]   These historians were Jean Hamelin, Fernand Ouellet, and later on, Marcel Trudel.

[**]   These historians were Michel Brunet, Guy Frégault, and Maurice Séguin.

believed that "the capacity to experience pain is inherent in every living creature . . . but not in collective realities. . . . Man, human personality is the supreme value, not the community, not collective realities."[62] He forcefully defended this view to the end of his life.

Two studies dealing with the relationship between Catholicism and the Quiet Revolution are worth mentioning because they bear upon Trudeau's part in it. The first one, co-authored by Martin Meunier and Jean-Philippe Warren and titled *Sortir de la "Grande Noirceur"*: *L'horizon personnaliste de la Révolution tranquille* [Beyond the Great Darkness: The Personalist Roots of the Quiet Revolution],[63] was originally published in 1999 and reissued in 2002. The second one is Michael Gauvreau's *The Catholic Origins of Quebec's Quiet Revolution, 1931–1970*, first published in English in 2005.

Meunier and Warren cogently argue that the fierce secularism and anticlericalism of the Quiet Revolution obscure the fact that those who brought about the revolution did so "not because the people then were no longer religious, but on the contrary because they were not religious enough."[64] Behiels had already made this point in 1985, although his work did not bear directly on this issue. Indeed, we have seen that the vast majority of contributors to *Cité libre* were fighting at once for the common good and for the good of the Church. Gérard Pelletier, for example, wrote that "our first concern is not the temporal sphere, over which the clergy are vying with us for authority; we are more concerned [with] the dangers our Mother Church may endure because of their encroachments."[65]

In *L'horizon personnaliste de la Révolution tranquille,* Meunier and Warren perceptively depict the emergence in France of "personalism" as a new left-wing Catholic current focusing on personal freedom and responsibility. Personalism therefore stood in stark contrast with Catholic traditionalists who advocated the respect and submission to authority, since both the "natural order" and the "social order" had been ordained by God. On the basis of solid research, Meunier and Warren examine the spread of personalism in Quebec and highlight the depth of the faith of many "architects of the Quiet Revolution."

We nonetheless find it surprising that nowhere do they mention Trudeau. They do not quote him or refer to his ideas or give any indication of his struggle. In the endnotes, his name appears only once, alongside Pelletier's, in reference to the article "Trudeau et Pelletier s'expliquent," which has nothing to do with personalism or the Quiet Revolution. This article was merely explaining their motives for moving into federal politics. In the bibliography, Trudeau's name is conspicuously absent.

We fail to understand how one can properly account for the struggle of the Catholic intelligentsia against clericalism while ignoring Trudeau. Few, if any, articles provoked the wrath of Church traditionalists the way Trudeau's did. In our view, he was the figurehead of the struggle, both through *Cité libre* and in Quebec society more generally. We have already noted that he fired a first blast in 1951, with his highly controversial comment about the divine right of priests, which led to his being summoned along with Pelletier before the Archbishop of Montreal. His trip to the Soviet Union in 1952 led to a long and vigorous debate with leading ecclesiastics, to the point where it became a *cause célèbre* in Quebec, involving, among many others, André Laurendeau and François-Albert Angers, two very well-known intellectuals. His struggle against clericalism continued unabated, such as, for example, in the collective work he edited on the Asbestos strike in 1956, where his denunciation of the many obstacles to Quebec's emancipation reverberated throughout the country.

Gauvreau approaches the subject from a different perspective and criticizes the various studies on the Quiet Revolution for having unduly marginalized Catholicism as a cultural phenomenon. By "cultural phenomenon," he means anything related to the major fields of the Church's social interventions such as the family, education, or health care. According to Gauvreau, stuffing all these activities into a grab bag called "clericalism" amounts to a distortion of historical reality and a mere caricature of the Church's essential role. Moreover, Gauvreau believes that by depriving the Church of her traditional areas of intervention the Quiet Revolution had a negative impact on Quebec.

And what does he make of Trudeau's role in all this? Unlike Warren and Meunier, Gauvreau believes he played an important role in this period of Quebec's history. He even goes as far as to criticize him for the part he played in bringing about a regrettable "revolution" that put an end to the Church's cultural role in Quebec. Specifically, he alleges that Trudeau and the *Cité libre* team turned their backs "on the social achievements of Catholic Action." Even worse, they displayed "an aggressive . . . spiritual elitism [according to which] working-class religion was vacuous and conformist and . . . too deferential to clerical leadership."[66] According to

Gauvreau, this elitism caused the working class to leave the Church in droves. In short, Quebeckers lost interest in the Church and religious rituals largely because of Trudeau and his allies.

We agree with Gauvreau when he says that Trudeau, Pelletier, and other Citélibristes considered the predominant form of Catholicism in Quebec to be ritualistic. True enough, they wanted to replace it with a more authentic form of Christianity. But did this really bring about the de-Christianisation of society? We will leave this question to specialists of Catholicism in Quebec. However, we do not see how Gauvreau can accuse Trudeau of being an aggressive elitist who held the working class in contempt. This accusation is simply not borne out by the facts. To the contrary, we have already seen some examples (and we will see many more) of Trudeau's spirited defence of the interests of the working class and of his solid commitment to unions. In fact, it wasn't just Trudeau but all Citélibristes who were strong supporters of workers and their organizations.

Trudeau could mock, ridicule, counter-attack; he could hurl a few pithy sentences at his opponents; but he never bothered to explain or justify the depth of his faith or that of other Citélibristes. He always spoke in his own name, using "I" – the first person singular. He never claimed to reflect *Cité libre*'s positions. Pelletier, by contrast, was overtly Catholic. Always the perfect diplomat, with carefully measured words he defended the magazine and proclaimed the authentic spiritual commitment of the entire team.

An example will highlight the stylistic peculiarity of each man. We earlier came across Marcel Clément who, along with François-Albert Angers, had submitted an action plan to the Association professionnelle des industriels API (the Professional Association of Industrialists) as a way of reinvigorating corporatism in Quebec. Clément was a French journalist who came to Quebec after the war and taught at the Faculty of Social Sciences at Université Laval. Until 1949, he was one of the progressives and joined Abbé Gérard Dion, director of the Department of Industrial Relations, in his attempts to get closer to the workers and the union movement. But in 1949 he switched sides, and according to Suzanne Clavette "he became [Quebec's] greatest defender of corporatism during the 1950s."[67] Accused of fanaticism, he was expelled from the university in 1950. He then became an extreme traditionalist and, in 1956, accused the *Cité libre* team of working "to establish a City free of God and of the fatherly authority of His Vicar on earth," and therefore of working "against God, the Church and the Holy See."[68]

Trudeau replied and, as could be expected, did not mince his words. In a television show watched by an audience of 250,000 people, he simply accused Clément of mouthing a lot of "crap." And in a short piece in *Cité libre,* he called him "a professional pope-worshipping devotee of corporatism."[69] Pelletier also replied to Clément's charges. Soberly, but forcefully, using "we" – the first person plural – on behalf of *Cité libre,* he declared: "We do not believe that Catholics can suffer in silence when they are slanderously portrayed as the enemies of the Church and of God."[70]

Trudeau's faith never wavered. Canadians may have long misunderstood the depth of his faith because he considered religion to be a private matter. To him, the separation of Church and State was essential because different principles underlay the spiritual and temporal spheres. In later years, as prime minister, Trudeau continued to hold the same view, as is shown by the following example, provided by David Seljak, professor of Religious Studies at St. Jerome's University in Ontario. In 1983, Canada's Catholic bishops issued a pastoral letter, "Ethical Reflections on the Economic Crisis," which criticized government policy on the 1982 recession and rising unemployment. "Trudeau dismissed the report and said the bishops should stick to religion, their sphere of expertise. They were not economists."[71] All his life, Trudeau acted according to what he believed were true Christian values, but matters of faith were an intrinsic part of his private life. It was only in 2004, with the publication of *The Hidden Pierre Elliott Trudeau: The Faith Behind the Politics,* that most Canadians discovered, with astonishment, this hitherto unknown dimension of his life.[72]

In the 1950s, Trudeau was part of a movement that strove to put an end to clericalism. But he went much farther. Not only did he fight for the separation of Church and State but, at the high point of the Cold War and the Red Scare, he criss-crossed the province promoting socialism and democracy, systems that were severely criticized by the Church. Finally, in spite of the prevalent anti-labour climate of the era, he worked tirelessly on behalf of workers and their organizations.

Trudeau sought to transform the outdated and counterproductive institutions and values of French-Canadian society, by encouraging workers to paddle with him against the current toward an open and democratic alternative. Quite the challenge!

Chapter 10

DEMOCRACY FIRST AND FOREMOST!

I would rather give up socialism than accept that it should be built on non-democratic foundations: Russia has shown us the path to totalitarianism.

— PIERRE ELLIOTT TRUDEAU,
Cité libre, 1958[*]

WITH DUE RESPECT TO FATHER BRAÜN, Father Desrosiers, Duplessis and many others, we maintain that Trudeau had no affinity whatsoever for Soviet-style socialist or Communist regimes. When, on returning to Quebec after his long journey abroad, he sang the praises of socialism, he meant *democratic and Christian* socialism, a system founded on the twin values of social justice and human dignity. In closing remarks Trudeau gave in June 1954, at the annual meeting of the Quebec Industrial Unions Federation in Champigny (now part of Quebec City), he explained that socialism respects the will of God: "God did not create one man rich and the next one poor. . . . Doesn't the world – and all its contents – belong to God? So if everything we own belongs to God, then it also belongs to our brothers in God's service."[1] And who are these brothers? Well, people of every creed and colour. Trudeau firmly believed that once French Canadians understood that socialism was the fairest and most Christian system, they would democratically endorse it. He knew, however, that from the cradle onwards, French Canadians had

---

[*] P.E. Trudeau, "Un manifeste démocratique," *Cité libre*, no. 22, October 1958, p. 20.

been served a diet of nationalism, corporatism, and authoritarianism, and they had repeatedly been warned that socialism was the work of the Devil. The way to change such deeply ingrained attitudes was to explain the true nature of democratic socialism.

He knew, moreover, that no matter how attractive great ideals seemed, they were useful only insofar as they were rooted in the social reality of a given time and place. He gave a first indication of this point of view in 1950, in a review of *L'unité européenne par l'intercitoyenneté*[2] [European Unity through Inter-citizenship], which he wrote while working at the Privy Council. The author of this book, the French jurist and historian Roger Picard, argued that nationalism was obsolete and would eventually be replaced by a kind of internationalism he called inter-citizenship. "If we could say that ideas rule the world," Trudeau argued, "then I would be the first to congratulate those who try to substitute the generous myth of universal brotherhood for the splintering of men into nation-states, which are self-centered concepts and tend to provoke wars. For my part, I tend to believe that an idea can only have an impact in historical terms if it meets a significant need."[3] And even then, for the idea to pursue its course, it must "start by accepting the kernel of truth lying at the heart of any movement." In other words, people needed to be addressed at their level and not have someone talking down to them. By starting with the people's "kernel of truth," one could stir in them a greater desire to participate in their milieu, which in turn will entice them to search for further truth, and so forth.

Clearly, Trudeau no longer believed that the people could be led to the truth only by an elite imbued with noble ideals. He now believed that "the people only learn about the common good when they draw subtle lessons from the interaction of history on ideas, and of ideas on history."[4] Moreover, he had come to believe that it was the working class that was the most receptive to his socialist ideals because it had a special interest in overcoming injustice. Convinced of the need of an ongoing dialectical interaction between ideas and social reality, he sought closer ties with the workers to help them in their search for truth while, in turn, benefitting from their life experience.

One may argue that it is all very well to engage in an educational project set in a dialectical process of mutual enrichment – but what about earning a living? How did Trudeau support himself? As is well known,

in the years between leaving the Privy Council in 1951 and his appointment as professor at the Université de Montréal in 1961, he held no full-
time job. To make a long story short, he lived comfortably off the
inheritance his father had left him. Which is not to say he didn't "work."
Quite the contrary. He was so busy that we had a hard time tracking
down all his activities.

One of his money-earning occupations was running a law firm,
located at 84 Avenue McCulloch in Outremont – coincidentally also his
home address. But charging legal fees was not his primary objective. He
was well known for taking up "interesting" cases whether the client
could afford to pay or not. He generally favoured cases involving personal liberty, human rights, and the defence of workers' rights. As could
be expected, he received numerous requests for assistance. Among them
was a letter from nudists who had been charged with indecency.[5]
Unfortunately we don't know the outcome.

True to character, Trudeau, much like Frank Sinatra's famous song,
"My Way," did things "his way." If a court appearance happened to
conflict with a trip he had already lined up, he made no bones about
asking for a postponement for as much as six months.[6] In spite of this
quirk, over the years his reputation as a brilliant, albeit somewhat eccen-
tric, intellectual and lawyer spread beyond Quebec. In the February 24,
1962, issue of *Maclean's* magazine, the celebrated journalist and future
radio personality Peter Gzowski wrote in "Portrait of an Intellectual in
Action": "In 1952, [Trudeau] moved to Montreal and opened a law office.
He has kept one open ever since, and from it has offered advice – often
free – to scores of people involved in everything from habeas corpus to
property suits."[7]

One example, among many, of his disregard for financial reward
occurred on January 26, 1958. Jacques Hébert, who had now become
Trudeau's close friend, asked him to help Robert Sauvé, a man unjustly de-
tained at Bordeaux jail in Montreal. Pierre Trudeau, Pierre Vadeboncoeur,
Frank Scott, and others formed an advisory committee to defend Sauvé
and succeeded in having him released in 1960. Trudeau's papers reveal his
serious work on this case for two years. And like the other committee
members, he earned the whopping fee of ten dollars.[8]

Clearly, he was not overly concerned about financial compensation,
whether for legal cases or for talks, courses, or speeches he was invited

to give. Sometimes he simply returned the cheque, with an elegant note, as in the following case: after a talk at Collège Basil Moreau, the Mother Superior sent him a thank-you letter along with a ten-dollar cheque. He sent the cheque back, suggesting the money be given instead to a charitable organization, the Society of St.Vincent de Paul. "I am sure they will make better use of it than I would," he wrote.[9] Sometimes Trudeau went as far as paying defence costs out of his own pocket. For instance, when Jacques Hébert got into legal trouble over his book *I Accuse the Assassins of Coffin,* Trudeau – now a professor at the Université de Montréal – took a month's unpaid leave to defend him, frequently travelling to Quebec City, where the trial was held.[10]

Some of Trudeau's professional activities had a more permanent character. For example, during the 1950s, he frequently worked as a union arbitrator in conjunction with companies such as the Aluminum Company of Canada Limited (Alcan), Campbell Chibougamau Mines Limited, Consolidated Papers, Guémont Mining, the newspaper *Montréal Matin,* Provincial Transport, and Radio-Canada (the French service of the CBC).[11] He meticulously prepared each case. He also frequently chaired arbitration tribunals, as for example in 1954 when Michel Chartrand – later a colourful separatist, well known for his radicalism and eloquence – filed a grievance against the Catholic Workers Confederation of Canada (CTCC). Chartrand accused the union's vice-president, Jean Marchand, of having eliminated his post in order to get rid of him. He provided evidence showing that other positions had been created, none of which had been offered to him. Marchand was one of Trudeau's good friends, and it was partly thanks to him that he had gained access to labour organizations. But Trudeau took his arbitration responsibilities earnestly, examing each case thoroughly, evaluating it on its merits. On October 7, 1954, the tribunal he chaired came down in favour of the plaintiff: "Mr. Michel Chartrand should be named to one of the positions that were open on May 1st 1954 and that have since been filled by candidates from outside the union."[12]

Chartrand and Trudeau were not friends, but they were well acquainted and both had belonged to the Bloc Populaire (a nationalist and anti-conscription party). We saw, in our first volume, that on November 25, 1942, their enthusiastic speeches in support of Jean Drapeau's candidacy had made the headlines of *Le Devoir.*[13] In the

1950s, they were both active within the Quebec wing of the CCF, which, starting in 1955, was called the Parti Social Démocratique (PSD). At first, Trudeau strongly supported the PSD, but for reasons that will be discussed in later chapters, he came to the conclusion that this party was not an appropriate vehicle for Quebec's emancipation. Chartrand, on the other hand, was a staunch supporter of the PSD. He succeeded Thérèse Casgrain as leader of the party in 1957. From 1958 onwards, although the two men continued to believe in socialism, they were no longer on the same political and philosophical path. They made a definitive break in 1970, at the time of the October Crisis. Chartrand was among the hundreds of innocent people arrested at the time, and he was jailed for four months. This proved to be the last straw in what had once been an amicable relationship. While Trudeau, as prime minister, fought forcefully against the separatists,* Chartrand enthusiastically endorsed their cause, going as far as supporting the Front de Libération du Québec (FLQ), the terrorist movement that brought on the October Crisis by kidnapping the British diplomat James Cross and Quebec Labour Minister Pierre Laporte. One of the FLQ cells assassinated Laporte.

We don't subscribe to the widely held view that during the 1950s Trudeau was a dilettante who never took up any serious task, apart from his writings in *Cité libre*. It is even claimed that at *Cité libre* he left the hard, unglamorous work to others. The facts tell a different story. They clearly show that he threw himself heart and soul into everything he did, be it in his intellectual, social, professional, or political endeavours. He focused on one overarching goal – the well-being of French Canadians – sometimes even to the point of obsession. That is why, among other things, he actively participated in the administration of *Cité libre,* and starting in 1955, he bore the major responsibility for bringing out the magazine. We should also keep in mind the articles he wrote from

---

* Today, when referring to the secession of Quebec from the rest of Canada, expressions such as "independence" and "sovereignty" are commonly used. But in the fifties the usual word was "separatism." In the sixties, one notices a move toward current usage. We will attempt to respect the historical record by using the expressions that best fit the era.

Ottawa, to share his newly acquired knowledge of the federal system as witnessed from within; his newspaper reports on his trip to Moscow, which went beyond the Cold War stereotype of the Soviet Union as the Devil's lair; and the ongoing struggle he waged against clericalism.

But this only amounts to scratching the surface. Trudeau seemed to be everywhere at the same time, a situation that presented us with quite a challenge. If we simply lined up his many activities in chronological order, we would risk confusing our readers. We have therefore taken a few liberties with the chronology and resorted to a thematic approach. In this chapter, we focus mainly on his "intellectual" activities bearing on the promotion of socialism and democracy, as well as his quest for a better understanding of the obstacles to a full democracy in Quebec. Chapter 11 will concentrate on his activities within the trade-union movement.

Trudeau wanted his fellow citizens to understand properly the notions of socialism and of democracy in order to make wise choices with respect to Quebec's social and political realities. This, he believed, required a basic knowledge of economic and political principles – something that French Canadians by and large lacked. So he offered free instruction to workers, students, people involved in politics, and the general public. He also made frequent radio and television appearances. In short, he was quite willing to speak to anyone who cared to listen. To give a sense of his message, we will give three examples of his talks: the first one within a left-wing political party, the second one during a radio debate, and the third in a university milieu.

On Friday, March 6, 1953, Trudeau was the guest speaker at a meeting of young CCF members at the home of Thérèse Casgrain, whom Trudeau had met on his return to Quebec. She had served as the leader of the Quebec wing of the CCF (Co-operative Commonwealth Federation) since 1951. Trudeau's speech on "economic and political aspects of socialism" and the subsequent discussion period filled up the entire evening.[14] Among the thirty-five to forty participants was Jacques Parizeau, future leader of the Parti Québécois and premier of Quebec from September 1994 to January 1996 and therefore, during the 1995 referendum. Trudeau announced forthrightly that his talk would focus on one single issue: demonstrating the urgency of understanding socialism, this "powerful theoretical model, the most coherent, the most rational, perhaps also the most Christian . . . of all systems."[15] Why the most Christian? First, because socialism gives primacy to the person. Second, because it seeks a fairer distribution of resources to achieve social justice. Trudeau was categorical: "Socialism is the only true form of democracy."[16]

However, although during his London sojourn Trudeau had been impressed by the Labour government's social policies, he didn't suggest that Quebec adopt the British welfare state. It was a risky business, he said, to import a social system on the grounds that it had succeeded elsewhere. Carrying out comprehensive reforms in a given society successfully requires being attentive to its history and its social and cultural contexts. Quebec had long been a breeding ground for right-wing ideologies, because it was shut off from the rest of the world and under the thumb of a traditionalist church. Proof of this was the powerful attraction corporatism and fascism exerted on the clerical-nationalist elite and the subsequent popularity of the social credit movement.

This doctrine, first developed in the 1920s by a British engineer, C.H. Douglas, met with considerable success in Canada, particularly in Alberta and Quebec. The basic idea was simple: a social dividend should be distributed to wean consumers from dependency on the financial system. Consumers could then buy goods, which would in turn increase production. In Quebec, this ideology was associated mainly with Réal Caouette, the founder in 1944 of the Union des électeurs (Union of Voters), Quebec's first "Creditist" party, and the only member of the Social Credit party with a seat in the House of Commons, which he won in 1946.

Trudeau attributed the emergence and success of Social Credit and other similar movements to "the void left by the defeat of fascism and the fear of the Left."[17] If many French Canadians found Social Credit appealing, he said, it was because they had an inadequate understanding of politics and economics. For example, they didn't know that "the state is a legal fiction which is the servant of all." In other words, they weren't aware that – as citizens and voters – *they* were the ones who chose the people and the institutions that made up the state.[18] This is why the state is accountable to *them* – rather than the other way round. Once they gained a better understanding of democratic principles, they would take their civic responsibilities more seriously and would be in a position to appreciate the coherent, rational, and Christian nature of socialism. Trudeau made it his personal mission to spread these ideas, as he did at Thérèse Casgrain's home, hoping perhaps that the people present would follow suit.

In November and December 1953, CBC-Radio Canada broadcast a series of three talks on the economy. Trudeau's talk on "Methods of Economic Stabilization" closed the series on December 8.[19] He was preceded by Roger Dehem, a professor of economics at the Université de Montréal. Dehem got his doctorate at the Catholic University of Louvain, then completed his training in Stockholm and Chicago on a prestigious Rockefeller Foundation fellowship, which helped him achieve an international reputation. In clear language, Trudeau presented the various tools available for minimizing the ill effects of economic cycles and explained the ABCs of what he called the "classical theory": "It was once thought that even a slight amount of unemployment would correct itself. The idea was that as the unemployed sought work, the ensuing competition would lead to a drop in wages, thereby reducing the cost of production. The rivalry between producers would then bring down prices, meaning that consumers would need less money, . . . the interest rate would therefore decrease, and new investments would become profitable. As a result, the unemployed would get jobs, and the economy would return to prosperity."[20] But he immediately followed up with a sharp critique of this model because it implicitly accepted the deterioration of the living standards of the most vulnerable people. He went on to argue that laissez-faire economics addressed only the symptoms, rather than the root causes of economic crises. History showed that cycles of growth and recessions regularly alternated in a capitalist system.

Trudeau argued forcefully that there was no need to put up with this situation, since techniques that could mitigate the extent of economic cycles were available. Adopting a Keynesian perspective, he explained that in times of crisis, the state can lower taxes and interest rates and increase spending. During a boom, it does the opposite. Targeting those self-righteously indignant people who "consider it intolerable that a government should deliberately take on debt," Trudeau retorted, "the government can borrow as much as it wants from the Bank of Canada, which will be only too happy to print millions of fresh banknotes. . . . If you want to smooth out economic cycles, you have to distinguish between national accounts and a grocery store ledger, and understand that a country will not be ruined just because it lends a lot of money to itself."[21]

He then wrapped up his talk and the series of three radio programs by stressing that economic science is no panacea. It "makes no claim to eliminate each and every bump along the road to progress; what it does is provide techniques for lessening fluctuations before they seriously undermine national prosperity. But it is vital that governments and citizens not be afraid to use them."[22] Economics can only provide good models; governments have to garner the courage to implement them.

Eager to spread the type of knowledge needed for enlightened political action, on February 2, 1954, the association of law students of the University of Montreal – named "Mignault Conference" in honour of the jurist Pierre-Basile Mignault – invited him to debate with the economist Roger Dehem, on the topic "Capitalism and Socialism." Unsurprisingly, Roger Dehem presented capitalism while Trudeau presented socialism.[23] Dehem's write-up of his talk, "A Constructive Critique of Capitalism," was published in Le Devoir on February 16, 1954. He argued that all over the world the standard of living had remained almost stationary for centuries. It was only through the mid-nineteenth-century Industrial Revolution that living standards improved significantly, particularly in Britain, the United States, and, more generally, countries with capitalist systems. Dehem acknowledged the negative aspects of capitalism but claimed that instead of rejecting it outright, efforts should be made to improve it.

Trudeau's combative speech contrasted sharply with Dehem's. To him, this was not just an intellectual exercise; he wanted to get his listeners to be aware of the advantages of socialism and democracy. Unfortunately, he exclaimed, in Quebec "fear and hysteria hinder the rational search for political truth."[24] The title of Le Devoir's report on the debate conveyed the gist of Trudeau's message: "Fear leads to fascism, and fascism leads to revolution."[25] He thus proceeded to examine socialism and democracy and right off the bat challenged a number of preconceived ideas. For example, socialism, so maligned by the Church, was not a new ideology. Rather, it was a conception "of society going back to classical Antiquity, which has been taught and applied differently in different historical periods. It is an economic, political, and social theory, found throughout the history of political thought," starting with Plato's "communist aristocratic republic."[26] Trudeau backed up his point with a learned account of different forms of socialism throughout history. Starting with the

Stoics of the third century BC, he proceeded to the Moravian Anabaptists in the sixteenth century, to Karl Marx in the nineteenth century, and finally to the Fabian Society and Social Democrats in the twentieth century. To him, these diverse interpretations of socialism had one important characteristic in common: they sought to "restore justice in society through a better distribution of wealth."[27] He then proceeded to attack another preconceived idea. History, he said, reveals that "none of these forms [of socialism] calls for violence."[28] Violence is sometimes fostered by historical conditions, not by socialism as such. In fact, "violence has attended the birth of liberalism and capitalism." Moreover, he continued, socialism does not deny the "historic benefits of liberalism and capitalism. . . . It seeks to extend these benefits along their historical trajectory."[29] Finally, he claimed that socialism promotes progress, because it "asserts its faith in man, and aims at freeing him from all forms of alienations."

In conclusion, Trudeau congratulated the organizers of the debate for their courage, since "the Université de Montréal must be one of the few universities where socialism is not taught." By helping "confused human beings" to seek the truth, the organizers showed they gave heed to the frightful biblical invocation: "I was hungry and you gave me no food, I was thirsty and you gave me no drink. Go away into eternal punishment."[30] The students at the time must have recognized this passage from Chapter 25 of the Gospel of Matthew in which Jesus differentiates between the righteous who give food and drink to the needy, and the unrighteous who are destined to hell. Trudeau believed that the students at the Université de Montréal who tried to make socialism better known deserved a place among the righteous.

Yet, as attractive and as Christian as socialism was, Trudeau did not recommend it for Quebec. Why? Simply, because French Canadians weren't ready; they had not yet properly understood the notion of popular sovereignty, which underlay democracy. This was fundamental to the establishment of a socialism founded on the primacy of the person and the respect of individual freedom. A socialism not rooted in democracy risked veering into totalitarianism: "When Quebec stops considering itself incapable of governing itself, when at last it becomes a little more democratic, only then will it be ripe for socialism and will adopt it wholeheartedly."[31] Only then, and not before. Why would Trudeau so resolutely affirm, in

1954, that this stage had not yet been reached in Quebec? To answer this question, we need to go back in time, more precisely to 1952.

———◦———

Three strikes will forever mark Quebec history: Asbestos, in 1949; Louiseville, in 1952; and Murdochville, in 1957. Once again, Trudeau was in the right place at the right time and was involved in each of them to varying degrees. We have already described his modest role in the Asbestos strike and will look at his involvement in the Murdochville one in Chapter 11. Here, we will briefly examine the Louiseville strike, which had a profound impact on Trudeau's political thoughts.

First, the facts. Employees of Associated Textiles of Canada Ltd. requested a wage increase of 20 cents an hour. The company countered with an 8½-cent offer. The union was on the point of accepting the offer when the company insisted that the employees abandon four clauses of the old collective agreement that were not on the bargaining table. This struck the employees as eminently unfair, and they rejected the offer. On March 10, 1952, after completing all the necessary procedures, they launched a perfectly legal strike. It lasted eleven months and proved one of the longest and harshest in Quebec history. It was also a defining moment in the history of the Confederation of Catholic Workers of Canada (CTCC), the union representing the more than eight hundred striking weavers. During the first months of the strike, as Duplessis was gearing up for the July 12, 1952, election, he seemed to side with the strikers: he accused Associated Textile of backing down on offers it had already accepted.

But by July, Duplessis had scored an election victory and the strike had taken a turn for the worse. He now switched to a radically different stand, accusing the strikers of anarchy since they were interfering with the employers' rights to conduct their businesses as they saw fit. The company, meanwhile, hired strikebreakers. When the strikers tried to prevent them from entering the plant, the police intervened several times, dispersing them brutally. The public and the clergy sided with the strikers. In August, even the Louiseville City Council passed a motion supporting the strikers. But the strike went on and the government did nothing to abate the violence, because as stated in *Histoire du Québec contemporain,* it was anything but neutral: "The collusion between the government and the company was flagrant and the provincial police protected the strikebreakers and repressed the strikers' protest marches."[32] Jean Marchand, vice-president of the CTCC, and René Gosselin, president of the Textile Federation, tried a new pressure tactic. On December 11 they organized a large peaceful rally. But it turned into a riot. The strikers threw projectiles at the police, who responded with tear gas, chasing the strikers into the union hall and beating them with clubs. During the ensuing hand-to-hand combat, shots were fired, and several people were injured, one of them seriously.

In desperation, the CTCC took a step that marked a milestone in the history of the labour movement. For the first time, this union, which had faithfully subscribed to the Church's social doctrine, took a more radical stance, akin to the "international unions" that the clergy so vigorously denounced: it called a general strike. Maurice Duplessis blamed the unions. On January 14, 1953, he reminded Quebeckers of their sacred duty of obedience: "Society rests upon two pillars: religious authority and civil authority. Any sabotage of one or the other leads to anarchy."[33] He warned that his government would not remain on the sidelines if the peace was breached. His message got across. Spooked by its own radicalism, the CTCC reluctantly announced on January 19, 1953, that it was calling off the general strike. The next day, the union publicly accused Duplessis of siding with Associated Textiles and of having politicized the strike by considering it as "a death struggle between organized labour and the government."[34] But the union had lost the battle. On February 10, 1953, after an eleven-month strike, the defeated workers headed back to work, with precious little to show for their effort.

———◦———

We have stated above that this strike had a significant impact on Trudeau's political views, but we haven't yet mentioned his name. We're getting there. On Tuesday, January 27, 1953, he gave a talk titled "Considerations on the Measures Needed to Avoid a Massacre"[35] on radio station CBF. This obscure title can be understood only when placed in context. The word "massacre" referred to both the Louiseville police forces and the strikers' recourse to excessive violence. He readily admitted that differences of opinion and divergent interests were to be expected in all social contexts. Moreover, he believed that there was no reason to take offence when workers resorted occasionally to tough actions, such as a legal strike. But every protest ought to fully respect the spirit of democracy, which had not been the case in Louiseville. This led Trudeau to outline the fundamental principles of democracy and in the process severely criticize all those who violated them.

Democracy, he said, was "a form of government based on the principle that agreement is sought by counting heads, not by cracking them open." Since the Quebec electorate had freely chosen the Duplessis government, it was a perfectly legal one, even if one disagreed with its policies. Any citizen dissatisfied with the result could always attempt to convince his fellow citizens to vote differently next time, "but in the meantime, he must respect any law that is not immoral." The smooth functioning of democracy depended above all on respect for the law. However, events in Louiseville had clearly shown that "democratic principles were applied . . . neither by the police nor by the government nor by the unions, nor by the vast majority of commentators." This was proof that "French Canada still needs an education in democracy." He went on to explain how each of these four groups shared the blame for what had happened.

First, the police. Its role, Trudeau reminded his listeners, is to enforce the law impartially. It must protect company property, but it must also respect picket lines and all actions and demonstrations of the strikers that were not illegal. However, in resorting to scare tactics, the police "needlessly drew pistols on people, whereas the law would at most have required that they be dispersed or arrested." Policemen are not above the law, and those committing excesses should be punished "to the full extent of the law." He moved on to the government's share of blame. It had "seriously failed in its duty" by tolerating and even encouraging the violent behaviour of the police. In a democracy the government itself is not above the law. "Theoretically," Trudeau roared, "the unions themselves could bring the perpetrators of these actions before the courts." But unfortunately, the unions – the third group at Louiseville – had lost confidence in the impartiality of the justice system and shunned this democratic course of action. In launching their call for a general strike, they had swept aside normal legal procedures. "With pointless bravado," they had decided "to act just like the police did, and placed themselves above the law."

The fourth group – "commentators" or "opinion makers" – were equally blameworthy in Trudeau's eyes. The newspaper *L'Action catholique* "evaded the issue by adopting the comfortable posture of otherworldliness," calling for "a prayer crusade to bring the crisis to an end." The magazine *Notre Temps,* meanwhile, called for tough government intervention to "quell malevolent employers and overzealous union officials." To Trudeau, these remedies were "reminiscent of fascism." As for pro-union commentators, he blamed them for approving an illegal general strike; that is, approving anarchy. To him, the conclusion was obvious: "For all intents and purposes, no one came out in favour of constitutional and parliamentary democracy."

He then explained that he was not criticizing for the sake of drawing up some "list of winners and losers, since we all deserved penalties for misconduct. . . . I just want to make one point: it is high time for French Canadians to overcome their political illiteracy." Where, he asked, could they find examples of a more enlightened behaviour? Well, among English Canadians. Trudeau was undoubtedly well aware that he was praising French Canada's archetypal and traditional enemy. But this didn't faze him. English Canadians "have much healthier political reflexes than we do. . . . Anglo-Saxons' superiority is not the result of some accident: it derives from a relentless civic education that starts on the school benches and continues day after day, thanks to those among them who think, write and talk." The reason for these healthy reflexes lay not in some genetic legacy, but rather in a solid civic education, which French Canadians could also acquire. But they had to choose: "In short, we must take sides for or against democracy, for or against totalitarianism." We can now understand why at the Mignault Conference of 1954 Trudeau did not recommend socialism even though he cherished it; the Louiseville strike had shown him that French Canadians had not acquired its indispensable prerequisite: democracy. Without democracy, socialism can all too easily degenerate into totalitarianism.

Since Duplessis had been elected through universal suffrage, some might argue that Quebec was already perfectly democratic. But clearly for Trudeau this was just one of the requirements of true democracy. On June 15, 1956, he explained on Radio-Canada why Quebec was not fully democratic: "In a parliamentary democracy, the role of the parties is to place before the electorate the true alternatives being proposed for the common good, so that the electorate can express its informed opinion."[36] But the Union Nationale didn't have the slightest intention of enlightening the electorate about its true plan of action. On the contrary.

Trudeau accused Duplessis of resorting to fraudulent political manoeuvring, building an entire system on lies, buying votes, manipulating electoral maps, punishing ridings that did not vote for him, doing nothing to prevent violence . . . and the list went on.

But why did French Canadians accept this sorry state of affairs? Since they were living in Canada, why didn't they fully adhere to democratic principles the same way English Canadians did? This question would preoccupy him for a long time. Two documents enable us to follow the evolution of his thoughts on this matter. On October 2, 1954, he took a first stab at the question in "Obstacles to Democracy," a speech given in the Laurentian resort of Sainte-Marguerite, north of Montreal. What was Trudeau doing in the Laurentians, and in what context was the conference held? To answer these questions, we have to travel back in time once again – to 1932 to be exact – and move west, to Ontario.

In 1932, at the height of the Great Depression, the National Council of the YMCA (the Young Men's Christian Association) founded the Canadian Institute on Public Affairs (CIPA) to provide a forum where well-informed people with different points of view would engage in vigorous debate.[37] The founding members were all devout Christians, critical of capitalism and the existing social order, as was manifested by the choice of the keynote speaker: J.S. Woodsworth, future founder of the CCF. The main and practically only activity of CIPA was an annual conference in August on the shores of Lake Couchiching in Ontario's idyllic Muskoka region. The location was no accident. A philanthropist had sold to the YMCA a summer cottage on a large estate, at an attractive price. Over the years, the institute acquired an outstanding reputation, with its high-calibre conferences drawing personalities from academia, politics, the arts, and the media. It came to be known as the Couchiching Institute of Public Affairs, and more familiarly "Couch" (pronounced "Cooch").

In 1952, the CBC decided to broadcast the proceedings of "Couch" on national radio, thereby giving a huge boost to the institute's visibility. The August conference that year was already making waves because of the national broadcast, but it also marked the first time the Canadian Institute on Public Affairs (CIPA) had held a joint meeting with the Canadian Institute of International Affairs (CIIA). This latter organization, renamed the Canadian International Council (CIC)/Conseil international du Canada in 2007, was even older than CIPA. Founded in 1928 and supported by private funds, the CIIA also promotes interdisciplinary debates on issues affecting Canada. These two organizations are complementary: one focuses on domestic policy, the other on international issues.

In 1952, CIPA officials were going flat out to set up this exceptional conference. Two of the conference organizers, Murray G. Ross, the sociologist and later the founding president of York University in Toronto, and Edgar McInnis, the renowned historian, specialist in international relations, and president of the CIIA, were hoping to finally succeed in establishing contacts with French-Canadian intellectuals who shared the "Couch" vision. This time they had in mind someone in particular. They got a fellow organizing committee member, Neil M. Morrison, director of Public Affairs at CBC, to invite one Pierre Elliott Trudeau, who seemed to fit the profile they were seeking. What a great idea! The only problem was to reach him – he seemed to have vanished in October 1951, after leaving the Privy Council. Where on Earth was he? And how could they reach him?

Time passed and the conference date drew closer. They finally tracked him down in Paris, where he had landed, after his recent trip to the USSR. On May 7, 1952, Frank W. Peers, of the Public Affairs department at CBC, wrote to him:

> You have been recommended to us as a person with independent views and one who is familiar with currents of opinion in Quebec. Would you be willing to participate in a panel discussion on this topic [Canadian Foreign Policy] with three other persons? We have in mind Edgar McInnis, chairman of the Canadian Institute of International Affairs; Mrs. Dorothy Steeves* of Vancouver and Max Freedman, Ottawa correspondent for the *Winnipeg Free Press.* . . .
>
> We should be able to provide for your traveling expenses and a small honorarium of $100. The dates of the conference this year are August 9–16, and the discussion on Canadian foreign policy will probably be on Monday evening, August 11.

---

* Dorothy Steeves had been an active member of the CCF since its creation.

We hope that you will be able to stay at Couchiching for at least a day and if possible for the entire week. Among others who will be speakers in attendance are the Right Honourable Hector McNeil of Great Britain; the Honourable Douglas Abbott;* Hugh Keenleyside,** etc.

Since we want to get our program arrangements completed as soon as possible, I would appreciate it if you would cable your reply collect.

Trudeau replied:

ACCEPTING COUCHICHING PROPOSAL STOP IF NECESSARY CAN BE REACHED PARIS TILL MID JUNE THEN 84 MCCULLOCH MONTREAL

TRUDEAU

Years later, the conference secretary Murray G. Ross still remembered Trudeau's dashing appearance at Couchiching, arriving "in a leather jacket on his motorcycle."[38] Trudeau's presentation turned out to be even more impressive. The topic of the session, "The Adequacy of Canadian Foreign Policy," was right up his alley. He had long taken a keen interest in the subject. He had left the Privy Council in part because of the silence imposed on civil servants. What position did he take at Couch? According to John English, "He was publicly and scathingly critical of Lester Pearson, who, he said, thought the role of Canadian policy was to interpret 'London to Washington & vice versa, as if they needed a despicable mouthpiece.'"[39] (Pearson was then Secretary of State for External Affairs – the title given at the time to the minister of foreign affairs.) In other words, Trudeau was contemptuous of Pearson whom he solely blamed for Canada's foreign policy woes. Trudeau's introduction, however, conveys a different message: "I would like to make clear . . . that no criticism of mine of Canadian foreign policy should be interpreted as directed personally against the

---

* The Hon. Douglas Abbott was minister of Finance from 1946 to 1954. In July 1954, he was appointed Justice of the Supreme Court of Canada.

** Hugh Keenleyside was an academic who had served with distinction in External Affairs and the civil service.

minister mainly responsible for it, and even less against a department of able civil servants. Canadians as a whole are responsible for the wishy-washiness of our government's policies, both at home and abroad."[40] The question, then, is how to explain this apparent contradiction.

Trudeau's notes show that he wanted to identify the weaknesses of Canadian foreign policy in order to suggest corrective measures. He began by presenting the criteria by which he assessed this policy: "I will argue that the adequacy of Canadian foreign policy should not be judged by the degree to which Canada fulfills the tasks assigned to it by senior nations, but rather by the degree to which our country fulfills itself as a united and autonomous nation." And here was the rub: "We have not yet found ourselves as such a nation." Since we Canadians have not succeeded in finding our own voice as a united and independent people, he said, we have nothing significant to offer the world, particularly in terms of human values. And we shouldn't tolerate this any longer.

In the second part of his speech, entitled "How Canadians Can Contribute to the Defence of *Human* Values,"* he outlined his vision of Canada's role in the world. We must, he said, be more than a post office between Great Britain and the United States. All Pearson is doing at the moment is "interpret London to Washington and vice versa, as if they needed a despicable mouthpiece." The adjective "despicable" comes as a surprise, since Trudeau had just pointed out he had no intention of criticizing the minister. Is it possible he used the word by mistake? Did he use a word he didn't fully understand? Quite possibly. This error could reflect the fact Trudeau thought first in French. Given the context, he likely meant to say "as if they needed a *subservient* mouthpiece." (The French word "servile" is "subservient" in English; whereas the word "vil" in French is "despicable" in English.) Could he have confused the translations of "vil" and "servile"? In his notes for the Couchiching presentation, we noticed several convoluted or awkward sentences, which suggests an imperfect command of English. People have always assumed that Trudeau was perfectly bilingual. In the period we have examined, we found that he certainly was bilingual but was always more comfortable – and more precise – when writing in French.

---

*   In the manuscript version of these notes, Trudeau underscored the word *Human*.

Whatever the reason, when he came back to the same idea further on in his talk, he used the correct word: "We have not yet proved to be a mature nation nor a useful contributor to international politics, due mainly to our *subservient* turn of mind." He underlined the word "subservient" twice. Nowhere else does he repeat the word "despicable" or a synonym. On the other hand, we noted earlier that when he was at the Privy Council, he criticized Pearson for lacking courage and obediently following American policy. In other words, for being *subservient* (*servile* in French).

In the international arena, Trudeau argued strongly that we Canadians should be true to ourselves. He claimed that three characteristics define us: first, our political principles and institutions are of British origin; second, our population is essentially bi-ethnic and bilingual; and third, our country is small, young, and wealthy. But in fact, he continued, "the first characteristic drowns the others" and permeates both our domestic and foreign policy. Our sources of information are mostly American and occasionally British. Why not consult *Le Monde* or the *Paris Herald Tribune*? We do not take advantage of our second characteristic on the grounds that Quebec is isolationist. But it isn't the case, he retorted: "Isolationism is a term which no longer applies to Quebec. Quebec strongly favours participating in world affairs, but feels that Canada should have more to give than armaments wherewith to destroy fellow men." As for the third characteristic: "Canada is the 3rd or 4th trading nation in the world, with the 2nd highest standard of living. . . . We don't have an axe to grind and should look more for truth and justice rather than opportuneness so called. . . . Unlike most countries of the world we don't have to go begging for funds from the U.S. or USSR." We do not make a difference at the international level, he said, because we do not use our other two characteristics. And why don't we? Because we lack self-confidence, we don't have a sense of national pride. We don't even have a flag of our own.[*] He was fully aware that Canada would never become a superpower capable of imposing its will: "We can't oppose a determined U.S./U.K. axis, but in undetermined matters we can construct." But we can play an important role with regard to human values. To do so, "it is necessary to define ourselves as Canadians if we are to act without wastages."

---

[*] Canada acquired its own flag on February 15, 1965.

We can well imagine his audience's bewilderment at hearing this French Canadian who had turned up in a leather jacket on a motorcycle. Here was a fluently bilingual speaker, well versed in Canadian foreign policy, who attributed Canada's insignificant impact on the world to the fact its citizens were not sufficiently patriotic. A Quebecker giving a lesson in Canadian patriotism. How unusual! The round table in which he participated proved to be the highlight of the conference. On September 22, 1952, Frank W. Peers, assistant supervisor, CBC Talks and Public Affairs, wrote to him:

> We very much appreciate the time and trouble you took to make both the conference and the broadcasts (as we are told) an outstanding achievement. There really has been quite an astonishing amount of comment from listeners, from those present at the Conference, and in the press. The general tone has been extremely favourable. We have had well over a hundred requests for copies of the main speeches, and they are still coming in.[41]

"Outstanding achievement . . . astonishing amount of comment . . . over a hundred requests for copies": Trudeau was a sensation. The historian Edgar McInnis, who was on the same panel, wanted to develop closer ties with this most unusual French-Canadian intellectual. As president of the CIIA (Canadian Institute of International Affairs), he was heading the Canadian delegation at the upcoming Commonwealth Conference in Lahore, Pakistan, from March 17 to 28, 1954.* He invited Trudeau to come along. Trudeau was quite interested, but requested more information. On January 11, 1954, McInnis wrote: "Indeed I am very pleased to learn that there is a good chance of your joining the delegation to Lahore. The enclosed material will answer a number of your questions, including your first one on the schedules and agenda of the Conference."[42] Satisfied with the information, Trudeau decided to join the group. Of the eight members of the Canadian delegation, three had attended the "Couch" conference: Edgar McInnis, Frank Peers, and Escott Reid, who was then High

---

* The official name of this meeting was the Fifth Unofficial Commonwealth Relations Conference.

Commissioner in India. It was a handpicked delegation, which included only one French Canadian: Trudeau.

We cannot resist the temptation of saying a few words about this trip. As we explained in Chapter 9, in lining up the required visas Trudeau got in trouble with the U.S. authorities. This is probably what prompted him to go to Pakistan via Europe. On March 11, he left for London. It took four days and several layovers, to get to Lahore, which he finally reached on March 15. Once the conference was over, he didn't particularly relish the idea of heading straight back to Montreal. Why not stay on and get to know this part of the world? But he was now travelling at his own expense, on the cheap, and complained that in one hotel bedbugs kept him awake. He struck up a friendship with the French commercial attaché, and together they visited the temples of Kanchipuram, one of the seven holy cities of India. On April 19, he was in Bali, once again in a third-rate hotel, sharing a room with two men – one Chinese and the other unidentified. And since he had already come this far, why not pop over to Australia? On April 26, he reached Sydney where he turned into a socialite, wining and dining with high society. Next, he made a side trip to Auckland, New Zealand, spent a few days at the beach in Waikiki, Hawaii, and flew on to San Francisco, then Chicago, arriving in Montreal finally on May 16. The next day, without missing a beat, he met Pelletier to discuss *Cité libre* matters.

Let us go back to Sainte-Marguerite on October 2, 1954. What was Trudeau doing in this little town in the Laurentians? Well, he was taking part in a historic meeting. From September 29 to October 2, 1954, the Institut canadien des affaires publiques (ICAP) held its inaugural conference at the Alpine Inn, on the theme of *The Sovereign People*.[43] Most observers, regardless of their political horizons, recognize the vital role played by this institute in bringing about the Quiet Revolution. Let us present a few testimonies.

In 1988, the sociologist Jean-Charles Falardeau wrote in a collective work marking the fiftieth anniversary of the founding of the Faculty of Social Sciences at Laval University that "perhaps the most important initiative during these years [the 1950s], was the Institut canadien des affaires publiques, which brought together diverse reform-oriented perspectives and channelled them into one productive course. . . . ICAP served as one of the primary conduits bringing fresh air into our society, which the French historian, Henri Marrou, described at the time as medieval."[44] Commenting on the Quiet Revolution, Jean-Paul Desbiens, wrote in *Le Devoir* of September 5, 2006: "[This revolution] has been a long time coming. A great deal of reflection had taken place in the 1950s. One has only to think of the newspaper *Le Devoir,* of the trade union activities of Gérard Picard and Jean Marchand, of *Cité libre,* and of the Institut canadien des affaires publiques." Jean-Paul Desbiens is widely recognized for his role in bringing about the Quiet Revolution with his 1960 best-seller *Les Insolences du Frère Untel,* which denounced the catastrophic state of the French-Canadian educational system.

In his 1981 biography of Marcel Rioux, who was director of the institute for four years, Jules Duchastel also stressed ICAP's "huge impact": "It is clear that the institute, alongside the *Refus global* and *Cité libre,* contributed to the critique of our traditional society and to the shaping of a progressive vision of Quebec which led to the Quiet Revolution."[45] In *Years of Impatience: 1950–1960,* Gérard Pelletier praised the high calibre of the institute's debates: "After each session we found ourselves better informed about our problems, less wanting in theoretical solutions, more up-to-date on the contemporary currents of thought."[46] In 1964, ten years after ICAP was founded, the institute president Guy Roberge proudly proclaimed that "ICAP conferences are true public confrontations, thanks to the coverage they get from the press, radio and television. All of Canada can follow them."[47]

While there is ample evidence that ICAP made a significant contribution to Quebec's transformation during the 1950s, strangely enough very little is known about the people who got the institute up and running. The abundance of acknowledgments of its importance contrasts with an astonishing muteness concerning its founding. Pelletier refers to "a few intellectuals." We occasionally see it portrayed as an initiative of unidentified *Citélibristes.* Curiously, there is no mention whatsoever of Trudeau's participation in launching it. In all the pages Pelletier devoted to the institute, he did not even mention his name. Yet we believe that Trudeau's close contacts with the key members of "Couch" most likely played an important part in the founding of the French institute.

One piece of evidence backing our hypothesis is the thank-you note Murray Ross sent Trudeau on August 20, 1952: "Your presence added greatly to the quality of our program." He added a handwritten note: "Hope we will see you during winter & we can organize a group from Quebec to come to Couch."[48] We don't know if Trudeau met with Ross. We do know, however, that on February 14, 1953, Maurice Lamontagne, in the name of a group of professors from the Faculty of Social Sciences of Laval University, sent a letter to Trudeau and a few other people inviting them to a meeting to study the founding of a French-Canadian institute with the same vocation as the Canadian Institute on Public Affairs. The sequence of events leads us to believe that it was Trudeau who was the source of this initiative. He couldn't launch such an institute himself since he was not attached to a university or to a research centre. So he probably got in touch with a group of professors receptive to the idea. And the ones he knew best were those of the Faculty of Social Sciences at Laval University. It is therefore unlikely that Lamontagne's letter of invitation coming just a few months after Trudeau's participation at "Couch" was a mere coincidence.

In any case, on February 28, 1953, the founding meeting of the French version of the Canadian Institute on Public Affairs was held in Quebec City. Léon Lortie was chosen president.[49] Since the new institute had to establish its credentials, a highly regarded president was essential. Léon Lortie nicely fit the bill. He was fifty-one, a professor at the Université de Montréal, and former president of French Canada's most prestigious scientific association, ACFAS (Association canadienne-française pour l'avancement des sciences). His well-known non-partisanship made him all the more acceptable. Pierre Trudeau, Maurice Lamontagne, and Marcel Faribault became vice-presidents.

The Institut canadien des affaires publiques' inaugural conference was held in Sainte-Marguerite, from August 29 to September 2, 1954. Significantly its main theme, *The Sovereign People,* was precisely Trudeau's pet subject at the time.[50] His address, "Some Obstacles to Democracy," turned out to be the springboard for a long-thought-out process, which played a major role in his political and intellectual endeavours for years to come.

In 1958, Trudeau published "Some Obstacles to Democracy in Quebec" in the *Canadian Journal of Economics and Political Science,* a fifteen-page article that made waves across Canada.[51] In Quebec, meanwhile, it infuriated some of his opponents, who blasted him for publishing his critique *"chez les Anglais"* – that is, in English Canada. The article reached the French-speaking public only in 1967, in Pierre Vadeboncoeur's translation.[52] Like many other people probably, we were originally under the impression that Trudeau had first expounded his views on the subject in 1958, and in English. Yet it was actually in Sainte-Marguerite, four years earlier, and in French, that he first presented his ideas on the subject. Sceptical readers have only to check for themselves – first in Radio-Canada archives on the Internet, where a recording of Trudeau's entire speech is posted (ICAP conferences were broadcast across Canada, just like CIPA's),[53] and second, in the report of the first annual conference of the Institut canadien des affaires publiques.[54]

Let us start with Trudeau's take on the question in 1954. He contended that historically, democracies went through two stages: combative democracy and established democracy. In the first stage, democracy struggles to establish itself: "Men bullied by a more or less despotic authority end up reflecting on the foundations of power. Adhering, somewhat confusedly, to the principle of the inviolability of the human person, they deduce that in civil society all men are fundamentally equal and none has the right to command others *against their will.* . . . And once the citizens as a whole no longer feel that they are justly governed, they have the right to change the government peacefully if they have the means to do so, and by force if they do not."[55] To Trudeau, the inviolability of the person and the fundamental equality of citizens were the core values of democracy. This is what led him to predict that citizens would not indefinitely accept being ruled against their will and would even resort to violence if peaceful change proved impossible. In this particular talk, he did not explain under what circumstances violence was justified. He took this matter up later, as we will see below.

Two kinds of obstacles stand in the way of combative democracy: concrete obstacles, which "are always present in the form of absolutist or oligarchic institutions, and ideological obstacles." The most important ideological obstacle is the idea that the human being "can only reach his full potential under the command of a leader (or of an elite). These theories amount to saying that one man knows what is good for the people."[56] Trudeau found this idea repugnant and consequently found ideological obstacles more insidious than concrete ones. The notion that one man has the right to impose on others his conception of the Good, rather than let people obey their own conscience, is not only false, it is immoral: "Such a man insults God because he tries to shape others in his own image."[57] This, of course, flew in the face of traditionalists who insisted adamantly that the elite – or the leader – knew better than the people what was good for them.

Established democracy also confronts obstacles, but of a different kind. These obstacles arise because democracy, like any social progress, is not acquired once and for all: "Freedom requires constant vigilance. Citizens should never stop improving the institutions through which they govern themselves, and adapting them to the ever-changing needs of society and men. . . . If people lose control of the machine of government for just a moment, or if they let themselves be overtaken by events, they will soon be swallowed up in the maelstrom of despotism or anarchy."[58] Trudeau gave several examples of democratic breaches in a number of countries, including the United States and Canada. How could they best be avoided? For Trudeau, "there is no universal recipe to preserve freedom in our hearts. . . . And every society must solve by and for itself problems that are in essence similar, but arise in different outlines, depending on the historical and geographical contexts."[59]

He then focused on the situation in Quebec: "We cannot overcome the obstacles to our own democracy without taking into account our society's evolution in time and space."[60] Which led him to the following hypothesis: "I contend that political difficulties specific to Quebec arise from the fact that our population has reached the stage of established democracy without first going through the combative stage."[61] The root of this situation lay in the very founding of Canada: "French Canadians are perhaps the only people known to history who enjoy democratic freedom without having struggled to acquire this freedom whether through their own efforts or those of their ancestors. . . . In 1763, we actually got rid of a corrupt and despotic authority, [and] we gradually benefited from democratic institutions." In other words, as a result of the 1763 Treaty of Paris, French Canadians inherited a ready-made democracy. Having never had to struggle to acquire it, they neither grasped its true value nor used it wisely. "*Individuals* didn't learn the value of the individual vote: they saw universal suffrage mainly as a truncheon or pressure tactic." French Canadians wanted, first and foremost, "to put the English in their place."[62] In other words, democracy was used to serve the group rather than the individual.

Trudeau went on to claim, "We [French Canadians] *don't really believe* in popular sovereignty."[63] He expounded the historical origin of this ideological obstacle to democracy: "Because as a people we were born weak, were orphaned early on in life, and are not prone to violence, we always feel the need for a protective father figure." Hence our habit of "taking authoritarian positions in politics: from Papineau to Duplessis we have never stopped asking Heaven to send us 'leaders.'" Barely rid of the seigniorial system, "many of our people, with terrifying coolness, wished for the triumph of fascism over the democracies, and especially over the English variety."[64] Unfortunately, said Trudeau with a hint of irony, "God – from whom authority flows – forgot to send us a Leader who would guide us to the Promised Land. . . . But in the meantime, it never dawned on the people that they must govern themselves through their representatives. . . . Could it be that our lack of passion about individual freedom derives from the fact that our ideologies, our institutions and our social environment have taught us how to obey rather than command?" This is why we occupy only subordinate positions: "Whichever way we look, we find ourselves today face to face with a destiny tragically devoid of grandeur."

Was it still possible to overcome these obstacles? Of course, answered Trudeau, with conviction. But "we will need to rediscover the missionaries,' the explorers,' and the fur traders' courage – to be just as ready as they were to risk everything."[65] Some encouraging signs gave him grounds for optimism: "There are still some places where the spark of freedom burns . . . I am thinking particularly of some Action Catholique militants, some artists, some writers, some union members, who seem determined to stake everything they've got on freedom." One big obstacle could, however, stop them in their tracks: Could the official elite, which "ostracizes its opponents, ever be convinced that the nation's salvation requires the rapid emergence of a social system founded on individual freedom and popular sovereignty?" Trudeau didn't know the answer. But he defiantly let out his battle cry: those who cherish freedom will not readily concede defeat. They would "do anything rather than let French Canada stagnate in its pathetic mediocrity."[66] Let the traditionalist and autocratic elite beware.

———◆———

Trudeau's 1958 article, "Some Obstacles to Democracy in Quebec," was published in the *Canadian Journal of Economics and Political Science,* a journal read by practically all the movers and shakers in economics and political science. It was a spectacular success, earning him the President's Medal from the University of Western Ontario as the best scholarly article of the year. This award outraged Robert Rumilly, an unrepentant Pétainiste, lifelong defender of Maurras, and chief propagandist of Duplessis and the Union Nationale. Rumilly penned a venomous article for the November 14, 1958, issue of *Noùvelles illustrées,* entitled "Pierre E. Trudeau Honoured for Insulting French Canadians." He himself went on to insult Trudeau and other like-minded individuals: "We find people like O'Neill[*] and Pierre Elliott Trudeau truly disgusting. But the Anglo-Canadian intellectuals who encourage such people demonstrate not just a lack of judgment or of respect. Their actions have weighty consequences. They are displaying their inability to understand French Canada, and their underlying desire to thrust upon us their own values. Moreover, they are providing ammunition to Quebec separatists, who are having a field day exploiting the natural and ongoing, albeit somehow unconscious, animosity directed towards us by the Anglo-Canadian 'elite.'"[67] But all this doesn't shed any light on what Rumilly found so "disgusting" in Trudeau's article. So let us have a closer look at it.

Trudeau had taken four years to deepen and refine the initial draft he had presented at Sainte-Marguerite: his new article was almost four times longer. It didn't focus exclusively on French Canadians,[68] but on Canada as a whole. He warned that "there exists an urgent need for a

---

[*] Father Louis O'Neill was Action Catholique chaplain at Université Laval and co-author with Father Gérard Dion, chair of the Department of Industrial Relations at the same university, of a pamphlet published by the Public Morality Committee, *Two priests censure political immorality in the Province of Quebec.* Excerpts of the original French-language version were published in *Le Devoir* on August 14, 1956.

critical examination of democracy in Canada," because the present obstacles will persist as long as one-third of the population – the French Canadians – simply do not believe in this system. Were they wrong not to? Hardly, "because to no small extent the remaining two-thirds – the English Canadians – provide them with ample grounds for distrusting it."[69] Trudeau set out to demonstrate to English Canadians in their own language their share of responsibility for this situation. His thesis was spelled out in the very first sentence: "Historically, French Canadians have not really believed in democracy for themselves; and English Canadians have not really wanted it for others."

He readily acknowledged that Canada owed its democratic system to the English Canadians who had struggled long and hard for it, and he provided many examples from Canada's history from the year 1763 on. He noted however that, starting with the 1792 elections, democracy had been twisted in English Canada's favour. In Lower Canada, where French Canadians were by far the most numerous, "they were quick to realize that, though their ethnic group made up 94 per cent of the population, it had elected only 68 per cent of the members of the Assembly."[70] The facts abundantly demonstrated that "the history of democracy in Lower Canada from 1793 to 1840 was the history of one long process of warping the very system."[71] All kinds of strategies were devised to "prevent the Assembly from being dominated by the French." The Act of Union following Lord Durham's report went even further – it sought the outright assimilation of the French: "A single Assembly was elected, with equal representation for Upper and Lower Canada, in spite of the fact that the latter province had 650,000 inhabitants against the former's 450,000. Moreover, English was to be the sole official language."[72]

To this day, Trudeau continued, English Canadians have two value systems. Whereas they vigorously denounce any violation of democracy across the country, they quite happily tolerate the corruption and authoritarianism of Duplessis. He indicted English-language newspapers in Quebec: "Perhaps the prime example of such political schizophrenia is found in the Montreal *Star* and the Montreal *Gazette*. Anti-parliamentary procedure at Ottawa or undemocratic practices perpetrated by national politicians are systematically denounced . . . but these same papers never write editorials on the innumerable cases of violation of parliamentary and democratic rights which are standard procedure for the [Duplessis]

Government."[73] Hence his conclusion: "To sum up, English-speaking Canadians have long behaved in national politics as though they believed that democracy was not for French Canadians."[74] And to think that Rumilly had accused Trudeau of insulting French Canadians!

But Trudeau was not finished. The English-Canadian elite kept the upper hand by colluding with the Church to suppress any inkling of the people for emancipation: "A long study would be needed to show how French-Canadian radicalism was crushed, mainly by the collusion between the English-Canadian governing class and the French-Canadian higher clergy.... Loyalty was bartered for religious freedom, and the Church was as good as her word. During the wars of 1775, 1812, 1914, and 1939, the Catholic hierarchy preached submission to His Majesty's government.... When the faith was safe, churchmen didn't care much about democratic liberty."[75] Thus, the Church never tired of teaching French Canadians to respect authority and to distrust democratic principles. Trudeau gave as proof an excerpt from the radio program, "Morning Prayer," broadcast on Radio-Canada the day of the June 1956 provincial elections: "Sovereign authority . . . is derived solely from God. . . . It is therefore an absolute error to believe that authority comes from the multitudes, from the masses, from the people. . . . This error, which dates from the Reformation, rests on the false principle that man has no other master than his own reason. . . ."[76] To those who might argue that the Catholic faith itself shapes this mindset, Trudeau countered in a footnote: "Many a Catholic would claim that democracy follows naturally from the Christian belief that all men are brothers and fundamentally equal."[77]

Trudeau's numerous examples were undeniable proof that authoritarian and anti-democratic stands were still common in Quebec. He particularly objected to the traditionalist Léopold Richer, who had published Trudeau's first articles from London in *Notre Temps*. But relations between the two men had since deteriorated. Trudeau now referred to this weekly publication as "supposedly 'social and cultural.'" He noted that Richer, who enjoyed the backing of much of the clergy, was systematically putting down "the new religion of democracy" and acted "in all circumstances as the champion of authority." As proof, Trudeau referred to Richer's frantic, over-the-top reaction when Gérard Filion wrote in *Le Devoir*, "Liberty can only exist when it is won over from authority." For Richer, this was "defiance of established authority.... It is sedition.

It is revolt. Gérard Filion has been reduced to preaching revolution openly.... One must regard him as an extremely dangerous journalist."[78] Unfortunately, wrote Trudeau, Richer was not an isolated case: "If I were to quote all the material proving that French Canadians fundamentally do not believe in democracy, and that ... not much is done to instil such a belief, I would 'exhaust time and encroach upon eternity.'"[79] This explains his heart-rending observation: "In 1958, French Canadians must begin to learn democracy from scratch."[80]

Clearly, Trudeau was rubbing people the wrong way, and he knew it: "I will perhaps have managed to displease all Canadians. Both French and English may claim that I put exaggerated blame on their particular ethnic group."[81] But they would be wrong, because "there is nothing easy about democracy, even in the best of circumstances." He added: "It is important for Canadians to become aware of their own pitfalls.... For as long as the people do not believe in democracy there is no reason for them to accept its ethics."[82]

In the years to come, Trudeau would develop and refine his thoughts on the notion of good government. Early in 1958, Jacques Hébert, publisher of the weekly *Vrai,* asked his friend Trudeau for a series of articles on political topics of his choice. Hébert was delighted when Trudeau agreed to provide twenty articles at the rate of one per week, in a special section entitled "Approaches to Politics."[83] These articles appeared between February 15 and July 5, 1958. This amounts to twenty-one weeks and Trudeau actually wrote twenty-one articles for *Vrai!* On June 14, 1958, he suspended the "Approaches" series in order to publish "Notes on the provincial Liberal Congress," which does not concern us here. In 1970, Hébert trusted that Trudeau's political thought deserved to be better known, especially since he had by now become prime minister, and he brought the other twenty articles together in a book, under the imprint of his own publishing house, Éditions du Jour (they also appeared, the same year, in an English translation under the title *Approaches to Politics*). Our references are drawn from the English publication.[84]

Approaches to Politics is one of Trudeau's notable works on political thought. Even the political scientist Léon Dion, who refused to grant Trudeau the title of "political thinker," recognized that these articles in

Vrai were his "meagre contribution to genuine political thought."[85] Some, like James Tully, an internationally renowned Canadian political scientist and philosopher, took a far more favourable view. In 2008, Tully included "the civic ethos of Pierre Elliott Trudeau" in a list of important thinkers, such as Hannah Arendt, Michel Foucault, Friedrich Nietzsche, Ludwig Wittgenstein, and Charles Taylor, who had influenced him.[86]

The articles in *Vrai* do illustrate Trudeau's civic ethos. They also show his ability to start with the real-life situation of his fellow citizens, then move on to address wider and more fundamental social and political issues. These articles are unlike most of his other writings, in the sense that they are more didactic than polemical, and generally more serene. But of course, Trudeau enjoyed polemics and did not always manage to hold back his biting irony. For example, he maintained that in granting favours, the Duplessis government worked against the common good: "But it is not the rascals who are to blame, but the politicians. (Mind you, the two terms are not mutually exclusive.)"[87] Sometimes he reserved bitter irony for people who had attacked him. André Dagenais, a traditionalist philosophy professor who later joined the separatist Rassemblement pour l'indépendance nationale (RIN), accused Trudeau in the newspaper *Salaberry* of being a "Rousseauiste" because he had quoted Rousseau's famous words "Man is born free." (Rousseau was roundly condemned by Quebec's clerical-nationalist elite.) Trudeau ridiculed Dagenais and his ilk: "Truth be told, I knew when I quoted even the most inoffensive of Rousseau's sentences that I was setting a snare for all the watchdogs of reaction. I should have known that I would find Mr. Dagenais in it, on all fours along with Léopold Richer."[88] But overall, Trudeau's main objective in *Approaches* was not to attack his opponents but to explain the basic principles of political life, with an emphasis on democracy.

His reflection revolved around the relationship between obedience and authority. "This is indeed the essence of politics," he wrote.[89] In social life, man is free, yet he must obey. But obey *whom*? And in what circumstances? Could he, should he, sometimes disobey? Under what circumstances? How could anarchy be avoided? Where does authority come from? These questions, he said, which have preoccupied philosophers for over a thousand years, have not yet been answered satisfactorily. Some people say, simplistically, that we must obey, because "authority comes from God." However, he countered, they "omit to explain why God conferred authority on a Stalin or a Hitler; or why, in our democracies, God would choose to express himself through the intermediary of electoral thugs and big campaign contributors."[90] Others argue, "authority is ordained by nature." So how is it that "in certain societies it is the grandfather who rules, in others it is the mother, in still others the queen's eldest son?"[91] Unsatisfied with these answers, Trudeau carried his analysis further.

He examined another misconception based on obvious facts: man lives in society, and "life in society cannot be pictured without subjection to an established order – that is, a government."[92] This leads some to argue that "because God has created man with a nature that compels him to live in society . . . political authority comes from God in the same sense as the queen's authority in the beehive comes from God."[93] The problem with this mode of reasoning, Trudeau retorted, is that "we are not bees, nor are we ants, and that is why this answer by itself is not enough. . . . Human society, then, differs from the beehives in that men are always free to decide what form of authority they will adopt, and who will exercise it (and not God, Providence or Nature)."[94]

The notion that obedience is ordained by God is used by people in positions of authority, none as masterfully as Duplessis: "Mr. Duplessis constantly teaches us that we must not criticize the authority that he exercises: firstly because this authority comes from God, and secondly because he rules in the name of the Province and the 'race,' values that none but a perverse spirit could assail."[95] Why, Trudeau asked, not question the very idea that we must obey? A common answer would be "Because the majority seek only their own comfort and pleasure. . . . Few men are aroused by an injustice when they are sure of not being its victims themselves."[96] They are misguided, he said, because "when authority in any form bullies a man unfairly, all other men are guilty," since by their silence they condone these abuses. "If they withdrew their consent, authority would collapse."[97] He thus concluded: "In the last analysis any given political authority exists only because men consent to obey it. In this sense what exists is not so much authority as obedience." And why wouldn't the citizen selfishly serve his own interests, while ignoring the fate of others? Because in the long run this attitude would backfire: "To remain free, then, citizens must seek their welfare in a social order that is just to the greatest number; indeed only great masses have the power to make and unmake governments. It follows that men can lead a free and peaceful life only if their society is just."[98] For Trudeau, like his mentor Laski, the notions of individual freedom and social justice would always be inseparable.

If citizens agree to obey freely in a just society, it follows that they can also disobey. How do they know when disobedience is justified? The only way, Trudeau answered, was "to examine their consciences on the quality of the social order they share and the political authority they acknowledge. If the order is rotten and the authority vicious, the duty of the citizen is to obey his conscience in preference to that authority. And if the only sure way of reconstituting a just social order is to stage a revolution *against tyrannical and illegal authority* – well, then, it must be done."[99] But citizens should beware, Trudeau warned: they should resort to disobedience only in exceptional circumstances. "Such a doctrine must be applied prudently and circumspectly or we shall have anarchy."[100] And it is precisely to avoid chaos that "most civilized peoples provide mechanisms whereby citizens can fight against laws they disapprove of without going outside the law or becoming conscientious objectors or political martyrs."[101] Needless to say, these "mechanisms" are the distinguishing features of democratic systems.

But to apply these mechanisms properly, one must first understand the role of the state. Unfortunately, he added, "we are used to identifying with the concept of the state all kinds of power that we dread: imperialism, statism, Freemasonry, Communism, atheism, and so on. . . . [102] Yet the state is by definition the instrument whereby human society collectively organizes and expresses itself."[103] But, careful, warned Trudeau, "if we were to extend the powers of the state without having multiplied our means of controlling its policy and limiting its methods of acting, we would tend to increase our enslavement. That is why I am wary of those who preach indiscriminate nationalization without setting themselves first to undermine the undue majesty of political power."[104]

Trudeau emphatically reminded his readers: "Liberty is a free gift – a birthright, which distinguishes man from beast. To allow human society to develop order and justice, men agree to some restrictions on their liberty, and obey the authority of the state."[105] In other words, it is not up to the state to grant liberties "sparingly" to the citizens, but rather up to the citizens to delegate powers sparingly to the state, so that order and justice shall prevail, for the good of all. However, although Trudeau was a forceful proponent of individual freedom and advocated delegating powers to the state "sparingly," he was no libertarian. As a matter of fact, he was neither a "communist" nor an "anarchist" nor a "libertarian." Unlike Communists, he rejected the idea of a ubiquitous state; unlike anarchists, he rejected the notion of a stateless society; and unlike libertarians, he did not believe in the doctrine of a minimal – or night watchman – state. "The democratic state is a strong state," he later wrote.[106] The state plays an important role, particularly in the promotion of fundamental values, such as "social justice." But in his view, its strength derives from the consent of citizens. By simultaneously emphasizing individual freedom and state intervention, Trudeau's political philosophy integrated conservative and liberal ideological perspectives. Small wonder that both the right and the left ferociously attacked him!

According to his conception of democracy, "the true statesman is not one who gives orders to his fellow-citizens so much as he is one who devotes himself to their service."[107] Moreover, "in a constitutional society it is not men, but rather laws, that control us. The rulers . . . can exert authority only as far as the law allows."[108] But Trudeau deplored the fact that the opposite prevailed in Quebec. Instead of putting the state at the service of the people, "we are that living absurdity – a craven people that makes itself the servant of the state; and this is the true definition of totalitarianism."[109] And Maurice Duplessis is the antithesis of the "good" statesman. His laws infringe on the freedom of citizens, and "he insults democracy in its most solemn sanctuary: the parliament. . . . The point is that in a parliamentary democracy the opposition is the last and most important bulwark against arbitrary tyranny. . . . And the Duplessis government, by buffoonery, contempt, accusation, insult, intimidation, illegality, and fraud, has prevented the parliamentary opposition from performing its functions and has therefore gagged the people in the persons of their best-accredited representatives."[110] The reason French Canadians didn't rise up against this state of affairs was because they had been taught "a morality in which insubordination is synonymous with infamy, and authority with infallibility."[111] In Quebec, "with very few exceptions . . . you find only distrust of freedom and hostility towards its exercise."[112]

But a system that respects the citizen, "that allows the people to choose and dismiss their rulers as peaceably as possible,"[113] does exist. It is none other than "true" democracy. Trudeau described its characteristics, insisting on the inalienable rights of individuals: "Certain political rights are inseparable from the very essence of democracy: freedom of thought, speech, expression (in the press, on the radio, etc.), assembly, and association."[114] Two additional rights naturally flow from these: "equality of all before the law, and the right not to be deprived of one's liberty or one's goods without recourse to a trial before one's peers, under an impartial and independent judicial system."[115] At this point, Trudeau returned to a dream he had long nourished and would bring to fruition only in 1982: "To guarantee that they will remain beyond the reach of the state, many democratic constitutions have felt the need to include a 'bill of rights,' treating these rights as in some sense anterior to the very existence of the state."[116] Trudeau was consistent in his beliefs – no doubt about that.

Trudeau was utterly fascinated by this model of government. The true democratic state "puts to good use the creative liberty of people living in society. . . . The state must go further than merely investigating their needs; it must also encourage them to demand what they consider just. . . . In such a state the liberty of citizens is an end in itself. The authorities don't think of it as an annoying phrase; on the contrary, they want it, and encourage it as the surest guide to the common good."[117] Trudeau was almost obsessed by his desire to bring about "true" democracy in Quebec, for the benefit of "his" people. Like the *Man of La Mancha* in 1965, he wanted to "dream the impossible dream . . . to reach the impossible star." But he was not naïve. He knew that ideal democracy does not exist anywhere: "That is not to say that democracy is a perfect form of government: you just have to look around you. . . . [Nevertheless] if the people use their sovereignty badly, the remedy is not to take it away from them (for to whom could we hand it over who would offer a better guarantee for *all* citizens?), but rather to educate them to do better."[118] So here was the program that all men of goodwill should take on: first, educate the people to understand the "true" nature of democracy; and second, work together to overcome the barriers on the long road ahead.

This is exactly what he set out to do, with great enthusiasm, especially once he became legal and technical counsel at the FUIQ (the Quebec Federation of Industrial Unions). He worked relentlessly for the advancement of the status of the workers and their unions, and they, in return, adopted him as one of their own. To follow him on this mission, let us return to 1952, the year the FUIQ was founded.

Chapter 11

WORKERS OF QUEBEC, UNITE!

The labour movement does not like violence. . . . What it wants is democracy.

– PIERRE ELLIOTT TRUDEAU,
"Scarecrows and Scared People," 1954[*]

THE DUPLESSIS GOVERNMENT, seemingly unbeatable since the tidal wave of 1948, was of course one of the obstacles barring the road to democracy in Quebec. In that election it had snapped up 51 per cent of the vote and eighty-two seats in the Legislature – thirty-four more than in 1944 – while the Liberals retained just eight of the thirty-seven seats they had previously held.

With the other parties virtually wiped out, Duplessis had no political opposition to fear. Some publications, such as *Cité libre* and *Le Devoir,* denounced his government's practices, but his most ferocious opponents were in the labour movement.

And for good reason. The unions accused him of systematically siding with the employers in all labour disputes. And while Adélard Godbout's Liberal government had maintained cordial relations with the unions, adopting laws that benefited them, Duplessis hounded them on the pretext that he was flushing Communists out of their ranks. In the early 1950s, for example, he tabled Bill 19, which allowed the government to deny – or revoke – the accreditation of any "organization that tolerates among its organizers or officers one or more persons adhering to a communist party

---

[*] Trudeau gave the speech "Épouvantails et épouvantés" or "Scarecrows and Scared People" at the second annual congress of the FUIQ (Fédération des unions industrielles du Québec) at Champigny on June 5–6, 1954.

or movement."[1] Since Bill 19, much like the infamous "Padlock Law" of 1937, did not define the words "communist" and "communism," the unions feared it would become "an instrument enabling unscrupulous bosses to delay the certification of unions."[2] Duplessis used force to break strikes, as was the case in Asbestos and Louiseville, or he sought to outlaw them through Bill 20, which was also tabled in the early 1950s. Once the bill was adopted, any public-sector association going out on strike would automatically be decertified. The bill would also be retroactive. It was an open secret that retroactivity would allow Duplessis to strike down a Supreme Court decision favouring the Alliance of Teachers of Montreal, which had gone out on strike in 1949. So the main opposition to Duplessis came from within the Quebec labour movement, and that is where we find Trudeau hard at work. It is worth examining the movement more closely to get a better idea of the context and impact of his actions.

From the beginning of the twentieth century, and particularly during the 1950s, North American unions underwent major changes and Quebec was no exception. Until the late 1930s, craft unions and industrial unions in the United States belonged to a single federation, the American Federation of Labor (AFL). Craft union members were mostly craftsmen proud of their skills. Members of industrial unions, meanwhile, lacked specialized skills, and most worked on assembly lines. Easily replaceable, they had come to realize that their strength lay in the unity of the working class and were more politically conscious. Thus, the AFL was an alliance of unions with divergent outlooks and interests. This unstable situation came to an end when the AFL, dominated by craft unions, expelled industrial unions from its ranks. In 1938, the latter created the Congress of Industrial Organizations (CIO).

In Canada, the labour movement followed the American pattern. Until the late 1930s, Canadian craft and industrial unions belonged to the Trades and Labour Congress of Canada (TLC). In 1939, the TLC was pressured by the AFL to expel industrial unions from its membership, who, in turn, formed the Canadian Congress of Labour (CCL) the following year. As was to be expected, the TLC in Canada maintained ties with the AFL in the United States, while the CCL remained close to the CIO. The labour scene in Quebec was more complex because of the religious factor and the national question. The Quebec Provincial Federation of Labour (QPFL) was affiliated to the Trades and Labour Congress of Canada and

the AFL in the United States. But there was no institution grouping industrial unions together.

Quebec alone had a faith-based union: the Catholic Workers
Confederation of Canada (CWCC), founded in 1921 by nationalist clergy
and laymen who saw "international unions" as a threat to French-
Canadian culture. This confederation based its positions on the Church's
social doctrine and promoted trade unionism steeped in both Catholicism
and French-Canadian nationalism. Unions within this confederation were
supervised by chaplains, and the Church hierarchy regularly reminded
workers of their duty to "respect authority" and not to meddle in politics,
while advocating close collaboration between employers and workers.
Until the 1950s, and despite the protests of several of its members, the
CWCC accepted only Catholic workers. For different reasons, the two
labour confederations in Quebec had hardly any political experience.

In the late 1940s and early 1950s, many factors impelled the AFL and
CIO – long-standing enemies within the American labour movement – to
lay down their arms. First, with the marked decline in craft unions, the AFL
and CIO had fewer organizational and ideological differences than before.
Then, this being the high point of McCarthyism, they believed that by
joining forces, they would be in a better position to detect the Communist
infiltration they both feared. Finally, by merging they would put an end to
inter-union raiding, which was draining considerable energy and money
without increasing the total union membership. In 1955, negotiations
bore fruit, and the AFL and CIO sealed their merger as the AFL-CIO.

As expected, the American pattern of reconciliation was adopted in
Canada. In April 1956, after several years of negotiations, over 1,500
delegates, "representing approximately one million members, met in
Toronto to bring about the merger of the TLC and the CCL, which ultimately led to today's Canadian Labour Congress (CCL)."[3] This new confederation faithfully adhered to the CCL tradition of giving the labour
movement an outlet for political action and chose as its political arm the
Co-operative Commonwealth Federation (CCF).

Things did not go so smoothly in Quebec. Although many unionists
sought a merger between the QPFL and the CWCC, this seemed unlikely,
especially because of the religious issue. (The CWCC lost its confessional
character only in 1960, to become today's Confédération des syndicats
nationaux or CSN.) The Church was concerned about a rapprochement

with the QPFL, which it considered "international," probably atheist, and certainly disrespectful of the Church's social doctrine. However, the Church realized that in order to avoid massive desertions, it had to tolerate the radicalism and militancy of the new CWCC leaders such as its president, Gérard Picard, and its secretary general, Jean Marchand. This explains, in part, why it supported the Asbestos strike.

But the confessional character of the CWCC was not the only obstacle to the unification of the Quebec labour movement. Before setting up an umbrella organization bringing together the QPFL (craft unions) and the industrial unions, it was essential first to regroup these unions. The Quebec Industrial Unions Federation (FUIQ) was created for this very reason. Its founding congress was held in Montreal on December 6 and 7, 1952. Political scientist Roch Denis writes in his study of the Quebec labour movement: "For the first time, 159 delegates from industrial unions, representing 30,000 members, were brought together in a common assembly."[4]

From the outset, it was understood that the FUIQ would be short-lived, since it was destined to merge with the QPFL to form a single federation. Yet it rapidly developed into a dynamic union, politically and socially. On February 9, 1956 – four years after the federation's inception – Le Devoir noted that it "participated actively in all economic, political, cultural and social controversies that animated public opinion in French Canada." And this happened to be the labour federation for which Pierre Elliott Trudeau worked as legal and technical counsel.

From its inception, the FUIQ undertook public education on a massive scale. It increased the number of schools for workers. It even produced a weekly radio show, "Les travailleurs au micro" [Workers at the Mike]. The FUIQ and Trudeau were a perfect match. Trudeau noted in Memoirs that in the 1950s he travelled widely "all over Quebec. Several times a month, I jumped on my motorcycle to go to Sherbrooke, Chicoutimi, Arvida, Shawinigan, Quebec, Joliette or Rimouski, where I gave classes at the labour action schools. . . . I taught them some basic economics, and enough accounting to be able to make sense of a company's balance sheet, and a bit of political science. . . . At the same time, I got to know union leaders all across the province."[5]

Indeed, Trudeau (the so-called high-flying playboy of legend) criss-crossed Quebec, giving numerous lectures in unglamorous little towns, and using these contacts to educate his audience about the importance of political involvement. For example, on December 12 and 13, 1953, he gave a talk on the causes of unemployment and the ways to combat it: he said loud and clear that the traditional elites were wrong to tell workers they should keep out of politics.[6] There were not two classes of citizens. The worker was a "first-class citizen" and as such had not only the right but also the duty to participate in political life. And when the Duplessis government claimed that unions hindered the freedom of workers, this was an outright lie designed to scare them. In a social and political framework favouring capitalists, workers needed – and had the hard-won legal right – to unite in order to protect their interests. How and where should they act? Trudeau gave practical advice for interventions at the municipal, provincial, and federal levels. The FUIQ leaders liked his message. Despite the long tradition of apolitical unions in Quebec, they stated publicly: "By definition, labour unions form a body which must defend the interests of workers in all areas. . . . We know that the working class needs to obtain justice in the economic, social and political fields."[7]

The workers appreciated Trudeau's ability to express complex ideas clearly and to speak in terms his audience could easily understand. Following Trudeau's course on economic fluctuations and the need for state intervention, Jean-Paul Desmarais, secretary of the workers' school of the Fédération nationale de la métallurgie, wrote to him:

> My dear Pierre,
>
> Your lecture came as quite a revelation and it is unfortunate that we could not spend a whole day on an extremely topical subject, presented by a speaker who has the ability to explain scholarly formulas in a clear language easily understood by the workers. . . .
>
> Please accept a cheque in the amount of twenty-five dollars ($25.00) to cover your travel costs.
>
> I hope we'll be lucky enough to return to this subject in the near future.
>
> Fraternally,
> Jean-Paul

Trudeau scribbled at the bottom of the letter: "Returned the cheque on February 3rd."[8]

The FUIQ actively participated in various political causes. In January 1954, it led the campaign against Bills 19 and 20, with the support of the CWCC and the Alliance of Teachers of Montreal – but without the QPFL. This latter union had already distanced itself from other workers' organizations in 1952, and especially from the CWCC, which it accused of harbouring a "revolutionary spirit."[9] In 1954, it publicly sided with the government; this explains why Duplessis personally met the QPFL chairman, the diehard anti-Communist Roger Provost, whereas he refused to meet delegations from the other trade unions.

The campaign against these bills included a big "March on Quebec" on January 22, 1954. Several thousand activists gathered at the Palais Montcalm to denounce the arbitrary measures of the Duplessis government. Trudeau was one of them.[10] But it was all for nothing: both bills were adopted on January 28. This failure convinced the FUIQ and the CWCC that political action was urgently needed. But which party should they support?

This issue of political affiliation was at the top of the agenda at the FUIQ's second annual congress, held in Champigny, near Quebec City, on June 5 and 6, 1954. And the keynote address was given by none other than Trudeau. In front of each delegate's seat was a card announcing the title of his speech – "Scarecrows and Scared People." He denounced every strategy meant to "scare" workers, reducing them to silence.[11] In Quebec, he said, "there are scarecrows just about everywhere. We see them in factories, at the Legislature, under bridges, etc. They are called communism, anarchy, socialism, etc." The workers were repeatedly accused of "no longer respecting authority, government, the clergy, traditions. . . ." But Trudeau retorted that this was simply false. You don't become an anarchist or a bad Catholic by criticizing the government: "God . . . has given us the power to choose our leaders, who in turn organize the life of the country. It is therefore our duty to scrutinize the laws they make, and to judge these laws as citizens." In a democracy, he maintained, sovereignty belongs to the people.

He then took on a second scarecrow: socialism. He argued that this venerable ideology actually went back to ancient Greece and in its current form "promotes much the same ideas as those of the labour movement. The ideal of this movement is to liberate man from the slavery of matter, and to distribute goods with greater justice." So there was no

reason to be afraid. Besides, he added, identifying directly with his audience, "we workers are not impressed by scarecrows." Pursuing this ideal
of justice required political and social action that was coherent, courageous, and sometimes even tough. But tough action does not mean violence: "The labour movement doesn't like violence. This is not what it
wants. This is something it uses only when forced to. What it wants
is democracy . . . the labour movement strives for democracy."

In *Histoire de la FTQ*, Émile Boudreau writes: "Trudeau's message
got across: the FUIQ set up a committee to formulate the federation's
guidelines for political involvement."[12] The document – called the
Manifesto – was presented on May 14, 1955, at the congress in Joliette.
It called for the establishment of a Quebec-based socialist party upholding the values of "democracy, private property and the traditions of the
French Canadian masses."

While Trudeau was not a member of the committee, his influence
appears in almost every line, as the following excerpts indicate. The signatories "affirm their faith in fundamental human rights as proclaimed
by the United Nations on December 10th 1948. . . . The recognition of
the inherent dignity of all members of the human family and their equal
and inalienable rights are the foundation of freedom, justice and peace
in the world."[13] Having listed the fundamental rights, the authors went
on to denounce the labour policies of the Duplessis government, demanding that the law deal severely with policemen who violate these rights.

The section on Canada's federal structure also reveals Trudeau's
influence: "The signatories of this manifesto want the province of Quebec
to remain part of Confederation with the explicit intention of repatriat-
ing the Constitution." They are in favour of repatriation "provided that
it includes an amending formula giving the provinces that make up the
Confederation a say in the matter. . . . This Constitution would include
a bill of rights pursuant to the proclamation of the United Nations previously mentioned."

This is vintage Trudeau! It is crystal clear that from the 1950s
onwards, he was nurturing the plan to repatriate the Constitution and
incorporate into it a declaration of inalienable rights. He would have to
wait until 1982 to achieve this goal. Regarding the protection of citizens,
"the signatories advocate a comprehensive social security programme,"
which they believed fell under provincial jurisdiction. "However, this

does not mean that the province of Quebec would object to a national health insurance plan, if the other provinces of Canada and the federal government proposed an agreement in this area." Trudeau acknowledged the division of powers, but welcomed any provincial-federal collaboration that enhanced the well-being of citizens.

The document presented by the Political Action Committee was adopted at the 1954 congress and was now referred to as the *Manifeste au Peuple du Québec* [Manifesto to the People of Quebec]. All recommendations were fully accepted, except for one, which happened to be the single most important recommendation: namely to create a political party. In fact, this proposal created a rift within the committee. Of the five members, four – all French-speaking – supported "the creation of a third political party in the Province of Quebec, a truly democratic party, controlled by its members."[14] The English-speaking fifth member called on the FUIQ to throw its support behind the CCF.

As for the delegates, not only were they torn about the choice of party, many of them rejected any form of political action. It was impossible to reach an agreement. Ultimately, the *Manifesto* clearly stated the FUIQ's ideological orientation: "We demand a democratic socialism respectful of private property and the faith and traditions of French Canadians." However, its political affiliation was simply dropped. In its place were the following words: "We publish our *Manifesto to the People of Quebec* in the hopes that it will stimulate fruitful discussions from which beneficial solutions will be found for the political problems of the Quebec people."[15] These high-sounding words fell short of a commitment to do anything.

Having witnessed the disagreements over the issue, Trudeau came to this inescapable conclusion: if the most dynamic trade union federation was not ready to get truly involved in politics, then French Canadians were even less ready. He was not about to give up, however. As we shall see in Chapter 13, he would continue his struggle by other means, committing himself heart and soul to a new movement: the Rassemblement.

One of the most important tasks the FUIQ assigned to its legal counsel was to write a brief on its behalf for the Tremblay Commission. The rationale behind the commission goes back to the Rowell-Sirois Commission, which had been established by the federal government in 1937 to address financial and social issues arising from the Great Depression of the 1930s. In 1941, following the recommendations of the Rowell-Sirois Commission, the provinces agreed to abandon some fields of taxation in exchange for federal grants. This unanimous agreement held up until 1947, when Ontario and Quebec decided to withdraw from the program. But in a dramatic turn of events in 1952, Ontario decided to opt into the agreement once again. The Duplessis government was now isolated and accused the federal government of violating the Constitution by encroaching upon fields of taxation that fell under provincial jurisdiction. In 1953, in order to put pressure on the federal government while bolstering his popularity among Quebec voters, Duplessis put in place the Royal Commission of Inquiry on Constitutional Problems – often referred to simply as the Tremblay Commission, after its chairman Justice Thomas Tremblay.

Trudeau fulfilled his task conscientiously. On March 10, 1954, four men presented the FUIQ brief to the Tremblay Commission: Romuald J. Lamoureux (the federation's president), Roméo Mathieu (the FUIQ secretary), Philippe Vaillancourt (organizational director of the Canadian Congress of Labour), and, of course, Trudeau. The brief consisted of two sections. The first one examined the Quebec workers' standard of living, noting that they had a lower quality of life than Ontario workers. Trudeau would take this analysis further in his introduction to *The Asbestos Strike,* which we will discuss in the next chapter. We focus here on the second part of the brief, which illustrates Trudeau's as well as the unions' conceptions of Canadian federalism.

The brief started out by stating that workers "are as keen as anyone to ensure the respect of all human values; and they lay down as the very foundation of civil or political society the premise of the inviolability of the person. . . . They believe deeply in the democratic system and its associated freedoms. . . . They affirm the equality of all before the law; and they believe that the reality of a nation based on the union of two major ethnic groups must be sanctioned by an intelligent and open federalism."[16] Even if we hadn't been told that Trudeau had penned these lines, we could have easily guessed it! Note in particular the reference to one Canadian nation, comprising "two major ethnic groups." Trudeau would never abandon this view. We should also note the reference to an intelligent and open federalism to ensure the well-being of all citizens. To this end, the brief suggested improvements to intergovernmental relations.

The first reform concerned the material well-being of workers. The very function of unions is "precisely to obtain higher wages for the workers compatible with social progress and justice."[17] However, in the federal system, inter-provincial rivalries could lead to a "premium on injustice." In fact, "since investments automatically flow where the greatest profits can be made, there is a danger that provinces might get into a bidding war, undercutting each other by keeping labour costs down. And since labour law falls under provincial jurisdiction (except for a few industries such as railways, etc.), a short-sighted government could be tempted to base its economic policy on overtly anti-worker legislation: the other provinces would be forced to lower their standard of living, or risk exclusion from capital markets. [The FUIQ] seeks to ensure a minimum of fairness in the wage system for the entire country, as a way of avoiding this premium on injustice. . . . Steps should be taken to adopt [labour] legislation that puts all Canadians on an equal footing."[18]

But rather than increase the powers of the central government, "the provinces should reach an agreement to adopt certain common standards."[19] In some cases, however, inter-provincial agreements might not be enough. A case in point was when companies with operations in several provinces had a disagreement with their employees: "In such cases, employers have an undeniable advantage over the workers [because] the right to strike is subject to varied regulations, and strikes have to comply with different deadlines in different provinces. Consequently, bosses can band together to force unions to give in one after the other."[20] It follows that "in addition to legislation specific to each province joint federal-provincial legislation is also needed."[21] Oddly enough, the brief noted, "the International Labour Organisation exists to ensure the coordination of laws of various countries, but nothing like this exists to institutionalize cooperation between provinces."[22]

As he would ceaselessly maintain throughout his life, Trudeau emphasized in this brief that the Canadian state consists of the central and the provincial states taken as a whole. This means not only that sovereignty is shared between the two levels of government but also responsibilities and fiscal resources. Hence the inevitable overlap between spheres of jurisdiction and the resulting conflicts between the two levels of government. An effective federal system transcends these divisions, with a view to establishing genuine and significant cooperation between the various governments. The whole thrust of the brief was to suggest concrete measures to achieve this type of cooperation.

From the earliest days of Confederation, the brief stated, sharing the tax base had been a constant bone of contention between the various governments, which only saw the problem according to their respective interests. A case in point was the Tremblay Commission itself, whose mandate was to study "the encroachments of the central government in the field of direct taxation." The implicit purpose of the commission was naturally to pressure the federal government to withdraw from this field. A section of the brief criticized this strategy, under the heading "A false solution: getting the federal government to abandon direct taxation." According to Trudeau, the recovery of direct taxation by the provinces is justified neither in law nor in practice. Legally, he wrote, "Sections 91 and 92 of the British North America Act clearly specify that the federal government has the power of direct as well as indirect taxation."[23] Provinces can levy direct taxes only within their jurisdictions. In practical terms, "even if the federal government voluntarily agreed to withdraw from the field of direct taxation, the results would be disastrous."[24]

Trudeau went on to explain why. On the reasonable assumption that the federal government would replace direct taxes by indirect taxes and on the basis of data for the fiscal year 1952–1953, he argued that the tax burden facing everyone in Quebec would increase by about 10 per cent. And the height of injustice is that since "direct taxes fall most heavily on the rich, whereas indirect taxes more often hit the poor . . . we would end up with a far more regressive tax policy than we have today."[25] The Tremblay Commission therefore needed to proceed with caution: "The idea is not to kick Ottawa out of the entire field of direct taxation, but only out of part of that field, giving the priority to Quebec. Well! The problem is to know exactly *which part* that is going to be."[26] The brief continued with a section entitled "Fiscal Cooperation," which explained how to "address this vital issue in a spirit of creative collaboration," based on three principles: (1) proportional taxation, (2) financial equalization, and (3) economic stabilization.

Trudeau examined first the principle of proportional taxation. When federalism is properly applied, he claimed, each government has to raise the revenue required to meet the needs that fall under its jurisdiction. As a result, "if a government has an overabundance of revenue such that it provides for the part of the common good outside its jurisdiction, this indicates that it may have collected more than its share of taxable capacity."[27] In other words, if a government could distribute services lavishly in an area outside its jurisdiction, this was no cause for celebration, for it meant the government was taxing citizens too heavily. Conversely, if a government used only part of its taxable capacity, thereby poorly fulfilling its responsibilities, then it was guilty of negligence toward the electorate. This was one of the most important aspects of Trudeau's vision of democracy in a federal system: every level of government has an obligation to provide for the "common good" within the powers conferred to it by the Constitution. In 1957, much to the horror of his usual allies, Trudeau applied this principle and supported Duplessis on the then burning question of federal grants to universities.

With regard to equalization, Trudeau believed that in a federal system, the reallocation of resources from rich provinces to the less fortunate ones was merely a question of social justice. As the brief put it: "The cohesion of a political entity depends on its will to ensure a minimum level of subsistence to *all* its members regardless of their geographic location." The principle of social justice was already central to Trudeau's political philosophy, and the pursuit of the "Just Society" was destined to become his mantra during his five terms as prime minister of Canada.

There remained the principle of economic stabilization, which particularly affected workers, because "they are the victims hardest hit during periods of crisis and unemployment."[28] It therefore comes as no surprise that a substantial part of the FUIQ brief was devoted to the subject. During a recession, the basic principles of classical political economy hold that the free play of supply and demand would restore things in the long term. The problem is that laid-off workers could not wait for the long term to feed their families. For this reason, the brief adopted the Keynesian view that "state intervention should curb the recession before it degenerates into a crisis."[29] It stands to reason that this model is easier to apply in a unitary political system, such as France, than in the Canadian federal system. In a unitary system, the government stabilizes the economy during a recession by lowering taxes and increasing spending, and it does the opposite during an inflationary period. Things get more complex in a federal system for three main reasons.

The first is that the two levels of government have conflicting rhythms: "The revenues of all governments fall off in times of crisis. But the central government can fight unemployment and stem the deflationary spiral by cutting taxes and increasing spending. On the other hand, a provincial government, left to its own devices, will be forced to do precisely what it should not do: it will increase taxes and cut spending."[30] Trudeau concluded: "This shows that the provinces are naturally forced to adopt a cyclical rather than an anti-cyclical fiscal policy, in other words, they tend to worsen rather than alleviate the impact of economic fluctuations and unemployment."[31]

The second source of complexity was that inflation or deflation did not necessarily hit all provinces at the same time or with the same intensity. The provinces "may for this reason have different views on the urgency to act, and even on how to act . . . to the point that the crisis ultimately spreads everywhere, and federalism becomes synonymous with chaos."[32]

The final difficulty is that the British North America Act (Section 91) specifies that the federal government has exclusive authority over a number of instruments including trade, banking, and credit, which are essential to achieve economic stabilization. Since the provinces have no authority in this area, the brief concluded that "economic stabilization and full employment are included in this part of the common good which falls under federal jurisdiction."[33] Trudeau insisted that this does not confer any superiority on the federal government with regard to sovereignty, since the objective is the purely pragmatic one of effectiveness. This explained not only that agreements between the provinces and the federal government were possible but indeed had been reached throughout Canadian history: provinces "rented" fields of taxation to the federal government in exchange for compensation. The brief therefore accepted the principle of fiscal arrangements but specified that they ought to be examined on a case-by-case basis. Regarding the most recent agreements: "The Quebec Industrial Unions Federation holds the view that the agreement formulas currently being proposed by the federal government should be modified in order to combine their stabilizing virtues with greater fiscal autonomy for the provinces."[34] The FUIQ then proposed means to achieve more equitable agreements. This, claimed the brief, is proof that it is possible to "develop theories acceptable to any government committed to federalism and democracy."[35] All it took was an honest endorsement of the principle of cooperation.

Cooperation is all the more necessary since the responsibilities and fiscal resources of each level of government cannot be allocated once and for all. Circumstances and issues change over time. Consequently, "there is no *adequate and definitive* division of functions between one government and the others in the Constitution, nor can there be in administrative practice. . . . Since cooperation is inevitable, it seems reasonable to try to make the most of it." But Trudeau had witnessed the power struggles at federal-provincial meetings when he worked at the Privy Council Office. A change of attitude was therefore needed, so that officials taking part in negotiations would not see them as "merely veiled opportunities to increase their own powers, something which can only lead to increased aggressiveness all round."[36] The brief then attacked the Duplessis government's autonomist policy. True autonomism does not consist in increasing the distance between the central and the provincial government, but in empowering citizens: "True autonomism . . . leaves the greatest number of responsibilities within reach of the people."[37]

With regard to the Constitution, the brief stated that the FUIQ "knows that the overriding need for daily bread affects the religious cultural and political evolution of a people more than constitutional guarantees; because living comes first, and philosophy comes later."[38] And in order to improve people's lives, reforms are better than grand schemes: "The Quebec Industrial Unions Federation has been less concerned with proposing constitutional amendments than with demonstrating how the current Constitution could enable citizens and governments to strive more effectively towards the common good."[39] However, if constitutional reforms are undertaken, then concessions would be needed on all sides.

For example, in the case of Quebec: "The Province could declare its willingness to accept the incorporation of a declaration of human rights into the Constitution, provided that the rights of disallowance and reservation were abolished. It could also propose a specific plan to repatriate the Canadian Constitution, including an amending formula, provided the Senate was transformed into a more federalist and less unitary institution, and provided the organization of the Supreme Court depended directly on the Canadian Constitution, rather than solely on federal statutes."[40] Here once again is Trudeau's vision of "fair" negotiation. Here too are values close to Trudeau's heart: the incorporation of a declaration of human rights, reform of the Senate, the independence of the Supreme Court from the political system . . .

The brief concluded with a lyrical and optimistic flight of oratory. The FUIQ hoped "that constitutional issues arising between the federal and provincial governments will be addressed with intelligence and without any sense of inferiority. Because confidence breeds confidence; and the labour movement knows enough about negotiations to realize that better results are achieved when the parties involved are treated as equals."[41]

It is in 1954, working as FUIQ counsel, that Trudeau made huge strides in his thinking on the subject of federalism. That same year, Les presses de l'Université Laval published *Le fédéralisme canadien: Évolution et problèmes*. Trudeau knew the author well. Not only had he rubbed shoulders with Maurice Lamontagne during his frequent meetings with the small circle of progressive intellectuals around Father Georges-Henri Lévesque at the Faculty of Social Sciences, but he had also had extensive and cordial exchanges with him about the trip to Moscow. Lamontagne had been director of the Department of Economics at Laval University, and by the time the book came out, he was a senior official in the federal government. Trudeau took the opportunity of the book's release to write "De libro, tributo . . . et quibusdam aliis"* in the October 1954 issue of *Cité libre*.[42] This title now seems obscure or pedantic, but would have been easy for readers of the time to appreciate. Latin played a prominent role in the curriculum of all classical colleges, and the title suited the content of the article: Trudeau dealt not only with Lamontagne's book (*de libro*), but also with tax (*tributo*) and various other topics, such as the FUIQ brief, the work of the Tremblay Commission, and other problems of the moment (*et quibusdam aliis*).

Lamontagne's basic premise was that following the economic crisis of the 1930s and the social problems resulting from the Second World War, "economic instability and social insecurity had suddenly emerged as serious threats to the population's welfare and the very foundations of political society."[43] A convinced Keynesian, he maintained that "only

---

* Concerning a book, taxes . . . and various other subjects.

the State, namely the federal government, could effectively undertake the fight against these two sources of instability arising from industrial development."[44] Moreover, the new responsibilities delegated to the central government "were freely and legitimately entrusted to it by the provinces."[45] Indeed, the fiscal agreements proposed by the federal government in 1941 were freely accepted by the provinces. Quebec, however, had opted out of them in 1947.

As Lamontagne had been ferociously criticized by the nationalist elite, Trudeau rose to the defence of this "perfectly serene and remarkably intelligent" book.[46] And why was Lamontagne attacked? For not being sufficiently nationalist: "Our outlandish elite lost no time in impressing upon the author that he had been unbearably pretentious to deal with ideas when race was the issue." Without batting an eye, Trudeau identified the culprits: "Condemned before it had even been written by the man who remains (in spite of all) our most lucid journalist, disavowed by the then rector of Laval University, misunderstood yet opposed by a professor of History at the University of Montreal,* this work met the only fate it could expect at the hands of our official intelligentsia." Trudeau quoted the Université de Montréal historian Michel Brunet verbatim – "The most serious charge that can be addressed to Mr. Lamontagne is to have forgotten that he is a French Canadian from Quebec"[47] – and then concluded: "It is inconceivable that a true scholar should use such arguments to discredit another scholar's work. And this is what makes me think that Professor Brunet, whom I do not have the honour of knowing, must, in his courses, occasionally mingle fancy with fact." In one fell swoop, Trudeau lashed out not only at Brunet but also at the editor of Le Devoir and a former rector of Université Laval. He accused them of resorting to ad hominem attacks rather than engaging in a reasoned debate about Lamontagne's ideas.

After castigating critics who had attacked Lamontagne's book on nationalistic rather than scientific grounds, Trudeau pursued his own analysis, starting with praise. He congratulated Lamontagne for

---

* The rector of Université Laval is Mgr. Vandry and the historian at l'Université de Montréal, Michel Brunet. Trudeau named them in a footnote. He didn't identify the journalist at Le Devoir. He was probably referring to Gérard Filion or André Laurendeau.

examining "Canadian federalism from the standpoint of modern economics. . . . This is what makes the reading of his historical chapters so
lively.[48] . . . And this is also what lets him give original and penetrating
views on a great variety of subjects.[49] . . . All this results in an irrefutable
demonstration of the absolute necessity for intergovernmental cooperation."[50] So much for the plus side.

And now the minuses. There is, continued Trudeau, "some good,
some bad, and some indifferent"[51] in this book. The bad elements could
be summed up in a few words: Lamontagne did not respect the fundamental principle of shared sovereignty between the two levels of government. "It seems to me rather strange," Trudeau wrote, "that an author
who has so knowledgeably established the absolute necessity for federal-
provincial cooperation . . . should come up, at the end of his book, with
a solution to the most crucial issue, that 'avoids discussion' between governments, forgets all about cooperation, and 'belongs to the most out-
moded of Canadian federal traditions.'"[52] Trudeau referred specifically
to the fiscal agreements. Lamontagne suggested that the central government could "simply advise the provinces that it was offering them an
unconditional annual subsidy (p. 270). . . . Should any of the provinces
manifest an obvious ill will, thereby threatening the national programme
of economic stability, the central government could always take measures against it (p. 271)."[53] While Trudeau was just as much a Keynesian
as Lamontagne, he was outraged: "No thank you!" he exclaimed: "This
is too much like arbitrary power for my taste."[54] He found this solution
all the more dangerous since "the gentlemen in Ottawa like to govern a
bit too much."[55]

Trudeau then discussed the dispute between Ottawa and Quebec
City, highlighting the wrongs committed by Ottawa. Taking advantage
of the fact that in 1947 Duplessis had opted out of an agreement accepted
by all other provinces, "Ottawa took exclusive control of income taxes
in all provinces *including Quebec,* and in return paid various sums to all
provinces *except Quebec.*"[56] Trudeau dismissed any excuse from the
federal government: "I am well aware this state of affairs resulted from
the Duplessis government's total incompetence in economic matters. . . .
But you cannot plead the victim's stupidity as an extenuating circum-
stance for the thief."[57] He was accusing Ottawa of theft. Nothing less.
According to him, "the federal government and its clever civil servants

accommodated themselves only too easily to a system that amounted to a manifest defrauding of the Quebec taxpayer," who bears the burden of double taxation.[58]

But for Trudeau, Ottawa's guilt did not exonerate Duplessis, who used demagogy as a strategic tool in negotiation. Duplessis knew the Constitution gives the federal government the right to levy direct taxes, but he had nonetheless mandated the Tremblay Commission "to study the encroachment of central authority in the field of direct taxation." By transforming "what had been an abstract conflict of constitutional rights into a heavy burden on the taxpayer, he managed to unite the entire Quebec electorate against Ottawa. From this position of strength he then proceeded to ask the federal government to modify its fiscal policy by allowing provincial income taxes to be deducted from the federal income taxes." True, Trudeau conceded, Duplessis "negotiated like a rascal, and probably like a coward; he negotiated without manners or dignity, through press conferences, . . . but, still, negotiate he did."[59] The federal government was therefore duty-bound to disregard his inelegant methods and to pursue negotiations in a spirit of justice for Quebec taxpayers.

Not only did the federal government manifest its disrespect for French Canadians, but it didn't play its hand well. Had federal officials been "more intelligent," interjected Trudeau, they would have realized the position taken by Duplessis was compatible with their own: "They could have pointed out that the tax abatement he requested was for a sum and for a period of time that were perfectly consonant with those originally planned in the fiscal agreements; and that this constituted tacit acknowledgement that decisions about the funds needed for macro-economic stabilization came under the jurisdiction of Ottawa."[60] All that would have remained to be done was to agree on the amounts involved.

"Many institutions," Trudeau wrote, "have rightly seen that the formula of tax deductibility could put an end to our current tax muddle." However, he added with a touch of pride, the FUIQ alone showed how to reconcile "the requirements of economic stabilization and provincial autonomy."[61] Trudeau could not miss the chance to promote the FUIQ's brief and devoted six pages to its recommendations. The most significant, he believed, were those meant to deprive the central government of the right to impose its will on the provinces. It could only encourage them to accept its proposals by offering them financial incentives. Hence the need to collaborate and to negotiate in good faith.

He then emphasized, once more, the complexity of a federal system: "Neither this article, nor the FUIQ brief, nor the whole body of other briefs, nor even Mr. Lamontagne's book have done more than scratch the surface of the immense problems of political economy faced by the Canadian federal system."[62] This was why he didn't expect that the Tremblay Commission, whose six members he described as "men of integrity," would do much to advance our understanding of federalism. What mattered most was for them not to be taken in by Duplessis's political game: "The Commissioners could write nothing more harmful than a narrow, provincial report rehashing the valour of French Canadians who defend their language, faith and rights against a centralizing oppressor. . . . And in the eyes of future generations, Messrs. Tremblay, Minville, Parent, Arès, Rowat and Guimont* will have much to answer for."[63]

Obviously, although Trudeau shared Lamontagne's Keynesian perspective, he disagreed with his conception of federalism. More specifically, he believed that the centralizing measures Lamontagne advocated were excessive and a violation of the principle of shared sovereignty enshrined in the British North America Act. In short, as he soon found out after reading the *Revue d'histoire de l'Amérique française,* his position was similar to that of the historian Michel Brunet. In this journal, Brunet articulated two fundamental criticisms of Lamontagne: first, in approving the federal government's centralizing policy, he was going against provisions of the British North America Act pertaining to the division of powers. Second, he did not take into account the special situation of French Canadians. Trudeau was obviously very sensitive to these arguments. As a result, a few days after his harsh criticism of Brunet, Trudeau sent him a letter that casts new light on his alleged arrogance and inability to admit mistakes. On October 20, 1954, he wrote:

I just read the review of Lamontagne's book you published in the *Revue d'Histoire de l'Amérique française* (September 1954). I must admit that if I had based my remarks on your review rather

---

* These were the six members of the commission.

than on the talk you gave on June 11th, I would have been less ironic about you in my *Cité libre* article of early August.

Your critique of his economic perspective would still have struck me as inadequate. However, the insight of your thought on the bicultural issue would certainly have commanded my respect. On several points, your ideas are akin to mine.

If we should remain adversaries, let us at least try to limit the damage.[64]

Trudeau was holding out an olive branch to Brunet, who ignored the gesture and bore a grudge against him all his life. Indeed, as quoted by Léon Dion, in a letter dated May 19, 1984, sent to the journalist and author Pierre Godin, Brunet wrote: "You may perhaps know what I think of this scatter-brained and evil being [Trudeau]. . . . I have always considered him a phony and I never took him seriously." According to Dion, Brunet's dislike of Trudeau "eventually turned into obsessive hatred."[65]

Although Trudeau criticized the nationalists who "had failed to examine properly the economic theories which constitute the core of Lamontagne's book," he nodded in the direction of "our comrade Gérard Fillion, who has initiated a discussion in the most courageous way."[66] Indeed, from July 21 to 24, 1954, Fillion published three articles in *Le Devoir* criticizing Lamontagne for advocating a rigid federalism, which he attributed to a dogmatic adherence to Keynes. While these theories were "certainly an improvement on the past," wrote Fillion, it was nonetheless dangerous "to build what Mr. Lamontagne calls the new Canadian federalism upon economic theories which will probably be outdated in a generation."[67] Trudeau agreed the theory would one day be obsolete. But what choice was there? "Economic problems have to be resolved today with the economic knowledge that we currently possess. And that is what Mr. Lamontagne attempted to do."[68]

Trudeau wrote the brief to the Tremblay Commission and the review of Lamontagne's book, which could both easily be described as odes to authentic and cooperative federalism, while working as legal counsel to the FUIQ. As noted above, this federation had been established for a limited duration. Its primary objective was to open the way to a single federation bringing together industrial unions (FUIQ) and craft unions (QPFL). Mission accomplished. In February 1957, at the FUIQ fifth and last congress, members voted to create the present-day FTQ (Fédération des travailleurs du Québec).

Nowadays, the FTQ is well known for its nationalism, its support of the Parti Québécois and of Quebec independence. It is hard to believe today that Quebec trade unions – and their leaders – were federalists well into the late 1960s. But they were. For example, Louis Laberge, elected president of the FTQ in 1964, who was given a state funeral in Quebec in 2002, declared at the time that nationalism was "an issue that interested pseudo-intellectuals far more than it did the workers."[69] In fact, until 1971, the FTQ promoted social democracy rather than nationalism, arguing that "French-speaking Quebec capitalists would not be more lenient towards Quebec workers."[70] Gradually, however, the FTQ changed, adopting business unionism and coming out increasingly in favour of Quebec independence. In 1976, it allied itself with a political party for the first time and played a big role in the Parti Québécois victory of November 15. In 1980 and again in 1995, the FTQ campaigned enthusiastically for the "Yes" side in the two referendums on Quebec secession. But in 1965, when Trudeau left for Ottawa to sit as a Liberal MP, he was on excellent terms with the unions, and the labour movement openly endorsed federalism.

In February 1957, at the congress in Quebec City dissolving the FUIQ, Pierre Dansereau, dean of the Faculty of Sciences at the Université de Montréal, was chosen as keynote speaker. Dansereau was also president of the Rassemblement, a political movement endorsed by the FUIQ.* But since, according to the newspaper La Presse, Dansereau had been "prevented from travelling to Quebec," he was replaced by the Rassemblement's vice-president, Pierre Trudeau.[71] Could this have been a diplomatic excuse? Or – as we suspect – an elegant way for Dansereau to make room for the highly regarded FUIQ legal and technical counsel?

In his speech, Trudeau once again promoted his beloved democracy. He also deplored Quebec's economic and social policies. Quebec natural resources, he said, were the most valuable in all of Canada. But they were often controlled by foreign companies, and not exploited with the

---

* We will describe the Rassemblement in more detail in Chapter 13.

common good in mind. He also bemoaned Quebec's lacklustre performance in education: "Except for Newfoundland, Quebec is the province
that spends the least per capita on education. Our shortage of engineers
and technicians is acute."[72] The same went for health: "We will probably
be the last [of all the provinces] to acquire health insurance." With
regard to politics, French Canadians "are guided far too often by passion
rather than by reason" and could easily be whipped up by references to
ethnicity. They were suspicious of democracy: "For us, democracy is a
kind of British institution tinged with doubtful and revolutionary liberalism. Yet true democracy is government by laws not by men."

The dissolution of the FUIQ did not end Trudeau's collaboration
with the labour movement, nor his struggle for a more democratic
Quebec, as we shall see in Chapter 13, when we discuss his involvement
in the Rassemblement and in the Union des forces démocratiques (Union
of Democratic Forces). But in 1956, before he got involved with these
two movements, and while he was still serving as FUIQ counsel, he
brought out the famous collective work *The Asbestos Strike*. Its first
chapter constituted his most comprehensive and vibrant analysis of
Quebec society. It exploded like a bombshell and its thunder rolled
across the province and the rest of Canada.

Chapter 12

AGAINST THE CURRENT

Our people have never accepted the nationalism of our official doctrine.

— PIERRE ELLIOTT TRUDEAU,
La Grève de l'amiante, 1956*

IN 1951, THE ASBESTOS STRIKE was still fresh in the minds of many Quebeckers. Frank Scott, the distinguished poet and McGill law school professor who was a co-founder of the study group *Recherches sociales,* planned to bring out a collective work on the subject. He brought together a group of like-minded contributors, including his own team and people from *Cité libre,* with the trade unionist Jean Gérin-Lajoie acting as coordinator. They drafted a work plan, identified potential authors, met again, updated their plan . . . but the project got nowhere. Gérard Pelletier was worried. He called the team members to a meeting in May and asked the authors who had already been designated – one of them Trudeau, then working at the Privy Council – to draw up "a fairly detailed plan of the work to be undertaken," because they had "no more time to waste now."[1]

Days went by, followed by weeks, months and years . . . By the end of 1953, only two chapters had been completed. The project was stagnating. Frank Scott and Jean-Charles Falardeau decided to entrust the

---

* Translator's note: In this chapter, we will refer to the collective work Trudeau edited as *La Grève de l'amiante,* since its real impact came from the initial French edition of 1956; the English translation only came out in 1974.

343

editing of the volume to someone else. That "someone" was busily engaged as union arbitrator and FUIQ legal and technical counsel and was just putting the finishing touches to the brief for the Tremblay Commission. He asked for time to think about the offer before giving his answer. "By February 1954, I accepted," Trudeau wrote in his personal notes, "provided that all the guys finished their chapter by the time I returned from India in May 1954."[2] As we have already seen, he was headed for Lahore with the delegates he had met at "Couch."

The authors agreed to submit their manuscripts by May but did not keep their promise. He had to hound them. He kept a record of the progress: "From May 1954 to December 1954, I push the guys and pick up the chapters, which all come in by Christmas. I correct them, edit them, send them back. . . . Last session, June 21, 1955. Everyone gets their chapters back, and reads my corrections, amendments, etc." When he took on this project, he was not only working on the FUIQ brief but was also writing an article for the March 1954 issue of *Cité libre,* on economic fluctuations and stabilization methods. And in October 1954, while hunting down the authors, he published "De libro, tributo . . . et quibusdam aliis" in *Cité libre,* as well as a review of *Essais sur le Québec contemporain,* a collective work edited by Professor Jean-Charles Falardeau at Laval University.

In December 1954 he had finished bringing together all the chapters of *La grève de l'amiante,* but still devoted a good part of 1955 to this project. In 1955, if Trudeau's name was conspicuously absent from the three issues of *Cité libre,* it is because he was busy editing the nine chapters written by the various contributors, plus the appendices. He was also writing the ninety-one-page first chapter, "La province de Québec au moment de la grève" ("Quebec at the Time of the Strike," ultimately running to eighty-one pages in the English translation), and the twenty-six-page epilogue. Not to mention his work as FUIQ counsel. Finally, in May 1956, Éditions Cité libre published *La grève de l'amiante* (which later appeared in English as *The Asbestos Strike*).[3]

This 430-page collective work consists of ten chapters, an epilogue, and four appendices. We will focus only on Chapter 1 – aptly titled "Quebec at the Time of the Strike" – since it was here that Trudeau expressed his own ideas, and quite forcefully at that.[*] As we will see, that

---

[*] The chapter is often referred to simply as the "Introduction."

chapter was a bombshell, one of the most important things Trudeau ever wrote. It established the context of the strike, by analyzing the evolution of Quebec society, particularly during the first half of the twentieth century. According to Trudeau, the most interesting feature of the strike was the date, rather than the place or the particular industry where it occurred. The strike, he claimed, "was significant because it occurred . . . precisely at a moment when our social framework – the worm-eaten remnants of a bygone age – were ready to come apart."[4] Interestingly, while these ninety-one pages unquestionably constitute his most thorough study of French-Canadian society, he produced them in record time, because his thinking on the subject had been maturing for several years. This introduction constitutes his sharpest critique of the fundamental premises of the nationalism endorsed by the French-Canadian elite at the time.

The chapter is divided into five parts, the three most important of which are "The facts," "The ideas," and "The institutions." Drawing from numerous studies, Trudeau briefly summarized the extent of Quebec's industrial transformation and its urbanization: "In 1941 Quebec was 63% urbanized, [which made it] the most urbanized province in the country. . . . In 1951 [more than] 67% of Quebec's population lived in urban areas."[5] Meanwhile, "at the turn of the century, the dollar value of agricultural production accounted for 65% of the total net commodities produced in Quebec, and in 1950 this percentage had fallen to 10.5. . . . On the other hand, the percentage . . . for the manufacturing industry rose from 4% to 65.3%."[6] Quebec had thus made a radical transition from an agricultural to an industrial economy. Trudeau then remarked that while Quebec was just as industrialized as Ontario, it lagged behind in two important respects: productivity and the living standards of its people.

Once he had presented the facts, he moved on to the "Ideas," which formed the crux of his chapter. He summarized his thesis as follows: if Quebec was in such a sorry state it was because "an entire people [had been forced] to choose one lifestyle . . . while all its intellectual and moral training urged it to cling to another."[7] To which he added, appropriately: "And this is precisely what I now have to demonstrate." Most of his analysis was devoted to what he called "this schizophrenia." It began with the intellectual disciplines.

"Nationalism," he said, was "up to the very end of the period studied in this book . . . the main focus of almost all French Canadian social thought."[8] As he had often argued, Trudeau readily acknowledged that after the Treaty of Paris in 1763, this nationalism was both understandable and beneficial for "a people who had been defeated, occupied, decapitated."[9] He also paid heartfelt tribute to the leaders of this people: "These men are, almost without exception, worthy of our respect. They have lacked neither honesty in their intentions, nor courage in their undertakings, nor firmness of purpose. . . . Confronted by politicians who were often shameless, the nationalist school was just about alone in constructing a *system of thought*. . . . Was it, perhaps, necessary first to 'save the race,' so that others might later find what was worth saving in man?"[10] While the "social theorists" were busy describing the fate of French Canada and its providential mission, "the people themselves were busy meeting the challenges of everyday reality. Individuals, after all, must first worry about making a decent living for themselves and their families, even if they have to upset a few mental constructs in the process."[11]

This explained the coexistence of two types of nationalism, which Trudeau called "de facto nationalism" on the one hand and "nationalism as an intellectual discipline" or "theoretical nationalism" on the other. He readily accepted the first type of nationalism, which he said was "only the concrete result of the virtue of patriotic piety exercised by an ethnic group."[12] We know that at least from the time he first read Berdyaev – and in fact up to his death – Trudeau considered this sense of belonging to a community quite normal. In 1996, he told us in an interview: "The existence of a sociological French nation, with its own culture, is a historical reality."[13] He didn't mind "de facto nationalism." Nationalism "as an intellectual discipline" was a different matter.[14] He strongly believed that this type of nationalism transformed the sense of belonging into a pseudo-science purported to be the only way to understand social problems and find appropriate solutions.

It is important to note that Trudeau was not yet referring to political nationalism – often called "neo-nationalism" – which blossomed in the sixties and will be discussed in Chapter 14. What he was rejecting was a system of thought. This nationalism, Trudeau wrote, was "formulated and dispensed by those among us who were professional writers and teachers, and who were generally accepted as our leaders and intellectual masters."[15] In his view, Mgr. Paquet's sermon of 1902 succinctly and forcefully summed up "this school of idealism" to which "our intellectuals had to subscribe."[16] As an elite people, Mgr. Paquet had declared, "our mission is not so much to manipulate capital, as to handle ideas. . . . While our rivals are laying claim to the hegemony of industry and finance, we shall strive above all for [respect] of the doctrine and the palms of apostleship."[17] French-Canadian intellectuals dutifully responded to the call: "One after the other they aspired to 'the honour of doctrine.' It reduced them to complete intellectual sterility in the end."[18]

This type of nationalism had two main features: the distrust of new ideas – especially ones held by "les Anglais" – and the search for unanimity, to which should be added basic premises such as the desirability of a return to the land. Any poor soul "whose thinking went beyond the limits of official nationalism . . . was automatically suspect"[19] and was brought back in line in no time. Trudeau cited the case of Édouard Montpetit, his former professor at the Université de Montréal. Like other young professors returning from Europe after graduation, he believed that French Canadians should enter the fields of industry and finance. "Greeted with hostility and suspicion, the young professors were accused of atheism, on the excellent grounds that they taught economic liberalism. Finally, they succumbed to attrition. By consenting to 'think nationally' in their scientific work, they arrested its development."[20] This was how, in an extremely urban and industrialized province, Montpetit ended up publicly maintaining that agriculture was the basic industry of Quebec. This anachronistic teaching did not in any way diminish his considerable fame in his province. To give but a few examples of the high regard in which he was held, a boulevard, a subway station, a Cegep in Longueuil, and a street in Laval have been named after him.

According to Trudeau, Esdras Minville provided another example of intellectual sterility. Minville is little known today, but during his lifetime he was one of the leading figures of French Canada. Much like Montpetit, the fact that Minville warped his scientific work by "thinking nationally" does not seem to have tarnished his fame. In 1995, Sylvain Guindon published a biography of Minville marking the centenary of his birth. He boasted that Minville, a former director of HEC (École des Hautes Études Commerciales) as well as the other professors there, were duty-bound to "develop in all their teaching the national point of view, to create an atmosphere conducive to the flourishing of a distinctly French-Canadian and ethnic intellectual personality, of a sense of patriotism, or national pride."[21] Clearly, nationalism has long-lasting allure! But Trudeau added it would be wrong to consider Minville and Montpetit as isolated cases. Virtually all "great" French-Canadian think-ers shared this view, as was clearly indicated by certain statements by Olivar Asselin, Victor Barbeau, Father Arès, and Abbé Groulx. Trudeau had heard, read, and admired all these nationalist leaders during his studies at the Collège Jean-de-Brébeuf and the Université de Montréal.[22] Now, in 1956, he deplored their "intellectual sterility." Nothing less. No wonder the published piece exploded like a bomb.

Trudeau pursued his line of reasoning. The problem with these think-ers was that after decrying all the perils of the city and explaining to the workers they were responsible for their own woes, "they had to suggest some cure for the 'ills' caused by industrialization."[23] Unfortunately, pre-cious few were qualified for the task because they knew nothing about the appropriate theories. He was appalled by such ignorance: "Our official thinkers, with amazing constancy, ignored all the social science of their day. To judge by their writings, we may say without exaggeration that until very recently, they knew nothing of universal legal thought, from Duguit to Pound; nothing of sociology, from Durkheim to Gurvitch; nothing of economics, from Walras to Keynes; nothing of political science, from Bosanquet to Laski; nothing of psychology, from Freud to Piaget; nothing of pedagogy, from Dewey to Ferrière."[24]

In order to find a remedy for the ills of industrialization, continued Trudeau, these thinkers had to find something to fill the gaps in their own knowledge, so they seized on the social doctrine of the Church or, more accurately, on their own particular interpretation of this doctrine. Because, he noted pointedly, this "social doctrine of the Church as it has been understood and applied in French Canada . . . is nothing more, in fact, than a continuation of our traditionalist assumptions, with a veneer of papal authority."[25]

This warped interpretation had an important consequence: "In other countries, the social doctrine of the Church did much to prepare the way for the democratization of peoples, the emancipation of workers, and the progress of society. In French Canada, it was invoked in support of author-itarianism and xenophobia."[26] Worse, "it rejected any solution which might have succeeded among our 'enemies': the English, Protestants, mate-rialists, etc."[27] This misguided attitude led to the rejection of democracy, an almost visceral distrust of any form of government intervention, even when aimed at solving dire social problems, the promotion of authoritarianism and fascism and the passionate quest for a "leader." Holding nothing back, Trudeau quoted statements by some of French Canada's major intellectual mentors, highlighting their undemocratic mindset. Esdras Minville, for example, praised the "peculiar qualities" of Quebec's popular mentality, which includes "an acceptance, spontaneous so to speak, of authority and hierarchy in the family, in society, and the State. *The French Canadians like to be governed.* . . ."[28]

This lack of openness meant these thinkers were unable to adopt reforms from anywhere else "for the irrefutable reason that liberal economic reforms were proposed by the 'English,' and socialist reforms by 'materialists.'" For this reason, Esdras Minville argued that French Canadians "can only expect to obtain a solution to their problems from no one other than themselves. For the past few years, instead of looking to the outside world for directives, an orientation, a system of thought, or a doctrine, they have set out to find these things within themselves, in their own social philosophy and in the examination of their actual situation."[29] And what were these native-born solutions, which Trudeau called "panaceas"? There were too many for him to tackle one by one, so he analyzed how "our nationalist 'social doctrine of the Church' proposed the renewal of economic and social life by five means: the return to the land, small business, the cooperative movement, the Catholic trade union movement, and corporatism."[30] Since he did not devote much attention to small business and the cooperative movement, we will only deal here with the three other means.

The first "panacea," according to Trudeau, was "agriculturism," a term popularized by Michel Brunet,[31] which constitutes "an integral part of our nationalism."[32] This misguided remedy not only involved settling young families on unworkable land, but also prevented any legislation to improve the sorry plight of workers. As proof, he cited the following statement by Minville: "Any measure *tending to improve the lot of the industrial worker even more,* or to give the illusion, at least, that the life of the urban worker is becoming more and more secure and easy, would almost fatally accelerate the movement *away from the countryside.*"[33] In other words, one of the foundations of traditionalist ideology at the time involved deliberately sacrificing the working class.

The second means was the Catholic trade union movement. Trudeau pointed out that this type of trade unionism was not "an offspring of liberal thinking, or an attempt to alleviate the real hardships afflicting our Catholic proletariat in Quebec. . . . One would almost be tempted to say that this result was a chance by-product. . . . Our ideas on trade unionism emerged from a nationalist reaction against reforms which arrived from the outside world, after we, in our indifference, had neglected to apply them in time."[34] "Outside" meant the international unions, which were viewed as dangerous. This fear was evident in J. Papin Archambault, whom Trudeau called a "tireless zealot of the École sociale populaire." Archambault claimed: "Without [the religious affiliation of these unions], *no authority will be able to enforce* the principles of Christianity in these organizations, where men of every opinion will come together."[35] According to Esdras Minville, international trade unionism had ideas that were carrying it "by a natural tendency as it were . . . towards communism."[36] Hence the necessity for Catholic unions to serve as a protective shield.

What objectives did these unions seek? What kind of struggle did they suggest to the workers? By way of answer, Trudeau said, "our social thinkers again retreated into the cozy myth of our providential mission."[37] For example, a self-assured Alfred Charpentier, president of the Confederation of Catholic Workers Federation of Canada from 1935 to 1946, said that "God, it seems, intended that our race should . . . become the purifying salt of the entire Canadian nation. . . . Providence calls upon our Catholic workers to do their part as well, namely, to lead a defence of this country's working class against the dangers which threaten it."[38]

The third and final means was corporatism. According to Trudeau, "Corporatism is without a doubt the most important reform to delight our social thinkers. The greatest variety of men, in the most different circumstances, and for the most opposed ends, proclaimed the gospel of corporatism. Their voices were as one, and they preached their futile homilies with unflagging enthusiasm. Nothing more starkly revealed the monolithic nature of our ideology."[39] As proof, Trudeau quoted an impressive number of statements, drawn from the most diverse sources. François-Albert Angers, one of the "social thinkers" mentioned in Trudeau's indictment, counted fifty-two well-known public figures who were "called to the defendants' dock" by Trudeau, not counting, he added, "the *Le Devoir* editorial team of yesteryear . . . , or all those who had ever given a lecture at the Semaines sociales, . . . the clergy and bishops throughout our entire history, and the members of L'Action Libérale nationale, with some exceptions."⁴⁰ But for Trudeau, this list of references only served to prove his point, because "one could add more names to it indefinitely."⁴¹

It may be worth noting that most of the people Trudeau accused of "preaching the corporatist gospel" were still alive when he wrote these lines. He was likely to run into them in the street or at social gatherings. After all, the French-Canadian elite of Montreal was a relatively tightly knit group. And the least we can say is that tact was never his strongest characteristic.

One surprising name stands out in the list: Father Georges-Henri Lévesque. Trudeau said he was also "one of the company since he had called for cooperative-corporate collaboration." But Trudeau was quick to pay tribute to the evolution of his thought: in 1938, upon his appointment as director of the School of Social Sciences at Laval University, "this Dominican was one of the rare examples among us of a man who, in his mature years, permits reflection and scientific research to overthrow the idols of his youth."⁴²

Inevitably, according to Trudeau, these ideologies, disconnected from reality, produced shaky institutions. These institutions tried to bridge the gap between the people, who "had suddenly, and as it were inadvertently, been thrust into the industrial era" and the theories of the doctrinarian thinkers, which were totally contradicted by this reality. To bridge the gap, Trudeau said, required them to do the splits. And he added ironically: "Such a posture is not conducive to energetic action."⁴³

Trudeau went on to examine the effects of "nationalism as an intellectual discipline" on several institutions and started with the Société Saint-Jean-Baptiste de Montréal: "This is a prime example of an institution where an obliging attitude to 'the doctrine' made it impossible to understand reality."⁴⁴ The École sociale populaire, meanwhile, should "assume a large share of the blame for the fact that, in contempt of reality, social thought in French Canada took a narrow nationalist path, blinkered by clericalism, agriculturalism, and a paternalistic attitude towards labour."

Let us recall that the slogan *l'achat chez nous* ("Buy from our own") was taught in schools, and that "our own" was clearly understood to refer to French Canadians, not to English-speaking or Jewish

Quebeckers. In his youth, Trudeau had been inspired by this type of economic nationalism in writing his high school play *Dupés*.* Now he was
denouncing the xenophobia of these economists. Blinded by their nationalism, they were headed in the wrong direction: "The common good
would doubtless have been better served if our researchers had studied
the unequal distribution of our provincial wealth less from the ethnic
point of view and more from the point of view of social classes and the
inequities inherent in economic liberalism."[45]

Trudeau then turned to educational institutions, recalling "the incredible struggle of the apostles of compulsory education against an entire
intelligentsia, which stubbornly refused to see this reform as anything but
a radical and atheistic measure."[46] He cited as an example the future
Cardinal Villeneuve, who had stated in 1923: "People are demanding a
compulsory school, a public school, a national school, a state school, as if
this were not tantamount to violating the family, and thereby enfeebling
society."[47] But in 1942, Villeneuve came out in support of Archbishop
Charbonneau's proposal on compulsory education. In 1943, a bill to that
effect met with the opposition of several bishops and of organizations such
as the JOC (Jeunesse ouvrière catholique) and the Société Saint-Jean-
Baptiste. Once the bill was tabled in the provincial legislature, Duplessis
and the entire Union Nationale came out against it. But the government
majority of Godbout managed to get the bill adopted: school attendance
became compulsory for children aged six to fourteen. However, Trudeau
added, "the Union Nationale came into power a year later, and has since
made hardly any efforts to enforce this law."[48] As a result, when Trudeau
wrote these lines in 1956, nothing had been done in this regard. It was
only in 1961 that Paul Gérin-Lajoie, a future Quebec minister of education, took steps to implement the law on school attendance and ensured
that textbooks would be distributed free of charge.

Trudeau noted that higher education also suffered the ill effects of
"theoretical nationalism." He juxtaposed two passages, written half a
century apart, in order to highlight the retrograde character of higher
education. In 1905, the French geographer and economist André Siegfried

---

* *Dupés* (literally "we've been had") was an anti-Semitic and nationalist play,
written by Trudeau and presented to mark the tenth anniversary of the founding of Collège Jean-de-Brébeuf, on May 16, 1938. See our first volume, p. 58.

had this to say about French Canada: "The university is far from being, as it is in some countries, a place where new ideas are in ferment, where future developments are in preparation; rather it is an effective instrument of conservation."[49] In 1954, the Université de Montréal submitted a brief to the Tremblay Commission, arguing that "research is not really an essential academic activity. . . . The role of the university is to preserve and transmit knowledge much more than to increase it."[50] Unbelievable but true! Trudeau knew he was not the only one to be appalled by this vision of the university: "No doubt, some professors at Laval and Montreal shuddered at these strange ideas. . . . Still, the above quotations are a painfully accurate reflection of the views of university administrations. Their systematic and persistent narrow-mindedness has produced generally poor results."[51]

Where the social sciences were concerned, Trudeau saw the Université de Montréal and Laval University differently. He pointed out that the Université de Montréal had set up the School of Social, Economic and Political Sciences in 1920, then given it the status of a faculty in 1942, and finally created the Institute of Sociology in 1943. But, he hastened to add, "this was a misrepresentation. In its brief lifetime, the so-called Institute hardly did any more sociology than the compilers of telephone directories. The 'Faculty' did not offer any instruction at the university level."[52] His remarks about the professors' competence were hardly more flattering, although he acknowledged recent and very solid research work conducted by a few priests. At Laval University, he saluted the work of Father Georges-Henri Lévesque, "now a liberal, [who] organized the teaching on a rational basis, fostered the intellectual development of his professors by giving them the opportunity to study abroad, and accepted the fact that science eliminates prejudice."[53] This praise did not prevent Trudeau from criticizing the Faculty of Social Sciences for not paying "enough attention to the problem of the *political* destiny of our people. In this field, the Laval school produced only vague and abstract notions and concentrated on attacking monolithic nationalism."[54]

Trudeau devoted twelve pages to the Church, which he said had "always been a distinctly national institution, inseparable from the basic structure of our society."[55] He cited as evidence the ubiquity of the clergy in the social and educational domains, and in various institutions, all of which bore witness to "the Catholic-nationalist alliance." Trudeau underlined the inadequacy of the Church's "traditional" stance on the challenges and social problems caused by the Industrial Revolution. He noted the Church's rejection of the CCF – which in 1961 would become the New Democratic Party (NDP) – its inordinate fear of Communism, and its concern about the popularity of international unions. He offered here and there a few words of praise for the "courageous and farsighted attitude" of Abbé Gérard Dion and a group of priests who, in 1944, had taken on the challenge of studying the problems linked with industrialization.

Trudeau then addressed political parties, which could be understood only if one grasped the pervasiveness of nationalism. He argued that all the established political parties could happily disregard all economic or social theories. Instead, they made abundant use of nationalism: "When political nationalism waxed virulent enough, it alone decided the outcome of elections; when it was dormant, a well-oiled political machinery assured success."[56] "Our political life," he continued, "by concentrating its energies on nationalism, has never evolved beyond the level of emotional response."[57]

To prove his point, he provided some examples of parties that had collapsed. Paul Gouin's Action Libérale nationale had initially been progressive. But in 1936, once its members formed an alliance with the conservative forces of Duplessis, their "programme of social reforms disappeared, for the most part, in a flood of nationalism and conservative verbiage."[58] A few years later, the Bloc populaire – for which Trudeau had campaigned – committed the same error. They had now disappeared, he said, because of "a curious mixture of conservative money and progressive hopes, all under the banner of nationalism."[59] And since the Communist Party and the CCF were both "forbidden by the theologians of nationalism and the politicians of clericalism," Social Credit filled the ideological vacuum, gaining ground "by thoroughly exploiting nationalist sentiment [and drawing] from time to time on anti-Semitism and union-bashing."[60]

Then in 1944, Maurice Duplessis was back on the scene. According to Trudeau, he "manipulated nationalism so successfully that social issues simply did not come to the fore. As a result, in the elections of July 28, 1948, the French Canadians still felt obliged to 'save the race' from the 'Ottawa centralizers' by electing eighty-two conservatives who claimed to be nationalists but were merely the representatives of high finance."⁶¹ Trudeau's conclusion was straightforward: nationalism permeated all parties. It muddied the water and prevented the serious reflection so essential if political action was going to be effective.

Trudeau argued that when political parties were able to meet the needs created by the industrialization of the province, it was not because they were inspired by "official social doctrines," but rather because they operated outside of these doctrines and were following the example of other provinces. None of these solutions were "made in Quebec": "In the great majority of cases, the Quebec legislator differed from those of other provinces only in his slowness and stinginess."⁶² For example, "in 1936, Quebec was the last of the provinces to agree to participate in the federal old age pension scheme, established in 1927. Our province was also one of the last to pass (in 1938) a needy mothers' assistance act."⁶³ Occasionally, Quebec led other provinces, for example in the case of the Workmen's Compensation Act of 1909.⁶⁴

Trudeau concluded his analysis by examining "the two main institutions in which the forces of industry have found their most eloquent expression: . . . capitalism and trade unionism."⁶⁵ Clearly, he said, "capitalist institutions in our province have developed in full contradiction to most of our nationalist assumptions (small business, cultural isolation, etc.)."⁶⁶ Noting that social thinkers claimed that French Canadians were "one big family . . . without . . . class rivalries," he remarked that, "capitalism was no more free of abuses in the Province of Quebec than elsewhere."⁶⁷ As proof, Trudeau cited the deplorable working conditions in many industries, which had been documented by numerous public enquiries. Trade unions were thus needed in Quebec just as much as anywhere else. Trudeau then proceeded to briefly sketch the history of trade unionism, demonstrating that there, too, social progress had come about not because of the social doctrine of the Church, but rather in spite of some of its exhortations.

At the end of this indictment, Trudeau asked the eminently reasonable question: "How have we managed to survive such torments?"⁶⁸ His answer: "Precisely by thumbing our nose at every ideology. Paradoxically, our ethnic group, though entrusted with a providential mission and the honour of doctrine, owes much of its survival to its 'materialism.' Peoples are not doctrinaire, thank God. . . . The imperious necessity of earning their living, of meeting their present needs, obliges them to rediscover practical possibilities by the constant application of the empirical method. . . . In the social field, this explains why the nationalism of our social thought, and its assumptions about society, were never accepted by our people in the half century preceding the asbestos strike. There was little return to the land and not much development of cooperatives. Small business became increasingly anaemic, corporatism remained in limbo, and Catholic trade unionism did not eliminate other kinds." Instead, "the province went through a period of intense industrialization, which bore a near-perfect resemblance to the industrialization of less messianic countries than our own."[69]

Trudeau was clearly paying tribute to the French-Canadian people, whose common sense had somehow enabled them to cope with the many challenges of life. In return, the people, this "silent majority," would see in him their champion. The people would remain loyal to him, supporting him at every election. And on his death, sixteen years after he left office, the people would once more show him both their recognition and their affection.

It is hard for us nowadays to imagine the courage it took for Trudeau to write such a devastating and public critique. By piecing together a few facts, we can however get an idea. In July 1956 – two months after the publication of La grève de l'amiante – André Laurendeau asked Gérard Bergeron, a political scientist at Laval University, to write some political analyses for Le Devoir. Bergeron used the pseudonym Isocrates. But why? Laurendeau explained to his readers: "The author . . . has every reason for not wanting to reveal his name."[70] In 1967, Bergeron wrote he was not "personally afraid of risking his 'livelihood.' [But] . . . several faculty members at my university had already been subject to undue pressure from the Premier of the time [Duplessis]. . . . I had no interest in having these disputes . . . affect my own modest position. . . . Nor did I want to . . . stake my scholarly future on occasional articles."[71] At about the same time, Le Devoir launched an investigation into provincial politics. Laurendeau highlighted a situation he found noteworthy: "More than half our correspondents refuse to identify themselves publicly. This is a profound reflection of the moral atmosphere of Quebec; people are not terrorized – no lives are actually at risk – but they are certainly afraid, because their livelihood is at stake. In many cases, this fear appears to be legitimate. In other cases, people are showing more prudence than courage: people in Quebec do not typically have a flair for danger."[72]

One can easily imagine, then, the upheaval Trudeau caused, in publishing such a scathing critique of the dominant ideology of Quebec elites, a critique aimed directly at the people in authority. It also helps us understand why some reactions were so extreme. Some readers were overjoyed that Trudeau had expressed publicly, in such brilliant and courageous language, what they felt deep down; they saw him as the champion of the voiceless in society. Others, particularly those who had borne the brunt of his attacks, were infuriated because they were unable to shut up this shamelessly self-assured critic. They did a good job of blocking his academic career, but they could not threaten his livelihood since his personal fortune placed him safely out of their reach. Still others saw Trudeau's words as the beginning of a new era, in which the search for truth would prevail over a system based on deceit. It therefore comes as no surprise that the publication of La grève de l'amiante was truly a phenomenon whose impact reached far beyond the borders of the province. Many reviews and articles appeared in both French and English. There can be no doubt that Trudeau's chapters, and particularly Chapter 1, drew the most admiring reviews and also the fiercest criticism. Trudeau methodically clipped and filed each article.[73]

Overall, the reviews in English were full of admiration. For example, the historian H. Blair Neatby described Trudeau's chapter as a "masterly analysis."[74] The political scientist C.B. Macpherson liked everything about the book and highlighted the exceptional quality of Trudeau's contribution. He saw La grève de l'amiante as "clearly a contentious book. One might almost say it is contentious because its analysis is so clear. . . . A work that gives unrivalled insight into both the problems of Quebec today and into the new spirit and intelligence that are at work there."[75] Anglican Outlook and News Digest – an English-language review published in Quebec – devoted both an editorial and a lengthy review to the work, noting Trudeau's "brilliant introduction of over ninety pages."[76]

For Quebec francophones, however, the work touched a raw nerve, which helps to explain the emotional nature of the reactions in French, something that was largely absent from those in English. Among the many accolades, both of the book and of Trudeau's contribution, let us note what Raymond Gérin, secretary of the Centre des Patrons Chrétiens, wrote in the September 1956 issue of the review *Relations industrielles:* "As paradoxical as it may seem, the turning point of the social history of our province has not, in our opinion, been so much the asbestos strike itself, as the publication of [this] book."[77] Gérin wrote that Trudeau's piece was "perhaps the most lucid and most honest analysis made in Quebec on the problems of industrialization." For this reason, he added, "we cannot blame him for the aggressive tone he sometimes uses and for claims that ought to have been more finely-shaded."

In *L'Actualité économique,* Roger Chartier said that Chapter 1 filled up a quarter of the whole volume, but "nobody would think of complaining because Trudeau has painted a raw and skilful portrait, in vivid tones, of the evolution of 'our social doctrine' over the past half century."[78] Like Gérin, Chartier forgave Trudeau for not sparing "anyone's sensitivities" given "the urgent clearing needed in our way of thinking." Solange Chaput-Rolland meanwhile wrote in her periodical *Point de vue* that the book was "one of the most important writings in French Canada on everything relating to our economic, political and labour situation, [which act as an antidote] to the stream of discreet and supposedly edifying lies we have been fed for years, as a way of lulling our national consciousness."[79]

Readers will surely have noticed that even when French-speaking critics praised Trudeau, they winced at some of his remarks. Just imagine the indignant reactions of devotees of nationalism and corporatism, whom Trudeau was taking on directly. Let us look briefly at three of them: first, the reaction of a "left-wing" nationalist, André Laurendeau; second, of a "right-wing" nationalist and corporatist economist, François-Albert Angers; and third, of a nationalist cleric, Father Jacques Cousineau. All three names come as a surprise, since up to now these people were his allies. Trudeau had known Laurendeau, assistant to the editor-in-chief of *Le Devoir,* since the 1940s. The two had maintained a friendly and mutually respectful relationship since that time. They had long been comrades-in-arms in the struggle against authoritarianism and clericalism. It will be recalled that, as we have seen in Chapter 9, in 1953, Angers, an economics professor at HEC (École des Hautes Études Commerciales), vigorously defended Trudeau from the withering attacks of Father Braün. As for

Father Cousineau, a regular contributor to the Jesuit review *Relations,* he had been a progressive in the 1940s and had come out supporting the strikers in Asbestos. Clearly, Trudeau's relentless public critique of the dominant ideology marked a first break with some of his allies.

André Laurendeau wrote three editorials in *Le Devoir* entitled "On Pierre Elliott Trudeau's one hundred pages."[80] He accused Trudeau of weakening his argument "with his non-stop aggression, with the quaking emotions and ferocious irony that have infused his writing, with his quasi absolute premises which he then uses to cast judgment on other premises. . . . He presents everything on the same plane; men and doctrines lack depth."[81] Laurendeau gave a few examples, suggesting that Trudeau had caricatured the reality he was analyzing, without giving due consideration to extenuating circumstances. "He is not being dishonest," Laurendeau wrote, "but is rather developing a passionate and in my opinion simplistic view."[82] For example, he wrote, Trudeau was right to recognize the poor quality of education in Quebec, but this was mainly attributable to "the intellectual poverty of [our] social environment and the financial scarcity of our 'cultural faculties.' . . . In a society that has always done without economists and sociologists, it is not easy to get people to see how important they really are."[83]

Laurendeau was not at all pleased that Trudeau accused his newspaper, *Le Devoir,* of increasingly "siding with conservatives" on social matters. He bristled that "Trudeau's simplifications border on the ridiculous."[84] He also rejected the very idea of a distinctly French-Canadian interpretation of the Church's social doctrine: "What Mr. Trudeau is discussing here is common to most social Christians nowadays: particularly corporatism, but also the return to the land, cooperation and trade unionism based on religious affiliation." Laurendeau conceded that French Canada had developed a few minor variations of this doctrine. "But for the rest, we were merely close imitators – which may not be glorious, but surely deflates Mr. Trudeau's claims about 'our very own' doctrine."[85]

While harshly criticizing some aspects of Trudeau's thesis, Laurendeau also drew attention to the text's real qualities: "This is polemical writing of the first water: well-informed, intelligent, competent, and expressed in nervous and quick-paced language. The author wields a sharp sword that comes crackling down like a blaze of lightning and leaves the ground littered with fifty severed heads." He also praised "the clear and lucid mind," "the acute and hard-edged analysis," the masterful synthesis "that often provides remarkable results." He even excused some of Trudeau's excesses: "The author has delivered an indictment, he wants heads to roll, and we have seen that his guillotine operates a little arbitrarily. But in pronouncing a judgment that is too severe has he not also revealed a new truth or at least [a reality] few people would have had the courage to expose? Which is why, in reading the introductory chapter straight through, we may feel either overwhelmed or liberated, depending on our state of mind. Both of these feelings flow from his incisive, sharp and indiscreet prose. . . . A remarkable personality has revealed itself."[86] With these words of admiration Laurendeau concluded his third and last editorial on the issue.

Trudeau – this "remarkable personality" – had undeniable qualities, but why did he also give in to excesses and oversimplification? Why did his sword slice the air, like a blaze of lightning? Why all the quaking emotion? Laurendeau suggested the answer lay in psychology. Trudeau "is a French Canadian disenchanted with his own people. His investigation has brought him into the presence of a 'monolithic mindset' which he rejects intellectually but which nonetheless wounds him to the very core: I think he is ashamed to be descended from such a people." This interpretation of the unacknowledged reasons for Trudeau's behaviour has gone down in history, while the rest of Laurendeau's harsh but balanced analysis fell into oblivion.

Some people even go as far as to say – wrongly – that in Laurendeau's view, Trudeau claimed not to belong to his ethnic group. For example, in a collection of Laurendeau's articles published in 1973, Claude Ryan wrote in the introduction that Laurendeau agreed with some aspects of Trudeau's critique, but "refused [to imitate Trudeau and] borrow a stranger's mask and judge men and institutions as though he has not been born in their midst."[87] Since then, several commentators have argued with great self-assurance that Trudeau's entire politics stemmed from his shame over being French Canadian. But who can penetrate deep into another person's heart and uncover that person's ulterior motives? In Trudeau's case, Ryan's explanation is simply contradicted by the facts. Whether in his writings or speeches, Trudeau always took for granted that he was part of the French-Canadian people. This is what we witnessed in the ten years we were friends with him. This also emerges clearly from all the documents we have consulted.

Laurendeau knew what he was talking about, in writing that "Trudeau is bound in solidarity to this not-so-distant past." Six years later Laurendeau himself felt duty-bound to justify the positions he had taken during the Conscription Crisis.[88] Indeed, during the 1940s, Laurendeau and Trudeau both shared in the nationalism, authoritarianism, corporatism, and anti-Semitism of their social environment, and they were opposed to conscription for overseas service, at the very time when fascism and Nazism were putting the world to fire and sword. Trudeau now rejected the ideology responsible for these failures of judgment, but he still stood with his fellow citizens in opposing conscription, on the grounds that governments had been hypocritical and had broken their promises. Moreover, and as we have seen, he paid tribute to past struggles of previous generations of French Canadians, acknowledging the real difficulties this French-speaking and Catholic community had faced in an overwhelmingly English-speaking and Protestant continent. He did not condemn the defensive nationalism of earlier generations. But times had changed. Now, these patterns of thought had become obsolete and were a significant obstacle to progress.

———————

Between September 1957 and September 1958, François-Albert Angers, director of L'Action nationale, wrote a series of six articles on La grève de l'amiante, focusing almost exclusively on Trudeau's Chapter 1 and epilogue. It was obvious to him that Trudeau had "put the basic tenets of L'Action nationale on trial."[89] Yet, while sharply critical, he maintained a respectful and courteous tone. He pointed out mistakes in Trudeau's analysis, but this did not prevent him from recognizing the competence of his opponent or the validity of some of his arguments. He was ten years older than Trudeau and considered it normal for young people – what he called "the New School" – to challenge traditional positions, like those defended by L'Action nationale. But he was convinced that "this new tide, no matter how furious it may seem, [will only succeed] in smoothing some edges a bit here and changing a contour line there."[90] As long as traditionalists kept their cool, they would emerge victorious in the end.

Where nationalism was concerned, for example, the New School, Angers claimed, felt "totally justified in seeing man in terms of humanity, rather than of nationality. Indeed, man is essentially man everywhere; but in fact he is conditioned above all by his heredity and temperament, his family and national homeland." It was only by reaching beyond this first level that man "attains true universality."[91] Angers also argued that this New School wasn't that "new"; it was actually part of a long-standing tradition: "Through Étienne Parent, the literary school of St. Hyacinthe, the Liberal Party of Laurier's younger years, the Liberal 'old guard' of T.-D. Bouchard, and the school of Jean-Charles Harvey and *Le Jour,* we finally reach *Cité libre,* the Rassemblement and the PSD [Parti social démocrate]." But the New School imprinted a new direction on this tradition. It was "more revolutionary than its predecessors in economic and social terms, according to the fashion of the day, but was in fact much less revolutionary in terms of fundamental ideas." Angers correctly noted that the school's anticlericalism was not antireligious. These young people, he continued, "are not seeking a substitute for Catholicism as the grounding value in our national life, but rather a deepening of the values Catholicism offers us."[92]

Why did Angers single out Trudeau's chapters for analysis? Because he unquestionably saw Trudeau as the figurehead of these Young Turks: "In recent years, views expressed by Trudeau have been circulating freely in the most varied milieus of society," such as radio, television, the annual conferences of the ICAP, and, Angers added, "even at *L'Action nationale.*"[93]

Angers then detected what he saw as a contradiction in Trudeau's ideas. Trudeau claimed to be fundamentally Christian and acknowledged that Christian values formed the basis of French-Canadian culture. If so, Angers argued, "fundamental Christian values [are] by definition imbued with a certain conservatism, traditionalism, and resistance to false modernism."[94] As a result, unless Trudeau was opposed to these values, he would be "singularly lacking in seriousness to call them into question as quickly and to treat them as contemptuously as he did in his famous chapter."[95] In other words, for Angers, when Trudeau rejected the conservatism and traditionalism inherent in French-Canadian culture, he was also rejecting Catholic values.

At first blush, Angers seemed receptive to Trudeau's criticism of nationalism: "It would be truly extraordinary if a clever young man, as Trudeau unquestionably is, were to prove wrong across the board, in lining up so many assertions about the faults and errors of our nationalism."[96] But he quickly added: "Is it not extraordinary, nevertheless, that someone claiming to be an impartial and objective observer should only see false and questionable aspects . . . in the entire range of the nationalists' economic-social positions?"[97] Trudeau claimed he wanted to describe society, "but practically his whole text seeks to prove the futility of nationalist thinking." Angers conceded that "the portrait Trudeau makes of the monolithic character of our society is not . . . completely false. . . . And there is no doubt that compared to most contemporary nations, French Canada has shown, at least until recently, a remarkable *unity of thought.** This unity stems . . . from its profound Catholicism (much more in fact than from its nationalism)."[98] Let us note the semantic refinement in Angers' distinction between "the monolithic character of our society" and "unity of thought."

For Angers, unity of thought is distinct from monolithic thinking in that it denotes the adherence to certain principles of life or action, but leaves "a lot of latitude in terms of application or interpretation."[99] Actually, if one applied this logic to Trudeau, he is the one guilty of "monolithic socialism," since he judges everything according to this ideology. As proof of this contention, Angers cited Trudeau's virulent criticism of corporatism, Angers's preferred doctrine. This helps explain his increasingly aggressive tone: "Since corporatism is not acceptable to the socialists, it obviously has to be excluded from the positive aspects of the nationalist position. It is even the worst aspect."[100] Angers writes: "Trudeau's whole thesis depends on the dialectical conception of historical materialism, according to which the passage through capitalism . . . [is] the temporary and necessary element of a synthesis whose final stage is socialism, which will save and redeem the proletariat and therefore the entire world."[101] In other words, Angers accused Trudeau of being Marxist. Failing to establish the proper distinctions between democratic socialism, Stalinism, Communism, and the various incarnations of Marxism, he simply failed to grasp that Trudeau's socialism was grounded in Christian values.

Then Angers flew off the handle, claiming that only a pamphleteer could use ideas like these "to pass the kind of peremptory judgments found in *La grève de l'amiante.* And for a Christian pamphleteer, this amounts to a serious sign of recklessness or thoughtlessness, since in matters of faith one has to be on one side or the other." In other words, by attacking

---

* Our italics.

corporatism, and by arguing that it was possible to be both Christian and socialist, Trudeau was leading the people astray and should not be trusted. Angers concluded that Chapter 1 of *La grève de l'amiante* was "a magnificent pamphlet. Possibly! But it was ultimately a dangerous pamphlet, since it spread the most fundamental kind of confusion!"[102] Angers recognized that Trudeau's analysis was accurate at times, but that was precisely what made it so dangerous: Trudeau's "argument is well-developed, as I have already said, and it could be accurate because it is plausible. But this very plausibility, combined with hasty but not totally wrong observations, give the argument an extremely perverse appearance of truth."

How did Angers explain all of Trudeau's excesses in his "famous chapter"? To him, this was simply a psychological trait typifying the entire French-Canadian community: "Deep down in Trudeau's thinking, I find that famous inferiority complex we [French Canadians] suffer from, and which incites us to accept as great and good anything coming from abroad, and to ridicule in extremely sarcastic terms everything that so-called 'dogmatic nationalists' think." Angers added that Trudeau "would have got closer to the truth if he had looked a little more sympathetically on a people forced by circumstances 'to choose one lifestyle . . . while all its intellectual and moral training urged it to cling to another.'"[103]

Although Laurendeau and Angers were critical of Trudeau, they still managed to detect some good points in his analysis. Father Jacques Cousineau, on the other hand, failed to see anything worthwhile in the various chapters of *La grève de l'amiante,* and even less in Trudeau's contribution. Between November 1956 and March 1957, he published four articles in *Relations.* And a year and a half later, he felt the urge to bring them together in a booklet published by the Institut social populaire.[104] This seventy-nine-page booklet includes the four articles from *Relations* as well as thirty-six pages of excerpts from reviews of *La grève de l'amiante* that had appeared in French and English in Canada and abroad. Note our deliberate choice of the word "excerpts." In reality, any interested reader can easily ascertain that although Cousineau's list of reviews and press references seems exhaustive, he picked his quotes selectively, then truncated them, as a way of bolstering his own point of view. Even a reviewer of *La grève de l'amiante,* writing for the Catholic publication *Revue*

Dominicaine, complained that Father Cousineau systematically truncated his own text in order to "beat Trudeau senseless."[105]

How are we to explain the fury of this Jesuit father who had supported the Asbestos strikers, much like Trudeau? At the time he was a
progressive member of the Church and had served as moral adviser to
the Conseil central des Syndicats de Montréal, under the auspices of
Archbishop Charbonneau. So why did he suddenly turn against his
former comrades-in-arms, and Trudeau in particular? Suzanne Clavette
provides an interesting answer in her doctoral dissertation *Les dessous
d'Asbestos.* In the chapter "Virage à droite de l'Église" [The Church
Repositions on the Right], she remarks that the sense of solidarity and
even unanimity that seemed pervasive during the strike was, in fact,
short-lived. As soon as the strike ended, the Church suffered profound
cleavages, and soon the conservative wing took over. In December 1949,
Mgr. Courchesne met with the highest authorities in Rome, and it is
alleged that he denounced the "pro-strikers" attitude of some members
of the Church. He would have had no problem getting a favourable
hearing, since the Vatican was repositioning on the right.

In 1950, Cousineau had to step down as moral adviser to the
Montreal unions, given that "his superiors had come to a decision that
called his social commitment into question." Was this a settling of
scores? Or was he being punished for advocating left-wing positions?
Whatever the case, he was sent off to teach in Quebec City.[106] By the time
he returned to social affairs after a six-year absence, the Church's repositioning on the right was solidly entrenched. This led Trudeau to claim
that Cousineau was now showing "excessive zeal in proving to his superiors that they had been right to call him back from exile by becoming
their rather exceptional champion."[107]

To get an overview of Cousineau's message, we have only to read the
subheadings of his critiques. For example: "The Significance of a Strike: A
Concocted Interpretation." Cousineau was setting out to destroy Trudeau's
credibility. He accused him of wilfully concealing some facts. "There is
method in his forgetfulness, and it is actually deliberate."[108] But rather
than directly accuse Trudeau of dishonesty, Cousineau wrote: "Trudeau
is both *sincere** and intelligent, so what could have motivated him to

---

* Our italics.

ignore basic realities to the point of completely failing to explain the Asbestos strike . . . and to have transformed it into a myth instead?"[109] He then took on Trudeau's critique of "the monolithic character of nationalism's official thinkers" and, playing on words, he accused Trudeau of never defining precisely who these *official* thinkers were. He found this "inadmissible in any court of law – even the court of public opinion."[110]

Cousineau's fury burst forth later on: "[Trudeau] has mentioned everything, but established nothing. I have identified bald faced lies in his text, both major and minor, systematic distortion of facts, dodges that fill entire pages and more than anything else a primitive work method: I must in good conscience say that his account has no historical value."[111] In conclusion, Cousineau pointed to the cause of these many errors: "Trudeau's account lacks any sympathy for the reality we live, for men, for institutions. . . . Truly, we cannot avoid concluding that worst of all, his entire *story* lacks a sense of the Church's temporal mission and actions!"[112]

Trudeau did not respond to Laurendeau or Angers. Nor did he respond to Cousineau's first set of articles in *Relations,* in 1956–1957. But with Cousineau's renewed onslaught in 1958, when the Institut social populaire brought out the booklet, Trudeau's blood was boiling. He wrote "Critique of a Critique" and informed Father Richard Arès, director of *Relations,* that he would be submitting it for publication. Arès replied that it would be too long for the review and suggested he "send a letter summarizing the main arguments of [his] critique."[113] Trudeau did so. He provided a summary by letter and informed Arès that "Critique of a Critique" would appear in the April 1959 issue of *Cité libre.*

March 17 brought the first dramatic turn of events. Arès said by telephone that Father Cousineau could not agree to *Relations* publishing "a letter summarizing an article in *Cité libre* which our readers wouldn't have seen."[114] Trudeau reminded Arès this had been his own idea. Adopting a conciliatory attitude, he proposed to amend the letter in order to overcome this problem and also to meet face to face to work things out. On March 19, the meeting took place, but Cousineau also turned up. Arès did not so much as open his mouth. During the discussion, Cousineau told Trudeau: "I was *very* nice to you. I could have smashed you. People asked me why I didn't crush you." After a vigorous exchange, Cousineau finally agreed that a letter appear in *Relations* – but it had to be amended according to his wishes.

But now came a second dramatic turn of events: Cousineau went back on his word, and the letter was not published.

"Critique of a Critique" appeared as an off-print of *Cité libre,* along with the rejected letter. Trudeau explained he readily accepted Father Cousineau's right to disagree with his thesis. "But his position as a Jesuit and the authority of the review for which he was writing brought a moral obligation to base his verdict on solid evidence. Instead, he relied on falsehoods."[115] Trudeau then established these "falsehoods" by systematically identifying, in his notes, each of Cousineau's logical fallacies, sophistries, errors of fact, pettiness, and other falsehoods, counting them and indicating where they appeared. He found thirteen contradictions, sixteen factual errors, and so on.[116]

For example, Cousineau accused Trudeau of quoting thinkers out of context or of singling out minor works, as a way of unfairly disparaging his victims, and of never bothering to "analyze the thinking of the masters, such as Minville and Groulx in their *ex professo* works on the issue, drawing instead on occasional speeches they gave."[117] Poor Cousineau had no idea that Trudeau had kept all his textbooks and lecture notes from his Collège de Brébeuf years. Trudeau could not resist using irony to teach Cousineau a lesson. He wrote: "The good Father will no doubt be interested to learn that an amusing coincidence partially dictated the choice of certain sources. . . . During the eight years I spent in a superb Jesuit college, the generous Fathers provided me with a huge number of nationalist books, pamphlets and 'occasional speeches'; I read and held onto them all, and I hardly had to leave my room to sketch out the recurring features of our traditional doctrine and institutions."[118] Trudeau knew what he was talking about: he had thoroughly studied and absorbed both the *ex professo* works and the "occasional speeches" of his former masters. He had no trouble backing up his critique of their thoughts with supporting documents.

Cousineau was outraged by Trudeau's bold claim that there was a distinctive French-Canadian interpretation of the Church's social doctrine: "So, according to T., . . . the bishops of French Canada apparently deceived us and guided us poorly for over fifty years. . . . Throughout the entire twentieth century, no charge as serious has been laid against the spiritual authority in our country."[119] Could Trudeau truly accept "the infallibility of the Church and the inspiration of the Holy Spirit" while arguing that the bishops had erred on social doctrines? Cousineau did not answer this question, but deferred on this matter to the judgment of "theologians and experts in canon law." As a devoted Catholic, Trudeau found this insinuation unacceptable. He took offence: "If I have committed heresy, Father Cousineau, then prove it outright. And if I did not commit heresy, why are you suggesting otherwise?"[120]

But there was more to come. In August 1959, Father Cousineau contributed a "clarification" to *Relations,* to which Trudeau replied in the January–February 1960 issue of *Cité libre:* "I didn't think it was possible, even for a Jesuit, to build up in a few short lines such inexhaustible reserves of bad faith and good conscience."[121] Evidently, some struggles go on and on.

———

Were Trudeau's main criticisms justified? With regard to form, there can be no doubt about the matter. Diplomacy was not exactly his strong point. No matter how well known his opponents were, he made no attempt to spare their sensitivities. Every reviewer rightly noted the aggressive tone and the irony in his writing. With regard to content, however, he is often right. Let us take a closer look at some of his criticisms.

For example, support for corporatism. This was, to him, an outstanding example of nationalist-bred monolithic thinking. But why was he referring to corporatism? While it is true that in his student years in Montreal, all his teachers had promoted this doctrine, it is also well known that the experience of war had put an end to its great appeal. From 1944 to 1949, corporatism had lost much of its allure, since it was now identified with fascist regimes. Does this mean that Trudeau was drawing an example from the remote past, in order to strengthen his thesis? If this were the case, how is it that none of the three critics – Laurendeau, Angers, and Cousineau – called him out on this score?

The reason is that corporatism had made a comeback in Quebec, just as it had in the Vatican. Indeed, as Suzanne Clavette convincingly demonstrates, corporatism had been dormant since the end of the war but surged in popularity starting in 1949. In July that year, Archbishop Courchesne of Rimouski criticized the Commission sacerdotale d'études sociales (a progressive group of clerics) for neglecting corporatism, which was an essential element of Pius XI's encyclical *Quadragesimo anno.*

Once Mgr. Paul-Emile Léger was installed as Archbishop of Montreal, "this new corporatist wave began to swell."[122] François-Albert Angers and Marcel Clément became the doctrine's leading advocates, as we saw in Chaper 9.[123] During much of the 1950s, Clavette writes, "the advocates of corporatism had the support of the majority of Quebec bishops."[124] *Notre Temps, L'Action catholique,* and the *Front ouvrier** promoted it enthusiastically. In 1951, Father Richard Arès came out in favour of corporatism too, promoting it in the pages of *Relations.*

The corporatist wind was blowing on the Vatican as well. On January 31, 1952, in addressing Catholic employers in Italy, Pope Pius XII spoke out explicitly in favour of corporatism. He deplored the distorted vision some people had developed of "Our glorious predecessor, Pius XI . . . ignoring the essential section of the Encyclical *Quadragesimo anno,* which actually contains . . . the idea of an occupational corporate order of the entire economy."[125] Henceforth, he declared, corporatism was to be "the focal point of the social doctrine of the Church with regards to the organization of labour in industry."[126] As a result, when Trudeau published his text in 1956, corporatism was the new mantra of the Church's social doctrine.

Corporatism in Quebec was closely aligned with Rome's instructions. But does it follow, as Laurendeau and Father Cousineau argued, that the social doctrine of the French-Canadian church was in no way distinguishable from that of the Church as a whole? This would be the case if corporatism were the only issue. But in the case of nationalism, for example, the Vatican traditionally opposed it, because it was considered contrary to the universal mission of Catholicism. For example, in 1927 the Vatican condemned the *Action française,* which had been built up by Maurras in France, on the grounds that it was nationalist. In Quebec, Henri Bourassa was rebuffed for the same reason. Despite these stern warnings, the French-Canadian Church systematically incorporated nationalism into its social doctrine.

Trudeau accused *Le Devoir* of increasingly "siding with conservatives" on social matters, and Laurendeau retorted that "Trudeau's simplifications border on the ridiculous." Who was right? Once again, Suzanne Clavette provides the answer. She demonstrates how the shift

---

* A publication promoting Catholic workers' action.

toward corporatism diverted attention from labour problems and harmed the cause of trade unionism. The editors of Le Devoir had supported the strikers at Asbestos, she notes, but from 1950 to 1954 they abandoned social issues to concentrate on the national question alone. "The columnist Fernand Dansereau was the only one focusing on labour issues on a daily basis."[127] Thus, this recent well-researched book supports Trudeau's thesis.

We have to admit, nonetheless, that Trudeau the pamphleteer was overwhelmed sometimes by his emotions. Ignoring nuance, he made some sweeping generalizations. Take the example of his critique of the monolithic mindset. It was certainly dominant. But were there really no dissenting voices? According to Clavette, "the new corporatist wind blowing across the province – with the approval of Pius XII – marked a sharp setback for progressive Catholics." But that doesn't mean these progressive people had suddenly ceased to exist. Trudeau should have mentioned and honoured them. After all, they were digging a breach in the monolithic wall, which took courage and determination, and they did continue "until the next wave of popular protest broke out, which led to the Quiet Revolution and the advent of the Welfare State."[128]

There can be no denying that there were weaknesses in Trudeau's argument. The polemicist sometimes won out over the impartial observer. But we should note the originality and strength of his central thesis, especially since it is often misunderstood. He has been accused of such visceral anti-nationalism that his darkened mind could not come up with a reasoned judgment. Yet we have seen that he readily accepted what he termed "de facto nationalism," that is, the sense of belonging to a community. At this stage of his life, he was sharply critical of what he termed "nationalism as an intellectual discipline," since it resulted in intellectual sterility and prevented French Canadians from fulfilling themselves. Trudeau had no qualms in granting that after the defeat of France in America, French Canadians "were members of a nation in ruins." Indeed, he paid tribute to those public figures who had guided the people under these difficult conditions.

But in his view, the "Conquest" of 1760 belonged to a distant past that did not lead inexorably to the present situation, because men have the power to transform their living conditions. As he wrote in the epilogue of *La grève de l'amiante:* "I must confess that I am only interested in the past as a means of acting upon the future.... We, French Canadians, have a social history rich in errors which we must not repeat. The first chapter in this book has been especially devoted to pointing them out."[129] His message was clear: Let's learn appropriate lessons from our past mistakes, let's turn the page, roll up our sleeves, and prepare to live fully and democratically in today's world.

This thesis flew in the face of what was commonly called "The Montreal Historical School" – whose three leading advocates were Guy Frégault, Michel Brunet, and Maurice Séguin – all disciples of Abbé Groulx. It is beyond the scope of this book to focus on their views. But two excerpts, one from Frégault and the other from Brunet, provide a glimpse of their perspective. In writing *La guerre de la conquête* in 1955, Frégault acknowledged "the obvious crisis of French-Canadian society," along the same lines as Trudeau did. But for Frégault, "this was not a crisis arising from circumstances, but rather from structure, from a structure that was destroyed and was subsequently never properly built up again."[130] In 1957, one year after the publication of *La grève de l'amiante,* Brunet wrote: "The historian who neglects or refuses to see in the Conquest of 1760 the single most important fact in the history of French Canada . . . displays his incompetence or his lack of objectivity."[131] And he added, referring directly to Trudeau's text: "In his exciting and passionate indictment against the sociologists and economists of the traditional nationalist school, . . . the author [Trudeau] suggests that these men of thought and action were mistaken because they were nationalists. . . . If their economic and social ideas were wrong or deficient, it was because they were members of a subjugated nation in ruins, not because they were nationalists. . . . We must never forget that the fundamental weakness of French-Canadian thought arises from the inability or unwillingness to understand the true meaning of the Conquest of 1760."[132] So, for the Montreal Historical School and its followers, Trudeau may well have been fascinating and passionate, but he did not understand that the Conquest was no mere historical phenomenon: it was the key to explaining the current situation of French Canada. This thesis would prove highly popular in Quebec.

All his life, however, Trudeau rejected the myth of victimization. He saw it as his duty to convince his fellow citizens to practise self-criticism.

He wanted them to face up to their weaknesses so they would overcome them. At times, his sarcasm and irony brimmed over: he wanted to scream in anger against those who led the people in the wrong direction, preventing them from fulfilling themselves. This is why he wrote "with quaking emotion," this is what made Chapter 1 fascinating and passionate. Trudeau acknowledged he sometimes went too far: "When I critiqued our traditional ideologies and venerable institutions in *La grève de l'amiante,* I expected a lot of reactions. And there were many, sometimes very sharp ones. I'm glad, because these reactions helped provide some balance where I had gone too far in expressing my disappointment over half a century of misguided social options."[133]

The motto "Reason before passion" is generally taken as emblematic of Trudeau's outlook. Some biographers have depicted him as cold and unfeeling. Stephen Clarkson, for example, considered him "the least sentimental of men."[134] The truth, as it emerges from our research of his writings, is much more complex. In his youth he had been passionate about the ideals promoted by his masters, but he later rejected these ideals by reasoning his way through. And now he passionately wanted his fellow French Canadians to learn to use their reasoning abilities, rather than their passions. He was sure that if they did so, they would see that democracy and federalism offered the most advantageous conditions for their development. Passion and reason were deeply mingled in all his thoughts and actions.

Indeed, Trudeau was paddling against the current when he stood up against nationalism as an intellectual discipline. As might be expected, some of his allies in the fight against clericalism and the authoritarianism of the Duplessis government started to distance themselves from him. But Trudeau was determined to state his position, loudly and clearly, whether it was consistent with that of his allies or of his opponents. As we mentioned earlier, we find a striking example in 1957, when Louis Saint-Laurent's federal government offered university grants to all provinces: he took the side of Duplessis and the nationalists.

Trudeau was well aware of this paradox: "Something is wrong somewhere. On the question of university grants, I find myself in disagreement with my friends and with people whose ideas I usually find congenial. On the other hand, I quite approve of some of the attitudes taken by Mr. Duplessis and the nationalists, with whom I am not in the habit of agreeing."[135] Most of his allies were shocked. Frankly, if they had paid more attention to the brief he had written for the FUIQ, to his review of Lamontagne's book, or to his many other writings on federalism and democracy, they wouldn't have been at all surprised. He could be criticized for his inflexibility or for his lack of appreciation of the dire financial situation of French-Canadian universities, but not for the consistency of his thought.

In "Federal Grants to Universities," Trudeau restated his conception of representative democracy within a federal system. In the Canadian state, he insisted, sovereignty is shared between the central government and the ten regional governments, "each of which is responsible for a specific part of the common good."[136] He further specified that each of these governments should "look after its share of the common good *as it sees fit.*"[137] Education, he reminded his readers, lay within provincial jurisdiction, and both the St. Laurent government and French Canadians favouring these grants were aware of this key fact. So they tried to justify their stand by claiming that these grants did not infringe on the principle of shared sovereignty. Trudeau examined seven arguments invoked for this purpose, refuting each one of them. By way of example, we will note a few. Some people, like Jacques Perrault (in the November 10, 1956, issue of *Vrai*), appealed to the principle of equalization: these grants enabled poor provinces – such as Quebec – to offer a university education comparable to that in other provinces. Trudeau retorted that these grants "were offered to universities of *all* the provinces whether rich or poor . . . for a purpose that does not fall within the central government's jurisdiction. This may be called centralization, but certainly not equalization."[138]

Others, such as Léon Dion (*Le Devoir,* November 5, 1956) or Maurice Blain (*Le Devoir,* November 2, 1956), wondered whether the provinces should be responsible for university education. To this Trudeau replied: "I am not saying, *a priori,* that education (at least university education) should never fall under concurrent federal jurisdiction. . . . But this needs to be proved. Above all, as a citizen I would require that such a revolutionary interpretation of our constitution be made the object of a conscious choice."[139] Political parties would have to take a stand on the issue, he said, and the electorate would have to decide. Furthermore, if the federal government wanted to follow this path it should have done so "openly and with the authorization of the sovereign people." It should either have proposed a constitutional amendment or "invoked a national emergency using the appropriate powers." However, he continued, St. Laurent's position, in his speech of November 12, 1956, was the exact opposite. He reaffirmed that "the provinces have the exclusive right to legislate in matters concerning education."[140]

Some intellectuals pleaded the argument of starvation. French-Canadian universities were in such a weakened state that they were on the point of collapse. Trudeau answered: "I must admit this is a moving argument. . . . Someone dying of hunger is justified in seizing whatever food he can find, regardless of laws governing property." But he hastened to add: "Allow me to distinguish between men and culture. . . . We must therefore be dealing with a case of 'dying culture.' But shouldn't we rather speak of suicide? From a judicial point of view, education is strictly the responsibility of the Quebec government; from a democratic point of view, this government is entirely the responsibility [of the Quebec people]. . . . Which is to say that if teaching is scorned and intelligence humiliated in our noble province, the fault lies very specifically with those who live in it. Under the circumstances, the very thing we must *not* do is run and beg Ottawa to alleviate our famine by giving us a bit of our own tax money."[141]

For Trudeau, the solution was political: "Take up the cudgels, for goodness' sake! If our culture is in such pressing danger that you feel justified in bypassing the constitution, why not begin by ignoring the law: go on strike, refuse to pay your taxes . . . write articles . . . engage – Yes! Engage – in political action."[142] In other words, it is up to the people to fight for better-funded universities at the provincial level, because education is a provincial responsibility.

Trudeau also examined the federal government's recourse to the argument of the "spending power." This very complex issue lies beyond the scope of our work. Interested readers should consult Trudeau's article, which was later reprinted in *Federalism and the French Canadians*.[143] Let us say in general that this is where interpretations diverged. On the one hand, the debate revolved around the kind of money the federal government had the right to distribute as grants to the provinces and, on the other hand, the jurisdictions it invaded by making these donations. Trudeau laid out all the arguments supporting the various positions. Ultimately, he recognized it was impossible to establish a rigorous division of powers: "Even the most scrupulous refutation of every argument put forward in favour of the grants still leaves one reason for permitting the federal government to give and the provinces to receive university grants."[144] Indeed, "any attempt to arrange 'spheres of influence' in water-tight compartments only leads to absurdity." Hence his conclusion: it is definitely "permissible to make moderate donations even outside one's own jurisdiction. But the nature of the donation must be such that its recipient does not have grounds to suspect that charity is being given to him out of his own pocket."[145] Trudeau and *Cité libre* have often been accused of being "centralizing federalists." Here is proof of the contrary, at least as far as Trudeau is concerned.

———————

In Chapter 1 of *La grève de l'amiante,* Trudeau defended a position directly confronting not only traditionalist nationalists, but also so-called neo-nationalists like the professors of the Montreal Historical School. In his review of Lamontagne's book, he came out against the idea of centralizing federalism. In "Federal Grants to Universities," he opposed his own close colleagues, argued against federal grants, and denounced lax interpretations of the division of powers between Ottawa and the provinces when the federal government's largesse proved tempting. Given his unwillingness to compromise on his values, Trudeau understandably made few friends and could not found a school of thought. But he didn't really care about that; he strongly believed that the well-being of French Canadians depended on a federalism that was both well understood and properly applied. He also attributed many of Quebec's problems to internal causes. This is where the battlefield lay – and all progressive forces should rally together in the fight to redress the situation. To this task, he would now devote all his energy, inspiring some people and alienating others.

Chapter 13

THE END OF AN ERA

The Liberal Party was alone in waging the decisive battle for
our freedom, and I take my hat off to it.

— PIERRE ELLIOTT TRUDEAU,
Cité libre, 1960[*]

ON APRIL 14, 1956, about eighty intellectuals and trade unionists "interested in building truly democratic structures in the province of Quebec" met in Montreal. The meeting was jointly chaired by Pierre Trudeau, at the time still FUIQ counsel, and lawyer Jacques Perrault, who also served as chairman of the board of *Le Devoir*.[1] The timing of the meeting was noteworthy: *La grève de l'amiante* had been sent to press and would be out in May, and a provincial election had been called for June 20. Barring a miracle, Duplessis was expected to sweep the province once again. No specific decision was taken on the election proper, but the attendees agreed to meet again on June 23, for a post-mortem of election results. Most importantly, they agreed to consider launching a "Rassemblement provincial des citoyens" or province-wide citizens' rally.[2] An organizing committee was set up, and it should come as no surprise that Trudeau was one of the members.

While awaiting this meeting, Trudeau campaigned heart and soul for the Parti social démocrate (PSD), travelling over six hundred kilometres to support Jean-Robert Ouellet, a candidate in Rouyn-Noranda in the Abitibi

---

[*] P.E. Trudeau, "L'élection du 22 juin 1960," *Cité libre*, August–September 1960.

region northwest of Montreal.[3] On June 15, he vigorously supported the party on Radio-Canada. In Quebec, he told his listeners, "if you are 'bleu' [blue] or 'rouge' [red], this means you belong to the Union Nationale or the Liberal Party. And you may not realize it, but indeed . . . you belong to politicians who, in turn, are bound to the financial interests that have filled the party coffers. In other words, you live in servitude, because you obey leaders who do not depend on you."[4] He reminded his listeners that for sixty years now, no matter which party governed, all elections had been tainted by fraud and by the exploitation of the basest passions. He urged people to vote PSD on June 20, since it was the only way to get rid of "venality and corruption in the province of Quebec," because "if you are social democrats you don't belong to the party, rather, the party belongs to you." Both in structure and ideology, he argued, this party was truly democratic.

To no avail. On June 20, 1956, the Union Nationale won an even greater victory than it had in 1952, snapping up seventy-two of ninety-three seats (four more than in 1952), whereas the Liberal Party was cut back to just twenty seats (three fewer than in 1952). However, these results did not reflect the distribution of the popular vote, which was more evenly matched: the Union Nationale got 51.8 per cent, and the Liberals 44.9 per cent. The PSD was obliterated, garnering an incredibly weak 0.6 per cent of the popular vote: all the party's candidates, including the leader, Thérèse Casgrain, were defeated. It is important to note that, at the time, corruption was rampant, and two priests, Gérard Dion and Louis O'Neill, had deplored the situation in *Political Immorality in the Province of Quebec.*[*] Many citizens were understandably appalled by this dire situation and wanted to join forces in order to do something. But do what, exactly?

On June 23, 1956, about a hundred people turned up for the meeting convened the previous April. Many people were invited to attend, and whether they attended or not, it is clear they came from diverse backgrounds, both socially and politically. Some, like Thérèse Casgrain and Michel Chartrand, were leaders of the PSD; others, such as Gérard Filion and André Laurendeau, were standard-bearers for the progressive and nationalist newspaper *Le Devoir;* still others, like Pierre Laporte, were close to the Liberal Party; Jean Marchand and Marcel Pépin, meanwhile, were active in the labour movement. All were united in their opposition

---

[*]   See Chapter 8, above.

to the Duplessis regime, but most of them believed the time wasn't ripe to create a new political party. Instead, they saw the first priority as educating the people.

Did Trudeau have something to do with this decision? Now that he had witnessed first-hand the FUIQ's reluctance to create or even support a political party, could he have felt that an education in democracy was an essential first step? Whatever the case, the people attending the June 23 meeting elected a provisional executive committee made up of five persons, which – not surprisingly – included Trudeau. The committee was mandated to prepare a declaration of principles and a draft constitution for the September 8 general meeting. It was left to Trudeau to draft these documents.[5] Typically, he was criss-crossing the province seeking new recruits even before this movement had been officially established. For example, on July 10 he participated in a public meeting in Shawinigan Falls – 150 kilometres northeast of Montreal – to publicize the creation of a "movement of citizens ready to work voluntarily . . . towards education in democracy and political action."[6]

In Trudeau's absence, the committee met again on August 27, 1956, and adopted the draft declaration of principles he had prepared. By now he was far, far away in the North-West. He had found out that Frank Scott, twenty years his senior, was headed for an expedition along the Mackenzie River in Canada's Far North, and he could not resist the urge to join him. Nearly thirty years later, Trudeau explained to Scott's biographer, Sandra Djwa, what motivated this decision: "[Frank] was a great hero of mine. . . . It's been [from] my contacts with Frank . . . that I absorbed much of my constitutional thinking, . . . almost as much by his poems, by his being and by his actions as by his writings. . . . So going on the Mackenzie with him wasn't just another adventure, of which I had many and which I like. . . . It was a chance also to be exposed to Frank Scott for days and weeks."[7]

On August 13, the two companions set out on their journey.[8] Once they reached the Canadian Shield, Trudeau told Frank Scott: "There's nothing between you and the North Pole, Frank."[9] And as soon as he caught a glimpse of rapids, huge surges of water, and tossing waves, he said: "I'm going in."

"Here, don't be silly," replied Scott, "you can't go into that."

"Oh, I'm going in."

Scott was fascinated by Trudeau's fearlessness and snapped a photograph just as he waded into the threatening waves. He later immortalized this challenge of one man standing up to the forces of nature in his famous poem "Fort Smith":

We climbed to the Slave
To the rock polished by ice
And the roar of the great rapids.
This is the edge of the Shield –
Eastward, away to Labrador
Lies the pre-Cambrian rock,
While North and South and West
Stretches the central plain
Unbroken from Gulf to Arctic
Hemmed in by the western hills. . . .
Pierre, suddenly challenged,
Stripped and walked into the rapids,
Firming his feet against rock,
Standing white, in white water,
Leaning south up the current
To stern the downward rush,
A man testing his strength
Against the strength of his country.[10]

Continuing their expedition, the two travellers reached Inuvik, where they met Gordon Robertson, Trudeau's old boss at the Privy Council, who was now commissioner of the Northwest Territories. And by the kind of lucky coincidence that always seemed to come Trudeau's way, he and Scott attended the very first session of the Territorial Council to be held north of the Arctic Circle.[11]

Shortly after their return to Montreal, Scott invited a few friends over, including the great literary critic Northrop Frye, for a slide show of the expedition. When a photograph of a naked athlete seen from behind suddenly flashed on the screen, "someone" jumped up and turned off the slide projector. At that moment, a bemused Scott discovered his companion's shy side.[12] In 1968, when several people were pressuring Trudeau to run for the leadership of the Liberal Party of Canada, Scott wrote him: "Just summon up the courage that led you to wade out into the fierce rapids of the Slave River!"[13] Shortly after

Trudeau became prime minister, Scott sent him the famous slide, along with his best wishes.[14]

On August 29, 1956, Trudeau returned to Montreal, and without breaking stride attended all his scheduled meetings the next day.[15] On September 8, the movement adopted Trudeau's draft Declaration of Principles and formally took on the name of "Rassemblement." It is likely that Trudeau had been the instigator of this movement, or at least one of those most involved in getting it going, but as usual he did not run for president, deferring instead to Pierre Dansereau, a well-known ecologist and dean of the Faculty of Sciences at the Université de Montréal. Trudeau accepted the more convenient position of vice-president, which gave him the freedom to leave town whenever he pleased.

The Declaration of Principles Trudeau had drafted now served as the organizational foundation of the Rassemblement. What did it say? The seven-page document, which looked like a political platform, was divided into five parts covering most aspects of life in society. In terms of political organization, it asserted the unquestionable superiority of democracy. Just as importantly, it affirmed the primacy of the individual and the necessity to respect and protect human rights. In particular, it stated that every citizen "must always remain the depository of a number of inalienable rights which lie beyond the reach of the state."[16]

The economy "must be organized in such a way as to derive from available resources the best possible returns for the entire population" and to reduce unemployment as much as possible. This, claimed the Declaration, was the only way to put an end to the "exploitation of man by man." While such a system called for state intervention, Trudeau did not reject either "market forces" or the principle of private property. Adopting the fundamentally pragmatist view typical of his Harvard days, he asserted that "private initiative and private ownership, mutual initiative and cooperative ownership, public initiative and nationalization are only *means* serving economic and human goals, and should be assessed as such." If capitalism proved to be the most effective way of pursuing the common good, he wouldn't hesitate to adopt it.

As far as the social system was concerned, the declaration asserted once again that it should "fully respect the human person." And, in this

respect, it stressed that "everyone has the right to work." What did
Trudeau mean by this? Was he proposing communist-style planning?
Not in the least. The declaration recommended measures such as "the
equality of workers regardless of gender, religion and ethnicity; . . .
freedom of association in labour unions without hindrance; . . . unemployment insurance benefits indexed to the cost of living; . . . the democratization of companies." In short, these were moderate measures,
typical of a social democratic perspective. But in the traditionalist and
anti-statist Quebec of the day, they seemed quite radical.

The declaration didn't neglect education and culture. Far from it!
Every citizen, it affirmed, had "the fundamental right to access all levels
of education and all instruments of culture, according to his abilities and
talents, without any limitation due to financial means or marital status."
And in order to reach that goal, Quebec's classical colleges, which were
elitist, should be replaced by a "democratic system, reflecting the people's
will." Control of education, which up to now was in the hands of the
Church, should now be ceded to the state in order to "establish a Ministry
of National Education, and a Secretariat for the arts and culture, and
another one for science and technology." As we know, these were ideals
that flew in the face of those close to the clerical-nationalist elite.
Secondary education in Quebec became free only in 1961, once Jean
Lesage's Liberal Party had taken power, and the Ministry of Education
was not established until 1964. On the other hand, free higher education, also recommended in the declaration, has never been adopted in
Quebec or the rest of Canada.

The declaration's final section dealt with the national and international system and established as its founding principle the solidarity
of all human beings: "Whatever the motives that lead men to regroup
into separate social entities, each individual's ultimate allegiance is to
mankind. All the people of all countries must promote solidarity to one
another, and where necessary they must offer fraternal assistance." But
Trudeau was not naïve. He knew that at this stage of history "human
societies have adopted the state as their legal system of political organization, and they act within it." In a multinational society like Canada,
people should choose the system that best reconciles centralization,
which is often necessary, and decentralization, which "favours the free
development of cultures."

And which system is that? Not surprisingly, it is federalism.

If we weren't told who had written the declaration, it wouldn't have been difficult to guess. Trudeau had clearly incorporated all his favourite themes: the pursuit of the common good in its political, social, and economic dimensions; faith in democracy, respect for the individual; equality of opportunity; solidarity between all human beings; pragmatism in politics; federalism for Canada . . . With such invigorating principles, surely the Rassemblement would soon gain the support of all progressive people in Quebec, right? Indeed, shortly afterwards the FUIQ executive committee unanimously endorsed the Rassemblement,[17] and at about the same time, local chapters sprouted right across the province.

But the Rassemblement proved short-lived. Created in 1956, it had virtually disappeared by 1958. What brought on this collapse? Thérèse Casgrain, leader, at the time, of the Parti social démocratique (the new name of Quebec's CCF), offered in 1971 the following explanation: "The Rassemblement only had three presidents: Pierre Dansereau . . . , René Tremblay, a professor at Laval University and later a federal minister, and Pierre Elliott Trudeau. This latter was known at the time as something of a dilettante, and although a prodigious intellectual, he lacked perseverance. He liked launching ideas or movements, and then lost interest and turned to something else. This attitude – which I hope he has now outgrown – probably had something to do with the Rassemblement's disintegration. During his tenure as president, he made a trip overseas and by the time he returned, the Rassemblement had ceased to exist."[18]

So for Casgrain, the movement's collapse was largely attributable to Trudeau. We ought to be satisfied by her explanation, since she was actively involved in this movement. And yet, at the time she had a strikingly different view of Trudeau. Far from seeing him as a "dilettante lacking perseverance," she called him "one of our extremely promising young Canadians."[19]

In his classic *Prelude to Quebec's Quiet Revolution* historian Michael Behiels gives a better explanation of the Rassemblement's failure. He notes that originally recruitment had been successful, by April 1957 reaching 511 members distributed in thirty-eight chapters across the province. He then pointedly notes that "within weeks of its formation, the Rassemblement was wracked with internal dissension on the question of membership qualifications and party affiliation."[20] Indeed, on January 30, 1957, a bare few months after it was set up, the executive felt compelled to remind all members of the nature and goals of the movement.[21] It explained that because only "a new movement, absolutely independent of the existing parties . . . can enable the vast majority of Quebeckers to learn about democracy, . . . it is agreed that the Executive Committee shall not allow any person to join the Rassemblement who could cause it to be identified with any existing political parties."[22] In other words, here was a movement that sought to recruit people who were very politically committed, while prohibiting them from being involved in a political party.

Gérard Bergeron, a well-seasoned political analyst, lost no time pinpointing the incoherence of the principles adopted by the Rassemblement and predicted it was heading straight into a brick wall. Under the pseudonym Isocrates, he wrote in *Le Devoir* of April 12, 1957: "The Rassemblement brings together a group of exiles in search of a political homeland. Typically, . . . each member belongs to the Rassemblement by default, while awaiting the emergence of a party more to his liking."[23] He concluded: "Members won't be content to sit in the Rassemblement's 'waiting room' for long. They will ultimately have to choose between joining the PSD or creating a new political party out of the Rassemblement." This was a pessimistic prediction, but as subsequent events showed, it proved accurate in many ways.

Some members of the Rassemblement also suspected their movement either had to become a political party or simply disappear. The FUIQ had come out supporting the Rassemblement, but all the other trade unions were holding back, which meant the fledgling movement was doomed from the start. A letter from Gérard Pelletier to Trudeau, dated August 29, 1957, reveals they were both aware of the issues.[24] Pelletier reported that he had asked "comrade Marchand" if his trade union, the CCWC, would support the creation of a leftist pro-worker political party. Jean Marchand's response was discouraging: the CCWC was of two minds about the Rassemblement. As for other unions, he said, "if they get orders from the top union brass to join the CCF (Jean thought this was inevitable), they would drop [the Rassemblement] like a hot potato."

While very disappointed by this news, Pelletier wrote that at least he knew he was getting the straight goods from Marchand. He went on to suggest that if people no longer believed in the Rassemblement, it was "useless to continue caring for a stillborn child that risked poisoning the system." This raised, once again, the question of a political party. Without a new party, how could they keep the troops energized about a movement promoting education for democracy?

When the Rassemblement's first annual convention was held in Quebec City on November 30 and December 1, 1957, the number of members had risen to 624, but the gloom was palpable. Only 34 of the 624 bothered to show up and vote.[25] The Rassemblement president, Pierre Dansereau, gave a speech acknowledging in diplomatic terms that things were not going well. Then the vice-president presented the executive committee report.[26] Trudeau was very disappointed and did not mince words. Too many members, he thundered, "treated the Rassemblement like an insurance policy: they joined just in case its future prospects improved, but they remained completely committed to their own political party." The secretary-treasurer, Jean-Paul Lefebvre, who spoke last, proposed a "sabbatical" so "everyone could figure out what to expect."[27] We can just imagine the collective sigh of relief, as members quickly adopted the proposal, while stressing the importance of pursuing the objective of democratic education. The mandate of the first executive committee, which included Trudeau, expired at this convention. A new committee and several other working groups were set up, to investigate a number of issues.

As it turned out, the new president, René Tremblay, sent just one message to the members in the entire year 1958. The working groups did not produce any reports. Pierre Joncas concluded in his master's thesis on the Rassemblement that "the November 1958 convention was in fact a funeral service."[28] That is when Trudeau was elected president. How could he possibly have accepted the presidency of a moribund movement, when he never agreed to take the helm of organizations that were in good shape? We believe that he was simply not ready to throw in the towel. He accepted the position so as not to abandon the slightest hope of rallying members committed to the promotion of democracy. He was very apprehensive about the elections slated for 1960 and sought to build a new common front of progressive forces against Duplessis. In fact, by the time he attended the convention in November 1958, he had just published "A Democratic Manifesto" in *Cité libre*.[29]

We believe that these facts speak for themselves. If the Rassemblement fell apart, it wasn't because Trudeau was a dilettante or off travelling. So why did Casgrain blame him, in 1971, contrary to all the evidence? In the process of retracing the evolution of Trudeau's ideas, we will gradually piece together an explanation, in this chapter and the next. But the "Democratic Manifesto" (which we will analyze in detail later) already provides some important clues. Suffice it to say that Trudeau came to realize that the PSD – long led by Thérèse Casgrain – was doomed to irrelevance. He claimed that even though the party's platform offered "positive, clearly identifiable and generally coherent political views," the deplorable election results clearly showed that "the social-democratic perspective hasn't even established a toehold in our province." And the PSD's "minuscule gains have come at a staggering price, in terms of time and energy. It is not as if new teams were joining up with existing ones; instead, we have seen successive teams burn out one after the other, leaving behind a smoking ruin of valuable human potential completely wasted."[30] All of this had serious consequences, not the least of which was that "a party constantly rebuilt by neophytes risks being doctrinaire." Trudeau went on to say: "This is the only way I can explain why the provincial PSD, with just a handful of voters, even fewer members, and no presence whatever in the Legislature, obstinately blocked the Rassemblement from becoming anything other than an exact replica of the PSD."[31] As party leader, Casgrain must have found this merciless criticism hard to take. But even more devastating criticism was to follow.

Sociologist Dorval Brunelle wisely points out that one of the difficulties with contemporary history is that the researcher must "use the perspectives of the very people he is studying, in order to decode or interpret history."[32] Indeed, as we have found out ourselves, witnesses are both judge and party. The problem in this case is aggravated because Trudeau is a man who left no one indifferent. We have been struck by the number of eyewitness accounts that combine truths, half-truths, and the settling of accounts. In Thérèse Casgrain's case, her memories were probably coloured by Trudeau's harsh critiques of the PSD and later of the NDP (the New Democratic Party, which succeeded the CCF).

The Rassemblement was not Trudeau's only concern. In 1957, his reputation as a political analyst was such that he was eagerly sought out by French- and English-language media. He was often invited to discuss theoretical issues as well as current political events in Quebec and the rest of Canada.[33] He regularly commented on municipal, provincial, and federal elections, sometimes dashing from one studio to another in the same evening. On February 2, 1957, he was a guest speaker at a special day-long event put on by *Le Devoir*.[34]

That same month, two articles came out. In the first, Trudeau dealt with federal grants to universities.[*] In the second, "Note sur une guerre momentanément évitée" [Notes on a Temporarily Averted War], he examined the Suez Crisis and the role played by Secretary of State for External Affairs Lester B. Pearson in defusing the conflict.[35] Although the article appeared under the collective signature of the *Cité libre* editorial team, he is definitely the author.

The magazine gave its full and unreserved support to Canada's foreign policy: "In these grave times, it is important that the people of Canada unconditionally support the policy of peace, and more importantly, the policy of justice, which has currently been adopted by the government." On behalf of the magazine, Trudeau recalled that in an unsigned article of 1951, which we know he also wrote, *Cité libre* asked: "Will Canada ever be able to take advantage of its position as a small nation to develop and disseminate a foreign policy based on mutual aid rather than domination, exploitation or competition for business opportunities?" Well, he said, *Cité libre*'s hope was now fulfilled: "For some time now, Messrs. St. Laurent, Pearson and Martin – admirably backed up by Department of External Affairs – have begun to provide an honourable answer to this question." He proclaimed loud and clear: "We agree with Paul Martin. . . . We agree with Lester B. Pearson. . . . We particularly agree with Louis St. Laurent . . . [when] he tells the world that 'small nations are made up of human beings just like large ones.' We agree with the government as a whole . . . whose primary concerns are to preserve peace and pursue justice." Trudeau was elated. We can picture him almost jumping for joy.

Early 1957 marked the creation of the World University Service of Canada (wusc) / Entraide universitaire mondiale du Canada (eumc).

---

[*]   See Chapter 12, above.

This was a new incarnation of the International Student Service, active in Canada since 1939. The first objective of the new version of this non-profit organization was to arrange an international seminar in Accra, the capital of Ghana, June 16 to July 7, 1957. The choice of location owed nothing to chance. Ghana, a British colony formerly known as the Gold Coast, had acquired its independence on March 6, 1957. This young state was also one of the first African countries to become a member of the Commonwealth. Students and some university professors were hand-picked to attend the seminar.

Trudeau could not resist attending the meeting, which would provide an opportunity to discover a part of the world he did not know, to see first-hand a former British colony in Africa that had become part of the Commonwealth, and to take part in a high-powered activity focusing on international development. Several participants would prove influential in their respective countries, such as Olof Palme, later prime minister of Sweden. Trudeau paid the $1,000 registration fee out of his own pocket – a considerable sum at the time.[36] As later events showed, he did more in Ghana than broaden his knowledge and enjoy himself; he also established lasting relationships with other delegates. Indeed, once Trudeau became prime minister, three other WUSC delegates worked with him – Don Johnston and Robert Kaplan in his cabinet, and Tim Porteous as executive assistant for five years.

But Trudeau was Trudeau, so after the seminar in Ghana, there was no question of going straight back to Montreal. On July 10, he simply had to make stopovers in Europe, partly to meet friends. Reading the names of the people he spent time with gives the feeling of entering the anteroom of history: most of them became influential figures nationally and even inter-nationally. To the three individuals he saw in Ghana, we should add those he met in London: Jean-Luc Pépin, later a federal minister; Charles Taylor, later a world-renowned philosopher; and Sylvia Ostry, later a well-known economist. When he arrived in Paris, he met Judith Jasmin, the first major female journalist in Quebec. On August 2, he returned to Montreal, throwing himself back into the struggle, as usual.

On August 13, 1957, he went to Arvida in the Saguenay region – where Alcan operated the world's largest aluminium smelter – probably to work there as an arbitrator. On the 18th, he attended a meeting of the Rassemblement in Rimouski. And on August 19, at five o'clock in the morning, he turned up in Murdochville, to join the picket line of one of the most important strikes in Quebec history.[37] Whereas most other strikes had been about wages or working conditions, this one stands out, because it was about the right of association.

Since the early 1950s, workers at the mine had been represented by the Trades and Labour Congress of Canada (TLC). When the TLC merged with the Canadian Congress of Labour (CCL) to create the Canadian Labour Congress (CLC) in 1956, miners at the Gaspé Copper Mines dissolved their union and proceeded to set up a new one, to be affiliated with the United Steelworkers, commonly referred to in Quebec as the "Métallos." But the company, known for its anti-union positions, used all kinds of strategies to delay certification. The company management knew they had the support of the Duplessis government. Tension was rising. On March 8, 1957, the union president, Théo Gagné, was fired, along with a hundred trade union activists.

On March 11, the infuriated miners went out on a strike that was technically illegal, since their union had not yet been certified. The strike lasted seven months and is still remembered for its excessive violence and acts of sabotage. One man was killed and several were wounded. Under the headline "Meute de voyous à l'œuvre à Murdochville" [A Pack of Thugs at Work in Murdochville], a front-page story in the August 20, 1957, edition of La Presse reported that the day before, a convoy of dozens of cars and three buses of supporters, led by Claude Jodoin, president of the Canadian Labour Congress, and Gérard Picard, president of the Confederation of Catholic Workers of Canada (CCWC), arrived in Murdochville. Once all these people – including Trudeau – joined the picket line in front of the main entrance of Gaspé Copper Mines, "company employees, taking a position on a nearby hill, began to trade insults with picketers and then to stone them."[38] We'll let Émile Boudreau, one of the demonstrators, recount the rest of the story, as he did in L'histoire de la FTQ:

> A good dozen union members, including four strikers from Arvida, were hit, the provincial police simply . . . looked on!
>
> Given how passive the police were, the picketers decided to move up the hill to dislodge the stone throwers. A truck would open the way . . . But there was nobody to drive it, and the

windshield didn't offer much protection against stones thrown by the henchmen of the provincial police. That's when Pierre Elliott Trudeau said, with a superbly casual air, "I've already driven a truck like this," and promptly sat behind the wheel. And off the troops went, to attack the fortress! Meanwhile, cars driven by unionists were overturned, the police threatened marchers at gunpoint or with tear gas.[39]

As reported in *La Presse*, "Six strikers were injured and one of them was sent to the hospital in Ste. Anne des Monts, suffering facial lacerations. The union offices . . . were sacked shortly after the departure of 450 workers who had turned out to demonstrate in support of the strikers." Trudeau was caught in the scuffle. On August 19, he wrote in his diary: "I am hit with tear gas. 5:00 PM, I am attacked by [he did not finish the sentence]." On the 22nd, he added: "I receive death threats." On August 24, he left Murdochville.[40]

Deeply disturbed by all this hatred, he wrote a day later "A Talk by Pierre E. Trudeau."[41] On November 4, he gave a lecture on the Murdochville strike. Was he using his notes of August 25? Possibly. But there could be no doubt that he was upset. He wrote: "In Murdochville, I saw men wounding other men, sacking offices, destroying cars while the provincial police stood by, in benevolent neutrality. I lived in a city where men had to shoot other men who had come to attack their families right in their homes. I saw an atmosphere of terror engulf this remote village in the heart of the Gaspé region." He wondered how such violence could be justified, how the utterly passive attitude of the police could be tolerated in a society that called itself Christian and democratic.

The question struck him as especially worrying, since he found the strikers' demands legitimate, democratic, and Christian. Their struggle was justified since they were seeking a better distribution of wealth. Indeed, he said, experience worldwide shows that "the industrial revolution only began to benefit the majority of people when the workers formed associations and unions strong enough to negotiate with management on an equal footing." Steps had to be taken to prevent the people of the Gaspé from continuing to be exploited "by a company without heart or soul. And to that end, it is urgent to bring together all those whose hearts beat, whose minds think and whose hands work for justice and freedom." Evidently, his own heart wasn't just beating. It was also bleeding.

On September 7, after giving a course during the morning on political parties at the workers' school in Trois-Rivières, he took part in the famous march on Quebec City in the afternoon, which sociologist Guy Bélanger calls "the climax of the [Murdochville] strike." Bélanger goes on to explain that "organized jointly by the FTQ and the CWCC, the march brought together more than 7,000 workers from all over Quebec to protest against government inertia and the anti-union stance of Gaspé Copper Mines."[42] Unfortunately, this struggle ended in failure. As they found themselves unable to support their families, half of the strikers slowly headed back to work. These defections, added to the scabs hired by the company, meant that the mine continued operating almost normally. On October 6, after seven months of struggle, the four hundred remaining strikers voted to return to work. But the company only hired back two hundred of them, at lower wages. The others fell on hard times.

The fact Trudeau took such an active part in the workers' struggles, and took such risks, did not prevent Solange Chaput-Rolland, founder and director of the review *Perspectives,* from publishing in 1958 an "Open Letter to a Few Intellectuals and Pierre Elliott Trudeau, Director of *Cité libre.*"[43] She wrote: "My dear Pierre Elliott Trudeau . . . If God or fate had not bestowed on at least some of you an independent fortune, . . . would you be so eager . . . to ensure the success of your careers, riding on the backs of men whose tough and hard-working lives you will never share? You know union problems better than I do, . . . but tell me, do you really know, right up close, the workers whose defenders you pretend to be? . . . You would probably achieve a fairer distribution of financial resources and human values if your understanding of human beings owed more to brotherhood and less to bookish principles (you quote so many economists, thinkers and philosophers.)" If you read fewer books, she suggested, "you would end up rubbing shoulders with the people on whom you have based your erudite pleas."* No matter what Trudeau actually did, many people still saw him as a wealthy dilettante who had never

---

* Solange Chaput-Rolland herself belonged to a wealthy industrial family (Chaput). Her husband, André Rolland, was the son of Jean Rolland, president of Rolland Papers.

mixed with "real" people. This reputation followed him to the grave, and even beyond.

———— ◦ ————

Between September 25 and 29, 1957, Trudeau was in the Laurentian resort of Sainte Adèle, attending the Fourth Annual Conference of the Institut canadien des affaires publique (ICAP), of which he was a founding member. He gave a lecture entitled "On Economic Domination in International Relations": the numerous drafts and the wide range of sources he consulted indicate how carefully he prepared his lecture.[44] A revised version came out in the May 1958 edition of *Cité libre*.[45] Backing up his thesis with facts and figures, he bemoaned the weight of foreign capital on the Canadian economy. As a result, he asserted, "non-residents are in a position to make decisions contrary to the well-being of Canadians."[46] He then asked: "Can Canada free itself from the economic domination of foreign and particularly American interests?"

He examined the problems Canada would have to address to do so and the measures it would have to enforce. This led him to a somewhat pessimistic conclusion: "From the foregoing, it is clear that Canada will not emerge effortlessly from its state of economic subservience. To get out of it, one must first of all, will it. But it isn't at all certain that Canadians really want it. . . . Above all, nobody knows whether Canadians would be willing to accept the kind of economic interventionism that these reforms require."[47] Once Trudeau became prime minister, his government adopted measures to reduce the control of the Canadian economy by foreign capital, such as the Foreign Investment Review Agency created in 1973, and two measures to regulate the oil industry: the creation of Petro-Canada in 1975 and the National Energy Program in 1980. As he foresaw in 1957, many Canadians were not willing to accept these measures.

The year 1957 came to a close. As we noted above, the secretary-treasurer Jean-Paul Lefebvre had proposed a "sabbatical" at the first annual congress of the Rassemblement in order to encourage reflection and better identify the movement's objectives. In fact, as Joncas rightly noted, "no research was published."[48] The members all took the year off – all but one, that is.

———— ◦ ————

Trudeau devoted a lot of energy to theoretical endeavours. Nineteen fifty-eight turned out to be a particularly fertile year in this respect. Starting in January, he participated in a research group on Canadian politics organized by Professor Michael Oliver, a very active member of the CCF. In 1961, Oliver published a collective work under the title *Social Purpose for Canada*.[49] Trudeau contributed the article "The Practice and Theory of Federalism," which will be discussed in the next chapter. In May 1958, he published in *Cité libre* "On Economic Domination," a theme he had presented at the ICAP congress. In August, the *Canadian Journal of Economics and Political Science* published "Some Obstacles to Democracy in Quebec," which we have analyzed in Chapter 10. Furthermore, between February 15 and July 5, 1958, he devoted himself to writing *Les cheminements de la politique*, a series of twenty articles, which appeared in *Vrai*, a political and social weekly review published by his friend Jacques Hébert. On June 14, 1958, he took a short break from *Les cheminements* to bring out "Notes on the Provincial Liberal Convention." But how could Trudeau attend a party convention without being a member of the party? Simply because Jacques Hébert had named him "special correspondent for *Vrai*." This gave him the status he needed to attend all political events across the province.

In May, the Liberal Party held a leadership convention to replace Georges-Émile Lapalme. Trudeau's first-hand report was quite pessimistic. He found the party just as undemocratic as "our people taken as a whole." With few exceptions, the convention had unfolded "in an unruly climate ranging from a general din to a clamorous tumult." Delegates seemed to have no interest in the party program: "They went to Quebec City for one reason: to choose a leader, and they seemed to believe that everything would follow from that. Not a single structural reform, not a single article of the program, not a comma was discussed on the convention floor." The democratic character of a party can be established only from the ground up, he noted, but he saw no sign of this in Quebec City.

What did he think of Jean Lesage, who had just been elected Liberal leader at the convention? He was "a fighter, an energetic organizer, an ambitious and, all things considered, a charming man. . . . But what do we know about his commitment to democracy? Not much, except that he has never made any great show of it for the last thirteen years, with the federal government. But we should give him the benefit of the doubt."

After attending the convention, Trudeau doubted the Liberals would be able to defeat the "creeping dictatorship of the Union Nationale" in the elections slated for 1960. What should be done? His answer lay in the "Democratic Manifesto," which appeared in *Cité libre* in October 1958.[50] This long thirty-one-page article took up almost the entire forty-eight-page issue and incorporated a big section of the Rassemblement's Declaration of Principles as well as Trudeau's thesis on obstacles to democracy in Quebec. We will deal here only with the new ideas expressed in the manifesto.

Trudeau wondered whether any opposition party was democratic enough to deserve the support of progressives. He examined each one, before concluding that none were up to scratch. So what should progressives do? To him, the answer was obvious: "'Democracy First!' must be the rallying cry of all reformist elements in Quebec."[51] And for that to work, people of integrity had to go beyond the ideological preferences of their respective parties and come together to serve a common goal. Did such people exist? Of course, said Trudeau: "I can say that I personally know a number of men, whether members of political parties or not, who are upright, courageous, enthusiastic and selfless. . . . In this article I am addressing these worthy elements in particular."[52]

He wanted to convince the social democrats – in other words, the PSD – to join the union of democratic forces he was attempting to set up. He knew they were so committed to the purity of their doctrine that they were unwilling to compromise. He assured them that he shared their beliefs in social democracy. However, he added: "I prefer renouncing socialism than accepting that it should ever be built on undemocratic foundations; Russia has shown where the path of totalitarianism leads."[53] He warned them that in refusing to form an alliance with liberal democrats, they were committing a very serious strategic error: "Mussolini and Hitler's seizure of power was greatly facilitated by the divisions between anti-fascist forces."[54]

For him, the solution was obvious: "We should strive towards a new movement: a Democratic Union."[55] He went on to systematically examine eleven objections to the union he advocated, eliminating them one by one. He started with the first one: "Doesn't the Rassemblement's modest successes over the last two years prove the futility of attempting to unite democratic forces?"[56] His answer: the Rassemblement refused to admit any person associated with a party, whereas "the *sole* criterion for membership would be accepting the constitution and the democratic principles of the movement." Moreover, the new movement would seek the moral support of prominent politicians, by getting them to endorse a manifesto. This would encourage the progressive elements of the various parties to rally around a single objective: democracy.

When it came to the concrete actions for bringing about this goal, the manifesto became somewhat vague. Trudeau devoted only two pages to this issue, on the grounds that it was up to the people engaged in political action to find the formulas that best suited them. But he suggested a few.

For example, the Rassemblement could "take the initiative of organizing meetings between leaders of various parties."[57] Thus he reveals that when he agreed to serve as president of a moribund movement he believed that the Rassemblement could still fulfil a very useful function, such as getting leaders of opposition parties to talk to each other and devise common strategies. He also suggested establishing an electoral front whereby the various opposition parties would agree to name a single candidate who would be "the sole *bona fide* opponent of the Union Nationale." Trudeau was well aware that few people would be willing to sacrifice their candidacy for the common good if they thought they stood a good chance of winning the election. He wrote: "I remain convinced that this solution, assuredly ideal, is the only one that can set us on the pathway to . . . a true democracy. But implementing it may possibly require greater numbers of outstanding statesmen than are usually found in Quebec."[58] He could have added: "Or anywhere else in the world!"

The manifesto was published on November 27, 1958. One month later, Radio-Canada broadcast a televised debate between Pierre Trudeau, the lawyer Jacques Vadeboncoeur, the historian Michel Brunet, and Gérard Laganière of the Union Nationale. Interested readers can listen to the complete broadcast on the Web.[*] They will certainly agree that the show was aptly called "A Free-for-all Over Democracy." They will also agree that indeed Laganière became "almost hysterical." But we should have said that an "almost complete" version of the broadcast is available over the Internet, because Radio-Canada removed one particular comment. When Laganière candidly admitted not having read the article they had all been

---

[*]   http://archives.radio-canada.ca/politique/premiers_ministres_canadiens/
dossiers/2076/.

invited to discuss, Trudeau called him an "asshole" then and there, on the air. The *Journal des vedettes* seized on the incident to launch a "study" on the meaning of the word "asshole."[59] Many newspapers reported the incident, all of them sharply critical of Laganière.

All over Quebec, there was talk about the desirability and the possibility of bringing together a union of democratic forces, in newspapers, on the radio, and in various political and intellectual circles. But did this union ultimately see the light? When the FTQ held its third annual conference in November 1958, delegates came out in favour of creating a party like the CCF, but reflecting Quebec's specific character. Roch Denis writes: "Trudeau, who had hoped to bring the trade unions into the Democratic Union, undoubtedly suffered a major setback with the defection of the FTQ, which had 175,000 members at the time."[60] For its part, the PSD came out against an alliance with the Liberal Party at its May 1959 convention, since it could well lose "about half its members, with most defections coming from its more committed supporters."[61] The PSD rejected the very idea of democracy that Trudeau was defending: "Democracy in its purest form is only of interest to some university professors and fans of uncensored movies."[62]

No union of democratic forces was ever created. Michael Behiels attributes this failure to organizational, financial, and strategic shortcomings: "The procedural strategy had a bad taste of boy scout amateurism and a large dose of political naivety."[63] Indeed, political naïveté seems to permeate the whole text. The manifesto is one of the least convincing documents written by Trudeau, and one wonders how he could have thought this union – this "ideal," as he put it – could be realized. Since no one could possibly accuse him of being unintelligent or politically uninformed, this apparent naïveté begs for an explanation.

We have to keep in mind the paramount importance of the context. Remember that the Liberal Party lacked organization and resolve, and the PSD had completely failed to establish the slightest toehold in the province. None of them had a chance of beating the Union Nationale. Trudeau, as pragmatic as ever, realized that to get rid of the Duplessis regime one had to start from existing conditions and set realistic goals. While teaching democracy to the people, one had to somehow bring the scattered opposition groups together in a kind of strategic political alliance. Given Duplessis's hold on power and the poor record of the other political parties, it was just about the only thing that could be done. So he tried to create such an alliance with the Union of Democratic Forces, because he didn't want to leave a stone unturned. And when it failed, he was profoundly disappointed and worried. He would often bemoan the missed opportunities of the Rassemblement and the Union of Democratic Forces, strongly criticizing those he felt were to blame.

In 1959, progressive people were despondent. There seemed to be no hope of ever getting out of the existing political quagmire. They weren't aware that a series of events – some already in their early stages, others completely unexpected – would have a huge impact on the history of Quebec and all of Canada.

———◦———

The federal Liberals under Louis St. Laurent had been in power since 1948, but in the June 10, 1957, elections, they were defeated by the Progressive Conservatives under John G. Diefenbaker. Jean Lesage had been in charge of several federal departments since 1951 and had no interest in being relegated to the Opposition benches. He decided to move to provincial politics and challenge Georges-Émile Lapalme as head of the Quebec Liberal Party. But Lapalme, who had been leader since 1950, had no intention of yielding to Lesage. In his memoirs, Lapalme explains what made him change his mind: "One evening, Maurice Lamontagne and Father Georges-Henri Lévesque turned up at my home in Outremont. . . . Once the greetings were over, they began describing, in a remarkably well-coordinated fashion, my own situation within a divided party. . . . They named party members whose loyalty I felt I could count on, but who had now thrown their support behind Jean Lesage. They asked me not only to hand over the leadership to Jean Lesage, but also to come out openly in his support."[64]

Lapalme reluctantly agreed. Jean Lesage's election as the party leader on May 31, 1958 breathed new life into the Quebec Liberal Party, rekindling the enthusiasm of the party faithful. In Ottawa, meanwhile, Lester B. Pearson replaced St. Laurent as leader of the federal Liberal Party.

The minority Conservative government fell after one year. But the new elections in March 1958 gave Diefenbaker 208 out of 265 seats (which translates to 78.5 per cent of the seats and 53.7 per cent of the popular vote) compared to just forty-eight seats for the Liberals. This stands as the greatest landslide in Canadian history. (People often refer to Brian Mulroney's historic victory in 1984, which was indeed remarkable, but his Progressive Conservatives' gaining 211 out of 282 seats translates to 74.8 per cent of the seats and 50.0 per cent of the popular vote.) Diefenbaker's tidal wave can largely be attributed to overwhelming support from Quebec, and particularly to the Union Nationale's powerful electoral machine, which Maurice Duplessis had mobilized for the occasion. Diefenbaker won fifty of the seventy-five Quebec seats. And for the first time since Wilfrid Laurier's election in 1896, the Liberal Party of Canada failed to win a majority of seats in Quebec. The message from francophone Quebeckers was clear: they no longer saw the Liberals (then led by the anglophone Lester B. Pearson) as their natural ally. This gave Jean Lesage a free hand, since now he could distance himself from the federal Liberal Party.

Just when Lesage replaced Lapalme as party leader in 1958, something very favourable to the Liberals came out of the blue: "the natural gas affair." On June 13, 1958, Pierre Laporte, a journalist at *Le Devoir*, revealed a potentially explosive scandal. Several ministers, including two future Quebec premiers, Antonio Barrette and Daniel Johnson, several members of the Legislative Council (the upper house of Quebec's provincial legislature), Maurice Duplessis's chief of staff, and senior officials of the provincial administration allegedly profited from their privileged position to buy shares of the Natural Gas Corporation of Quebec cheaply. Some said the speculative gains amounted to $20 million. Robert Rumilly, long-time propagandist of Duplessis, asserted that no crime had been committed but he was well aware of its political consequences: "*Le Devoir* has handed Jean Lesage a weapon just as he became Leader of the Opposition. Jean Lesage naturally uses it."[65]

Poor Lapalme, who had been strong-armed into giving up the leadership of the party, could not contain his jealousy: "Have you ever seen anyone as lucky as Jean Lesage? He never lost an election. The day he finally lost his job as minister, he was offered the Quebec Liberal leadership on a silver platter. No sooner was he into his new job than this long-sought scandal broke out. Luck is stuck to his behind."[66] Lapalme did not yet realize that Lesage's run of good luck was hardly over, as will soon become apparent.

On December 28, 1958, French-speaking producers at Radio-Canada went out on strike. They wanted to unionize, but the English-speaking management at the Canadian Broadcasting Corporation claimed that since producers were running production teams they were managers and could therefore not unionize. For many French Canadians, the dispute took on symbolic proportions: they took it as proof they were treated as second-class citizens. Many French-Canadian personalities – writers, actors, and journalists – supported the strikers, including René Lévesque, who has often been depicted as the leading light of the strike.

Lévesque had been hosting the TV show *Point de mire* since 1956, a show that took on an almost mythical status as the years went by. Pierre Godin, author of the monumental four-volume biography of René Lévesque, notes, however, that "*Point de mire* was not as popular as journalists claimed. In a November 1958 poll, International Surveys ranked *Point de mire* sixth out of the twenty most popular current affairs programs on Radio-Canada."[67] Lévesque's show trailed André Laurendeau's *Pays et Merveilles* and Gérard Pelletier's *Les idées en marche,* to both of which Trudeau regularly contributed. Even so, Godin says, "the legend of the most popular show in town stuck. Claude Sylvestre [producer of *Point de mire*] later acknowledged that the show's success had been exaggerated."[68] As for Lévesque's role in the strike, Michel Vastel later cautioned: "René Lévesque had to have his arm twisted a bit before he would show up on the picket line. He was a freelancer who wanted to respect his contract, or, more likely, who was afraid of losing his job. But he eventually made it to the front lines."[69] Lévesque later remarked that the strike was a turning point in his political life.

Was Trudeau involved in the strike? It is often claimed he was conspicuously absent, since he was holed up in his room with a leg set in plaster strung up to the ceiling, following a skiing accident. This explanation falls short though, since the strike lasted from December 28, 1958, to March 7, 1959, when the producers got the right to unionize. Trudeau's agenda shows he was confined to his room for the first few days. But on January 14, as soon as the cast was taken off, he rushed out to show his support for the strikers.[70] On February 12, he attended a concert they organized. And on March 7, at a meeting marking the end of the strike at Radio-Canada, he partied with the strikers and their supporters until six in the morning.

Trudeau made a few other media appearances to promote the Union of Democratic Forces. And on April 15, 1959, he turned up in Japan, on the other side of the planet. He visited Asia, including Taiwan. This latter destination created problems for him the following year, when he wanted to visit mainland China. He also visited Iran and Israel.[*] From July 14 to 17, he attended the Sixth Congress of the Socialist International in Hamburg, returned to France, travelling here and there. He was back in Montreal on September 19, after a five-month absence. But the Quebec he found was not the same one he had left. The province was in a state of shock.

———————

On September 3, 1959, on a visit to the Schefferville iron ore mines on Quebec's North Shore, Duplessis smoked a cigar, chatted with friends, leaned against the window, and . . . collapsed. He died September 7. So he wasn't immortal after all, as some people feared. With eighteen years as premier, Duplessis still holds the record for longevity. Who would succeed him? "Paul Sauvé was tacitly considered the heir apparent," wrote Rumilly.[71] Paul Sauvé was the only minister Duplessis had completely trusted, and he took over the leadership on September 11, 1959, with the unanimous support of the Union Nationale. Surprisingly, the "heir apparent" launched a series of reforms that deviated significantly from the path set by his mentor. In a famous speech, in which he repeated the word "*désormais*" (from now on), over and over again, he charted a range of progressive new policy directions. Within months, he steered over sixty bills through the legislature, with a view to modernizing Quebec and improving relations with the federal government and the labour movement. In 2009, a Radio-Canada documentary marking the fiftieth anniversary of Paul Sauvé's government described him as "the unexpected hero of the Quiet Revolution."[72]

Quebec was rocked by the death of Duplessis, but now came a second earthquake. On January 2, 1960, Paul Sauvé died of a heart attack, after only 112 days in office. The man who could have engineered Quebec's much-needed modernization was fifty-two years old. Antonio Barrette succeeded him as premier on January 8, 1960. But

———————

[*] Trudeau's observations on Israel are found above, in Chapter 5.

Barrette lacked the force of character, the charisma, and the dynamism of his predecessors. He tried as well as he could to implement Sauvé's reforms. But when the June 22, 1960, election was called, a Union Nationale victory was anything but certain. The party had gone through three leaders in a few months; the "natural gas affair" reeked of corruption; its leader lacked charisma; and the party's great "electoral machine" was no longer running smoothly.

With all this excitement, one might think that Trudeau would stay in Quebec, at least until the elections. But no. He threw himself into a crazy scheme, dreamed up and meticulously organized by Alphonse Gagnon, director of Gagnon Frères, a Chicoutimi furniture store. On April 29, 1960, the *Key West Citizen* of Florida reported that three men – Alphonse Gagnon, Pierre Trudeau, and Val Francoeur – planned to take a canoe from Florida to Cuba in twenty-four hours: "The technique calls for one man paddling in conventional fashion while another lies backward in the boat and rows with oars attached to his feet. The third man rests. They plan shifts of two hours on the oars and one resting and will switch positions for each shift."[73] These daredevils fortunately took the precaution of being escorted by another boat. On Monday, May 2, the *Montreal Star* reported the adventure had come to an end: "They had covered 50 miles of the 90 miles distance across the rough Florida straights (sic) when they quit Saturday night. . . . The three said they would have continued if the salt water had not put their flashlights out of commission. They feared they might lose their escort boat in the darkness."[74] Trudeau returned to Quebec and became active once more in the struggle to bring about democracy in Quebec.

Two months after Duplessis's death, a series of articles, usually considered to have had an impact in the launch of the Quiet Revolution, appeared in *Le Devoir*. Between November 1959 and June 1960, a "humble Marist brother" teaching "ordinary people" in a remote Quebec region sent the newspaper a dozen letters for publication, signed "Frère Untel" – literally "Brother Anonymous." They were later brought together as a book titled *Les Insolences du Frère Untel* [The Impertinences

THE END OF AN ERA

of Brother Anonymous], published by Jacques Hébert's *Les Éditions de l'Homme*. It hit the shelves on September 6, 1960, and with more than 130,000 copies sold, became the biggest French-Canadian best-seller.[75] In this relentless indictment, Frère Untel (whose real name was Jean-Paul Desbiens) embarked on a withering attack on the entire French-language education system in Quebec. He targeted everything, from language classes to teachers and parents. He loudly proclaimed: "I work with an axe. . . . When everybody talks *joual*, it's no time to watch the fine points of grammar."[76] Born then, the word *joual* came to define the loose French language spoken by many French Canadians. And what is meant by it? To speak in *joual*, Desbiens explained, is "to say *joual* instead of *cheval* [horse]. It is to talk as horses would talk if they had not long plumped for the silence and smile of Fernandel."*[77] *Joual* caused a lot of ink to flow and took on political overtones. Léon Dion claimed that for some left-wing separatists, such as those of the review *Parti pris*, "*joual* is the most compelling manifestation of the French-Canadian loss of sense of self: its corrupting influence reaches even into their minds."[78] On the other hand, subsequently, many came to see *joual* as a source of national pride. Passionate debates continued for decades between the promoters of *joual* and the defenders of "international" French.

Frère Untel also forcefully denounced the fear paralyzing French Canadians: "We are afraid of authority. . . . The pervading fear in which we live sterilizes all our efforts." He went on to assert: "It is not Christianity that crushes us." The harshest fear "is the spirit of domination,"[79] and that has never been condemned from the pulpit. He followed this up with a scathing critique of the French-Canadian Church.

The impact of this book can well be imagined: here was a "humble" brother saying aloud, with considerable erudition and wit, what a lot of people secretly felt deep down. Undoubtedly, the book heralded a new era. Just three months before, the Liberal campaign slogan had been "*C'est l'temps qu'ça change*" (It's time things changed). But things did not change that quickly. "Shortly later," Jacques Hébert wrote, "Frère Untel was formally condemned by the Office of the Sacred Congregation

---

*   Fernandel was one of France's biggest post-war movie stars. Millions flocked to see the films of this very popular comic actor and singer, whose trademark was his "horse-like set of teeth."

for Religious in Rome. . . . For his punishment, he was sent to the Eternal
City, where he remained for three years as a silent recluse, in the shadow
of Roman disapproval."[80]

———◦———

When the elections were called, the defeat of the Union Nationale
seemed within reach. But the left was unprepared; the labour unions
hadn't managed yet to acquire a political voice, and the PSD, feeling
unprepared, decided not to nominate any candidates. The Liberal Party
was therefore, de facto, the only opposition to the Union Nationale.
Many progressives, catching a whiff of victory, joined Jean Lesage's
team with enthusiasm. Among them was René Lévesque, a candidate in
the Montreal riding of Laurier.

One month before the election, Lévesque, who was not a regular contributor to *Cité libre,* wrote one of the two articles he ever wrote for the
magazine a month before the election. His two-page article, "Pas plus bêtes
que les Arabes" [No Stupider than the Arabs], dealt with the exploitation
of natural resources in Quebec.[81] In writing this piece, Lévesque doubtless
knew Lesage was offering him the Ministry of Hydroelectric Resources in
the event the Liberals won. In the article, he laid his cards on the table,
while indulging in some irony. His thesis was that Quebeckers, unlike the
Arabs, didn't know how to take advantage of their huge natural resources.
The Arabs were poor, Lévesque argued, just like us. They had tremendous
natural resources (oil), just like us. These resources were controlled by foreigners, just like in Quebec. The difference was that the Arabs had learned
how to negotiate contracts with foreign capitalists, thereby deriving astro-
nomical profits from them. Lévesque provided some examples and listed
the social benefits accrued. It made him jealous: "You have to admit it's
enough to make you dream a little. The kind of dream that sets your teeth
grinding." Because we Quebeckers, he continued, are still poor: "All you
have to do is look at the Far North of Quebec to get a raging desire to go
ask the Iraqis for advice." His sarcastic conclusion: "I wonder if the Arabs
could lend us one of their sultans or even one of their colonels."

Lévesque was elected on June 22 and sworn in as minister of hydroelectric resources and public works on July 5. In 1961, he took over the
new Ministry of Natural Resources and fought hard, sometimes against
members of his own party, to push forward the nationalization of the

electricity sector. People often believe that this process started with him. In fact, it was the Liberal government of Adélard Godbout, who had created Hydro-Québec in 1944, by nationalizing one of the largest privately owned electricity companies.

In May 1960, Trudeau had a two-page article titled "De la notion d'opposition politique" [On the Idea of Political Opposition],[82] in the same issue of Cité libre that carried Lévesque's article. Clearly, his concerns were not Lévesque's. He could hardly contain what he called his "amazement" – we prefer to call it "anger" – over the fact some Opposition members had agreed "to be appointed by the Union Nationale to serve on the Superior Labour Council, the Commission of Inquiry into Montreal's Administrative System, the Commission of Inquiry into Hospital Insurance." He targeted these people, reminding them that "a member of the Opposition must systematically and mercilessly criticize the government's mistakes . . . so that eventually the people could put another party in office." This is how true parliamentary democracy works, he wrote. Whereas, by accepting these positions, the same people "who have been telling us for five, ten and fifteen years that it was *absolutely* necessary to get rid of the Union Nationale, who loudly denounced fascism and dictatorship," had become the government's accomplices.

As proof, he described what had just happened at the Supreme Labour Council. The council's role was to develop labour policy for the Union Nationale. But at the very first meeting of this council under his government, Prime Minister Antonio Barrette declared that any unanimous decision of the Supreme Labour Council would automatically become law. In other words, these decisions would not be submitted to the Legislature for adoption. "Yet," added Trudeau, "not one member of the Council objected to this statement, which – in the very best traditions of the Union Nationale – treats the Legislature and the people's representatives as non-entities." Moreover, "whereas the law prohibited any remuneration to members of the Council, they granted themselves" generous compensation for personal expenses. To Trudeau it was clear that "Council members . . . [were] embezzling public funds." As a result, "at their first meeting, former members of the Opposition were mired in antiparliamentarianism, lawlessness and extortion, they were becoming part of what is likely the most reactionary and corrupt government the Province has seen since Confederation."

Trudeau acknowledged that these appointments represented a "real coup" for the ruling party, which had thus reduced regime opponents to silence. Furthermore, by keeping them busy, it was preventing them from creating a true party of the Left. Trudeau's disappointment and concern were palpable. He resented the fact that some of his allies had so readily swallowed the bait of personal advancement, quickly abandoning the grand democratic principles they had previously upheld. His concern was heightened by the fact that he expected the election to be close, and he feared that any Opposition weakness would help entrench the Union Nationale in power.

A few days before the election, he published another article in *Cité libre:* "Notes sur l'élection provinciale" [Notes on the Provincial Election].[83] In this short piece, which ran to less than two pages, he explained why he planned to vote for the Liberal Party. His position was that since no left-wing party deserved to be supported, "the Liberal Party held a *de facto* monopoly of Opposition votes." Trudeau was pleased that in this situation, "someone like René Lévesque – who suddenly wanted to play a role in the election – could only act within the Liberal Party. Good for the party: I won't blame it for being so lucky." However, in the event the Liberals were elected, Trudeau feared that the still fragile base of democracy would be "crushed under the stampede of greedy opportunists rushing to the trough." And if the party were defeated, "then an attempt will once again have to be made to unite reformist forces. And I hope that this time people won't be so stubborn as to ignore for our Province the watchword 'Democracy First.'"

On June 22, 1960, the Liberal Party narrowly defeated the Union Nationale, putting an end to nineteen years of UN rule, sixteen of them consecutive. The Liberals won fifty-one of ninety-five seats, and the Union Nationale took forty-three. The popular vote, however, scarcely changed. The Liberals got 6.5 per cent more than in 1956 (51.4 per cent of the vote) and the Union Nationale 5.2 per percent less than in 1956 (46.6 per cent). Trudeau remarked that "if 2% of the electorate had voted UN rather than Liberal (that is, four people per polling station), the Union Nationale would have swept the province once again. . . . The Liberal victory hung by a thread."[84] This is confirmed by political scientist Réjean Pelletier, who points out that six Liberals won with very slim majorities (from nine to 149 votes). This group included René Lévesque, who got just 129 more votes than his opponent. Pelletier appropriately concludes: "Without these six members and these 462 votes, the Liberal Party would have found itself back in Opposition."[85]

But it was a victory nonetheless. And in "L'élection du 22 juin 1960,"[86] which appeared in the August–September issue of *Cité libre*, Trudeau paid tribute to the Liberals: "We must first salute those that delivered us from the scourge of the Union Nationale." Even though it was not alone in opposing the regime, "the Liberal Party was alone in waging the decisive battle for our freedom, and I take my hat off to it, while offering special greetings to the incorruptible Mr. Lapalme and the indefatigable Mr. Lesage who painstakingly built up a party that just ten years ago had only eight elected members." He noted, however, that the Union Nationale could never have remained in power "were it not for the cowardice and subservience of virtually everyone exercising authority. . . . Very few members of our 'elites' broke publicly with Duplessis." So we should beware, he warned, of people switching sides in order to be in the good books of the ruling party. In addition, Trudeau pointed out, these elections were not free of corruption, scandal, and confusion: "Which goes to show that a people who have never been told anything about democracy except that authority came from God, have very awkward reflexes when the time comes to change the party in power without the assistance of the Almighty."

Trudeau then praised the Liberal government for what it had already accomplished, after just over a month in power. He emphasized the party's "near miraculous" integrity, in "keeping on a short leash all the greedy opportunists rushing to the trough." In his comprehensive study of Quebec's political parties, Réjean Pelletier provides an impressive account of projects undertaken within the first month of the Liberals taking power.[87] To mention a few: the creation of several new ministries, including the Ministry of Youth, directed by Paul Gérin-Lajoie, which later became the Ministry of Education; the establishment of the Treasury Board to monitor government spending; the beginning of an offensive against patronage; a first call for tenders for public works; the reorganization of the provincial police; the creation of a commission of universities; talks with the federal government with a view to inaugurating hospital insurance on January 1, 1961. It is a very impressive list of initiatives.

But Trudeau was realistic. He knew the Liberal Party would face enormous challenges. Implementing its program "will take hard work and skill. . . . The educational revolution in particular will require daring, intransigence and almost genius."[88] Since people with such talents were few and far between in Quebec, Trudeau thought it would be necessary to search for them outside the province, because "if the party fails in its first years in power to build strong teams of competent and disinterested people, it risks slipping back, along with the entire Province, bloodless and breathless, into the cheap politicking that is one of the most enduring features of our history."

Trudeau doubted that one would find many experienced democrats in the ranks of the Liberal Party. Until recently, he recalled, most Liberals were undistinguishable from the Union Nationale: "While pretending to fight it on its own ground, they resorted sometimes to nationalism, sometimes to clericalism, in order to maximize their impact." We should remember, he said, that during the past fifteen years, the real opposition to the Union Nationale was not the Liberal Party but rather the leadership of the CCWC and the FUIQ, as well as *Le Devoir, Vrai, Cité libre,* and a few intellectuals. As for the Liberal campaign slogan, "It's time things changed," he remarked that these other opponents of Duplessis "had been clamouring for this change for the last fifteen years."

Trudeau explained he was not bringing up these facts, unpalatable for the Liberal Party, "for the foolish pleasure of belittling a team . . . which had the immense merit of organizing and winning the decisive battle." He was doing it "because they had extremely important strategic and ideological consequences." The Liberal Party had embarked on a program of reforms "that are not only far ahead of public opinion, but remain poorly understood even by the party's own supporters." Trudeau therefore called on all progressives to join them, in the hopes that "left-wing doctrinaires" would not sabotage their efforts, as they had already done in the case of the Rassemblement and the Union of Democratic Forces. (He doesn't seem to be able to get over his profound regret and frustration.) He warned that "if the programme of democratization and radicalization of the Liberal Party failed, in the 'worst' scenario, it would benefit the forces of autocracy and reaction rather than the Left." Without the support of the Left, the Liberals risked "veering to the Right, where reasonable alliances and a well-funded war chest would guarantee them future victories."

Trudeau identified another problem. Given the inexperience of the Liberal Party, a strong and vigilant opposition was needed. But the Union

Nationale could not fulfil this role: "Of course, the Union Nationale has quite a few members in the Legislature. . . . But a party which could only produce cowardly parliamentarians when in power, can hardly be expected to produce, on the Opposition benches, anything more than ridiculous hagglers." Effective opposition had to lie elsewhere. But where? "The current paradox of those in power," Trudeau wrote, "is that they must rely on the very people who may be their only effective opposition." In other words, the progressive Left. As a result, he recommended that "we come together in support of the new government, while acting as its only effective opposition. . . . Because the Liberals, who are not super-human, have committed themselves to a program that has something of the superhuman, considering our social context."

Thus, a few months after the Liberals came to power, Trudeau wel-comed them and incited the progressive Left to support them. But he also knew their path was strewn with obstacles; they would therefore need a strong opposition to keep them on track. His heart bursting with hope and full of apprehension, he wished them every success.

Chapter 14

THE NEW TREASON OF THE INTELLECTUALS

My priority: Turn this country into a free, open and strong
political society. And on this solid foundation, we could build
a radiant French culture.

— PIERRE ELLIOTT TRUDEAU, 1968[*]

JEAN LESAGE'S ELECTION MARKED THE beginning of a period of Quebec history that has fuelled – and will undoubtedly continue to fuel – many studies and debates. Should it be called *"La révolution tranquille"* (The Quiet Revolution)? The *Oxford English Dictionary* defines "revolution" as "a dramatic and wide-reaching change in conditions, attitudes, or operation." This definition certainly reflects the dramatic changes then sweeping Quebec. But like many others, we believe that while the adjective "quiet" properly reflects the absence of violence of the process, it does justice neither to the speed nor to the scope of these changes. We will use the expression nonetheless, since it is so widely accepted.

Opinions are also divided over how long this revolution lasted. Some people suggest it spanned the period between Lesage's election on June 22, 1960, and the Union Nationale's return to power under Daniel Johnson Sr. on June 5, 1966. According to the political scientist Léon Dion, it lasted a decade longer than that. The end of the Quiet Revolution, he wrote in his posthumous work, *La révolution déroutée: 1960–1976,*

---

[*] P.E. Trudeau. Speech given in Montreal on April 2, 1968, during the federal Liberal leadership campaign.

came on November 15, 1976, with the election of the Parti Québécois and the "political channelling of strong *indépendantiste* impulses."[1] Since our study ends in 1965, we will not delve deeper into this debate, which doesn't affect us directly.

In any case, some observers have suggested the revolution was already running out of steam by 1964, while others said it had deviated from its initial objectives. In the August–September 1964 issue of *Cité libre*, for example, the philosopher Charles Taylor described this ideological drift in "'*La révolution futile*' *ou* '*Les avatars de la pensée globale*'" ["The Futile Revolution" or the "Misadventures of Global Thinking"]: "We are today confronted by a new and systematic dogmatism that prevents us from seeing our problems as they really are. . . . It is therefore absolutely urgent that we once again take up our work of former days."[2]

In April 1965, *Cité libre* editor Jean Pellerin wrote an editorial entitled "*La réaction tranquille.*" As conclusive evidence the revolution had gone off the rails, Pellerin cited the strike at the daily *La Presse* from June 3 to December 23, 1964, and particularly Gérard Pelletier's dismissal as editor of the newspaper. The strike had lasted so long, he wrote, because the French-Canadian bosses of the *grande bourgeoisie* wanted to "break the back of the employees' union."[3] Pellerin believed Pelletier had been fired so cavalierly on March 30, 1965, because this same bourgeoisie wanted to regain power and put an end to freedom of expression: "For the *grande bourgeoisie*, there is only one 'reaction' – and this reaction is anything but 'quiet.'"[4] Consequently, he said, "we must return to the *maquis*" (in other words, resume the fight against the government).[5] So by the time the "Three Wise Men" of Quebec – Jean Marchand, Gérard Pelletier, and Pierre Trudeau – went into federal politics, the boundless optimism of the early 1960s had already waned.

Trudeau wrote in his memoirs that after the death of Duplessis in 1959, "the political situation took an entirely new and very positive turn, at least for the first two years. I was one of the very first beneficiaries of this change."[6] Indeed, the Université de Montréal offered him a permanent job as professor and researcher, ending the saga of his appointment, which had started in 1952. In February that year, while in Paris on the way to Moscow, he had received a letter from the dean of the Faculty of

Social Sciences at the Université de Montréal, Esdras Minville, offering him a position "leading possibly to a permanent professorship in 1953–1954."[7] Strangely enough, the position Minville actually offered him on October 18, 1959, was not as a tenure-track professor, but rather as an adjunct lecturer on contract, teaching a course called "Issues of Domestic Policy." Trudeau was outraged by the offer, which he considered degrading, and turned it down. He received several similar offers after that, all revised downwards, and rejected them all.

Reading Trudeau, one could imagine that with the death of Duplessis in 1959, the obstacles barring his appointment simply vanished. In fact, as late as April 14, 1960, *Le Devoir* reported that "after Trudeau had been invited to teach at the Université de Montréal, he was still denied entry." According to the newspaper, Trudeau had been offered four positions over eight years, by two different deans (Esdras Minville and Philippe Garigue). Yet each time, the full-time position on offer was replaced by an adjunct lectureship teaching night courses on subjects that were not within his main area of interest. On May 5, André Laurendeau came to his friend's defence in *Le Devoir,* revealing that after being invited to teach at l'Université de Montréal, Trudeau was in fact shut out. On May 13, the Ottawa newspaper *Le Travail* (where Gérard Pelletier was editor-in-chief) backed up Laurendeau's position. And in June, 125 social science students sent a petition to the university Board of Governors, "demanding that Pierre Elliott Trudeau be appointed as a professor."[8]

But support for Trudeau was by no means unanimous. The *Montréal Matin* of May 17, 1960, rejoiced that he had not been hired: "We don't see why, in the name of liberty, anybody has the right to teach whatever they want at the university." The tabloid quoted some of Trudeau's statements out of context, suggesting he was a socialist, if not an outright Communist. Clearly "the Trudeau Affair" was becoming a *cause célèbre*. The rector of the university, Mgr. Lussier, felt compelled to justify his decision. He sent a letter to Trudeau insinuating that it was he who had turned down the tenure-track position he had been offered on the recommendation of the dean, Philippe Garigue. With a touch of irony, the rector wrote: "I understand the serious grounds you mentioned, that prevented you from accepting a teaching post this year. I hope that on your return from the upcoming journey . . ." In other words, Trudeau was a frivolous man who had turned down the position for the sake of travel abroad. True,

Trudeau was heading with a small group on an exclusive trip to China in September 1960, at the invitation of the Chinese government. He later recounted this experience in *Two Innocents in Red China*.[9]

But this was not why he had refused the job, and since Trudeau had no tolerance for half-truths, on September 6, with one foot in the plane, he wrote a reply to the rector. In no uncertain terms, he told him he knew first-hand from the dean that it was the rector himself, and nobody else, who had not followed up on the offer, because he had seen which way "the wind was blowing." In other words, since the "authorities" were not supporting Trudeau's candidacy, Mgr. Lussier had advised Garigue against pursuing any job offer "under the circumstances." Trudeau continued: "It is true circumstances have now changed. But I would find it just as unpleasant to work for the university because you felt the wind had changed direction, as to be denied a job for such arbitrary reasons." He mentioned something else that had come up in their meeting: Mgr. Lussier had offered him an hourly wage. He was well aware this was a device allowing the rector to sound out opinion and fire him if he wanted to, merely "on the dean's say-so." There was no way Trudeau would accept such an insult: "Monsignor, I am neither of an age, nor of a mind, nor by training, willing to accept such weak offers, which seem to show little respect for the academic career. Especially since . . . less than six months ago, the Dean of Social Sciences in Montreal offered me a tenure-track professorship, which I duly accepted – only to find myself shut out from the position, as you know." He concluded: Unless he were offered a position "in the manner prescribed by the university Charter for a tenure-track appointment, namely with the approval of the Board of Governors," there was no need to pursue the discussion further.

Trudeau eventually accepted a teaching position in the Faculty of Law. On May 29, 1961, he was also appointed "a research associate working half-time at the new Public Law Research Institute at the Faculty of Law."[10] He had finally become a professor and researcher at the Université de Montréal. Between 1962 and 1965, he taught two courses per year: "Constitutional Law and Administrative Law" and "Civil Liberties." It is clear from his course notes that he prepared each class thoroughly. As usual, he made the connection between theory and practice. In teaching civil liberties, for example, he cited newsworthy cases reported in the press.

John English writes that Trudeau accepted the professorship "half-heartedly." A little later he adds: "Certainly Trudeau was not ready to settle in the classroom."[11] Other commentators claim Trudeau did not enjoy teaching. We do not agree, and nor did Trudeau. In an interview with Peter Gzowski in 1962, he said he was enchanted with teaching and research: "What could be better for me? I am working in the field I know best, and this will give me a chance for a few years to read some books and replenish my stock of ideas."[12]

But was he a good prof? Norm Goldman, one of his students in Constitutional Law in 1963, told us: "Trudeau was a very good professor, interested in both his subject and his students."[13] When we asked Goldman whether students challenged Trudeau in the classroom, he answered without hesitation: "No more than other professors and less than some. Keep in mind that students challenged everything at the time. We had a strike almost every week. Trudeau never talked about politics in class. And if someone challenged one of the ideas in the course, he always answered patiently and respectfully. They say he was arrogant. But I didn't see any arrogance in his classes. He enjoyed the company of students. During breaks, he often stayed with us, joining in our discussions, whether on film or anything else." Goldman recalled that Trudeau spoke with fascination of Declarations of Rights: "When I saw his Charter of Rights in 1982, I said to myself: 'This is exactly what he was talking about in class!'"

Among Trudeau's students was one Bernard Landry, who asked him for a letter of recommendation. Landry later became one of the leading lights of the pro-independence Parti Québécois. Trudeau wrote: "From the academic point of view, the candidate is only *average*. But as an organizer, a polarizer, a man of action, the candidate is *brilliant*. . . . He is a man who . . . keeps a tolerant frame of mind, and a critical perspective." Trudeau recommended the candidate be admitted to graduate studies "because our society must encourage these future men of action to base their judgment on reason not emotion."[14]

<hr />

Trudeau was very active at the new Public Law Research Institute. On July 12, 1961, he was appointed for a four-year term as a "member of the committee assisting the director in administering the Institute."[15]

His mandate was renewed in 1965 for another four years, but he took an unpaid leave of absence to run as Liberal candidate in the November 1965 federal elections. He worked hard drafting the February 26, 1962, speech that the guest of honour, Paul Gérin-Lajoie (the Quebec minister of youth and later minister of education), would be giving at the institute's official inauguration.[16] Trudeau was clearly both a research associate and an administrator.

In his committee work, he collaborated closely with Marc Lalonde, who later played a very important role in his cabinet. Starting in 1962, Trudeau was part of a group of four professors in charge of producing a textbook of public law. He was responsible for the chapters on the state, power, and political systems as well as the concluding chapter on political freedoms. The director of the institute was Jean Beetz, a Rhodes Scholar and Oxford graduate, eight years younger than Trudeau. The two men got along very well, appreciated each other, and cooperated closely. When Trudeau became prime minister, he appointed Beetz as a special adviser on constitutional affairs. And in 1974, he appointed him Justice of the Supreme Court of Canada, a position Beetz held for fourteen years.

Trudeau regularly attended scholarly conferences, both in Canada and Europe. He received dozens of invitations from all over. For example, in April 1962, the University of British Columbia asked him to present a paper at a major symposium on constitutional affairs, scheduled for July 3 to 6. But Trudeau was unsure of himself and refused at first, saying he had no time to prepare. He explained in rather awkward English (a language he had still not fully mastered in the written form): "I am but four months going in my academic career, and I have not yet accumulated the fund of knowledge that permits older minds to prepare a good paper in a short time." The university insisted reassuringly. Trudeau agreed and asked them if they could arrange a trip for him up to Alaska. It was a deal. Trudeau went to Vancouver and presented "The Meaning of Federalism in Canada." The paper of the other guest speaker, Georges-Émile Lapalme, Quebec minister of cultural affairs, dealt with "French Canada Today." Once Trudeau boarded an Alaska Cruise Line ship, he wrote a draft of the article "About the June 18, 1962 Elections," which appeared in the August–September 1962 issue of *Cité libre*.[17]

Trudeau's fame as an intellectual was well established and now spread well beyond the borders of Quebec. He was invited to meet with several leading figures in Canada and the United States and to participate in major conferences. In 1962, he was part of a group of "a dozen distinguished Montreal leaders" invited by the Consul General of the United States to visit the Plattsburgh Air Force base.[18]

On November 6, 1963, Guy Sylvestre, president of the Royal Society of Canada, informed Trudeau that his candidacy as a Fellow had been approved but he had to consent to being nominated. Trudeau knew nothing about this venerable society, founded in 1882, which recognizes excellence in learning and research and exceptional accomplishments in a variety of areas. He had no idea he was now being offered one of Canada's most prestigious scholarly honours. He tried to find out more about the society and wrote to Sylvestre: "I wonder who the Fellows are, and what my obligations would be. I do not know how many candidates are running, nor how many positions are open, nor whether I have the slightest chance of being elected."[19] One can well imagine Sylvestre's bemused smile as he reassured Trudeau: "I would not have approached you unless I knew your chances were very good." Sylvestre laid it out for Trudeau: "When the nominating committee makes a unanimous recommendation, the candidates are always voted in." On April 4, 1964, Trudeau was formally elected a Fellow of the Royal Society of Canada. This very same year, the well-known journalist Peter C. Newman described him as "one of his province's most influential thinkers."[20] So, by the time he took a leave of absence to enter federal politics, his reputation was well established in Quebec as well as in the rest of Canada. Clearly, he was well suited to his academic career.

———

In 1960, before starting work at the Université de Montréal, Trudeau made a trip to China, later made famous by the book *Two Innocents in Red China,* which he co-authored with Jacques Hébert. To what extent did they share authorship? The manuscript reveals which sections each man wrote, but there is no need for any complicated calculation. Systematic as ever, Trudeau made it for us: he had written two-fifths of the book. Readers of Trudeau's other works will probably be surprised by the anecdotal tone of this book, so different from his usual style. With good reason. Hébert dealt with everyday life, telling various anecdotes or bringing out the amusing side of situations. Trudeau wrote the analytical sections on the economy and politics: he dealt with facts and figures, reported discussions with intellectuals, and described working conditions in factories. He was also mainly responsible for the preamble and epilogue.

Hébert and Trudeau drew a particularly insightful conclusion from their journey: "So the real threat is not the Yellow Peril of our nightmares; it is the eventual threat of economic rivalry in the markets of the world, and the nearer threat of an ideological success that is already enabling China to help – with its capital, its technicians, and above all its example – the even poorer countries of Asia, Africa and Latin America."[21]

In fact, Trudeau could have written a book all his own, based on the seventy-five pages of his travel diary.[22] It probably would have been less entertaining but would have conveyed a truer image of the socio-political reality than *Two Innocents in Red China*. His notes contain no anecdotes, but they provide abundant information on economics, politics, and philosophy – he was the one in the group confronting the Chinese about their ideology, and he noted that their answers inevitably came back in "official jargon."[23] While he was impressed by China's remarkable progress in many areas, he was by no means blind to the regime's shortcomings.

The book was a huge success and provoked strong reactions. It convinced many people it was time to initiate diplomatic relations with China. In the Thursday, April 6, 1961, issue of *Le Devoir,* André Laurendeau wrote: "After reading [Trudeau and Hébert], one no longer finds the American position on China unfair or awkward, but ridiculous and even farcical." The trip would have a major impact on Canadian foreign policy. On October 13, 1970, the Trudeau government officially recognized the People's Republic of China. Canada joined the Netherlands, Britain, and France as one of the few Western nations – and the only one in the Americas, apart from Cuba – to develop closer ties with Communist China. This clever Canadian diplomatic move angered the United States. President Richard Nixon and his Secretary of State, Henry Kissinger, were quietly preparing a Chinese diplomatic overture of their own and never forgave Trudeau for upstaging them. Nixon visited China in 1972, but it was not until 1979 that the United States finally broke with Taiwan and established formal diplomatic relations with Beijing.

On September 10, 1960, three months after Jean Lesage's victory, and while Trudeau and his group were visiting China, a new nationalist movement burst onto the scene in Quebec: the Rassemblement pour l'indépendance nationale (RIN). Léon Dion saw it as "one of the first fruits" of the Quiet Revolution.[24] According to Réjean Pelletier, who devoted his doctoral dissertation to this movement, "the RIN roused the sense of a Québécois community, just as the 'Quiet Revolution' had."[25] About thirty people were involved in founding the RIN, and they named André D'Allemagne president and Marcel Chaput vice-president. Chaput became president a year later.

The RIN was propelled – maybe unintentionally – to the forefront of public awareness by the Congress on Canadian Affairs. In November 1961, the congress organized a debate under the honorary patronage of the Governor General of Canada on the question "The Canadian Experiment: Success or Failure?" The association invited the new RIN president, Marcel Chaput, who had just published his sensational *Pourquoi je suis sépara-tiste*. Chaput was then a federal government employee working for the Defence Research Board. As might be expected, his employer was dead-set against his taking part in the debate, but Chaput went anyway. And the RIN benefitted from the resulting publicity, especially when Chaput was fired.

In 1961, the movement stated its *raison d'être* in Article 1 of its Constitution: "The RIN is a cultural and political organization whose goal is . . . to promote the creation of a sovereign French state." In 1963, it became a political party whose sole objective was Quebec's independ-ence. The movement brought together people from very different ideo-logical horizons. Six of the founding members came from the Laurentian Alliance, which was, according to Léon Dion, a "right-wing, corporatist and quasi-fascist" organization.[26] On the other hand, the great orator Pierre Bourgault, who became the longest-serving RIN president, was avowedly socialist. As for Andrée Ferretti, who became vice-president in 1967, she was the leader of a fringe radical left wing. Not surprisingly, the movement was shaken by constant infighting and many defections from the very beginning.

Réjean Pelletier considers D'Allemagne as "one of the leaders of the party"[27] and the RIN top theorist. D'Allemagne had been strongly influ-enced by the Montreal Historical School, which was the topic of his doc-toral dissertation. Like this school and especially his professor Guy

Frégault, D'Allemagne attributed the current inferiority of French Canadians to the Conquest of 1763 – when France was defeated by Great Britain. However, whereas the school saw no way out of this "legacy of misery," the Rassemblement pour l'indépendance nationale sought to overcome this pessimism by struggling for Quebec's independence. In this sense, the RIN was the political arm of the school.

As we noted above, the party was plagued by internal conflicts from the start. Pierre Bourgault and Andrée Ferretti were sworn enemies. In 1967, when Ferretti became vice-president, she radicalized the RIN. This led to a fierce struggle between Bourgault and Ferretti, and the latter resigned. Her departure marked the victory of the RIN's pro-independence faction over the leftist one. Then, in October 1968, the Ralliement national, a right-wing Social Credit party, merged with René Lévesque's Mouvement Souveraineté-Association to form the Parti Québécois. At this point, the RIN dissolved, leaving its members free to join the new party if they wished. This is how the different pro-"sovereignty" factions came together within the Parti Québécois.

Jean's Lesage election in June 1960 marks the emergence of a new nationalism in Quebec. This "neo-nationalism," as it is often called, had two branches: one was "federalist" and sought to keep Quebec within Canada – although on a profoundly different basis that would recognize the "special," "distinct," or even "national" status of Quebec. The other was "separatist." It rejected federalism and, while hoping to maintain cordial relations with the rest of Canada, advocated Quebec's secession. With RIN's help, political terminology went through some changes: *séparatisme* was soon replaced by *indépendantisme*. Once René Lévesque's Mouvement Souvrainté-Association and the Parti Québécois were created, *indépendantisme* gave way in turn to *souverainisme*. We will continue to use the term "separatism" most of the time, since it was the most prevalent one in the early 1960s.

Initially, Trudeau was gratified to see the Liberal Party win, since he believed it marked the advent of democracy in Quebec. But by January 1961, the party had already begun to disappoint him. In "The Restoration," an unsigned article in *Cité libre* that he unquestionably wrote, he laid out his reservations and a few concerns.[28] He compared the Liberal Party's return to power to the restoration of the Bourbon monarchy after the French Revolution of 1789. The French "were quick to note that 'the Bourbons, on returning from exile, had forgotten nothing and learned nothing.'"[29] He worried that "on their own return from exile, the Liberals, like the Bourbons, have forgotten nothing and not learned much. . . ."[30] He recalled that "in June 1960, the *Cité libre* team had no choice but to support the Liberals as a lesser evil. . . . After the elections, we welcomed the liberal Restoration but had some reservations, given the 'need to support the Liberals, while acting as an opposition in order to develop an alternative ideology.'"[31]

According to Trudeau, it turned out *Cité libre*'s reservations were fully justified. He identified significant weaknesses in the Liberal Party, sometimes exaggerating them. He blamed Jean Lesage for "hasty and irresponsible" statements, asking indignantly: "What person, in what country in the world would have been foolish enough to declare: 'There is no question of my administration ever creating a Ministry of Public Education?'"[32] But Trudeau was coming on too strong. He forgot Lesage had to compromise and delay reforms, in the face of the Church's vigorous opposition. Trudeau was exaggerating because he truly believed in the crucial role of the opposition, which had to "develop an alternative ideology." But which one?

The New Democratic Party (NDP) was founded in August 1961. Progressive circles in Quebec were eagerly awaiting the arrival of this party, still unnamed but which they called The New Party. Was this the alternative ideology that the opposition could support? Not according to Trudeau, who attacked Marcel Rioux for encouraging *Cité libre* readers to support the party. Trudeau warned: "It happens that this friend is a regular contributor to *Cité libre*, so his opinion is likely to be mistaken for the magazine's position as a whole: let's be clear that it is not."[33] For Trudeau, a progressive party could not just be set up any old way or any place: "We are thinking, not without bitterness, of the lost years from 1956 to 1959, when the Union Nationale was falling into decrepitude and the federal Liberal Party was reeling from defeat: the Rassemblement and later the Union of Democratic Forces sought to consolidate left-wing elements, which could eventually have led to a new party. . . . But now, *now*, what is the urgency of setting up a new party? Because that's what it's all about. . . . It is about a *new party* which must be founded in Quebec right now, for the very good reason that other men in other jurisdictions have decided the time had come to establish such a party there!"[34]

Clearly, Trudeau had not yet come to terms with the failure of the Rassemblement and the Union of Democratic Forces. He simply could not understand that the people responsible for this failure were now rushing to the New Party. He suggested they "make sure this Party doesn't end up being a bunch of ideologues without roots and union leaders looking for a place to hang their political hat."[35] To distance himself from this new Left, he would, from then on, describe *Cité libre* as a magazine on the "liberal Left" or "non-partisan Left."[36]

"The Restoration" raised an additional concern, which was "the remarkable revival of Quebec nationalism, especially among the younger generations." Trudeau felt the Left had to resume dialogue with the nationalists: "It is in this spirit and to stimulate debate that *Cité libre* will publish an article by Jean-Marc Léger in its next issue."[37] Indeed, the February 1961 issue contained an article by the journalist Jean-Marc Léger titled "*Urgence d'une gauche nationale*" [The Urgent Need for a Nationalist Left]. It was the first neo-nationalist article to appear in *Cité libre* and was followed in March 1961 by "*Lettre d'un nationaliste,*" signed "G.C." Trudeau replied to both in the March 1961 issue.

In "The Urgent Need for a Nationalist Left," Jean-Marc Léger criticized the Left's anti-nationalism. He also attacked *Cité libre* and, more particularly, Trudeau, without naming them.[38] In Léger's view, objectives such as the primacy and dignity of the individual, equality, and the common good "that our official Left claims as its own are nothing but a big hoax if, because of a pathological anti-nationalism, the national tragedy of the French Canadians is ignored. Given the actual situation of our people, an anti-nationalist Left, or even a Left that doesn't pay attention to nationalism, deceives the masses by turning itself into either straight reformism or crass opportunism."[39]

G.C. went further in his "Letter from a Nationalist."[40] He announced loud and clear that "the absolute independence of Quebec [and] the establishment of a socialist system" were needed to emancipate "this people who demand to live, to live in peace with everyone and who '*have the right to do so.*'" He asked his fellows citizens bluntly: "Are you concerned about the debasement of our methods of education, the language we speak?" His solution was straightforward: "Let us close the borders, proclaim unilingualism – and overnight the French language will become a golden value."[41]

Trudeau responded to the two authors in "*L'aliénation nationaliste.*" He wanted to keep the dialogue going, but he also wanted to criticize them. From the outset, he admitted candidly, "there has been a tendency at *Cité libre* to consider Quebec nationalists as alienators," even if, like them, "we are painfully aware of Quebec's shortcomings in all areas."[42] The difference, however, is that "we consider some claims of our nationalists awfully exaggerated, for example when they blame practically all the backwardness of our society on '*les Anglais.*' . . . Whether the Conquest was or was not the root of all evil, whether the *Anglais* were or were not the most treacherous occupying force in living memory, the fact remains that the French-Canadian community holds in its hands, here and now, the main instruments of regeneration. Through the Canadian Constitution, the Quebec government can exercise extensive powers over the souls of French Canadians and the territory where they live, the richest and largest of all Canadian provinces."[43] So for Trudeau, all French Canadians had to do was use the powers conferred on them by the British North America Act of 1867. And retorting to G.C., who wanted to close borders in order to save the French language, Trudeau concluded sharply: "Let's open the borders; the people are suffocating to death!"[44]

Trudeau maintained an ambiguous relationship with the socialists. He didn't hold back on criticism of the Left but was still part of their circle. An example of this ambivalence is found in his participation in 1958 in a research group in Canadian politics, set up by Professor Michael Oliver, an active member of the CCF. In 1961, the CCF was transformed into the NDP, led by former Saskatchewan premier Tommy (T.C.) Douglas, and Oliver became its first president. In 1963, he served as research director of the famous Royal Commission on Bilingualism and Biculturalism – commonly known as the "B&B" or the Laurendeau-Dunton Commission. In 1961, Oliver brought out a collective work, *Social Purpose for Canada,* to which Trudeau contributed "The Practice and Theory of Federalism," an English-language article that appeared in 1967 in the French edition of *Federalism and the French Canadians.*[45] In this article, Trudeau criticized the CCF/NDP for promoting ideals out of sync with Canadian reality.

Whether they liked it or not, he said, Canada was a federation and not a unitary state: "But unfortunately socialists in Canada have seldom been guided in their doctrine and their strategy by a whole-hearted acceptance of the basic political fact of federalism."[46]

He was well aware that "no national party can keep its integrity while preaching a gospel that varies as it moves *a mari usque ad mare.*" Yet, because of the diversity of regions, "it is folly to endorse strategies that are devised to swing the whole country at the same time and in the same way into the path of socialism.[47] . . . If the party preaches the same gospel everywhere, its partisans in some areas will desert it for being too reactionary, whereas in other areas the party will fail to find adherents because it appears too revolutionary."[48] Socialists also had to understand that the perception of the central government varied by region. Moreover, if they gave due consideration to the bi-ethnic nature of Canada, they would see that "central government encroachments, which are accepted in other provinces as matters of expediency, cannot be so viewed in Quebec."[49] He gave as a telling example Quebec's refusal of federal grants to universities.

Clearly, Trudeau chose this example less as a way of justifying the political and strategic refusal of Duplessis than to explain his own reasons for opposing them: "From the Quebec point of view, the most serious objection to the federal grants to universities was obviously not that the universities had enough money or that federal money had a peculiar odour; it was that once the universities had their bellies filled with provincial grants they would see no reason to oppose that provincial government which had persistently failed in its constitutional duties by leaving education in such an impoverished state."[50] Trudeau also pointed out that the true socialist was necessarily a humanist and a democrat, and therefore had to be a pluralist. He had to understand that "some people like to live by the sea, some in the plains, and that some prefer to speak French."[51] In other words, a socialist party had to recognize that Canadian pluralism necessarily included the French fact.

For Trudeau, federalism required collaboration between various levels of government. That is why he devoted several pages to this principle, noting that it was enshrined in the Constitution. He also stressed the importance of maintaining a balance between centralization and decentralization, a balance that seemed threatened, at the time he wrote the article, by a tendency to "an extreme provincialism. . . . There is a greater need than ever for an enlightened socialist approach to the fiscal problems of a federal form of government."[52] Some people, he said, believe that socialism "within a federal structure of government is not as pure, as exciting, and as efficient as socialism in a unitary state." Trudeau retorted: "That may be so, just as democratic socialism may be less efficient and far-reaching than the totalitarian brand. But just as democracy is a value in itself, which cannot be sacrificed to considerations of expediency, likewise at certain times and in certain places federalism may be held to be a fundamental value, and the penalty for disregarding it may well be the complete collapse of socialism itself."[53]

Starting in 1960, given the groundswell of support for neo-nationalism among young people, it comes as no surprise that *Le Quartier Latin*, the student newspaper at the Université de Montréal, devoted many articles to Quebec's independence and held debates on the issue. It is worth noting that almost all of these debates were not about whether Quebec's independence was needed or even appropriate, but rather about whether it was feasible.

For example, in the February 23, 1961, issue of *Le Quartier Latin*, RIN president André D'Allemagne called for "complete independence . . . insofar as reality permits." On March 7, Walter O'Leary, founding member of the Knights of the Round Table of a Free Quebec, claimed: "There are two free peoples in Canada, two proud nations, two universal cultures and two national states: one in Ottawa representing the '*Canadian*' people and nation, and the Quebec state representing the 'Laurentian' people and nation." Other public figures came out in favour of Quebec's independence, even when they doubted it would ever become a reality. For example, on March 9, André Laurendeau said he shared the ideals of the nationalists, while believing "that separatism is not possible." On March 14, Michel Brunet argued that independence would be a very good thing, although it posed significant economic problems. On April 6, Jacques-Yvan Morin, destined to play an important role in the Parti Québécois, wrote that independence was desirable but that "most French Canadians are unwilling to assume these risks." The students invited Trudeau to give his point of view, but he turned the offer down.

He needed some fresh air. On May 25, 1961, he boarded the *Homeric*, in first class, on his way to Paris. It was during this trip that he joined the crowd running just ahead of the bulls in Pamplona.[54] He also made a leisurely stop on the Côte d'Azur, travelling afterwards through Italy and Yugoslavia. One evening in Peć, Kosovo, as the hotels were full, he slept in the park. On September 8, he returned to Paris and a few days later, he and his friend, Caroll Guérin, celebrated her twenty-fifth birthday at the Lido, the famous cabaret on the Champs-Élysées. The following day, he invited her again, this time for dinner at the exclusive restaurant La Pérouse. He then hopped across to the London School of Economics, and back again to Paris from September 22 to 29, to attend the congress of the International Political Science Association. The next day, on returning to Montreal, he found that separatism was gaining ground in the province day by day.

As we noted above, *Cité libre* wanted to encourage dialogue with Quebec's youth, who were particularly attracted to the notion of independence. Once the magazine opened its pages to them, contributions poured in. According to Gérard Pelletier, the response was so overwhelming that in "the first month, we had a problem with space that only got worse as time went by."[55] One of these young people was Pierre Vallières, who wrote his first article in the February 1962 issue of *Cité libre*, and his second in March. He was twenty-four years old.

As their articles showed, these young contributors all had different expectations of what independence should achieve. For example, André Major came out "both for independence and for a secular state."[56] Vallières, on the other hand, couched his support for independence in a kind of religiosity reminiscent of the clerical-nationalist elite of the 1930s and 1940s. A worried Vallières asked: "Where are our thinkers? Where are the leaders? Where is The One who will get us all standing firmly on our own two feet?"[57] In March, he rejoiced that the idea "to carry the torch of Catholicism in America" had become obsolete and that French Canadians had become free. What should they do with their newfound freedom? To him the answer was clear: "Our authentic freedom will start with fair-minded questioning of the meaning of our presence on earth."[58] He also declared that young people were right to want a revolution, since this was the only way to get rid of "the inefficiency and current decay of liberal democracy."[59] What a strange mixture of mysticism, neo-nationalism, and revolutionary fervour!

The struggle between neo-nationalists and "federalists" was waged in the columns of *Cité libre*. In April 1962, the magazine devoted a special issue to separatism. The two Breton brothers – both became renowned social scientists: Raymond as a sociologist, and Albert as an economist – noted that if "support for separatism comes and goes in waves, it can't be because *les Anglais* periodically change their attitudes towards French Canadians."[60] Waves in separatist support must be explained in socio-economic terms. Separatist movements, they added, relied on different economic theories. For example, the "Alliance Laurentienne is corporatist. Action socialiste is fighting capitalism. The Rassemblement pour l'indépendence nationale does not advocate any particular ideology."[61] Did separatism have a future? To which they replied confidently: "Once institutions become less rigid, separatism will disappear."[62]

———◆———

Trudeau unquestionably penned the most powerful article in this special April 1962 edition of *Cité libre*: "*La nouvelle trahison des clercs*" [The New Treason of the Intellectuals].[63] This article is not only very sound, scientifically; it also constitutes, in our view, one of Trudeau's best-ever polemical pieces. Understandably, this issue had "the largest circulation since the founding of the magazine – 9,500 copies."[64] No doubt this was partly due to the theme of separatism, but Trudeau's article greatly contributed to this success. We will quote here from the version later published in English in *Federalism and the French Canadians*.[65] We should note at the outset that it is difficult to do justice to this remarkable text, which combines passion, reason, and erudition.

The title is deliberately reminiscent of the French philosopher and writer Julien Benda's 1927 masterpiece, *La trahison des clercs* (later appearing in English as *The Betrayal of the Intellectuals*). In this merciless indictment, Benda castigated the intellectuals of France and Germany, who had abandoned the world of selfless thought and universal values to embrace political passions such as race, nationalism, or anti-Semitism (Benda was of Jewish origin and had been very affected by the Dreyfus Affair). The "intellectuals" Trudeau denounced were the separatists. He knew the neo-nationalists drew inspiration from the decolonisation movements around the world, particularly the liberation of Algeria. When he wrote this article, the Evian Accords had just been signed on March 19,

1962, bringing the Algerian War to an end. The GPRA (Le gouvernement provisoire de la république algérienne), which was the political arm of the National Liberation Front (FLN) during the war, negotiated peace terms with France. (This explains why Trudeau referred to the GPRA in his article.) At the same time, Frantz Fanon's 1961 best-selling book, *Les damnés de la terre* [The Wretched of the Earth], a powerful plea for anti-colonial struggle and the emancipation of the Third World, was hugely popular in separatist circles.

Trudeau's first sentence aptly encapsulates the key theme of the article: "It is not the concept of *nation* that is retrograde; it is the idea that the nation must necessarily be sovereign."[66] At the theoretical level, Trudeau claimed, the separatists fail to make the proper distinction between the concepts of *nation, state, people,* and *sovereign people.* This results in faulty reasoning, with serious consequences. He illustrated the problem with a telling quote: "Marcel Chaput writes: 'Since the end of the Second World War, more than thirty countries, formerly colonies, have been freed of foreign tutelage and have attained national and international sovereignty. . . . And today it is the people of French Canada who are beginning to rouse, and they, too, will claim their place among free nations."[67]

False, countered Trudeau: none of these countries had acquired "national" sovereignty. Almost all of these thirty countries had become states, "in the same way as Canada is a state. They have acceded to full sovereignty just as Canada did in 1931. In no way are they nations in the sense that French Canada might be a nation. Consequently, putting the independence of Quebec into this particular historical context is pure sophistry."[68] He continued: "As for Algeria, which our *indépendantistes* are always holding up as an example, there is no doubt what kind of state she is seeking to become. Besides inhabitants of French, Spanish, Italian, Jewish, Greek and Levantine origin, in this particular country we must count Berbers, Kabyles, Arabs, Moors, Negroes, Tuaregs, Mzabites, and a number of Cheshire cats."[69] With all this diversity, argued Trudeau, it was clear that Algeria was not seeking to become a *nation* but rather a *state.* He then cited another case: "The state of India is a sovereign republic. But there are no less than four languages officially recognized there. . . . There are eight principal religions, several of which are mutually and implacably opposed. Which nation are we talking about? And just what independence should we take as an example?"[70] Trudeau concluded: "What emerges from all this is that promoting independence as an end good in itself, a matter of dignity for all self-respecting peoples, amounts to embroiling the world in a pretty pickle indeed."[71]

Trudeau was well aware that summarizing "some seven thousand years of history in three paragraphs, is, of course, a little short." Nevertheless, it allowed him to draw three observations, which deserved consideration: "The first is that the nation is not a biological reality. . . . Except for a very small fraction of his history, man has done very well without nations." He said he was emphasizing this fact "for the benefit of our young bloods, who see the slightest dent in the nation's sovereignty as an earth-shaking catastrophe."[72] The second observation was the following: "The tiny portion of history marked by the emergence of the nation-states is also the scene of the most devastating wars, the worst atrocities, and the most degrading collective hatred the world has ever seen."[73] He provided many examples to support this statement.

Why was he fighting tooth and nail against this idea "that corrupts all," to use his expression? "What worries me," he explained, "about the fact that five million Canadians of French origin cannot manage to share their national sovereignty with seven million Canadians of British origin, beside whom they live and who they know, in general, have no fleas, is that this leaves me precious little hope that several thousand million Americans, Russians and Chinese, who have never met and none of whom are sure the others are not flea-ridden, will ever agree to abdicate their piece of sovereignty in the realm of nuclear arms."[74] Let us point out that, at the time, Trudeau was not alone in worrying about the prospect of a nuclear conflict. He shared this feeling with much of the planet.

His third observation: History shows that "the very idea of the nation-state is absurd. To insist that a particular nationality must have complete sovereign power is to pursue a self-destructive end. Because every national minority will find, at the very moment of liberation, a new minority within its bosom which in turn must be allowed the right to demand its freedom. . . . That is why the principle of nationality has brought to the world two centuries of war, and not *one single final* solution."[75] Once again, he backed up this statement with many examples.

He then asked: Why is it that the idea of nation-state, "absurd in principle and outdated in practice," has enjoyed and still enjoys "extraordinary favour"? The reason is that strong states have used this concept, dressing it up with appealing names such as "the white man's burden, civilizing mission, pan-Slavism . . . and all the other rubbish by which the strong justify their oppression of the weak."[76] This, in turn, gave rise to a defensive nationalism of "nations that were dominated, dismembered, exploited and humiliated."[77] For Trudeau, it was "into the depths of this world-wide nationalist phenomenon that we must delve in examining the sub-sub-species Quebec of the sub-species Canada."[78] Indeed, he said, "however outworn and absurd it may be, the nation-state image spurred the political thinking of the British, and subsequently of Canadians of British origin. . . . Broadly speaking, this meant identifying the Canadian state with themselves to the greatest degree possible."[79] From an economic standpoint, English Canadians had tried in vain to assimilate the French Canadians; they then used their strength in numbers to dominate them. "In social and cultural matters, Anglo-Canadian nationalism has expressed itself simply by disdain. Generation after generation of Anglo-Saxons have lived in Quebec, without getting around to learning three sentences of French."[80]

Trudeau claimed that French Canadians could respond in one of two ways to the idea of an Anglo-Canadian nation-state: they could counter with the idea of a French-Canadian nation-state, or they could reject the concept of nation-state altogether, making Canada a multinational state. The first choice, that of the separatists or *indépendandistes,* was "an emotional and prejudiced choice." Trudeau went on to assert that "Constitutionalism" offered a much better choice. We saw, in Chapter 2, that Trudeau first encountered this notion at Harvard. Over the years, it became the foundation of his political philosophy. He appreciated particularly the fact that it integrated the two fundamental notions characteristic of any civilized society: respect for the individual, and the rule of law. In his 1962 article, he also argued that Constitutionalism was founded on the repudiation of the self-destructive idea of the nation-state "in favour of the more civilized goal of polyethnic pluralism" of the multinational state.[81] Moreover, he said, the struggle for independence was actually waged against "a largely imaginary adversary." Separatists did not realize that because of the threat of American domination "Anglo-Canadian nationalism has never had much of an edge." Whether they liked it or not, English Canadians had "to take cognizance of the French-Canadian nation."[82]

As a result, the strength of English Canadians, he argued, was only due to the weakness of French Canadians, who had marginalized themselves by not taking their rightful place and had consequently contributed little to the destiny of Canada. He deplored the fact that all the energy devoted to "bewailing our misfortunes, denouncing our enemies, and avowing our independence" did not make "one of our workers more skilled, nor a civil servant more efficient, a financier richer, a doctor more advanced, a bishop more learned." He then made the following calculation: "There is probably not one French-Canadian intellectual who has not spent at least four hours a week over the last year discussing separatism. That makes how many thousand times two hundred hours spent flapping our arms?" He then explained the title of his article: "This is what I call *la nouvelle trahison des clercs* [the new treason of the intellectuals]: this self-deluding passion of a large segment of our thinking population for throwing themselves headlong – intellectually and spiritually – into purely escapist pursuits."[83]

In Trudeau's view, separatists claiming to be on the Left were no less reactionary: "Just because their social thinking is to the left, and they are campaigning for secular schools, and they may be active in trade union movements, and they are open-minded culturally, they see their national-ism as the path to progress. What they fail to see is that they have become reactionary politically." Indeed, since they give a political dimension to the idea of nation, "they are surely led to a definition of the common good as a function of an ethnic group, rather than of all the people."[84]

Trudeau ridiculed those who believed Quebec's independence would unleash supernatural powers. They imagine, he said, "that the realization of our nation-state will release a thousand unsuspected ener-gies. . . . In other words, there is supposed to be some sort of creative energy that will bestow genius on people who have none and give courage and learning to a lazy and ignorant nation."[85] That amounted to believing in magic. Fortunately, he added, "the backbone of our people . . . shows more common sense than do our intellectuals and the *bourgeoisie*. The province's major trade unions have come out categori-cally against separatism."[86]

Instead of putting their hopes in the magical virtues of independence, French Canadians should be making better use of what they already have. The Canadian Constitution gives Quebec all the political powers it needs to develop its human and national values. As a case in point he referred to the main thesis of *Why I Am a Separatist*. He wrote: "On pages 98–99 of his book, Mr. Chaput proposes sixteen items of economic reform which could be undertaken by an independent Quebec. Except for the first, which would abolish taxes levied by Ottawa, all these reforms could be undertaken under the present constitution!"[87]

In order for French Canadians to preserve their cultural values, they should, instead of resorting "to the ridiculous and reactionary idea of national sovereignty . . . separate once and for all the concepts of state and of nation, and make Canada a truly pluralistic and polyethnic society. Now in order for this to come about, the different regions within the country must be assured of a wide range of local autonomy." English Canadians also had to do their part; they had to be willing to change their idea of Canada and accept the obvious: "The die is cast in Canada: there are two main ethnic and linguistic groups; each is too strong and too deeply rooted in the past, too firmly bound to a mother-culture, to be able to engulf the other."[88]

Trudeau was brimming over with idealism. He had big plans for his province and concluded his article with a clarion call to excellence: "If Quebec became such a shining example, if to live there were to partake of freedom and progress, if culture enjoyed a place of honour there, if the universities commanded respect and renown from afar, [then] French Canadians would no longer need to battle for bilingualism [and] the ability to speak French would become a status symbol. . . . Even in Ottawa, superior competence on the part of our politicians and civil servants would bring spectacular changes." Of course, he continued, such an undertaking is immensely difficult. It is possible, nevertheless. And it is at least as "inspiring" as separatism.[89]

As expected, this indictment provoked many reactions. For example, Raymond Barbeau, leader of the corporatist Alliance Laurentienne, wrote that Trudeau should have called his article "The Last Betrayal of *Cité libre*"; he called the magazine's attitude "reactionary and, in political terms, twenty years behind the times."[90] In most cases, critics attacked the messenger, not the message. But Hubert Aquin, a RIN member, took a more measured approach in a review article for the May issue of *Liberté*, "*La fatigue culturelle du Canada français.*"[91] He explained that "since Pierre Elliott Trudeau couches his analysis in terms of reason, it is at this level that I will try to engage the dialogue with him."[92]

Aquin argued that Quebec separatism was not the result of national-ism: "In fact, there is no French-Canadian nation any longer; instead, there is a homogenous cultural-linguistic group based on a common lan-guage.... French Canada is multi-ethnic.... What differentiates Canada from French Canada is not that Canada is multi-ethnic whereas French Canada is mono-ethnic, the difference is that Canada is bicultural while French Canada is culturally homogeneous."[93] Aquin went on to say that it was tiresome to see that the minority, which was accused of being a dead weight, was accepting this role "with ever-increasing pain." He continued, this was indeed "a bad role," which entailed psychological consequences such as "self-inflicted punishment, masochism, self-depre-cating thoughts, 'depression,' . . . all of which are sure signs of what anthropologists have called 'cultural fatigue.'"[94] In Aquin's view, this fatigue explained the contradictions and ambiguities in the minds of French Canadians. Their culture "has all the symptoms of extreme fatigue: it seeks both strength and rest, existential intensity and suicide, independence and dependence."[95] He considered this situation tragic, and Quebec could get over it only by becoming independent.

Aquin found fault with Trudeau's dialectics – for example, when he assumed there was "a causal link between war and nationalism. [This, he claimed, was] a flimsy argument minimizing the significance of the phenomenon of war."[96] Trudeau would most likely have agreed with this statement since, as we have seen, he recognized that summarizing "some seven thousand years of history in three paragraphs, is, of course, a little short." Let us note, moreover, that Trudeau was arguing neither that all wars were caused by nationalism, nor that all nationalisms led to war. As for the difference Aquin set out between a bicultural Canada and a linguistically and culturally homogeneous Quebec, we have refuted this perspective – in our view, surprisingly simplistic – on many occa-sions.[97] Moreover, even the most die-hard separatists nowadays would not accept Aquin's description of Quebec and Canada. We will leave it to readers interested in the subject to pursue this debate, in order to return to our own narrative: the evolution of Trudeau's political ideas.

Before moving on, a few words about Hubert Aquin may be of some interest. Two years after writing his rebuttal of Trudeau's article, he went into hiding and endorsed terrorism as a means of achieving Quebec's independence. He was arrested and interned in a psychiatric hospital. He subsequently wrote several notable novels, becoming a major figure in the world of Quebec literature. In 1969, he turned down the Governor General's Award for his book *Trou de mémoire* [Blackout]. His professional and social life was marked by constant conflicts. He became increasingly isolated, managed his financial and personal affairs poorly, and took his own life in 1977. The Université du Québec à Montréal honoured his memory by naming a building after him.

––––––⦿––––––

In "The New Treason of the Intellectuals," Trudeau pointed out that the major unions had come out strongly against separatism. This may come as a surprise today. But when these lines were written in 1962, the unions were staunchly anti-separatist. According to Jacques Rouillard, the renowned Quebec labour historian, "For the FTQ and the other unions, calling for provincial autonomy did not imply supporting Quebec's accession to sovereignty. . . . At every convention from 1963 to 1967, separatism was strongly condemned as being contrary to the interests of workers."[98] A concrete example of this stance is found in the brief the labour unions presented to the Parliamentary Committee on the Constitution set up in 1963 by the Quebec Legislative Assembly. Three unions – the FTQ (Fédération des travailleurs du Québec), the CSN (then known in English as the CNTU or Confederation of National Trade Unions), with Jean Marchand as president, and the UCC (Union of Catholic Farmers) – decided to present a joint submission. They mandated Pierre Trudeau to write it – he was then working at the Université de Montréal's Public Law Research Institute. The fact they chose Trudeau, whose constitutional positions were well known, clearly indicates what position they planned to take. In their study of the FTQ, François Cyr and Rémi Roy note that "in 1966, the anti-separatism and federalism of FTQ leaders reached a climax." They add: "The policy on 'constitutional' problems is best embodied in the joint FTQ-CSN-UCC[*] brief presented to the constitutional committee of the Quebec Legislature in April 1966." The brief "mainly reflects Trudeau's positions on constitutional matters."[99]

Oddly enough, the working document for this brief appeared in 1967 as the first chapter of Trudeau's *Federalism and the French Canadians,*

––––––––––––––––––––

[*] The Union catholique des cultivateurs.

under the title "Quebec and the Constitutional Problem." Without identifying the unions that had commissioned it, Trudeau said he wrote the study
in February, March, and April 1965 "as a working document for some
popular movements." He added, "I have decided to publish it under my
name," and specified that the opinions expressed were his alone.[100] How
can the contradiction between Cyr and Roy's statements and Trudeau's be
explained? Was a brief presented by the unions? Let's shed some light on an
ambiguity that persists to this day.

First, let us note some factual errors in Cyr and Roy's statements.
A brief was presented not in April 1966, but on September 28, 1966,
and not to the Constitutional committee – which no longer existed with
the dissolution of the Legislative Assembly on April 18, prior to the
June elections – but directly to the government of Daniel Johnson Sr. of
the Union Nationale. Let us now move on to the substantive points. When
Trudeau was elected as a federal member of Parliament, on November 8,
1965, separatism was increasingly popular in Quebec, especially with
young people. However, the three workers' federations had not yet embraced this ideology so, at first, they approved Trudeau's draft.

Ironically, it is Trudeau's childhood friend and former Citélibriste,
Pierre Vadeboncoeur, by then a die-hard separatist, who turned things
around. Interpreting Trudeau's document as "a virulent pamphlet against
Quebec's independence,"[101] he attempted to convince a reluctant Marcel
Pepin, then president of the CNTU, to reject Trudeau's views. However,
under the combined pressures of Vadeboncoeur, André L'Heureux, who
became vice-president of the CNTU in 1976, and Jacques-Yvan Morin,
who occupied various ministries when the Parti Québécois came to
power, Pepin eventually gave in. So on September 28, 1966, the three
federations presented a modified version of Trudeau's text, without any
reference to his contribution.

The differences between Trudeau's text and the brief that was finally
submitted bear essentially on the notions of federalism and independence.
The brief insists on the idea that "Canadian federalism must be tested"
and "adapted to reality."[102] For Trudeau, on the other hand, Canadian
federalism needs no testing whatsoever: "it is evolving – radically – and has
been for a hundred years"[103] and is therefore very well adapted to reality.
Moreover, it is particularly well suited to French Canadians' needs since
"in a great number of vital areas, and notably those that concern the

development of particular cultural values, Quebec has full and complete sovereignty under the Canadian constitution."[104] As for independence, Trudeau categorically rejects it and demands that "people who wish to undermine or to destroy the Canadian federal system must define clearly the risks involved."[105] Like Trudeau, the authors of the brief are against Quebec's independence. However, instead of referring to the risks that could "undermine" or "destroy" the Canadian federation, they state that the virtues of independence have not yet been established. They add: "As long as the required studies have not been undertaken and discussed, independence will remain to us a hypothesis insufficient not only to merit adoption, but even to be the basis of worthwhile discussions."[106]

In this subtle way, the independence "hypothesis" infiltrated the workers' movement and gradually won it over. Rouillard writes: "After the conventions of 1967 and particularly of 1969, the FTQ changed its political allegiance. . . . With René Lévesque's creation of the Movement Sovereignty-Association in 1967, the independence project took on an air of respectability."[107] Rouillard adds that in 1970, FTQ president Fernand Daoust said 50 per cent of union members voted for the Parti Québécois. Gradually, the unions completely reversed their political positions. Once strong supporters of federalism, they became unshakable advocates of independence, throwing their weight behind the Yes side in the 1980 and 1995 referendums on sovereignty.

We won't dwell here on the substance of Trudeau's text, which reflects his views of federalism, the Constitution, and social justice. One passage, however, is worth noting: "Our existing constitution, skillfully exploited, modified if need be (but in such a way that the division of power between the two levels of government is the same in all provinces), would create a country in which Quebec may call upon nine allies to protect provincial autonomy, and thus struggle on a level playing field against the federal government in order to nurture the development of French culture in North America."[108] This is a clear expression of a central dimension of Trudeau's conception of Canadian federalism: Quebec had no reason to demand a "special status"; it already had the means to protect its interests. In its fight against the central government, it could "protect provincial autonomy" by forming alliances with some or all of the other nine provinces. Moreover, with regard to language, it wasn't just Quebec, but French Canadians, more generally, who had to partake in the struggle to ensure the equality of

French and English. Trudeau provided examples to illustrate what he meant by linguistic equality: "At the federal level, the two languages must have absolute equality. . . . Any text or ruling is invalid if English and French texts are not published side by side. . . . In the civil service and the armed forces, the two languages must be on a basis of absolute equality."[109] The least we can say is that Trudeau was persistent in the pursuit of his ideals.

This brief, published as a book chapter, shot us ahead to 1967. Many things happened before 1967. So let us go back to 1962, when Trudeau wrote "The New Treason of the Intellectuals." In the early 1960s, despite the rise of neo-nationalism, Trudeau was in general pleased by the evolution of Quebec society. He had fought hard for democracy – we have only to remember his mantra "Democracy First!" – and found reason to believe democracy had finally reached Quebec. This optimism sometimes led him to hasty judgments.

In "Note sur la conjoncture politique" [Note on the Political Situation], he declared right at the start: "The federal elections of 1958 and 1962, and the provincial election of 1960, strike me as harbingers of the first turning-point in our political mentality in two centuries. I now believe we have witnessed the birth of democracy in Quebec and heard its first babblings in these elections."[110] He then set out to show how each of these elections indicated French Canada's growing maturity with regard to democracy.

First, he examined the 1958 federal election, which had handed John Diefenbaker's Conservatives a landslide unsurpassed to this day. He wrote: "On March 31, 1958, for the first time since 1891, Quebec did not send a majority of Liberal MPs to Ottawa." He interpreted this dramatic change as an indication that French Canadians no longer voted along nationalist lines. He wrote: "In March 1958, the electorate felt that by voting Conservative they could finally get rid of MPs so secure in their jobs they had become pretentious, tyrannical, backward and incompetent. . . . Quebec had finally learned the first premise of any democratic action: when a government claims to be irreplaceable, that is a sure sign it must be replaced."[111]

In the provincial elections of 1960, Quebeckers demonstrated they had learned a second lesson: "By driving the wretched Union Nationale from power, they showed once again they no longer intended to respect traditional authorities." But there was more. By voting for a party with a forward-looking program rather than one frozen in the past, Quebec indicated it had learned the second premise of any democratic action: "Elections are not just a matter of substituting one elite for another: They are about substituting one political ideology . . . for another."[112]

His final proof: "On June 18, 1962, Quebec completed its primer in Democracy." In this federal election Diefenbaker's Conservatives were returned to power, but as a minority government (winning 116 seats out of 265 against ninety-nine for the Liberals). A key factor in this outcome was the staggering performance of the Social Credit Party in Quebec, where it won twenty-six seats. (Surprisingly, this party – originally from Western Canada – got only four seats outside Quebec.) Trudeau interpreted these results as follows: "By giving a quarter of its votes and one third of its seats to Social Credit, Quebec – for the first time in its history – proved it was possible for a third party to rise, in opposition to the traditional parties."[113] Trudeau took these three election outcomes as proof Quebec had acquired the basics of the democratic process.

How could a skilled analyst like Trudeau fail to notice many basic facts that could have been interpreted differently, leading to an assessment in total contradiction to his own? Gordon O. Rothney, a professor at Memorial University of Newfoundland who knew Quebec well, took on the challenge and wrote Trudeau a personal three-page letter, dated September 18, 1962. His analysis of each of these elections led him to challenge Trudeau's hypothesis.[114] This is Rothney's interpretation: "Why did Quebec return fifty Progressive Conservatives out of seventy-five members of parliament in 1958? Because of French nationalism. . . . The Union Nationale organization was thrown behind Mr. Diefenbaker. . . . Quebec in 1958 really voted, not Progressive Conservative, but Union Nationale." As for the Liberals' success in 1960, Rothney argued that with Duplessis and Sauvé now dead, "the way was completely open to the Liberal Party to become the party of provincial autonomy and nationalism in Quebec." As for Social Credit's extraordinary gains in 1962, Rothney continued, they were simply because "Réal Caouette was 'un des nôtres' (one of us). Diefenbaker, Pearson, and Douglas had no such leaders in French Canada. . . . My conclusion, then, is not that there has been a new birth of democracy in French Canada, but that Quebec still votes, as always, for reasons of sentimental linguistic nationalism."

Professor Rothney's reputation was well known. That's why Trudeau paid close attention to his letter, making copious annotations in the margins. He replied in his somewhat awkward English: "It is an honour to receive a long and thoughtfilled letter from one whose writings I had often times had [sic] occasion to admire in the past." Trudeau realized Rothney had pinpointed some weaknesses in his argument. He tried nonetheless to defend his position, at least in part. He started by criticizing what he believed were some exaggerations in Rothney's analysis but eventually admitted: "There remains much to be said for your interpretation, and I agree . . . with many of the things you wrote in your letter. As you may know, your explanation of Quebec's behaviour in terms of political nationalism is not at all one I would repudiate, *au contraire*." Thanks to Rothney's critique, Trudeau realized his own optimism had coloured his interpretation of the facts.

As the November 14, 1962, elections were approaching, Trudeau examined the political landscape. He thought the Liberal Party had done a relatively good job managing the province and deserved to be re-elected. The problem was on the Left. Given the narrow victory of the Liberals in 1960, he feared the New Party (NDP) would split the progressive vote and help return the Union Nationale to office. In "L'homme de gauche et les élections provinciales" [Leftists and the Provincial Elections], published by *Cité libre* shortly before the elections, he accused the NDP of being "so concerned about being the one and only left-wing party, that they forgot the need to make this Left a reality, and to build it up."[115] He added: "What bothers me particularly is that the NDP takes its own exclusive stand for revolutionary purity, whereas it is simply sheer ignorance." Moreover, he continued, the socialists' strategy clearly "demonstrated their utter incompetence in practical terms. And what's worse, they demonstrated it *once again*."[116] According to him, these "perfect little leftists" had already failed twice to create a leftist movement, first by not agreeing to join the Rassemblement, and second by cold-shouldering the Union of Democratic Forces.

In the same article, Trudeau enthusiastically supported the Liberal Party and expressed great admiration for René Lévesque. The major issue in the November 14, 1962, elections was the nationalization of electricity, a policy vigorously defended by René Lévesque as minister of natural resources. Although Trudeau did not agree with this most important measure of the Liberal platform, he couldn't fathom how a single democrat could consider voting for any party other than the Liberals. In his view, there was no justification for the nationalization of electricity "either economically or politically. . . . Ultimately, if we need to nationalize electricity, it is mainly for an entirely different reason: for thirty years, the Right as much as the Left has seen in this policy (wrongly or rightly) a symbol of our political virility." Trudeau did not think either that "this party had very good future prospects." So why vote Liberal?

There were three reasons. The first was to prevent an alliance of Social Credit and the Union Nationale from taking power. The second was that the Liberal government had done more in two and a half years than "the previous government in sixteen." The third was that "even though it had its share of cowards and lackeys," the Liberal Party was "open enough to have appointed a leftist minister in 1960 . . . [and] progressive enough to put its survival on the line by focusing on the very policy promoted by this same minister."[117] Was Trudeau really praising Lévesque? Some may be surprised to learn there was a time when Pierre Trudeau and René Lévesque were allies and held each other in mutual esteem. Yet they did. Trudeau's article reveals a great admiration of Lévesque. It may even be that Lévesque's important stature within the Liberal government was one of Trudeau's main reasons for backing this party. In fact, Lévesque often sought out Trudeau's advice. For example, in early 1960, he solicited Trudeau's advice on the issue of natural resources.[118] In 1962, he asked him to comment on the electricity nationalization policy.[119]

Gradually, however, their political views diverged. In the June 5, 1966, elections, the Liberal Party got only fifty seats. The Union Nationale returned to power with fifty-six seats. (The distribution of seats was markedly different from the popular vote: the Liberal Party got 47.3 per cent of the vote, against just 40.8 per cent for the Union Nationale. That the Liberals should lose while garnering 6 per cent more of the popular vote than the Union Nationale was due to Quebec's peculiar electoral map and the disproportionate weight given to rural voters.) Once the Liberal Party was back on the Opposition benches, it was forced to reconsider its entire program, including Quebec's place within Canada.

The October 1967 Liberal Party congress witnessed a confrontation between two mutually exclusive visions for Quebec. The first one called for recognition of Quebec's "special status" within the Canadian federation and was supported by a majority of delegates. Ever since then, the Quebec Liberal Party has consistently sought a "special status" or some other form of recognition of the Quebec people. At one time it was as a "distinct society," now it is as a "nation." René Lévesque articulated the other vision, of a sovereign Quebec in economic association with the rest of Canada. When his proposal was voted down, he resigned from the party and the following month founded the Mouvement Souveraineté Association (MSA), which became the Parti Québécois in October 1968.

René Lévesque's MSA proved a virtual magnet, attracting left-wing, right-wing, and "neutral" separatists. By that time, Trudeau was already in Ottawa, working hard to improve federalism and maintain Canadian unity. At this juncture, the former brothers in arms had become sworn enemies locked in an epic struggle that eventually culminated in the May 1980 referendum and the April 1982 repatriation of the Constitution. Yet, in spite of their diametrically opposed visions of Canada, they were both supported and admired by francophone Quebeckers.

———◦———

In 1962, when Trudeau and Lévesque were still friends and allies, neo-nationalism was making significant gains. Even the "federalist" Jean Lesage capitalized on the catchy slogan *"Maîtres chez nous"* (Masters in our own house) during the 1962 election campaign. Separatist movements were multiplying and diversifying. In February 1963, the Front de libération du Québec (FLQ) was born. This movement advocated and practised political terrorism, a hitherto unknown phenomenon in Canada. They set off bombs in barracks, mailboxes, foreign consulates, monuments, and stores* (over two hundred bombs went off between 1963 and 1970), resulting in several deaths and dozens of injuries. When the first victim was killed on April 21, 1963, a horror-stricken André Laurendeau wrote: "With this fireball of hatred, the FLQ has resorted to

---

* On February 16, 1965, the FLQ joined the Black Liberation Front in trying to plant a bomb at the base of the Statue of Liberty. FLQ member Michèle Duclos was arrested in New York City with sticks of dynamite in her car.

the ultimate crime."[120] Twenty-three suspected terrorists were arrested. "They were young, mostly in their twenties," Léon Dion wrote, "and most were RIN members."[121] They got widespread public support, and many people regarded them as "political prisoners." The FLQ would later bring on the October Crisis of 1970, kidnapping the British diplomat James Cross and the Quebec minister of labour, Pierre Laporte, and murdering the latter.[122]

A few events marking the rise of separatism are noteworthy. The RIN was created in September 1960; Marcel Chaput's *Pourquoi je suis séparatiste* made a sensation in 1961; the FLQ was set up in February 1963. October 1963 marked the birth of the review *Parti pris,* which rejected the Quiet Revolution and liberal democracy, while advocating a "real" revolution. But "how could this be achieved?" asked Pierre Maheu, founder of the review. His answer: "Our task is clear: we should spread word of the revolution, call for it unceasingly, say, and write things that are not quite true now, so they become true some day."[123] Questionable ethics, to say the least.

In 1963, the issue of Quebec separatism crossed the Atlantic. On October 9, the French daily *Le Monde* published an article by D'Allemagne, one of the leading lights of the FLQ.[124] On October 11, Claude Julien, the paper's foreign news editor, with some urgency called on his friend Trudeau to send him a rebuttal. "I am sure," he wrote, "that you will readily agree to write this piece, in order to explain to our French readers that the problems are probably less straightforward than some people seem to believe."[125]

Julien had no doubt Trudeau would send the article. After all, *Le Monde* was not any old newspaper. It was – and still is – read by most French intellectuals and has an international reputation. Most people would have been honoured to be asked for an article and would have rushed to write it. But not Trudeau. On October 16, he replied:

> I still think nationalism is harmful, and I maintain that the exaggerated importance given to everything "national" has been a major cause of all kinds of degeneration in French Canada. For this reason, I want to avoid whenever possible entering sterile discussions on the subject. I have said once or twice what I thought of Quebec nationalism, in *Cité libre* and *La Grève de l'amiante.* Enough already.

Would you be willing, for your part, to get involved constantly in the most basic debates? It seems to me this would amount to a waste of time, and to think nothing new.

We don't know whether Claude Julien fell off his chair when reading Trudeau's letter but we do know by the sarcastic tone of his reply that he was quite angry:

> I have no idea how many Le Monde readers saw the two articles you mention. But surely you won't be surprised to learn that they were no more than a handful. That's why I asked you to write an article responding to D'Allemagne for our very sizeable readership. Turn the offer down if you like, but I don't think there is anything sterile in all this, to use your own word.
>
> I am more than willing to write for you an article for Canadian readers on problems I have often written about for readers in France.[126]

Trudeau realized he had unwittingly offended his friend, and he hastened to apologize, assuring Julien how much he respected Le Monde. His answer revealed why he was so irritable: "I must have struck you as very foolish. And I really was, by giving you the impression I was snapping at you, rather than at Quebec separatists. . . . It would clearly be hard to demonstrate that Claude Julien or Le Monde are responsible for the revival in Quebec of the most dangerous kind of political twaddle."[127]

Trudeau thought that by giving space to the separatists, Le Monde was helping their cause, but he felt frustrated because he couldn't prove it. Moreover, he did not want to get involved in "sterile discussions" that would help spread their ideology. He may have also turned down the opportunity because his university duties took a lot of time and energy and, as he wrote in "The New Treason of the Intellectuals," he was appalled to see intellectuals going round in circles discussing the same topic, over and over again.

How did Cité libre react to this rising tide of separatism? Events actually plunged the magazine into a major crisis. Some Citélibristes, like Gérard

Pelletier and Albert and Raymond Breton, saw separatism as a passing phenomenon but one the magazine could not ignore. As we have seen, *Cité libre* brought out a special issue on separatism in 1962, in which Trudeau denounced "The New Treason of the Intellectuals." By way of reply, many of the magazine's opponents simply wrote off Citélibristes as "old men" incapable of adapting to modern ideas. But these "old men" resolutely took part in public debates and had evidently lost none of their punch.

In November 1963, for example, students at the Université de Montréal organized a debate between, on one side, two "old men" (Gérard Pelletier and Pierre Trudeau) and, on the other side, André D'Allemagne and Pierre Bourgault (representing "youth"). Unsurprisingly, the November 26, 1963, edition of *Le Quartier Latin* reported the debate as the "clash of two generations." The article was less about the arguments developed by each side than about the author's own impressions: "Overall, the federalists struck me as marked by fatalism and pessimism stemming from their experience with the old regime.... Can we blame the *indépendantistes* for being confident about the future?"[128] In other words, the article cast the debate as a struggle between the pessimism of the older generation and the optimism of young people.

Another article appearing in the November 21 issue of *Le Quartier Latin* offered a completely different perspective. The author rightly noted that "it was a foregone conclusion the crowd supported the separatist thesis ... which was to D'Allemagne and Bourgault's advantage," yet, paradoxically, the federalists won the debate. This obviously threw the author into a state of confusion: as hard as he tried he still couldn't understand why the federalists had won.[129]

As *Cité libre* editors, Trudeau and Pelletier realized that their supposedly "advanced" age – they were, after all, in their forties! – made them an easy target. Moreover, they had been at the helm of the magazine for thirteen years now. It was time to pass on the torch to the next generation, so they resigned as editors, formally agreeing not to comment "on the orientations of the magazine, to enable the new team ... 'to get into the swing of things.'"[130]

With the January 1964 issue, two new managing editors – Jean Pellerin and Pierre Vallières – were now in charge and were soon joined by new contributors. This was also the first of three issues taken over by the separatist-revolutionary Left. Several of the new contributors later made a name for themselves as leading *indépendantistes*: the writer Jacques Ferron; the poet and future Parti Québécois minister Gérald Godin; and the future FLQ member and Marxist-Leninist, Charles Gagnon, who became the comrade-in-arms of Pierre Vallières. Yes, the same Vallières who replaced Trudeau and Pelletier as co-editor of *Cité libre.*

When he joined *Cité libre,* Pierre Vallières seemed at first to subscribe to "personalism," but when he became co-editor he was to be found defending extreme left-wing ideas. He asserted that "the 'Quiet Revolution' was the tool of budding capitalists, businessmen and merchants who would soon be, and may already have started to be, the first to exploit us in the name of tradition." He included in this group "liberals and conservatives just as much as separatists." He even accused the RIN of harbouring "a so-called-progressive, but in fact reactionary, mentality."[131] He was adamant: there was "only one way to be creative, namely by being revolutionary."[132]

Vallières became one of the FLQ's leaders. In 1966, he was charged with participating on May 5 in a bomb attack that killed one woman and wounded three other people. His 1968 best-seller *Nègres Blancs d'Amérique* [White Niggers of America],[133] written while he was in prison, compared the situation of French Canadians to that of American Blacks and advocated armed struggle "to liberate Quebec." However, in *L'urgence de choisir*, published in 1971 by Éditions Parti Pris, Vallières severed his ties with the FLQ and asked that "an end be put to all forms of FLQ activities, be they in actions or words." According to the biographical notes provided by his publisher, VLB, Vallières was "a very marginal individual [living] his rebellion and spirituality with painful intensity." He switched causes and perspectives several times, dying in 1998 a "tormented man."[134]

The original editorial team must have been stunned by the magazine's about-face. They most likely asked themselves in horror how on earth *Cité libre* had repositioned itself as a nationalist, separatist, revolutionary, and extreme left-wing magazine. They rushed to straighten things out. In "Pour clore un incident" [Putting an End to an Incident], Pelletier explained the new team had embarked on a path diametrically opposed to the one *Cité libre* had consistently followed. The magazine, he wrote, had "always refused to focus on ethnicity, to consider the nation as the primary value of its philosophy and its activities. . . . *Cité libre* has always fought and is still fighting all totalitarian tendencies in politics. The magazine believes in democracy and personal freedom."[135]

Interestingly, Pierre Vadeboncoeur, a member of the old guard, wrote in the February issue of 1964: "It is wrong to undermine the current nationalist movement. . . . On the contrary, we should understand this revolution, and shed light on what it will become. We shouldn't turn our backs on it."[136] Vadeboncoeur, who had probably written the fiercest anti-nationalist articles in *Cité libre,* couldn't resist the call of neo-nationalism. He became the only member of the original editorial team to move over to *Parti pris,* which he did with enthusiasm.

In April 1964, the founding team regained control of *Cité libre,* while the young dissident faction headed over to *Parti pris,* with Pierre Vadeboncoeur in tow. Gérard Pelletier devoted a six-page article titled "*Parti pris,* ou la grande illusion" to tear apart the new review. It was evident, he wrote, that *Parti pris* had thrown out Christian dogma, replacing it by political dogma, and this new religion was "more dangerous than the one before."[137]

In the May 1964 issue, two further articles rebutted the separatists: the first by a group of intellectuals including Trudeau, and the second by Trudeau alone. The first, entitled "Manifeste pour une politique fonctionnelle," was jointly signed by Albert Breton, Raymond Breton, Claude Bruneau (a lawyer), Yvon Gauthier (a doctor), Marc Lalonde (a lawyer who later served as minister of several departments in the Trudeau government), Maurice Pinard (a sociologist and anthropologist), and Pierre Elliott Trudeau.[138] Interestingly, this article was the only one to be published simultaneously in French and English. The English translation appeared in the Toronto review *Canadian Forum,* under the title "An Appeal for Realism in Politics." It had a huge impact in both languages. The English version specified "This is not a 'French Canadian Manifesto' but a 'Canadian Manifesto.'" This "Committee for Political Realism" (made up of the authors of the first article) brought out two further important articles in *Cité libre.* Once Trudeau became prime minister, he called on the talents and intellectual rigour of these old comrades-in-arms, particularly on Marc Lalonde and Albert Breton.

The authors stated their position clearly: "We declare our disagreement with most of the panaceas in vogue at present among our politicians. Canada, today, is a country in search of a purpose. Emphasis on regional interests and the absence of leadership from the central government could lead to the utter disintegration of the Federal state. In the Province of Quebec, the 'Quiet Revolution' – while it has a number of achievements to its credit – has, nonetheless, been limited oftentimes to a mere waving of symbols, and, in some areas, has come to a complete halt, already exhausted. The reform movement appears compromised, and is in danger of deviating badly."[139] They stated their faith in the person and called for policies based on pragmatic and human principles.

Canada, they continued, was facing real problems that called for urgent solutions. For example, they cited the increase in unemployment between 1957 and 1964, caused by a protectionist policy that discouraged foreign investment; the unacceptable distribution of wealth among social groups and Canada's different regions; the poor administration of justice; the lack of health insurance, although hospital insurance was a step in the right direction; the inappropriate division of fiscal powers between the provinces and the central government, with regard to their constitutional responsibilities. Internationally, the authors believed "we must gradually but resolutely move towards free trade."[140]

The Committee for Political Realism rejected the concept of the nation-state as obsolete. It also held that "to use nationalism as a yardstick for deciding policies and priorities is both sterile and retrograde."[141] This criticism was addressed to English-Canadian nationalists just as much as to Quebeckers brandishing the slogan *"Maîtres chez nous."*[142] The authors argued that "nationalistic policies in Canada or in Quebec are by and large advantageous to the bourgeoisie; they run counter to the interests of the majority of the population, more particularly of the economically disadvantaged."[143] They wrote: "The nationalist alienation manifests itself today through the exaggerated importance given by our elite to constitutional problems." Echoing the arguments Trudeau had already developed elsewhere, they argued that "the obstacles to economic progress, to full employment, to an equitable welfare scheme, or even to the development of French culture in Canada, are not principally the result of the Canadian Constitution. . . . The effort devoted at the present to debating such a reform takes up a great deal of energy that could be profitably spent in solving much more urgent and more fundamental problems in our society."[144]

The authors rejected separatism categorically: "We refuse to let ourselves be locked into a constitutional frame smaller than Canada. To take it apart would be to run away from the real and important tasks that lie ahead. . . . The challenge is for a number of ethnic groups to live together. It is a modern challenge, meaningful and indicative of what can be expected from man."[145] They advocated instead political realism, based on reason, intellectual rigour, the search for truth, and a sense of responsibility: "The challenge we have to face consists in defining and implementing a policy made up of precise objectives, practicable and based on the universal attributes of man. . . . Democratic rule must be maintained at all costs. It is a matter on which we will not compromise."[146] The authors then concluded by making public their readiness to work for the common good: "It is subject to these conditions that we wish to work for the good of the community."[147]

In the same May 1964 issue, Trudeau signed alone another article in which he tore into leftist separatists claiming to be revolutionaries. In "Separatist Counter-Revolutionaries," he was no doubt addressing those *Cité libre* contributors who had recently gone over to *Parti pris,* but also what he called the entire "nationalist brood." He reminded them that both revolutions and counter-revolutions are characterized by profound change. What distinguishes the two is the central place given or denied to respect for the person and democracy. He explained: "True, freedom is often less effective than authority as the basis of short-term organization. That is why . . . some men came along, claiming exclusive possession of political truth. . . . As soon as they could, . . . they abolished the opposition and installed the one-party system. . . . They murdered liberty and enthroned themselves as dictators. . . . These dictators were called Hitler and Mussolini. There were others called Stalin, Franco, and Salazar. It cannot be denied that they all claimed to be serving the destiny of their respective national communities. . . . But who would call the whole of their work revolutionary? . . . They abolished personal freedom, or at least prevented it from growing; that is why history classes them as counter-revolutionaries."[148]

A real revolution in Quebec, he continued, would have seen the triumph of the inalienable rights of human beings, protecting them against capital, against the nation, against tradition, against the Church, and even against the state.[149] In 1960, such a revolution could have come about in Quebec, but this unique opportunity had been missed: "The dogmatism of Church and State, of tradition, of the nation, had been defeated. . . . In 1960, everything was becoming possible in Quebec, even revolution. . . . A whole generation was free at last to apply all its creative energies to bringing their backward province up to date. Only it required boldness, intelligence and work. Alas, freedom proved to be too heady a drink to pour for the French-Canadian youth of 1960. Almost at the first sip it went at top speed in search of . . . some new dogmatism."[150] Freedom of the person, which is the ultimate goal of social organization, was totally forgotten: "When personal freedom exists, it would be *inconceivable that a revolutionary should destroy it* in the name of some collective ideology. . . . That is why in Quebec today you have to speak of separatist counter-revolution."[151]

Trudeau was quite troubled by the attitude of many students: "Today, scarcely a week passes without a handful of separatist students coming to tell me they are against democracy and for a single-party system; for a certain totalitarianism and against the freedom of the individual."[152] This led him to write, with biting irony: "The truth is that the separatist counter-revolution is the work of a powerless *petit-bourgeois* minority afraid of being left behind by the twentieth-century revolution. Rather than carving themselves out a place in it by ability, they want to make the whole tribe return to the wigwams by declaring its independence. . . . Inside the tribe the counter-revolutionaries will be kings and sorcerers."[153] And Trudeau concluded, with a thundering blast: "Separatism a revolution? A counter-revolution; the national-socialist counter-revolution."[154]

Although Trudeau was vehemently opposed to separatist ideology and urged French Canadians to stop whining and take charge of their own affairs, he nonetheless believed many of their grievances were legitimate. In particular, he denounced the limited place French Canadians held in the federal civil service in Ottawa and the lack of bilingualism in federal institutions. Reforms were definitely needed. His friend André Laurendeau thought along the same lines. Although a nationalist, he wrote, "Confederation is better than separation, provided it is completely renewed."[155] To this end, Laurendeau suggested in the January 20, 1962, edition of *Le Devoir* that a commission of inquiry on bilingualism be set up "to overcome the overwhelming inferiority of French Canadians in the federal government."

Let us describe the kind of bilingualism Laurendeau had in mind: "I am speaking of the country, its political institutions, not of each inhabitant." How could this bilingualism be achieved? Laurendeau proposed three measures he considered "feasible": first, "recognize French as the official language in all provincial legislatures"; second, "use both languages in all official documents"; and third, "complete the establishment of a French radio network so that people can listen to the state radio in French, almost everywhere in Canada."[156] Laurendeau knew these measures would not satisfy the separatists, but he was sure they would be welcomed by the majority of French Canadians. These three reforms would pave the way for the *real* reforms, which "would require a tremendous amount of good will."[157]

Laurendeau began to dream about the nature of these "real reforms": "I am thinking, for example, of the gradual recognition of French as a working language in the federal civil service . . . and in the provinces where the French-Canadian minority is large enough. In another vein, I am thinking of the progressive and effective recognition of the right of French Canadians to be educated in their language, wherever possible, in public schools."[158] But these reforms would require the assent of eleven governments (ten provinces and the central government). He wondered, pessimistically: "Doesn't this amount to admitting at the outset that these [reforms] are completely unrealistic? . . . Is there, in English Canada, a sufficient number of enlightened individuals willing to take a closer look at this 'utopia'?"[159] Young Canadians nowadays may smile in reading these lines, since most of Laurendeau's "utopia" has long been an everyday reality. They may not realize, however, how hard it was to achieve, or that it was Trudeau who launched the "real reforms" Laurendeau could only dream about.

Laurendeau proposed establishing a royal commission on bilingualism in 1962, but the Conservative prime minister, John Diefenbaker, a staunch defender of a Canada loyal to the British "mother country," showed little interest in the idea. In contrast, Lester B. Pearson, who led the Liberals to victory in the April 8, 1963, elections, was quite concerned by the rise of separatism. He adopted Laurendeau's suggestion and established the Royal Commission on Bilingualism and Biculturalism on July 19, 1963. The commission was jointly chaired by a francophone, André Laurendeau himself, and an anglophone, Davidson Dunton, president of Carleton University and former president of the Canadian Broadcasting Corporation.

It is important to note the inclusion of the word "biculturalism" in the official name of the commission. According to Léon Dion, who served as "special adviser" to the commissioners, two competing visions clashed within the commission from the start, one focused on the community and the other on the person. In *La révolution déroutée*, he explained that, as a long-standing nationalist, Laurendeau defended the first of these visions and advocated recourse to "political measures to protect the French culture in Quebec. [He insisted on] the need to give Quebec a very special constitutional status."[160] Many other commissioners, including Jean-Louis Gagnon and Frank Scott, defended the second vision focusing on the primacy of the individual, which they insisted was the cornerstone of liberal democracy.

The commission undertook extensive research, held hearings across the country, and provoked emotionally charged reactions for and against bilingualism, for and against biculturalism. On February 1, 1965, it issued a preliminary report (generally referred to as the Blue Pages). In December that year, the remaining members of the Committee for Political Realism published an analysis of this report in *Cité libre*.[161] By that time, Trudeau was no longer a committee member. He had been elected MP for Mount Royal but had yet to take up his seat. In "Bizarre Algebra," Albert Breton, Claude Bruneau, Yvon Gauthier, Marc Lalonde, and Maurice Pinard sharply criticized the report. They depicted the commission's research methods as "naïve and confused."[162] They questioned "the main thrust of the mandate, which calls for the equality of Canada's two peoples." What did the commission mean by that? "The idea of equality between individuals is well established in political thought," they wrote, but what was the equality of two peoples, of two cultures? How could this kind of equality be legally implemented? "It is hard to see how the penal code, for example, could be adjusted to meaningfully take into account the involvement of an accused person in one of the two cultures. . . . What would be the relative weight of a federal official mastering Shakespeare, compared to another official who only knew Feydeau and Claude-Henri Grignon?"*[163] The Committee for Political Realism also noted that the report contained "no idea which had not already been repeated ad nauseam in nationalist circles and writings," well before the separatist crisis.[164]

The *Final Report* of the Royal Commission on Bilingualism and Biculturalism ran to six volumes, but only the first, dealing with official languages, had any political effect. Léon Dion wrote: "The Official Languages Act, adopted [by the Trudeau government] on July 9, 1969, grew out of the Commission's first volume. The federal government and administration, federal courts and Crown corporations in the capital and all provinces became officially bilingual." And he added, admiringly: "This represented a huge gain for the French language."[165] Dion went on to say that Prime Minister Trudeau "eagerly embraced the recommendations about bilingualism that fell under federal jurisdiction, but he coolly dismissed the notion of biculturalism."[166]

Why did Trudeau adopt the recommendations about bilingualism but not biculturalism? His opponents have put forward various arguments, such as his supposed contempt for French-Canadian culture or his supposed desire to treat the French-Canadian community as an ethnic group, one among many others in Canada. The answer lies elsewhere. One can find it, at least in part, in the article of the Committee for Political Realism: whereas the equality of languages could be translated into legal terms, the equality of cultures raised insurmountable legal problems. Moreover, how could it be claimed there were only two cultures in Canada? Furthermore, did all French Canadians share exactly the same culture? And what about the English-speaking Canadians? Most importantly, we know that Trudeau passionately defended the primacy of the individual, as did Maritain, Berdyaev, Frank Scott, and his professors at Harvard, the LSE, and even Sciences Po, to name a few.

---

* Georges Feydeau (1862–1921) was a French author famous for his light comedies. Claude-Henri Grignon (1894–1976) was known above all for his novel *Un homme et son péché,* published in 1936, which was adapted as a long-running radio series from 1939 to 1952, and then as a hugely popular television series from 1956 to 1970, *Les Belles Histoires des Pays-d'en-Haut.* *Un homme et son péché* was eventually translated into English as *The Woman and the Miser* (1978). Despite his popularity, Grignon is not generally considered a "great" French-Canadian author.

We noted above that when "Bizarre Algebra" was published, Trudeau was actively engaged in politics – *and* at the federal level. His decision to enter the fray has never ceased to intrigue political analysts, who have often interpreted it as opportunism. Even Trudeau and Pelletier's close associates at *Cité libre* expressed mixed feelings about their plunge into federal politics. In the October 1965 article "Marchand, Pelletier, Trudeau et le 8 novembre," the editorial team – namely Jean Pellerin (editor), Maurice Blain, Jacques Tremblay, and Charles Taylor – wrote that with this decision, the two men "seem to have broken with convictions developed during fifteen years of collective collaboration, and to have turned their backs on their former ideas and associates."[167] The authors tried somehow to explain this about-face: Trudeau, Marchand, and Pelletier had a sense of urgency; they felt that Canada was in danger; they had therefore decided to defend federalism against the separatist threat.

Of course, the editorial team wrote, "English Canada" would find their presence in Ottawa reassuring, but they worried that their departure could weaken Quebec. With all three running under the Liberal banner, they feared "a further splintering of the Left in Quebec."[168] They wanted to express their disappointment. So they announced publicly: "The editors of *Cité libre* wish to make clear they are in no way bound by the decision of three of their members." They nonetheless wished their former comrades-in-arms good luck.

If even their close associates could be so uncomfortable with the Liberal candidacies of Marchand, Pelletier, and Trudeau, it's not surprising that their opponents reacted even more strongly. To cite a single example: Trudeau received a newspaper clipping, with an anonymous annotation in the margin: "Pierre Laval* was convicted of national indignity and sent before the firing squad for much less than that!"[169]

Now that the dust has settled, how can this departure for Ottawa be explained more objectively?

---

* Pierre Laval (1883–1945) was second in command in Pétain's Vichy Regime. A staunch admirer of Nazi Germany, he enthusiastically collaborated with the Germans. Sentenced to death for "high treason," he faced the firing squad on October 15, 1945.

After gaining power in 1963, Pearson's minority government was confronted by the spectacular rise of separatism. This created a climate of anxiety, which the Royal Commission on Bilingualism and Biculturalism hearings did nothing to dispel. On the contrary. So Pearson urgently sought to strengthen the Quebec wing of the Liberal Party by recruiting well-known "federalist" figures, and Jean Marchand seemed the ideal candidate. On July, 2, 1960, just days after the Quebec Liberal victory, Marchand, then Secretary General of the CTCC, publicly declared that his union would work with the government "to implement its program to the extent that it coincides with [their] own."[170] Although Marchand worked passionately within the labour movement, he was by conviction a liberal, in the philosophical sense. He indicated as much in an article in the December 1960 issue of Cité libre, where he stated: "Since in political terms the common good cannot be identified with the interests of a specific social class . . . I don't see how a workers' party could be morally justified."[171]

In the same article, Marchand praised the Liberal Party of Canada. And on returning from the "Symposium on National Problems" organized by the party in Kingston, he said that what he had heard gave him "hope for a revival in Canadian politics." This helps explain why the struggling Liberal Party was particularly interested in recruiting Marchand, and why the latter, who was troubled by the rise of Quebec separatism, judged the time ripe for the switch to Ottawa. But he set his conditions: he refused to go without Gérard Pelletier and Pierre Trudeau.

The Liberal Party was willing to accept Pelletier, but Pelletier had never shown any particular interest in active politics, and even less at the federal level. However, since he had just been fired from La Presse, Marchand's offer was tempting.

Trudeau's case was more complex. In April 1963, he had published "Pearson ou l'abdication de l'esprit" [Pearson or the Abdication of the Mind] in Cité libre. The article's title said it all. An epigraph signed P. Vadeboncoeur referred to Lester B. Pearson as "the unfrocked advocate of peace." This was a scathing criticism of the Liberal leader, who had won the Nobel Peace Prize in 1957. Trudeau accused him of flip-flopping on the acquisition of nuclear weapons by Canada. He began by reminding his readers that Pearson had categorically stated since 1961 that if the Liberals regained power, they would never equip Canada with nuclear warheads. Trudeau continued: "The Leader of the Opposition took the trouble, on November 14, 1962, to reaffirm his unshakable faith in his party's policy, stating firmly: 'I have always maintained that . . . Canadians should not accept nuclear weapons either under national control or jointly with the United States.'"

Now suddenly, wrote Trudeau, on January 12, 1963, Pearson declared before the Liberal Association of York-Scarborough that the Canadian government "should stop shirking its responsibilities and agree to equip its strategic weapons with defensive nuclear warheads that cannot be used effectively without them. . . . As a Canadian I am ashamed when we make commitments and then refuse to fulfill them."[172] Trudeau had trouble reining in his indignation: "So, the same man who had denounced NORAD commitments and refused to be bound by them, . . . the man who repeated this position on November 14, 1962 . . . felt bound less than two months later by an unexpected sense of honour."[173]

Trudeau explained this about-face. The Pentagon, who wanted to get rid of the Diefenbaker government – which was opposed to American policy – offered to help Pearson beat the Conservatives, provided that he "betrayed the party program, as well as his own long standing ideal."[174] Since opinion polls showed that "a pro-nuclear policy would not bother a majority of voters unduly," Pearson yielded to temptation. "Power was offered to Mr. Pearson, who had nothing to lose, save his honour. He lost it, and so did the rest of the party."[175] Trudeau concluded: "In the elections of April 8, I plan to vote NDP."[176] He campaigned for his friend Charles Taylor, then running for this party in the riding of Mount Royal. Taylor was defeated, but ran in the same riding in the 1965 elections.

No wonder Pearson was not keen on recruiting Trudeau! So why did the Liberals approach him in 1965? Simply because Pearson really wanted Marchand, and without Trudeau there was no Marchand. Thus Trudeau entered the Liberal Party through the back door. When he learned that he was being offered the riding of Mount-Royal – where he would be running against his friend Charles Taylor, who campaigned under the NDP banner – he had such qualms that he tried to back out of the race altogether. But Marchand convinced him to stay in.

But why did Trudeau decide to take the plunge into politics? Why into federal politics? And finally, why with the Liberal Party, which he had so harshly criticized just two years earlier? Trudeau and Pelletier were very aware that their allies and opponents alike were asking themselves these questions, and asking them to explain their behaviour. The two men responded in "Pelletier et Trudeau s'expliquent"[177] [Pelletier and Trudeau Make Themselves Clear]. We will let them state their case, wherever possible, adding details and comments that seem relevant.

To the first question, they answered: "There are two ways to be involved in public affairs: from the outside, by analyzing critically the ideas, institutions and men who together make up political reality; or from the inside, by becoming a politician oneself. . . . After spending fifteen years telling others what to do and how, is it really that surprising that one day we should want to *do* things ourselves?"[178]

But they provided an additional reason: the rise of neo-nationalism. For them "the most effective way to heal the nationalist alienation is to establish a better system. We want to set ourselves to this task."[179] In other words, they wanted to fight separatism while trying to meet the legitimate demands of French Canadians.

The second question – "Why federal politics?" – was all the more relevant since their political battles had all taken place in Quebec. They answered that they had consistently defended "constitutionalism and the federal form of government." When Quebec was stagnating under the Union Nationale, their struggle had to be waged in Quebec. But since 1960, "Quebec has become strong and the central power has weakened. Quebeckers are increasingly turning to the provincial sphere . . . [and] are less and less present [on the federal scene,] be it intellectually, psychologically or even physically. . . . However, this kind of political vacuum cannot last, and . . . power always finds a taker. If honest people don't take it, then inevitably the rabble will. This is one of the surest theorems of political science."[180] They also had another motivation: "Without indulging in alarmism . . . the undersigned believe that a certain state of emergency exists in Canada."[181] Because it misunderstood Quebec's new nationalism, the federal government was not up to the challenge. This could rapidly have dire consequences on the Canadian political union.

And, finally, why the Liberal Party? Weren't they both men of the Left? Yes, they answered unhesitatingly. But the Left and the NDP were not one and the same. Trudeau, we should note, never became a member of the NDP. In fact, for several years he had been denouncing its dogmatism and poor understanding of the Canadian reality. This, he said, explained the NDP's inability to garner significant electoral support.

In effect, the NDP offered "anyone who wants to act meaningfully on the Canadian political scene, particularly in Quebec, the prospect of 'dying with honour' but very few opportunities of 'saving the proletariat,' that is, of exercising timely and effective influence on Canadian politics."[182]

Given the urgency of the situation, it made sense to work within the party that stood the best chance of taking corrective action. Pelletier and Trudeau said there was no question of joining the Conservatives: "Not only is Mr. Diefenbaker's party nonexistent in Quebec but he has abundantly demonstrated his inability to understand the Canadian problem and to govern Canada." As for the Créditistes, "it is obvious they have no political thought, and the disintegration of their party in recent weeks has confirmed that you can't use demagoguery as a substitute."[183]

That left the Liberal Party. But, skeptics would say, hadn't Trudeau viciously attacked the Liberals just two years previously? Pelletier and Trudeau had an answer for that too. They explained that those who choose to focus on politics as public intellectuals "have to see their thinking through to the end. If they feared creating enemies with their critiques . . . they would lose their independence, and with it, their usefulness. This is why . . . we have said and written a lot of sharp things about all Canadian political parties, without exception."[184] The critiques they had made about the Liberals "long and not so long ago" should therefore be seen in this light.

<hr />

Trudeau was elected MP for Mount Royal in the general election of November 8, 1965. His many talents were soon recognized. After serving as minister of justice, he was encouraged to run for the Liberal leadership. In the course of this campaign he delivered a speech in Montreal on April 2, 1968, before a French audience, titled "Of Truth and Freedom in Politics: French Canadians and the Federal Challenge."[185] We will quote extensively from this speech, since it articulates his philosophical and social credo, and the building blocks of his political program:*

---

* We have shortened some passages and changed the punctuation, to make this speech easier to read.

You will not be astonished if I affirm my faith in a form of government called federalism. I would like to state precisely that, as far as I am concerned, federalism is not an expedient, nor is it a compromise. Far less is it a makeshift, as some people believe it to be. On the contrary, it is an avant-garde political formula, to which I would subscribe even outside the Canadian context. Why?

The great advantage of federalism is that it brings the state and the citizen closer, it allows for local legislation for local needs, regional for regional needs, and federal for confronting global problems. But rapprochement, pooling, unity, do not mean uniformity. Some people dream of an international society where everybody would speak the same language, would live in the same way, would eat the same meals, and would watch the same television programs. This type of world would have certain advantages, but chances are that we would die of boredom. It remains certain that we are evolving toward a closer union among peoples. Now, federalism is the very political system which allows for union in freedom and for unity in diversity.

As French Canadians, we have not yet given the quarter of our true capacities. Some people assert that Quebec's progress is incompatible with Canada's. I propose that we start with a contrary hypothesis, namely that the safest token of progress for Canada is a strong and dynamic French Canada, sure of itself, freed from fear, and thoroughly involved in all aspects of Canadian life.

The first priority, when we choose a political system, is the human person. Not the person as an abstract notion; what is of prime importance is concrete human beings, you, me, the farmers, the workers. . . . I would like to quote Frère Untel here: "Socialism, capitalism, social doctrine . . . I have a criterion for judging them: the poor that I know. If a social measure translates, or could have been translated, into a little more security or dignity for the poor people that I know, it has my support." That is my conviction as well.

But if you asked me now which is my first priority, here is my answer: to make out of this country a free political society, open and strong, which could in the first place erase from our cities and rural districts the shame of misery in the midst of wealth. And on this solid foundation we could build a radiant French culture, creative, freed from the most terrible of oppressions: insecurity and fear.

Masters in our own house? I agree.

But our own house is the whole of Canada, from Newfoundland to Victoria, with its immense resources which belong to all of us and of which we should not give up even a patch.

And, as the saying goes, "The rest is history." As prime minister, Trudeau adopted the Official Languages Act, forever changing Canada's political and linguistic landscape. His government sought to bring about the "Just Society." By promoting multiculturalism as a key factor in Canada's development, he helped turn this country into a model of tolerance and peaceful coexistence recognized throughout the world. He repatriated the Constitution, which finally made Canada a fully independent country. He enshrined the Charter of Rights and Freedoms in the Constitution, protecting bilingualism and the French language, strengthening individual liberties and creating a truly new Canadian identity. This son of Quebec has become the father of a new Canada.

Whether we revere him or revile him, the fact remains that today's Canada is the Canada of Pierre Elliott Trudeau.

ACKNOWLEDGMENTS

This book could not have been written without the cooperation of many people. We are fortunate to have benefited from the expertise and encouragement of many friends and colleagues.

We would like to express our sincere thanks to the Honourable Marc Lalonde and Alexandre Trudeau for giving us privileged access to Pierre Elliott Trudeau's private papers. We can't avoid thinking sadly that Pierre himself would have done it in 1995 if circumstances had been different. But these were troubled times in Quebec: the separatist wind was blowing at full force, and for us to embark on this big and fascinating project would have meant giving up the directorship of *Cité libre*. We were torn between the two options. We chose *Cité libre* on the insistence of Pierre, who repeatedly claimed that there was no urgency for his biography. Well, there was. In 2000, just as the political climate had cooled down and we were ready to tackle our project, Trudeau passed away, and we, like most Canadians, found ourselves mourning his death.

But perhaps the delay in completing this project turned out for the best. Now that the dust has settled and the political landscape has considerably changed, it is probably easier to re-examine the Quebec of the 1950s and 1960s more dispassionately.

We have very much appreciated the help of the staff at Library and Archives Canada (LAC). The skilful help of Christian Rioux, in charge of the Trudeau Papers, has made our work more efficient and pleasurable. He went beyond our requests, in particular when he directed us to Maurice Lamontagne's correspondence with Trudeau. This allowed us to shed a new light on Trudeau's trip to the Soviet Union. When Christian

Rioux retired, Geneviève Couture very ably took his place. And like him, she went well beyond the call of duty to assist us.

Publishing the French and English versions of this book simultaneously was quite a challenge and required a lot of cooperation and goodwill. We are grateful to Les Éditions de l'Homme for their continued confidence in us. Monique Perrin-d'Arloz did an exceptional job in translating the English quotations for the French version. Our seasoned editor and friend, Doug Gibson, has given us his unfailing support during all these years. We are very grateful not only for his wise advice, but also for his words of encouragement, especially when our spirits were low. Wendy Thomas has very ably assisted Doug in the editing of the book. Doug Pepper, Elizabeth Kribs, Bhavna Chauhan, and their team at McClelland & Stewart have worked miracles in order to publish the English version in record time. George Tombs has shown considerable understanding and patience in translating a work in progress. He also made numerous suggestions that enriched our manuscript. Thanks to his collaboration, we can confidently claim that the English version faithfully reflects the French original. Thank you, George!

Our book is based first and foremost on Trudeau's private papers and writings, but also on other primary sources. Experience has shown us that, unlike the recollections of witnesses, documented sources are not affected by the passing of time or by personal or political factors. Nevertheless, we undertook a number of interviews. Roger Rolland was kind enough to spend many hours with us recounting memories and anecdotes about his good friend Pierre. He also very generously gave us access to his private correspondence with him, which reveal new facets of Trudeau's personality. The late Jacques Hébert described for us, in his legendary humorous and biting style, their many fights against the reactionary forces in Quebec. He also put at our disposal his complete collection of his weekly magazine *Vrai*, in which Trudeau wrote some of his most incisive articles. Micheline Legendre, now deceased, was an active member of Le Rassemblement who witnessed Trudeau's important role in launching and maintaining this movement. She has provided us with the rich documentation she had meticulously kept for almost half a century. After all these years, she still vividly, and fondly, remembered the enthusiasm of the progressive elite for this avant-garde movement. Norm Goldman shared with us his recollections of his professor of constitutional law at l'Université de Montréal, Pierre Trudeau. His testimony runs counter to some common views on Trudeau's level of comfort with academic life.

We were sometimes overwhelmed by the breadth of the scientific knowledge we had to attempt to digest in order to follow this man who seems to have been everywhere, seen it all, and witnessed some of the most decisive events in the twentieth century. Fortunately we could count on the scholarship of friends who generously shared their expertise with us. Edelgard Mahant (York University, Toronto) used her long teaching experience to alert us to some of the comprehension problems facing anglophones unfamiliar with Quebec's history; Jean-Pierre Derriennic (Laval University) has very generously shared his remarkable knowledge of contemporary political history; Michael Behiels and Réjean Pelletier (Laval University) have published notable scholarly studies of this period. And Marc Lalonde, better known for the very important role he played in Trudeau's government, in fact, fought alongside Trudeau in the 1960s in Quebec. He was, to us, an invaluable witness of that epoch. Our sincere thanks to each and every one. Needless to say, we are solely responsible for any remaining errors or omissions.

Most of all, we consider ourselves very fortunate to have had the opportunity to write an intellectual biography of Pierre Elliott Trudeau, an exceptional man who sought the truth throughout his life in order to improve the well-being of his people.

NOTE ON THE BIBLIOGRAPHY

This book could not have been written without the cooperation of many people. Normally, at this stage of a book like *Trudeau Transformed*, the reader might expect many pages of bibliography, listing the hundreds of books and articles by or about Pierre Trudeau that we have consulted. We followed that predictable pattern with our first volume, *Young Trudeau*.

For this second volume, although we gratefully acknowledge the contribution of the many authors who have preceded us and helped us in the complex and fascinating task of understanding Trudeau, we were compelled to proceed differently. We wanted to avoid, on the one hand, the Scylla of too much information in the form of a very lengthy list, which would unavoidably include many obscure titles when abstracted from their contexts, as well as numerous well-known and readily accessible Trudeau writings in several editions and different collected works. On the other hand, we wanted to stay clear of the Charybidis of the attempt to identify the "most important" sources – a somewhat blurred notion in this volume. Well-known classics were often less "important" than a letter, or an obscure but revealing document, long or short. Consequently, we have decided to restrict ourselves to two statements that may hopefully guide other scholars.

First, in this volume, *Trudeau Transformed*, we have given primary importance to Trudeau's own writings. But the numerous reactions of his opponents as well as his allies to the positions he was defending at the time, and Trudeau's responses to them are, we believe, also crucial if we are to follow the development of his political thoughts. These interactions must been seen in their context to be fully appreciated.

Second, we have gone to great lengths to make our notes for each individual chapter as complete and as true to the context as possible, and our references as precise as possible. The following index will, of course, provide additional information. We hope that this will answer the needs of our readers.

NOTES

Chapter 1: IN SEARCH OF THE STATESMAN (pages 1–10)

1   G. Radwanksi, *Trudeau,* Macmillan of Canada, 1978, p. 26. Radwanski is here quoting an anonymous Liberal insider.

2   P. Green, in N. Southam (ed.), *Pierre,* Toronto, McClelland & Stewart, 2005, pp. 292–293.

3   Reported by J. English, *Just Watch Me,* Toronto, Knopf Canada, 2009, p. 98.

4   Reported by D. Somerville, *Trudeau Revealed by His Actions and Words,* Richmond Hill, ON, BMG Publ. Ltd., 1978, p. 33.

5   LAC, vol. 13, f 11. All citations in archival documents will use this style. We will give details of this attempted crossing to Cuba in Chapter 13.

6   1961 Agenda, LAC, vol. 39, f 5. We should note that Trudeau was thirty-two years old when he visited Pamplona.

7   J. English, R. Gwyn, and W. Lackenbauer (eds.), *The Hidden Pierre Elliott Trudeau: The Faith Behind the Politics,* Ottawa, Novalis, 2004.

8   N. Southam (ed.), *Pierre,* McClelland & Stewart, 2005, Chapter 1, "Faith," pp. 1–30.

9   Agenda, LAC, vol. 39, f 6.

10 Trudeau was secretary of the Bloc Populaire's Education and Politics Committee at the party congress of February 3 to 6, 1944.

11 E. Amyot, *Le Québec entre Pétain et de Gaulle. Vichy, la France libre et les Canadiens français 1940–1945,* Montreal, Fides, 1999, p. 191.

12 S. Clarkson and C. McCall, *Trudeau and Our Times,* vol. 1: *The Magnificent Obsession,* Toronto, McClelland & Stewart, 1990, p. 70.

13 G. Radwanski, *Trudeau,* op. cit., pp. 80–81.

14 M. Vastel, *The Outsider: The Life of Pierre Elliott Trudeau,* translated by Hubert Bauch, Toronto, Macmillan of Canada, 1990, p. 85.

15 J. English, *Trudeau, Citizen of the World: The Life of Pierre Elliott Trudeau,* vol. 1: *1919–1968,* Toronto, Alfred Knopf Canada, 2006, p. 252.

16 Ibid., p. 254.

17 Quoted by Edith Iglauer, "Prime Minister – Premier Ministre," *The New Yorker*, July 5, 1969, p. 36.

Chapter 2: THE SHOCK OF HARVARD (pages 11–48)

1   Letter to Thérèse Gouin, October 11, 1945. In J. English, *Citizen of the World: Trudeau*, vol. 1: *1919–1968*, Toronto, Alfred A. Knopf Canada, 2006, p. 138.

2   P.E. Trudeau, *Memoirs*, Toronto, McClelland & Stewart, 1993, p. 38.

3   Letter to Roger Rolland, December 9, 1945. Private collection of R. Rolland.

4   Testimony of several of Trudeau's former classmates. C. McCall and S. Clarkson, *Trudeau and Our Times*, vol. 2: *The Heroic Delusion*, Toronto, McClelland & Stewart Inc., 1994, p. 42.

5   On December 9, 1945, he wrote to R. Rolland: "I always prefer writing to friends than doing anything else." Private collection of R. Rolland.

6   This was the name given to the Harvard students' newspaper, *Crimson Daily*, during the war years. For a history of this newspaper, see Greg Lawless, *The Harvard Crimson Anthology: 100 Years at Harvard*, Boston, Houghton Mifflin, 1980, 378 p.

7   "Alumni in U.S. Forces Included Total of 22,620 Men," *Service News* (name of the *Harvard Crimson Daily* during the war), August 25, 1944.

8   "Wild Heads New Veterans' Bureau," *Service News*, October 6, 1944.

9   "Harvard Changed by War But Returning to Normalcy," *Service News*, July 6, 1945.

10 "Next Fall's Influx of Freshmen Will Approach Normal," *Service News*, March 19, 1946.

11 "Law School, Business Schools Hit Record-Breaking Totals in Enrollment," *Service News*, October 23, 1946.

12 A. Burelle, *Pierre Elliott Trudeau, l'intellectuel et le politique*, Montreal, Fides, 2005, p. 70.

13 D. Somerville, *Trudeau Revealed by His Actions and Words*, Richmond Hill, BMG Publishing Ltd., 1978, p. 19.

14 Vol. 39, f 1.

15 Letter of February 25, 1945. Private collection of R. Rolland.

16 Letter to Roger Rolland, dated April 15, 1945. Private collection of R. Rolland.

17 "Van Doren Slams United Nations, Calls World Government Essential," *Crimson Daily*, May 4, 1946.

18 "U.N. or You Ain't," *Crimson Daily*, May 7, 1946.

19   Alfred Cobban, *Dictatorship, Its History and Theory,* New York, Scribner, 1939, p. 283. Alfred Cobban was a professor of history at University College, London.

20   C.J. Friedrich, *The New Belief in the Common Man*, Boston, Little, Brown, 1942. Vol. 39, f 2.

21   W.Y. Elliott, *The Pragmatic Revolt in Politics: Syndicalism, Fascism, and the Constitutional State,* New York, The Macmillan Company, 1928, p. 218.

22   For an excellent analysis of this issue, see J. Cornwell, *Hitler's Pope,* New York, Viking, 1999, p. 148 et seq.

23   Vol. 7, f 25.

24   MG26, Series 03, vol. 24 f 3. Interview with Thomas Axworthy, conducted in 1993 for the television series based on Trudeau's memoirs. Thomas Axworthy was formerly senior policy adviser, principal secretary, and speechwriter for Prime Minister Pierre Trudeau and was then a professor at Harvard. He is now president of the Centre for the Study of Democracy at Queen's University, Kingston, Ontario.

25   J. English, *Trudeau, Citizen of the World: The Life of Pierre Elliott Trudeau,* vol. 1: *1919–1968,* Toronto, Alfred Knopf Canada, 2006, p. 125.

26   Vol. 7, f 22.

27   http://en.wikipedia.org/wiki/Joseph_Schumpeter.

28   Vol. 7, f.16.

29   C. H. Kisch and W. A. Elkin, *Central Banks,* London, Macmillan, 1928.

30   P. Einzig, *The Theory of Forward Exchange*, London, Macmillan, 1937. Notes by Trudeau, vol. 7 f 13.

31   MG26, Series 03, vol. 24, f 3. Interview with Thomas Axworthy, 1993, op. cit.

32   Vol. 7, f. 14.

33   Vol. 7, f. 14.

34   See, for example, E. Feser (ed.), *The Cambridge Companion to Hayek,* New York, Cambridge University Press, 2007.

35   G. Dostaler, *Keynes et ses combats,* Paris, Albin Michel, 2005, p. 386.

36   Ibid., p. 390.

37   MG 26, Series 03, vol. 24 f 2. Interview conducted in 1993 with Michael Ignatieff, former Harvard professor and former leader of the Liberal Party, for the television series on Trudeau's memoirs.

38   MG 26, Series 03, vol. 24, f 3. Interview with Thomas Axworthy, 1993, op. cit. Trudeau actually said White. But this was a mistake, since he had mixed up the names of the head of the delegation and of his teacher.

39   MG 26, Series 03, vol. 24, f 3. Interview with Thomas Axworthy, 1993, op. cit.

40 Trudeau's private library, Pine Avenue West, Montreal. On the first page, Trudeau wrote: January 1945.

41 J.M. Keynes, *The General Theory of Employment, Interest and Money,* New York, Harcourt, Brace, 1936, p. 379.

42 Ibid., p. 379.

43 Ibid., p. 378.

44 Ibid., p. 381.

45 Vol. 39, f 1.

46 J.K. Galbraith, "Citizen of the World," in N. Southam, *Pierre,* Toronto, McClelland & Stewart Ltd., 2005, p. 209.

47 C.H. McIlwain, *Constitutionalism Ancient and Modern,* Ithaca, Cornell University Press, 1940, p. 143.

48 Vol. 7, f 17.

49 MG26, Series 03, vol. 23 f 3. Interview with Ron Graham, conducted in 1993 for the television series on *Memoirs.* The person who did the transcript wrote "Mackelrane" instead of McIlwain – a good phonetic transcription!

50 Vol. 39, f 8.

51 P. Gzowski, "Portrait of an Intellectual in Action," *Maclean's,* February 24, 1962, p. 29.

52 The importance of this work is indicated by the fact that a posthumous edition (Fainsod died in 1972) was prepared by Jerry F. Hough and published in 1979 under the title *How the Soviet Union Is Governed.*

53 Vol. 7, f 22.

54 Vol. 7, f 22.

55 Vol. 7, f 19.

56 W.Y. Elliott, *The Pragmatic Revolt in Politics. Syndicalism, Fascism, and the Constitutional State,* New York: The Macmillan Company, 1928, pp. 224–225.

57 Ibid., p. 241.

58 For more details on the revolutionary manifesto, see our Volume I, p. 226.

59 Vol. 7, f 23.

60 Louis Hartz, *The Liberal Tradition in America: An Interpretation of American Political Thought Since the Revolution,* New York, Harcourt, Brace, 1955, 329 p. A new edition appeared in 1991.

61 John Dewey, "Force and Coercion," *The International Journal of Ethics,* vol. xxvi, No. 3, April 1916, pp. 359–367.

62 For details of their revolutionary movement, see our Volume I, Chapter 9, pp. 212–245.

63   J. Dewey, "The Need for a Recovery of Philosophy," in *The Political Writings*, Indianapolis, IN, Hackett Publ. Co., 1993, p. 8.

64   J. Dewey, "The Problem of Truth," in *The Political Writings*, op. cit., p. 19.

65   "The Public and Its Problems," in R.B. Westbrook, *John Dewey and American Democracy*, Ithaca, Cornell University Press, 1991, p. 229. This excellent work clearly presents the importance of democracy and democratic education in the philosophy of Dewey.

66   J. Dewey, "Force and Coercion," op. cit., p. 361.

67   Trudeau cited as an example the Russian revolutionary manifesto of 1879.

68   S. Clarkson and C. McCall, *Trudeau and Our Times*, vol. 1: *The Magnificent Obsession*, Toronto, McClelland & Stewart, 1991, pp. 47–48.

69   N. Ricci, *Extraordinary Canadians: Pierre Elliott Trudeau*, Toronto, Penguin Canada, 2009, p. 119.

70   Twenty-four pages of this monumental introduction appear in P.E. Trudeau, *Against the Current: Selected Writings, 1939–1996*, edited by Gérard Pelletier, Toronto, McClelland & Stewart, 1996, pp. 42–66.

71   The famine of 1944–45 caused 20,000 deaths in the Netherlands. The Dutch still express their gratitude to Canada.

72   Letter to R. Rolland, April 13, 1945. Private collection of R. Rolland.

73   J. English, *Citizen*, op. cit., p. 126. The date of the letter is not indicated.

74   Ibid. The block capitals are Trudeau's own.

75   Lecture notes entitled "Centralized Planning Totalitarian Gosplan," vol. 7, f 24. Unless otherwise noted, all excerpts cited in the following paragraphs are from this folder.

76   All notes in this section are from vol. 39, f 8.

77   M. Radin, *The Day of Reckoning*, New York, Alfred A. Knopf, Inc., 1943.

78   For example, it was reviewed by F. L. Schuman in the *California Law Review*, vol. 31, no. 4 (September 1943), and by R.B. Schlesinger in the *Columbia Law Review*, vol. 43, no. 6 (September 1943), pp. 960–966.

79   M. Radin, *The Day of Reckoning*, op. cit., pp. 10–11.

80   Ibid., p. 68.

81   Ibid., p. 125.

82   Ibid., p. 126.

83   Ibid., p. 144.

84   Vol. 7, f 21.

85   J.T. Shotwell, *Governments of Continental Europe*, New York, The Macmillan Company. The first edition, entitled *Contemporary Governments of Europe*, appeared in 1940. This is probably the one

that Trudeau read. We were only able to consult the 1952 edition,
881 p.

86 P.E. Trudeau, "Quand les Canadiens français réclamaient un Mussolini,"
    Vrai, vol. 2, no. 41, July 28, 1956, p. 6.

87 P.E. Trudeau, "Le syndicalisme catholique et le corporatisme," *Vrai*, vol.
    3, no. 3, September 15, 1956, p. 8.

88 C.J. Friedrich, *Constitutional Government and Democracy: Theory and
    Practice in Europe and America*, Waltham, Massachusetts, 4th edition,
    1968 (1st edition 1941), p. 4.

89 P.E. Trudeau, *The Essential Trudeau*, edited by Ron Graham, Toronto,
    McClelland & Stewart, 1998, p. 168.

90 C.J. Friedrich, *Constitutional Government*, op. cit., p. 8.

91 P.E. Trudeau, *Memoirs*, op. cit., p. 46.

92 Vol. 7, f 24. Unless otherwise stated, all excerpts quoted in the following
    paragraphs are from this folder.

93 Vol. 8, f 23.

94 Vol. 8, f 3.

95 According to INSEE (the Institut national de la statistique et des etudes
    économiques), 50,000 francs in 1946 had approximately the purchasing
    power in 2004 of €3,546.50, or CA$5,542.37 (given an exchange rate of
    1 euro = $ 1.5628).

Chapter 3: **PARIS, JE T'AIME!** (pages 49–80)

1   LAC, vol. 8 f 2.

2   Quoted by John English, *Citizen of the World: Trudeau*, vol. 1: *1919–
    1968*, Toronto, Alfred A. Knopf Canada, 2006, p. 143.

3   LAC, vol. 9, f 2. We found this hand-written note on the letterhead of the
    Privy Council of Canada, and therefore believe it to date from 1949 or 1950.

4   Letter of July 24, 1946, addressed to Trudeau by René de Messières,
    cultural attaché at the French embassy in Canada. LAC, vol. 8, f 4.

5   The detailed official list is found in LAC, vol. 8, f 4.

6   Letter of September 16, 1946, from Yvette Gouin. LAC, vol. 8, f 8.

7   Official attestation of the Consulate General of France, issued September
    17, 1946, LAC, vol. 8, f 4.

8   LAC, vol. 5, f 15.

9   The dates of all Trudeau's activities in Paris are detailed in his agenda,
    LAC, vol. 39, f 1.

10 For more information on Hertel's influence on young people in Quebec,
    see our first volume.

11 F. Hertel, "Lettres à mes amis," *Cité libre,* February 1951, pp. 34–35.

12 P.E. Trudeau, "Les séparatisties: des contre-révolutionnaires," *Cité libre,* May 1964. Reproduced in *Federalism and the French Canadians,* Toronto, Macmillan, 1968, p. 207.

13 S. Veil, *Une vie,* Paris, Stock, 2007, p. 82.

14 Ibid., p. 99.

15 Ibid., p. 117.

16 C. Tatilon, *La soupe au pistou,* Paris, Éditions France Loisirs, 2008.

17 I. Némirovsky, *Suite française,* Paris, Éditions Denoël, 2004.

18 Quoted by T. Judt, *Un passé imparfait – Les intellectuels en France, 1944–1956,* Paris, Librairie Arthème Fayard, 1992, pp. 85–86.

19 M. Winock, *Le siècle des intellectuels,* Paris, Éditions du Seuil (2nd edition), 1999, p. 474.

20 For more information on Maurras and the way the French-Canadian intelligentsia admired him, see our first volume.

21 Quoted by M. Winock, *Le siècle,* op. cit., p. 448. Captain Alfred Dreyfus was a Jewish military officer, unjustly convicted (and only rehabilitated many years later). Toward the end of the nineteenth century, the "Dreyfus Affair" divided France into two camps: the "Dreyfusards," such as Émile Zola, who were convinced that Dreyfus was innocent, and the "anti-Dreyfusards," such as Charles Maurras, who believed he had to be guilty, since he was Jewish.

22 T. Judt, *Un passé imparfait,* op. cit., p. 61.

23 Some people challenge this figure. According to Winock, in *Le siècle des intellectuels,* op. cit., p. 514, "This figure does not correspond to reality."

24 Quoted by Richard Arès, *Plans d'étude sur la restauration sociale,* 3rd edition, 1941, p. 11. For the position of the Catholic Church on Communism, see our first volume.

25 For more information on requests for permission to read works pro-hibited by the *Index,* see our first volume, pp. 53–54.

26 LAC, vol. 14, f 12. Trudeau's letter of January 20, 1950; Mgr. Vachon's reply of January 28. The 1948 version of the *Index* prohibited Catholics from reading works by authors such as Blaise Pascal, Denis Diderot, Honoré de Balzac, Émile Zola, Victor Hugo, Jean-Paul Sartre, Sigmund Freud, and even Pierre Larousse, for his *Grand Dictionnaire universel.* (The *Index* was abolished in 1966.)

27 M. Winock, *Le siècle,* op. cit., p. 526.

28 E.-M. Meunier and J-P. Warren, *Sortir de la "Grande noirceur,"*

L'horizon "personnaliste" de la Révolution tranquille, Sillery, Les Cahiers du Septentrion, 2002, 210 p.

29 In *Mounier et sa génération,* quoted by M. Winock, *"Esprit," les intellectuels dans la cité, 1930–1950,* p. 253.

30 E. Mounier, "Suite aux maladies infantiles des révolutions," *Esprit,* December 1944. In M. Winock, *Esprit,* op. cit., p. 272.

31 E. Mounier, "Y a-t-il une justice politique?", *Esprit,* August 1947, in M. Winock, *Esprit,* op. cit., p. 276.

32 E. Mounier, "Le Casse-cou occidental," *Esprit,* November 1945, in G. Boudic, *Esprit – 1944–1982, Les métamorphoses d'une revue,* Éditions de l'IMEC, 2005, p. 59.

33 G. Boudic, *Esprit – 1944–1982,* op. cit.

34 P.E. Trudeau, *Memoirs,* Toronto, McClelland & Stewart, 1993, p. 44.

35 G. Pelletier, *Years of Impatience: 1950–1960,* Toronto, Methuen, 1984, pp. 18–19.

36 Ibid., p. 19.

37 P.E. Trudeau, *Memoirs,* op. cit., pp. 40–45.

38 S. Veil, *Une vie,* op. cit., p. 115.

39 LAC, vol. 8, f 24. Letter of April 1, 1947, from L.G. Robinson, dean of Graduate Studies.

40 LAC, vol. 8, f 24. Letter of April 7, 1947, from L.G. Robinson. It is amusing to note that after two years of study at Harvard, Trudeau's written English still came off as so French: "I interested myself, I did not pass any exams."

41 All documents relating to Sciences Po are found in LAC, vol. 8, f 13.

42 Quoted in A. Kaspi, *Les juifs américains: Ont-ils réellement le pouvoir qu'on leur prête?* Paris, Plon, 2008, p. 11. This quote can also be found in the English version of André Siegfried's work *America Comes of Age: A French Analysis,* p. 20.

43 A. Kaspi, p. 11 and the English translation of Siegfried's *America Comes of Age,* p. 20.

44 A. Kaspi, pp. 11–12, and the English translation of Siegfried, p. 25.

45 LAC, vol. 8, f 19, P.E. Trudeau, "La promesse du Québec," April 3, 1947.

46 P.E. Trudeau, *Memoirs,* op. cit., p. 44.

47 N. Berdyaev's book *De l'esclavage et de la liberté de l'homme* (1946) was found in Trudeau's private library, Pine Avenue West, Montreal.

48 Interview with Roger Rolland, who was present at this meeting.

49 For more information on this subject, see our first volume.

50 LAC, vol. 8, f 19. P.E. Trudeau, "La promesse du Québec."

51 LAC, vol. 39, f 10.

52 Trudeau's private library. This 412-page book, inscribed "November 1945, Harvard," is underlined and annotated in several places.

53 Dr. Charles Odier, *Les deux sources – consciente et inconsciente – de la vie morale*, Ed. de la Baconnière, Neuchâtel, 1947 (2nd edition, 1st edition: 1943). Trudeau's private library, with the inscription: "Pierre Elliott Trudeau, avril 1948."

54 Study by Germain Lesage, 1962. Published in G. Lesage, *Notre éveil culturel*, Montreal, Rayonnement, 1963, pp. 135–148.

55 Trudeau's letter to Thérèse Gouin of November 22. In J. English, *Trudeau, Citizen*, op. cit., p. 150.

56 Letter of Thérèse Gouin of February 15, 1947, and letter of Trudeau of February 22, 1947. In English, *Trudeau, Citizen*, op. cit., p. 152.

57 Dreams and interpretation. All quotes are from LAC, vol. 39, f 10.

58 Undated manuscript, LAC, vol. 22, f 2.

59 Letter of Guy Jasmin of June 7, 1947. LAC, vol. 22, f2.

60 P.E. Trudeau, *Memoirs*, op. cit., p. 40.

61 Trudeau had a French edition of N. Berdyaev. The English edition quoted here is *Slavery and Freedom*, Centenary Press, 1943.

62 Ibid., p. 28.

63 Ibid., p. 136.

64 Ibid., p. 167.

65 Ibid., p. 103.

66 Ibid., p. 105.

67 P.E. Trudeau, "Separatist Counter-Revolutionaries," in *Federalism and the French Canadians*, op. cit., pp. 204–212.

68 N. Berdyaev, op. cit., pp. 171–172.

69 Ibid., p. 18.

70 Ibid., p. 250.

71 P.E. Trudeau, *Memoirs*, op. cit., p. 48.

72 LAC, vol. 8, f 19. Unless otherwise noted, all quotations on this subject are from this file.

73 N. Berdyaev, op. cit., pp. 166–167.

74 M. and M. Nemni, "A Conversation With Trudeau," *Cité libre*, February-March 1998, p. 101.

75 P. Trudeau, "La nouvelle trahison des clercs," *Cité libre*, April 1962, translated as "The New Treason of the Intellectuals" and reproduced in P.E. Trudeau, *Against the Current: Selected Writings, 1939–1996*, edited by Gérard Pelletier, Toronto. McClelland & Stewart, 1996, p. 151.

76 For more information on the Catholic Church's position on the CCF, see our first volume, pp. 129–130.

77 P.E. Trudeau, "La nouvelle trahison des clercs," op. cit., p. 158.

78 P.E. Trudeau, *The Essential Trudeau,* edited by Ron Graham, Toronto, McClelland & Stewart, p. 101.

79 For more information on the "national revolution," see our first volume, pp. 212–273.

80 Letter of February 11, 1949 from Laurendeau, LAC, vol. 8, f 19.

Chapter 4: "BRITISH-STYLE" SOCIALISM (pages 81–115)

1 Thérèse Gouin later married Vianney Décarie, a future professor of philosophy at the Université de Montréal. Trudeau remained friends with the couple all his life.

2 Letter of July 10, 1947, to Lomer Gouin. In J. English, *Trudeau, Citizen of the World: The Life of Pierre Elliott Trudeau,* vol. 1: *1919–1968,* Toronto, Alfred Knopf Canada, 2006, p. 163.

3 BAC, vol. 11, f 12. One of Trudeau's hiking companions, Jacques Dubuc, told the epic tale of this long walk in *Jeunesse canadienne,* May 1948.

4 Max and Monique Nemni, "Entretien avec Marc Lalonde sur la crise d'Octobre," *Cité libre,* vol. 38, no. 4, Autumn 2000, p. 50.

5 Letter of September 26, 1947, from Claude Ryan, BAC, vol. 8, f 30.

6 "Jeunes Canadiens au Vieux Monde," *Jeunesse canadienne,* November 1947, p. 14. After this description of Trudeau appear the initials "C.R." although on his personal copy, Trudeau wrote the name "Claude Ryan."

7 A. Potvin, M. Letourneau, and R. Smith, *L'anti-Trudeau, Choix de textes,* Montreal, Éditions Parti Pris, 1972, p. 8.

8 The controversy was actually over conscription for service overseas, but has come to be known as "the Conscription Crisis."

9 A. Twigg, "The Achievements of F.R. Who?", *The Province,* March 1, 1981, in S. Djwa, *A Life of F.R. Scott: The Politics of the Imagination,* McClelland & Stewart, 1987, p. 332.

10 W. Churchill, Speech of May 13, 1940.

11 M. Charlot, *L'Angleterre: 1945–1980, Le temps des incertitudes,* Paris, Imprimerie nationale, 1981, p. 12.

12 W.D. Rubinstein, *Twentieth-Century Britain: A Political History,* New York, Palgrave Macmillan, 2003, p. 227.

13 Ibid., p. 232.

14 M. Charlot, *L'Angleterre: 1945–1980,* op. cit., p. 64.

15 Ibid., p. 52. From this point onwards, the British lost the habit of eating bread to accompany meals.

16 Ibid., p. 147.

17 Ibid., p. 81.

18 Ibid., p. 84.

19 Ibid., p. 101.

20 Quoted in M. Charlot, *L'Angleterre: 1945–1980,* op. cit., p. 101.

21 W.D. Rubinstein, *Twentieth-Century Britain,* op. cit., p. 241.

22 Letter of June 17, 1948, from the Dean of Post-Graduate Students. BAC, vol. 8, f 24.

23 Thesis topics, BAC, vol. 39, f 8.

24 P.E. Trudeau, *Memoirs,* Toronto, McClelland & Stewart, 1993, p. 47.

25 Letter of June 22, 1948, from Laski, vol. 11, f 23.

26 M. Vastel, *The Outsider: The Life of Pierre Elliott Trudeau,* translated by Hubert Bauch, Toronto, Macmillan, 1990, 266 p.

27 M. Vastel, "La minable série de la CBC sur Trudeau," *Le Soleil,* April 3, 2002. Part of this article appears on p. 42 of *The Outsider.*

28 I. Kramnick and B. Sheerman, *Harold Laski: A Life on the Left,* London: Hamish Hamilton, 1993, p. 2.

29 A remark by Justice Felix Frankfurter quoted in I. Kramnick and B. Sheerman, *Harold Laski,* op. cit., p. 332.

30 I. Kramnick and B. Sheerman, *Harold Laski,* op. cit., p. 332.

31 Ibid., p. 587.

32 H. Laski, "The Crisis in the Theory of the State," introduction to the 1937 edition of *A Grammar of Politics.* This is the edition Trudeau read at Harvard, with great attention. We have consulted the 5th edition, of 1967, p. xiii.

33 Lectures given by Raymond Aron on April 29 and 30 and May 4, 1948. BAC, vol. 8, f 29.

34 Class notes, BAC, vol. 8, f 26. Unless otherwise indicated, quotes from this course are from this particular file.

35 I. Krammick and B. Sheerman, *Harold Laski,* op. cit., p. 232.

36 Ibid., p. p. 323,

37 P.E. Trudeau, *Memoirs,* op. cit., p. 47.

38 P.E. Trudeau, *Approaches to Politics,* Toronto, Oxford University Press, 2010, p. 36. This book brings together most of Trudeau's articles from *Vrai.*

39 H. Laski, "The Crisis in the Theory of the State," p. iii, introductory chapter to the 4th edition of *A Grammar of Politics,* London, George Allen & Unwin Ltd., 1937.

40 H. Laski, *The State in Theory and Practice*, op. cit., pp. 219 and 320.

41 P.E. Trudeau, *Memoirs*, op. cit., pp. 46–47.

42 H. Laski, *The State in Theory and Practice*, op. cit., p. 82.

43 P.E. Trudeau, *Approaches to Politics*, op. cit., p. 36.

44 Trudeau's notes, BAC, vol. 8, f 28.

45 T.S. Axworthy and P.E. Trudeau (eds.), *Towards a Just Society: The Trudeau Years*, Toronto, Viking, 1990, p. 357.

46 Ibid., p. 358.

47 Ibid., p. 360.

48 Notes on *Liberty and the Modern State*, BAC, vol. 8, f. 29.

49 J.M. Robertson, *An Introduction to English Politics*, New York, New Amsterdam Book Company, 1900.

50 Martin Page, *Britain's Unknown Genius – An Introduction to the Life-Work of John Mackinnon Robertson*. London, South Place Ethical Society, 1984, p. 9. We should note two other important works on Robertson: Odin Dekkers, *J.M. Robertson: Rationalist and Literary Critic*. Brookfield, VT, Ashgate, 1998, 281 p. Chris R. Tame, *The Critical Liberalism of J.M. Robertson*. London, Libertarian Alliance, Occasional Paper No. 19, 1998, 20 pp. (First published in 1987.)

51 J.M. Robertson, *A Short History of Christianity*. Third Edition, Revised and Condensed. London, Watts & Co., 1931 © 1902.

52 P.E. Trudeau, *Memoirs*, op. cit., p. 46.

53 J. R. Spencer, "Obituary: Professor Glanville Williams," *The Independent*, April 17, 1997.

54 P.E. Trudeau, *Memoirs*, op. cit., p. 46.

55 Trudeau's notes on Kant, BAC, vol. 8, f 25.

56 Draft of "Des avocats et des autres, dans leurs rapports avec la justice," BAC, vol. 22, f 30. *Notre Temps* published this article on December 27, 1947.

57 A. Perrault, "Plaidoyer pour la justice, le droit, les juges et les avocats," *La Revue du Barreau de la province de Québec*, vol. 8, no. 1, January 1948, pp. 1–5. In BAC, vol. 22, f 30. There are many indications that Trudeau read this article carefully.

58 Trudeau kept a copy of this article in *Notre Temps*, BAC, vol. 22, f 29. The article appeared in the November 1947 issue of *Notre Temps*.

59 P.E. Trudeau, "Some Obstacles to Democracy in Quebec," a 1958 article reprinted in *Federalism and the French Canadians*, Toronto, Macmillan, 1968, p. 113, although Trudeau uses the hybrid English-French phrase

"self-styled 'hebdomadaire social et culturel,'" which is here translated as "a self-styled social and cultural weekly."

60 Letter of February 15, 1948, from Richer, BAC, vol. 22, f 28.

61 Letter from Arcand, BAC, vol. 22, f 31.

62 E. Delisle, *Essais sur l'imprégnation fasciste au Québec,* Quebec City, Les Éditions Varia, 2002, p. 83.

63 J. English, *Citizen,* op. cit., p. 191.

64 Notes taken in Laski's course, BAC, vol. 8, f 28.

65 J. English, *Citizen,* op. cit., p. 213.

66 J.H. Newman, *The Present Position of Catholics in England,* 1851. Quoted by The Newman Association: http://www.newman.org.uk/.

67 J.H. Newman, *University Sermons,* London, Longman Green, pp. 82–83.

68 J.H. Newman, *Apologia pro vita sua,* London, 1864. The following year a new edition of this work came out under the title *History of My Religious Opinions.* All our references are drawn from the version edited by Wilfrid Ward, revised in 2002: http://www.newmanreader.org/works/apologia/index.html.

69 M. Trudeau, *Beyond Reason,* New York, Paddington Press, 1979, p. 60.

70 Association française des Amis de Newman. http://www.jhnewman-france.org/cardinal/index.htm.

71 The International Centre of Newman's Friends.

72 "Politique canadienne," BAC, vol. 5, f 7. Unless otherwise indicated, all quotes from this text are from this file.

73 *Le Soleil,* December 23, 1947, BAC, vol. 8, f 7. Trudeau noted that the article had been sent to him by Ernest Lavigne.

74 The Senate now consists of 105 members, who must retire on reaching the age of seventy-five.

75 From Laurier's time onwards, Canada had actually had five prime ministers and nine governments: Sir Wilfrid Laurier (July 11, 1896–October 6, 1911), Sir Robert Borden (October 10, 1911–July 10, 1920), Arthur Meighen (July 10, 1920–December 29, 1921, and June 29, 1926–September 25, 1926), William Lyon Mackenzie King (December 29, 1921–June 29, 1926, September 25, 1926–August 6, 1930, October 23, 1935–November 15, 1948), Richard Bedford Bennett (August 7, 1930–October 23, 1935). We should note, however, that in 1896, two governments preceded Laurier: Sir Mackenzie Bowell (December 21, 1894–April 27, 1896) and Sir Charles Tupper (May 1, 1896–July 8, 1896).

Chapter 5: A POLITICAL GLOBE-TROTTER (pages 116–156)

1   P.E. Trudeau, *Memoirs,* Toronto, McClelland & Stewart, 1993, p. 47.

2   C. McCall and S. Clarkson, *Trudeau and Our Times,* vol. II, *The Heroic Delusion,* Toronto, McClelland & Stewart, 1994, p. 48.

3   S. Clarkson and C. McCall, *Trudeau and Our Times,* vol. I, *The Magnificent Obsession,* Toronto, McClelland & Stewart, 1991, p. 51.

4   G. Radwanski, *Trudeau,* Toronto, Macmillan of Canada, 1978, p. 69.

5   J. English, *Trudeau, Citizen of the World: The Life of Pierre Elliott Trudeau* – vol. 1, *1919–1968,* Toronto, Alfred Knopf Canada, 2006, pp. 166 and 168.

6   Letter to Grace Trudeau, Bangkok, July 18, 1949. LAC, vol. 11, f 22.

7   LAC, vol. 11, f 22. Our italics.

8   G. Radwanski, *Trudeau,* op. cit., p. 69.

9   C. McCall and S. Clarkson, *Trudeau,* vol. II, op. cit., p. 48.

10 See M. and M. Nemni, *Young Trudeau,* vol. I: *1919–1944,* Toronto, McClelland & Stewart, 2006, pp. 75 seq.

11 N. Berdyaev, *Slavery and Freedom,* Centenary Press, 1943, p. 251.

12 P.E. Trudeau, *Memoirs,* op. cit., p. 48.

13 Travel notes, LAC, vol. 11, f 21. Unless otherwise indicated, all quotes from Trudeau in this chapter are from this file.

14 LAC, vol. 11, f 1.

15 R. Rolland, "Pierre Elliott Trudeau," *Le Petit journal,* June 12, 1949. LAC, vol. 11, f 15.

16 Letter to Grace Trudeau, Kabul, December 2, 1948. LAC, vol. 11, f 22.

17 Letter to Grace Trudeau, Nanchang, March 10, 1949. LAC, vol. 11, f 22.

18 Letter to Grace Trudeau, Bangkok, January 28, 1949. LAC, vol. 11, f 22.

19 Letter to Grace Trudeau, Kabul, December 2, 1948. LAC, vol. 11, f 22.

20 Letter to Grace Trudeau, Bangkok, January 28, 1949. LAC, vol. 11, f 22.

21 T. Judt, *Postwar. A History of Europe Since 1945,* New York, Penguin Books, 2005, p. 19. This book is to be highly recommended; it won the Hannah Arendt Award in 2007. Tony Judt's acceptance speech is also worth reading: "The 'Problem of Evil' in Postwar Europe," in *The New York Review of Books,* February 14, 2008, pp. 33–35.

22 LAC, vol. 11, f21.

23 For more details, see our Volume 1, p. 209.

24 T. Judt, *Postwar,* op. cit., p. 16.

25 Ibid., p. 23.

26 Ibid., pp. 28–29.

27 Ibid., p. 32.

28 Please note that unless otherwise indicated, all quotes from Trudeau's journey are in LAC, vol. 11, f 21.

29 Since Trudeau wrote these lines, the figure of 5 million people exterminated at Auschwitz has been revised downwards. A current estimate is about 1,100,000. The figure of 5 or 4 million was long considered accurate, and certainly was accepted when Trudeau wrote these lines. (This figure refers to people exterminated at Auschwitz alone, and not in camps as a whole.)

30 LAC, vol. 11, f 16.

31 The question mark is Trudeau's own. He realized he was hazy about the details.

32 P.E. Trudeau, *Memoirs,* op. cit., p. 50.

33 Ibid.

34 Ibid., pp. 51–52.

35 LAC, vol. 11, f 24.

36 The article appeared in *Le Devoir,* July 23, 1949.

37 Trip to Israel, LAC, vol. 13, f 5.

38 A penetrating analysis of this problem is found for example in *Moi, juif arabe en Israël,* by Mordecai Soussan, Encre, 1985, 231 p.

39 According to the 1941 census, Canada's population was 11.507 million.

40 Letter to Grace Trudeau, Kabul, December 2, 1948. LAC, vol. 11, f 22.

41 Notes taken during Professor Meneges's lecture before a Catholic Action group in Bombay. LAC, vol. 11, f 21.

42 Letter to Grace Trudeau, Kabul, December 2, 1948, LAC, vol. 11, f 22.

43 Ibid.

44 Ibid.

45 M. Enright, *Ideas,* CBC Radio One, May 18, 2008.

46 Letter to Grace Trudeau, Bangkok, January 28, 1949, LAC, vol. 11, f 22.

47 Ibid.

48 J. English, *Citizen,* op. cit., p. 192.

49 See our Chapter 4 above, p. 104–107.

50 J. English, *Citizen,* op. cit., p. 192.

51 Ibid.

Chapter 6: LET THE FIGHT BEGIN! (pages 157–188)

1   LAC, vol. 11, f 21.

2   "Mr. Trudeau who has just returned from a two-year trip around the world has shared his impressions of this journey with us." Jeunesse indépendante catholique of Montreal. Report of the second civic summer

school held in the Eastern Townships, from June 18 to 22, 1949. LAC, vol. 11, f 18.

3   R. Rolland, "Pierre Elliott Trudeau," *Le petit journal,* June 12, 1949, LAC, vol. 11, f 5.

4   This summer school was held from June 18 to 25, 1949. The report on Trudeau's talk of June 22, "Where Is the World Headed?" is found on pp. 16–17, LAC, vol. 11, f 18.

5   *Le Devoir,* April 13, 1949.

6   *Le Petit Journal,* June 12, 1949.

7   "Where Is the World Headed?" op. cit.

8   Letter in *Le Devoir,* published December 5, 1950.

9   Letter to *Le Devoir,* January 22, 1951, LAC, vol. 22, f 7.

10 G. Filion, letter of January 31, 1951, LAC, vol. 22, f 7.

11 P.E. Trudeau, "Matériaux pour servir à une enquête sur le cléricalisme," *Cité libre,* May 1953, p. 29.

12 Report on "Where Is the World Headed?"

13 P.E. Trudeau, *Memoirs,* Toronto, McClelland & Stewart, 1993, p. 61.

14 R. Rumilly, *Maurice Duplessis et son temps,* Montreal, Fides, 1973, and C. Black, *Duplessis,* Toronto, McClelland & Stewart, 1976, and *Render Unto Caesar – The Life and Legacy of Maurice Duplessis,* Toronto, Key Porter Books Ltd., 1998.

15 G. Boismenu, *Le duplessisme: Politique économique et rapports de force, 1944–1960,* Montreal, Presses de l'Université de Montréal, 1981.

16 G. Boismenu, "Le duplessisme: substrat social d'une alliance politique de classe," in A. Gagnon and M. Sarra-Bournet (eds.), *Entre la Grande Noirceur et la société libérale,* Montreal, Québec-Amérique, 1997, p. 283.

17 A. Gagnon and M. Sarra-Bournet (eds.), *Entre la Grande Noirceur,* op.cit.

18 LAC, vol. 11, f 21.

19 P. Laporte, *The True Face of Duplessis,* Montreal, Harvest House, 1960, p. 19.

20 Ibid., p. 50.

21 Ibid., p. 47.

22 J. Hébert, *Duplessis, non merci!* Montreal, Les éditions du Boréal, 2000, p. 168.

23 P. Laporte, *The True Face of Duplessis,* op. cit., p. 75.

24 J.-F. Nadeau, "50 ans après la mort de Duplessis: l'homme de l'arbitraire," *Le Devoir,* September 5, 2009. See also R. Comeau and J.-F. Nadeau, "Actions de Jacques Perrault," in A.-G. Gagnon and M. Sarra-Bournet, *Duplessis,* op. cit., pp. 121–143, in which the authors accuse

Duplessis of having indirectly caused the suicide of one of his major opponents, the prominent lawyer and activist, Jacques Perrault.

25 P. Laporte, *The True Face of Duplessis,* op. cit., p. 41.

26 G. Boismenu, "Le duplessisme: substrat social d'une alliance politique de classe," op. cit., pp. 299–300.

27 R. Pelletier, *Partis politiques et société québécoise: de Duplessis à Bourassa, 1944–1970,* Montreal, Québec/Amérique, 1989, p. 38.

28 P. Laporte, *The True Face of Duplessis,* op. cit., pp. 86–87.

29 P.E. Trudeau, "L'homme d'État, un serviteur," an article appearing in *Vrai* in 1958. Translated by I.M. Owen and published as part of *Approaches to Politics,* Toronto, Oxford University Press, 2010, p. 65.

30 *Le Devoir,* July 23, 1948, in R. Pelletier, *Partis politiques,* op. cit., p. 43.

31 G. Boismenu, *Le duplessisme : Politique économique et rapports de force,* op. cit., p. 219.

32 J. Rouillard, *Le Syndicalisme québécois, deux siècles d'histoire,* Montreal, Boréal, 2004, p. 122.

33 *Le Devoir,* January 14, 1954. Quoted by D. Monière, *Le développement des idéologies au Québec,* Montreal, Éditions Québec/Amérique, 1977, p. 301.

34 *Le Soleil,* July 26, 1948, in R. Pelletier, *Partis politiques,* op. cit., p. 43.

35 P.-A. Linteau, R. Durocher, J.-C. Robert, and F. Ricard, *Histoire du Québec contemporain – volume 2: Les Québec depuis 1930,* Montreal, Boréal, 1989, p. 208.

36 M. Sarra-Bournet, *L'affaire Roncarelli, Duplessis contre les Témoins de Jéhovah,* Quebec, Institut québécois de recherche sur la culture, 1986, p. 101.

37 Ibid., p. 103.

38 P.E. Trudeau, *Memoirs,* op. cit., p. 62.

39 The full text of *Refus Global,* in both French and English, can be freely accessed on several websites.

40 *Le Devoir,* September 28, 1948.

41 *Histoire de la FTQ – des tout débuts jusqu'en 1965, des milliers d'histoires qui façonnent l'histoire* [Émile Bourdreau] Quebec Federation of Labour (FTQ), 1988, p. 109.

42 J. Rouillard, *Histoire du syndicalisme au Québec, Des origines à nos jours,* Montreal, Les Éditions du Boreal, 1989, pp. 38–39.

43 P.E. Trudeau (ed.), *The Asbestos Strike,* translated by James Boake, Toronto, Lewis & Samuel, 1974.

44 Joint declaration of François Vaudreuil and Rodrigue Chartier in *Le Devoir,* February 13, 1999.

45 J. Rouillard, *Le Syndicalisme québécois, deux siècles d'histoire,* op. cit., p. 132.

46 Ibid., p. 135.

47 Ibid., p. 135.

48 I. Abella, *On Strike: Six Key Labour Struggles in Canada 1919–1949,* Toronto, James Lorimer & Company, Publishers, 1975 (first edition 1974), pp. xiii–xiv.

49 M. Behiels, *Prelude to Quebec's Quite Revolution, Liberalism Versus Neo-Nationalism, 1945–1960,* Montreal and Kingston, McGill-Queen's University Press, 1985, p. 5.

50 G. Bergeron, *Du Duplessisme à Trudeau et Bourassa, 1956–1971,* Montreal, Éditions Parti Pris, 1971 (2nd revised and enlarged edition of *Du Duplessisme à Johnson, 1956–1966*), p. 123. According to Bergeron, the first case of "public furor" came·in 1935–1936 when the Taschereau government collapsed, the second was the virtual unanimity in Quebec during the Conscription Crisis, the third was the Asbestos strike, while the fourth was the Dion-O'Neill declaration of 1956, when they jointly published a forty-seven-page pamphlet on political immorality in Quebec.

51 J-P. Warren, *L'engagement sociologique. La tradition sociologique du Québec francophone,* Montreal, Boréal, 2003, p. 255.

52 E. Delisle and P. Malouf, *Le Quatuor d'Asbestos,* Montreal, Éditions Varia, 2004, p. 20.

53 G. Beausoleil, "History of the Asbestos strike," in P.E. Trudeau (ed.), *The Asbestos Strike,* op. cit., p. 144.

54 J.-P. Geoffroy, "Le procès Rocque: une abstraction," in *Cité Libre,* May 1951, p. 12.

55 Ibid., p. 13.

56 E. Delisle and P. Malouf, *Le Quatuor d'Asbestos,* op. cit.

57 P.E. Trudeau (ed.), *The Asbestos Strike,* op. cit., p. 199.

58 Ibid., p. 203.

59 See the leading role E. Delisle and P. K. Malouf attributed to Burton LeDoux in *Le Quatuor d'Asbestos,* op. cit.

60 Chapter VI, Gérard Dion, "The Church and the Conflict in the Asbestos Industry," in P.E. Trudeau, *The Asbestos Strike,* op. cit., p. 205.

61 J. Rouillard, *Le syndicalisme québécois, deux siècles d'histoire,* op. cit., p. 110.

62 Gérard Dion, "The Church and the Asbestos Conflict," op. cit., p. 214.

63 Ibid., p. 210–211.

64 Ibid., p. 222.

65 This sermon was reported in *Le Devoir* on May 2, 1949, and quoted by G. Dion in "The Church and the Conflict in the Asbestos Industry," op. cit., p. 211.

66 *La documentation catholique,* vol. 47, 1950, columns 613–616. Claude Bélanger, Marianopolis College, 2001. http://faculty.marianopolis.edu/c. belanger/quebechistory/docs/asbestos/index.htm.

67 *Le Devoir,* March 23, 1949, in G. Dion, "The Church and the Conflict in the Asbestos Industry," op. cit., p. 221.

68 G. Beausoleil, chapter IV, "History of the Strike at Asbestos," op. cit., p. 164.

69 Ibid., p. 164.

70 *1949 Diary,* LAC, vol. 11, f 20.

71 H. Brown, "A report on the Asbestos strike," in G. Dion, "The Church and the Conflict in the Asbestos Industry," op. cit., p. 165.

72 G. Boismenu, *Le Duplessisme,* op. cit., p. 348.

73 Ibid., p. 349.

74 G. Dion, "The Church and the Conflict in the Asbestos Industry," op. cit., p. 252.

75 Letter to Roger Rolland, April 19, 1950. Private collection of R. Rolland. In this passage, Trudeau himself underlined the word "completely."

76 Draft dated May 1950, LAC, vol. 20, f 1.

77 *Cité libre,* June 1950, p. 39.

78 Letter to *Le Devoir* dated May 12, 1950. LAC, vol. 9, f 12.

79 P-A.Linteau, *Histoire de Montréal depuis la Confédération,* Montreal, Éditions du Boréal, 2000, p 346.

80 R. Lapointe, *L'histoire bouleversante de Mgr Charbonneau,* Les Éditions du Jour, 1962, chapter 2, "Une victime de son milieu."

81 M. and M. Nemni, "Entretien avec le révérend père Georges-Henri Lévesque" [A Conversation with Father George-Henri Lévesque], *Cité libre,* Fall 1999, p. 22 (translated by J-P. Murray).

82 Ibid., p. 22.

83 *1949 Diary,* LAC, vol. 11, f 20.

84 M. Lamontagne, *Le fédéralisme canadien: évolution et problèmes,* Quebec City, Presses Universitaires Laval, 1954.

85 Simon Fraser University, *Canadian Election Results: 1867–2000.* www.sfu.ca/~aheard/elections/1867-present.html.

86 *Le Devoir,* June 28, 1949. LAC, vol. 22, f 6.

87 *Le Devoir,* July 6, 1949. Letter sent on July 2 from Mont-Rolland (where Roger Rolland lived). LAC, vol. 22, f 6.

88 J. English, *Trudeau, Citizen of the World: The Life of Pierre Elliott Trudeau*, vol. 1: *1919–1968*, Toronto, Alfred Knopf Canada, 2006, p. 203.

89 Ibid., p. 209.

90 M. and M. Nemni, *Young Trudeau*, vol. 1: *1919–1944*, Toronto, McClelland & Stewart, pp. 308–309.

91 Draft letter in the file containing his application to join the civil service. LAC, vol. 9, f 4.

92 Letter from Pierre Dumas, June 2, 1949. LAC, vol. 9, f 4.

93 Letter from Pierre Dumas, June 8, 1949. LAC, vol. 9 .

94 Letter Pierre Dumas, dated "Friday morning." LAC, vol. 9, f 4.

95 *Diary.* LAC, vol. 39 f 2.

96 Letter of August 31, 1949. LAC, vol. 9, f 7.

Chapter 7: GRADUATE COURSE IN APPLIED FEDERALISM
(pages 189–215)

1   J. Duchastel, *Marcel Rioux, Entre l'utopie et la raison*, Montreal, Les éditions Nouvelle Optique, 1981, pp. 46–47.

2   Ibid., p. 83. Trudeau teases his friend by writing "anthropophagite" instead of "anthropologist."

3   M. Rioux, "Idéologie et crise de conscience du Canada français," *Cité libre*, December 1955, p. 21.

4   Ibid., p. 29.

5   J. Duchastel, *Marcel Rioux*, op. cit., p. 108.

6   Ibid., p. 115.

7   Ibid., p. 115.

8   M. Rioux, *Pour prendre publiquement congé de quelques salauds*, Montreal, L'Hexagone, 1980.

9   Letter dated Ottawa: September–October, 1949. Private collection of R. Rolland.

10 For more details on the love affair between Trudeau and Helen Segerstråle, see J. English, *Trudeau, Citizen of the World: The Life of Pierre Elliott Trudeau*, vol. 1: *1919–1968*, Toronto, Alfred Knopf Canada, 2006, pp. 231–235.

11 Letter to Rolland, September-October 1949. Private collection of R. Rolland.

12 Letter to Rolland, October 7, 1949. Private collection of R. Rolland.

13 "On Price Support for Commodity Surpluses," September 21, 1949, LAC, vol. 9, f 17.

14 "Notes on Compact Theory," LAC, vol. 10, f 15. Trudeau put "autumn" on this document, without providing any specific date.

15 Letter of Maurice Duplessis to Louis Saint-Laurent in *Le Devoir* of September 24, 1949, quoting Duplessis.

16 A. Laurendeau, Editorial: "La conférence fédérale/provinciale s'ouvre demain," *Le Devoir,* January 9, 1950.

17 Notes on Gérin-Lajoie's dissertation. LAC, vol. 10, f 10.

18 In "Notes on the Compact Theory," Trudeau quoted *Confederation Debates,* p. 30. LAC, vol. 10, f 15.

19 Talk by Gérin-Lajoie, quoted in the daily *Le Canada,* December 28, 1949. LAC, vol. 10, f 22.

20 "Federalism Revisited." LAC, vol. 9, f 9.

21 Letter of thanks from Jules Léger. LAC, vol. 9, f 9.

22 The complete title of the document is *Cabinet Committee on the Constitutional Conference. Programme for the Second Session of the Constitutional Conference.* LAC, vol. 9, f 10.

23 P.E. Trudeau, "Quebec and the Constitutional Problem." This text serves as an introduction to *Federalism and the French Canadians,* a compendium of his articles and essays published in French in 1967, and in English translation the following year, when Trudeau was a member of Lester Pearson's Cabinet and a few months before he became prime minister. This book and the introduction in particular, which focuses on constitutional issues, provide a good overview of his thought at a critical juncture in his political life.

24 Letter to Roger Rolland dated April 19, 1950. Private collection of R. Rolland.

25 "Theory and Practice of Federal-Provincial Cooperation." LAC, vol. 10, f 6.

26 "Federal-Provincial Cooperation." LAC, vol. 9, f 20.

27 "Theory and Practice," op. cit. LAC, vol. 10, f 6.

28 Ibid.

29 Ibid.

30 Ibid.

31 Ibid.

32 Ibid.

33 Officially known as the Royal Commission on Dominion-Provincial Relations.

34 "Federal-Provincial Cooperation." LAC, vol. 9, f 20.

35 "Theory and Practice," op. cit. LAC, vol. 10, f 6.

36 Ibid.

37 Ibid.

38 P.E. Trudeau, *A Mess That Deserves a Big No,* Montreal, Robert Davies Publishing, 1992, p. 32. Trudeau was referring to the referendum across Canada on the so-called Charlottetown Accord Consensus.

39 On September 27, 1984, Trudeau recalled his admiration for the actions
    of Frank Scott in an interview with Sandra Djwa. In S. Djwa, *The
    Politics of Imagination,* Toronto, McClelland & Stewart, 1984, p. 319.

40 Letter from Father Cousineau. LAC, vol. 9, f 3.

41 Memo to Robertson. LAC, vol. 9, f 23.

42 P.E. Trudeau, "Pearson ou l'abdication de l'esprit," *Cité libre,* April 1963,
    pp. 7–12.

43 Draft of a letter to Jules Léger. LAC, vol. 9, f 10.

44 "Canadian Foreign Policy in a Two-Power World." LAC, vol. 10, f 11.

45 Letter to Douglas Lepan and to a colleague of his, April 28, 1951. LAC,
    vol. 10, f 7.

46 "Positions sur la présente guerre," *Cité libre,* May 1951, p. 1.

47 Ibid., p. 4.

48 Ibid., p. 7.

49 Ibid., p. 9.

50 Ibid.

51 Ibid.

52 Ibid., p. 10.

53 Ibid., p. 11.

54 Letter to Norman Robertson. LAC, vol. 9, f 2.

55 P.E. Trudeau, *Memoirs,* Toronto, McClelland & Stewart, 1993, p. 65.

Chapter 8: THE BIRTH OF CITÉ LIBRE (pages 216–253)

1   L. Dion, *Québec, 1945–2000,* vol. 2: *Les intellectuels et le temps de
    Duplessis,* Quebec City, Les presses de l'Université Laval, 1993, p. 271.

2   In M. Cardinal, V. Lemieux, and F. Sauvageau, *Si l'Union nationale
    m'était contée . . . ,* Montreal, Boréal Express, 1978, p. 236.

3   G. Pelletier, *Years of Impatience: 1950–1960,* Toronto, Methuen, 1984,
    p. 126.

4   G.-E. Lapalme, *Mémoires,* vol. II: *Le vent de l'oubli,* Leméac, 1971, p. 87.

5   L. Dion, *Québec, 1945–2000,* vol. 2: *Les intellectuels,* op. cit., p. 279.

6   G. Bergeron, *Notre miroir à deux faces: Trudeau, Lévesque et, forcément,
    avec bien d'autres . . . ,* Montreal, Québec-Amérique, 1985, p. 81.

7   Ibid., p 83.

8   Ibid., p. 84.

9   Ibid., p. 82.

10 C. Ryan, "L'Universitaire tiraillé entre l'étude et l'action," in R. Hudon
    and R. Pelletier (eds.), *L'engagement intellectuel, Mélanges en l'honneur de
    Léon Dion,* Quebec City, Les Presses de l'Université Laval, 1991, p. 540.

11   G. Cormier, "Un théâtre d'ombre," *Le Devoir,* January 14, 1978.

12   G. Pelletier, *Years of Impatience,* op. cit., p. 114.

13   Ibid., p. 114.

14   J.-P. Warren, "Gérard Pelletier et *Cité libre,*" op. cit., p. 315.

15   Ibid., p. 334.

16   G. Pelletier, *Years of Impatience,* op. cit., p. 115.

17   Ibid., p. 126.

18   G. Pelletier, "*Cité libre* confesse ses intentions," *Cité libre,* February 1951, p. 4.

19   G. Pelletier, "Histoire de collégiens qui ont aujourd'hui 30 ans," *Cité libre,* June 1950, p. 6.

20   G. Pelletier, "Crise d'autorité ou crise de liberté?", *Cité libre,* June–July 1952, p. 2.

21   G. Pelletier, "Réflexions sur l'état de siège," *Cité libre,* February 1957, p. 40.

22   "Histoire de collégiens qui ont aujourd'hui 30 ans," op. cit., p. 8.

23   J. English, *Trudeau, Citizen of the World: The Life of Pierre Elliott Trudeau,* vol. 1: *1919–1968,* Toronto, Alfred Knopf Canada, 2006, p. 241.

24   Trudeau's personal library, Pine Avenue West, Montreal.

25   "Mounier disparaît," *Cité libre,* June 1950, p. 37.

26   E. Mounier, "Entretiens VIII," November 22, 1934. Quoted by E.-M. Meunier and J.-P. Warren, *Sortir de la "Grande noirceur," L'horizon "personnaliste" de la Révolution tranquille,* Montreal, Les Cahiers du Septentrion, 2002, p. 408.

27   G. Pelletier, "Mounier et les dialogues d'*Esprit,*" *Le Devoir,* April 15, 1950. In Warren, "Gérard Pelletier et *Cité libre,*" op. cit., p. 338.

28   In M. Winock, *Le siècle des intellectuels,* Paris, Éditions du Seuil (2nd edition), 1999, p. 404.

29   Ibid., p. 403.

30   "Blum et Laski," *Cité libre,* June 1950, p. 38.

31   Ibid., p. 38.

32   Ibid.

33   Ibid.

34   J.-P. Warren, "Gérard Pelletier et *Cité libre,*" op. cit. p. 313–346.

35   E.-M. Meunier and J-P. Warren, *Sortir de la "Grande noirceur," L'horizon "personnaliste" de la Révolution tranquille,* Montreal, Les Cahiers du Septentrion, 2002.

36   J.-P. Warren, "Gérard Pelletier et *Cité libre,*" op. cit., p. 339.

37   A. Burelle, *Pierre Elliott Trudeau: L'intellectuel et le politique,* Montreal, Éditions Fides, 2005, p. 23.

38 P.E. Trudeau, "The Values of a Just Society," in T.S. Axworthy and P.E. Trudeau, *Towards a Just Society: The Trudeau Years,* Toronto, Viking, 1990, p. 363.

39 P.E. Trudeau, *Memoirs,* Toronto, McClelland & Stewart, 1993, p. 40.

40 Ibid.

41 E. Mounier, *Manifeste au service du personnalisme,* Fernand Aubier, Éditions Montaigne, 1936, p. 9.

42 Interview conducted in 1993 by J.-M. Domenach with P.E. Trudeau, for a television series. LAC MG 26, Series 03, vol. 24, f 4.

43 G. Boudic, *Esprit, 1944–1982: les métamorphoses d'une revue,* Institut Mémoires de l'édition contemporaine, 2005, p. 50.

44 J. Hellman, "Maritain and Mounier: A Secret Quarrel over the Future of the Church," *The Review of Politics,* vol. 42, no. 2 (April 1980), pp. 152–166.

45 M. Winock, *"Esprit," des intellectuels dans la cité: 1930–1950,* Éditions du seuil, 1996, p. 375.

46 Ibid., p. 378 *et seq.* For more details on Winock's point of view on this subject, see the section "Jésus + Marx" in this same work, pp. 375–383.

47 J. Lacroix, "De la démocratie libérale à la démocratie massive," *Esprit,* March 1946, in T. Judt, *Un passé imparfait – Les intellectuels en France, 1944–1956,* Paris, Librairie Arthème Fayard, 1992, p. 56.

48 G. Boudic, *Esprit,* op. cit., p. 57.

49 E. Mounier, "L'homme américain," *Esprit,* November 1946, pp. 208–211, in Judt, *Un passé,* op. cit., p. 236.

50 "Éditorial," *Esprit,* June 1952, in Judt, *Un passé,* op. cit., p. 236.

51 "Éditorial: Les flammes de Budapest," *Esprit,* December 1956, p. 773, in Judt, *Un passé,* op. cit., p. 236.

52 For a more comprehensive look at Maritain's position, see our first volume, particularly pp. 239–245.

53 In this English translation, the quote is taken from J. Maritain, *The Twilight of Civilization,* New York, Sheed & Ward, 1943, p. 55.

54 Likewise, in this English translation, the quote is taken from J. Maritain, *The Rights of Man and Natural Law,* New York, Charles Scribner's Sons, 1943, p. 2.

55 J. Maritain, *Humanisme intégral. Problèmes temporels et spirituels d'une nouvelle chrétienté,* Aubier, Éditions Montaigne, 1968 (1st edition 1936), p. 170.

56 In this English translation, the quote is taken from J. Maritain, *Man and the State,* Chicago, University of Chicago Press, 1951, pp. 5–6. This passage is also quoted in Burelle, *Pierre Elliott Trudeau,* op. cit., p. 39.

57 F. Mauriac, *Journal*, quoted in Winock, *Le siècle*, op. cit., p. 527.

58 J. Maritain, *Humanisme intégral*, op. cit., p. 172.

59 *Esprit*, No. 192, July 1952.

60 Interview with J.-M. Domenach. LAC MG 26, Serie 03, vol. 24, f 4.

61 R. Boisvert, "Domiciles de la peur sociale," *Cité libre*, June 1950, p. 13.

62 Ibid., p. 16.

63 Ibid., p. 14.

64 P. Vadeboncœur, "L'irréalisme de notre culture," *Cité libre*, December 1951, pp. 20–21.

65 P. Vadeboncœur, "Le sort fait à la révolution," *Cité libre*, no. 3, May 1951, pp. 17–20.

66 Ibid., p. 19.

67 G. Cormier, "Petite méditation sur l'existence canadienne-française," *Cité libre*, June 1950, p. 36.

68 Ibid., p. 29.

69 Ibid., p. 30.

70 Ibid., p. 26.

71 Ibid., p. 28.

72 Ibid., p. 35.

73 Ibid., p. 35. Cormier was obviously referring to Maurice Duplessis.

74 Ibid., p. 35.

75 G. Pelletier, *Years of Impatience*, op. cit., p. 121.

76 M-J. d'Anjou, *Relations*, Xth year, no. 117, September 1950, p. 277.

77 Ibid., p. 278.

78 Letter of Father d'Anjou to Trudeau, October 7, 1950. LAC, vol. 21, f 9.

79 P.E. Trudeau, "Politique fonctionnelle I," *Cité libre*, June 1950, p. 21, quoted in P.E. Trudeau, *Against the Current: Selected Writings, 1939–1996*, edited by Gérard Pelletier, Toronto, McClelland & Stewart, 1996, p. 28.

80 P.E. Trudeau, "Politique fonctionnelle II," *Cité libre*, February 1951, pp. 28–29.

81 Letter from G. Pelletier, February 28, 1951. LAC, vol. 21, f 21.

82 G. Pelletier, *Years of Impatience*, op. cit., p. 119.

83 M-J. d'Anjou, "Le cas de *Cité libre*," *Relations*, XIth year, no. 123, March 1951, p. 69.

84 Ibid., p. 70.

85 Letter from Father d'Anjou, February 21, 1951. LAC, vol. 21, f 9.

86 Letter from Father d'Anjou, March 2, 1951. LAC, vol. 21, f 9.

87 F. Hertel, "Lettre à mes amis [subtitled:] Refusé un peu partout," dated August 15, 1950, *Cité libre*, February 1951, p. 34.

88 R. Rolland, "Interview imaginaire avec François Hertel," *Cité libre*, February 1951, p. 38.

89 M-J. d'Anjou, "Le cas de *Cité libre*," op. cit, p. 70.

90 Interview with J.-M. Domenach, op. cit.

91 P.E. Trudeau, "Politique fonctionnelle," *Cité libre*, June 1950, pp. 20–24, some of which appeared in English translation in P.E. Trudeau, *Against the Current*.

92 Ibid., p. 21.

93 Ibid., p. 21.

94 Ibid.

95 Ibid., p. 22.

96 Ibid., p. 23.

97 P.E. Trudeau, "Politique fonctionnelle II," *Cité Libre*, February 1951, p. 24.

98 Ibid, p. 25.

99 Ibid.

100 Ibid.

101 Ibid., p. 27.

102 Ibid., p. 28.

103 Ibid.

104 Ibid., pp. 28–29.

105 Ibid., p. 29.

106 See for example Jean-Baptiste Boulanger's insulting remarks about Harvey, in our first volume, pp. 178–179.

107 G. Bessette, L. Geslin, and C. Parent, *Histoire de la littérature canadienne-française par les textes*, Centre éducatif et culturel, Inc., 1968.

108 Ibid.

109 Letter of Alan Thomas Jr., February 25, 1951. LAC, vol. 20, f 2.

110 "Note liminaire," *Cité libre*, December 1952, p. 1.

111 Ibid.

112 C. Lussier, "Monsieur Pat Walsh, les communistes et *Cité libre*," *Cité libre*, May 1953, p. 44.

113 Ibid., p. 45.

114 P.E. Trudeau, "Réflexions sur la politique au Canada français," *Cité libre*, December 1952, pp. 53–70.

115 Ibid., p. 53. Once again, some of this article appeared in English translation in P.E. Trudeau, *Against the Current*.

116 Ibid.

117 Ibid., pp. 62–63.

118 Ibid., p. 63.

119 G. Dion and L. O'Neill, priests, *L'immoralité politique dans la province de Québec,* Comité de Moralité Publique de la Ligue d'Action Civique, 1956. The quotes here are from the English edition, *Two Priests Censure Political Immorality in the Province of Quebec,* Public Morality Committee of the Civic Action League, 1956.

120 Ibid., p. 8.

121 Ibid., pp. 10–11.

122 Ibid., pp. 15–16.

123 Ibid., p. 16.

124 Ibid., p. 17.

125 P.E. Trudeau, "Réflexions sur la politique au Canada français," op. cit., p. 54.

126 Ibid., p. 55.

127 Ibid.

128 Ibid.

129 Ibid., p. 56.

130 Ibid., p. 60.

131 Ibid., p. 59.

132 Ibid., p. 65.

133 Ibid., p. 60.

134 Ibid., p. 61.

135 Ibid., p. 65.

136 Ibid., p. 66.

137 Ibid., p. 59.

138 Ibid., p. 65.

139 P.E. Trudeau, "L'élection fédérale du 10 août 1953: prodromes et conjectures," *Cité libre,* November 1953, pp. 1–10.

140 Ibid., p. 1.

141 Ibid., p. 2.

142 Ibid., p. 3.

143 Ibid.

144 Ibid.

145 Ibid., p. 4.

146 Ibid., p. 5.

147 Ibid.

148 Ibid., p. 7.

149 Ibid., p. 8.

150 Ibid.

151 Ibid., p. 9.

152 Ibid., p. 9–10. Our italics here reflect Trudeau's underlining the phrase.

153 Ibid., p. 10.

Chapter 9: THE HELLISH STRUGGLE OF ANTICLERICALISM
(pages 254–285)

1   G. Pelletier, *Years of Impatience: 1950–1960*, Toronto, Methuen, 1984, p. 131.

2   L. Dion, *Québec, 1945–2000*, vol. 2, *Les intellectuels et le temps de Duplessis*, Quebec City, Les Presses de l'Université Laval, 1993, p. 196.

3   C. McCall and S. Clarkson, *Trudeau and Our Times*, vol. II: *The Heroic Delusion*, Toronto, McClelland & Stewart, 1994, p. 75. They cite Ramsay Cook as a reference.

4   Agenda 1951. LAC, vol. 39, f 2. On November 23, he wrote that the Naples museum was "wonderful."

5   "Évitez d'être Anglais . . .," *Le Devoir*, February 1, 1952.

6   "Les Anglais auraient tort de s'obstiner," *Le Devoir*, February 2, 1952.

7   "Notes sur une guerre," *Cité libre*, February 1957, pp. 1–2.

8   "Le Soudan aux Soudanais," *Le Devoir*, February 5, 1952.

9   "À propos de missions." LAC, vol. 11, f 15.

10 Letter from Helen Segerstråle, January 26, 1952, quoted by J. English, *Trudeau, Citizen of the World: The Life of Pierre Elliott Trudeau*, vol. 1: *1919–1968*, Toronto, Alfred Knopf Canada, 2006, p. 234.

11 Agenda 1952. LAC, vol. 39, f 3.

12 Ibid.

13 Pelletier, *Years of Impatience*, op. cit., pp. 131–133.

14 Ibid., p. 138.

15 Letter from Alfred Sauvy, dated October 4, 1951. LAC, Fonds Maurice Lamontagne, MG32, B32, vol. 12. All correspondence related to the Moscow Conference is contained in this file.

16 Letter from Lamontagne to Sauvy, October 15, 1952.

17 Letter written by Trudeau from Florence, November 12, 1951. Fonds Maurice Lamontagne, op. cit.

18 S. Clavette, in *Les dessous d'Asbestos, une lutte idéologique contre la participation des travailleurs*, Quebec City, Les Presses de l'Université Laval, 2005, p. 394.

19 Message published in *l'Action catholique de Montréal*, vol. 7, no. 4, December 1950. Quoted by S. Clavette, *Les dessous*, op. cit., p. 407.

20 S. Clavette, *Les dessous*, op. cit., p. 406.

21 Ibid., p. 356.

22 Ibid., p. 357.

23 The series published in *Le Devoir* can be found in LAC, vol. 12, f 13.

24 P.E. Trudeau, "L'auberge de la grande URSS," *Le Devoir,* June 14, 1952. LAC, vol. 12, f 13.

25 Ibid.

26 "Premières rencontres," *Le Devoir,* June 16, 1952.

27 "Un peuple sympathique, mais conventionnel jusqu'à la nausée," *Le Devoir,* June 17, 1952.

28 "Le citoyen soviétique demeure un 'cochon de payant,'" *Le Devoir,* June 18, 1952.

29 "La conférence commence . . ." *Le Devoir,* June 19, 1952. "Les conclusions de la Conférence," *Le Devoir,* June 20, 1952.

30 "Est-ce pour ça qu'on a fait trois révolutions?", *Le Devoir,* June 21, 1952.

31 "Un mois en URSS," fourth talk given on CBF, the French network of the Canadian Broadcasting Corporation, Thursday September 25, 1952, entitled "Aux prises avec le Politbureau." LAC, vol. 12, f 16.

32 CBF, "Un mois en URSS." The first talk, given on September 4, was "J'ai fait mes Pâques à Moscou"; the second, given on September 11, was "Staline est-il poète?"; the third, given on September 18, was "Au sommet des Caucases"; the fourth, given on September 25, was "Aux prises avec le Politbureau." Vol. 12, f 16.

33 *Le Quartier Latin,* October 23, 1952, p. 5. LAC, vol. 12, f 12.

34 *Nos cours,* vol. XIV, no. 8, November 15, 1952, pp. 15–28; LAC, vol. 12, f 14. Unless otherwise noted, all quotations regarding this debate are to be found in LAC, vol. 12, f 14.

35 Letter to André Laurendeau of November 17, 1952.

36 Handwritten note at the bottom of the letter of December 1, 1952, addressed to Louis-Philippe Roy.

37 *Nos cours,* vol. XIV, no. 13, p. 29.

38 Trudeau's personal notes. LAC, vol. 12, f 14.

39 A. Laurendeau, "La chasse aux sorcières est-elle commencée?", *L'Action nationale,* January 1953, pp. 78–82.

40 F-A. Angers, "Au nom de l'honnêteté et du bon sens!", *L'Action nationale,* January 1953, pp. 37–60.

41 F-A. Angers, "Comment on a dénaturé le reportage de P.E. Trudeau," *Le Devoir,* February 21, 1953.

42 "Enquête sur le cléricalisme, *Cité libre*," May 1953. The first part, on pages 29–37, is signed P.E. Trudeau, while the second part, on pages 38–43, is signed R. Rolland.

43 Ibid., pp. 40–41.

44 Ibid., p. 34.

45 Ibid., p. 29.

46 Ibid., p. 37.

47 Ibid., p. 32.

48 Ibid., p. 37.

49 Ibid., p. 35.

50 Ibid., p. 36.

51 Ibid., p. 36.

52 Ibid., p. 34.

53 Ibid., pp. 35–36.

54 Ibid., p. 36.

55 Ibid., p. 37.

56 Letter from McInnis of January 11, 1954. LAC, vol. 12, f 18.

57 Immigration, March 9, 1954. LAC, vol. 12, f 18.

58 Letter to Mgr. Pelletier of June 6, 1960. LAC, vol. 21, f 35.

59 Letter from Mgr. Pelletier of June 20, 1960. LAC, vol. 21, f 35.

60 P.E. Trudeau, "De l'inconvénient d'être catholique," *Cité libre*, March 1961, p. 21.

61 M. Behiels, *Prelude to Quebec's Quiet Revolution: Liberalism versus Neo-Nationalism, 1945–1960*, Montreal and Kingston, McGill-Queen's University Press, 1985, p. 71.

62 N. Berdyaev, *Slavery and Freedom*, Centenary Press, 1943, p. 28.

63 J-P. Warren and E.-M. Meunier, "L'horizon 'personnaliste' de la Révolution tranquille," in *Société*, nos 20/21, Summer 1999, pp. 347–448. Subsequently re-issued under the title *Sortir de la "Grande noirceur." L'horizon "personnaliste" de la Révolution tranquille*, Les Éditions du Septentrion, 2002, 310 pp.

64 Ibid., p. 32.

65 G. Pelletier, "Crise d'autorité ou crise de liberté?", *Cité libre*, June–July 1952, p. 6.

66 M. Gauvreau, *The Catholic Origins of Quebec's Quiet Revolution, 1931–1970*, Montreal and Kingston, McGill-Queen's University Press, 2005, p. 355.

67 S. Clavette, *Les dessous*, op. cit., p. 418.

68 G. Pelletier, "Les accusations de M. Marcel Clément," *Cité libre*, February 1957, p. 52.

69 P.E. Trudeau, "Le père Ledit et la délectation morose," *Cité libre*, February 1957, p. 69.

70 G. Pelletier, "Les accusations de M. Marcel Clément," op. cit., p. 52.

71 D. Seljak, "Trudeau and the Privatization of Religion," in N. Southam, *Pierre,* Toronto, McClelland & Stewart Ltd., 2005, p. 55.

72 J. English, R. Gwyn, and P. Whitney Lackenbauer, (eds.), *The Hidden Pierre Elliott Trudeau: The Faith Behind the Politics,* Ottawa, Novalis, 2004.

Chapter 10: DEMOCRACY FIRST AND FOREMOST (pages 286–320)

1   Handwritten notes for the closing address, Annual Meeting of the Quebec Industrial Unions Federation (CTC) at Champigny, June 1954. LAC, vol. 15, f 10.

2   R. Picard, *L'unité européenne par l'intercitoyenneté,* Paris, Éditions Spid, 1948, 117 pp.

3   P.E. Trudeau, *L'actualité économique,* Autumn 1950, p. 562. In LAC, vol. 22, f 1.

4   Ibid., p. 563.

5   Letter from nudists, dated August 31, 1951. LAC, vol. 14, f 2.

6   Court appearance delayed, letter of March 7, 1953. LAC, vol. 14, f 2.

7   P. Gzowski, "Portrait of an Intellectual in Action," *Maclean's,* February 24, 1962, p. 23 and pp. 29–30.

8   Sauvé Affair, handwritten note by Trudeau dated November 4, 1961. LAC, vol. 14, f 5.

9   Letter of May 26, 1955. LAC, vol. 14, f 10.

10 Authors' interview with Jacques Hébert, December 10, 2002.

11 Union arbitrator. LAC, vol. 18–19.

12 Chartrand case. LAC, vol. 18, f 4.

13 See our first volume, pp. 118–119.

14 The details about this evening are to be found in LAC, vol. 26, f 1.

15 Speech to young CCFers. LAC, vol. 26, f 1.

16 Ibid.

17 Ibid.

18 Ibid.

19 Radio-Canada, December 8, 1953. LAC, vol. 25, f 6.

20 Ibid.

21 Ibid.

22 Ibid.

23 Mignault Conference. LAC, vol. 26, f 7.

24 Ibid.

25 G. Duguay, "La peur conduit au fascisme, le fascisme à la révolution," *Le Devoir,* February 6, 1954.

26 Mignault Conference. LAC, vol. 26, f 7.

27 Ibid.

28 Ibid.

29 Ibid.

30 Ibid.

31 Quoted in *Le Devoir,* February 6, op. cit.

32 P. Linteau, R. Durocher, J.-Cl. Robert, and F. Ricard, *Histoire du Québec contemporain.* vol. ii : *Le Québec depuis 1930,* Montreal, Les Éditions du Boréal, 1989 (revised edition), p. 315.

33 Duplessis Speech at the Legislative Assembly January 14, 1953, as reported in *L'Action catholique,* January 15, 1953, p.18.

34 Statement published in the press. Quoted in R. Denis, *Luttes de classes,* op. cit., p.139.

35 Louiseville Strike. LAC, vol. 25, f 5. All quotes are taken from this document.

36 LAC, vol. 28, f 16.

37 Patricia Pearson, with the contribution of Barbara C. Eastman, *Couchiching: The First Sixty Years, 1932–1991,* Willowdale, Ont., Couchiching Institute on Public Affairs, 1991, 67 pp. The facts presented in this chapter are drawn from this work.

38 Ibid., p. 17.

39 J. English, *Trudeau, Citizen of the World: The Life of Pierre Elliott Trudeau,* vol. 1, *1919–1968,* Toronto, Alfred Knopf Canada, 2006, p. 276.

40 Couchiching. LAC, vol. 25, f 41.

41 Letter from Peers. LAC, vol. 25, f 4.

42 Letter from McInnis. LAC, vol. 12, f 18.

43 Report of the First Annual Conference of the Institut canadien des affaires publiques. Organized with the assistance of Radio-Canada. *Le peuple souverain.* Alpine Inn, Ste-Marguerite. From September 29 to October 2, 1954. Trudeau's talk is found on pages 36–40. LAC, vol. 26, f 18.

44 A. Faucher (ed.), *Cinquante ans de sciences sociales à l'Université Laval. L'histoire de la Faculté des sciences sociales (1938–1988),* Quebec City, Faculté des sciences sociales de l'Université Laval, 1988, p. 28.

45 Jules Duchastel, *Marcel Rioux. Entre l'utopie et la raison.* Montreal, Les Éditions Nouvelle Optique, 1981, p. 82.

46 G. Pelletier, *Years of Impatience: 1950–1960,* Toronto, Methuen, 1984, p. 149.

47 G. Roberge, "L'ICAP, lieu de réflexion," in *Le Canada face à l'avenir : un pays qui s'interroge,* Conférence annuelle de l'Institut canadien des affaires publiques (ICAP), 1964, Montreal, Les Éditions du Jour, 1964, pp. 11–12.

48 Letter from M. Ross. LAC, vol. 25, f 41.

49 Meeting of the French section of the Canadian Institute on Public
    Affairs, February 28, 1953. LAC, vol. 26, f 17.

50 Report of the First Annual Conference of the Institut canadien des affaires
    publiques. Organized with the assistance of Radio-Canada. *Le peuple
    souverain.* Alpine Inn, Ste-Marguerite. From September 29 to October 2,
    1954. Trudeau's talk is found on pages 36–40. LAC, vol. 26, f 18.

51 "Some Obstacles to Democracy in Quebec" in *Canadian Journal of
    Economics and Political Science,* vol. XXIV, no. 3, August 1958, pp.
    297–311. This article also appeared in Mason Wade (ed.), *Canadian
    Dualism,* Toronto, University of Toronto Press, 1960; and in John
    Saywell (ed.), *Federalism and the French Canadians,* Toronto,
    Macmillan, 1968.

52 P.E. Trudeau, "De quelques obstacles à la démocratie au Québec," *Le
    fédéralisme et la société canadienne-française,* Montreal, Éditions
    HMH, 1967, p. 107–128. (Translated from English by Pierre
    Vadeboncœur.)

53 Radio-Canada Archives. http://archives.radio-canada.ca/politique/
    droits_libertés/clips/12901/.

54 P.E. Trudeau, "Obstacles à la démocratie," Report of the First Annual
    Conference of the Institut canadien des affaires publiques. Organized
    with the assistance of Radio-Canada. *Le peuple souverain.* Alpine Inn,
    Ste-Marguerite, from September 29 to October 2, 1954, pp. 36–40.
    Trudeau kept a copy of this document. LAC, vol. 26, f 18.

55 Ibid., p. 36.

56 Ibid.

57 Ibid., pp. 36–37.

58 Ibid., p. 37.

59 Ibid., p. 38.

60 Ibid.

61 Ibid.

62 Ibid., pp. 38–39.

63 Ibid., p. 39.

64 Ibid.

65 Ibid., p. 40.

66 Ibid.

67 *Nouvelles Illustrées.* LAC, vol. 14, f 38.

68 All quotations from this article are taken from Saywell, *Federalism and
    the French Canadians,* Toronto, Macmillan, 1968.

69 J. Saywell, *Federalism and the French Canadians,* op. cit., p. 103.

70 Ibid., p. 104.

71 Ibid., p. 116.

72 Ibid., p. 117.

73 Ibid., pp. 121–122.

74 Ibid., p. 120.

75 Ibid., pp. 106 and 108.

76 Ibid., p. 110.

77 Ibid., p. 111, footnote 12.

78 Ibid., p. 114.

79 Ibid.

80 Ibid.

81 Ibid., pp. 122–123.

82 Ibid., p. 123.

83 This fact was reported to us by Jacques Hébert, whom we knew well.

84 Since Jacques Hébert gave us access to his own collection of the weekly *Vrai,* we were able to check this personally. This is how we discovered the practically unknown article on the Liberal Party congress.

85 L. Dion, *Québec, 1945–2000,* vol. 2: *Les intellectuels et le temps de Duplessis,* Quebec City, Les Presses de l'Université Laval, 1993, p. 279.

86 J. Tully, *Public Philosophy in a New Key,* vol. 1: *Democracy and Civic Freedom,* New York, Cambridge University Press, 2008, as summarized in Bonnie Honig, *Perspectives on Politics,* June 2010, vol. 8, no. 2, p. 656.

87 P.E. Trudeau, *Approaches to Politics,* Toronto, Oxford University Press, 2010, p. 71.

88 Ibid., p. 57.

89 Ibid., p. 25.

90 Ibid., pp.27–28.

91 Ibid., p. 28.

92 Ibid., p. 30.

93 Ibid.

94 Ibid., p. 31.

95 Ibid., p. 33.

96 Ibid., p. 32.

97 Ibid., p. 34.

98 Ibid., pp. 31 and 37.

99 Ibid., p. 36.

100 Ibid., p. 38.

101 Ibid., p. 39.

102 Ibid., p. 43.

103 Ibid., p. 44.

104 Ibid.

105 Ibid., pp. 49–50.

106 Ibid., p. 78.

107 Ibid., p. 63

108 Ibid., pp. 63–64.

109 Ibid., p. 70.

110 Ibid., p. 79.

111 Ibid., p. 75.

112 Ibid., p. 78.

113 Ibid., p. 76.

114 Ibid., p. 80.

115 Ibid.

116 Ibid., p. 81.

117 Ibid., p. 78.

118 Ibid., p. 87.

Chapter 11: **WORKERS OF QUEBEC, UNITE!** (pages 321–342)

1   L-M. Tremblay, *Le syndicalisme québécois. Idéologies de la C.S.N. et de la F.T.Q. 1940–1970,* Montreal, Les presses de l'Université de Montréal, 1972, p. 134.

2   Quoted in FTQ, *Histoire de la FTQ – des tout débuts jusqu'en 1965, des milliers d'histoires qui façonnent l'histoire* (Émile Bourdeau was commissioned to write this book), Montreal, Fédération des travailleurs et travailleuses du Québec (FTQ), 1988, p. 148.

3   Ibid., p. 157.

4   R. Denis, *Luttes de classes et question nationale au Québec. 1948–1968,* Montreal, Presses socialistes internationales, 1979, p. 141.

5   P.E. Trudeau, *Memoirs,* Toronto, McClelland & Stewart, 1993, pp. 65–66.

6   École ouvrière de Saint-Jean, Saturday December 12 and Sunday December 13, 1953. LAC, vol. 26, f 21.

7   *Les nouvelles ouvrières,* in L-M. Tremblay, *Le syndicalisme québécois,* op. cit., p. 132.

8   École de métallurgie, course offered on January 23, 1954. Letter from Jean-Paul Desmarais, January 28, 1954. LAC, vol. 15, f 6.

9   H. David, *L'état des rapports de classe au Québec de 1945 à 1967,* in

F. Harvey, *Le mouvement ouvrier au Québec*, Montreal, Boréal Express, 1980, p. 241.

10 Émile Boudreau mentions Trudeau's presence in FTQ, *Histoire de la FTQ*, op. cit., p. 147.

11 All quotations here from Trudeau's talk are found in LAC, vol. 15, f 10.

12 FTQ, *Histoire de la FTQ*, op. cit., p. 154.

13 D. Latouche and D. Poliquin-Bourassa, *Le manuel de la parole, manifestes québécois*, vol. 2: *1900 à 1959*, Montreal, Éditions du Boréal Express, 1978, pp. 291–295. All quotations from this manifesto are from the version digitized by Igor Tchoukarine on the "Bilan du siècle" website at the Université de Sherbrooke.

14 R. Denis, *Luttes de classes*, op. cit., p. 165.

15 D. Latouche and D. Poliquin-Bourassa, *Le manuel de la parole*, op. cit.

16 *Mémoire de la Fédération des Unions Industrielles du Québec*, p. 7. LAC, vol. 16, f 4.

17 Ibid., p. 22.

18 Ibid.

19 Ibid., p. 23.

20 Ibid.

21 Ibid.

22 Ibid., p. 24.

23 Ibid., p. 29.

24 Ibid.

25 Ibid., p. 31–32.

26 Ibid., p. 32.

27 Ibid., p. 33.

28 Ibid., p. 37.

29 Ibid., p. 25.

30 Ibid., p. 28.

31 Ibid.

32 Ibid., p. 36.

33 Ibid.

34 Ibid., p. 38.

35 Ibid., p. 41.

36 Ibid., p. 45.

37 Ibid., p. 43.

38 Ibid., p. 8.

39 Ibid., p. 42.

40 Ibid., p. 46.

41 Ibid.

42 P.E. Trudeau, "De libro, tributo . . . et quibusdam aliis," *Cité libre*, October 1954, pp. 1–16. This article was reproduced in P.E. Trudeau, *Federalism and the French Canadians*, Toronto, Macmillan, 1968, pp. 63–78.

43 M. Lamontagne, *Le fédéralisme canadien. Évolution et problèmes.* Quebec City, Les presses de l'Université Laval, 1954, p. vii.

44 Ibid., p. 86.

45 Ibid., p. 89.

46 This quote is taken from a talk by Michel Brunet entitled "The Federalism of Maurice Lamontagne," given on Friday, June 11, 1954. LAC, vol. 20, f 10.

47 P.E. Trudeau, *Federalism and the French Canadians*, Toronto, Macmillan, 1968, p. 64–65.

48 Ibid., p. 65.

49 Ibid., p. 66.

50 Ibid., p. 64.

51 Ibid., p. 66.

52 Ibid., pp. 66–67.

53 Ibid., p. 67.

54 Ibid.

55 Ibid., p.68

56 Ibid.

57 Ibid., pp. 68–69.

58 Ibid., p.69.

59 Ibid.

60 Ibid., pp. 70–71.

61 Ibid., pp. 75–76.

62 Ibid., p. 78.

63 Letter of October 20, 1954 to M. Brunet. LAC, vol. 20, f 10.

64 Quoted in L. Dion, *Québec, 1945–2000*, vol. 2: *Les intellectuels et le temps de Duplessis*, Quebec City, Les Presses de l'Université Laval, 1993, p. 303.

65 P.E. Trudeau, Federalism, op. cit., p.77, note 12.

66 Ibid.

67 Ibid.

68 F. Cyr and R. Roy, *Éléments d'histoire de la FTQ : la FTQ et la question nationale*, Laval, Éditions coopératives Albert Saint-Martin, 1981, p. 102.

69 F. Cyr and R. Roy, *Éléments d'histoire de la FTQ : la FTQ et la question nationale*, Laval, Éditions coopératives Albert Saint-Martin, 1981, p. 102.

70 Ibid., p. 15.

71 *La Presse,* February 14, 1957. LAC, vol. 15, f 11.

72 Ibid.

Chapter 12: AGAINST THE CURRENT (pages 343–375)

1   Letter of April 30, 1951, from G. Pelletier. LAC, vol. 23, f 15.

2   Handwritten notes. LAC, vol. 23, f 15.

3   This collective work was edited by P.E. Trudeau. Montreal, Les Éditions
    du Jour, 1970 (First edition, Les Éditions *Cité libre,* 1956). We quote here
    from the English edition, translated by James Boake. It was published by
    James Lewis & Samuel of Toronto, in 1974.

4   Ibid., p. 67.

5   Ibid., p. 2.

6   Ibid., p. 6.

7   Ibid., p. 7.

8   Ibid.

9   Ibid.

10 Ibid., p. 8.

11 Ibid., pp. 7–8.

12 Ibid., p. 8.

13 M. and M. Nemni, "A Conversation with Pierre Elliott Trudeau," *Cité
    libre,* February–March 1998, p. 92.

14 P.E. Trudeau, (ed.), *The Asbestos Strike,* translated by James Boake,
    Toronto, Lewis & Samuel, 1974., p. 9.

15 Ibid., p. 8.

16 Louis-Adolphe Paquet, priest, was a professor at Laval University for nearly
    sixty years. He was French Canada's "national theologian" and defined
    the church's position on public policy, shaping the somewhat defensive
    "messianic nationalism" of his day (*The Canadian Encyclopedia*).

17 Ibid., p. 9.

18 Ibid.

19 Ibid.

20 Ibid., p. 10.

21 S. Guindon, *Esdras Minville: l'homme, son action, sa pensée.* Research
    work presented December 6, 1995. Department of History of the
    l'Université de Montréal. http://www.histoirequebec.qc.ca/publicat/
    vo12num1/v2n1_4es.htm.

22 We have dealt with this subject in detail in the first volume.

23 P.E. Trudeau, Chapter 1 of *The Asbestos Strike,* op. cit., p. 12.

24 Ibid., pp. 12–13.

25 Ibid., p. 12.

26 Ibid., p. 14.

27 Ibid.

28 Ibid., p. 17.

29 Ibid., pp. 17–18.

30 Ibid., p. 18.

31 M. Brunet, "Trois illusions de la pensée canadienne-française." Lecture reported in *Le Devoir*, June 2, 1954.

32 P.E. Trudeau, *The Asbestos Strike,* op. cit., p. 19.

33 Ibid., p. 19.

34 Ibid., p. 21.

35 Ibid., p. 23.

36 Ibid.

37 Ibid.

38 Ibid., p. 24.

39 Ibid.

40 F-A. Angers, "Pierre-Elliott Trudeau et La grève de l'amiante. Deuxième partie. Confusions et généralisations hâtives." In *L'Action nationale,* October 1957, p. 90–91. Documents digitized by Claude Bélanger, Marianopolis College © 2001.

41 Ibid., p. 25.

42 Ibid., p. 40.

43 Ibid., p. 26.

44 Ibid., p. 27.

45 Ibid., p. 31.

46 Ibid., p. 34.

47 Ibid., pp. 34–35.

48 Ibid., p. 35.

49 Ibid.

50 Ibid., p. 36.

51 Ibid.

52 Ibid., p. 39.

53 Ibid., p. 40.

54 Ibid., p. 41.

55 Ibid.

56 Ibid., p. 50.

57 Ibid.

58 Ibid., p. 51.

59 Ibid.

60 Ibid., p. 52.

61 Ibid.

62 Ibid., p. 55.

63 Ibid., p. 54.

64 Ibid.

65 Ibid., p. 56.

66 Ibid., p. 57.

67 Ibid.

68 Ibid., p. 65.

69 Ibid., pp. 65–66.

70 A. Laurendeau, quoted in G. Bergeron, *Du duplessisme à Trudeau et à Bourassa, 1956–1971*, Montreal, Éditions Parti pris, 1967 et 1971, p. 14.

71 G. Bergeron, op. cit., pp. 14–15.

72 A. Laurendeau, quoted in G. Bergeron, op. cit., p. 17.

73 LAC, vol. 23, f 17.

74 H.B. Neatby, "Turning New Leaves," *The Canadian Forum*, October 1956, pp. 162–163.

75 C.B. Macpherson, *The Canadian Journal of Economics and Political Science*, May 1967, pp. 268–269.

76 *Anglican Outlook and News Digest*, vol. 11, no. 9, August–September 1956.

77 R. Gérin, *Relations industrielles*, September 1956, pp. 306–307.

78 R. Chartier, *L'Actualité économique*, July–September 1956, p. 354.

79 S. Chaput-Rolland, *Point de vue*, "Les livres," p. 14., LAC, vol. 23, f 17.

80 A. Laurendeau, "Sur cent pages de Pierre Elliott Trudeau," *Le Devoir*, I, October 6, II, October 10 and III, October 11, 1956. These articles can be found on the excellent website created by Claude Bélanger at Marianapolis College: *Documents sur la grève de l'amiante de 1949 / Documents on the 1949 Asbestos Strike.* © 2001 Claude Bélanger, Marianapolis College.

81 A. Laurendeau, "Sur cent pages de Pierre Elliott Trudeau," *Le Devoir*, October 6, 1956.

82 Ibid., October 10, 1956.

83 Ibid.

84 Ibid., October 11, 1956.

85 Ibid.

86 Ibid.

87 P. Stratford (Essays selected and translated by). Introduction by Claude Ryan. *André Laurendeau: Witness for Quebec.* Toronto, Macmillan of

Canada, 1973, p. xi.

88 A. Laurendeau, *La crise de la conscription–1942*, Montreal, Éditions du Jour, 1962.

89 F-A. Angers, "Pierre-Elliott Trudeau et *La grève de l'amiante*. Première partie. Réflexions préliminaires," in *L'Action nationale*, September 1957, pp. 10–22. In *Documents sur la grève de l'amiante de 1949 / Documents on the 1949 Asbestos Strike*. © 2001 Claude Bélanger, Marianopolis. http://faculty.marianopolis.edu/c.belanger/quebechistory/docs/asbestos/. All future reference to these articles by F-A. Angers are taken from this website.

90 Ibid.

91 Ibid.

92 Ibid.

93 Ibid.

94 François-Albert Angers, "Troisième partie. Les défauts de notre société," in *L'Action nationale*, November 1957, pp. 291–304.

95 Ibid.

96 François-Albert Angers, "Deuxième partie. Confusions et généralisations hâtives," in *L'Action nationale*, October 1957, pp. 87–99.

97 Ibid.

98 François-Albert Angers, "Troisième partie. Les défauts de notre société," op. cit.

99 Ibid.

100 François-Albert Angers, "Cinquième partie. Mais ils n'étaient pas socialistes," in *L'Action nationale*, May–June 1958, pp. 570–585.

101 Ibid.

102 Ibid.

103 F-A. Angers, "Troisième partie. Les défauts de notre société," op. cit.

104 J. Cousineau, *En marge de "La grève de l'amiante,"* Montreal, *Les Cahiers de l'Institut social populaire*, September 1958. LAC, vol. 23, f 20.

105 P.E. Trudeau, "Le père Cousineau, s. j., et *La grève de l'amiante*," *Cité libre* off-print, April 1959, p. 4.

106 S. Clavette, *Les dessous d'Asbestos. Une lutte idéologique contre la participation des travailleurs*, Quebec City, Les presses de l'Université Laval, 2005, p. 397.

107 P.E. Trudeau, "*Le père Cousineau, s.j., et La grève de l'amiante*," op. cit., p. 4.

108 J. Cousineau, *En marge de "La grève de l'amiante."* op. cit., 2. 21.

109 Ibid., p. 22.

110 Ibid., p. 25.

111 Ibid., p. 38.

112 Ibid., p. 40.

113 P.E. Trudeau, "*Le père Cousineau, s.j., et La grève de l'amiante,*" op. cit., p. 2.

114 LAC, vol. 23, f 20.

115 P.E. Trudeau, "*Le père Cousineau, s.j., et La grève de l'amiante,*" op. cit., p. 2–4.

116 LAC, vol. 23, f 20.

117 J. Cousineau, op. cit., p. 26.

118 P.E. Trudeau, "*Le père Cousineau, s.j., et La grève de l'amiante,*" op. cit., p. 15, note 4.

119 J. Cousineau, op. cit., p. 34.

120 P.E. Trudeau, "*Le père Cousineau, s.j., et La grève de l'amiante,*" op. cit., p. 6.

121 P.E. Trudeau, "Mauvaise foi et bonne conscience: l'argumentation selon Saint Ignace," *Cité libre,* January–February 1960, p. 25.

122 S. Clavette, *Les dessous d'Asbestos,* op. cit., p. 422.

123 Ibid., p. 424.

124 Ibid., p. 446.

125 Ibid., p. 421.

126 Ibid., p. 427.

127 Ibid., p. 428.

128 P.E. Trudeau, "Epilogue," *The Asbestos Strike,* op. cit., p. 330.

129 G. Frégault, *La guerre de la conquête,* Montreal, Fides, 1955.

130 M. Brunet, *La présence anglaise et les Canadiens,* Montreal, Beauchemin, 1964, pp. 116–117. This work takes up again the "Essai d'histoire intellectuelle" published in *Écrits du Canada français,* 1957.

131 Ibid., p. 116.

132 P.E. Trudeau, "*Le père Cousineau, s.j., et La grève de l'amiante,*" op. cit., p. 4.

133 S. Clarkson, "An Explicit Destination?", in J. English, R. Gwyn, and P. W. Lackenbauer, (eds.), *The Hidden Pierre Elliott Trudeau: The Faith Behind the Politics,* Ottawa, Novalis, 2004, p. 34.

134 P.E. Trudeau, "Federal Grants to Universities" in *Federalism and the French Canadians,* Toronto, Macmillan, 1968, p. 79.

135 Ibid., pp. 79–80.

136 Ibid., p. 80.

137 Ibid., p. 82.

138 Ibid., p. 83.

139 Ibid.

140 Ibid., p. 91.

141 Ibid., pp. 91–92.

142 Ibid., pp. 92–93.

143 Ibid., pp. 79–102.

144 Ibid., p. 98.

145 Ibid., p. 99.

Chapter 13: THE END OF AN ERA (pages 376–407)

1   Letter of invitation quoted by Pierre Joncas in *Essai sur le Rassemblement: mouvement d'éducation et d'action démocratiques.* Master's dissertation, Laval University, 1959. Trudeau read this document and made annotations. LAC, vol. 28, f 7.

2   LAC, vol. 27, f 1.

3   LAC, vol. 28, f 16.

4   Notes for a talk given by Trudeau on Radio-Canada, June 15, 1956. LAC, vol. 25, f 14.

5   This is revealed by a letter of August 20 notifying the committee of the August 27 meeting. The secretary, Jean-Paul Lefebvre, wrote they would discuss "the Declaration of Principles of the Rassemblement . . . per se, drafted by Pierre Trudeau." LAC, vol. 27, f 1.

6   Stencilled message dated July 3, 1956. LAC, vol. 14, f 10. Jacques Perrault and Jean-Paul Geoffroy, technical adviser of the Confederation of Catholic Workers of Canada (CCWC) also participated in this meeting.

7   S. Djwa, *The Politics of the Imagination: A Life of F.R. Scott,* McClelland & Stewart, 1987, p. 326.

8   Agenda. LAC, vol. 39, f 4.

9   S. Djwa, *The Politics of the Imagination,* op. cit., p. 324.

10   "Fort Smith," *The Collected Poems of F.R. Scott,* McClelland & Stewart, 1981, p, 227. In 1981, Scott received the Governor General's Award for his *Collected Poems.*

11   S. Djwa, *The Politics of the Imagination,* op. cit., p. 332.

12   Ibid.

13   Ibid., p. 336.

14   Ibid., p. 332.

15   Agenda. LAC, vol. 39, f 4.

16   LAC, vol. 27, f 1.

17   *Le Devoir,* December 3, 1956. LAC, vol. 27, f 14.

18 T. Casgrain, *Une femme chez les hommes,* Montreal, Éditions du jour, 1971, p. 211.

19 Letter of April 16, 1954, from Thérèse Casgrain to CCF leader Tommy Douglas. Quoted in J. English, *Trudeau, Citizen of the World: The Life of Pierre Elliott Trudeau,* vol. 1: *1919–1968,* Toronto, Alfred Knopf Canada, 2006, p. 296.

20 M. Behiels, *Prelude to Quebec's Quiet Revolution: Liberalism versus Neo-Nationalism, 1945–1960,* Montreal and Kingston, McGill-Queen's University Press, 1985, p. 252.

21 *Déclaration de l'exécutif général du Rassemblement:* précisions sur la NATURE et les BUTS du mouvement (the words "nature" and "buts" are capitalized in this text). The late Micheline Legendre, a well-known Quebec puppeteer, graciously provided us with this document on November 13, 2006.

22 Ibid.

23 G. Bergeron, "Le Rassemblement et les partis," *Le Devoir,* April 12, 1957. In LAC, vol. 27, f 14.

24 Gérard Pelletier's letter of August 29, 1957, LAC, vol. 27, f 8.

25 LAC, vol. 27, f 8.

26 This report was provided by Micheline Legendre.

27 Secretary-Treasurer's report quoted by P. Joncas, in *Essai sur le Rassemblement,* op. cit., p. 50.

28 P. Joncas, op. cit., p. 53.

29 P.E. Trudeau, "Un manifeste démocratique," *Cité libre,* October 1958, pp. 1–31.

30 Ibid., p. 8.

31 Ibid., p. 9.

32 D. Brunelle, *Les trois colombes,* Montreal, VLB éditeur, 1985, p. 15.

33 LAC, vol. 25, f 16.

34 Agenda. LAC, vol. 39, f 4.

35 "Notes sur une guerre momentanément évitée," *Cité libre,* February 1957, pp. 1–2.

36 Ghana seminar. LAC, vol. 13, f 4.

37 Agenda. LAC, vol. 39, f 4.

38 *La Presse,* August 20, 1957. LAC, vol. 15, f 13.

39 É. Boudreau, FTQ, *Histoire de la FTQ – des tout débuts jusqu'en 1965, des milliers d'histoires qui façonnent l'histoire Montreal,* Fédération des travailleurs et travailleuses du Québec (FTQ), 1988, p. 231.

40 Agenda. LAC, vol. 39, f 4.

41 LAC, vol. 15, f 13.

42 G. Bélanger, "*La grève de Murdochville*," in the e-journal *Labour/Le Travail* at www.lltjournal.ca.

43 S. Chaput-Rolland, "Lettre ouverte à quelques intellectuels et à Monsieur Pierre Elliott Trudeau, directeur de *Cité libre*," *Cité libre*, May 1958, pp. 18–21.

44 LAC, vol. 26, f 19.

45 P.E. Trudeau, "À propos de domination économique," *Cité libre*, May 1958, pp. 7–16.

46 Ibid., p. 11.

47 Ibid., p. 15.

48 P. Joncas, op. cit., p. 52.

49 M. Oliver, (ed.), *Social Purpose for Canada*, Toronto, University of Toronto Press, 1961.

50 P.E. Trudeau, "Un manifeste démocratique," op. cit.

51 Ibid., p. 21.

52 Ibid., p. 16.

53 Ibid., p. 20.

54 Ibid.

55 Ibid., p. 22.

56 Ibid., p. 28.

57 Ibid., p. 30.

58 Ibid.

59 *Le journal des vedettes*, December 7, 1958. Trudeau filed a copy of this article and many others besides. LAC, vol. 28, f 9.

60 R. Denis, *Luttes de classes et question nationale au Québec, 1948–1968*, Montreal, Presses socialistes internationales, 1979, p. 194.

61 Ibid., p. 200.

62 Ibid., p. 201.

63 M. Behiels, *Prelude,* op. cit., p. 254.

64 G-É. Lapalme, *Le vent de l'oubli. Mémoires*, vol. 2, Montreal, Les Éditions Léméac, 1970, p. 223.

65 R. Rumilly, *Maurice Duplessis et son temps*, vol. 2 (1944–1959), Montreal, Éditions Fidès, 1978, p. 651.

66 G-É. Lapalme, *Le vent de l'oubli,* op. cit., p. 233.

67 P. Godin, *René Lévesque: un enfant du siècle*, Montreal, Boréal, 1994, p. 323.

68 Ibid.

69 M. Vastel, *The Outsider: The Life of Pierre Elliott Trudeau,* translated by Hubert Bauch, Toronto, Macmillan, 1990, p. 87.

70 Agenda. LAC, vol. 39, f 4.

71 R. Rumilly, *Maurice Duplessis,* op. cit., p. 648.

72 This documentary by Paul Carvalho was broadcast on Radio-Canada's show *Zone Doc* on Friday, December 25, and Sunday, December 27, 2009. It was adapted from Paul Labonne's work *Paul Sauvé: désormais, l'avenir, 1907–1960,* Montreal, Éd. Point de fuite, 2003.

73 *Key West Citizen,* April 29, 1960. LAC, vol. 13, f 11.

74 *Montreal Star,* Monday, May 2. LAC, vol. 13, f 11.

75 J.-P. Desbiens, *The Impertinences of Brother Anonymous,* translated by Miriam Chapin, Montreal, Harvest House, 1962, p. 23.

76 Ibid., p. 27.

77 L. Dion, *La révolution déroutée: 1960–1976,* Montreal, Boreal, 1998, p. 153.

78 J.-P. Desbiens, *The Impertinences,* op. cit., p. 58.

79 J. Hébert, "La petite histoire des Insolences," preface to the 1988 edition of J.P. Desbiens, *Les insolences du Frère Untel,* Montreal, Éditions de l'Homme, p. 16.

80 R. Lévesque, "Pas plus bêtes que les Arabes," *Cité libre,* May 1960, pp. 17–18.

81 P.E. Trudeau, "De la notion d'opposition politique," *Cité libre,* May 1960, pp. 13–14.

82 P.E. Trudeau, "Notes sur l'élection provinciale," *Cité libre,* June–July 1960, pp. 12–13.

83 P.E. Trudeau, "L'élection du 22 juin 1960," *Cité libre,* August–September 1960, p. 4.

84 R. Pelletier, *Partis politiques et société québécoise: de Duplessis à Bourassa, 1944–1970,* Montreal, Québec/Amérique, 1989, p. 243.

85 P.E. Trudeau, "L'élection du 22 juin 1960," op. cit, pp. 3–8.

86 R. Pelletier, *Partis politiques,* op. cit., pp. 194–195.

87 P.E. Trudeau, "L'élection du 22 juin 1960," op. cit.

Chapter 14: THE NEW TREASON OF THE INTELLECTUALS
(pages 408–456)

1 Léon Dion, *La révolution déroutée: 1960–1976,* Montreal, Boréal, 1998, p. 254.

2 C. Taylor, "La révolution futile ou Les avatars de la pensée globale," *Cité libre,* August–September 1964, p. 22.

3   J. Pellerin, "La réaction tranquille," *Cité libre,* April 1965, p. 6.

4   Ibid., p. 7.

5   Ibid., p. 8.

6   P.E. Trudeau, *Memoirs,* McClelland & Stewart, 1993, p. 71.

7   Letter of E. Minville, February 14, 1952. LAC, vol. 33, f 3. Unless otherwise specified, the references are found in this file.

8   *Le Devoir,* June 6, 1960.

9   J. Hébert and P.E. Trudeau, *Two Innocents in Red China,* translated by I.M. Owen, Vancouver, Douglas & McIntyre, 2007.

10 Letter from Jean Beetz, director of this institute. LAC, vol. 33, f 19.

11 J. English, *Trudeau, Citizen of the World: The Life of Pierre Elliott Trudeau,* vol. 1: *1919–1968,* Toronto, Alfred Knopf Canada, pp. 170 and 171.

12 P. Gzowski, "Portrait of an Intellectual in Action," *Maclean's,* February 24, 1962, p. 30.

13 Interview with Norm Goldman, Montreal, November 13, 2006.

14 Letter of reference for Bernard Landry, dated "January" but without indicating the year. LAC, vol. 33, f 16.

15 Public Law Research Institute. LAC, vol. 33, f 19. Unless otherwise indicated, the references to Trudeau's work at this institute are found in this file.

16 The manuscript handwritten by Trudeau and a typed version are found in LAC, vol. 33, f 19.

17 The draft of this article was written on the Alaska Cruise Line letterhead. LAC, vol. 20, f 34.

18 Letter from Jerome T. Gaspard, Consul General of the United States, dated August 13, 1962, inviting Trudeau to visit Plattsburgh Air Force Base. LAC, vol. 13, f 15.

19 Letter to G. Sylvester of November 13, 1962. LAC, vol. 31, f 15. All correspondence pertaining to the Royal Society is found in this volume.

20 P.C. Newman, "Quebec Made the Scapegoat," *Montreal Star,* September 1964. LAC, vol. 33, f 6.

21 J. Hébert and P.E. Trudeau, *Two Innocents,* op. cit., pp. 209–210.

22 Travel diary. LAC, vol. 24, f 7.

23 For example, on October 10 he noted a discussion on Marxism and Leninism that got nowhere. LAC, vol. 24, f 7.

24 L. Dion, *La Révolution déroutée,* op. cit., p. 107.

25 R. Pelletier *Les militants du R.I.N.,* Ottawa, Éditions de l'Université d'Ottawa, 1974, p. 11. Pelletier defended his doctoral dissertation on the RIN in Paris, in May 1972. This book proved very useful to us in writing this chapter.

26 L. Dion, *La Révolution déroutée,* op. cit., p. 110.

27 R. Pelletier, *Les militants du R.I.N.,* op. cit., p. 25.

28 [P.E. Trudeau], "La Restauration," *Cité libre,* January 1961, pp. 1–3.

29 Ibid., p. 1.

30 Ibid., p. 3.

31 Ibid., p. 1.

32 Ibid., p. 3.

33 Ibid., p. 2.

34 Ibid.

35 Ibid.

36 Ibid., p. 3.

37 Ibid.

38 J.-M. Léger, "Urgence d'une gauche nationale," *Cité libre,* February 1961, pp. 12–13.

39 Ibid., p. 13.

40 G.C., "Lettre d'un nationaliste," *Cité libre,* March 1961, pp. 6–8.

41 Ibid., p. 7.

42 P.E. Trudeau, "L'aliénation nationaliste," *Cité libre,* March 1961, p. 3.

43 Ibid.

44 Ibid., p. 5.

45 P.E. Trudeau, "The Practice and Theory of Federalism," in M. Oliver (ed.), *Social Purpose for Canada,* Toronto, University of Toronto Press, 1961, p. 371–393. Our citations here are from P.E. Trudeau, *Federalism and the French Canadians,* Toronto, Macmillan, 1968, pp. 124–150.

46 Ibid., p. 124.

47 Ibid., p. 128

48 Ibid., pp. 127–128.

49 Ibid., p. 140.

50 Ibid., pp. 139–140.

51 Ibid., p. 150.

52 Ibid., p. 144.

53 Ibid., p. 150.

54 See Chapter 1, above.

55 G. Pelletier, "Un silence provisoire," *Cité libre,* January 1962, p. 1.

56 A. Major, "Problème bicéphale," *Cité libre,* January 1962, p. 5.

57 P. Vallières, "Nous éveiller à la profondeur," *Cité libre,* February 1962, p. 18.

58 P. Vallières, "Premières démarches de notre liberté," *Cité libre,* March 1962, p. 4.

59 Ibid., p. 5.

60 R. and A. Breton, "Le séparatisme ou le respect du statu quo," *Cité libre,* April 1962, p. 28.

61 Ibid., p. 22.

62 Ibid., p. 28.

63 P.E. Trudeau, "La nouvelle trahison des clercs," *Cité libre,* April 1962, pp. 3–16.

64 *Cité libre,* June–July 1962, p. 48.

65 P.E. Trudeau, "New Treason of the Intellectuals" in *Federalism and the French Canadians,* op. cit., pp. 151–181.

66 Ibid., p. 151.

67 Ibid., p. 152.

68 Ibid.

69 Ibid., p. 153.

70 Ibid., pp. 152–153.

71 Ibid., p. 154.

72 Ibid., p. 157.

73 Ibid.

74 Ibid., p. 158.

75 Ibid.

76 Ibid., p. 161.

77 Ibid.

78 Ibid.

79 Ibid., p. 164.

80 Ibid., p. 163.

81 Ibid., pp. 164–165.

82 Ibid., p. 165.

83 Ibid., pp. 167–168.

84 Ibid., pp. 168–169.

85 Ibid., p. 173.

86 Ibid., p. 176.

87 Ibid., p. 180.

88 Ibid., pp. 177–178.

89 Ibid., p. 180.

90 *Le Nouveau Journal,* April 14, 1962.

91 H. Aquin, "La fatigue culturelle du Canada français," *Liberté,* May 1962, pp. 299–325. This article later reappeared in H. Aquin, *Blocs erratiques,* Montreal, Quinze, 1977, pp. 69–103.

92 Ibid., p. 71.

93 Ibid., p. 82.

94 Ibid., pp. 88–89.

95 Ibid., p. 97.

96 Ibid., p. 72.

97 Readers may consult the many articles we wrote for *Cité libre,* when we served as editors from 1995 to 2000.

98 J. Rouillard, *Histoire du syndicalisme au Québec, Des origines à nos jours,* Montreal, Les Éditions du Boreal, 1989, p. 323.

99 F. Cyr and R. Roy, *Éléments d'histoire de la FTQ : la FTQ et la question nationale,* Laval, Éditions coopératives Albert Saint-Martin, 1981, p. 95.

100 P.E. Trudeau, "Quebec and the Constitutional Problem" in *Federalism and the French Canadians,* op. cit., p. 51.

101 R.P. Güntzel, "The Confédération des syndicats nationaux (CSN), the Idea of Independence, and the Sovereigntist Movement, 1960–80," in L.S. MacDonnell and I. Radforth, Canadian Working-Class History: Selected Readings, 3rd Edition, Toronto, Canadian Scholars Press Inc. 2006, p. 392.

102 C. Bédard, "Pour un régime federal adapté à la réalité," *L'Action* (formerly *L'Action catholique*), September 29, 1966, p. 18.

103 P.E. Trudeau, "Quebec and the Constitutional Problem," op. cit., p. 37.

104 Ibid., p. 33.

105 Ibid., p. 18.

106 C. Bédard, "Pour un régime fédéral adapté à la réalité," op. cit., p. 18.

107 J. Rouillard, *Histoire du syndicalisme,* op. cit., p. 324.

108 P.E. Trudeau, "Quebec and the Constitutional Problem," op. cit., p. 42.

109 Ibid., p. 49.

110 P.E. Trudeau, "Note sur la conjoncture politique. À propos des élections du 18 juin 1962," *Cité libre,* August/September 1962, p. 2.

111 Ibid.

112 Ibid.

113 Ibid., p. 3.

114 Letter from Gordon O. Rothney, September 18, 1962. LAC, vol. 21, f 3.

115 P.E. Trudeau, "L'homme de gauche et les élections provinciales," *Cité libre,* November 1962, p. 4.

116 Ibid.

117 Ibid., p. 5.

118 For example, when Trudeau took part in a Canadian conference on natural resources in 1961, René Lévesque sent him a note of congratulations. LAC, vol. 26, f 26.

119 LAC, vol. 30, f 20.

120 A. Laurendeau, quoted by L. Dion, *La Révolution déroutée,* op. cit., p. 170.

121 L. Dion, *La Révolution déroutée,* op. cit., p. 170.

122 For a serious study of this crisis, see W. Tetley, *The October Crisis, 1970, An Insider View,* Montreal and Kingston, McGill-Queen's University Press, 2007.

123 P. Maheu, "Que faire?", *Parti Pris,* vol. 1, no 5, quoted in L. Dion, *La Révolution déroutée,* op. cit., p. 161.

124 Trudeau kept a copy. LAC, vol. 33, f 5.

125 Letter from C. Julien, October 11, 1963. LAC, vol. 33, f 5.

126 Letter from C. Julien, October 22, 1963. LAC, vol. 33, f 5.

127 Letter from Trudeau, October 24, 1963. LAC, vol. 33, f 5.

128 *Le Quartier Latin,* November 26, 1963. LAC, vol. 31, f 17.

129 *Le Quartier Latin,* November 21, 1963. LAC, vol. 31, f 17.

130 G. Pelletier, "Pour clore un incident," *Cité libre,* April 1964, p. 1.

131 P. Vallières, "Sommes-nous en révolution?", *Cité libre,* February 1964, p. 9.

132 P. Vallières, "Les 'plorines' au pouvoir," *Cité libre,* March 1964, p. 2.

133 P. Vallières, *Nègres blancs d'Amérique, autobiographie précoce d'un "terroriste" québécois,* Montreal, Éditions Parti pris, 1968. This book was published in English by Monthly Review Press in 1971, then by McClelland & Stewart the following year, under the title *White Niggers of America: The Precocious Autobiography of a Quebec Terrorist.*

134 Biographical note about Pierre Vallières published by Éditions VLB: www.edvlb.com.

135 G. Pelletier, "Pour clore un incident," op. cit., p. 2.

136 P. Vadeboncoeur, "Les amiables compositeurs" (This was not a typo. In Latin "amiable" means "who seeks to conciliate"), *Cité libre,* February 1964, p. 12.

137 G. Pelletier, "*Parti pris* ou La grande illusion," *Cité libre,* April 1964. p. 8.

138 A. Breton, R. Breton, Cl. Bruneau, Y. Gauthier, M. Lalonde, M. Pinard, and P.E. Trudeau, "Pour une politique fonctionnelle," *Cité libre,* May 1964, pp. 11–17. We quote here from the English translation appearing in the May 1964 issue of *Canadian Forum.*

139 Ibid., p. 29.

140 Ibid., p. 32.

141 Ibid.

142 Ibid.

143 Ibid., pp. 32–33.

144 Ibid., p. 33.

145 Ibid.

146 Ibid.

147 Ibid.

148 P.E. Trudeau, "Separatist Counter-Revolutionaries" in *Federalism and the French Canadians*, op. cit., pp. 204–205.

149 Ibid., p. 205.

150 Ibid., p. 206.

151 Ibid., p. 209.

152 Ibid., p. 210.

153 Ibid., p. 211.

154 Ibid., p. 212.

155 A. Laurendeau, *Ces choses qui nous arrivent: chronique des années 1961–1966*, Montreal, éditions HMH, 1970, p. 60.

156 Ibid., p. 61.

157 Ibid., p. 62.

158 Ibid.

159 Ibid.

160 L. Dion, *La révolution déroutée*, op. cit., p. 204.

161 A. Breton, Cl. Bruneau, Y. Gauther, M. Lalonde, and M. Pinard, "Bizarre algèbre," *Cité libre*, December 1965, pp. 13–20.

162 Ibid., p. 13.

163 Ibid., p. 14.

164 Ibid., p. 17.

165 L. Dion, *La révolution déroutée*, op. cit., p. 211.

166 Ibid., p. 202.

167 Editorial team, "Marchand, Pelletier, Trudeau et le 8 novembre," *Cité libre*, October 1965, p. 1.

168 Ibid., p. 2.

169 LAC, vol. 34, f 5. We were unable to identify the source and date of the article, or the person who wrote these words.

170 *La Presse,* July 2, 1960, p. 30, in D. Brunelle, *Les trois colombes,* p. 153.

171 J. Marchand, "L'évolution des partis," *Cité libre,* New Series, December 1960, p. 18.

172 P.E. Trudeau, "Pearson ou l'abdication de l'esprit," *Cité libre,* April 1963, p. 8.

173 Ibid., p. 9.

174 Ibid., p. 10.

175 Ibid.

176 Ibid., p. 12.

177 G. Pelletier and P.E. Trudeau, "Pelletier et Trudeau s'expliquent," *Cité libre,* October 1965, pp. 3–5.

178 Ibid., p. 3–4.

179 Ibid., p. 4.

180 Ibid.

181 Ibid., p. 5.

182 Ibid.

183 Ibid.

184 Ibid.

185 This speech is published in French and English in J. Peter Meekison, *Canadian Federalism: Myth or Reality?* Toronto, Methuen Publication, 1968 (English text pp. 396–406).

INDEX